Sociology
An Introduction and Beyond

John T. Pullinger

ISBN 10: 1903-499-984
ISBN 13: 978-1903-499-986

Printed and bound in the United Kingdom by 4edge Ltd, 22 Eldon Way Industrial Estate, Hockley, Essex, SS5 4AD.

Contents

Preface

The aim of this text is to offer a broad based and sound academic guide to those studying sociology at the pre-university stage and / or during their university studies. It is also intended to assist the inquisitive mature reader to adopt a reflective and insightful outlook on society through the lens of sociological theories and concepts.

Making no assumptions about the reader's prior knowledge in the subject area, the text is written in a direct and accessible style which enables the reader to develop a complex understanding of the subject area. This is assisted by the structure of each chapter which:

- is introduced by an abstract overview that is designed to orientate the reader to the forthcoming chapter content
- provides an introduction to the terrain of the topic area of the chapter
- alerts the reader to the challenges faced and typical preconceptions that need to be confronted in making a successful transition to a sociological view of the topic area
- with the exception of chapters 1, 14 and 15, highlights and defines key terminology that will be used in the chapter
- is divided into subheadings which identify both the scope and key theme or message of each subsection.

By such means, the reader is gradually immersed into the challenges of the subject, led to examine and deconstruct common preconceptions about society, and armed with a number of key concepts that form the basis for reconstructing their understanding sociologically.

The book is designed in such a way that the entire text or chapters can be approached sequentially, or the reader can dip in and out by taking guidance from sub-headed sections regarding specific areas of interest or through passing curiosity. Diagrams are occasionally used to provide variety of communication and assist in different learning styles. Key referencing within the text and a reference list are provided to guide students into follow up research.

No assumption is made of previous knowledge in the subject, but the diligent reader should feel that they are sufficiently challenged and supported by the text to be making rapid academic progress. The text is aimed at:

- those studying A Level Sociology and equivalent Scottish Highers and looking for a text that adopts a reflective approach to the subject area and covers a majority of the content of A Level Sociology syllabi, without being tied to the content of any single one;

- Access to Higher Education sociology students who are looking for a text that covers a very broad range of Access unit topic areas, is unintimidating, but can nevertheless provide a guide to a challenging level of study;
- university foundation level sociology students who are looking for a broad based introductory text;
- remaining a good companion into degree level studies for all of the above groups or for those starting their degree in sociology;
- higher education students in allied subject areas whose studies require incursions into sociology;
- the general reader who is interested in benefiting from viewing contemporary issues through the lens of sociology and is looking for an approachable text through which to do so.

Although the text is primarily aimed at a British market, given the universal by nature of many of the topic areas it is expected that sociology students and general interest readers in other countries that are looking for an English written sociology text will find this book to be of interest.

Finally, the author hopes that through this work he has been able to make a contribution to a rewarding intellectual venture for the reader.

*To my wife Suzanne, for your patient
support and understanding.*

Chapter 1
Sociology and Becoming a Sociologist

Abstract

In this chapter, a brief introduction to what sociology is about is followed by definitions of the related subject areas of psychology, social anthropology, social policy, politics, criminology, economics and history. Throughout the chapter, the newcomer is alerted to a number of challenges that becoming an effective sociologist poses. Of primary importance is the need, through open mindedness, to suspend acceptance of everyday common sense knowledge and to develop the capacity to see society anew. The chapter also attempts to allay and reverse some of the negative preconceptions that commonly abound regarding the subject.

Reference is made to the need to cultivate what C Wright Mills refers to as the sociological imagination. This is explained as the development of the ability to recognise that personal experiences can be related to the impact of broader social forces and structures on people's lives. These effects can be analysed and formulated as public issues for the purpose of promoting social change. Mills' example of viewing the personal troubles of unemployment through the application of the sociological imagination is introduced, and further examples are developed by the author with reference to the collapse of financial institutions, job insecurity, the housing market, image anxiety, child carers and mental health.

Having identified some of the challenges, difficulties and rewards that await the student new to sociology, the author identifies a number of guidelines to help point the newcomer in the right direction. One pointer is to do with acquiring familiarity with sociological perspectives. The guidance here is that although the theoretical perspectives may offer new understandings of society, they should be used selectively and themselves evaluated critically.

Further guidance relates to the need to be aware of the influences of the social environment on behaviour, even where convincing explanations can be put in the form of genetic predispositions. Similarly, one should always be very wary of attempts to explain behaviour as the outcome of apparently fixed properties of human nature.

Another point relates to the need to contextualise the profiles that people's lives take within the broader constraints of socially structured life chances.

Reference is also made to the importance of avoiding the pitfall of being ethnocentric. Avoiding being ethnocentric is about avoiding working on the assumption that the ways of one's society are natural and provide a superior vantage point from which to judge other societies.

Finally, the issue of causality in sociology is raised. The key point here is that care needs to be taken in how causality is viewed in sociology. Whilst social influences on behaviour can be measured, in studying society the type of absolute causality which is seen to operate in the physical world is not appropriate.

What is sociology about?

Very briefly introduced, sociology is the study of patterns of behaviour amongst individuals that are shaped by social influences. As social beings, individuals live in a social environment which influences and shapes their behaviour; an environment which, to some extent, they are also able to influence. The society that individuals are born into predates their lives and is shaped by its own history. Social relationships therefore take place within a context of pre-existing cultural values, social institutions and economic relationships etc. It is in this sense that society is 'out there'.

It provides a mediating environment of influences which are internalised into the minds of individuals. Therefore, as well as being 'out there', it is also 'in here'. This internalisation of society's ways and values by individuals is referred to as 'socialisation'. It provides the basis for a degree of predictability in patterns of behaviour which are the subject matter of sociology.

How does sociology compare to related academic disciplines?

Sociology can also be defined by comparing it to certain subject areas that it runs up against. For example, psychology is also a subject which explains human behaviour. However, whereas psychology looks primarily at explaining behaviour in terms of personality traits, thought processes, perceptions, feelings and attitudes through studying the internal workings of the mind, the focus of sociology falls primarily on understanding external social influences that pattern the behaviour of groups of people.

The focus of social anthropology is on understanding the culture, customs, beliefs, traditions and ways of life of social groups that may be very different from those that seem familiar to people in the contemporary western world. Such societies were often once referred to as 'primitive'. By contrast, the attention of sociologists is on the study of the contemporary world. However, the findings of anthropologists have sometimes assisted sociologists in achieving insightful understanding of contemporary society – as, for example, we will see in a later chapter with reference to Durkheim's sociological study of religion.

Policy refers to an intended course of action. Social policy focusses on government intervention in society to achieve policy ends, such as the form that health care provision takes or the reform of education and training with the needs of the economy in mind. The ends of social policy interventions tend to be steered by a mixture of political party ideological reference points and practical options available for their realisation. The means of social policy delivery are through the passage of legislation and the shaping of institutions.

In theory, sociology, through its understandings of the workings of society, could provide a useful guide to the policy making process, but its findings are frequently ignored by policy makers for reasons that will become apparent throughout this text.

Politics tends to be conventionally viewed in terms of political parties, elections, formal political institutions of government and constitutional issues. Central to politics is therefore the acquisition and use of power and authority through these means. Sociology's interest in politics is to look behind the formal institutions of political processes. It analyses the social origins and distribution of power which is defined in terms of the capacity that some people have to exercise their will over others, providing a more socially rooted view that recognises a political dimension in all social relationships.

The subject area of criminology is to do with the study of offending. It looks at how the institutions of the criminal justice system work. Criminologists study data on crime levels and trends. Through explanations of the causes of criminal behaviour in terms of individual and social influences, its findings, within a particular political climate, can impact on crime policy. Sociology tends to study crime from a more critical perspective. It raises such questions as whose interests the law tends to uphold, how public perceptions of certain types of crime are shaped by the media and the dynamics of how particular groups may become defined as deviant.

Economics is essentially about the creation of value through productive activity and the study of how people act in their capacity as producers, consumers, investors, lenders and borrowers etc. Through the study of forces of supply and demand, it focusses on the materialistic motivations and actions of people within society. There is much dispute within sociology as to the extent to which social behaviour is primarily shaped by economic forces.

A key area of interest to sociologists is an understanding of how societies are changing and what forces are influential in this process. Sociologists may therefore be reliant on historical data. Viewed simplistically, historical data may be regarded as facts about events upon which sociologists can construct theories of social change. We will see later, however, that this view of historical fact is problematic for the sociologist.

These, of course, are academic distinctions. Their phenomena are very much intermixed in the world of social reality.

Sociology is not a pushover

Sociology has often faced image problems. There are those who doubt the academic credentials of the subject and others who dismiss it as merely subversive. It is hoped that in following this and other sociology texts, the reader will agree with the author that sociology is not an academically lightweight discipline at all. Indeed, sociologists face highly complex problems and successful application requires great dexterity of thinking. As for the subversion criticism, if this amounts to a distorted expression of 'encourages critical awareness', then the author would argue that the rephrasing should be taken as a compliment to the capacity of the subject.

To the newcomer, sociology is likely to appear to be a bewildering discipline. Students often initially experience confusion and frustration in trying to get onto the wavelength of the subject. Why is this so? There are a number of reasons. Firstly, it is a discipline of vast magnitude which studies highly complex phenomena by using a broad range of technical concepts that require precise understanding and careful application. This takes time and requires much patience. Secondly, there exists no single indisputably correct theory of society, but rather rival perspectives that require rigorous evaluation in their competition to explain this complex and constantly changing reality.

Developing the ability to move between and compare alternative theories and explanations and use them selectively will therefore be necessary. Thirdly, to pursue the subject effectively requires certain psychological and intellectual qualities. The sociology student must be prepared to suspend and re-examine much that they may have taken for granted about society. This requires the development of mental flexibility and a predisposition of open-mindedness to unexpected findings. The budding sociologist needs to be motivated by a social curiosity to nurture a scepticism regarding common sense outlooks and to be prepared to patiently embark on a long voyage of intellectual discovery.

To clarify, the student new to sociology will bring with them to the subject their everyday knowledge about society through their involvement in family life, friendship groups, the education system, the workplace, exposure to and use of the media etc. Surely, it may be asked, sociology is simply about adopting a more organised approach to what we already know as members of society? Surely, it is common knowledge that the education system offers all children an equal opportunity to prove themselves, that the rich are rich through their capacity for hard work and endeavour and the poor are poor through their inherent laziness, that people's health and longevity is conditioned by their biological makeup, and that we live in a classless society?

These commonly held views of society, and many more, have been investigated by sociologists who have found strong evidence that they are at least highly questionable. It is the task of the sociology student to take a step back and be prepared to question such apparently obvious assumptions about society that are held by many people in their everyday lives. The student must be open-minded to new insights and prepared to make qualitative leaps in thinking based on an assessment of sociological research findings and theoretical reasoning, the outcome of which may fly in the face of widely held common sense knowledge.

The aim of this chapter is to give some idea of the scope and nature of sociology, raise some important implications regarding the subject, and alert the reader to key difficulties and challenges which lay ahead.

The sociological challenge

1. Developing your sociological imagination

American sociologist C Wright Mills first published a work entitled 'The Sociological Imagination' in 1959. He was writing at a time when he believed that rapid social change was leaving people in a state of vague uneasiness whilst also often being devoid of the ability to relate this personal experience to an understanding of the broader social changes that were its origin. For Mills, the risk in this situation was the emergence of a widespread feeling of indifference to public issues, with individuals retreating into a preoccupation with their private worlds and problems.

Whilst the development and application of the physical sciences had accelerated the pace of technological and social change, Mills argued that these subject areas were not equipped to help people to deal with the difficulties of not coping with the resulting experience of disorientation. For Mills, only sociology, undertaken in the right way, could offer the prospect of acquiring an understanding of broader social and historical processes and promote a needed reengagement of people in social policy issues. Central to this approach was the need for a widespread cultivation of the 'sociological imagination'. But what did Mills mean by this term?

Mills viewed the sociological imagination as the development of the capacity to view and understand personal experiences within the broader canvas of society that was undergoing change. This requires individuals to acquire an intellectual dexterity to think in an upward and downward direction between the experiences of their personal world and an understanding of the constraints bearing down on it from the broader social structure.

But what do we mean by the term 'broader social structure'? It can be visualised as a type of social architecture which holds together the actions of individuals into a degree of patterned regularity. Key components of social structures are social roles, rules, the law, institutions and social hierarchies and these are embedded in social cultures, norms and values.

As individuals, we experience personal problems or troubles. Mills argued that people frequently view, blame and seek remedy for their troubles within themselves or people within their immediate social environment. However, the origin of troubles can often be traced to the impact of the broader social structure. This, therefore, is the level at which we can more fruitfully engage our viewpoint and analysis as the basis for informed action and it enables us to represent personal troubles in terms of public issues that require attention.

As Mills (1975, p.22) eloquently put it, the sociological imagination:

'... is a quality of mind that seems most dramatically to promise an understanding of the intimate realities of ourselves in connexion with larger social realities'.

The nurturing of the sociological imagination can thus be both intellectually and practically liberating. Mills' essential ideas are summarised in figures 1 - 3.

Figure 1

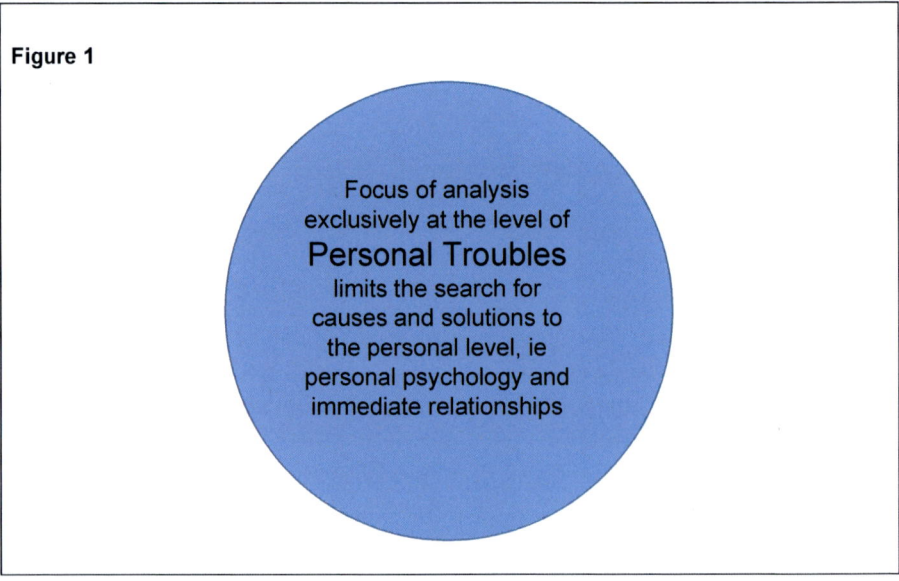

Focus of analysis exclusively at the level of
Personal Troubles
limits the search for causes and solutions to the personal level, ie personal psychology and immediate relationships

Figure 2

Social Structure

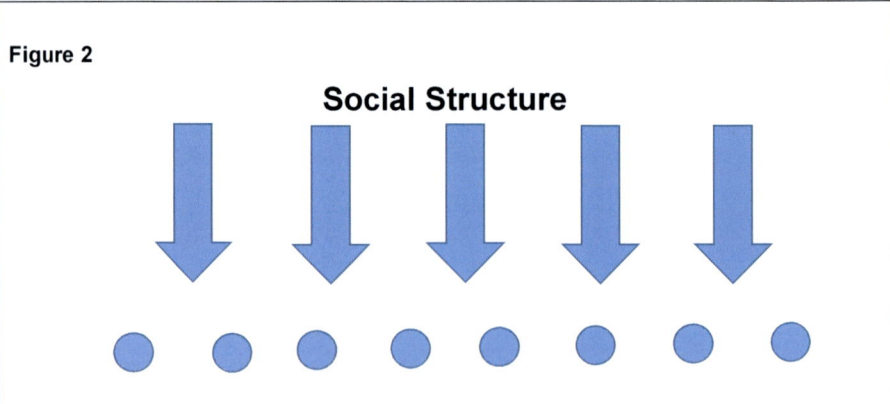

Through the application of the sociological imagination, people can recognise the influence of the broader social structure on their experience of personal troubles.

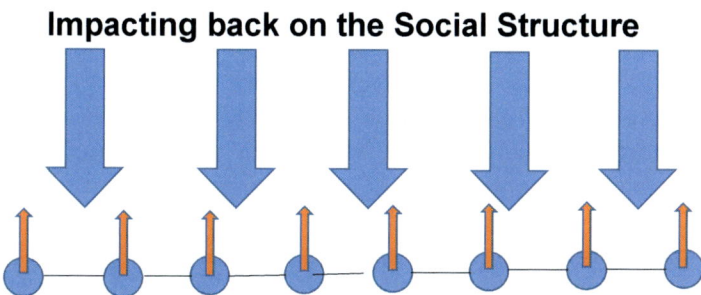

Figure 3

Impacting back on the Social Structure

Using sociological imagination and engaging with others sharing similar personal troubles, these can be raised to the level of public issues. Acting to influence political and social policy decisions that work back down through the social structure can bring about improvements in personal well-being.

How did Mills illustrate the beneficial use of the sociological imagination? The examples that he provided included reference to unemployment, war, marriage and urban life (Mills, 1975, pp.15-17). Here, the author will focus on the personal trouble of unemployment and, through paraphrasing Mills, show how he related this to the sphere of public issues.

Mills provided the example that if in a city of 100,000 people, only one person is unemployed, this is a personal trouble. The focus of solving that trouble would rightly fall on the character of that individual, their skills and the opportunities available to them for gaining employment. If in a nation of 50 million employees 15 million people are unemployed, at one level this is experienced as 15 million personal troubles. However, sociologically, this should be viewed as a public issue and analysed at the level of a social structure within which opportunities for employment have collapsed. The range of solutions then remains within an analysis of society's economic and political institutions, not just the personal characteristics or circumstances of a large number of unemployed individuals. Thus, Mills argues, all the time that the broader economy remains arranged in such a way that economic slumps or recessions occur, the problem of unemployment cannot be solved at the personal level.

So what was Mills' central message? It was that people often individualise their experiences and problems. As such, they tend to look to themselves and known others for blame or remedy, and examine experiences in terms of individual abilities or shortcomings. This may sometimes be an appropriate level of analysis for viewing and tackling problems. However, by itself it is a viewpoint that may also often be misplaced and debilitating. A preoccupation with explaining problems in terms of individual characteristics or the little picture of our immediate environment is likely to blind us to asking more searching questions and raising important social issues. These issues only become evident when we develop the ability to relate immediate experiences to broader social structural influences through having developed our sociological imagination. This is not to deny individuals responsibility for their actions, but to generate insight into the reasonable limits of that responsibility given the broader constraints (which now may be taking an increasingly global dimension) that shape their lives and the options available to them. Analysis may then lead to the practical option of pressing for social reform to improve people's lives.

Taking up Mills' reference to unemployment, one view often encouraged by certain sections of the mass media is that people who are out of work are lazy and become dependent on welfare benefit when they should do more about remedying their personal situation. Indeed, we may know of particular instances where we believe this to be so and individual case studies have been used within the media to try and substantiate the view that this is a very general phenomena. The focus of the problem is then fixed on what is regarded as the moral deficiencies of a large number of individuals who are simplistically labelled as inherently lazy.

Using the sociological imagination raises new vantage points on the problem of unemployment. If individual laziness is essentially at the heart of the problem, the question arises as to why there are so many more inherently lazy people when 3,000,000 people are unemployed than when 1,000,000 people are unemployed? Posing this simple question shifts the focus of attention to recognising the relative powerlessness of individuals in the face of a malfunctioning economy. The broader public issues related to this immense number of personal troubles would then be to do with not just questioning how the economy is run that produces this outcome but also why certain sections of society and the mass media prefer to focus attention at the level of individual shortcomings instead.

To pause and recap, Mills posits that if a large number of people experience similar individual problems, it is likely that the broader social environment is the common originating factor. It is the task of the sociologist to understand the structures and forces that are at work within society and how they penetrate right down to the lives of individuals. Using the sociological imagination for this purpose is both a rational and logical exercise but also requires the capacity for insightful thinking.

Let us examine this a little more carefully with some more examples.

- The collapse or near collapse of a number of financial institutions between 2007 and 2008 (and major threats to the entire global banking system in 2008) can be viewed at the level of a multitude of personal troubles, particularly threats to savings, loss of jobs, loss of homes and delayed retirement. Millions of people in many countries also faced a decline in their standard of living for years afterwards. These mass personal troubles can be traced back to political decisions made during the 1980s in a number of countries to deregulate the financial sector. Deregulation enabled financial institutions to incentivise high risk speculative ventures without the need for sufficient reserves to cover possible losses. The precariousness of the situation became evident when panicking investors rushed to withdraw savings from banks that they feared might go bust, a situation which overstretched the financial cover of many institutions. To avoid a collapse of globally interconnected financial institutions, governments put in place massive financial rescue packages. The resultant disaster of a lengthy recession and severe austerity measures raised public issues regarding the national and global reforms to financial and regulatory structures that need to be instituted in attempts to avoid the possibility of mass personal troubles of this type in the future.

- A common contemporary experience is that of job insecurity. Although directly experienced as a personal trouble by very many individuals, analysing job insecurity sociologically could place it within the very broad context of the forces of highly mobile global capital. To compete for inward capital investment, governments may feel impelled to encourage flexible labour markets. As a consequence, workers can face increasing risk of redundancy, reduced redundancy payment or the uncertainties involved through employment on zero hours contracts. Analysis of job insecurity therefore needs to be framed in terms of the range of policy options open to governments working within the pressures and constraints of global capitalism. It may also raise issues about conditions of employment in other parts of the world and that of ethical trading.

- Staying at home later into life is a personal problem for many young people and their families in the UK. This problem is often not due to lack of personal willingness to live independently but to lack of availability of affordable independent housing options. The public issue here is to identify deficiencies in the housing market that indicate policy reforms necessary to tackle the problem.

- Personal experiences of image anxiety appear to be a growing feature of many contemporary societies. Associated with image anxiety are illnesses such as anorexia and bulimia and there is also evidence of more people resorting to the use of plastic surgery to imitate the looks of celebrities. An examination of the origin of and possible responses to such matters would need to focus on the public issue of the values of consumerist aspirational celebrity culture and the role of mass and social media in their promotion.

- Child carers take varying levels of responsibility for looking after parents and families in need of help. In extreme cases, some take on the burden unassisted by and invisible to the authorities, often through fear of being taken into care if their plight becomes known. The personal troubles that they experience are likely to include lack of leisure opportunities, educational underachievement and blighted future employment prospects. To tackle these personal troubles, issues of deficiencies in the community care support system would need to be raised and remedied.

- There has been a significant increase in the number of youngsters suffering mental health issues in recent years. Responses are mainly focussed at the individual or at best micro social level. Whilst these approaches may help to provide individual coping mechanisms, they avoid the need to look at and address the nature of broader social pressures which the upward trend suggests. As Mills might have put it, when almost a quarter of girls self-harm by the age of 14, yes, we need to improve resources for mental health support, but we need to look at ourselves as a society where mass and social media image has become so important.

There are many other areas in which the experience of personal troubles can be studied within the context of broader social structures and raised in the form of public issues. It would be a valuable exercise for the reader to pause and in pursuing other examples, some of which may relate to their personal experiences, develop their sociological imagination. The purpose of applying sociological thinking to raise public issues for debate is to encourage changes to improve people's lives. However, the political problem regarding possible reforms may be that of tackling vested interests.

2. Making the transition from everyday citizen to sociologist

What does making the transition from the vantage point of the everyday citizen to that of sociologist entail? It essentially requires a person to be prepared to examine their taken for granted assumptions about society and contemplate whole new social panoramas. Accepting a common sense outlook may offer the comfort of familiarity and easy answers, but such a viewpoint can provide illusions which sociology is able to penetrate. Comfort in illusion is the easy option, but in taking this option, we may be unwittingly conspiring against ourselves since sociology can reveal much that the powerful would prefer to remain hidden. The subject can therefore expect no favours from these quarters.

To achieve this critical stance, it is necessary to work toward a mental position of standing back from the very society that a person has been brought up in and feels so familiar with. For the sociologist, the citizen's familiarity with society through their everyday life assumptions may be misleading compared to the findings of academic sociology. For the student initially studying sociology, the experience of stepping back from a taken for granted world may, at least at first, feel disconcerting. But to be an effective sociologist, this step needs to be taken. A key aim of this text is to offer guidance in this process.

Why, then, is everyday knowledge likely to be inadequate for purposes of sociological analysis? There are many reasons. Perhaps the first question to ask is where does the everyday observer of society obtain his or her working knowledge of society from? This knowledge is likely to come from a variety of sources including media information, the opinions and experiences of others that we converse with and our own personal experiences. It may often be adequate for everyday purposes, but would not stand up to the criteria of scrutiny required in academic sociology. Knowledge of society gained in the above ways is likely to be biased, unsystematic, and unrepresentative, and, in the light of sociological scrutiny, the self-evident may turn out to be misleading.

Consider, for example, how one may relate to the tabloid press. The everyday reader may be susceptible to such newspapers shaping what they believe to be important and influencing their opinions and common sense outlook on society. Through their choice of tabloid media, they may be conspirators a process where their outlook is reinforced.

The tabloid press may also be of interest to the sociologist. However, the purpose will be a different one. By stepping back, the sociologist may study how the tabloids attempt to manipulate readers' common sense through the use of stereotypes, emotive language, positioning of articles etc. and raise questions and analyse whose interest this serves. By contrast, governments, not always great supporters of subjects like sociology, may have a vested interest in promoting that everyday citizen activity of restricted common sense thinking on social issues.

Acquiring insights into society by adopting an analytical distance can take various forms. For example, people may develop different insights into cultures that are unlike their own than people who live their everyday lives within those cultures, and this is likely to work both ways. The risk, though, is of simply being judgemental of other cultures from the point of view of one's own – otherwise known as being ethnocentric. This type of distancing does not achieve the degree of open mindedness which is required of the sociologist.

Another type of distancing is historical. This may enable the contemporary observer to look back and recognise in ways that were not obvious to those of former times how, for example, religion was used as a form of social control or that, from a contemporary viewpoint, past political leaders owning slaves and professing allegiance to the view that all men are born equal involves a contradiction.

However, developing insights into past times is fraught with problems. Through the process of socialisation, people internalise an outlook of their times, particularly shaped when they were young and impressionable. As Raymond Williams has pointed out (Barlow, 2009, Ch.20), because society changes all the time, the socialisation of successive generations provides new lenses through which the past is viewed. It is therefore of no surprise that people from different generations may find it difficult literally seeing eye to eye. No generation looking back into the past will be able to capture an identical understanding of the times to that of those who lived during that period. Social change can therefore result in constant reinterpretations of history, which brings the idea of a single correct understanding of the past very much into question.

But sociology is not just an academic exercise. Sociological insight and analysis can be a prerequisite for intelligent intervention to change society through persuasion and action. Consequently, we may at least have some power to influence those who have the power to change society. That being said, sociology does not offer us solutions for the creation of a perfect society. If this was once the aim of some early social theorists, who by the way differed fundamentally in their images of what constituted an ideal society, the disappointments of the twentieth century and the social complexity and relentless change of the contemporary world have curbed such expectations.

However, for those who are dissatisfied with everyday knowledge of society, sociology offers new insights and a more exacting level of analysis to help us formulate broadly considered and academically based views of society. It is the aim of the following chapters to assist the reader in this direction.

Some fundamental implications and guidelines

Sociology is a complex and sometimes illusive subject for the beginner to grasp. A number of important implications and guidelines can be summed up at this point to help provide more substantial guidance for the prospective sociologist:

1. Use theories critically and selectively

The scope and complexity of sociology is massive, ranging from the study of the smallest social environments of friends, families and partners, through to broader communities and right up to the societal and global level. No single all-embracing theory holds a monopoly of understanding, but numerous theories compete for plausibility and demonstrate strengths and weaknesses in different areas. In this text, a number of theoretical perspectives will be reviewed, from those of the founding theorists through to the ideas of more contemporary thinkers.

Using theory can have a liberating effect from the intellectual constraints of conventional wisdom and common sense dogma. A key capacity for a sociologist is to apply theories critically and selectively to develop insights into the workings of society. It is therefore important to remain vigilant that the potential intellectual liberation which theory provides is not itself closed down by one's dogmatic adherence to a particular perspective.

Furthermore, whilst studying sociological theory may assist the budding sociologist in acquiring a more rigorous and analytic view of society, it is important to be aware that theory is shaped by the time and place of the theorist. As society changes, old theory, particularly when viewed through the eyes of a younger generation, can appear to be deficient in the task of explaining contemporary times. One needs to continuously assess what is and what is not salvageable and remain attuned to the emergence of new perspectives.

2. Consider environmental explanations, even when genetic explanations may seem to be obvious

Sociologists challenge the view that our makeup and behaviour is largely the outcome of innate and fixed capacities residing within individuals – the 'nature' argument. Rather, it is primarily viewed as a product of socialisation and the restrictions and opportunities that derive from the social environment – the 'nurture' argument. Consider, for example, evidence which may suggest that levels of intelligence run in families. A simple nature interpretation, once emphasised by psychologists of the eugenics movement such as Francis Galton, is that such evidence is proof that intelligence levels are genetically inherited.

Sociologists, in emphasising nurture explanations, do not deny that people are born with different intellectual capacities and potentials. However, the same evidence on intelligence would be studied more in terms of the influence of the social environment on educational opportunity and the development of individual intellectual potential. Interest would focus on a different type of inheritance – the inheritance of socially structured different 'life chances' that people are born into, affording varying environmental opportunities for nurturing intellectual success, rather than explanations emphasising fixed and genetically transmitted intellectual qualities.

3. Question explanations of behaviour that are put in terms of human nature

We should beware of explanations of behaviour couched in terms of 'human nature'. This term can be, and has been, used as a largely vacuous justification for almost any particular type of behaviour. When behaviour is explained in terms of human nature, it tends to be assumed that the latter is a narrow and fixed innate human capacity, determining certain behaviour as inevitable. However, even a casual survey across societies and history would reveal a very broad and varied range of human behaviour, influenced by different social and cultural contexts. Viewed sociologically, human nature provides a very broad canvas of behavioural potentials, the outcome of which society shapes.

As a single example, to say that it is human nature to be materialistic and individually competitive is to: a) ignore the evidence of cultural diversity as many cultures have at one time or another held more communal and co-operative based values, b) apply a fatalistic attitude to possible alternatives, and c) ignore the key message of sociology that human nature is malleable through socialisation within different social environments. To say that materialism and individual competition are fundamental values of contemporary western capitalist society that we are socialised into and thus strongly influence behaviour is much nearer to the mark. To put this more provocatively, when people's minds become the receptacles of the trash of contemporary advertising and celebrity culture, the sociological question is not what is human nature but what have we become by the type of society that we (and who are the we here?) have created.

Although we are biological beings, our actions are not, as in the case of animals, narrowly determined by our biology. Although we have instincts, our actions are not just instinctive. And although we may refer to our human nature, this provides a propensity for a very broad range of action. Our action is largely the outcome of a mixture of constraints and influences from our social environment and individual reflection on potential courses of action.

4. Think about life profiles as related to socially structured life chances and opportunities

As individuals, sociologists or otherwise, we may occasionally reflect on the profile that our lives have taken. Perhaps they could have gone, to some extent, in one direction or another based on circumstances and decisions taken at different points in time. How can we best analyse this? The major influences on our lives are likely to include a mixture of individual abilities, chance circumstances and social environment.

Sociologists do not deny that to some extent our path in life may be influenced by our innate makeup, for example in the form of personality characteristics and physical and intellectual capacity. Without ability, a person cannot become a university professor. Further, a mixture of chance encounters, lucky decisions and the ability to take advantage of situations can be important factors in the way that our lives unfold. Indeed, the idea of chance or luck may itself act as a motivating factor, keeping dreams alive of winning a fortune in such competitions as the National Lottery in the face of otherwise limited or bleak life alternatives that many people face. In this case, chance is random and, per unit expended, the entrants all face equal and extremely thin odds of winning a fortune.

However, chance and luck are clearly not equally distributed in society. Lottery type luck finishes at or before birth. Sociologists emphasise that from birth our individual life course is powerfully influenced by the social environment. It can shape our personality and nurture or impede the development of our intellectual capacity. The types of inequality that the social structure imposes, particularly but not exclusively economic, can influence the type of education that we may have access to, the type of people that we are likely to associate with and the chances of living a healthy, rewarding and successful life. These chances are socially loaded in favour of some and against others through the effects of socially structured inequalities. This reality is expressed in sociology by the concept of life chances – socially structured differences in, for example, material and cultural resources within the backgrounds that people are born into and grow up in and which continue to influence the opportunities that they are likely to have access to.

A key area of debate within sociology is the extent to which individuals can overcome unfavourable circumstances of the social environment that they have been brought up in. To put it another way, how strong is the influence of these life chances in determining our opportunities and course of life or to what extent are we alternatively able to create our own life chances, opportunities and outcomes, by, for example, overcoming disadvantage through individual ability and determined action? And, very important to reflect upon sociologically, which institutions may enhance or impede this process?

People sometimes view their life experiences in terms of fate. Bound up with belief in fate is often the idea that society is an impenetrable mystery and even that there are mysterious forces at work that we cannot understand but should resign ourselves to. In any society where people experience restricted opportunities, belief in fate can provide consolation; our fortune is in the lap of the gods. But such an outlook is likely to be debilitating. One of the tasks of sociology is to reveal through analysis the degree to which societies, including the one that we live in, offer equality of opportunity for individual achievement, whatever is claimed by politicians or believed by the public.

5. Stand back and be prepared to question society's and your own common sense views

As members of society, our everyday worlds comprise our outlooks based on the social influences and experiences that we have been exposed to. However, given the diversity of societies and cultures that exist throughout the world, as well as groups within our own society, it is clear that our world view is only one of many. Difficult as the socialisation process implies that it may be, we must make every effort to suspend what we take for granted about people and society if we are to attempt to understand this diversity in an open minded way and become effective sociologists.

This issue can be related to the problem of ethnocentricity. Being ethnocentric is taking the dominant world view of one's society as by definition a superior starting point against which different societies can be judged. As Anthony Giddens has argued, through an awareness of cultural diversity demonstrated by anthropologists, 'the exercise of the sociological imagination makes it possible to break free from the straightjacket of thinking only in terms of the type of society we know in the here and now' (Giddens, 1982, p.26).

6. Think of 'causality' appropriately

How is the issue of causality addressed in sociology? If one is to apply the term causality to the study of society, it needs to be used in a less hard sense than in the physical sciences. Sociologists look for patterns in behaviour which point to underlying social influences, but we must remember that these influences are complex and that individuals often act through reflection rather than stimulus and response. For example, it may be demonstrated that people in different positions within the social structure tend to have different voting preferences. This of course does not mean that there is an absolute causal effect impelling all people occupying a similar position in the social structure to vote the same way. Evidence from studies of voting behaviour shows that this is clearly not the case. However, it also shows that, compared to those in the higher professions, there is frequently a greater tendency for people employed in lower level occupations to vote for political parties of the left. In this case, the task for sociologists is to identify an often complex range of social influences which result in such patterns of voting behaviour as well as the voting behaviour of those who do not follow the dominant pattern.

In conclusion

Sociology is not likely to appeal to those who fear stepping outside of conventional wisdom, who place a mental block on ways of thinking that they are unfamiliar with, or who find it difficult to relate personal experiences to a far larger social canvas. It will not appeal to those who expect to find singularly right or wrong answers to the questions that it raises.

The purpose of this text is to encourage the reader to make a transition in thinking about society from that of the common sense and often restricted thinking of the everyday citizen to that of the more sophisticated and analytical approach of a sociologist. This may not be a simple task. It is not uncommon for newcomers to the subject to find the early stages of their studies to be disorientating. The subject seems to fall into place for different people at different stages. In anticipation of these early difficulties, the reader is alerted to the need for patient commitment to this subject.

Chapter 2
Sociology: Society and the Individual

Abstract

In this chapter, a distinction between human and animal behaviour is made which emphasises both the human capacity for independent action and the need for social constraint. A definition is provided of the meaning and purpose of concepts and a number of key sociological concepts — socialisation, culture and subculture, values, norms, moral pressures, roles, institutions and the law - are introduced which explain the makeup of the social fabric. It is through this social fabric that the forces of social constraint bear down on the actions of individuals and make patterned social order possible. This particular emphasis is pointed out as a predominant feature of the functionalist perspective and taken up in the next chapter.

However, it is emphasised that social structures are not static. Moral values change over time and individuals, often through collective social action, challenge social structures. This chapter concludes that in fact there exists a two way relationship between the individual and society in the formation of each other, locating purposeful individual action within the context of social constraint; an emphasis which will be shown in the following chapter to be more closely aligned to Weber's social action theory.

The meaning of concepts

All academic subjects have their own concepts. A concept is an abstract idea, the purpose of which is to offer ways of conceiving reality. Concepts help us to make sense of reality, structure our observations, communicate our understanding with others and assist our analysis. The purpose of the next section is to introduce a number of concepts that assist in conveying an understanding of the way in which society is structured and the behaviour of its constituent individuals patterned and, to some extent, controlled.

A number of sociological concepts such as socialisation, culture and role will be introduced. The reader should also be aware, however, and will see later, that as sociological concepts need to correspond as closely as possible to reality, new ones may need to be devised as society changes. Indeed, some of the concepts and theoretical foundations upon which the subject was developed have increasingly come into question as being inadequate for the task of understanding contemporary times and sociologists are struggling to develop improved alternatives.

Society as constraint and control – introductory concepts

Human behaviour is sometimes compared to animal behaviour to justify it as somehow 'natural'. Clearly, the problem here is that any behaviour from the diversity available in the natural world can be selected for this purpose, providing justifications to back up almost any type of human behaviour. An important starting point for the sociologist is the realisation that instinctive pre-programming of behaviour constitutes an extremely small element of the human condition compared to that of animals and that our capacity for learning is much superior. Nature locks the range of animal behaviour into narrow channels. This behaviour is highly stimulus and response based and the capacity for passing on any learning is very limited.

By contrast, humans are able to engage in abstract thinking and symbolic communication, making sophisticated understanding and communication in the form of written and spoken language possible, along with the passage of learning on to successive generations to build on. Throughout the world, as humans we have developed a diversity of social and cultural environments, belief systems and institutions in response to problems encountered. Within these environments, we are able to contemplate the consequences of our own and others' actions, consider and weigh up options available and engage in conscious decision making. Human capacities thus 1) liberate our behaviour from the narrow constraints of the animal world and enable choice of action. But 2) as individual behaviour is largely not predisposed into narrow channels by the constraints of instinct, something else must be responsible for co-operative co-existence to be possible. This realm is the subject matter for sociology in the understanding of human action – it is 'society'.

As individuals, we are born into pre-existing society. As we awaken to society, we encounter an environment which we tune into through our senses and adjust to through our experience of the responses of others. In so doing, we learn and internalise features of this environment and respond to it. The extent to which the individual engages in a relatively active or passive relationship with the social environment has been much debated within sociology and this capacity will vary from individual to individual. However, sociologists emphasise that socialisation – the influence on individual consciousness and identity of culture, social values, norms, social roles, moral pressures and laws etc. - will be profound during our early years (referred to at this stage in life as primary socialisation) and accompany us throughout our lives. Let us briefly define some established sociological concepts which comprise the mainstays of the social environment.

The term culture, as used in sociology, has a rather different meaning from the judgement of sophistication with which it is more commonly associated. In sociology, culture refers to the beliefs and values that make up a common way of life. It becomes internalised through our capacity to learn the meaning of sounds, gestures and symbols in the form of language. Culture also includes commonly recognised ceremonies, dress, rituals, traditions and artefacts which may substantially pre-date the lives of individuals in any contemporary society. It may be bound up with belief systems about the supernatural which we refer to as religion. Whilst socialisation into culture is a universal feature of human life, there is much diversity of culture between societies. However, through socialisation, at a general level individuals tend to take their own culture as their universal reference point.

The term subculture has been used to refer to social groups who share a set of values which are distinct from and may be in opposition to the values of the dominant or mainstream culture. For example, dominant social values in contemporary western societies emphasise the importance of individual application and material success. In the context of school culture, when embraced, these values promote academic application and striving for exam success. However, sociological research has shown that subcultures have emerged within schools (sometimes referred to as counter cultures) which hold academic success in disdain and powerfully influence deviant behaviour, often leading to poor academic performance of group members.

Cultural diversity refers more to the degree of co-existence within a society of different cultural groups, usually distinguished by their own religious and ethnic cultural traditions. There is strong evidence that through migration contemporary western societies are becoming internally more culturally diverse. This growing diversity can on the one hand enhance tolerance and social harmony between cultural communities or on the other promote intolerance and conflict.

Social values are a part of culture. They relate to belief systems which offer general guidelines by which action is judged as desirable or undesirable. Despite their frequent multi-cultural diversity, societies tend to have dominant overarching value systems. For example, contemporary western societies value highly opportunities for individual achievement based on personal merit. A society which operates in accordance with these values is referred to as a 'meritocracy'. Evidence, however, may indicate that institutions and action which depart from dominant values are quite widespread. Regarding meritocratic values, some sociologists point to significant disparities between these values and what happens 'on the ground', particularly in the spheres of educational and occupational opportunity and achievement, where it appears that some people have far greater opportunities than others with little reference to individual merit. In sociology, social values which provide a systematic distortion of reality are referred to as ideology, the main purpose of which is social control.

Norms relate to values but provide more clearly defined expectations of behaviour in regard to conventions. They specify what is deemed to be normal and acceptable within society. Thus, norms regarding family life in Britain in the 1950s emphasised a uniform model of a married male and female partnership for the upbringing of children, with primary financial support provided by the male breadwinner and domestic chores and childrearing the responsibility of the housewife. These norms were powerfully supported by moral pressures upholding separate and clearly defined male and female roles, stigmatising cohabitation, illegitimacy and divorce, and imposing sanctions against offenders. Norms of contemporary household life indicate the acceptability of much greater diversity of lifestyle and arguably reflect a liberalisation of social and moral values associated with a more tolerant society.

In a formal sense, social roles are social niches which specify to individuals who occupy them standard expectations and constraints on their action vis-à-vis the actions of the occupants of other roles. This type of role relationship through which the interaction of individuals is structured is referred to as role reciprocity. The relationships between people in different roles, such as doctor and patient, when mutual expectations are shared, integrates the action of the participants. Task orientated role relationships, such as between managers and workers within the workplace, may be set within highly formalised and hierarchical organisational power structures, in which entitlements and responsibilities of participants are prescribed by job descriptions and backed up by legally binding contractual obligations. These relationships may also be set within a broader social power structure. By contrast, leisure roles, such as between a host and visitors at a dinner party, are likely to be much more informal, but could include subtle expectations regarding etiquette.

Individuals live their lives within externally imposed social roles. As Peter Berger explained

'A role, then, may be defined as a typified response to a typified expectation. Society has predefined the fundamental typology. To use the language of the theatre, from which the concept of role is derived, we can say that society provides the script for all the dramatis personae. The individual actors, therefore, need but slip into the roles already assigned to them before the curtain goes up. As long as they play their roles as provided for in this script, the social play can proceed as planned' (Berger,1974, p.112).

This conformity may be superficial though, perhaps out of perceived necessity. Furthermore, through the roles they occupy, individuals may engage in image manipulation to influence others. However, Berger goes on to show that by acting out roles, these roles come to enter the internal constitution of the individual.

'Roles carry with them both certain actions and the emotions and attitudes that belong to these actions. The professor putting on an act that pretends to wisdom comes to feel wise. The preacher finds himself believing what he preaches. The soldier discovers martial stirrings in his breast as he puts on his uniform' (Berger, 1974, p.113).

The characteristics of social roles, which exist external to the individual, become to some extent internalised through the process of acting them out.

Overall, each individual will occupy many roles, which engage them in a variety of social relationships, each comprising reciprocal expectations between themselves and others. Therefore, within some situations, individuals may face conflicting role requirements, such as the expectations associated with the role of employee and wife, which can be difficult to resolve. Key roles, such as those linked to domestic and work life, were relatively fixed for individuals in the post war decades. Now, arguably, society is more rapidly changing and people have to develop the skills to navigate their way through many role changes throughout their lives.

Institutions also structure social action. They may take the form of formal organisations which can prescribe the roles of participants and impose rules and regulations through authority structures, whilst sometimes being themselves controlled by oversight from external regulatory apparatuses. At one extreme are institutions within which, through choice or compulsion, individuals find their lives confined. These would include psychiatric hospitals, prisons, monasteries and boarding schools. Such institutions are referred to as 'total institutions' within which the capacity for control over the individual can be extreme, at times even leading to very serious cases of personal abuse. Other formal institutions would include educational establishments (excluding the above) and various workplaces. However, institutions can govern behaviour in a broader sense when they uphold traditions, such as 'the institution of marriage'.

The law formalises sanctions and imposes controls which tend to uphold dominant social and moral values and norms, but in a codified form. Changes in the law often synchronise with parallel changes in social norms and values. For example, in Britain and many western societies, a liberalisation of norms and values regarding family life has been accompanied by a liberalisation of divorce laws and more liberal sexual morals has led to changes in the law whereby homosexuality ceased to be a crime and, more recently, same sex civil partnerships and marriage have become possible through legislative change. The enactment of legislation and regulatory reform can also be partly fuelled by a response of moral outrage to the infringement of social norms and values, as in the case of public response to the reckless behaviour behind the banking crisis of 2008 and its subsequent economic consequences.

Individual compliance with behavioural constraints may not always be embraced but sometimes pursued, even grudgingly, out of practical necessity. Thus, the need to work to obtain an income is for many a necessity so that bills can be paid to provide at least food, shelter and a degree of comfort as well as acquiring a standard of living and quality of life that we (are encouraged to) aspire to. To some extent, the need for this type of compliance may be born out of our inability to extract ourselves from being victims of enticed material aspiration in which the mass media may have a powerful controlling effect.

The above mainstays structure the actions of individuals within society. The degree to which they are synchronised with each other provides a framework of consistency that orders the behaviour of individuals. We have now reached the position where the problem is not that of explaining how social action is ordered, but explaining levels of individual freedom, choice of action and diversity, as well as conflict and disorder encountered in contemporary societies. We will later see that emphasising the importance and explaining the basis of social order or conflict in society was a fundamental dimension of dispute between the different founding theoretical perspectives of functionalism and Marxism respectively.

Society, social structure and individual action

That society is possible at all is based on human capacity for intelligent communication, co-operation and organisation. Social groupings and societies emerge from the capacities of humans living in aggregates. Once formed, society reacts back on its participants through developing structure and providing an environment of constraints and opportunities. We have identified above some of the social influences and constraints that shape the actions of many individuals. These influences exist externally to individuals. Customs, moral values, institutions and laws etc. exist outside of individuals in the sense that they predate our existence, will continue to operate long after we are gone, and for most of us, whether we were ever here or not will make little overall difference to them. We are swept along by them, often unaware of their influences because we live in a social world where we take much for granted. These external social influences are internalised through the process of socialisation.

However, it would be far too strong to say that social structures and processes precisely 'determine' the behaviour of individuals. Although society has structure and structure shapes action, it does not just call forth socially regulated responses from individuals in some mechanical type fashion. If it did so, the effect of society on humans would be much like that of nature in animals. By contrast to animals, the human condition includes the capacity for reflection, attribution of meaning and symbolic communication and conscious decision making which enable in individuals a degree of free thought and independent action. Viewed sociologically, the action of individuals is the outcome of a delicate and shifting balance between the effects of social constraints and the capacity for individual choice. The effect of an element of free choice by an individual on society as a whole is usually infinitesimal, but multitudinous effects of individual choices, especially when acting with a common purpose, can react back into society which will change as a consequence.

Society can be viewed in terms of its constraints and structures, but a rebalancing of outlook is now required. These should be seen as the medium within which purposive individual actions takes place. For example, institutional structures, such as those through which healthcare and education are delivered, whilst regulating the behaviour of professionals and clients, are designed and changed through human agency. Moreover, individuals and groups resist social pressures, break rules and the law and engage in protest movements, legal or illegal. Not all social guidelines and constraints are clear and unambiguous and different individuals may make different interpretations of them. And as society undergoes change, the guidelines of expected behaviour may become confusing.

The operation of the free market provides a good example of the precarious balance between social constraints and purposive action. The free market encourages active entrepreneurship and innovation but within the constraints of legitimate action, ultimately backed up by the forces of law and order. Yet these very values of free enterprise and the competitive drive for profit can lead to actions of dubious business legitimacy or moral ethicality and law breaking activity.

And so on to sociological theory

Sociological theorists differ substantially in terms of the extent to which they view society as a formation that bears down on individuals and structures their actions or as built up from the actions of purposive individuals. As we shall see in the next chapter, Emile Durkheim adopted a structural functionalist position which regarded society as a powerful external force that constrained the actions of individuals for the collective well-being.

Karl Marx also adopted a structuralist position. However, in his case the structuring of society was heavily influenced by inequalities of wealth and power which constituted the basis for socially structured conflict between social classes. Each of these theoretical perspectives have been criticised for underrepresenting the extent to which society is also the product of more free and intentional action of individuals. Max Weber, in adopting a social action approach, arguably attempted to theorise a more nuanced balance between the impact of social structure and the input of individual action, a quest which we will see was later taken up by Anthony Giddens in his structuration theory approach.

Chapter 3
Sociological Perspectives

Abstract

This chapter explains what is meant by sociological concepts and theories and introduces the reader to some founding theoretical perspectives in sociology. It does not attempt a critical evaluation of these theories, but rather locates them as responses to the challenge of radical social transformations which were taking place from the late eighteenth century.

The founding perspectives provide an underpinning to sociology as it emerged in the context of nineteenth century modernisation. 'Modern' sociological theory is thus explained to date from this period. Other key concepts relevant to this phase of theory construction are identified and explained.

Some key features of French and English of modernisation, in terms of the French and Industrial Revolutions respectively, are sketched to provide a contextual background to pioneering attempts to develop sociological theory. The early theoretical responses to the process of modernisation – St.Simon's and Comte's positivism, Spencer's evolutionism, and Marxism being included here – are presented as attempts to provide an understanding of a much changed social environment to that of traditional society by offering rational and scientific explanations of social change. It is shown that each of these theoretical approaches claimed that society operated in terms of social scientific laws and that understanding of these laws would explain the transition from traditional to modern society as well as anticipate the features of the type of society that would emerge in the future. The author further suggests that these theorists used the appeal of science to justify the inevitability of their own future social utopias.

For those interested in studying the above theorists in a little more detail, the author has included an extension chapter at the end of this text.

The key characteristics of functionalist theory are introduced with reference to the ideas of Emile Durkheim. Growing out of the French positivist tradition, this perspective retains faith in the possibility of social scientific intervention to improve society through 'social engineering'.

Weber's social action theory is presented as a perspective which emphasises the importance of understanding behaviour at the micro (small scale) level as well as the macro (large scale) level. The author shows Weber to be critical of various aspects of the pioneering approaches. Weber attempted to counter what he felt to be an overemphasis on explaining society in terms of economic factors (Marxism) and an inappropriate application of science to study social life (positivism). Social action theory paves the way for a more 'subjective' approach to sociology by emphasising that a full understanding of action must take the perceptions of actors into account.

The perspectives of Spencer, Marx and Weber are briefly taken up as broad frameworks to see what light they might shed on a more contemporary issue - the financial and economic crises following 2007.

Micro orientated theoretical perspectives with a subjective emphasis are taken up next. One such approach that is introduced is symbolic interactionism. This perspective originated through the works of Mead, relatively independently from the influence of Weber's social action theory. From this perspective, the distinguishing feature of social life is the human capacity to communicate meaning through the use of symbols and the author picks up on the important insight of the shaping of self-identity through social interaction with others.

An introduction to phenomenology and ethnomethodology is included. These perspectives offer a radical challenge to the assumption of conventional sociology that society is a structure in its own right which exists external to individuals and can be understood scientifically. They argue that a sense of social order is actively constructed by people in their everyday life engagements and that sociology should focus solely on how this is achieved.

A multiple choice exercise with answers is provided to give the reader an opportunity to assess their recollection of the main features of the perspectives introduced in the chapter and to backtrack over any areas of uncertainty. This is followed up by the introduction of a key theme that preoccupied the thinking of a number of founding sociological theorists – the view that the constitution of society in the modern capitalist unban world of the west had brought with it a sense of the loss of community.

The author reiterates that the main purpose of sociological theory is to act as a guide in the insightful understanding of society. It is therefore important to remember that developing sociological understanding should remain a live activity in which theories act as touchstones but not as fixed and final explanations. Indeed, the idea of the need to rejuvenate the subject as a result of far reaching changes in contemporary society is introduced. Postmodern and high modern perspectives, to be reviewed in more detail throughout the text, are identified as contemporary responses.

The sociological challenge

One of the difficulties frequently experienced by the newcomer to sociology is an unfamiliarity with the concepts used in the subject and the level of abstraction that they will need to work at. Having taken the initial step of standing back and questioning the picture of society seen through the everyday citizen lens, the next step involves the patient acquisition of a familiarity with new concepts, theories and perspectives that abound within the discipline. In time, it should become appreciated that compared to the insights generated by sociological thinking, non-sociologists come to appear to be either in a state of sleepy acceptance or if critical of society ill-equipped to develop penetrating insights and analyses of society and social issues.

However, sociology does not provide a single infallible alternative viewpoint. Instead, it offers various theoretical perspectives. Theories are made up of logically interconnected concepts. A concept is an abstract idea which stands for something in the real world. For example, in sociology, social class and political power are concepts which explain social layering (stratification) and the capacity to influence respectively in the real world.

Concepts are combined in sociological theories which can be tested through the findings of research. A theoretical perspective is broader than a theory. Perspectives offer different vantage points from which to view society and they act as interpretive and filtering devices through which to see and understand society. The plurality of competing theoretical perspectives reflects the near infinite complexity of society which can be plausibly represented in many different ways. Theories and perspectives are also likely to relate to the different values and vantage points of the theorists who develop them.

The process of utilising different theoretical perspectives can be likened to that of trying on different pairs of glasses, each of which equips the wearer with an alternative view of society. Each perspective, through its interconnected concepts, offers a filter through which the observer is equipped with a simplified view of society. Each simplified view offers its own patterned understanding. It is through working with a number of sociological perspectives that new windows of awakening on society can be developed and the transition from everyday citizen vantage point to sociologist made.

The aim of this chapter is to outline a number of sociological perspectives, whilst alerting the reader that they should ultimately be applied reflectively, selectively and critically rather than acting as straight-jackets to thinking.

Definition of main concepts

In anticipation of the challenges that the theoretical perspectives covered in this chapter are likely to pose, particularly to the newcomer to the subject, a clarification of some key constituent concepts will first be undertaken.

The term **feudalism** is used to characterise the key features typical to many societies that existed long prior to industrialisation. Within such societies, agriculture was the main form of production and the majority of the population lived in small communities located in the countryside. Life for the majority was very harsh and governed by the routines of the seasons, customs and religion. Privileged noble elites dominated the social hierarchy, their power deriving from the inheritance and acquisition of land and noble title, the ability to raise militia and support from the established religious authorities. The height of feudalism in most European societies is recognised to be around the twelfth to thirteenth centuries and societies have existed in similar form in other parts of the world.

Modern industrial society was the result of the application of science and technology to the process of mechanised mass production which replaced agriculture and craft work as the main form of employment. Associated with the rise of industrial societies was an exodus of people from rural communities and into rapidly expanding urban centres – a process referred to as **urbanisation**.

Capitalism refers to a form of industrial (and now arguably post-industrial) society within which productive enterprise is privately owned and the economy is geared to a large extent around the competitive quest for profit within free markets.

Two central concepts that were embedded in the works of early theorists were those of **progress** and **evolution**. The concept of progress refers to some measure of social betterment, but theorists often profoundly disagreed on how they viewed and defined betterment. The concept of evolution is closely related to that of progress, and the two can easily be confused. Strictly speaking, evolution is a process of change in the form of growth whereby an inner potential unfolds over time.

Both of these concepts are suggestive of social dynamism and early theorists were keen to identify the forces that drove social change. In their search, they tended to adopt a positivist view that in a scientific sense it was possible to identify the laws or mechanics of social change. In searching for laws of change, some theorists (especially Saint Simon and Comte) adopted an idealist stance. Here, theorists give priority to belief systems in explaining the social order and as the driving force of social change.

By contrast, from a **materialist** position (as particularly in the works of Marx) the structuring of society and driving force for change is seen to be located in the economy. Within this context, the term **economic determinism** emphasises that social relationships are determined by economic factors.

Other key concepts that are located within the Marxist perspective include the following. The **means of production** are the combined technological and human means by which economic production takes place, whereas the **relations of production** are the broader social relationships, in the form of opposing social classes, that have their origin in work relationships. Under capitalism, Marx referred to these opposing classes as the **bourgeoisie**, who own the productive technology and are hence the capitalist class, and the **proletariat**, a **working class** who sell their labour for wages in employment to the bourgeoisie.

Through the productive process, value is created. From the Marxist perspective, **surplus value** is a measure of the value created, as established by the price at which goods are sold, which is not returned to workers but is extracted by capitalists as profit. The extraction of profit takes the form of **exploitation** of workers when they are not apportioned their rightful share of the surplus value created by their labour input. For Marx, it is around the allocation of value between capitalists and workers that class conflict has its origin.

The concept of **alienation** refers to an absence of fulfilment and experience of estrangement. For Marx, alienation is endemic to capitalism which is a system that imposes a form of workplace discipline that reduces the worker to the condition of an object of other's profit.

Ideology, from a Marxist perspective, refers to a systematically distorted image of reality. The consequence of ideology, a phenomena natural to capitalist societies, is to hide an underlying reality of injustice from view so that a subject class gains a **false consciousness** of their situation as fair and acceptable.

Functionalist theory in particular makes use of a **biological analogy**, the purpose of which is to improve the understanding of society by comparing it to a biological entity. As the analogy suggests, functionalism is a **holistic** perspective, meaning that understanding the way that any part of the social system works must always be framed within an overview of society as a whole.

The term **anomie** was used by Durkheim to identify an ailment of the modern condition which he argued takes the form of a dangerous slackening of moral guidelines and norms that can leave individuals in a state of aimlessness.

Weber used the term **rationalisation** to identify an advance in the culture rational thinking which he closely related to the emergence of modern western capitalism. The organisational accompaniment of rationalisation was a process of **bureaucratisation**, the expansion and spread of formal organisational hierarchies as the means to most efficiently put rational plans into practice. For Weber, the consequence of these developments was an experience of **disenchantment** – from the scientific understanding of, systematic dominance over and extraction of life from nature and into man made institutions and routines, life loses its charming mysteries.

For phenomenologists, the quest for **ontological security** refers to the human need to construct stable meaning systems through which sense can be imposed on an otherwise meaningless world.

Modernisation as the context for founding social theory

Before reviewing a number of the major founding perspectives of sociology, it is important to pause and consider the social context of their origin which made the quest for a new understanding of society so necessary.

The major perspectives comprising the early theoretical foundations of sociology were developed during the nineteenth and early twentieth centuries. The impulse for social theorising came from rapid and far-reaching social, political and industrial change, which, related to the advance of rational and scientific thinking, was challenging the traditions and religious outlooks upon which the old social order had been based. The idea of social progress – the belief in ongoing betterment, accompanied by optimism in its continuation into the future – was taking root.

In France, eighteenth century Enlightenment thinkers applied rational scrutiny to traditional ideas and institutions. This helped to undermine the legitimacy of the remnants of an old feudal order of fixed social ranks, privileges and duties and contributed toward the dramatic events of the Revolution of 1789. The revolutionary values of liberty, equality and fraternity were now associated with the idea of progress toward a new type of society where reason would prevail at the expense of religion. However, liberation from the old social constraints brought protracted social and political turmoil and instability.

In England, Enlightenment thinking focussed more on economic matters, explaining how the advance of science and technology would be applied to new ways of working and producing goods for a free market. New machinery and sources of power were introducing new types of work specialization and early mass production. In concentrating workers in ever larger numbers in factories, these changes were setting in motion large scale rural to urban migration and the unprecedented growth of towns and cities. England's late eighteenth century revolution was an industrial one but the changes were also very much social. In promoting urbanisation and the factory system, it undermined the ways and traditions of rural life and enhanced the wealth and power of factory owners.

Throughout the nineteenth century, advances in science – especially geological – were increasingly throwing the literal interpretation of creation derived from the Bible into question. Fatalistic religious attitudes toward illness were being challenged within learned circles as medical science grappled to eradicate contagious diseases which ravaged populations living in overcrowded and squalid urban environments.

During the nineteenth century, these forces of modernisation were bringing about a new type of society in which the power and values of the old landed elite were being challenged by the growing power of industrialists. A common viewpoint of the latter was that power in the new order should be based on economic wealth derived from industriousness rather than from inherited privilege. But the new society was also spawning a mass urban working class and generating problems of mass poverty, disease, social polarisation, economic destabilisation, and social unrest. How could these problems be addressed? As science and rational thinking were at the centre of progress, it was reasonable to be optimistic that science and rational thinking should have the capacity to tackle the problems that progress had brought.

In such modernising societies, there had emerged a context of both belief in and need for the capacity of 'man' to rationally understand and control the conditions of modernisation. The term 'modern' sociological theory is thus used to refer back to theory originating in this context and those who still retain faith in its quest. Unlike their more common everyday use, modern sociological theory and modern society are not usually used in sociology as synonymous with 'contemporary'. Indeed, some theorists believe that the most advanced contemporary societies have more recently undergone changes every bit as profound as those associated with the earlier revolutions and are entering a 'postmodern' era for which a new postmodern approach to social theory is necessary.

Founding social theorists: scientific laws of social change toward utopian futures

By the early nineteenth century, social theorists were struggling to understand the nature and causes of the social and intellectual conditions of change touched on above. Given the protracted upheaval of the French Revolution, was a return to the past possible or desirable? Could past levels of social order be re-established? How could we know what form a society of the future might take? Some key ideas of two French pioneers in the history of sociology who attempted to answer such questions, Henri Saint Simon and Auguste Comte, will be sketched shortly.

The works of these pioneering social theorists often took the form of social philosophy rather than sociology. Their theoretical schemes were very broad ranging and not grounded in their own empirical research. All of this can make the understanding of their schemes quite challenging.

A common theme of these theorists was the belief that society operated in a causal way and was thus amenable to scientific understanding. This faith in science led these founding theorists to gaze back through history in an attempt to extract laws of social change which they believed explained the durability and eventual collapse of the old feudal order, elucidated the problems of the new emerging society, provided a compass bearing for the transition to a future stable society, and would assist in guiding social reconstruction through rational intervention that went with the natural grain of progress. Their ideas began to establish some of the important themes of what in sociology would become the functionalist perspective.

The belief that scientific laws of social change could be revealed and provide certainty of future social stability may have been very appealing during times of social instability. However, pioneering theorists often held utopian images of their ideal future societies. These acted as frames of reference against which social change could be judged as progressive (or otherwise). It could therefore be argued that each of these early theorists utilised the idea of social laws in such a way as to show that progressive social change would impel society toward their own ideally visualised future.

Although they claimed scientific credentials, it may be suspected that to some extent their personally desired societies of the future shaped their reading of history and that laws of change were enlisted to demonstrate the future certainty of their social utopias. In this sense, it is informative to contrast the future societies envisaged by Comte, Spencer and Marx, their contrasting evaluations of what constitutes progress, and the forces of change that each believed would bring their ideal society about. Some of the key points are sketched in table 1 on utopianists and elaborated in the text.

Table 1	Utopianists		
Social Theorist	Auguste Comte 1798-1857	Herbert Spencer 1820-1903	Karl Marx 1818-1883
Family Background	Catholic family background. Father orderly government official	Family of religious nonconformists who questioned social conventions	Father Jewish lawyer and influenced by Enlightenment thinkers
Social Context of Works	Social instability in the wake of the French Revolution during the late eighteenth and early nineteenth centuries	The achievements of free enterprise capitalism in mid nineteenth century England following the Industrial Revolution	The ravages of free enterprise capitalism in mid nineteenth century England following the Industrial Revolution
Features of Utopian Future	Positivist society – interventionist form of capitalist industrial society regulated by social scientific technicians	Non-interventionist free enterprise, free trade capitalist industrial society, harmonised through enlightened individualism	Communist industrial society in which the means of production are commonly owned and co-operation replaces class conflict
Forces of Social Change	Intellectual progress determines social progress through law of three stages and the hierarchy of the sciences	Social and moral evolution follows the same formula as evolution throughout the rest of the natural world	Economic relations determine social relations. Economic based class conflict drives social progress

Early positivism: the problem of re-establishing social order

In its simplest form, the term 'positivism' refers to the view that social phenomena operate according to laws which can be discovered through a rational and scientific study of society. This positivist quest gained impetus in French social thinking during the decades following the French Revolution of 1789. This section will touch on the ideas of two French theorists of this period – Henri Saint Simon and Auguste Comte – whose mission was to uncover laws of social change. The practical social purpose of this quest was to rationally guide the process of social rebuilding and reorganisation following the socially destructive effects of the Revolution.

A pioneering response was provided in the early 1800s by Henri Saint Simon. For Saint Simon, the condition of belief systems has a powerful effect on the condition of society. During feudal times, Catholic religious dogma provided potent support for a rigid social hierarchy within which people knew their place. However, belief systems change. When the religious Reformation and the advance of science came to challenge medieval religious dogma, they eroded the belief system which had propped up the feudal social structure and the power of the nobility. This process eventually culminated in the collapse of the old feudal order in the form of the French Revolution, the consequence of which was social chaos and uncertainty.

How would this unhealthy social condition be terminated and social order re-established? Saint Simon argued that the only social elites that were worthy and capable building and leading a new society would be scientists and industrialists. In this industrial society, the idle nobility who had inherited their social position through the privilege of birthright, would be replaced by those appointed for their scientific expertise and industrial capacity to organise society and its productive forces.

Table 2	Henri Saint Simon's Theory of Social Progress	
Old Social Order →	**Collapse of Old Order** →	**Future Social Order**
Dominant belief system – Catholic religious dogma	Reformation and scientific progress undermined Catholic dogma	Dominant belief system – Scientific and industrial outlook
Feudal social structure, headed by elite nobility of hereditary privilege	Revolution – feudal hierarchy overthrown. Nobility lose control	Industrial society, headed and regulated by new elite of scientists and industrialists appointed on merit

Saint Simon's ideas are developed in greater detail in chapter 15 at the end of this text.

Auguste Comte's view of social progress and the human capacity to understand it and prepare for the future was strongly influenced by the ideas of Saint Simon. Comte agreed that the state of knowledge and belief systems strongly impact on the social condition. For Comte, all phenomena operated according to their own scientific laws. However, before these laws are discovered, the phenomena in question are explained through theological and then metaphysical (philosophical) systems. Scientific understanding had already been reached in the physical sciences, for example physics and astronomy, as the laws by which their phenomena operate can more easily be reduced to mathematical formulae. Yet, the most challenging laws were still to be discovered. These are those which govern the structure and progress of society, since as related to the highest life form these laws will be the most removed from the direct application of mathematics.

Theology had already given way to the critical philosophical doctrines that fomented the French Revolution. But Comte argued that since the life science of biology had already been developed, the time was approaching whereby a science of society will be available to assist in the much needed task of social reconstruction and regulation. This science, named by Comte as 'sociology', would post a new elite of sociologists as social scientific experts at the helm of a 'positivist' society, regulating society through the knowledge of social laws, independently from political advantage.

Table 3	Auguste Comte's Theory of Social Progress	
Old Social Order →	**Collapse of Old Order** →	**Future Social Order**
Dominant belief system – Catholic religious dogma	Critical philosophical doctrines emphasising individual rights undermined Catholic dogma	Dominant belief system – Scientific outlook
Feudal social structure, headed by elite nobility of hereditary privilege	Revolution – feudal hierarchy overthrown. Nobility lose control	Positivist society, headed and regulated by new elite of social scientists

Comte's ideas are developed in greater detail in chapter 15 at the end of this text.

Herbert Spencer: social evolutionism brings social order through deregulation

The idea of the scientific understanding of society also loomed large in the works of Herbert Spencer. However, in the context of English modernisation, the future society toward which he believed it pointed was a very different one from the regulated societies variously anticipated by Saint Simon and Comte.

Spencer attempted to link social progress to the view that a singular universal law of evolution applied to all phenomena. Evolution refers to the unfolding of an outcome through a process of growth. Such a law can be detected in biological evolution whereby individual organisms grow in size and complexity of structure and collectively mutually adjust to their environment to survive.

For Spencer, feudal societies exist within a broader environment of barbaric conflict. Social survival under these conditions required the development of oppressive and highly regulated social structures. However, Spencer argued that as in the case of biological evolution, the natural path of evolution for society is to grow is size and advance in specialisation of institutions and the division of labour. For Spencer, the outcome of this evolutionary process is the flowering of an industrial society of freely interacting individuals, who as specialists in their occupations rely upon the mutual exchange of goods and services within a society that is self-regulated and free from state interference.

Table 4	Herbert Spencer's Theory of Social Evolution	
Old Social Order →	**Gradual Evolutionary Change** →	**Future Social Order**
Feudal society – militant type		Capitalist industrial society
Moral condition barbaric, warlike		Moral condition – peaceful enlightened individualism
Environment of international hostility		Environment of free trade
Survival of the fittest requires oppressive military organisation throughout society		Survival of the fittest transmutes to economic competition. Self-regulated free enterprise societies are best adapted

Spencer's ideas are developed in greater detail in chapter 15 at the end of this text.

Karl Marx: from unstable capitalism to communism

For Marx, the driving force of social change was not belief systems but economic forces. Indeed, dominant belief systems often impeded change.

In his critique of capitalism, Marx identified an essential relationship of conflict in which those who own the means by which production takes place – the 'owners of the means of production' – will have the power to use the labour of others to create value in the production of goods and services and to retain an excessive proportion of that value at the expanse of relatively powerless and poorly rewarded workers. It is this relationship between capitalist and worker, referred to as the 'relations of production', which shapes antagonistic social class relationships in society at large.

How is this class conflict contained? One element of containment is the use of coercive power by the state in the form of the police, the legal system and the armed forces. However, if the nature of capitalism as conceived by Marx remains transparent, open class conflict and its suppression are likely to be endemic. It is through ideological domination that open conflict is minimised. From a Marxist perspective, a dominant ideology is the existence of a belief system that provides a systematically distorted picture which hides the true nature of an underlying reality. Through the process of socialisation, the effect of ideology is to create a 'false consciousness' of reality with the effect of dissipating conflict. The table overleaf sums up some key points of contrast between reality and its ideological representation from a Marxist Viewpoint.

Table 5　　　Reality	Ideology
Work, wages and profit Workers exploited 'Freedom' to leave employer = only freedom to move from one situation of exploitation to another The concept of profit is used to sanitise and legitimise expropriation of value from the labour of workers	**Work, wages and profit** Fair day's pay for a fair day's work Workers are free to leave an employer if dissatisfied Profits are just reward for risk and effort and necessary for innovation and business growth
Law and the state The law primarily protects the interests of the powerful and the purpose of the state is to shore up capitalism	**Law and the state** The law is applied equally and impartially to all and the state acts in the national interest
Education Education restricts critical and insightful thinking. It serves the interests of employers for efficient and exploitable labour, keeping workers in their subordinate class position	**Education** Education provides opportunity for all to achieve in life in terms of personal merit through ability and effort
Representative democracy Political choice and influence available to the electorate are largely illusory as power originates in the ownership of means of production, not government	**Representative democracy** Opportunity to vote for a party of personal choice enables input into the political system by holding governments accountable to the electorate
Religion Belief in an afterlife is an unsubstantiated myth to encourage conformity and make the tribulations of life under capitalism more bearable	**Religion** Religious belief provides ethical guidance, solace and support
Mass media The media distracts the populace by promoting as ideology of consumerism which helps to keep capitalism buoyant. It shapes political outlook within a narrow 'conservative' range	**Mass media** The media is informative. It must be politically responsive to the changing balance of popular opinion to be profitable

There are, however, times when capitalism may be vulnerable. This is because it cannot avoid periodic economic crises which can become social crises. In the struggle of capitalist against capitalist for profit, survival and growth, the inbuilt dynamics of capitalism are to competitively depress wages and maximise profits and production. As a result, a periodic build-up of overproduction leads to economic slumps and mass unemployment. It is at such times that the ideological veil which distorts reality can become transparent. Glimpsing the underlying reality may assist workers to collectively make the psychological transition from a state of false consciousness to that of class consciousness which is a prerequisite for common class action. This action will only be revolutionary when it takes the form of the mass seizure of the means of production into common ownership. At this point, a transition will be under way from a capitalist to communist society within which the economic basis for class conflict disappears.

Table 6	Karl Marx's Theory of Social Progress	
Capitalist Social Order →	**Collapse of Capitalism** →	**Future Social Order**
Economic system capitalist – means of production owned by capitalist class	Revolution – means of production expropriated from capitalist class	Economic system communist – means of production commonly owned
Inbuilt class conflict suppressed	Open class conflict turns to revolution	End of class conflict
System driven by profit motive		System driven by collective good
Power concentrated in capitalist class		Power ultimately diffused throughout society

Marx's ideas are developed in greater detail in chapter 15 at the end of this text.

Emile Durkheim – functionalism and the science of social engineering

Originating in Auguste Comte's more philosophical writings, which dated from the 1820s, functionalism in this French tradition found its sociological formulation from the late nineteenth century in the works of Emile Durkheim. These early functionalists were preoccupied in demonstrating the normality of social order whilst explaining the tribulations experienced by individuals in the modern age. For Comte, concern had been with terminating the social destabilisation of the post-Revolution decades. For Durkheim, it was the very nature of the new social order that had emerged which introduced new vulnerabilities to the well-being of both society and individuals. For both thinkers, the development of social science held the practical usefulness of assisting policy makers to rationally intervene in society so as to promote social consensus and order.

The organic analogy

Durkheimian functionalism used a biological or organic analogy to assist in the understanding of society. An analogy aids understanding through the process of comparison. Through analogy, the understanding of one area of knowledge can be enhanced by indicating similarities to another area which is already better understood. The biological analogy did not mean that society was literally viewed as an organism, but that the understanding of society could best be advanced by comparing it to that of a living body. Sociology could advance as a science of society on this basis because biology was also a science of life but a more advanced one. Sociology could haul itself up by the insights derived from the biological analogy – an observation derived from Comte's hierarchy of the sciences.

In what ways is it beneficial to view society as like an organism? To answer this question, the term function firstly requires definition. A function is a recurrent activity of a part of an integrated body which operates for the benefit of that body. For example, the beating of the heart is of crucial functional importance for the well being of the human body. In this sense, it is a 'functional prerequisite' – its working is a pre-requirement for the very life of the body. Other organs play their own allocated functions. They are each interdependent, and the health and vitality of the entire human body relies on each organ performing its appropriate function effectively.

Within society, formal institutions, especially those of business and the state, are the key functioning apparatus. Like the organs of the body, they need to be mutually integrated and synchronised for the whole entity of society to operate efficiently. Social institutions comprise structured frameworks within which individuals occupy roles which are interconnected. These roles specify and constrain the institutional activities of individuals.

Roles also govern individual activity outside of formal institutions, as do shared values, norms and obedience to rules and laws. For Durkheim, together, these various aspects of society are external to individuals and constrain their behaviour. They provide a type of constraining social architecture. Society is therefore viewed as more than an aggregate of individuals, but as an ordered entity in its own right with its history of change, its present and its future, preceding, superseding and succeeding the lives of its individual members. Individuals are absorbed into this social realm through socialisation.

The biological analogy can be suggestive of conditions of social good or ill health. Like the organs of a body, social institutions perform functions for the health and well being of the entire society. For example, the family rears the next generation and socialises them into the values and expectations of broader society, hence shaping law abiding citizens and contributing to social harmony and order. As well as instilling academic knowledge, the education system imposes on pupils the need to abide by institutional rules and regulations, the habit of regularity, and the acquisition of work related skills, all of which are functional for the efficient participation of individuals in the workplace. The workplace enables resources to be provided for society, incomes for families, and taxation for public services such as education. At the extreme, without social order and the routines of productive activity, modern society would soon cease.

Some of the essential features of Durkheimian functionalism are presented in figure 1 below. The black arrows indicate functional exchange between institutions. The blue arrows show the predominant influence of broader social norms, values and laws on institutions and individuals. The green arrows demonstrate that roles constraining individual behaviour are framed by institutional authority structures.

Figure 1   **Basic Functionalist Consensus Model of Modern Industrial Society**

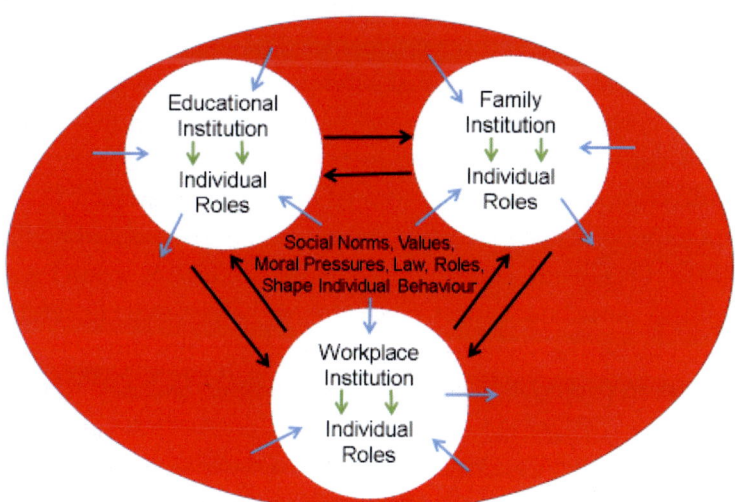

This organic analogy would suggest that society should be viewed as a whole entity. By this, it is meant that the purpose of the parts of society – its various institutions which bring together individuals to structure and regularise their actions – can only be understood through firstly obtaining an overview of society in its entirety. Just as it would be insufficient to try and understand the workings of an organ within a human body in isolation from the whole body, so it would be insufficient to start with an analysis of individual social institutions in an attempt to build up an understanding of the functioning of society. As in the case of the human body, so in the case of society, an overview must first be acquired. From this, one is able to understand the functional workings of its different elements such as the family, educational institutions, the workplace, etc. and how they relate to each other. This vantage point is referred to in sociology as 'holism' and it makes functionalism a 'macro' theory – one which focuses on the broad dimensions of society. Furthermore, functionalism traditionally equated society with nation as a discrete entity of analysis.

From mechanical to organic social solidarity

Durkheim viewed societies as evolving like organisms. As societies grow and advance, they develop more complex forms of organisation. Primitive societies, like primitive organisms, are made up of simple structures – they are small, they exhibit a very low level of technological advance and will have developed only a very limited division of labour. Communities tend to be segmented into small groups, for example in the form of clans. Given the limited division of labour, 1) there is a low level of interlocking of activities or exchange of goods or services that bind people into society, 2) harm to one part of the community will therefore have limited repercussions for the functioning of the whole community, and 3) there is much commonality of life across the community. For societies of this type to cohere, they must bind their members together with a powerful feeling of common collective identity which Durkheim referred to as the 'collective consciousness', imposing strong sanctions against transgressive behaviour. He referred to social integration by the term 'social solidarity' and this form that social integration took in primitive societies as 'mechanical solidarity' (Durkheim, 1964a).

As societies evolve, they develop higher levels of technology and grow in size and dynamic intensity of life. Under these conditions, specialised institutions emerge along with specialist roles within them. These institutions come to perform increasingly specialised functions. They become integrated on a larger scale as the whole of society develops a sophisticated interconnection between them. As institutions become increasingly interdependent, each becomes more highly reliant on the others performing their necessary functions.

In modern industrial societies, a new form of social integration is therefore present. The need for a powerful collective consciousness to oppressively control behaviour to hold society together diminishes as advances in institutional specialisation and the division of labour perform an interlocking function through mutual interdependence and exchange. Modern societies of this type, characterised by the advance of individual diversity and freedom, exhibited a different form of integration referred to by Durkheim as 'organic solidarity' (Durkheim, 1964a).

For Durkheim, the specialisation, diversity and exchange that accompany modernisation bring a new form of societal precariousness. Given the complex interdependency of institutions in modern industrial society, it is more vulnerable to the widespread consequences of the malfunctioning of any of its institutions. This, and social conflict or factionalism, can be highly damaging to society. A faction ridden society is one where order and collective consensus have broken down and people put their factional interests ahead of broader social needs. The effects of disruption to society through, for example, high levels of strike activity by workers, are likely to widespread. From a functionalist perspective, such activity would be a sign of a condition of social ill health which needs to be remedied. At the extreme, revolutionary change would be a condition of chronic ill health. The natural and healthy state suggested by the organic analogy is that societies grow and evolve through a process of gradual change and adjustment.

The malady of egoism and anomie

Any major social change can be socially destabilising and also dangerous for the well-being of individuals. In particular, there is the risk of the emergence of a disconnection between the individual and society within the more liberal social environment which accompanies the development of organic solidarity in modern society. Durkheim pointed to the twin dangers of 'egoism' and 'anomie', especially during the period of early modernisation when old social structures and norms had broken down, new institutions were still emerging and social norms to guide individual behaviour appeared uncertain. In this environment, there is a risk of widespread egoism; an excessive preoccupation by individuals with the self, resulting from their detachment from the constraints of social groups. Furthermore, anomie is a condition of loss of moral certainty and clear norms to guide behaviour. In a society of greater freedom and diversity, the guiding environment of social norms can become so slackened that individuals can feel left in a directionless state of aimlessness. This, within Durkheim's functionalist theory, bears some similarities to the malady of alienation in Marx's theory.

Functionalists maintain that social hierarchies are a natural and inevitable feature of all societies, although the principles around which they are organised change over time. They argue that in modern industrial societies, the functional importance of institutions provide the framework of the social hierarchy and that ability is the main criteria for the allocation of individuals to roles in their occupational capacity and position in the social hierarchy. This enables the efficient utilisation of a range of abilities available in society to take place for the general social benefit. However, the prospect of individual achievement through merit, combined with the advancing capacity of society to generate wealth, can raise unbounded individual expectations. When combined with conditions of egoism and anomie associated with the slackening of social constraints, such expectations can result in chronic levels of personal dissatisfaction and provide a socially based explanation of contemporary levels of suicide (Durkheim, 1970).

The new social order

The term 'analogy', when the biological analogy is used, does not literally mean sameness between a biological organism and society. For example, although countries may maintain the right to control immigration, a society does not have the physical boundary as a bodily form – people can migrate between societies. So what is it, other than a growing level of mutual interdependence that holds a modern society together and provides the framework for social order and cohesion? Durkheim's answer to this essential question was very different from that of Spencer. He argued that Spencer's model of an industrial society of self-motivated and self-supporting individuals provided insufficient social fabric to constrain the disunity resulting from individual self-interest. It would rest on 'the vast system of particular contracts which link individuals as a unique basis …… Social solidarity would then be nothing else than the spontaneous accord of individual interests' (Durkheim, 1964, p.203). Durkheim went on to ask

'Is this the character of societies whose unity is produced by the division of labour? If this were so, we could with justice doubt their stability. For if interest relates men, it is never for more than some few moments……when the business has been completed, each one retires and is left entirely on his own……. For when interest is the only ruling force each individual finds himself in a state of war with every other since nothing comes to mollify the egos, and any truce in this eternal antagonism would not be of long duration. There is nothing less constant than interest. Today, it unites me to you; tomorrow, it will make me your enemy. Such a cause can only give rise to transient relations and passing associations' (Durkheim, 1964, pp. 203-204).

Durkheim's classic functionalist statement argues that an enduring society cannot just be the sum total of freely entered into agreements between self-interested individuals. Society is something which exists externally to the individuals that make it up and must provide a fabric of its own to order and structure individual behaviour through the constraints of institutions, roles, rules, regulations, norms, moral pressures and laws etc. For Durkheim, society acts as an integrating force through imparting shared values via the processes of socialisation and education and by the pressures toward conformity imposed by moral constraints. Shared values promote broadly recognised norms of behaviour, social consensus and a degree of harmony which bind individuals to society. An integrated and smoothly functioning society represents a condition of social good health from which all, as members of society, benefit. By contrast, Durkheim argued that the type of industrial society envisaged by Spencer would be nothing more than an unstable aggregate of self-interested individuals who would be highly exposed to suffering the despair of extreme egoism and anomie.

Engineering the new social order

Bound up with the functionalist perspective in sociology has been the development of positivism – the view that society could ultimately be understood in scientific terms. If this were to be the case, for Durkheim, sociologists would be able to act as 'social engineers', assisting policy makers in their reforms from a position of scientific neutrality as opposed to factional interest or political bias. Policy interventions could then engineer institutions in such a way as to promote social harmony, integration and consensus and counter the maladies of excessive egoism and anomie in a way analogous to a doctor or surgeon using scientific medical knowledge to cure an ill patient.

It is clear that functionalism (as consensus theory) and Marxism (as conflict theory) are diametrically opposed perspectives. But they do have one important characteristic in common. They are both macro perspectives which emphasise the downward impact of socialisation in moulding the consciousness and behaviour of individuals to the dominant norms and values of society. For Durkheim, this moulding process is positive, whereas for Marx, under capitalism, it is viewed negatively. However, they each offer little insight into the potential of individuals to act as free and wilful agents whose activities contribute to the shaping society itself. Max Weber's social action theory was an attempt to counter this imbalance.

Max Weber – social action theory – social science and contingency

Max Weber was a German theorist and contemporary of Durkheim, producing his major works between the late nineteenth and early twentieth centuries. Weber developed a theoretical approach which is more difficult to tie down than Marxism or Durkheimian functionalism. This is partly because the academic scope of his work was immense (covering sociology, philosophy, economics, politics and history) and also because his sociological perspective was relatively open. The perspective that Weber developed is referred to as social action theory. An introduction to social action theory will be presented by summarising a number of its key features.

Firstly, Weber was keen to emphasise the two way relationship which exists between the impact of society on the individual and the shaping of society by the interpretations, motivations and actions of individuals. He opposed approaches to sociology which 'reified' society. Reification of society is the view that society has a purpose and independent life of its own. The analysis of society as such a powerful entity, a characteristic of both functionalist and Marxist theory, loses focus on and understates the importance of the input of individual action to the form that society takes.

Secondly, Weber recognised the importance of contingency in social change. The existence of chance events, inventions, and complex social interactions mean that the application of a scientific approach and the possibility of predicting the social future must be taken through painstaking research and with great caution. Social change could not be explained in terms of the types of scientific laws developed by positivist thinkers and through social contingency and complexity the future remained more open and uncertain.

Thirdly, Weber contested the Marxist view that social conflict and change are invariably driven by economic and material factors and that belief systems are shaped by economic forces and social inequalities which they exist to justify. For Weber, cultural ideas, such as religious belief systems, can be more independent of economic forces and can at times be powerful forces of social and economic change.

Fourthly, Weber argued that for social action to be fully understood, the study of actors within their micro environments and the apprehension of the subjective motives behind their actions is as important as recognising the influences of the broader social structure upon individuals.

The following diagram, figure 2, illustrates the complex interplay between the purposeful independent action of individuals, cultural values and economic forces.

Figure 2   Diagram illustrating interconnection between cultural values, economic forces and individual actions in Weber's social action theory

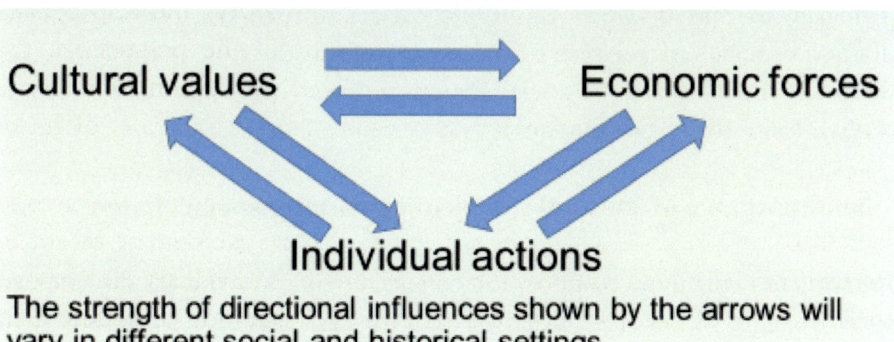

Cultural values   Economic forces

Individual actions

The strength of directional influences shown by the arrows will vary in different social and historical settings.

For Weber, the study of social action can be approached as an academic venture and as a science of a sort. Here, though, Weber was critical of the positivist position which maintains that approaches relevant to the physical sciences can be adopted in or adapted to the study of social action. For Weber, social 'science' is the systematic study of social action. But social action is the outcome of conscious decision making undertaken by actors in terms of meanings, interpretations and motives. These lie behind observed behaviour within the subjectivity of the actor's consciousness, rendering useless analysis of behaviour in strictly cause and effect terms. In emphasising the difference between causality in the physical realm (and the largely stimulus and response behaviour of the animal world), and conscious human choice, freedom of action and contingency of social action, Weber's approach to understanding society strongly departs from the positivistic emphasis in the works of Comte, Durkheim or Marx where individuals are seen as highly controlled and constrained by external social forces bearing down on them and shaping society in law like ways.

Although generally viewed as a conflict theorist, Weber's position is strongly at odds with the conflict approach of Marx. When viewing society at the macro level, Weber maintains that social groups tend to compete for power and resources and that those who hold these assets will usually attempt to retain exclusive control through erecting barriers to access by others. However, whether, and if so how, this leads to conflict in particular societies and at particular times in history and whether conflict primarily takes the form of class conflict is regarded as a matter open for analysis. It is therefore not appropriate to refer to either consensus or conflict as natural to societies in the way that functionalists and Marxists respectively do. For Weber, it is also misleading of Marxists to reduce social conflict primarily to that between economic classes and to use economic class defined in terms of relation to the means of production as the single key with which to explain the social structure, the distribution of power and motive force for social change.

The importance of cultural values in explaining social change

In trying to explain the composition of social structures and the direction of social change, Weber argued that it is not the case that economic forces will necessarily have a determining effect. As he demonstrated in his comparative study of religions, belief systems and cultural values can sometimes be relatively independent and more important influences on the extent and direction of social change (or of social stagnation) than economic factors. Cultural values can indeed be the driving force behind people's actions and these can have economic consequences – a proposition which gives cultural values a potentially dynamic role to play in promoting social change and therefore potential prominence in analysis. It is ultimately for the analysis of particular societies in specific periods of history to uncover the complex and contingent influences on social conflict, consensus and social change.

In Weber's social action theory, cultural value systems provide an influential broader context for the motivations and actions of social actors. These value systems form an important part of the social backdrop to action and can themselves change over time. Weber viewed the major change in cultural values associated with capitalist modernisation in the west in terms of the process of 'rationalisation'. To clarify this process, Weber employed the device of 'ideal types'. An ideal type is a pure intellectual construct. It models essential characteristics of a type of society in a pure and uncontaminated way. The pure type probably never exists in the highly complex real world but nevertheless it assists the analyst in understanding the essential social features of societies that can be classified under different types.

Weber distinguished between two main ideal type cultural value systems which he classified as the traditional and the rational. The traditional value system largely provided the broader framework for social action in much of western pre-capitalist society. In this context, the actions of individuals were guided largely by custom and tradition. Traditional ways tended to be justified as appropriate in their own right, without a need for the rational appraisal of information regarding alternative and potentially more efficient courses of action. People lived their lives according to customary ways which were often followed relatively uncritically.

However, cultural values can change, providing a changing context guiding social action. Weber (1978) identified the emergence of certain religious belief systems (Calvinism and puritanism) as providing a challenge to the traditional outlook. These belief systems, in part the product of individual intellectual input, were able to germinate and gather following within the environment of relative religious tolerance in pre-industrial England. Calvinists, following the religious teachings of John Calvin, felt it their duty to devote their energies exclusively to a life of hard work and application as their beliefs led them to conclude that achieving material success could be taken as a sign of their righteousness and salvation. These religious beliefs provided a powerful incentive to achieve economic and business success through weighing up different ways of working and introducing those which were likely to be more effective in producing economic reward. This religiously sanctioned rational evaluation of the means to efficiently achieve material ends, along with other fortuitous conditions that were present in England, was setting a dynamic in place whereby the utility of traditional ways would be questioned and upon which the values and material basis of modern western capitalism could grow. In contrast to Marx, therefore, Weber assigned a substantial role to the emergence of religious cultural and belief systems within traditional society that were conducive to rational calculation and focussed industrious action. These cultural values were significant factors influencing the actions of many individuals whose input provided the dynamic for eventual emergence of a capitalist economy first in England.

Weber argued, though, that with the emergence of western capitalism, the work ethic and quest for rational efficiency would gradually detach itself from its original religious sanction. This is because the extension of rational thinking undermines religious superstition. Society would thus come to correspond more closely to Weber's ideal type in which a culture of rational calculation based on scientific and technical knowledge and practical rational action is applied to achieve profit maximisation. But through the self-destruction of the religious sanction behind materialistic aspiration and the advance of secularisation (the decline of religion), the religious compass bearing of moral rectitude may be lost as the acquisition of wealth becomes seen as an end in itself rather than a passport to heaven. To achieve the end of rational efficiency, organisational structures increasingly take the form of large, impersonal bureaucratic power hierarchies which progressively formalise social relationships. However, of course, in the real world, some remnants of traditional value systems and action are likely to remain in the social and cultural mix.

Given Weber's academic caution and antipathy toward theories that refer to laws of change and the dominance of society over the individual, it is ironic that his studies led him to conclude that the real danger accompanying modern western capitalism is the bleakly inescapable march of rationalisation (rationally constrained thinking and action) and bureaucratisation (the spread of bureaucratic organisations throughout society where human relationships are governed by rules and regulations) which he believed would constrain individual freedom and reduce individuals to little more than cogs within efficient social machinery. Worse than this, coldness and formality in social relationships would crush the human spirit. Technological dominance over nature would replace enchantment with the mysteries of the world with a feeling of disenchantment – a sense of spiritual loss which is a counterpart in Weber's theory to that of alienation in Marxist theory and the modern malaise of moral anomie in Durkheimian functionalism.

The importance of purposive individual action

The analysis of social action, however complex, would be incomplete if it were only seen as being shaped by broad cultural and belief systems and social and economic institutions. This emphasis tends to be a weakness of the functionalist approach which reifies society and its 'needs' to such a level that individuals seem as if to be just passing through it. For Weber, although society and its cultural systems and institutions exist outside of individuals, it is also the case that institutions are consciously planned, created and changed and value systems challenged through purposive action by individual actors.

The difficulty of extracting subjective meaning

This means that the study and understanding of social action can only be complete if an analysis of broader macro influences on individuals is complemented by knowledge of action in micro settings through the use of direct observation. To understand action in this setting, account must be taken of the meanings and motivations which reside behind it in the consciousness of social actors. These individual meanings and motivations are likely to be shaped by broader cultural and belief systems. However, the difficulty facing the observer is that of being sure that they have correctly uncovered the subjective motives that lie in the minds of the actors and behind the observed action. To do so, the observer must attempt the challenging process of engaging in empathy – understanding the motives of the actor(s) being observed by putting oneself in their position. This process Weber referred to as 'verstehen' and we may take a very simple example from football to illustrate the difficulty.

On observing the ball hitting the hand of a player, the referee has to make a key decision as to whether or not the contact was intentional. He observes a physical process, but from that observation he has to try and read into the mind of the player. In some cases, the evidence may appear to be clear cut and the interpretation of the referee is likely to be correct. In other cases, he may be unsure and his decision runs a greater risk of being incorrect. And in further cases, a footballer may be able by his actions to 'con' the referee by feigning unintentionality.

This difficult issue of interpreting the meaning behind action is a reminder that to practice social science requires acknowledgement of the gulf that exists between the physical processes of the natural sciences and the subjective element in the study of social action.

A more contemporary application of perspectives

For the purposes of this section, the author will suggest how some of the perspectives covered can be applied to shed light on the financial crisis and economic recession following 2007.

Some key points will first be sketched as a background to this crisis. In essence, various policies and circumstances conspired to bring about a precarious buoyancy in the housing market and consumer spending in the late twentieth and early twenty first centuries. Arguably, the main impetus for the collapse came from the United States, but the pursuit of similar policies in other countries such as Britain during this time period prior to the collapse and effects of global financial and economic interconnectedness facilitated the global contagion of events.

Following the economic stagnation of the 1970s and the recession of the early 1980s, a number of governments took the decision to deregulate financial institutions, enabling easier consumer access to credit and mortgages. Increased consumer debt therefore provided an economic stimulus, but also led to an inflated and overvalued pricing of property assets. This deregulated financial sector became an expanding part of modern economies. However, over time many financial institutions had put themselves in a vulnerable position through developing complex and high risk financial products which incentivised the pursuit of short term gain. They also overstretched themselves by providing speculative loans without sufficient capital reserve to cover potential losses.

When interest rates increased in the United States, more vulnerable mortgage holders defaulted, properties were repossessed and property prices collapsed. This precipitated the financial crisis of 2007-2008, in which it became clear that sub-prime loans (more risky mortgages to people on lower incomes) had been overvalued.

Financial institutions faced panics from investors who were keen to withdraw savings from banks that they feared might go bust. As a result, national governments had to bail out banks that held insufficient capital to cover excessive withdrawals in fear of the collapse of the entire banking system. Interest rates slumped, credit availability virtually dried up and the world stock markets fell dramatically. The financial contagion spread to much of the world economy with a steep recession in national output in many countries. Greece in particular hovered on the verge of national bankruptcy and the economy had to be kept on life support through loans from international organisations which had conditions of severe austerity measures attached to them.

In sum, the millions of 'personal troubles' which ensued from this catastrophe have included: loss of homes, unemployment, a decline in wages and standard of living, delayed retirement, a decrease in public expenditure and an increase in the tax burden.

In consideration of the above perspectives, one may recall that for Spencer a viable social structure is dependent on the (modifiable) moral nature of individuals, the social units that make up that structure. Applying a Spencerian approach, the damage to the financial sector and economy caused by the banking crisis cannot be explained in terms of the inherent weakness of capitalism as a system. Instead, it can be broadly viewed in terms of rapid financial deregulation running ahead of a necessary corresponding advance in the moral condition toward enlightened individualism. Without sufficient social constraint, the advance of individualism without enlightenment is likely to equate to purely self-serving action and self-centred greed without concern for the consequences of one's actions for others. Within this context, the existence of high financial incentives can lead to reckless risk taking. In a highly integrated global economy, any destructive consequences will be widespread. In Spencerian terms, the need for state intervention and regulation to save the banking system from collapse and the introduction of control measures to help avoid irresponsible individualism in the future were retrograde but necessary steps to enable social institutions to become re-attuned to the reality of the prevailing moral condition of self-centred as opposed to enlightened individualism.

A diametrically opposed viewpoint of the crisis stems from the Marxist perspective. Despite disagreements between Marxists on just how Marxist theory should be interpreted, it is generally agreed that such crises are the inevitable product of capitalism as a system. In the competitive pursuit of survival and profit maximisation, private enterprises must innovate to increase productivity, steal a temporary advantage over their competitors, and reduce labour costs. Whilst of short term benefit to particular enterprises, the overall and longer term consequences are a crisis of overproduction as, with a tendency toward rising unemployment and lower wages, there is a decline in the consumer spending power available to buy the surplus of goods produced. This will lead to economic depression, a crisis tendency which Marxists argue cannot in the long term be solved within capitalism (Smith, 26/11/2013).

However, governments and private enterprise will attempt to counter such crises and prop up the system. Credit can be made available to keep capitalism buoyant. Government spending, leading to an increased debt burden, can increase demand. Seductive advertising of products to consumers who are also given access to easy credit will also increase demand, but with it personal indebtedness increases. Large financial institutions, which themselves, from a Marxist perspective, do not create value, become a growing part of the economy, and should they malfunction the consequences are likely to be catastrophic for the 'real economy'. Under such conditions, measures to stimulate the economy, such as quantitative easing, may prolong the life of capitalism, and government regulation of the financial sector may be introduced in an attempt to save capitalism from itself, but its economic forces are too powerful to be everlastingly held in check. Consequently, its collapse is likely to be all the more dramatic, eventually with one such crisis leading to both its collapse and the overthrow of capitalism itself.

As working people have suffered the pains of the post 2008 financial crisis and deep economic recession, public anger can be easily focussed on the greed of a few high profile individuals as the cause of the problem. But the problem is a systemic one and, in contrast to Spencer, Marx claimed that it is the institutions of capitalism that corrupt human nature. Marxists argue that the attribution of personal blame conveniently distracts public attention away from recognising a systemic problem at the heart of capitalism. Such personalization provides a false consciousness of the problem.

From the broad contours of a Weberian perspective, a greater emphasis is placed on the importance of cultural values and rational social action. Weber argued that a powerful motive force behind the emergence of capitalism was a religiously sanctioned work ethic of sobriety, rectitude and austerity. For example, Barclays Bank was run on such principles of business integrity by its Quaker founders. However, Weber has argued that the forces of rationalism that accompanied the advance of capitalism undermined religion and its moral sanctions. Consequently, capitalism would become a system in which the pursuit of wealth, increasingly unbounded by religious ethical constraints, would become an end in itself. Within this context, deregulation of financial institutions would clearly run the risk of encouraging the unbounded pursuit by institutions and individuals of material wealth.

The rational pursuit of material gain cannot explain the whole picture though. Part of the crisis stemmed from feelings of panic as investors rushed to withdraw their savings, creating a run on the banks.

The emergence of micro perspectives

Although variations on the founding perspectives retained an influence in sociology for much of the twentieth century, new perspectives were developed, some of which focussed on explaining social action wholly or largely at the micro level. These perspectives - symbolic interactionism, phenomenology and ethnomethodology - are generally referred to as 'interpretive' sociology. At a general level, they hold in common the view that society is founded on shared meaning, that social action can only be understood through grasping the subjective meanings that actors hold, and that the study of micro social environments is the more fruitful way for sociologists to approach an understanding of social behaviour.

1. Symbolic interactionism – social self-identity

Symbolic interactionism was a perspective developed in the United States during the early decades of the twentieth century and in this section some of the key ideas of the founding theorists, G.H. Mead and C.H. Cooley, will be explored.

Society, from the point of view of this perspective, is the product of purposeful actions of individuals, and interaction with others in small scale situations provides the most important contexts in which individuals live their daily lives. Central to this perspective is the importance of symbols as a means of communication and shared understanding.

Despite this emphasis on purposeful social action and the micro dimension, symbolic interactionism developed relatively independently from the influence of Weber's social action theory. It was indebted more, both culturally and academically, to the American tradition of pragmatism (Ritzer, 2008, pp. 347-348). Briefly, this academic tradition held that ideas and actions relate to practical purpose. People understand situations in ways that are sufficient for practical action, and to engage in practical action, individuals must negotiate with others.

Central to Mead's interactionism is the emphasis that human capacity to think in terms of symbolic meaning separates human kind from animals and makes self-consciousness uniquely possible. Symbols include written and spoken language, gestures, signs and body language. They provide a medium for shared communication, making reflection and interpretation an on-going feature of social life. For example, a teacher writing on a white board is essentially making black marks on a white background. It is through the acquisition of shared language that the ability to extract meaning from the configuration of the marks on the white board is possible. When the teacher speaks to the class, he / she is essentially just making sounds. Again, it is through the medium shared language that meaning can be derived from these sounds. When it is announced that the class will break at 11.00 a.m., the clock on the wall provides its own symbolic communication of time.

It is this constant monitoring of meaning which distinguishes reflective and purposeful social action from the largely automatic stimulus and response behaviour of animals who lack the human capacity for sharing this level of symbolic meaning. Far more than this, the social world provides an environment which has a profound effect on the individual sense of self. Self-identity is therefore not something which is biologically pre-determined but is a construct of social interaction.

The social development of the self

Mead proposes a developmental model which locates self-identity within social processes and relates it to the maturation process. From early childhood, children learn social roles by copying the actions of 'significant others' in their immediate environment, especially their parents and siblings. Later, they come to develop the capacity to relate to other individual roles and eventually to people in multiple roles in larger organised settings. For example, the child needs to develop such an awareness within the environment of the school. This is referred to by Mead as the development of an awareness of the 'generalised other' and through this a perception of the attitude of the group. By this process, the mature individual becomes aware of how they are seen by others and of the requirement for social compulsion.

Mead viewed the self as composed of 'me' and the 'I' characteristics. The 'me' refers to the social self, built on the capacity that the individual has to see oneself through taking on the viewpoint and attitudes of others. Awareness of the social self requires the capacity for 'representation' – the mental ability to step outside of ourselves to contemplate how others see us. Such self-consciousness is enhanced during the process of our interaction with others. The formation of the 'me' aspect of the self is based on the appraisal of ourselves by others and the values and expectations of the community. Within this context, the individual learns how to project a public image, shaped by the perceptions of what others think about his or her actions and judgements on how they are likely to respond. This part of the self is stabilised through the social environment but one also learns how to work that environment through the manipulation of self-image.

In distinction to the 'me', the 'I' element of the self refers to the more subjective inner self. It is that part of the self which retains spontaneity and the capacity to react back against society. An individual's angry outburst, despite knowledge of the rules of etiquette of a social situation, is a rather extreme example of the capacity of the ever lurking 'I' to at least momentarily overwhelm the socially fashioned 'me'. Individual action is therefore a combination of the 'me' and the 'I' and is: a) not biologically pre-determined and b) although socially shaped, not socially pre-determined.

Further insights within this perspective were developed by Charles Cooley, most notably his concept of 'the looking glass self' (Coser, 1977, pp. 305-307). For Cooley, the capacity for reflection enables individuals to view themselves through how they attribute others to see them. The components of this process are the imagination of how we appear to others, the imagined judgement of others based on that appearance, and the consequent positive or negative self-feeling. Rather than an imposing structure, society is the interweaving of such self-reflections and provides an environment in which individuals attempt to manage the promotion of their external self.

This perspective reveals potentially liberating practical implications for the individual. If we have been negatively viewed by others, this can lead to low self-esteem. We may act in confirmation of these views and retain an identity conveyed to us by others. However, as symbolic interactionism reveals, social interaction does not have to be just a one-way process of passive acceptance of others' judgements. We can initiate a change toward a more positive self-identity, but this is not just a private matter. By learning the changes that are necessary in the way that we project ourselves to convince others that we are not as they see us, we can assert to them a new image. If successfully carried off and sustained, through their modified responses to us, this new positive image can become stabilised and internalised in a changed sense of self as it is reflected back to us. Ultimately, one may decide to turn one's back on certain significant others whose negative view of us cannot be changed.

Symbolic interactionism suggests that individuals have a degree of freedom and responsibility and a significant element of say in their self-identity through their capacity to manipulate their own image. Figures 3-5 below show this relationship between the self and significant others (SOs), with strength of arrows indicating predominant influences.

Symbolic interactionist models of social self-concept

Figure 3   Self concept / identity socially shaped

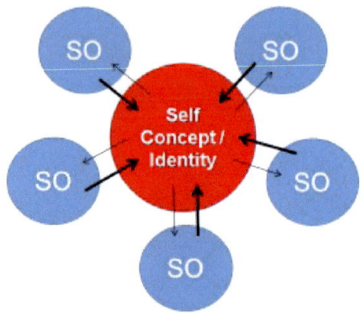

Figure 4   Establishment of image change

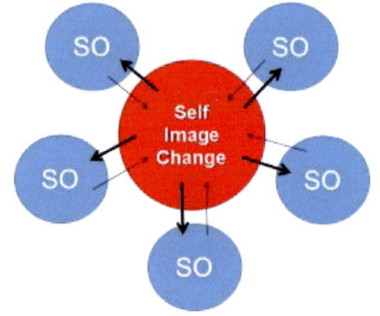

Figure 5   Social stabilization of new self concept / identity

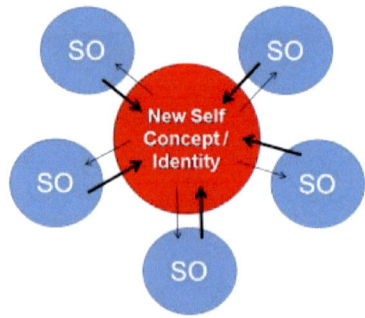

In sum, symbolic interactionists tend to view society as being in a state of flux. It is not a hierarchically imposed structure and overpowering identity moulding entity as portrayed in functionalist theory, but rather the creation of the actions of numerous individuals, mutually orientated through the looking glass self. This is all possible through the medium of the shared understanding of symbols and the capacity for representation and it remains open as to whether social relationships are of co-operation or conflict between individuals or groups.

2. Phenomenology and ethnomethodology – the subjectivity of social structures

Phenomenology is distinct from and a more radical theoretical approach to that of symbolic interactionism, but at a general level there are certain similarities between the two perspectives. They both emphasise the importance of understanding action through actors' subjective meaning and both focus on the centrality of symbolic communication between social actors. Both perspectives emphasise the importance of a micro approach to understanding social action and view social action as essentially a fluid process rather than the outcome of constraints originating in the social structure. Both perspectives are commonly referred to as 'interpretive' sociology – they adopt the view that an understanding of social action requires the study of the meaning frameworks adopted by actors.

In his development of phenomenology between the 1930s and the 1950s, Alfred Schutz built on the broader philosophical works of Edmund Husserl and the sociology of Max Weber. Weber recognised the importance of grasping the subjective meanings and motives of actors that lie behind and therefore give meaning to action for the observer. However, he did not provide a systematic theory of subjective meaning. In applying the philosophical insights of Husserl to social phenomena, Schutz attempted to construct a more systematic approach to subjective meaning to develop a foundation for sociology, one which would provide an understanding of the subjective processes involved whereby actors develop the perception of an ordered and structured social world.

A basic premise of phenomenology is that phenomena hold no intrinsic meaning, only that attributed by humans in their capacity to do so. In the social world, actors have to provide meaning to what their sensory perceptions reveal to make sense of their environment and enable them to engage in purposeful social action. The way that the social world is viewed is therefore actively defined as such by its participants. Meaning is assigned to behaviour through shared language and reality is structured through the classification of like labelled phenomena in the form of 'typifications'. A social typification assigns meaning to a category of behaviour, as for example that of a 'thief' or 'poet'. Such typifications provide the building blocks of a shared common sense view of a structured social world and enable assumptions to be made about how society works in a predictable way.

Working through the medium of shared common sense, the world of subjective meaning is intersubjective; subjective communication is able to take place on the reciprocal assumption that we all tend to view the world similarly. For Schutz, the 'life world' is an intersubjective and continuous flow of daily experience, framed by a shared common sense, in which each participant strives to make sense of the actions of others. The meaning framework provided means that this process often takes place quite automatically, but behaviour can be misunderstood and meaning is constantly open to change.

Subjectivity operates at various levels. Individuals have their own biographical profile of subjective experience. Subjective interchange takes place in close relationships which Schutz refers to as 'we' relationships. We may also subjectively relate to people in a more formal way or even anonymously, referred to by Schutz as 'they' relationships. The task of the sociologist from a phenomenological perspective is to understand the subjective meanings that people use in their daily lives. The aim of researchers is to apprehend the subjectivity of those observed to the extent of seeing the world as they do.

From a phenomenological viewpoint, society does not exist as a 'thing' in its own right. Although not intrinsic to the social world, the appearance of social structure is a consequence of the imposition of meaning onto behaviour through typifications and a common sense which in daily life become taken for granted. This sense of an external social structure is essentially an illusion, but is real to the extent that it is commonly believed and acted upon. Society thus comes to be seen as a thing in its own right by its creators.

For phenomenologists, functionalists mistakenly reproduce this viewpoint. They take this creation as an entity in its own right, thus reifying society. Society is taken as a starting point, providing the constraints of concrete structures, cultural consensus and socialisation to integrate individuals. Strongly positivist approaches to sociology are guilty of viewing society in terms of its own intrinsic and independent structures and processes which can be analysed in terms of their own causes and effects with individuals comprising the data of solid facts.

Phenomenologists such as Peter Berger argue that people seek 'ontological security'; 'a stable mental state derived from a sense of continuity and order' (Bilton, 2002, p.545). The alternative to this is the experience of the mental anguish of chaos. However, at times the necessary sense of ontological security can come under threat. For example, many of those, particularly in United Kingdom, who were shocked and surprised by the outcome of the 2016 Referendum on whether or not the UK should leave the European Union, will have experienced a degree of ontological insecurity that their familiar world had changed, especially given the dire warnings of the consequences of a leave vote conveyed by political, financial and economic elites and the expectation of a vote to remain. The immediate shock of the exit vote to the stock market and the value of the pound seemed to confirm these fears. But ontological insecurity is intolerable in the longer term. How can a sense of security be regained? The author suggests that the answer can be found in a combination of: psychological adjustment to the new reality, belief that warnings had been massively exaggerated as stock markets and the pound recovered and re-stabilized and hope that the government may be able to negotiate a smooth transition.

In comparison, imagine the extent of ontological insecurity experienced by people who have lived through revolutionary change. If familiar old structures and ways have been swept aside, how can the resultant confusion be replaced by a new ordered understanding of the world? Arguably, the very emergence of sociology as an academic discipline and the positivist and structural forms it often took can be explained as responses to the need for ontological security following the French and Industrial Revolutions.

The fundamental points are that for the phenomenologist, the social analyst needs to 1) suspend the common sense viewpoint and classificatory framework adopted by the lay person for everyday practical purposes and instead study the subjective processes involved by actors in arriving at the common sense viewpoint in the first place and 2) avoid the practice of functionalist / positivist sociologists of building on the common sense world and viewing structure and order as intrinsic to society. Action is not the product of the constraints of external structures but is guided by the conscious interpretations placed upon situations by actors in their need to perceive structure and order.

Ethnomethodology – how people establish a sense of order

Ethnomethodology shares the same philosophical terrain as phenomenology, but in making the transition from phenomenology to ethnomethodology, we are moving from a social philosophy to sociology. We have seen that Schutz's phenomenology theorised about the intersubjective creation of a sense of a structured world. Based on the same philosophical premises, the aim of ethnomethodology was to reveal the methods used by people (referred to as members) to build a sense of meaning and order through the activities of their everyday lives. This approach was pioneered in the late 1960s by Harold Garfinkle.

Following the outlook developed by Schutz, for Garfinkle members tend to share common understandings and mutual expectations which provide a framework for the routines of everyday life. All the time that shared meanings and routines remain undisturbed, members adopt a taken for granted stance; they are often hardly aware of them. It is only when disruption of the meanings and conventions which provide a sense of order takes place that awareness of them is raised and members engage in attempts to re-establish a sense of order.

As a very simple example, consider the following situation. Imagine that you have just moved into a neighbourhood and are getting to know local people. In the street, you acknowledge a person that you have come to recognise as a local, but find that your acknowledgment is sometimes returned and on other occasions you are completely ignored. This is not what you expect from the rules of etiquette in these everyday encounters. How do you respond to this apparently random behaviour? You will probably try to attribute sense to it by considering plausible reasons for the behaviour: perhaps he didn't hear me? perhaps he didn't remember me? perhaps he was preoccupied in thoughts or worries? If this behaviour should persist, there is likely to come a time when you will attempt to impose a new interpretation on the situation – this is an ill mannered person that I cannot be bothered to acknowledge any more. You have actively resolved the ambiguity by interpreting behaviour and imposing meaning on it to make it understandable and manageable.

Or consider the experience of disorientation that occurs when a supermarket that you regularly shop at changes the layout of its products and sections from that which you are familiar with. Part of the reason behind such changes may be the motive of enticing customers into new spending habits by buying products that they unexpectedly find in front of them. But what would happen if such change took place frequently? Loss of customers, who may experience greater familiarity of layout by shopping elsewhere, may be the outcome.

People actively strive to achieve a sense of order and structure in their daily lives. But given the taken for granted stance which commonly accompanies the routines of everyday life, how can this process be teased out by sociologists? To study the process of the construction of meaning and a sense of order, ethnomethodologists set up experiments in natural settings. These often take the form of 'breaching experiments' in which the aim is to break the rules and conventions of certain situations. The purpose of this approach is to 1) bring into relief what was taken for granted within the situation in the first place and 2) especially to study the methods that actors employ to reconstruct meaning and a sense of order from the confusion caused so that they can make sense of the situation. Such experiments were pioneered by Harold Garfinkle (1984) and it may be helpful at this point for the reader to pause and study those referred to in Chapters 4 and 5 of this text.

Through constructing breaching experiments, ethnomethodologists are able to demonstrate how members play an active role in constructing a sense of social meaning and structure. From the findings of his experiments, Garfinkle developed concepts which he claimed reveal the processes by which members create a sense of order in their everyday activities. Through the 'documentary method', members select certain features from a mass of information and events to establish a sense of patterned meaning. Through 'reflexivity', an ongoing process of confirmation of this patterned meaning is established. Reflexivity works through a two way process. The established pattern helps the actor to select and make sense of further information and the meaning ascribed to this information provides confirming evidence of the pattern itself. Further, through 'indexicality', understanding of behaviour is influenced by the context within which the action takes place, with similar behaviour interpreted differently in different contexts.

Ethnomethodologists follow the criticisms of functionalist and positivist approaches that are made by phenomenologists. They argue that there are no social structures existing externally to and independently of people and imposing social conformity on relatively passive individuals. Sociologists who take these structures as real in their own right as the basis for sociological analysis are therefore mistaken. They are ignoring what ethnomethodologists claim that sociology should be all about – a study of the methods by which a sense of structure is actively achieved by members.

Having mentioned the general similarities between symbolic interactionism and phenomenology at the beginning of this section, we are now in a better position to make a precise distinction between them. From a phenomenological and an ethnomethodological perspective, although symbolic interactionism adopts a subjectivist approach, in attempting to view the world as through the eyes of the participants in micro situations, it only builds its concepts on the common sense definitions provided by the actors. It does not reveal the active methods that they employ in the construction of a sense of order in the first place.

Recap on the founding theories

The following exercise has been designed to assist the reader in gauging their recollection and understanding of the founding theories touched on in this chapter. For each statement presented, there is strictly speaking only one correct choice of theoretical perspective. Phenomenology and ethnomethodology are coupled, as they are in the chapter, but a finer distinction within this choice is underlined in the answers. The statements are randomly ordered with regards to the perspectives to which they apply.

Using the coding system below, designate one of the following codes to each of the statements. The codes for the correct answers are given on the following page. It is hoped that this will assist the reader in establishing areas of strength and weakness and revisiting sections of the text to clarify understanding.

EP = Early positivism
SE = Spencer's evolutionism
DF = Durkheim's functionalism
M = Marxism
SAT = Social Action Theory (Weber)
SI = Symbolic interactionism
PE = Phenomenology / ethnomethodology

1. Social consensus is the normal and healthy social state.

2. Social change is viewed both in terms of progress and evolution.

3. Conflict is built into the social and economic structure of capitalism.

4. Social science is the key to the building of a new social order following the disorder of the French Revolution.

5. Social classes are identified in relation to the means of production.

6. Excessive social conflict indicates the ill health of society.

7. Social change is driven by class conflict.

8. The future high point is a society based on enlightened individualism.

9. Social classes are essentially in antagonism to each other.

10. Self-identity is influenced by the labelling process.

11. Taken for granted meaning is sufficient for people in their everyday worlds.

12. The new industrial society should be regulated by scientific and industrial elites.

13. The industrial society will ultimately be one of deregulated free enterprise.

14. The observer of social action needs to effectively engage in 'verstehen' to understand the action of others.

15. There are many contributory causes of broad social change, different ones being of greater significance in different societies at different times.

16. The conditions of survival of the fittest change through evolution from warfare to peaceful production.

17. The process of rationalisation is key to the development of modern capitalism.

18. Cultural values can be as important as economic factors in explaining social change.

19. It is of benefit to society that the individual is moulded and constrained by external social forces.

20. Personal identity is a product of the looking glass self.

21. The broad direction of social change cannot be understood by applying the causality of the physical sciences and the future cannot be predicted by laws of change.

22. Political power derives from economic power.

23. Efficient bureaucratic organisations proliferate in modern legal rational societies.

24. Social change is driven by economic forces.

25. This approach analyses how actors construct meaning and order in their everyday lives.

26. People both meaningfully create their society and are constrained by it.

27. Oppressive authority is necessary in societies in a state of mechanical solidarity.

28. Individuals can challenge the labelling process and negotiate their identity.

29. The history of thinking can be divided into three stages, the first two of which are the theological and the metaphysical.

30. As well as the social world impacting on the individual, individuals retain the capacity to change the social world.

31. Society is not intrinsically structured.

32. A full understanding of social action must complement macro and micro analysis.

33. With some regret, there is an increasing tendency for people's lives to

become constrained by large impersonal institutions.

34. Systems of thinking govern the condition of society.

35. The advance of formality, bureaucratisation and rationalisation can lead to the experience of disenchantment with the world.

36. Private ownership of the means of production enables exploitation of the subject class.

37. The act of meaning construction can be best observed in the context of breaching experiments.

38. The decline in oppressive authority is a key feature of societies in a state of organic solidarity.

39. Economic life is the determining force around which the rest of society is organised.

40. Social inequality is not inevitable.

41. Shared values promote social integration.

42. The 'I' is the inner self which may react on the social environment.

43. The scientific understanding of society is the last to be revealed as its subject matter is the least reducible to mathematics.

44. Self-identity is shaped in the process of interaction.

45. Anomie is an ailment of modern industrial societies, especially during times of major change.

46. Social communication and understanding is mediated by a shared understanding of symbols.

47. Capitalist society is organised primarily for the benefit of one class who will exploit another.

48. Society is beneficially structured by institutions, roles and rules to constrain individual behaviour.

49. The 'me' is both a product of and manipulator of the social environment.

50. Understanding the meanings that people exchange in social interaction is as important as recognising the constraints of the broader social structure.

Answers to multiple choice exercise

1	DF	14	SAT	27	DF	40	M
2	SE	15	SAT	28	SI	41	DF
3	M	16	SE	29	EP	42	SI
4	EP	17	SAT	30	SAT	43	EP
5	M	18	SAT	31	PE	44	SI
6	DF	19	DF	32	SAT	45	DF
7	M	20	SI	33	SAT	46	SI
8	SE	21	SAT	34	EP	47	M
9	M	22	M	35	SAT	48	DF
10	SI	23	SAT	36	M	49	SI
11	PE	24	M	37	PE	50	SAT
12	EP	25	PE	38	DF		
13	SE	26	SAT	39	M		

Loss of community, a key theme in the establishment of sociology

At the forefront of eighteenth century Enlightenment rationality were attacks on the mysticisms of religion, the dogma of religious authorities and the confining social structure of feudal hierarchies. Enlightenment writers applied reason to attack and undermine the old order and looked forward to a society in which institutions could be fashioned on rational principles. Such attacks helped to precipitate revolutionary change and the emergence of capitalist industrial societies.

However, in the aftermath of the French and Industrial Revolutions, concern about dislocation from the past and the effects of rapid social change on the fabric of society were profoundly felt by many people across modernising societies. Indeed, it was these social changes that provided the backdrop to the ideas of founding sociologists in formative phase of sociology as they attempted to understand the social condition of the emerging urban, industrial and capitalist world. Within this context, the concept of community became one of the fundamental units in the development and establishment of sociology (Nisbet, 1970, Ch3).

The concept of 'community', as traditionally conceived, is not a difficult one to envisage. It tends to be associated with small groups of people amongst whom close and intimate social relationships abound. There are likely to exist shared experiences, ways of life and outlooks. Such communities are often associated with life in rural settings or small towns which enable members to frequently meet face to face and know much of the details of each other's lives. Mutual support and reciprocal obligations tend to tie people into community life. This concept of community may thus conjure up a positive response, made all the more so by the feeling of something that was being lost in the impersonal relationships of the contemporary urban world.

Classical social theorists – particularly Tonnies, Marx, Weber, Durkheim and Simmel – were particularly interested in the ways in which modernity was undermining communities and were grappling to identify the nature of new forms of social relationships that were emerging. The re-emergence of interest in community in social thinking during the nineteenth century can be seen against the backdrop of the new social order within which the loneliness of individual rationalism sometimes encouraged a nostalgia for a lost communal past.

Founding sociological perspectives on community and urbanisation

A major contribution to the debate can be found in the works of Ferdinand Tonnies. For Tonnies, communities comprised closely bound social relationships within which people developed a sense of belonging. Nostalgia for a lost past was captured in Tonnies view that competitive and coldly calculating individualism of modern capitalism and urban life was undermining such communities. It was fragmenting societies into more superficial contacts between people based simply on the sharing of common interests or purposes.

Tonnies developed a typology by which the process of social modernisation was viewed in terms of a transition from the personal intimacy of small scale rural communities to that of large scale and impersonal urban society – a transition of social relationships from those of community to association. In this process, he argued that socially designated and relatively fixed status within the confines of community life gives way to a more atomistic society of individual contractual relationships which are superficially forged out of economic convenience. This change is accompanied by a

73

decline in the importance of religion and a growing preoccupation with the practical. Thus, a society formed of intimate communities (referred to as Gemenischaft) gives way to a more impersonal society, resting on an association of individual interests (Gesellschaft). However, in extreme associational conditions, attempts may be made to recover lost communal security through engineering pseudo gemeinschaft conditions. We might see this stage exemplified, for example, in the emergence of welfare state apparatus as a form of pooled protection from the insecurities of extreme individualism and free market forces of the associational form.

As we have seen, for Durkheim, primitive societies comprised small gatherings of people who were tightly integrated into communities of like others through the bond of a powerful collective consciousness. Life for most in feudal societies remained localised, the division of labour was still limited, guilds provided a strong form of occupational identity, and powerful local community sanctions and constraints governed people's lives. However, in time, scientific and technological advances increased occupational specialisation and shaped unlikeness between individuals. These changes eventually culminated in social, political and industrial revolutions that swept away the local institutions and social constraints of feudal society.

Durkheim was concerned that the erasure of the confining social institutions of feudalism and the advancing division of labour that accompanied modernisation would lead to a dangerous slackening of moral guidelines and social bonds. Economic self-interest, even in the context of interdependent relationships of economic exchange, would not alone provide an adequate moral basis for communal life. For Durkheim, it was within the modern urban environment that the forces of social and moral dislocation were heightened. It was particularly in the city and urban world that was located the malady of anomie; an unhealthy sense of normlessness. Within the urban environment, official statistics of higher suicide rates than in rural settings provided Durkheim (1970, p.70, p.353) with evidence of these social forces at their most destructive.

Having diagnosed this social malaise, the urgent task for sociology was that of providing guidance to policy makers to refashion society so that a sense of collective identity and social integration could emerge. New individual liberties needed to be accommodated within a system of shared moral constraints and institutional structures that were appropriate to the new society. For Durkheim, a state education system geared toward nurturing individual talents, complemented by an emphasis on national identity, good citizenship and social duties and responsibilities would, it was argued, help to satisfy these requirements. However, the void between the growing state apparatus and the lives of individuals that was left by the demise of occupational guilds and the decline of local communities needed to be filled. Guided by the new science of functionalist sociology, the engineering of new social institutions, operating at this intermediate position, was a necessary response to this need. Although left rather vague, Durkheim argued (1970, pp. 378-381) that new communities of occupational groupings would provide an intermediate social context for improving the integration of individuals and stabilising society.

To Marx, the emergence from feudalism of free enterprise capitalism was tending to replace old community bonds with new relationships of naked self-interest, as epitomised in the ways of the entrepreneurial classes. However, Marx was more condemnatory of past rural and communal life than the mainstream of classical sociologists tended to be. There was no nostalgia for a lost past of communal relationships which he saw as socially and intellectually confining and being founded on old superstitions, small mindedness and rural idiocy.

For Marx, the transition from feudalism to capitalism brought a heightening of the process of commodification, whereby, through the development of the means of production, goods and services are produced for their exchange value as a source of profit in capitalist markets. Urban life was logically part of this process, enabling an intensification of the productive process to be possible with workers crowded into physical settings close to their place of work and concentrated within workplaces where their labour was itself treated as a commodity. For Marx, therefore, capitalism and urbanism created squalor and the experience of alienation.

However, from the class divided societies which had emerged, Marx argued that a progressive form of community could materialise through a common class consciousness developing amongst the exploited class that would hold the potential for future revolutionary transformation and new communal relations in a communist society. Thus, Marx argued that capitalism was clearing the way for a higher form of community life that would emerge through the advanced means of production being taken into common ownership (Hoey, in Matthweman ed. Ch.19).

Max Weber (1958) provided a detailed historical analysis of classical and medieval cities. Important to the latter were market settlements of trade and commerce in which free trade and commercialism, relatively free from feudal restrictions, were able to flourish and provide a dynamic for urban growth. These would become the defining features of capitalist society, and it may be for this reason that Weber had little to say about the modern city itself, recognising that its features were those of capitalist society as a whole (Parker, 2004, Ch.2).

In his view of the modernisation process Weber owed a substantial intellectual and largely unacknowledged debt to Tonnies. In Weber's works, we see the impersonal forces of rationalization undermining feelings of community belonging which prevailed in traditional society. The concern of Weber was that capitalist modernisation, in the quest for rational efficiency, was taking the form of bureaucratic regulatory institutions of hierarchical social relationships that were dominated by experts and governed by principles of cold calculation. As in the case of Tonnies, for Weber a society governed by rationally motivated self-interest, whilst economically efficient, was tending to become barren of subjective empathy, and the world fabricated by man experienced as detached from nature and disenchanting.

The classical theorist who wrote most directly about the modern city was Georg Simmel. In his essay on the metropolis (1903), Simmel provided a remarkably perceptive analysis of the metropolitan human condition. Here, the meeting of the exterior social world with the inner world of the individual psyche was analysed with profound insight.

For Simmel, the rural pre-industrial context of social life provided for the individual a small circle of close acquaintances and a close affinity to the routines of nature. This enabled and required individuals to invest a high degree of their subjectivity and emotional self into their social relationships. The agricultural worker would follow the routines of the seasons and the craft worker would be making products for a known customer.

However, eighteenth century Enlightenment thinking challenged the injustices placed on the individual by the claustrophobic social constraints of the remnants of the feudal structure. It led the way to greater individual freedom, the advance of the division of labour associated with industrialization, and the capacity of individuals to increasingly distinguish themselves from each other in terms of greater opportunity to realize their uniqueness and special talents. For Simmel, it was the city environment which had achieved the 'escape velocity' from the relatively static life traditional of pre-industrial rural society (Parker, 2004, p.5).

In the metropolis, mechanization and the money economy were accompanied by an 'objectification' of human relations. The city was both a liberating and constraining bustling centre of industriousness, commerce and finance. It aggregated masses of individuals into close proximity and, through numbers and pace of life, forced fleeting and superficial relationships where meetings are precisely scheduled by the imperatives of clock time.

Simmel argued that it would be psychologically and emotionally destructive for individuals to invest the degree of subjective and emotional involvement that was more typical of rural and even small town life into their relationships in the metropolis. Here, in an environment of fast moving stimuli, social contacts were high in frequency and brief in endurance. The defensive adaptation necessary for the individual in this environment also suited the needs of metropolitan life. Thus developed an attitude of 'reserve', with the intellect providing a protective shield for the emotional world of the individual, screening out stimuli that is not important to the task at hand. However, as others such as Milgram have shown in experiments (Hubbard, 2006, p.17), one consequence of this screening process is a greater degree of bystander indifference to criminal acts compared to that found in rural settings. In the city, for each individual there exists the rationalization for non-action given the presence of numerous other individuals who could help.

Behind this blasé exterior stands in the minds of individuals a calculating and rational mentality. This is a world of hard headed rational intellectualism and free market relationships constituting a battle between individuals within a man-made environment. The craftsman who once produced for a known customer would be replaced by the worker who produces to satisfy the impersonal market of consumers whom he would never meet.

Enmeshed in this impersonal world in which the individual made a specialized contribution, the broader personality tended to become neglected. Qualitative social relationships would tend to become hollowed out into a quantitative form with each individual relating to a far greater number of others but within the context of more anonymous and often fleeting specialized relationships, constrained by the precise quantification of time and money. Although liberating from the constraints of traditional rural life, the confines of punctuality rein in the potential for spontaneity and life is shaped to 'serve the calculative imperatives of money' (Hubbard, 2006, p.18), making intimate relationships very difficult to sustain.

Combining purposive individual action and social structure

Returning to our earlier themes, an enduring rift within sociological theory developed between macro and micro approaches. This rift has been between those perspectives through which society is viewed as an external constraining force, existing independently of individuals and operating as a system regulating and constraining their behaviour, and those which portray it as the product of purposive individual action based on shared meaning and understanding. We have seen that the former approach is allied to the macro perspectives of both Marxism and functionalism and the latter to such micro approaches as symbolic interactionism, phenomenology and ethnomethodology. Weber attempted to combine both aspects in his social action theory, but others (see Slattery, 2003, pp. 274-275) have argued that the differences between the approaches are too fundamental to reconcile.

a) Norbert Elias' figurational sociology

Norbert Elias developed an approach of sociology which tended to sidestep the problem of social structure versus individual agency and combined insights from the tradition of macro sociology and Freudian psychology. Elias looked at how long term historically changing networks of social bonding shaped behaviour by entering individual consciousness and the personality structure. He argued that with the development of market economies, advances in the division of labour and functional specialisation extended chains of mutual interdependence between individuals. Individual awareness of the extended chain of relationships has a civilising effect on individual behaviour in the sense that the free flow of emotions and passions became curbed in the personality structure by people's mutual need for management of self-restraint through self-awareness of the complex chain of effects of behaviour on others (Kilminster & Mennell in Ritzer ed. 2003, Ch.7, Calhoun et al ed. 2002, Ch.29).

b) Anthony Giddens' structuration theory

In his theory of 'structuration', Giddens viewed social structures as constraining environments for but nevertheless modifiable through meaningful individual and collective action.

For Giddens, society is ultimately made from the actions of individual human beings, without whom it clearly would not exist. However, society is ordered behaviour; it reacts back on individuals to restrict their freedom of action. Social institutions and structures comprise various rules, regulations and power relationships which are necessary to mobilise collective action in the productive process. In doing so, they constrain the range of free action open to individuals. Social structures develop over time, both pre and post existing the lives of individuals who make up society. As such, they can be experienced as if they are external regulatory forces with a life of their own.

Giddens challenges approaches that singularly emphasise this degree of social structuralism. For Giddens, societies carry individuals, who through their own or collective input can meaningfully modify systems and structures. Although they work within structures, individuals engage with them reflectively and ultimately have the freedom to challenge the legitimacy of even the most repressive political regimes. External to and overpowering of individuals as they may sometimes feel to be, social structures cannot exist independently of meaningful social action - they may restrict the scope of individual actions to varying extents but are always also the product of social action. People therefore, although having the range of their free action prescribed by the constraints of social structures, have the capacity to self-consciously control and shape those social structures by which they feel controlled. This is the duality of social life which Giddens explained as follows:

'By the duality of structure I mean that social structures are both constituted by human agency, and yet at the same time are the very medium of this constitution' (Giddens, 1976, p.121).

Sociological theory – the way ahead

Without the discipline of theory and evidence, the sociological imagination remains speculative and subjective. On the other hand, as mentioned at the beginning of this chapter, whilst theories equip the sociologist with the tools for perceiving and analysing society, being an effective sociologist is not just about uncritically applying theory to society. Instead, theory must be a living thing in the sense of being applied reflectively to society and modified whenever evidence suggests that it is necessary.

With this caution in mind, and without making any claim that the previous pages comprise anywhere near to a comprehensive history of sociological theory, this chapter will be concluded with brief reference to three main ways ahead for sociology. The first position refers to sociologists who still largely adhere to one or more of the founding perspectives, if in somewhat modified form. However, the basic viability of these perspectives to explain the social world early in the twenty first century has been increasingly called into question. How can functionalism adequately explain how societies function when through the processes of globalisation societies are no longer, if they ever were, sealed and separately functioning entities? How can Marxist analysis, rooted in mid nineteenth century industrial capitalism with clear divisions between owners and non-owners of the means of production, explain the workings of post-industrial service and information based societies which have arguably undergone the reforms of becoming a widespread share and property owning form of popular capitalism? Can Weber's theory of bureaucratisation remain relevant to contemporary capitalism in which organisational structures need to be highly flexible and responsive to rapid change? And to what extent can the symbolic interactionist view of the development of self-identity remain a plausible model in a society where 'interaction' is increasingly mediated through technological communication?

A second and radical position is adopted by a range of theorists referred to as postmodernists, including writers such as Jean-Francois Lyotard and Jean Baudrillard. They define the 'modern' period as that emerging from the eighteenth century Enlightenment and now ending. This period was dominated by the discourse of science and the aspiration to use science and rational thinking as the method to achieve absolute truth and to assist progress. Sociology itself emerged during this period to analyse society in scientific terms, in, for example the positivistic writings of Comte, Durkheim and Marx.

Postmodernists argue that the brutal track record of dominant science and the creation of a world devoid of emotional intelligence are leading to the abandonment of science as the dominant quest for absolute truth. As a consequence, contemporary society comprises competing belief systems, each of relative worth, and it is becoming realised that neither founding social theory, nor in the extreme any social theory, is equipped to offer a single explanation of society which is superior to any other explanation. For postmodernists, 'truth' in the contemporary fast changing world of media created images is becoming illusive and with it sociology as a superior discipline for rationally understanding and organising society is becoming redundant.

Thirdly, are those such as Ulrich Beck and Anthony Giddens, who respectively view contemporary society as having reached a stage of second modernism or high modernism. They maintain that major changes have taken place in contemporary society such as the erosion of the confines of traditional family life and the social class structure, these within the broader social context of increasingly rapid social change. Enhanced global interconnectedness has brought such new risks as global financial instability. For the individual, these changes can lead to the experience of greater uncertainty and insecurity. However, high modernists argue that it is still possible to intelligently guide practical intervention to protect societies and individuals from the negative consequences of these newly created risks. Indeed, rational guidance through sociological theory is much needed, but new approaches and concepts are required to reconnect sociology with a rapidly changing and globalised world.

Postmodernist and high modernist approaches will be explored further at the end of a number of topic chapters and developed in chapter 14 on Developments in Sociological Theory.

Chapter 4
Sociological Research Methods

Abstract

This chapter begins by alerting the reader to the problem of the intrusion of personal bias into everyday knowledge about society and emphasises that sociology requires a methodical approach and a sound evidential base for the study of society which is able to justify claims to academically superior knowledge. It is also emphasised, however, that for a number of reasons, sociologists must be cautious about their findings. A limited number of key terms and concepts central to research methods are then introduced and clarified.

Research methods are the means by which sociologists obtain information about society. A simple classificatory framework is adopted to cover a range of research methods that sociologists have at their disposal. This framework classifies methods in terms of whether information is gained primarily through asking questions, through making observations, or through utilising documents. However, it is also explained that, by their very nature or through their varied applications, methods may be located in other than just their primary category and that some methods may overlap with and even be used within other methods. The methods are explained in terms of how they are used, examples of their use are provided and some of their strengths and weaknesses are considered. In these sections, reference is also made to the positivist or interpretive features of the methods outlined and a classification table combining this dimension with the three criteria of the above mentioned framework is provided.

The sociological challenge

In our daily situations, we all hold a stock of knowledge about the social world. This knowledge may seem to be self evidently correct and adequate for our everyday purposes. It may be only when events take place which challenge it that we are likely to engage in more thoughtful scrutiny of what we have previously taken for granted. In sum, in our everyday lives we are likely to hold a pragmatic view of society – what we take as true or adequate remains relatively unchallenged all the time that it gets us by.

But from where do we acquire our everyday knowledge about society? Its main sources will include our immediate experiences, hearsay information from other people, and information from the mass media; sources which vary in their impact, may overlap, and can complement or contradict each other. By such means, our attitudes and opinions are formed and influenced. We may be vulnerable to misrepresentation and manipulation but we are also likely to be conspirators in the process to the extent that we select information and interpret the world to confirm our beliefs through our choice of friends and associates, newspapers, television programmes and internet information.

Further consideration of the influences contributing to our everyday knowledge reveals how unreliable this may be as a basis for understanding society. For example, experiences vary from individual to individual and the world of our immediate social experiences is very small. How far, therefore, is it valid to generalise our knowledge of society from these limited experiences? They may be quite unlike the experiences of people of different gender, social class, ethnicity, age, and life chances, etc. Nevertheless, our immediate experiences help to form our attitudes and opinions and these in turn frame our interpretations of our experiences. We may share similar opinions and interpretations with those who we choose to be our friends and acquaintances. The potential for selective reinforcement of our attitudes and opinions can therefore be great, and these are the means through which we filter our understanding of broader society.

We also need to rely on the mass media for helping us frame the bigger picture – for example on global events. Even if we are cautious, suspecting that information is being distorted or that we are being manipulated, the key question to ask is how can we check the truthfulness of what we are being told? Is it enough to review alternative sources of media information when we cannot check hardly any of this information by direct experience? Furthermore, if the media is an important vehicle of agenda setting in the public domain, what can we know about issues or events that tend to remain off the agenda altogether?

Most sociologists would agree that as an academic subject, sociology can not be just an assemblage, even a well organised one, of the stock of everyday knowledge that exists about society. To be so would often be to reproduce everyday bias, subjectivity and selectiveness and it would not be possible to assess the relative worth of one person's viewpoint on society to that of another. Most sociologists adopt the position that sociology must generate its own superior findings through procedures which stand up to rigorous scrutiny even though these findings can never be taken as foolproof or undisputed or final truths. The findings may be of varying levels of interest for people in their everyday lives or even fly in the face of common sense knowledge or assumptions. However, it is the educative role of sociology to feed back its findings not just to its own academic community but to members of society and to encourage people to examine their taken for granted assumptions. Sociology therefore has a broader enlightening role to play.

So just where do we place sociology in providing a sound understanding of society? Having emphasised the superior academic credentials of sociological knowledge to that of common sense knowledge, some cautionary points need to be raised:

1. There is much debate within sociology over which aspects of rigour (in particular, reliability or validity) are the most important, as well as the uses, virtues and limitations of different methods of obtaining information.

2. Rarely is there any single method by which a particular area of study can be uniquely and conclusively researched.

3. In the study of any single topic area, different methods can provide different types of data and lead to different or contradictory findings. How can this be interpreted?

4. Often reality is multifaceted. Research may show that the reality of a situation is viewed differently by different groups of participants.

5. However well established and conclusive the findings of a piece of research may be at a particular point in time, the fact that society is constantly changing necessitates the need for ever new research and explanations.

6. A particular difficulty for sociology is that sociologists, as people, are deeply implicated in society, the subject of their studies. As well as being sociologists, they are also everyday members of society about which they are likely to hold their own values, attitudes and prejudices. These can intrude, possibly subconsciously, into the researcher's choice of topic area and various aspects of the research process including the choice of methods used, the type of information acquired and how it is evaluated. The claim to objectivity and superior academic credentials of the findings must therefore be at least moderated.

The purpose of this chapter is to examine a range of approaches and methods that sociologists use to obtain information about and develop an understanding of society. This examination will indicate some of the strengths that sociological research offers in obtaining reliable and valid information compared to the epistemological (knowing) basis upon which everyday knowledge rests. It will also touch on the relative strengths and weaknesses of the methods themselves and encourage the reader to apply critical assessments.

Definition of main concepts

In sociology, a fundamental distinction in research methods can be made between whether the sources of information used are of a primary or secondary nature. **Primary** information is that which has been compiled by the researcher in the form required for the research. This may include, for example, information obtained through social surveys or participant observation. **Secondary** sources of information are those which have been compiled by others, often originally for non-sociological purposes. Official statistics, for example compiled by Her Majesty's Revenue and Customs (HMRC) or the Home Office, and personal documents, such as diaries or letters, are examples of types of information which fall into this category.

Sociologists can use various forms of **interviewing** to obtain information from others. The terminology applicable to the participants is dependent on the style of interviewing. Some interviews follow a highly structured approach. Here, a standardised document in the form of an **interview schedule** is used by the person eliciting verbal feedback, the **interviewer**, to closely guide the process and record the answers given. Delivering a formalised approach through which short answers are required to the questions is typical of interviews within large scale social surveys. The formality of this style of interviewing is related to the importance of focussing responses to questions deemed by researchers to be specifically relevant to the research. When this interviewing style is adopted, the person (or people) providing verbal answers is usually referred to as a **respondent(s)**.

The term respondent is also applied to those providing information in survey research which does not involve a verbal interview. In this case, the standardised document used to elicit information, which may be identical to that used in an interview, is referred to as a **questionnaire**. The key distinction between a questionnaire and an interview schedule is that the former may be taken away by the respondent themselves to be filled in or delivered through mail or internet surveys, whereas the latter structures an oral communicative process.

Returning to face-to-face interviewing, some styles are less formal and allow the person(s) interviewed to more fully participate in elaborating their answers or even influencing the sequencing of the interview. For this approach to interviewing, the terms **interviewer** and **interviewee** are more appropriate. Sometimes, the interviewee is referred to more specifically as an informant when their role is one of guiding the interviewer toward other sources of information, as is more likely to be the case during the exploratory phase of research.

The technical terms 'population' and 'sample' are closely connected. In sociological research, the term **population** refers to a clearly defined category of people to which the research applies. Research into voting behaviour may take the 'British electorate' as the relevant population. Alternatively, a study of the causes of homelessness may define its population as 'those living without access to accommodation in Nottingham'. A **sample** is a small selection from an identified population for purposes of inclusion in the research. The aim of taking a sample is to make the research process efficient, or in many cases even possible at all, usually by aiming to obtain a precise fractional replication of the characteristics of the population for analysis. Two key points emerge from this: 1) the sample should ideally be selected so that it is as representative as possible of the profile of the population relevant to the research from which it is drawn, and 2) the findings of the research based on the sample can then be generalised back to the population from which the sample was taken, but not beyond. Thus, it would not be methodologically sound to assume that the findings from a Nottingham study of those without access to accommodation would apply to those without accommodation in, for example, Glasgow.

In fact, there are a variety of approaches to sampling that have been used by sociologists and, dependent on the type chosen, are likely to lead to the selection of more or less representative samples.

In Chapter 3, a distinction was made between **positivist** and **interpretive** perspectives. A sociologist's orientation toward one of these broad perspectives may influence their research methodology, strategy and choice of methods used. Briefly, the term **methodology** refers to different research procedures, strategies and preferred methods which are often guided by underlying theoretical assumptions. Ultimately, different theoretical and methodological approaches are rooted in different **epistemological** (way of knowing) assumptions. These more abstract issues will be investigated in more detail in the following chapter, but they will be touched on here as they from a dimension of the framework by which methods will be classified in this chapter.

Positivist methodology emphasises that society is little different from the natural world and can therefore be similarly analysed in quite hard scientific terms. Sociologists who incline toward positivism will be looking to demonstrate that natural scientific method and precision has been undertaken in their research. Consequently, they will tend to devise precisely pre-planned and tightly controlled research strategies to obtain the type of information that they know they want. To assist in the precision of measurement, they will prefer to use methods which can supply **quantitative** information – that which is viewed as hard data and can be expressed in numerical form, often with the purpose of identifying trends, correlations and cause and effect relationships. Methods which can be used in this way and supply this type of information include the social survey and the analysis of official statistics.

When research procedures have been precisely specified and controlled, their use can be carefully **replicated** by others in further research. It is frequently suggested that in the social sciences, as in the physical sciences, this means that a researcher should be able to repeat the same controls and procedures and obtain the same results. This is an over simplistic and incorrect assertion. It would be more accurate and precise to say that positivist type methods such as the social survey or laboratory experiments should provide the same findings when repeated if it were possible that another researcher had used the identical method and procedures on the same participants at the same time. Consequently, confidence in the comparability of findings between different research projects can be high. If this is so and if researchers apply the same methods and procedures at different times or places and obtain different results, it is likely that the difference is substantial (it may provide a reliable measure of social change or diversity) and not due to the vagaries of the method or the way in which it has been used.

Research which emphasises natural scientific procedures and the possibility of precise replication is considered to be high in **reliability**. This criterion of rigour is of primary importance to and viewed as a strength in positivist methodology and quantitative research.

By contrast, **interpretive methodology** is related to an approach to sociology which posits that understanding society can only be possible through more subjective means. Theorists who tend to identify with an interpretive stance will emphasise the importance of gaining insight into the meanings behind people's actions rather than attempting to measure behaviour in terms of causes and effects. Interpretive type research will more likely take the form of a continuous learning process. The methods and strategy used will therefore allow researchers to constantly review procedures and evidence and enable refinement of insight to take place. The preferred methods will tend to be those which generate **qualitative** information – that which is aimed at promoting quality of insight into the worlds of others and which may lend itself more to narrative than to quantitative expression. Methods particularly suitable for interpretive type research are sometimes broadly referred to as ethnographic and include participant observation, unstructured and in-depth interviewing and the study of personal documents.

Interpretive sociologists emphasise that in terms of rigour, priority should be placed on establishing certainty that the researcher is measuring what they claim to be measuring. Research procedures must therefore allow the researcher greater flexibility to engage in a learning process whereby closeness to the outlook of social actors can be established. If this is achieved, then rigour takes the form of establishing a high level of **validity** in the findings, which provides a key strength in interpretive methodology and qualitative research.

Positivist approaches tend to be weaker in establishing the validity of their findings. This is because they usually pre-structure research around researchers' meanings and adopt a greater clinical distance from the subjects of the research. By contrast, interpretive approaches, in prioritising validity, can be criticised for lacking sufficient reliability as each piece of research relies heavily on the subjective judgements and interpretations of the researcher and cannot be precisely replicated by others to provide a sound basis for the comparison of results.

Range of research methods

The methods of research used by sociologists are many and varied. It is rarely the case that any area of study can only be approached by using a single method which is deemed to be exclusively suitable. Various factors can influence the methods(s) used and the way in which they are used. As well as the theoretical and methodological leanings of the researcher, these factors can include the amount of time, funding and manpower that is available and ethical guidelines and researcher judgements. Moreover, as all methods have their strengths and weaknesses, it is quite common for sociologists to utilise more than one method in a research project in an attempt to maximise overall rigor. This approach has been referred to as 'triangulation'.

As well as potentially combining both the rigour of reliability and validity, using a variety of methods enables the research to establish a closer and more subtle approximation to reality than when being grounded in just one. Society may be viewed as a multi-layered and sometimes contradictory reality, the complexities of which are often only apprehended through the use of a rich variety of research methods.

Research methods themselves can be classified in various ways. One common approach has been to notionally construct a linear scale with positivist and interpretivist ends and locating the methods accordingly on the scale. Although this dimension can rarely be completely ignored, other approaches have been adopted. For example, McNeill and Chapman (2005) comprehensively organise methods into the following chapters: social surveys, experiments and comparative method, ethnography, and secondary data.

The author of this text will apply two levels of organisation to a range of research methods. The first level will refer directly to the methods themselves as practical ways of acquiring information and the categories employed will be derived from answering the simple question 'how do the methods enable sociologists to obtain information?' The resulting categories used will be: through asking questions, through observing behaviour, and through utilising documents. Methods will be classified in terms of these above categories within which they can be primarily but not necessarily exclusively located. As research methods can be applied in a variety of ways, some will also require mention in more than one of the above categories. Methods may also overlap, as could unstructured interviewing and oral history; or one broad method, for example ethnography, can encapsulate others, in this case often participant observation, itself possible employing unstructured interviewing.

The second level of organisation will be guided by methodological classification in terms of positioning on a positivist and interpretivist scale. Together, these two levels will enable the positioning of a number of research methods on a classificatory grid which will be presented at the end of the chapter.

How do sociologists obtain information?

1. Primarily through asking questions

The social survey

Most people have had experience of being interviewed, for example through participation in market research. Such an encounter is usually within the scope of a social survey, which is a highly pre-structured research method. By this is meant that the parameters of the research, the type of information elicited, the wording of questions, the size and type of sample selected, and the procedures employed by interviewers (when interviewing takes place) are precisely defined at the start by researchers. The interview schedule / questionnaire (a distinction between which is made earlier in this chapter) is a key tool, not a method itself, which is invariably used within the social survey method.

It comprises a standardised list of questions which are finely tuned to gain information on a particular topic area under investigation from a relatively large number of people. Used in sociology, the focus of social survey research is usually designed to test a speculated explanation (hypothesis) and statistical analysis of data derived from the survey provides the means by which this can take place. However, it is important to be aware that in reality the process of designing the research and interpreting data is not just mechanical and always requires a degree of researcher insight, creativity and judgement.

Where face-to-face interviewing is used, the location of survey interview situations is likely to vary with the topic of the research and could take place, for example, in the street, the respondent's home, the workplace or in an office of the interviewer. Much depends on the nature and sensitivity of the topic area. In the context of much survey research, the respondent is simply restricted to answering pre-set questions and the encounter is quite brief and formal. This enables a large number of people, usually constituting a sample, to be interviewed within the constraints of time and resources available, with the aim of generating a mass of information in the form of numerical data which can be statistically analysed and from which conclusions can be drawn.

Supporters of the social survey point to statistical sampling, structuring, formality and standardisation as virtues of this method in the quest to obtain quantifiable and reliable information, with the possibility of generalising research findings from a sample to a broader population from which it was drawn. Within a social survey, interview schedules / questionnaires are designed as precision instruments for gathering focussed information on the area of interest. Care in the design and use of these instruments is therefore crucial. It is standard practice that the wording of questions must not be leading but must be clear, precise and absolutely relevant to the research. More than this, interview schedule / questionnaire design is of vital importance to encouraging the participation of respondents and to eliciting honest and accurate information. To assist this process, most surveys include a pre-test of the schedule / questionnaire in which colleagues are invited to review it and suggest improvements that can be made, for example in wording, style and sequencing of questions. This may be followed by a pilot survey, delivered to a very small sample of the population and run in advance of the full survey with the purpose of acquiring feedback on the clarity of the questions and instructions as well as information regarding the interview process (if used) itself as perceived from the viewpoint of both interviewer and respondent. The aim at this stage is therefore that of further fine tuning rather than providing survey data from the answers. Interviewers themselves have to be carefully prepared to deliver interviews in a standardised and non-directive way - there should be no intimation to the respondent of preferred answers. If, in addition to the above preparations, the privacy and anonymity of respondents is guaranteed, respondents should feel that they are in a position to answer honestly, accurately and impartially – if they are so inclined!

Survey questions are not only delivered in the form of face-to-face interviews. Other approaches include allowing respondents to take away, fill in and return the questionnaire themselves, telephone interviewing, mail questionnaires, newspaper and magazine surveys, and e mail surveys.

Telephone interviewing has been assisted through the use of computer software such as CATI which guides the interviewer on screen as answers to questions are typed in, instructions are adapted according to answers given, and data is immediately processed.

These alternative survey approaches may offer economical access to a broadly geographically spread sample of respondents compared to the option of using face-to-face interviewing, but they raise a range of other problems which could undermine the reliability of the research. For example, when respondents take questionnaires away for completion, there is a high risk that, unknown to the researcher, other people may influence the answers given. Furthermore, a significant proportion will not be returned, impacting on what is referred to as the 'response rate'. These are problems which are often exacerbated in the case of mail surveys. The problem is that however representative the original sample may have been of the population from which it was drawn, a low response rate may itself be unrepresentative of the sample, thus distorting the findings. For example, people holding strong views on the topic of the research may be more likely to be motivated to respond than others, thus underrepresenting information from those who hold moderate opinions. Moreover, without the presence of the interviewer, there is no opportunity for the respondent to ask for clarification of the questions (although this may be possible in the case of e mail surveys), and it cannot be certain that the selected person has filled in the questionnaire, or if so has answered the questions in the required order and with diligence.

A number of these problems can be in large part combatted through the administration of questionnaires in collective settings. Examples of such settings include classrooms and the workplace. Here, questionnaires can be distributed, instructions clarified, uncertainties addressed, and time allocated for questionnaires to be completed and collected during the sitting.

Linked to the formality of this method and the quest for quantifiable data is the typical style of questioning. In many surveys, a large proportion of the questions take a closed ended form – they only offer the respondent choice from a range of pre-determined categories in selecting their answer(s). The purpose of such questions is to provide pre-coded data in which answers classified into categories can be structured for statistical analysis. This data, of course, will lack the subtlety of response which is the aim of open ended questions which ask the respondents to answer at greater length, in their own terms and in each answer provide detail which is unique to themselves. However, when used within the context of the social survey, open ended questions are still invariably part of a heavily pre-structured and often formally delivered method. Furthermore, the quality and diversity of information gained by answers to open ended questions is often at least partially compromised by the process of 'post-coding'. This is a procedure whereby, for purposes of assisting the quantification of the unique, rich and complex information, researchers look through the varied answers and construct a limited number of categories into which they can then be pigeon holed for a more statistical analysis.

Interviews used in social surveys can take the form of **semi-structured** encounters which offer the interviewee (not now respondent) some feeling of control or, at the extreme, with unstructured interviews even more control. However, logistically, interviews of the latter type are likely to be restricted to very small scale surveys within which both the size of the sample and type of information acquired would substantially diminish the scope for using statistical analysis. Most social surveys are of a large scale and standardised nature in the quest to obtain a mass of data. This requires the interview to remain a tightly focussed, efficient and strongly interviewer guided process.

An alternative approach to questioning which is sometimes employed within the social survey is the **'vignette technique'** through which hypothetical situations in the form of cameo scenarios are presented to respondents to elicit their responses. The technique can be useful to measure attitudes and anticipated practical responses toward various specified social situations and can be a beneficial approach when it is suspected that a question may be interpreted in different ways by different respondents, thus invalidating question standardisation. For example, in their survey into family responsibilities, Finch and Mason (1993) employed this technique to help them compare participants' anticipated actions with norms of expected behaviour. The following is an example of a scenario from their research:

'Jane is a young woman with children aged 3 and 5. She has recently divorced. She wants to go back to work and she needs the money. But if she has a job she must find someone to mind the children after school. Her own family live far away but her former mother-in-law Ann Hill is at home all day and lives near by. Jane has always got on well with her former mother-in-law. Should Ann offer to look after Jane's children?' (cited in Devine and Heath, 1999, p.50).

The answer to such a question could then be probed further with the use of closed and / or open ended questions to obtain more detail from the respondent.

The social survey is a well-established research method. It has been applied in various ways and across a broad range of topics. One form that it takes is the descriptive survey. The aim of such a survey is to measure the extent of social phenomena rather than to test sociological theory. The most comprehensive descriptive survey in terms of its numerical size is the government census which, once every ten years, aims to achieve a 100% response rate from the British population, particularly to provide demographic information (information about the makeup of the population) to assist government planning and social policy regarding such matters as educational and health service provision and road building. However, the census may fall short of complete coverage of the population. For example, some of the homeless population are likely to be overlooked. For others, there may be a vested interest in evading inclusion. Such groups may include illegal immigrants, or, as was the case in 1991, many who were avoiding payment of the local authority community charge (poll tax) and did not want their whereabouts to become known to the local authorities.

Poverty has been frequently studied through the social survey method. Although essentially descriptive surveys, the pioneering work of Charles Booth (accounts published between 1889 and 1907) and Seebohm Rowntree (1899) provided compelling evidence of the widespread extent of absolute poverty in parts of England, challenged attitudes that had blamed the poor for their plight, and provided an impetus for the introduction of social security reforms during the early twentieth century.

Social surveys often take the form of **cross sectional studies**; they are one off pieces of research, gaining information from a sample of a population at a particular point in time. However, some are repeated at quite lengthy time intervals. These surveys are referred to as **repeated cross sectional surveys** as they do not track a particular group of people over the time period. An example of this type of survey is National Survey on Sexual Attitudes and Lifestyles, conducted by researchers from the London School of Hygiene and Tropical Medicine (National Survey on

Sexual Attitudes and Lifestyles, 22/6/2018). The research was initiated over concern regarding the spread of the HIV virus and the first run in 1990 – 1991. From a sample of almost 30,000 people, 18,876 completed the 40 – 60 minute interviews. A second survey was undertaken in 1999 – 2001 and more recently one in 2010 – 2012.

Regarding the sensitivity of the subject matter of this particular survey, a number of important points can be brought out. Great care had to be taken over choice of wording and sequencing of the questions. Pilot interviews were therefore an important prelude to the survey. Interviewers had to be carefully prepared in the way that they approached respondents so as to maximise both the response rate and respondent honesty. During the face-to-face interviews, self-completed questionnaire sections were included regarding questions in the most highly sensitive areas. Also, from the main sample, a smaller sample was selected to provide more qualitative information and obtain a greater depth of insight into sexual experience and practices. This process is referred to as multi-stage sampling.

Overall, by comparing the findings of the surveys, it was possible to identify social changes in sexual attitudes and lifestyles over an extended time period.

When cross sectional surveys are repeated, it is sometimes the aim that the wording of all or a significant proportion of the questions is held constant between the surveys so that direct comparisons of information can be made over time to measure social change. An example of such a survey of a descriptive type is the Crime Survey for England and Wales which started as the British Crime Survey in 1982 and became conducted biannually. The survey now operates on a rolling basis, interviewing people throughout each year on their experiences of being the victims of crime during the previous twelve months, as well as on matters such as their perceptions of and attitudes toward crime and the Criminal Justice System and their experiences of the police.

For this survey, Royal Mail lists are used as a sampling frame from which addresses are randomly selected. A large main sample of approximately 50,000 households was selected for 2018 – 2019 face-to-face interviewing of a randomly selected person from each household amongst those aged 16 or over. Also from the main sample, a smaller sample of over 3,000 10 to 15 year olds was selected for inclusion in shorter 15 to 20 minute interviews. The selected households received in advance a letter and leaflet providing information about the survey to enhance understanding and encourage voluntary co-operation. Response rates have usually attained close to 75% (Office for National Statistics, 22/6/2018).

In this survey, the responses to questions are recorded on interview schedule tablets. However, to help maximise information on very sensitive areas, such as those in the section which asks questions about sexual abuse and domestic violence, respondents are handed the tablet and are able to complete their own answers which then become hidden to the interviewer.

A key aim of the Crime Survey has been to establish a more reliable measurement of the extent of different types of crime than official statistics derived from crime reported to and recorded by the police can alone reveal. However, when interpreting information on crime trends, the Office for National Statistics tends to take a holistic view by incorporating both types of information as there are different strengths and weaknesses to each set.

To assist in the comparability of information over time, the victimisation section of the interview schedule has remained relatively unchanged. However, the nature of crime itself changes with social and technological change. Thus, fraud and computer misuse questions to be trialled in 2015, subsequently to be fully incorporated and then awarded National Statistics status in 2018.

Government funding constraints have further impacted on the survey, requiring from October 2017 a small reduction in the sample size and the removal of some questions relating to the Criminal Justice System.

Although such descriptive surveys are not conducted originally for sociological purposes, the results, often in the form of official statistics, can be utilised, but with a degree of caution, as secondary information by sociologists for more analytical purposes and related to sociological theory.

A further example of the repeated cross sectional survey is the study of voting behaviour carried out in the British Election Studies which dates from 1964. The survey (headed in 2015 by Curtice et al) now uses a mixture of face-to-face interviewing, mail questionnaires and internet surveys and includes a sample of approximately 30,000 respondents per run to obtain information on why people vote the way that they do and to ascertain factors that have affected the outcome of elections. Some examples of the type and structuring of questions are provided in box 1 overleaf.

Box 1   Sections from the interview schedule / questionnaire used in the British Election Studies, 2015

pp. 26 - 27

SINGLE CHOICE W1W2W3W4W5
Generally speaking, do you think of yourself as Labour, Conservative, Liberal Democrat or what?

1 ○ Conservative
2 ○ Labour
3 ○ Liberal Democrat
4 ○ Scottish National Party (SNP) Show if country==2
5 ○ Plaid Cymru Show if country==3
6 ○ United Kingdom Independence Party (UKIP)
7 ○ Green Party
8 ○ British National Party (BNP)
9 ○ Other party (open [partyIdOth1])
10 ○ No – None
9999 ○ Don't know

SINGLE CHOICE W1W2W3W4W5
Do you generally think of yourself as a little closer to one of the parties than the others? If yes, which party?

1 ○ Conservative
2 ○ Labour
3 ○ Liberal Democrat
4 ○ Scottish National Party (SNP) Show if country==2
5 ○ Plaid Cymru Show if country==3
6 ○ United Kingdom Independence Party (UKIP)
7 ○ Green Party
8 ○ British National Party (BNP)
9 ○ Other (open [partyIdSqueezeOth1])
10 ○ No – None
9999 ○ Don't know

SINGLE CHOICE W1W2W3W4W5

Would you call yourself very strong, fairly strong, or not very strong
$party?

1 ○ Very strong
2 ○ Fairly strong
3 ○ Not very strong
9999 ○ Don't know

p.36

SINGLE CHOICE W4   Do you think the number of immigrants
from foreign countries who are permitted to come to the United
Kingdom to live should be increased, decreased, or left the same as it
is now?

1 ○ Decreased a lot
2 ○ Decreased a little
3 ○ Left the same as it is now
4 ○ Increased a little
5 ○ Increased a lot
9999 ○ Don't know

SINGLE CHOICE W4 How necessary do you think it is for the UK
Government to eliminate the deficit over the next 3 years - that is
close the gap between what the government spends and what it raises
in taxes?

4 ○ It is completely necessary
3 ○ It is important but not absolutely necessary
2 ○ It is not necessary but it would be desirable
1 ○ It is completely unnecessary
9999 ○ Don't know

SINGLE CHOICE W4 If the government does cut the deficit over
the next 3 years, should it do so mainly by increasing taxes, by cutting
public spending, or by a mixture of both?

1 ○ Only by increasing taxes
2 ○ Mainly by increasing taxes, but also by cutting spending
3 ○ An equal balance of spending cuts and tax increases
4 ○ Mainly by cutting spending, but with some tax increases
5 Only by cutting spending
9999 ○ Don't know

Answers to questions such as those selected above are related to information on a variety of social and demographic type respondent characteristics including occupation, parent's occupation, country of birth, highest education level, left-right values, ethnicity, religious beliefs, etc. Although highly structured and providing quantifiable information, the aims of this survey go somewhat beyond that of just assembling descriptive data (British Election Study, pp. 26-27, p.36, 22/6/2018).

An example of primary research that aimed to test a sociological hypothesis is provided in Goldthorpe and Lockwood's (1969) classic social survey into changes in the class structure. The purpose of the survey was to test the validity of the 'embourgeoisement thesis' - the theory that modern societies are becoming increasingly middle class – in Britain. Within this survey, conducted in the Luton area, 229 married blue collar workers, who were purposely selected in income terms as affluent workers (referred to as a purposive sample), and 54 white collar workers were interviewed. Lengthy interviews, which the relatively small sample size made possible, took place within the workplace regarding work related issues, and at home with reference to politics and leisure etc. Since the blue collar workers were not exhibiting strong signs of middleclassness, Goldthorpe and Lockwood argued that their evidence disproved the broader theory of embourgeoisement (see the Social Stratification chapter for findings).

As a cautionary point, care should be taken not to over stereotype the survey approach. Surveys are likely, to a greater of lesser extent, to be supported by ethnographic (study of everyday life) information, especially if researchers live amongst the people that they are interviewing and conduct daily observations as part of their research. For example, living within the vicinity of the community that they were researching supplemented Young and Willmott's social survey research into family life in the East End of London (1957) with further insights. However, overall, survey procedures are claimed to match up to traditional canons of scientific objectivity and tend to be preferred by positivist orientated sociologists who strive to obtain factual data, either at a descriptive level or to test hypotheses and theories.

Longitudinal surveys differ from cross sectional surveys in that researchers return to the same people (if the participants are selected in terms of being born within a specified date range, they are referred to as a 'cohort') at key points over a protracted period of time, often many years, to acquire more information from them. Such surveys, like the cross sectional, tend to be large scale, work with mainly quantitative information and are generally seen, due to the continuity of participants, as superior to a series of snap shot surveys for the purpose of tracing social processes that operate over lengthy time periods.

One example of a longitudinal survey is that conducted by the Office for National Statistics which, from 1971, used census returns from which it obtained a 1% sample and followed up the information on these people with that obtained in subsequent censuses and related it to information from other sources such as the Registrar of Births and Deaths. The aim of this research was to study the relationship between social class, illness and death rates (McNeill & Chapman, 2005, p.54).

The North West Longitudinal Study (Parker, 1999) provides a further example of longitudinal research. This research was conducted in the Manchester and Merseyside districts and ran between 1991 and 1995. The focus of interest was to discover more about the growth of drug use amongst youngsters into a mainstream activity. A cohort of 776 youngsters aged 14 was selected from eight state schools. The participants were asked to complete a confidential self-report questionnaire annually. To help interpret the broad data acquired from the questionnaires, the researchers selected a sample of 86 seventeen-year-old participants for in-depth interviewing to provide qualitative data on attitudinal development.

In 2000, the survey had been able to acquire further information from 465 participants who had by that time become young adults. It concluded that "sensible' recreational drug use is becoming increasingly accommodated into the social lives of conventional young adults' (Parker et al, 22/6/2018).

Traditionally, the term **panel survey** originated in the study of political opinion, with the purpose of understanding why people change their attitudes over time or their vote from one election to another. Being of a longitudinal nature, for this research to be effective, the same people are re-interviewed at relevant periods of time, for example at successive elections.

Anthony Heath et al (1994) have conducted extensive panel studies of this type in Britain.

On the general theme of attitude change, de Vaus (1999, pp.37-40) has likened the panel survey to a type of incomplete experimental laboratory approach (see under section on observing behaviour) with the aim of measuring changes in attitude in a natural rather than artificial setting before and after an intervention, to test the impact of that intervention. He has provided an example of such a survey in the following form. If one were to measure the religious beliefs of a new intake of university students and do the same again at the end of their studies, it may be deduced that any measured decline is attributable to the experience of university life having a 'secularising' influence on students. We will later identify weaknesses in making such a deduction.

One source of terminological confusion derives from the fact that the term 'panel survey' has often become applied more generally to longitudinal surveys. For example The British Household Panel Survey, which was first run in 1991, was set up to look into social and economic change in people's lives, including areas such as housing composition, health, and labour market behaviour. This research provided a good example of the dynamics of longitudinal samples. 5,500 households, comprising 10,264 individuals, participated in the first 35-60 minute face-to-face interviews in 1991. As many participants as possible were to be re-interviewed on an annual basis and contact in the meantime was maintained through letters, but within eight years the number of respondents had fallen to 6,080 – this despite the fact that as the family was the unit of analysis, new members could be included. This problem of dropout rate, otherwise known as 'attrition', is characteristic of longitudinal research. It can be caused by losing people who move, who die and who refuse to continue their participation. From 2008, this survey was subsumed into the UK Household Longitudinal Study which comprised 40,000 households and looked at changing fortunes, attitudes and circumstances within families.

We have established that social surveys invariably require the use of interview schedules / questionnaires as a tool to gather standardised information. When face-to-face interviewing is used, the encounter is likely to be experienced as a formal and highly structured one. However, alternative uses of interviewing may employ far more open approaches to interviewees. One could construct a scale of interviewing techniques ranging from structured to unstructured approaches as follows:

1. Highly pre-structured, using closed ended questions only.
2. Highly pre-structured, but also introducing some open ended questions.
3. Semi-structured, employing mainly open ended questions and allowing some latitude to the interviewee in terms of input and sequencing.
4. Unstructured, comprising open ended questions and allowing the interviewee substantial personal input into the content and some influence on both the sequencing and direction of the interview.
5. Conversational, in which technically an interview may be taking place but the form that it takes is experienced by the 'interviewee' as if it were or very close to that of a spontaneous conversation.

Whilst the first two styles of interviewing tend to be characteristic of social surveys, types 3, 4 and 5, whilst sometimes comprising a component within social surveys that add more qualitative information, move increasingly toward research which is likely to be undertaken on a smaller scale and from an interpretive perspective. Seen from this perspective, the degree of pre-structuring typical of the social survey can be viewed as a barrier to understanding the world of the subject since the interests and definitions of researchers are imposed on the respondents from the start.

If interviewing is to be used, interpretive sociologists are likely to prefer to engage in relatively unstructured interviewing (categories 4 and 5) which might be used alongside other methods as part of a broader ethnographic (studying people's lives through their first-hand accounts) approach or within the method of participant observation (see under section on observing behaviour), all of which claim high validity to their findings.

Unstructured interviewing

Unstructured interviewing (often synonymous with the term in-depth interviewing) is usually far more time consuming per interviewee than formal style social survey interviewing. This is because the purpose of this type of interviewing is to acquire greater insight into the world of the interviewee. To assist in the process, it is important for rapport to be achieved between interviewer and interviewee (or informant). Although the interviewer will be working within some degree of pre-specified areas of particular interest, the interview encounter will be far less formal and less obviously pre-structured than that experienced in a large scale social survey. Topic areas and general questions are likely to be formulated in advance of interviewing to assist research focus and achieve a limited degree of standardisation between the work of different interviewers, but the questions may be referred to by the interviewer more as a guide and not necessarily followed as a sequential list. The interviewee may be offered significant latitude in answering questions in ways that they see fit and even given some input into the order and direction of the interview.

In some cases, interviewing may appear to be so unstructured to the interviewee that it is experienced as if it were a spontaneous conversation. In fact, strictly speaking, this will rarely be the case as the 'conversation' is likely to be gently manipulated to the needs of the interviewer. If covert (undercover) research is being carried out, the interviewer is likely to have little other option than to disguise the interview within a conversational style. And unlike the social survey interview, which is likely to take place at an appointed time and place, through the conversational interview, the researcher may have to adapt their interviewing to the opportunities which arise spontaneously if it is part of a broader strategy of participant observation.

It is likely, furthermore, that interviewees may be interviewed numerous times at length as rapport is gradually built up and they are guided toward the interests of the researcher, whilst the interviewer becomes attuned toward the ideas that are emergent from the interviewee feedback. This two way process involved in engagement between interviewer and interviewee is the basis for the development of what Strauss and Corbin (1998, pp.12-14) refer to as 'grounded theory'. Whilst early exchanges are likely to be of a highly conversational type, unstructured and even semi-structured interviews may follow as the interviewer is able to ground more refined questions in a growing awareness of the reality of the interviewee.

A limited degree of structuring can also be enhanced through a 'structure layering technique' whereby at the start of an interview the interviewer summarises what he / she believes to be essential understandings from previous interviews. These understandings can be corrected if necessary by feedback from the interviewee and also provide a focus to build on in the forthcoming interview.

It is clear that the interviewer in the unstructured interview situation will need to apply quite different qualities and skills to those of the survey interviewer. They will need to remain alert and open minded to the emergence of unexpected information and respond with appropriate questions, often off the cuff, as well as being able to retain an overview of the whole interview process whilst it is in progress to establish whether areas of importance to the research have been covered. Interviewers will need to decide on ways in which the interview may have to be shaped to bring the interviewee round to any areas which have been missed. And whilst remaining mindful of the theoretical issues and focal areas of the research, interviewers will need to translate these into everyday language to connect with the interviewee and bring out information from them at their own level. Subtlety, sensitivity and flexibility are therefore key qualities required of the in-depth interviewer, qualities which can be professionally enhanced through filmed role play interview training played back to the interviewer for analysis.

In contrast to the typical social survey interview, unstructured interviewing increases the potential for a rich flow of information, but also introduces the risk of the interview being too open and the interviewer developing a too close affinity with the interviewee and exhibiting subjective bias. The interviewer can also be faced with certain dilemmas in recording information. Taking notes is likely to 1) interfere with the free flow of the interview and 2) lead to difficulty of keeping up with everything that is going on, with consequent loss of important detail. Making notes after the interview should overcome the first of these problems but would probably exacerbate the second due to selective memory recall and possible distortion. Using a recording device to capture the details may therefore be the preferred alternative. However, such devices are likely to be inhibiting for the interviewee who may take longer to feel relaxed, making a series of lengthy interviews necessary before much headway is possible. A methodological case can therefore be made for the covert recording of interviews, although this practice runs strongly counter to the ethical guidelines of the British Sociological Association regarding the acquisition of informed consent. Issues relating to the use of covert approaches will later be discussed under the broader method of participant observation.

Despite these dilemmas, research using a relatively unstructured approach to interviewing offers greater opportunity for the researcher to be open to the emergence of unexpected insights. Elizabeth Bott used in-depth interviewing of 20 London based married couples in her pioneering 1957 research into the family roles adopted by husbands and wives (conjugal roles). Bott often made initial contact with couples through a person known to them. Field workers explained the general nature of the research and conducted between eight and nineteen interviews per couple. The interviews would usually begin with about 30 minutes of general talk before moving on to cover a broad range of pre-established topic areas, but in no particular order. Interviewers would raise topics to engage the couples in discussion, take notes in the process and if the couples wandered from the topic at hand, subtle guidance to redirect them would be applied. Researchers also conducted observational studies of the families when the children were present at the weekends. Although the findings were of a qualitative nature and not amenable to statistical analysis, Bott discovered that the pattern of roles adopted by partners within the family bored a relationship to the different types of friendship networks engaged in by the partners outside of the family.

A further advantage of unstructured interviewing is that it may be a more suitable way of engaging with groups who would normally shy away from the use of more formal methods that could be suggestive of officialdom, a classic example being Howard Becker's 1953 study of 50 subjects who used marihuana as a recreational drug (Becker, 1973). The sample comprised approximately 50% musicians and 50% from a broad range of other occupations. In probing into each interviewee's history of the use of the drug, Becker conducted most of the interviews himself and used the jargon of the users where he could. Although he has told us very little about the method used, it is clear from the detailed information provided that Becker used unstructured interviews to develop an understanding of the steps that users typically go through in their career of using the drug.

Another classic example of the use of unstructured interviewing is that of Ann Oakley's research into household task allocation and also her study of the experiences of transition to motherhood. In the latter research, Oakley (1979) found that a collaborative approach with the interviewees resulted in highly co-operative levels of response. Four interviews of approximately two hours each, two before the birth and two after, were planned for each of the 66 women at the start of the interview process. Of these, 55 interviewees completed all four interviews and only one of the women who dropped out did so voluntarily (Oakley, cited in Lincoln and Denzin, 2003, p.255). The reasoning behind the method adopted by Oakley holds many similarities to that justified by interpretivists but with a particularly feminist twist which will be picked up on in the following chapter.

Semi-structured interviewing

A semi-structured approach to interviewing is more flexible than the pre-structured approach of survey interviewing. It is likely to employ a mixture of closed and open ended style questions. Although the interview will be steered by the interviewer in terms of a research framework established prior to the interview, some latitude will be available in the sequencing of the interview and the improvisation of more specific questions to follow up information which may emerge in the course of the interview. Hence, the semi-structured interview attempts to combine some of the virtues of structured survey interviewing and unstructured in-depth interviewing by combining opportunities for qualitative insight with a degree of standardisation and comparability between interviews.

Although the boundaries between unstructured and semi-structured interviewing are not always easy to establish, the interviewing of the marriage and grammar school samples in Young and Willmott's 1955 research into family life in East London would seem to provide a good example of semi-structured interviewing. This sample was taken from their broader survey sample to add a qualitative dimension to their research. In contrasting the interviewing approach in these smaller samples with that of the main survey, Young and Willmott stated that

'the interviews with the marriage samples in both borough and housing estate and the grammar school sample......were relatively 'intensive'. They varied in length from one to three hours, and we called back for further interviews on a number of informants......We used a schedule of questions, but the interviews were much more informal and less standardised than those in the general survey. Answers had to be obtained to all the set questions listed (though not necessarily in the same order), but this did not exhaust the interview. Each couple being in some way different from every other, we endeavoured to find out as much as we could about the peculiarities of each couple's experiences and family relationships, using the set questions as leads and following up anything of interest which emerged in the answers to them as the basis for yet further questions. After each interview we wrote up, from our notes, a full interview report, including where possible people's verbatim remarks' (Young and Willmott, 1974, pp.206-207).

Characteristics of the interview types touched on above can be summarised as follows in table 1:

Table 1	Summary of Types of Interviewing			
	Interview Type	Scale	Structure	Personalised Input
Formality ↕	Survey	Large	High	Low
	Semi-structured	Moderate	Moderate	Moderate
	Unstructured	Small	Low	High
Informality	Conversational	Small	Very Low	Very High

A particular form of unstructured interviewing is taken in the form of oral histories. In this case, the interviewee is recounting past events such as the experience of emigrating to and settling down in a new country, explaining what life was like within a particular community, or providing unofficial accounts of working within an institution. Such research provides a particularly valuable record of past events if a community is faced with a major change such as rehousing or the decline of an industry such as the coal mining industry. This method enables first-hand accounts of past experiences of people to be documented before getting lost along with the lives of the interviewees. The method is of course highly subjective and in reality oral histories are usually prompted, contextualised and checked through the use of personal and official documents within the broader method of life histories which will be reviewed later under the heading of case studies.

The term longitudinal research has already been referred to within the context of social surveys. Since the key characteristic of this method is the tracing of change over long periods of time by periodically collecting more information from the same participants, the scale of the research does not necessarily have to be of social survey proportions. It may adopt a small scale and qualitative approach which uses a more open ended interviewing style. This was illustrated in '7 Up' – a television series commissioned in

1964. The study selected 21 seven year old children from a broad cross-section of social backgrounds but only focussed on 14 who filmed well. This process of selection, of course, would not be acceptable for sociological research purposes as those included were not likely to be a representative selection from the original 21. From the starting age of 7, and returning at seven yearly intervals to re-interview those participants who were prepared to remain in the project, the series traced, through information provided from an open style of questioning, their individual life course experiences, outlooks and fortunes against the backdrop of their varied life chances in an attempt to document the long term effects of social class background on their lives.

An alternative approach to the on-going longitudinal method is found in retrospective longitudinal research which allows measurement to be taken at one point in time. The classic example of this is that of oral and life history methods mentioned elsewhere in this chapter where the longitudinal dimension comprises reflections on the past and the use of personal and public historical documents.

2. Primarily through observing behaviour

Participant observation

Methods which rely heavily on direct observation, of necessity tend to limit research to quite small scale dimensions. The classic sociological observational method is participant observation, a method which often incorporates the use of interviewing, either semi-structured or unstructured or that disguised as every day conversation. The purpose of participant observation is to capture the meanings of behaviour as it takes place rather than provide a mass of statistical data to study broader social patterns or processes. Participant observation is therefore a micro and interpretive type method which produces qualitative information that is rarely amenable to statistical analysis. It is usually the primary method used by ethnographers who adopt a method or approach which will be introduced later in this section.

To uncover a detailed and accurate picture of life as it is, participant observation is usually a very time consuming method. Research employing this method is often of lengthy duration, but is not usually recognised as longitudinal because involvement of the researcher with the group is a relatively intensive and continuous process rather than one of periodic touchdowns.

Participant observation has been used in sociology in a variety of ways. One way of distinguishing different uses of the method has been with reference to a classificatory scale ranging from high involvement of the researcher with those being observed to a stance of complete detachment. Gold (cited in McCall & Simmons (ed.), 1969, pp.33-37) has constructed such a scale of researcher stances comprising the following: 1) complete participant, 2) participant as observer, 3) observer as participant and 4) complete observer. The extreme position of non-participant complete observer is, strictly speaking, not participant observation at all since the researcher has no involvement in the activities of those observed. This stance is one of the detached observer whose observations may be known to the observed, as in the case of a classroom observer, or unknown to the observed, and thus conducted 'covertly', as in the case of hidden CCTV observation. By contrast, the complete participant researcher would be so fully immersed in the activities of a group that he / she is able to pass themselves off as a group member. For Gold, this stance is also likely to require that the research is carried out covertly, as any knowledge by members of the group of the participant's true researcher role would be likely to invalidate the group's full acceptance of them and distort group members' behaviour. The more central positions on the scale involve research which is likely to be carried out overtly (with the knowledge of the group) and this tends to comprise the mainstream use of this method. Different issues arise for the researcher to confront dependent on the position adopted, but however used the essential feature of this method is that it attempts to study behaviour as it naturally takes place, and is hence referred to as a 'naturalistic' approach.

Using participant observation raises a number of questions and difficulties. For example, if entry to a group is necessary, which it usually is, how does the researcher gain access? When access and entry are achieved, what type of stance or role can the researcher adopt? How is it possible to capture information which is constantly flowing, especially in hectic situations? And how can the researcher minimise the impact of their presence on the spontaneity of the behaviour observed? Such issues will be touched on throughout this section.

In sociology, participant observation has been particularly useful, and sometimes the only realistic approach available, to study life within social groups that engage in law breaking activities or are viewed as deviant by the majority in mainstream society. This method has thus been used to study, amongst other groups, street corner gangs (Whyte, 1993, Liebow, 1967), criminal gangs (Patrick, 1973), life on the wards of a psychiatric hospital (Goffman, 1968), religious groups (Festinger, Riecken, and Schachter, 1956), the behaviour of prisoners (Kaminski, 2004) and fringe political organisations (Fielding, 1993). These groups would almost certainly be highly defensive against being studied by formal methods such as structured interviews which smack of officialdom. They may well refuse to co-operate, or if research is possible, participants would be likely to be highly selective in what they are prepared to reveal. Furthermore, pre-structured surveys have proved to be of limited worth in providing detailed ethnographic (first hand study to understand cultural meaning) material and are of no use in attempting to understand behaviour as it takes place. Through participant observation, the researcher usually blends in with the group and typically adopts a non-judgmental approach. Deviant groups may therefore be prepared to allow research of this type to be conducted if group anonymity and that of individual members is guaranteed. In this case, researchers can adopt an overt approach by revealing their research intentions to the group.

Before research can get under way, the difficult issue of gaining entry to the group has to be carefully considered. Groups may be more or less inviting to or suspicious of an outsider entering their midst to study them. On the matter of planning to enter a group, Schatzman and Strauss (1973, Ch.2) have provided important guidance. They suggest that careful preparatory research and hands on reconnaissance should be undertaken since there may be only one opportunity to make favourable contact. Reviewing similar research may give pointers to successful approaches, whilst low key preliminary reconnaissance (often adopting a total observational role) may reveal some of the routines of the group, key potential contacts and how the researcher might advantageously present themselves.

Initial contact with the group can sometimes be initiated by use of a trusted intermediary and the most advantageous entry point may be through a group leader or a prestigious group member. The priority of the initial contact would be to develop an amicable relationship and, with careful timing, float the idea of research to the contact person in the hope that they will vouch for the researcher to the rest of the group.

William Whyte's research provided an excellent example of this strategy. To gain access to an Italian street corner gang in an urban slum area referred to as 'Cornerville', Whyte used a contact worker in the Norton Street settlement house to introduce him to Doc, a street gang leader. Through striking up a relationship, Doc took Whyte under his wing, offering that "I can take you around to the street corners. Just remember that you're my friend. That's all they need to know" (Whyte, 1993, p.291).

Schatzman and Strauss point to the importance of providing a document which states in simple terms a request for research to be conducted and spells out the aims of the research, the fact that the researcher is a learner and will not be there to pass judgement, that anonymity will be guaranteed, and that the group will eventually be provided with feedback from the research. The intention would be for this document to be used by the contact person in discussion with group members to establish an understanding through which research can be undertaken. However, even on gaining successful entry, researchers would need to recognise that this may be at the sufferance of the group and that it could be terminated at any point, making the research at times an exercise in treading on egg shells.

It must be recognised that given the nature of the target groups, gaining access to conduct research overtly may not always be possible. Where gaining access by overt means is unlikely, an alternative strategy available is to infiltrate the group to be researched covertly. However, the British Sociological Association's ethical guidelines caution against such an approach which breaches the normal requirement of obtaining the informed consent of the subjects of research. Ultimately, the ethical decision lies with the researcher.

Planning for successful covert entry to a group will require particularly painstaking preparation for the sociologist. This is because the very reason why covert research is necessary is likely to be due to the fact that the group may be engaging in activities that make them suspicious of infiltration by certain outsiders such as the police or journalists. A good example of the care that may be necessary to enter such groups is provided by the journalist Donal MacIntyre (1999), whose aim was to enter the world of the Chelsea Headhunters, a group of violent football hooligans.

For MacIntyre, preliminary archive research was necessary. Police files were studied to obtain the names and pictures of those who were to be 'befriended'. Research of newspaper articles provided names and information relating to past cases of violence implicating members of the group. The history of Chelsea Football Club also had to be carefully studied. Preliminary observations of football hooliganism were made at a distance in the bars and on the streets during the 1998 World Cup in France. Back in Britain, to be eventually accepted into the group, conveying the right appearance was necessary. MacIntyre needed to learn how to smoke convincingly and had to acquire a Chelsea tattoo. Although he knew the locality of one of his key targets, MacIntyre had to hang around the streets to find out where he lived. He was then able to move into the same block of flats and watch out for his target's routine. Designer clothes were worn, an expensive car was hired out for show and every effort was made to be seen about. Eventually, first contact was made at a fast food outlet, with MacIntyre equipped with his hidden recording devices.

A further example of journalistic use of covert participant observation is provided by Jason Gwynne (2004, 24/6/2018) who gained access to British National Party meetings through a disillusioned Party member. His covert recording of speeches and conversations by leading figures in the BNP provided both material for a BBC television documentary 'The Secret Agent', and evidence that was used as prosecution material.

Although covert participant observation may be used in virtually identical fashion by journalists and sociologists, it is important to distinguish between their respective aims. When journalists use this approach to attempt to uncover the actions and identities of those engaging in deviant or illegal acts, it is less likely to be guided by the quest to enhance sociological understanding and more for the purpose of public entertainment, raising moral questions, bringing about a public response and even providing evidence for the punishment of identified culprits. By contrast, when sociologists engage in covert participant observation, their aim is to provide information to test and particularly develop theories which will advance sociological understanding of behaviour. Any value judgements that the researcher might hold need to be carefully monitored and held in check and the anonymity of subjects guaranteed.

Covert sociological research can sometimes by carried out under cover of an officially designated role. Thus, research by Goffman (1968) into life on the wards of a psychiatric hospital, that was covert to the patients and most of the staff, was undertaken, with the agreement of the hospital authorities, under the guise of Goffman working in the official role of an Assistant Athletics Director.

Jacobs (1969) conducted covert participant observation under the cover of a case worker in a social welfare agency. His findings, in common with those of Goffman, reveal an important advantage of the method used. In each case, the covert participant observer was able to penetrate the veneer of conformity which participants within institutions conveyed when they suspected that they were under the scrutiny of officialdom. Using this method, the studies revealed the unofficial practices which are part of the normal way of life within such formal organisations. It is unlikely that these practices would have been revealed by using more conventional methods such as social surveys.

Whether conducted overtly or covertly, the aim of participant observation is to accurately portray the lives of people and understand the meanings of their actions. Whether more fully participatory or detached observational stances are adopted may depend on the situations involved, the topic at hand and the subjects in question. A relatively detached observational role may be possible if the study is of people in public places such as museums or fairgrounds where research could be conducted relatively covertly. From such a stance, there is very little risk of the research becoming biased through one's subjective involvement. However, the problem with the highly observational role comes with the attempt to understand behaviour at a distance. Here, the problem of 'Verstehen' arises – how can we be sure that the meanings that we attribute to the observed behaviour correspond to those in the minds of the participants since we are not able to engage with them to check?

To combat this problem, most researchers will prefer to adopt a more participatory stance. Those who advocate a highly participatory approach argue that via a high level of immersion into the group, empathy with the participants can be maximised and insights into their lives generated, often through the personal experiences of the researcher as a group member, which may not be accessible by other methods. But if the research is being undertaken covertly, it may necessary for the researcher to offer proof of their worthiness to be a group member through engaging in an initiation process and it will be very difficult to avoid taking a fully participatory role in a range of activities when participation is the expected behaviour of all group members. As part of the preparation process, the researcher would need to anticipate such scenarios as far as possible and think about where to draw the line on the type of behaviour he / she is prepared to be involved in. If situations arise where non-involvement is decided upon, great care would have to be taken to justify non-participation without arousing suspicion amongst group members and risk having one's 'cover blown', especially given the dangers that this could pose to the safety of the researcher. In this context, Howard Parker (1974) felt it necessary to engage in criminal activities to retain his cover in the covert study of a juvenile gang. By contrast, William Whyte (1993), who conducted overt participant observation of a street corner gang, was able to justify his non-participation in acts of violence.

A different type of risk resulting from high participation is a methodological one. It is the negative side of the high level of subjective involvement invested by the researcher; he / she may become so close to the lives of the subjects of the research that a healthy degree of clinical detachment is lost and the research becomes value biased and distorted by the researcher's close identification with his / her subjects of study. When complete absorption into the group compromises researcher objectivity, this phenomena is referred to as 'going native' – a term which indicates the early origins of participant observation in the field work of anthropologists.

Cases where a highly participatory role is necessary may therefore require periodic extraction of the researcher from the group to 'cool off' and review information and experiences at a more objective distance. Ideally, it would seem that the judicious balance would be a form of participation in which the researcher is able to at times manoeuvre closer to the subjects to enhance insight into the meaning of their behaviour and on other occasions stand back to ensure that a healthy degree of detachment is achieved to protect the objectivity of the research.

However employed, participant observation is not usually as tightly a pre-structured method and research strategy as are more positivist approaches such as the social survey or the shortly to be reviewed experimental laboratory approach. By contrast, the researcher could well start in the field with quite a loose focus on the research. Open minded as to what he or she might find, the early stages of the research are likely to be exploratory with the researcher acutely preoccupied in watching and listening. Part of the early tuning in process could involve overcoming a degree of culture shock if the culture of the group is substantially different from that with which the participant observer is familiar. Only over a period of time, as the researcher becomes sensitised to the life of the group, may relevant questions and categories of analysis become formulated. These will enable more focussed observation to take place. By this process, participant observation offers much more opportunity for the researcher to obtain a grounding in the reality of the group (providing grounded research) than if a rigid but alien framework of researcher pre-defined categories and structured analysis were imposed from the start. The fundamental aim of participant observation is to develop a sociological understanding and exposition of behaviour which the group members would themselves recognise as valid.

The participant observer is likely to need to use some form of interviewing as part of their method. During the early stages of the research, interviewing may be of a conversational or unstructured style to help the researcher to make sense of situations. However, in time, to test the validity of the researcher's understanding or acquire more precise and detailed information on areas of particular interest, a more focussed and semi-structured approach is likely to be more appropriate and possible if the research is being conducted overtly. The style of interviewing, nevertheless, is usually relatively informal and the form that the questions take is only likely to have emerged within the research process. For example, during his overt research into the activities of a street corner gang, William Whyte (1993) developed questions based on his observations and would interview members of the gang to help clarify his own understanding of their behaviour.

By contrast, when covert participant observation is used, such focussed questioning would be virtually impossible since it would be unnatural and reveal to the group the presence of a covert researcher whose cover would be blown. Anything approaching interviewing would need to be conducted in a carefully disguised and highly conversational style. This necessity is explained effectively by Riecken (1956, cited in McCall and Simmons (ed.), 1969, pp.39-42) in an article entitled 'The Unidentified Interviewer'. Riecken, Festinger and Schachter covertly infiltrated a small religious group who assembled at the house of a prophet of doom by presenting themselves as ordinary enquirers. To reduce the influence of their presence on the behaviour of others, they adopted a relatively low key role of 'sympathetic listeners' who were keen to learn. In fact, disguised in a casual and conversational style, they were covertly interviewing members of the group.

In summary, table 2 highlights some of the relative advantages and disadvantages involved in comparing overt and covert approaches in the use of participant observation.

Table 2		Participant Observation		
Overt Conducting research on and recording information openly to all participants.			**Covert** Researcher role in hidden to participants and information about their behaviour is recorded without their knowledge.	
	Advantages	**Disadvantages**	**Advantages**	**Disadvantages**
1	No ethical dilemma	Takes a long time for participants to feel more comfortable in presence of observer	Careful preparation enables gaining of participants' trust	Ethical dilemma – professional and personal
2	Can avoid involvement in 'dubious activities'	Observer presence restricts spontaneity – 'Hawthorne effect'	Less distorting effect of observer presence, but must select role carefully	Difficult to avoid involvement in 'dubious activities' – how and where to draw the line?
3	No risk of cover being blown as no cover required	Researcher entry may be prohibited by some groups	May be only method of entry to some groups	Risk of cover being blown
4	Less chance of 'going native'	More distance between observer and world of observed	Gets closer to seeing world through eyes of participants through similar experiences	More chance of 'going native
5	Can interview to find out specific information without arousing suspicion	Imposes a degree of structure on research	Less structured	'Interviewing' must be disguised as natural conversation
6	Can record information	Open recording of information	Can follow more spontaneous flow	Difficulty of covert recording – time,

The main criticism of participant observation is likely to be that of its questionable reliability. The question of reliability could be put as follows: could other researchers precisely reproduce the research and have confidence that the method provides a sound basis for comparison of findings, uncontaminated by the vagaries of the method or the actions and interpretations of the researchers? How can studies be replicated and meaningful comparisons between them made when: 1) different sociologists may select different features from their observations which are important specifically to them or 2) differ in terms of their memory recall of events and 3) another researcher may have elicited different behaviour from the same group or interpreted the same behaviour differently?

These weaknesses in reliability tend to be inherent in the subjective nature of participant observation, but supporters of the method argue that they are a worthwhile trade off to achieve a close and valid representation of the world as experienced and understood by individuals, groups and communities. Moreover, the criticisms regarding weak reliability can be answered to a limited extent in the following ways.

Firstly, a number of observers of a group may be employed, as in the above mentioned research conducted by Riecken et al. Their findings can be compared to help produce a balanced and comprehensive overview of events. In the case of a mixed sex group, it may be particularly valuable to include both male and female researchers where possible as a female observer may pick up on the meaning of a female's actions in a way that may be overlooked by a male observer, and vice versa.

Secondly, observers can be prepared so as to work within a common framework through using standardised observation manuals.

Thirdly, as the focus of the research develops, it may be possible to use 'structured protocol sheets', which concretely define those activities and situational features to be documented in every case (Flick, 2011, p.227).

Fourthly, detailed exposition of the processes involved in the research should be documented in the writeup, partly to show researcher reflexivity (ongoing critical self-awareness) to the dynamics of the research situation, but also to allow other researchers to evaluate and follow or modify them in their own research.

Research conducted by Roseneil sheds further light on the versatility of participant observation and ethnographic research. Her research was into life at the Greenham Common peace camp during the early 1980s. What is unusual about this research, and perhaps contentious, is that Roseneil only decided to conduct her research years after her involvement in the peace camp. In other words, information that she gained as an everyday participant, she later reviewed as a researcher. Backed up by open-ended interviewing of other participants at this later time and the retention of various personal and public documents from the past, Roseneil refers to her approach as 'retrospective auto-ethnography' (Devine & Heath, 1999, pp.180-187).

Ethnography

Ethnography refers to the study of ways of life. The emphasis of this approach is for researchers to immerse themselves into the everyday life of social groups with the purpose of learning the codes of understanding through which people communicate in their cultural environment. Unsurprisingly, within sociology ethnography has often found favour with symbolic interactionists and is often primarily undertaken through participant observation. However, the broad emphasis on apprehending the cultural world of participants means that participant observation often has to be supplemented by unstructured interviewing, conversation, the life history approach and the study of documents and artefacts. The common umbrella term used for this approach is 'fieldwork' and it is argued that only through this broadly grounded approach will the subtlety and complexity of social life viewed from the different angles of various participants be recognised.

Ethnographic research was pioneered by anthropologists during the early twentieth century, classically requiring extensive periods of immersion into the life of people in traditional non-western cultures to enhance the researcher's understanding. The method emerged in the sociology of the Chicago School of urban sociologists who, led by Robert Park, were by the 1930s looking to ground their models of city growth and zonal areas through more micro and qualitative studies of community life, sometimes taking the form of what will later be identified in this chapter as the case study approach.

Many of the studies previously referred to as providing examples of the use of participant observation were also more broadly ethnographic studies, the classic one being Whyte's Street Corner Society. More recently, Buscatto (Silverman ed., 2011, Ch.3) has adopted an ethnographic approach to reveal the ways in which women tend to become marginalised in the predominantly male world of trade union representatives and in the world of jazz. Buscatto found that it was only through an ethnographic approach to her study areas that insights, such as the working milieu and social networks that operated to the benefit of males, that would not be fully visible to the researcher through interviewing alone, were revealed. Furthermore, ethnographic study was argued to be necessary to expose aspects of their environment that interviewees themselves may not have been aware of.

The best ethnographic studies employ a high level of reflexivity. Applied in this context, reflexivity refers to the constant re-evaluation and questioning of research methods and interpretation of findings by the researcher. This should be sufficiently detailed to be published as part of the research to assist others in their evaluation of the validity of the findings. Thus, although ethnography has frequently been criticised as a too subjective approach to sociological research, it has been counter argued (Buscatto, in Silverman ed. 2011, p.49) that reflexivity provides a form of 'scientificity' which makes the method more rather than less rigorous in a way that is most appropriate to the study of human cultural life.

Focus groups

The focus group method brings together small groups, typically of five to ten participants, who respond to issues within a framework clearly set by the researcher. The method can be applied at different levels. It can be used simply for revealing information that is not likely to be forthcoming through direct interviewing, or it may focus more on the group dynamics themselves to study the ways in which the information emerges.

Focus groups bring together people who are required to focus on topics of interest to the researcher. The researcher, referred to as the 'moderator', needs to create an environment which 1) provides a structured framework for the group interaction through exposing all group members to standardised communication, such as questions and film clips and 2) sets key ground rules for participation. Within these constraints, the aim is to provide an open and unintimidating environment that encourages group interaction and discussion, with the moderator acting as facilitator of the process.

The approach has been frequently used by political parties, not just with the aim of measuring opinion, but with obtaining a more in-depth understanding of the responses to political messages which emerge within group settings, studying how messages are picked up and attitudes influenced. So whilst, for example, attitudes toward immigration may be measured through a social survey, a focus group may prove to be a superior method to study communication and group dynamics behind such attitude formation.

Likewise, those working in advertising and market research have been interested in the potentials of this method in the study of consumer reception of symbolic messages.

Given the fluidity of the processes to be observed, interaction is usually electronically recorded for replaying and analysis. Such analysis can take a more or less quantitative approach. For example, content analysis (explained in the next section) may be used to apply a classificatory framework through which a numerical count of events or comments can be made. On the other hand, whilst still working within a classificatory structure, a qualitative approach will present findings in a more literary form, illustrating instances of types of contributions made through frequent use of quotations.

However, for Wilkinson (ed. Silverman, 2011, pp. 173-181), an alternative purpose for the focus group method can be to study the social dynamics of the group and the linguistic devices used by the participants to manage the situation as an end in itself, largely irrespective of the topic at hand. This is a more ethnographic based approach which holds some common ground with the theoretical perspective of ethnomethodology.

Focus group studies have investigated topic areas such the withdrawal of adolescent girls from sports activities (Slater & Tiggermann, 2010) and how older people are perceived in television commercials (Ylanne & Williams (2009).

Although the aim of focus group research is to provide a window of understanding into the lives of people in the outside world, such insights into natural everyday settings may be precarious given the artificiality of the focus group setting. However, in this on-line age, focus group research can be applied to the study of virtual focus groups in a natural cyber space field work setting.

Experimental method

A quite different approach to observation than that of participant observation is used in the experimental method which may be conducted within laboratory or field environments (although in some applications the observational element is limited or even non-existent). In its most rigorous form, the **experimental laboratory approach**, more often used by psychologists but in areas of topic interest to sociologists, claims scientific credentials through the setting up of a social equivalent to controlled scientific laboratory conditions. The method is therefore strongly positivistic and is claimed to have a very high level of reliability.

The logic of a scientific laboratory can be summed up simply as follows. Controlled conditions are created whereby a cause, referred to as an independent variable (for example the application of heat) can be introduced and its effects measured on the dependent variable (for example, the application of a measured amount of heat to an iron bar and the measured effect of its expansion). Following the hypothesis (theorised prediction) that iron expands by a certain amount when heated to a certain degree, the above test situation can be designed whereby the dependent variable (the iron bar) is measured before and after the application of the independent variable (heat). The difference in the measurements is deduced to be the effect of the application of heat onto the iron bar and provides evidence by which the hypothesis (predicted outcome) can be tested.

There are various ways in which controlled measurements have been devised to attempt to follow a similar logic when applied in social settings. As a simple example, if one wanted to measure the amount of learning that had taken place by students attending classes on an elementary mathematics course, the following experiment could be set up. A test paper could be given before the course to measure the knowledge that each of the class members started out with. A test paper could then be set at the end of the course in which each of the questions on the first test paper could be matched with different questions measuring the same areas of mathematical performance and with equal degrees of difficulty. The difference between the two scores would measure the amount of learning (the dependant variable) that had taken place in between by each individual and for the group as a whole as a direct result attending classes (the independent variable).

Or would it? There are at least two problems here. Firstly, however unlikely it may be, it cannot be logically ruled out by this experiment alone that mathematical ability may not have naturally improved over the course of this time period. To allow for or eliminate this possibility, a comparison would need to be made with the measured performance of a matched group who did not attend classes at the beginning and end of the same time intervals. Secondly, since people do not live their entire lives in laboratories (or in this case the classroom) we cannot be sure that some students will not have benefited from receiving access to external tuition rather than or as well as classroom teaching.

The reader is now referred back to the example in the previous section and the comment that the panel survey is 'a type of incomplete experimental laboratory approach'. The problem with the pre-test, intervention and post-test design in the social sciences is that it cannot necessarily be deduced that the independent variable is the single cause of the differences measured at the two points. As de Vaus points out (1999, p.38) in the example of a measured decline in religious beliefs amongst students after studying at university compared to when starting, unless measurements are made at the same time intervals with a matched sample not attending university and a similar degree of decline in religious belief is not found, we cannot have confidence that the experience of university life alone is the cause of such a decline in belief amongst students.

To apply the logic of the experimental laboratory in the social sciences in its simplest form therefore usually requires the use of two groups. Prior to the experiment run, the composition of these two groups is matched as closely as possible regarding the size of the groups and their internal makeup in terms of gender distribution, age range, ethnic composition and social class spread etc. The purpose of matching the groups is to make the experiment as watertight as possible. It is an attempt to isolate the singular effect of the independent variable by screening out the effects that any of these other characteristics may have on the outcome of the research if the groups were not matched.

The two matched groups are placed in closely controlled and matched environments. Just one factor (the independent variable), the influence of which is to be measured, is then introduced into the environment of one of the groups. This group is referred to as the experiment group. The other group, the control group, is not exposed to this influence. Before, sometimes during, and after the experiment, the behaviour, attitudes or knowledge etc. of members of the two groups is measured. Any measurable differences which are detected between the groups are deduced to be attributable to the influence of the independent variable that was introduced into the experiment group but not into the matched control group. By such means, the precise influence of a number of individual factors can be measured by introducing new independent variables each time.

In one example of such a tightly controlled artificial laboratory experiment, Eysenck and Nias (1978) demonstrated that, compared to control groups that weren't exposed to television violence, experiment groups that were showed greater signs of aggression. From these findings, the researchers deduced that similar effects may be taking place when people viewed television violence in the broader setting of their everyday lives – a dubious conclusion but one that could provide fuel for groups in favour of the censorship of sexual and violent content in the media.

Although experimental laboratory research should be easily replicable and the findings of replicated studies directly comparable, the artificiality of the situation invariably means that the research is conducted overtly and participants' knowledge of their own participation in the research is likely to affect their behaviour in ways that it is difficult to know about or allow for. They may look for clues as to what they think that the researchers deem to be preferred or acceptable behaviour – a phenomena referred to as 'demand characteristics'. However carefully the laboratory research is conducted, this artificiality also usually limits the potential for generalisation of the findings – it is questionable how far findings can be applied to natural settings where there is no similar consciousness of being observed. Furthermore, under experimental laboratory conditions the time span over which influences are assessed is often limited to a stimulus response framework which may reveal little about the effect of exposure to long term influences in the natural setting. The information obtained from such studies also sometimes takes the form of quantified physiological data (for example a monitored change in heart rate or level of perspiration etc.) which gives the appearance of hard science. However, it is difficult to translate such data unambiguously into the meaning behind it. Heightened rates in an experiment group who were exposed to images of violence could denote feelings of aggression but could alternatively relate to excitement.

The degree of artificiality involved in laboratory experiments can introduce other uncertainties regarding the effect which knowledge of being observed can have on the behaviour of the participants. This contaminant is referred to as the 'Hawthorne effect', the name origin of which will shortly be explained. Some laboratory research attempts to get around this problem by use of unobtrusive observation. For example, attempts have been made to measure the impact of exposure to violence in the mass media under controlled laboratory conditions with the researchers observing behaviour from behind two-way mirrors.

In a more complicated version of the experimental laboratory approach, the psychologist A. Bandura, (1965), studied levels of imitative aggression acted out by children who had been exposed to film of adult aggression toward a bobo doll. The control group were just shown this film, whereas one experiment group was also shown the adult being rewarded for the aggression and another group shown the adult being punished for it. Afterwards, the behaviour of each child toward toys including a bobo doll was observed and levels of aggressive behaviour recorded.

An alternative approach to the experimental laboratory has been to introduce controlled intervention into more natural settings. This variation is referred to as the **field experiment**. The logic of this approach remains the same as the laboratory version but the intention is to overcome the criticism of lack of generalizability from the laboratory to natural settings. For example, the classroom may provide an example of a natural field setting. We previously introduced the idea of pre-testing and post-testing a single group of students to measure the amount of learning that had taken place on a course. Let us suppose that this course had been delivered by traditional lecturing methods and one wanted to measure the comparative effectiveness to learning when adopting a student centred approach which involved more student participation. As suggested before, pre-testing and post-testing by matching the test questions could be used to measure learning. Students would need to be allocated to classes in such a way that matched control and experiment groups could be set up. The traditional lecturing method would be continued with control group but, following the same syllabus, more participatory teaching methods would be used in the experiment group. The comparative effectiveness of the two teaching approaches to the learning outcomes could be measured by the pre-testing and post-testing performance differences, and if researchers were present explanations could be supplemented by observational material.

There would of course be weaknesses in and limitations to the use of such a method. One weakness would be that although one is attempting to isolate the comparative effectiveness in promoting measurable learning by changing one variable in the experiment group – introducing a different teaching method - one cannot exclude the possible contaminating effect of different teacher personalities on the outcome of the experiment. And given the emphasis that is placed on numerical measurement in the use of this method, it may be easier to quantify progress in a subject such as mathematics than in a more discursive subject like English literature.

A pioneering piece of research which adopted the field method was conducted in the USA at the Hawthorne plant of the Western Electrical Company between 1924 to the early 1930s. The study attempted to measure the impact of changes in the work environment on the output levels of production line workers. By using an experiment and a control group, efficiency experts started by comparing the effect on the productivity of the experiment group of improving the level of illumination in their environment whilst leaving that of the control group as it was. Elton Mayo was then brought in to test the effect on productivity of other changes imposed on the experiment group such as changes to heating and humidity levels, changing the rest periods, the introduction of company lunches and shorter working weeks, etc.

It should be noted that only the effects of one independent variable at a time can be measured. Thus, if testing the effect of introducing a shorter working week on productivity level were to follow the testing of different illumination levels, the illumination level of the experiment group would first need to be returned to the same as that of the control group to ensure that what was being measured in its effect on productivity levels was the shorter working week alone. This procedure would be followed with the testing of each single successive independent variable.

Surprisingly for the researchers, during the research the productivity levels of workers in both control and experiment groups increased, whilst it was expected that the output of the control group would remain at a relatively consistent level. Indeed, even when changes were introduced into the environment of the experiment group which were anticipated to reduce productivity levels, such as a reduction of illumination to just the equivalent of full moonlight, output increased! The researchers realised that by knowing that they were being studied, the workers' behaviour was being affected by their desire to please the researchers, as well as their improved sense of self-worth as a result of their regular consultation. This phenomenon confounded the original aims of the research since the independent variable of overriding effect on productivity levels was in fact the workers' awareness of their involvement in the research itself. It made precise measurement of the variables that the researchers were attempting to isolate impossible. The effect of such awareness by participants on their behaviour has subsequently become referred to as the Hawthorne effect.

Not all field experiments have a high researcher observational element, as the following examples illustrate. Research led by Ariel et al (2016) was set up to measure the effect of the introduction of police camera use on police and public interaction. This experiment included police from forces in the West Midlands, West Yorkshire, Northern Ireland, Cambridgeshire and California. From the almost 2,000 police involved, each week during the year of the research officers were reallocated to shifts with or without use of cameras in roughly equal numbers – i.e. all officers experienced both scenarios.

The most striking outcome was a 93% reduction in complaints against the police in situations where the camera was used compared to the previous year when cameras were not used. Even in those research situations where cameras were not used, complaints against the police significantly declined. These findings were essentially interpreted as follows:

> The cameras introduced an external 'observer effect' which provided transparent evidence of the encounter and cooled down the interaction of police and public participants and put off the public from making dubious complaints.

The improved policing carried out in filmed situations became carried over into encounters with the public where cameras were not used, a phenomena referred to as 'contagious accountability'.

A Danish field experiment reported by Wiking (Blair, 25/6/2018, Cremer, 25/6/2018) aimed to test for any relationship between life satisfaction and use of Facebook, here without observational presence. In this research, 1,095 daily Facebook users were divided into roughly equal groups. The control group continued their normal Facebook use for the one week duration of the experiment and the experiment group went off Facebook for the week. At the start and end of the run, satisfaction ratings were measured on an ascending ten point scale. The results of these measures were as follows:

Table 3	Life Satisfaction Scores / 10		
	Before the test	**Intervention**	**End of the test**
Control group	7.67	X Remain on Facebook	7.75
Experiment group	7.56	✓ Off Facebook	8.12

Wiking interpreted the significant improvement in the happiness of the experiment group to be a consequence of their withdrawal from an activity in which most participants convey and play up the bright sides of their lives, providing other users with a false image against which they may evaluate the happiness of their own lives. Whether there are similar long term effects is of course not established.

To more fully utilise the benefits of the field experiment, some researchers have hidden or misrepresented the nature of their research to participants. For example, D. J. Smith (1977) set up a field experiment to measure the extent of racial discrimination in the labour market. Actors of different ethnic backgrounds but with otherwise matched CVs were used to apply for jobs; ethnicity was isolated as an independent variable whose effects on potential employers' decisions were to be measured. Measurements were taken of the written responses by employers and where interviews were obtained covert recording took place. Clear evidence emerged that employers were discriminating against ethnic minority applicants.

Overall, there tends to be a trade off between the different uses of experimentation in the social sciences. Using the experimental laboratory method, the investigator is able to apply tight but artificial controls. Although logically the effects of variables can be isolated and precisely measured, there are likely to be major doubts about the effect of the artificial environment on participants' behaviour and thus the validity of the findings, as well as the possibility for their generalisation to natural settings; the external validity of the findings is questionable. By contrast, in attempting to overcome these difficulties and enhance the validity of the findings, the more naturalistic the field experiment becomes, the more difficult it may be to impose tight experimental controls and the reliability of the research becomes more questionable.

A different approach to experiments is unique to ethnomethodologists and is referred to as **breaching experiments**. The theory behind this research method has been touched on in chapter 3 and will be explained in more detail in the following chapter. Essentially, the purpose of breaching experiments is to illustrate that everyday life is dependent on shared understandings between participants in situations which are so routine that participants lose awareness of this structured understanding upon which ordered interaction takes place. Breaching experiments are set up to break rules and cause disorder. By doing so, the nature of the taken for granted rules and understanding becomes highlighted and attempts by participants to reconstruct meaning can be observed. In one such experiment, Harold Garfinkle (1984, pp.47-49) prepared some students to act like paying lodgers for a short period of time on their return home at vacation and to record the responses they received. The aim of the research was to lay bare the taken for granted rules concerning appropriate interaction between family members and to document the way in which attempts were made by puzzled members of the family to re-establish a sense of meaning and order into the situation.

3. Primarily through utilising documents

Official documents

Various types of document are available to sociologists, usually but not exclusively in the form of secondary research material – material which already exists independently of the research being conducted and will not have been originally compiled with the specific needs of the researcher in mind. A distinction can be made between sources in the form of personal 'life documents' and official documents which emanate from a variety of private and public organisations. Official documents may be held in archives to which there will be a greater or lesser degree of accessibility to the public and sociologists, as can be seen in comparing newspaper articles and medical records respectively.

Official documents have been extensively used in pioneering sociological research. For example, Frederick Engels, in his study of working class life in England in 1844 entitled 'The Condition of the Working Class in England', relied heavily on the reports of Royal Commissions and newspaper reports.

When, in the mid-nineteenth century, Tocqueville studied the origins of the French Revolution of 1789, he relied quite heavily on gaining access, through having been a member of the French Chamber of Deputies, to official government archives. Although overstating his case, Tocqueville maintained that:

> 'in a country where a strong central administration has gained control of all the national archives there are few trends of thought, desires or grievances, few interests or propensities that do not sooner or later make themselves known to it, and in studying its records we can get a good idea not only of the way in which it functioned but of the mental climate of the country as a whole' (Tocqueville, 1966, pp. 24-25).

Research into social history may be reliant on accessing official historical records. In this case, parish and census records may be useful. For example,

Peter Laslett (1972) utilised information gleaned from parish records in his study of family life before the Industrial Revolution.

Official documentation is stored by a broad range of public and private organisations, but access is usually denied to information held in the form of personal details and that which is deemed to relate to national security. Where information is accessible, the advantages of cheapness and immediacy of access may be available, especially through use of the internet. However, the introduction of computer technology has also meant that documents can be lost through being overwritten when updated.

Sociologists are usually cautious in their use of official documents. They will need to consider the social context and processes behind their production, asking which organisation produced them, how they were produced and what the purposes were behind their production. These sources are often the product of a process of sanitization from the point of view of practitioners and organisations. Motivations for this could include the covering up mistakes or misdemeanours that have been made in a professional capacity, such as police tampering with witness statements, putting a particular political slant on events or erasing 'sensitive' material in state documents deemed to be in the interests of national security. Information may also be presented to generate a favourable public image of an organisation to maximise sales and income. Official minutes of meetings will not contain off the record comments, which if made available through a more ethnographic approach may have been very revealing. There may also be a substantial difference between official records and action itself, as for example in comparing lesson plans with what transpires in classrooms. In this case, a more valid approach would be to supplement the study of official records with observation.

A common approach to the study of official documents is the procedure of content analysis (introduced later in this section); a form of scrutiny which applies a coding system from which a numerical count of particular significant words and phrases takes place. However, as noted above, this process alone is likely to be of limited use in disclosing the place of the document amidst the social processes and contexts of its creation. Prior (ed. Silverman, 2011, Ch.6) suggests that a more revealing ethnographic approach would be to scrutinise how official documents are embedded as part of the interaction process which drives and routinizes social actions within organisations.

Life documents

These types of document usually relate to people's lives in a more personal and intimate way than official sources usually do. Sources may include personal diaries, letters, e mails, photographs, videos, and even autobiographies. As such, they will tend to supply detailed qualitative information and lend themselves to small-scale in-depth research or form part of case studies (see later in this section). Information gleaned from these documents, along with oral histories, may contribute to a broader life history approach in which family photograph albums as well as household objects may be referred to during in-depth interviews to spur the recollections of the interviewee. Plummer (cited in Seale (ed.) 2004 pp. 282-290) even refers to a search through the attic as a potential source of rich documentary and interview material. In historical research, documents may also be the only source of information available of course if the person concerned and their friends and close relatives are no longer alive.

Some life documents in particular need to be reviewed with a degree of caution. A key factor here is whether the information was originally recorded on a strictly private basis, as in most personal diaries, or written with an audience in mind, as in the case of letters. In the latter form of document, the writer may well have chosen to put a particular angle on events to influence the recipient. The researcher may therefore be keen to investigate the understanding of the communication by the recipient and their response. Moreover, the letters and diaries of public figures may have originally been carefully written with the expectation of future publication to a broader audience in mind. Autobiographies that further select and sanitise this information therefore introduce at least two levels of distortion into the material and may consequently be of doubtful validity. And it may not just be the small scale of the research and the availability and selection of documents through which we may question the representativeness of these materials, but also the fact that they disproportionately focus on the lives of the more powerful, literate or articulate.

In an electronic age, records of e mails sent and received and activity on social media are likely to be replacing letters, thus providing a source of more ephemeral personal document.

Time budgeting

Not all research that uses life documents is dependent on documents that already exist. A form of primary research documentation is used to provide sociologists with time budgeting material. This method requires the participants to keep a detailed diary of activities or events for use as research material. A good example of the time budgeting method was employed in Young and Willmott's (1973) study of family life where participants were asked to keep a detailed record of the domestic activities and tasks that they engaged in at points in time throughout the day. A further example of the application of this method is provided within research conducted by Oscar Lewis (Seale, 2004, p.283) into the lives of a small number of Mexican families. Compared to personal diaries, the entries within which are often intimately selected by the author, key differences in time budgeting diary content include the structuring of material within a time frame provided by the researcher, the recording of information that is relevant to the research and, through awareness of participation in the research, a possible change in the behaviour of the informant and / or distortion in the accuracy of its recording.

Content analysis and semiotics

Often but not exclusively applied to the study mass media output, broadly speaking a content analysis approach studies the use of words and phrases in a communication by applying a classificatory system to group those that come within particular meaning ranges into appropriate categories. This method therefore largely lends itself to a form of quantitative analysis of a document or communication. In its simplest form, the analysis of a message may be based on a count of words or phrases deemed to be of key significance to the research or the incidence of coverage of particular news items. Political parties may use this approach to scrutinise the output of television channels. In the case of the BBC, content analysis has been used to check that the broadcaster has fulfilled its statutory requirements of engaging in overall balanced and objective political coverage.

Content analysis has been applied to studies in topic areas such as racism and sexuality. As an example of the latter, Stokes (ed. Stokes & Reading, 1999, Ch.14) conducted research to measure the extent of sexual content within girls' magazines against the backdrop of claims that girls were being exposed to too much of this type of material. For the purposes of the research, seven different magazines for girls aged under 18 were selected, with three consecutive issues taken of each magazine. The time period covered was from 31 December 1997 into the early months of 1998. Stokes found that reference to sex was surprisingly low, thus questioning the worries of those regarded as moralizers. Sections that could be classified under the heading of sex, sexuality and sexual health comprised, depending on the magazine in question, between 0% and 7% of the content. Rather than promoting sexual promiscuity, the content of the magazines was found to be more geared toward promoting conspicuous consumption.

Within social surveys, sociologists will either formally or informally apply content analysis when they categorise the answers provided by respondents to open ended questions into a limited number of types for post coding. This structuring of responses assists in providing a more quantitative measure of qualitative material. Content analysis has also been applied to the study of personal documents for the purpose of gaining insight into a person's frame of mind or their attempt to influence others.

The effectiveness of content analysis is dependent on a number of factors. One is that the coding system applied needs to be reliable. This would mean that a number of coders of some particular material that use the coding system should make the same classificatory decisions. Another relates to the coder. A person coding scripts may over time through growing familiarity with the system gradually change the way that they classify content. To avoid the effects of such changes or variation between coders, computers can be used. However, computers have so far been fallible in lacking the human capacity to extract the precise contextual meaning of words with multiple meanings.

A more subtle approach to content analysis might look at the positioning of articles and / or pictures in relation to each other and attempt to decode underlying messages and identify intended reader manipulation. Such analysis might reveal, for example, the intentions behind newspaper articles on unemployment and immigration that are placed in close proximity, leaving the reader to make the desired connection – an insight that is unlikely to develop through simple content analysis. This approach borders into **semiotics** (the study of signs and codes) which analyses communication with the purpose of revealing underlying or hidden meaning. For example, semiotics has been used to reveal techniques involving the transference of symbolic meaning into products in advertising by connecting them with an appropriate image of a well-known celebrity which draws in the potential purchaser through connecting the purchase of the product to their aspirational lifestyle (Leiss, et al, cited in Seale (ed.), 2004, pp.341-344).

Semiotics was applied in a broad range of research conducted by the Glasgow Media Group, including television coverage of strikes in the 1970s and more recent research into the Arab and Israeli conflict. In the former case, although equal coverage may have been given to both sides in disputes, it was argued that the symbolic context of interviews - smartly dressed management located within offices, perhaps stocked with authoritative texts, compared to dishevelled workers standing near to a burning brazier on a picket line – was likely to convey a message of legitimate authority and worthiness of respect toward management as opposed to that of a disregard for rightful authority by a rabble of strikers who should be condemned.

It is therefore clear that semiotics moves the analysis of communication in a more qualitative and insightful direction. However, it should be noted that whatever analysis of content reveals, it would be a shortcoming of this approach if it were assumed that a similar standardised interpretation was made by all recipients of the message. Stuart Hall argued that this was often not the case and David Morley (1992) substantiated Hall's position in his research.

Comparative and historical research

A method which ranks amongst the largest in scale and grandest in sociology is that of comparative and historical research. It utilises information from historical events and therefore relies heavily on various sources of historical documentation. The method adopts a form of experimentation, but unlike the field experiment the effects of social causes are not revealed through the manipulation of the situation. Instead, a deduction of influences is made by process of controlled comparisons. Through making systematic comparisons between societies or social groups within societies, this method aims to tease out key causal influences on social change or behaviour by identifying factors that are more prominent in some societies or groups than in others.

A simple example can be provided in the area of education. Sociologists who are interested in explaining the different educational performance levels between different ethnic minority groups might engage in a comparative study of social, economic and cultural differences between the ethnic groups, as well as the treatment of different ethnic minorities within educational establishments. By painstaking comparisons, it may be possible to tease out the impact of specific influences on the varied performance of different ethnic minority groups.

The comparative and historical method was comprehensively adopted by the founding theorists in sociology. For example, Durkheim used this method very effectively in his 1897 landmark study of the social causes of suicide (Durkheim, 1970) by applying painstaking comparative analysis to official statistics on suicide rates between European societies and communities within them going back many decades. From this study, he was ultimately able to deduce a link between the weakness of regulatory norms and higher levels of suicide, thus analysing suicide rates in terms of the social condition rather than focussing on individual psychological factors.

During 1904 – 1905, Max Weber (Weber, 1978) applied the comparative and historical method to identify key influences contributing toward England being the first country to experience the transition to modern capitalism. Clearly, a study of English modernisation alone would have been insufficient to identify influences which were present there and assisted the process but were relatively absent in countries that made the transition to capitalism later. Only careful historical comparison brought into relief an important connection between the religious ethic of Calvinism and its associated work ethic cultural values which enhanced the modernisation process.

In a somewhat more recent piece of research, Skocpol (1979) engaged in a comparative analysis of the French, Russian and Chinese Revolutions in an attempt to develop a general theory of the origins of revolutions. This makes an interesting comparison with Tocqueville's research. However insightful, the latter was only based on the study of events leading up to the French Revolution. It was effectively a large-scale case study (see below) and therefore, as it stood, Tocqueville's theory could only legitimately be applied to the French case. By engaging in comparative analysis, Skocpol was able to tease out influences for which she could claim a greater degree of universality for her theory than Tocqueville could.

A further example of the application of the comparative and historical method is evident in the research of Barrington Moore (1969). Moore was interested in explaining the circumstances through which agrarian societies modernised either into representative democracies or fascist or communist dictatorships. To achieve this, he compared the role of the peasantry and the upper landed orders across a number of societies in their agrarian past.

Moore was able to link, for example, the emergence of fascist dictatorships to a process of modernisation forced from above by elites of societies with intensely feudal social structures.

The application of the comparative and historical method was pioneered and usefully applied during times when nations were viewed and could be analysed as relatively enclosed entities for comparative purposes. One may speculate that the extent to which processes of globalisation are diluting national boundaries may at least complicate the way in which this method can now be used. Furthermore, with any historical research, it is worth being wary of viewing history in terms of simple facts. As Raymond Williams observes (ed. Barlow & Mills, 2009, Ch.20), social historical research is a complex process of piecing together, analysing and interpreting information from a number of sources. Since this information is always viewed from within new and changing social and historical contexts, recovering the past is never finalised and always different from the outlook of those who lived in it.

Official statistics

Official statistics are, strictly speaking, statistics provided by the government and its agencies. The state has both the power compel and the resources to compile information on a national scale. This information is vital for social policy planning and implementation; social engineering which relies on accurate and comprehensive data. As noted above, a key source of information in Durkheim's study 'Suicide' was official suicide statistics available from a number of European countries.

In Britain, statistical information is accessible from a variety of official bodies, such as the Office For National Statistics, the Home Office and Gov.UK. Official statistics are available on a broad range of phenomena including health, crime rates, strike activity, the distribution of wealth and income, school examination performance, unemployment levels, births, deaths, marriages, and divorce rates. This information will have originally been compiled through a variety of methods. Some organisations must record certain information. For example, schools are obliged to provide information on the educational attainment of their pupils so that league tables can be compiled to show the relative performance of different institutions and assist parents and children in their choice of schools. Educational performance data is also compiled at a national level to show trends in exam performance and used at an international level for comparative purposes. All births, deaths and marriages have to be officially registered. Government surveys, in particular the national census which it is a legal requirement to complete, provide detailed demographic information.

Official statistics provide sociologists with a convenient source of information which has already been gathered by others. As such, it provides a cheap and easily accessible means by which large scale social patterns and trends can be identified. Nevertheless, this type of data has well recognised limits. Reliability may be an issue. Because official statistics are presented to the public, they may be prone to political manipulation. In particular, sociologists would need to be vigilant to detect whether there have been changes over time in the categories used to compile the statistics, sometimes with a political motive in mind. If these changes have taken place, questions of comparability in the data arise, as has been the case with unemployment figures, NHS performance figures and crime statistics. Sociologists using these figures will have to somehow factor in these changes and adjust the data to be able to realistically study trends over time.

The validity of official statistics may also be questioned; do they really measure what they claim to measure? On this dimension, the validity of government unemployment statistics as a measure of all people who are not employed or are underemployed and seeking work is open to doubt since it is based on eligibility to claim benefit to which some who are seeking work may not qualify, whilst some who claim may not be actively seeking work.

There may be powerful influences on the organisation providing the information, such as performance targets, sometimes related to funding, which distort the statistics provided. Educational institutions and the police service are organisations which have each found ways to work the system in the statistics that they provide. In the latter case, in the interests of improving clear up rates, police forces have commonly adopted the process of not vigorously pursuing certain reported crimes and subsequently reclassifying them as 'no crime' in those cases such as alleged rape and domestic violence where there is a high incidence of victims later withdrawing charges.

It is also well known by comparing official statistics to information gained from surveys that statistics in many areas underestimate the extent of the phenomena measured. This uncertain degree of underestimation is referred to as a 'dark figure', in which the official statistics are likened to that part of an iceberg which is visible above the surface of the water and the dark figure that which is submerged. Since the extent of the dark figure is uncertain, there may be doubt as to whether an increase or decrease in measurements through official statistics represents a real change in the incidence of the phenomena or, by analogy, the visible proportion of the iceberg increasing or decreasing. For example, a 177% increase in the recorded incidents of rape in England and Wales between 1980 and 1990 would need to be interpreted against the backdrop of Home Office recommendations to police forces in 1986 to restrict their 'no crime' practice and a likely increased willingness of victims to come forward given a more victim centred approach adopted by the police (Edwards, cited in Stephens & Becker (ed.), 1994, pp.134-139).

Another problem is that there may not be official statistics readily available in the form in which or from areas that the sociologist is interested in. Such areas of interest may include unofficial work stoppages, membership of new religious movements, marriages in a state of separation, people working in the black market and undetected and unreported crime. In the latter area, government crime surveys have attempted to fill the gap and provide more valid and reliable data on crime rates than that provided by official statistics based on crime known to and recorded by the police.

A criticism specific to ethnomethodologists is that the factual appearance of data in the form of official statistics masks the fact that it rests on official interpretations and classifications of behaviour in the first place. Thus, it has been suggested that figures showing a high incidence of working class juvenile delinquency are to some extent the consequence of stereotypical judgements made by officials, especially but not exclusively police officers, who may view and classify similar behaviour by middle class participants from 'good family backgrounds' more leniently. Number crunching sociology based on such data is therefore seen from this perspective as a spurious science.

Despite their many weaknesses and limitations, of all the methods so far mentioned, the use of official statistics offers one key advantage over others such as interviewing and most observational methods – the sociologist is unobtrusive, thus avoiding the influence of demand characteristics and the Hawthorne effect on the data.

Library and online research

Under this section of the chapter can also be included an approach that has been traditionally referred to as library based research. A library as a resource centre provides access to various forms of document for research purposes. The documents and information accessed may be in the form of physical copies of texts and journals etc. or research information may be electronically generated, thus often liberating the researcher from the need to visit to physical library location. Whether in physical or e form, the required information might be of a raw secondary nature, such as official documents or statistics, to be used for research purposes, or pre-existing research and theories which form the body of academic sociology and provide sources for further theoretical analysis. Researchers who utilise information of the latter type are sometimes referred to disparagingly as 'armchair theoreticians', but some of the greatest contributions to sociology, such as Durkheim's 1912 study of religion (Durkheim, 1976), have relied heavily on the study of other academic sources.

As people increasingly communicate **online**, new opportunities have been opened up to research other than the collection of written information, allowing the adaptation by sociologists of their research methods. For example, face-to-face interviewing can be conducted through Skype. Questionnaires can be completed interactively at a great distance allowing the respondent to pause and amend answers and contact the researcher for clarification. At another level, as people are increasingly engaging in social media friendship networks, ethnographic studies may take the form of cyber observation or participant observation of chat room communication to study the ways in which such online groups form and develop.

Ethical guidelines, such as those for informed consent, were developed in sociology before the internet age. Although the ethical foundations may remain, guidelines on their application will need to evolve. This can be briefly illustrated through the issues raised by online research conducted at Harvard University. To study how friendships emerge, sociologists at the University in 2006 accessed 1,700 Facebook profiles. However, access had taken place without students' knowledge. Moreover, as research assistants were used to download the data, even when privacy settings limited access to friends, if the research assistant was a friend that access could be gained. Having arguably breached ethical guidelines of student privacy at the research stage and released part of the information in 2008, Michael Zimmer (Parry, 2011) has argued that a) given the uniquely titled courses referred to, the data can be seen to refer to Harvard undergraduates and b) it would be possible in some instances to establish the identities of particular students.

An example of the problem of applying informed consent in the study of online discussion sites is highlighted by Markham (ed. Silverman, 2011,

Ch.7). These groups are quite fluid; they comprise a continuous through flow of participants leaving and entering, thus informed consent of all group members at one point in time will quickly become outdated.

Case study – no simple classification

The case study approach often combines a range of methods from this and the two previous sections of this chapter, thus defying simple classification. A case study is the study of a 'bounded system' (Stake, 1995, p.2) - a single unit of working parts with its own identity and sense of boundary. The unit of the research could be, for example, a person, a group, a neighbourhood, an institution or even a country. The case study approach often entails detailed and protracted study providing depth of insight into the subtle complexities that make up the subject area. The use of multiple methods enables multiple viewpoints and contradictory information to emerge. Advocates of the case study argue that rather than being problematic, this reflects the complexity of social life which may be viewed differently from the vantage point of different participants. Thus, within a college, one should not be surprised to find different vantage points on reality experienced by students, lecturers and managers.

The case study method can be used to follow and document social change in detail as it takes place. A community about to undergo urban development or a school about to go through an inspection may provide fertile ground for the case study approach. In the study of any institution, background information can be trawled, for example on the internet, before contact and, hopefully, entry is made. This information, of course, in providing a public image of the organisation, is likely to be highly partial. The aim of the case study would be to delve below this one dimensional exterior. Upon entry, early contacts that engage informants in a conversational style of interviewing will be useful for getting a feel for issues that concern them and provide a starting point from which the researcher can pick up on leads and move on to other people. Observations can provide another source of information, as would gaining access to institutional documents. Later, the use of semi-structured interviewing and even survey questionnaires may help to provide more information on areas that are coming into focus as the research progresses. Using such a broad range of methods, the end product is likely to be a highly complex and multi-faceted account of institutional life.

A number of ethnographic studies are in effect case studies. The same could be said about most participant observation studies, although these may tend to lack the rich combination of methods that characterise the use of the case study method at its best. Again, Tocqueville's (1966) study of the causes of the French Revolution was a case study, but a rather one dimensional one through its heavy reliance on the use of official documents.

Although generalisation of case study findings is not sustainable beyond the individual case, insights provided may be useful for guiding further detailed case study research in similar areas. Furthermore, it only takes the findings of one case study to disprove a hypothesis and undermine the theory from which it is derived. Thus, Goldthorpe and Lockwood's (1969) study of affluent workers primarily working at the Vauxhall Motors car plant in Luton, previously referred to as employing the social survey method, provided case study evidence which was taken to disprove the broad theory that affluent manual workers throughout society were becoming middle class.

Researchers may also bring together a range of case studies carried out by other researchers to develop a broader understanding of social phenomena. In his work 'Communities in Britain', Frankenberg (1973) drew on a variety of case studies of community life from which he was able to distil the key features necessary to construct a rural and urban classificatory scale.

Some case study work adopts a retrospective approach. If the focus of a retrospective case study is on the individual, it may take the form of a life history approach which often combines the use of life documents and oral history. In such studies, the participant is gently guided by the researcher to provide biographical details of their life, often with the purpose of identifying the formative experiences that have influenced the type of person that they have become. Oral reflections are often supplemented by personal and public documents - which can themselves be used as prompts - and interviews with family, friends and acquaintances can provide a check on the reliability of the interviewee's memory and the validity of the information provided. Life history information is likely to be of a highly personal, descriptive and qualitative nature, which for positivist minded sociologists makes it too subjective and unrepresentative to be of much worth.

An example of the life history case study focussing on the individual is Clifford Shaw's 'The Jack Roller' which documented the life of a delinquent boy, 'Stanley', in 1920s Chicago. Through the use of autobiographical material, diary entries and interviewing, Shaw was able to offer, much through Stanley's own words, a case study of the circumstances which led to the development of his delinquent behaviour.

It is argued by advocates of the life history approach that micro case study research can provide a very rich source of information from which can emerge a detailed understanding of the experiences of such groups as immigrants and delinquents which would otherwise not emerge through the use of more pre-structured methods such as the social survey. The life history case study may therefore provide very fruitful leads for further research.

Life history research may also form the basis of a larger scale case study of a neighbourhood or community. Amongst the most comprehensive of such examples is Thomas and Znaniecki's extensively cited 1919 study of 'The Polish Peasant in Europe and America'. This work looked at the culture of Polish immigrants and their integration into American society during the early twentieth century. The documentary evidence utilised by Thomas and Znaniecki comprised 750 letters provided by members of the Polish community.

To grasp the potential of the case study approach, it is worth pausing to consider the range of methods employed, the strategy adopted and the general sequencing of the methods used. One might consider, for example, how these may be applied in the following areas:

- What goes on within a school in preparation for an Ofsted inspection.
- Gender role relationships within a coal mining community.
- The culture and life of a group of football hooligans.
- The formation of social relationships on a new housing estate.
- An urban protest movement or riot.

Research methods – an overview

In reality, much research conducted by sociologists applies a number of methods to obtain information, an approach referred to by Denzin (1978) as 'triangulation'. The case study approach potentially carries this to the extreme. Ethnographic approaches may for example employ participant observation, unstructured interviewing and the study of official and life documents. In this type of research, the methods which complement each other are mainly of a qualitative type. Sometimes triangulation combines quantitative and qualitative methods in an attempt to maximise both the reliability and validity of the findings, as indicated in table 4 below.

Table 4	Triangulation	
	Positivist / Quantitative	**Interpretive / Qualitative**
Reliability	High	Low
Validity	Low	High

   To add to the different viewpoints which different participants may bring to an understanding of a situation, the information derived from different methods may not match well or can even appear to be contradictory. At the end of the day, much will rely on researchers applying what C. Wright Mills termed 'intellectual craftsmanship' in their struggle to best represent the complexity of social reality through their research.

   Table 5 provides a breakdown of the main research methods covered in this chapter and offers a classification through the three main categories employed and approximate positioning on the positivist and interpretivist scale.

Table 5	Classificatory scale of research methods	
	Positivist Methods Methods which deal with quantitative data to establish cause and effect relationships. Strong in **reliability**	**Interpretive Methods** Methods which use qualitative data to study the meanings behind actions. Strong in **validity**
Primarily Asking Questions	Social Survey, Cross Sectional *Interviews* *Closed ended questions* *Open ended questions* *Semi-structured* *Unstructured Conversational Oral history* Longitudinal Survey / Panel Survey	Longitudinal In-Depth
Primarily Observing Behaviour	Experimental Field Laboratory Experiments	Participant Observation *Complete observation* *Complete participation* Ethnography Breaching Experiments Focus Groups
Primarily Utilising Documents	Official documents Content Analysis Comparative and Historical method Official Statistics	Life Documents Time Budgeting Semiotics

Chapter 5

Theory and Research Methodology in Sociology

Abstract

The chapter opens with a brief consideration of the challenge that the sociologist faces in terms of popular misconceptions about science as the expectation against which sociology should be judged. This is followed by definitions of a small number of key concepts that relate to sociological theory and methodology. Research methodology is explained as something more theoretically based than just the practical use of research methods as tools for acquiring information.

A plurality of methodological approaches exist within sociology, each resting on different theoretical and philosophical assumptions about how truth can be most effectively established when studying social phenomena. The methodological positions of positivism, social action theory, symbolic interactionism, phenomenology and ethnomethodology are reviewed and explained in terms of their theoretical and philosophical underpinning and the methodological procedures of induction and deduction are introduced.

A key question that has plagued sociology is that of whether it can or should rightfully claim scientific status. This question runs explicitly and implicitly through the methodologies and epistemologies touched on in this chapter. Furthermore, the extent to which science itself lives up to some of its commonly held strictures is briefly considered with reference to the Popper versus Kuhn debate.

Some more contemporary approaches to sociological research are introduced in the form of critical theory, feminism and postmodernism. These approaches raise a number of fundamental questions regarding established canons of sociological research, including the questions of the certainty of knowledge, the nature of researcher and subject relationships, the possibility of value neutrality and the very status of sociology. The more extreme position of some postmodernists even dismisses the possibility of establishing the truth and challenges the traditional assertion that sociological knowledge is superior to any other knowledge about society. This claim is seriously questioned by the author.

The sociological challenge

Sociology is sometimes criticised from the viewpoint being too soft a subject to be a 'real' science and thus not worthy of academic credentials. The common sense view of real science is likely to include the process of objective truth seeking whereby a theory can be proven to be correct through the acquisition of hard evidence. Judged by this criteria, sociology, within which there exists a variety of theories and perspectives which are often at odds with each other, some of which emphasise the importance of studying subjectivity, cannot be considered as a science.

Those versed in the physical sciences and, in terms of the above stereotype, expecting to find singularly correct and indisputable evidential support for theories, are likely to find sociology a disconcerting subject. But is the gap between the physical sciences and sociology quite as wide as this view suggests?

1. It is important to question whether those subjects that are commonly regarded as hard sciences, for example astronomy, physics and chemistry, do actually conform to these commonly perceived scientific strictures.
2. Given that the subject matter of sociology, people in society, must take account of human consciousness, should sociology even aspire to the type of science which is more appropriate for the above subjects in which there is no subjectivity in the phenomena to study?

Definition of main concepts

Research methods used in sociology operate in the front line of practical research with the aim of providing information. The term **methodology** refers to more than just the aggregate of methods used in research. It is about strategies and justifications for using chosen research methods in particular ways in research investigations to obtain certain types of information. But what guides the methodological procedures and the type of information that sociologists are looking for is more than just a practical question. There are theoretical and philosophical dimensions that lay behind methodological choices.

As noted in the previous chapter, positivist and interpretive perspectives incline methodological strategies and choice of methods in different directions. This is because they make different **philosophical assumptions** about the society. Philosophy questions the nature of reality and what we can know about it. A key philosophical question running through sociology is how knowing about society can compare to knowing about the natural world and consequently how society can best be studied and understood. This question of knowing is referred to in philosophy more specifically as **epistemology**. Epistemology is concerned with the question of how knowledge is acquired, how we can know whether it is trustworthy and what actually counts as evidence. It is important therefore to apprehend the philosophy and epistemology that reside behind the sociological perspectives that guide research methodologies.

Research methodology may tend to take a predominantly deductive or inductive form. When conducted **deductively**, the primary aim of research is to logically draw hypotheses from pre-existing theory that allow predictions to be made and evidence gathered by which the theory can be effectively tested. Put simply, if the evidence supports the theory, then the theory is verified, but if it contradicts it, the theory is disproved or falsified. Positivists claim that such processes and scientific credentials can be applied to the social as well as the natural sciences.

By contrast, an **inductive** approach is more exploratory. It begins with open minded collection of data upon which new theory is developed. Through a lengthy process, it is claimed that theory can be effectively built on and grounded in the data.

In reality, the approaches tend to complement each other. For example, whilst a largely inductive methodology may be used in qualitative research, it would seem difficult to identify the type of information looked for without some type of theoretical starting point, even very loosely formulated or operating at a subconscious level.

The term **empiricism** refers to the epistemological position that a direct apprehension of reality can be acquired through the senses. Empiricists therefore tend to believe in the straightforward factual certainty of information obtained in this way. The philosophy of nineteenth century **positivism** tended to be built on the foundations of empiricism, claiming that is was possible to acquire objective knowledge as the basis for the demonstration of social causes and effects, for the building of social theory, and ultimately the uncovering of social laws.

The procedures of science have however been much disputed. An alternative view to that of constant theory testing is that scientists work in professional communities that tend to adopt a common **paradigm** – that is, as a professionally trained community, they routinely conduct their scientific work through common practices and shared theoretical outlooks which guide regular scientific activity.

Given the diversity of theoretical perspectives in sociology, a key question is whether sociology can or should claim scientific status.

Classical positivist methodology – an empirical knowledge base for social causality

The study of positivist methodology provides a point of departure for this chapter against which social action and interpretive views of appropriate methodologies can be compared. The philosophical position behind positivist methodology is essentially that the means by which the social realm can be understood are similar to and take their lead from those by which the physical sciences have been successful in revealing the processes involved in the physical world. The study of the physical world by scientific means has shown that its workings can be understood in terms of causes and effects and ultimately firmly established laws such as those of planetary motion. Sociological positivism is therefore premised on the view that causes and effects and even social laws operate in their own way in the social world. As is the physical world, the social world is amenable to understanding in these terms and the methods of science are the means by which this understanding can be revealed.

Anthony Giddens has defined the epistemological basis of nineteenth century positivism in the following way: it concerns a 'conviction that all 'knowledge', or all that is to count as 'knowledge', is capable of being expressed in terms which refer in an immediate way to some reality or aspects of reality that can be apprehended through the senses' and 'a faith that the methods and logical structure of science, as epitomised in classical physics, can be applied to the study of social phenomena' (Giddens, 1976, p.130).

Positivist social theorists tend to view society in terms of broad social structures which impose patterns of regularity on the lives of individual members. The behaviour and consciousness of individuals is seen as strongly determined by social structures and forces which exist external to them. This structural determinism can be seen in the works of Comte, Durkheim and Marx and is a feature of the macro theories of functionalism as a consensus perspective and Marxism as a conflict view of society.

Positivism as a systematised social philosophy can be traced back to the work of the pioneering French social thinker Auguste Comte who first coined the term. According to Comte, the absence of the effective application of science to the study of society during the first half of the nineteenth century was not to do with its inapplicability to this area of study but because of the unique complexity of social phenomena. This complexity provided science with its greatest challenge, but it was argued that social causes and effects could be revealed through factual data provided by direct observation, experimentation and careful comparison of societies, either contemporary to each other or through historical comparison (Comte, in Thompson, 1976, pp.101-114). Once this was achieved, social science would come to eclipse religion and philosophy and provide the rational means for both analysing society and organising intervention to improve its condition – a fundamental hallmark of modernist thinking.

For Comte, social scientists must remain objective and impartial analysts. He argued that people's individual consciousness could only be objectively understood as shaped by observable social forces that existed externally to them and were internalised through socialisation. As internal processes were of a subjective nature and unobservable, they, and psychology as a subject, were thus not, according to Comte, amenable to scientific understanding.

A clear link exists between Comte's positivist methodology and the functionalist perspective. Durkheim, a functionalist in the positivist tradition, emphasised that social processes exist in a realm that is external to individuals and impose constraints on their actions. For Durkheim, society was viewed as an entity which imposes patterns of regularity on individuals in the form of its legal constraints, roles, institutions, moral pressures and customs. Durkheim referred to these external social forces as 'social facts' (1964b, Ch1) which, it is important to emphasise, he maintained could not be changed by the action of individuals. It would therefore be inappropriate to view society as an aggregate of freely acting individuals. Instead, it was a realm in itself, the structured influence of which on individuals could be measured through the patterns revealed in statistical data. Durkheim applied this methodology in his study of suicide in which he used official statistics on suicide rates and adopted a comparative and historical approach to evidence the effects of the condition of the social environment on individual behaviour.

Durkheim's reliance on official statistics raises important issues regarding the development of positivism. Firstly, it indicates a departure from Comte's empiricist emphasis on direct observation. Whilst the statistics formed the basis for quantitative and scientific analysis through the use of comparative method, they were the outcome of the perceptions and classificatory decisions of others. Secondly, for Durkheim suicide statistics were not themselves seen as social facts but rather provided a statistical index of the social forces that brought them about. This is an important point to recognise because more contemporary positivism tends to emphasise the numerical factuality of the data itself.

Inductive and deductive methodology

Inductive and deductive approaches have been briefly defined earlier in this chapter. Early positivists such as Comte regarded inductive methodology, whereby the accumulation of evidence provides the basis for social theory in the form of cause and effect relationships and the discovery of social laws, as the key to social scientific progress.

Durkheim's 1897 study of suicide (1970) is regarded as a classic example of the application of inductive methodology. Built on scrupulous comparative analysis of official statistics on suicide rates, Durkheim was able to 1) eliminate non-social causes of the patterns that emerged and 2) develop a classificatory system of social influences that explained the data. He showed that in traditional societies, forces of excessive social integration were responsible for types of suicide that he referred to as altruistic and fatalistic. By contrast, Durkheim found that in modern societies, anomic and egoistic forms of suicide resulted from slackness of social integration. Durkheim thus believed that he had established the existence of social laws that related suicide types to the social condition.

However, Comte was no naïve empiricist, recognising that the very perception and selection of data is likely to be influenced by one's preexisting theoretical orientations. Thus, pure inductive method is an extreme methodological position which would appear difficult to realise and it seems clear that in their use of data to verify their analysis of social laws, Durkheim, and especially Marx, were guided by theoretical predispositions. Thus, in 1893, four years before it became a central concept in his study of suicide, Durkheim (1964a) had already theorised about anomie in terms of an abnormal lack of social regulation. Deduction accompanied induction.

In fact, positivist methodology has often now become more closely linked with deductive methodology and it is interpretivists who apply a more inductive approach.

The focus of contemporary positivist methodology is often to structure research to acquire data to specifically test speculated patterns of social cause and effect and establish the truth through theory testing. To test a theory, it must be formulated in such a way as to generate 'hypotheses' which are smaller theoretical offshoots of a theory. Hypotheses enable social predictions deriving from the theory to be made based on speculated social causes and their effects. The data of science must be that of observable or measurable facts. This requires hypotheses to be 'operationalized', a process whereby they are converted from theoretical level statements to concrete statements referred to as propositions that enable predictions to be made. Appropriate observations can then be made or data collected based on the provisional assumption that the theory is correct. Measured facts and observations enable these predictions to be tested and the outcome to be fed back to the originating theory to assess its truthfulness or correspondence with reality.

Viewed in terms of deductive methodology, the progress of social science takes place through endless cycles of theory guided research, a process sometimes referred to as the hypothetico-deductive model (Worsley, 1970, pp. 69-71, with an adaptation of Worsley's model, p.70, in figure 1 overleaf). Research findings fed back to theories help theories to become more finely tuned, and finely tuned theories more precisely steer research. If analysis of the research information proves the hypothesis to be incorrect, both theory and hypothesis must be modified to take on board the refuting evidence and new research set up to test the new or modified theory. If analysis of the new information leads to confirmation of the hypothesis, the theory is substantiated, but only ever, according to Popper (1972), until further notice.

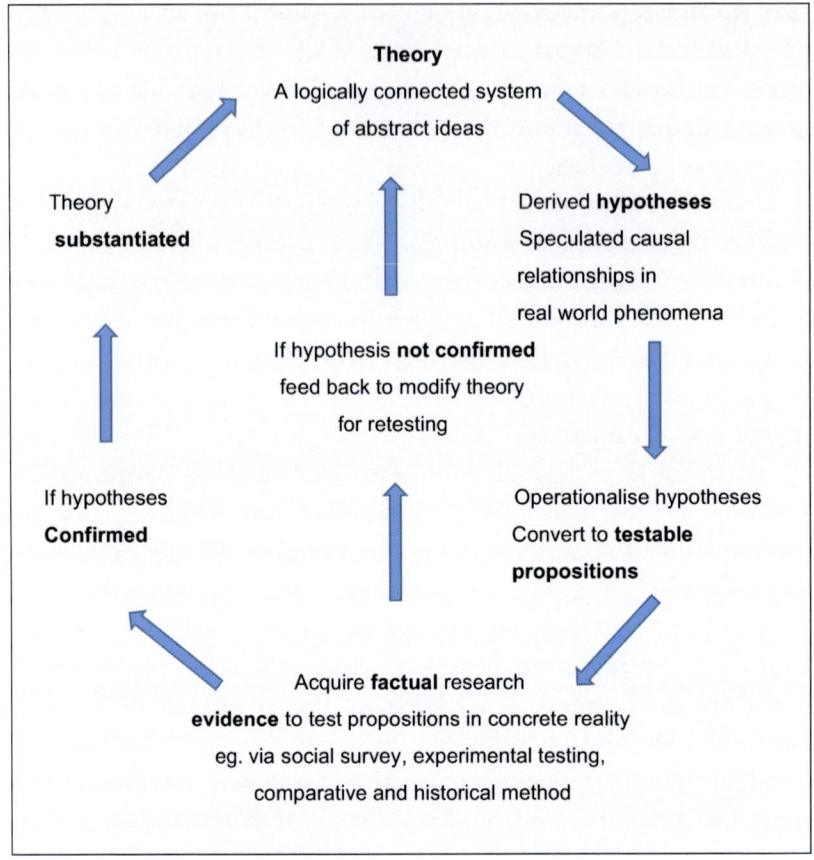

For example, one might want to test Durkheim's theory that low social integration is a social malady with damaging effects on individual well-being. As well as hypothesising higher suicide rates, one might speculate that other aspects of well-being would be affected. These might include levels of self-esteem, satisfaction, loneliness, worthwhileness, anxiety and stress etc. Social environments of low and high social integration levels would need to be identified, such as anonymous urban environments compared to small and closely knit communities respectively. Structured social surveys could be used to acquire quantifiable data on the degree of integration of individuals into social groups and dimensions of well-being to test the theory.

Despite what would seem through the hypothetico-deductive model to be a very mechanical approach to sociological research, high levels of creativity and insight are required to speculate on theoretical issues, to convert theories into hypotheses and to design research programs. However, to provide a rigorous test of a theory, highly pre-structured procedures are likely to be followed. Social phenomena must be reducible to hard data which can be precisely measured. Appropriate methods need to be chosen to provide the required quantifiable data and procedures for their application precisely specified. Regarding research methods, those which provide data which can be quantified and statistically analysed to demonstrate levels of correlation (association) or, ideally, causality at work within society are strongly preferred.

In the attempt to apply the rigours of scientific laboratory conditions to the study of human behaviour, the observational method of the experimental laboratory approach rests well within positivist methodology. However, this method is essentially restricted to micro level research. Positivists prefer to use methods which enable causality to be studied in society at a macro level. Such methods would include highly structured social surveys, the use of official statistics, and comparative and historical method. For example, if a social survey is used, a questionnaire will be predesigned to elicit the precise information required, a sample of respondents will be selected according to statistical sampling techniques and interviewers will be prepared to interview in a uniform and non-directive way. The quantified data will then be analysed to establish whether the anticipated cause and effect relationship is present.

In summary, the methodological basis of positivism is the belief that through the application of research methods of observation and comparison and the acquisition of quantifiable data, clinical analysts, adopting a social scientific approach, can establish truth about an objective reality. Early positivists claimed to be following an inductive methodology, even though implicitly against a background of theoretical knowledge. Positivist inclined sociologists now tend to adhere to a hypothetico-deductive approach through which theoretical speculation is regarded as necessary to guide and structure the research process. From theories are generated hypotheses which, when converted to the level of concrete predictions, can be precisely tested through quantifiable measurement in research findings. The structured procedures used enable positivist researchers to claim that their methods are highly reliable; they can be replicated and the findings checked or compared against other research that follows these procedures.

Social action theory – an interpretive social science

This and the following sections signal a progressive move away from positivist methodology. The methodological position of social action theory, as developed by Weber, is arguably a complex one regarding methodology and is quite open with respect to research strategy. Whilst recognising that the action of individuals is in part constrained by social structures, social action theory challenges the view that it can be adequately understood as resulting from social structural constraints alone and through the application of cause and effect analysis. This does not mean that the quest for impartial analysis and academic rigour has to be abandoned. It does mean that the sociologist has to take account of micro and macro contexts of action, of individual free will as well as social constraints and the influence of cultural meaning within a broad social context as well as the internal subjective meaning held by individuals when they engage in social action. Consequently, a different approach to 'science' will be necessary for studying society than that advocated by positivists.

A fundamental distinction in social action theory is made between behaviour and action. Strictly speaking, behaviour refers to highly pre-programmed or stimulus response activity, whereas action is activity which is mediated by meaning and conscious individual decision making based on choice. Human action is neither predetermined in the way that behaviour is in the animal world nor simply the outcome of imposed social constraints. It is meaning directed and meaning ultimately rests in the consciousness of individuals. Weber thus rejects all approaches which view society as an entity with a law like direction of change of its own, carrying along relatively passive individuals. Society is not an entity in its own right and the idea of such irresistible social laws is sterile, shallow and offers an incomplete understanding of social action as it ignores the capacity to change the social structure through meaningful and wilful actions resulting from subjective interpretations and motivations of individual actors. The challenge for Weber was to reconcile individual subjective meaning behind social action with the possibility of developing a scientific sociology.

Viewing society at the macro level, the details of social life throughout history present the sociologist with a virtual infinity of phenomena. To assist in making sense of this extraordinary amount of detail, Weber argued that sociologists have to develop theoretical concepts and 'ideal types', the latter being organisational devices for selectively identifying social patterns through the template of prefect logical constructs. These ideal types can never replicate the detail of the real world but should be seen as orientation devices for sociologists to help them to grapple with a much greater level of social complexity. Those developed by Weber for this purpose included traditional and rational-legal social types, used to help frame an understanding of what Weber argued were the essential features of pre-industrial and modern capitalist societies.

For Weber, action is bounded by social influences and cultural value systems. Nevertheless, it is the outcome of conscious choices which are ultimately made by individuals as free agents and whose actions feed into society. If we are to establish the 'causes' behind action, we must look to the meanings, motives, means and ends envisaged by individuals. This is only possible through the process of 'verstehen' whereby through the observer's own capacity for meaningful action they can attempt to empathise themselves into the subjective world of the observed to uncover the meanings and motives which are at work behind that action. Understanding social action must thus take account of the complex interplay between the influence of broader cultural values and social structure and the micro level context of everyday action which is ultimately determined by the conscious decision making of the participating actors which itself feeds back into the broader social and cultural domain. An excellent example of this complex relationship is provided in Weber's 1905 study of the Protestant Ethic and the Spirit of Capitalism which shows the importance of a set of religious cultural values and subjective individual motives to the process of economic modernisation.

The implications of Weber's position for research methodology are vast and just how to combine the micro and macro in research is left open by Weber. The range of potential methods is all embracing. At the micro level, ethnographic approaches including participant observation and the study of personal documents will be important methods to get to personal meanings. At the other extreme, Weber himself utilised comparative and historical studies to help tease out key social 'influences', terminology which is about as close as can be approximated to 'causes', behind broad social change. Weber was also aware that since sociologists are also everyday members of society, it is inevitable that what they study and the way that they study it will be influenced by their personal values. However, in conducting their research, he insists that they must strive to adopt a value free approach – a matter of fact intellectual predisposition of academic neutrality. They must be clear in their use of methods and avoid biasing their findings toward how they would want the world to be – taken to be a condemnation of what was seen by Weber as the politically biased approach taken by Marxists.

In summary, social action theory rejects positivist approaches to social science but still claims that a science of a sort appropriate to the study of society is possible. Realistically, one should remain cautious about the findings of social science. For one thing, there will always remain uncertainty as to whether an observer of action has accurately interpreted the motives that reside behind it in the mind of the actor. For another, even if something approaching causality can be accurately attributed to action which has taken place, one can only talk in terms of probability in predicting future action since people have the capacity to learn from their experiences and modify their actions in similar future situations.

As sociology developed in the twentieth century, the early positivist emphasis was retained in functionalist and Marxist perspectives, if a little less naively. Other developments concentrated more exclusively on the micro and subjective dimension also emphasised by Weber. These interpretive approaches include symbolic interactionism, phenomenology, and ethnomethodology.

Micro action approaches – interpretive methodology

Interpretive approaches that developed after Weber's social action theory tended to focus more exclusively on micro contexts of social interaction at the expense of an interest in the broader social structure. Some took a key extra step away from positivist methodology in abandoning the search for a causal understanding of the social realm altogether. This was because the phenomena of the physical world and social phenomena were seen to be so fundamentally different that to explain regularities in each required fundamentally different approaches.

The nature of this break was highlighted in the work of Peter Winch (Cuff et al, 2001, pp.116-120). For Winch, the search for causal and law like regularity in the physical world is appropriate there as laws demonstrate that the regularities which exist are impelled regularities. An example can be used in the fact that the movement of planets is absolutely impelled by forces and can be explained in terms of gravitational laws. By contrast, regularities in the social world are a consequence of following rules and conventions and are underpinned by symbolic meaning to which analysis in terms of causality is not appropriate.

To illustrate this distinction, Cuff et al provide the example of rules of the road. When stopping at a red traffic light, it is not the colour red that has a direct physical effect of invariably making traffic stop. Instead, stopping at a red light is a consequence of a shared cultural understanding of what the red light symbolises within the context of rules of the road. It is the meaning attributed to the red light which induces regularity of behaviour. To apply a physical science approach to explaining this type of regularity would be blind to the fact that it was based on meanings and rules which could be broken by mistakes or circumvention by the purposeful action of individuals – for example by jumping the lights.

The important point is that there is nothing intrinsic to red which means stop. A different colour could have been used to symbolise the rule 'stop'. It is the common interpretation which brings about the regularity of behaviour. If we broaden out this example, since different cultures provide different meaning contexts for behaviour, to understand the regularities of behaviour in an unfamiliar cultural environment, one would need to live in that environment and by observation and questioning learn the symbolic meanings behind the behaviour.

Symbolic interactionism – a humanistic methodology

Symbolic interactionism was pioneered as a social philosophy by a number of American theorists writing in the early decades of the twentieth century, a key figure amongst whom was G. H. Mead. From these more philosophical foundations was developed a theoretical perspective which challenged approaches that tended to view individual behaviour as governed by commanding social structures and powerful external forces. Instead, action could be best understood at the level of interaction between individuals in face-to-face small group situations.

The underpinning of this interaction is the exchange of meaning through shared understanding of the meaning of cultural symbols (speech, written language and body language in particular) which act as a medium of communication. Social situations are viewed as fluid encounters in which images of self and others are created, manipulated and imposed and identities and meanings are negotiated amongst participants. For symbolic interactionists, the extent to which society is structured and ordered (the acknowledgement of which varies between different theorists) is largely the emergent outcome of these fluid micro level meaning sharing and negotiating processes. Indeed, a key criticism of interactionism is that it tends to lose sight of broader social structures and power inequalities through which some have far greater capacity than others to shape meaning systems.

Whilst social interaction can be observed, the meanings and definitions exchanged between the participants may be uncertain to the researcher. The actual exchange of meanings between the actors in such encounters can only be revealed through painstaking micro level study. It is therefore the task of the researcher to prioritise understanding the participants' meanings and this can only be achieved through an open minded quest to gain intimate familiarity with their reading of the situation in question. By so doing, an insider's view can be achieved which will reveal some of the subtleties of the interaction process which would be missed if one were to adopt the more distant and clinical methods of positivist methodology which are only likely to touch the surface and achieve a distorted outsider's view of the situation.

Symbolic interactionism formed an important theoretical backdrop to much small-scale ethnographic work carried out by the Chicago School of sociology in the United States during the 1920s and 1930s, and much micro research since. For example, Goffman (1968) was able to discover through largely covert participant observation the operation of unofficial practices within an asylum which would probably not have been revealed by adopting a more overt and pre-structured positivist approach to the research. And although this research took the form of a case study, it was suggestive of such practices in other institutions awaiting to be revealed by the use of similar methods of research.

Although there are differences of position between symbolic interactionists on the question of the possibility of developing causal explanations of behaviour, generally, this is the less radical of the main micro interpretive perspectives in its criticism of social causality. However, interactionists commonly reject the theoretical focus and research strategies adopted by positivists. It is argued that positivists place an excessive emphasis on the impact of the broader social structure and constraints in determining individual behaviour. Likewise, interactionists criticise in positivist research the tendency to impose researcher definitions and highly structured procedures from the start of research programmes. These are seen to act as barriers to understanding the social interaction experienced by the participants. To avoid this, and achieve a close correspondence between the research findings and the world as viewed by the participants, and thus a high level of validity for the research, interactionists advocate the need for researchers to 'sensitise' themselves to the world of social actors. The favoured methods for achieving this include ethnographic approaches of lengthy participant observation, in-depth and unstructured interviewing and also the study of personal written materials – all of which provide qualitative information. Interviews are much more likely to be collaborative than hierarchical and the interviewer is regarded as more the novice than the expert.

It is seen as advantageous that the focus of research may start out as vague. This more inductive approach can help to attune the open mindedness of the researcher to the world of the participants. In contrast to deductive approaches, in interactionist research hypotheses are often generated and fine-tuned during the course of the research from the information that emerges, rather than set beforehand for testing. The research process is therefore more creative, enabling theory to be naturally grounded in the everyday meaning of the participants and sociological knowledge to grow bottom up through the accumulated findings of very many micro studies.

The interactionist approach usually approximates the qualitative research process identified in figure 2 below.

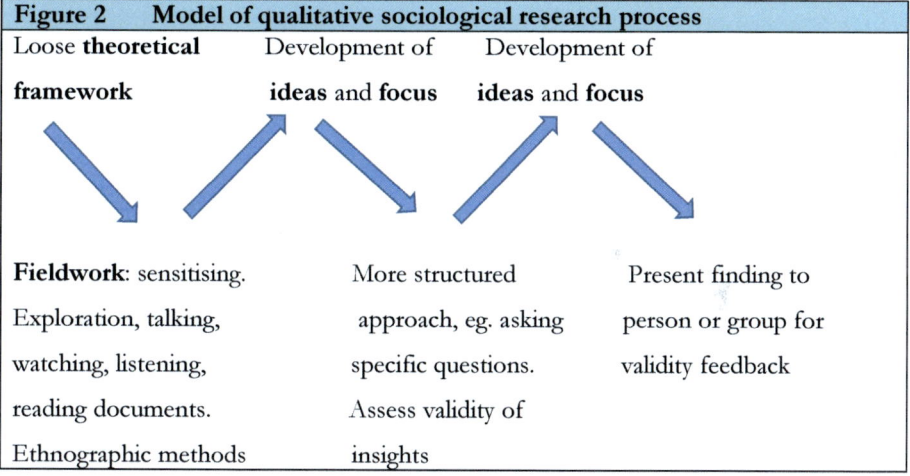

Figure 2	Model of qualitative sociological research process	
Loose **theoretical** framework	Development of **ideas** and **focus**	Development of **ideas** and **focus**
Fieldwork: sensitising. Exploration, talking, watching, listening, reading documents. Ethnographic methods	More structured approach, eg. asking specific questions. Assess validity of insights	Present finding to person or group for validity feedback

A more radical criticism of positivist methodology was adopted with the emergence of the interpretive perspectives of phenomenology and ethnomethodology.

Phenomenological methodology – the study of subjective meaning

The perspective of phenomenology was pioneered by Alfred Schutz between the 1930s and 1950s and provided a philosophical backdrop for the approach to sociological research later taken up by ethnomethodologists (indeed, the positions of the two perspectives are so overlapping that the work of some theorists such as Aaron Cicourel has been variously classified within either approach). Taking Weber's emphasis on the importance of subjective meanings which reside behind social action as his starting point, Schutz (1974) attempted to develop a more systematic understanding of the subjective construction of meaning. Subsequently, sociologists working within this perspective have launched powerful attacks on positivist methodology, especially in positivists' use of official statistics as if they were objective factual data and their overlooking of subjective meaning.

For Schutz, to engage in their practical everyday activities, people adopt a structured understanding of the world. Structured understanding is possible through the development of classifications which derive partly from past personal experiences and largely from socially shared meaning systems and taken for granted assumptions. This all provides a sense of social predictability and order which is required for engagement in daily routines. Schutz refers to the daily experience of order and routine as living in the 'natural attitude' in which assumptions of order and regularity are a necessary requirement for practical action. Although shared meaning is the active product of social interaction, when it is not disrupted by unexpected events the sense of structure and order which it creates appears to exist independently as an objective reality in its own right.

We have seen that in their criticism of positivist methodology, symbolic interactionists focussed on the nature of the social world as one of shared symbolic meaning. Criticism from phenomenologists of positivist methodology is more radical. They deny the possibility of causal explanations of social phenomena and adopt a subjectivist approach in criticism of what positivists take for granted – the existence of an objective social reality external to, independent of and constraining the behaviour of individuals, and making causal explanations possible. Instead, what appears to be an objective and factual reality is subjectively constructed.

The methodological position of phenomenology is based on the view that the existence of external social structures is the product of the subjective imposition of classifications and definitions on reality and nothing more. Consequently, there are no independent and externally existing social facts that are awaiting scientific discovery. All that those who engage in the scientific study of 'factual' data are doing is to quantify the products of subjective judgements and give them a spurious status of objective social facts.

The subjective process by which people apply meaning systems to classify and interpret behaviour is a process engaged in equally by the person in the street and people in official capacities. All official statistics are therefore the consequence of official classifications based upon shared meanings applied by people in their official roles. Phenomenologists are therefore particularly critical of the way in which positivists tend to take official statistics as if they are hard scientific facts. Research undertaken from a phenomenological perspective has questioned the factuality of such statistics as measurements of suicide (Atkinson) and the apparently high level of working class juvenile delinquency (Cicourel). In each case, researchers have demonstrated that official statistics are the outcome of decisions made by officials in the classification of behaviour and are subjectively based on the application of stereotypes and common sense judgements. Those who use this data as if it were hard fact are thus basing their analysis, which has the appearance of objectivity, on data which is itself the product of subjective constructs.

For phenomenologists, since there is no stand-alone objective reality to society, the aim of sociology must be restricted to the study the subjective processes involved whereby people classify behaviour to provide a sense of structure and order. Thus, rather than adopt a stance of detachment from phenomena to analyse it as is possible when dealing with material objects in the physical sciences, phenomenology requires the researcher to be subjectively engaged with subjects in order to document the processes by which they order the world. The methods employed are therefore highly likely to be of a qualitative type. Indeed, in his study of the work of officials in the classification of deaths as suicides or otherwise, Atkinson engaged in observations at inquests, and within the workplace of a coroner's office held discussions with coroners and studied a coroner's record. Atkinson's writeup is a description of the processes involved in arriving at decisions on the cause of death, and thus the creation of statistics, in contrast to Durkheim's positivistic study which deals with official statistics on suicide as if they are simply objective facts.

Ethnomethodology – facts are provisional; just the means by which they are constructed should be studied

Out of the more philosophical origins developed by phenomenology, the closely linked sociological perspective of ethnomethodology developed during the 1960s and 1970s. The radicalism of this perspective takes the form of the questioning of any certainty in sociological knowledge. This puts it at loggerheads with positivist methodology and reflects the spirit of times when the authority and certainties of the 1950s came under great challenge in society. Although not itself a contemporary perspective, the attack launched by ethnomethodologists on the scientific orthodoxy of positivism with its claim to superior and reliable knowledge about society indicates some very general similarities with more contemporary postmodernism perspectives.

For ethnomethodologists, knowledge and behaviour is understandable relative to its meaning context. The aim of sociology is to research into small-scale everyday social encounters to understand how people make sense of each other's actions. The methods applicable are therefore likely to include participant observation and in-depth interviewing.

Contrary to a more positivist approach which looks at small-scale situations as structured by broader social constraints, ethnomethodologists view such situations as social encounters which people navigate their way through, sometimes in an improvised way, based on and leading to the emergence of a level of mutual understanding which is actively constructed by participants. For ethnomethodologists, the focus of sociology should therefore be exclusively on identifying the methods that people use to achieve the sense of shared meaning necessary to everyday life for ordered and purposeful action to take place.

A key research method pioneered by Garfinkle to study the process of the construction of shared meaning is the breaching experiment. This method relies on the setting up of small-scale experimental situations where, through the disruptive actions of a prepared participant in the research, the background behavioural expectations of the other participants are violated. The aim of the research is to study the methods used by the participants to re-establish a shared sense of meaning and social order.

An example from Garfinkle's research employing a breaching experiment was referred to in the previous chapter. In this piece of research (Garfinkle, 1984, pp.47-49), on returning home, a number of students acted like lodgers in their own home for a short period of time and reported back the responses of family members to Garfinkle. The extent of members' reliance on shared understanding of behaviour between family members was demonstrated by their confused and even hostile responses to the lodger type behaviour and attempts by members of the family to shore up their shared expectations of family interaction by searching for reasons by which they could rationalise the odd behaviour where the taken for granted rules were broken. For example, it was reasoned that perhaps the student was feeling unwell or had been overworking.

Another breaching experiment (Garfinkle, 1984, pp.79-94) involved one to one counselling sessions where undergraduates were told that they should prepare their questions to counsellors in such a way that advice could be given in the form of just 'yes' or 'no' answers. What the subjects did not know was that the 'counsellor' was in fact an experimenter who was reading off answers to each question asked from a pre-prepared randomised list of 'yes' or 'no' answers. Garfinkle found that students tended to report after the interview that although often initially confused, their questions had been answered and useful advice given. They had constructed their own sense of meaning out of randomised disorder.

Ultimately, through detailed analyses of numerous such processes, ethnomethodologists believe that it is possible to extract general rules on the methods that people use in social situations to develop a shared structured understanding. Identifying the rules of the construction, negotiation and imposition of meaning should be the goal of sociology, nothing more.

As conversation is a key means of communication, conversational analysis has been an important research method for ethnomethodologists. Conversations are viewed as improvised activities of reciprocal sense making and are accomplishments of the participants. For ethnomethodologists, conversational analysis requires detailed study of not just words but inflections, pauses, breathing sounds and non-verbal communication etc. Detailed analysis of conversations has led ethnomethodologists to identify how fit takes place as conversation progresses and to show that participants tend to share an understanding of conversational rules and structures, such as appropriate introductions and terminations of conversation. Ethnomethodologists study these communicative exchanges to show how shared taken for granted understanding of conversational rules and processes is demonstrated in a variety of settings such as job interviews (Button, 1987), telephone conversations (Schegloff, 1979) and political speeches (Heritage and Greatbatch, 1986). They also study processes of breaching repair, should a participant stray from the rules.

What is so important about this seemingly trivial enterprise? The following points are worthy of mention.

Firstly, ethnomethodology breaks down the barriers raised between the sociologist and the everyday citizen that are erected in more positivist research. The traditional status and expertise of the specialist sociologist over the everyday person is undermined as ethnomethodologists recognise that the sociologist is encapsulated in the world of everyday meanings which he / she is trying to understand just as much as the people whose interactions are the object of study. Even the activities of sociologists, engaged in research or otherwise, can be studied in the same way as other everyday social encounters. Sociology is thus 'disprivileged.'

Secondly, the perspective recognises that practical sociology is conducted all the time in the everyday encounters of ordinary people as they interpret meanings and rules.

Thirdly, the sociologist takes the lead from those being observed, rather than vice versa as is the case in more positivist approaches.

Fourthly, all social encounters are of equal worth for study – establishing the relative truth of different groups' views is not the purpose of research, but simply the processes involved in the emergence of shared meaning.

Ethnomethodologists have pointed out fundamental weaknesses in the tendency of positivists to base causal explanations on the analysis of supposedly hard scientific data such as official statistics or that derived from survey interviews. For ethnomethodologists, official statistics are themselves the outcome of judgements, interpretations, definitions, stereotypes, etc. made by officials. The task of sociology should therefore be to analyse the encounters and judgements through which interpretations of the behaviour of others by officials are made. This would show that the resulting social statistics, such as those indicating juvenile delinquency rates, are highly provisional. When positivists base their research of the uncritical acceptance of official statistics, which are viewed as if they are hard facts, the causal theories that they build on them are likely to distort social reality to that which reflects official viewpoints.

This perspective was applied by Cicourel in his 1976 study of juvenile delinquency in two American cities. Cicourel found that judgements made by officials – particularly police and probation officers – were key to decisions over whether or not a person had officially engaged in delinquent behaviour. If a youngster who had engaged in anti-social behaviour exhibited those characteristics which officials stereotyped as associated with juvenile delinquency – for example were black, or working class, or from run down areas – they were more likely to be viewed as delinquent than others from white middle class backgrounds who had engaged in similar behaviour. The different rates of juvenile delinquency which the figures show are therefore not objective facts but the product of subjective judgements influenced by the application of common stereotypes. Theories of delinquency which are based on treating the resulting official figures as facts are therefore reducing the study of reality to the status of an uncritical reflection of stereotypes used to interpret behaviour by officials. From an ethnomethodological perspective, studies of delinquency should be examining the different capacities which different groups have for imposing definitions and negotiating justice.

Likewise, in the case of social survey interviews, rather than trying to understand society in terms of the apparently hard data provided, the object of study should be the interview process itself and an examination of how this particular encounter is based on shared or constructed assumptions about how the process is conducted (for an overview, see figure 3).

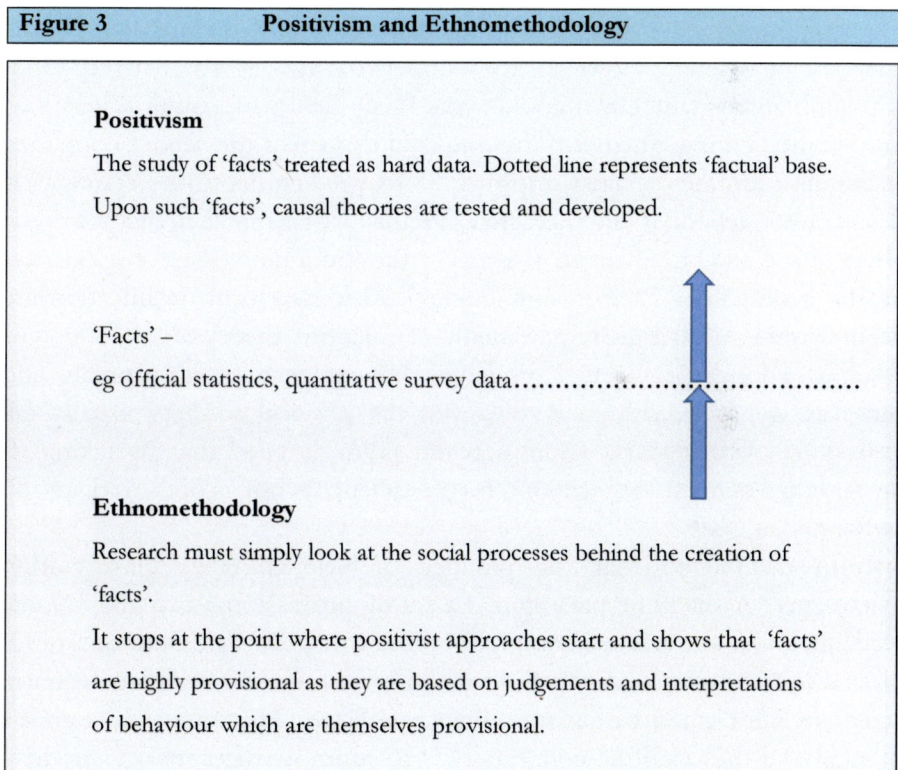

| Figure 3 | Positivism and Ethnomethodology |

Positivism

The study of 'facts' treated as hard data. Dotted line represents 'factual' base.

Upon such 'facts', causal theories are tested and developed.

'Facts' –

eg official statistics, quantitative survey data......................................

Ethnomethodology

Research must simply look at the social processes behind the creation of 'facts'.

It stops at the point where positivist approaches start and shows that 'facts' are highly provisional as they are based on judgements and interpretations of behaviour which are themselves provisional.

What defines science and how does it progress?

For Karl Popper, the hallmark of any scientific theory is that it must be convertible into testable hypotheses or propositions, and that rather than looking to prove a theory correct, testing should always be vigilant for evidence whereby it can be falsified. Furthermore, however much evidence is found to substantiate a theory, there always remains the possibility that some may be found to refute it – hence Popper's caution that even the most highly substantiated scientific theory should be seen as provisional. Overall, by such means, scientific progress is an open, continuous, incremental and evolutionary process.

Popper has argued that any theory that cannot be held to account through evidential testing or avoids the openness of potential disproof cannot be regarded as scientific. On this count, Marxism was one particular sociological theory that Popper clearly had in his sights (Popper, 1974). Classical Marxism claimed scientific credentials by claiming to have uncovered laws of social change from which predictions were made regarding the future overthrow of capitalism. Establishing laws and making predictions are seen as the hallmark of science. However, for Popper, the theory was hedged about with ambiguities whereby it could avoid being held to account in terms of precise predictions. Furthermore, one could add that the theory contained an inbuilt immunity against disproof of its predictions in the concept of false consciousness; if the predicted overthrow of capitalism did not come about, this could be explained in terms of the continuing false consciousness of the masses. For Popper, ambiguities and immunity to falsification are disingenuous and fail the requirements of scientific theory.

Whilst Popper provided a model of how science should operate and progress, it has been argued that even the physical sciences usually fall well short of this ideal. Thomas Kuhn (1962) argued that by taking its professional context into account, mature science is not as open to disproof as Popper suggests.

Kuhn maintained that the practice of science takes place within 'paradigms'. A scientific paradigm is a set of professional and institutional guidelines that provide an acceptable framework for legitimate questions, procedures and outlooks for those working within a scientific community. Scientists are trained within prevailing paradigms. The effect of scientific training and the scientific community is to promote theoretical orthodoxy and the conservative comfort of professional self-interest. Thus, evidence that challenges dominant theories and conventional working frameworks is regarded as potentially subversive and tends to be put on one side as anomalous, unimportant or a result of questionable measurement. However, over time, the accumulation of evidence which doesn't fit the working paradigm will lead to a paradigm crisis. This crisis can only be settled by an imaginative leap that enables the replacement of one paradigm by another that is able to explain the anomalous evidence and provide a new framework for scientific orthodoxy.

For Kuhn, scientific progress is not a continuous and incremental process of refinement but involves only periodic but major revolutionary shifts. Moreover, in reality, in the sense of openness to disproof, the physical sciences often fall well short of the ideal advocated by Popper.

More contemporary approaches to sociological research methodology

Despite disputes between positivists and social action theorists over questions of subjectivity, methodology, and the actual research methods preferred, there tended to be agreement that a basis for truth could be established, that explanations in terms of causality should be aimed for, and that it was the role of the researcher to be a neutral analyst. What distinguishes some contemporary from these more established approaches is the calling into question of these fundamental canons of science. A major departure from positivism has already been signalled in the approaches of phenomenology and ethnomethodology. In this section, approaches will be introduced which radically challenge the assumptions of positivist sociology and may even question the possibility of achieving objective knowledge.

Critical theory – neo-Marxist methodology and consciousness raising

Critical theory is based on insights derived from Marxism, but revised to accommodate the circumstances of the twentieth and twenty first centuries. Marx had developed a critical theory of capitalism which aimed to enlighten working people as to their plight and enhance the potential for political liberation through enlightened collective action. From this perspective, it is argued that all research takes place within power structures and so, even from a position of supposed methodological 'neutrality', the views of the powerless are unlikely to come through. Regarding the alliance between positivist methodology and functionalism, scientific social research, often funded and framed by governments, is seen to be used as a tool for government intervention in support of capitalism. As such, value freedom and scientific neutrality are used as a cloak whereby the interests of the powerful can be supported, but covertly.

For Lee Harvey (1990), it is more appropriate to refer to 'oppressed groups' rather than 'the working class'. Given the inequalities of power and influence, truth from the point of view of oppressed groups tends to be suppressed. To counter this, the role of critical sociology is through research to articulate truth from their perspective(s). The aim of critical methodology is to promote social improvement for oppressed groups by using research to reveal how they are oppressed in terms of broader social structures and through their adoption of dominant social values. Sociological theory and research can be used to encourage such groups to acquire new insights through which they may be able to improve their lives. Critical theorists usually agree with more established methodological traditions that research can uncover truth. However, they argue that truth can be selective and partial and serve the interests of different social groups. Moreover, they oppose established approaches by maintaining that the role of the researcher is not just that of revealing the truth but crucially also that of using research findings to encourage action amongst oppressed groups to improve their lives.

To a limited extent, critical methodology has affinities with interpretive approaches. It opposes the hierarchical nature of positivist research procedures and engages the subjects of the research in discussions of findings to assist validity. Research may often be small-scale, study the life of the underdog, and prefer to use qualitative methods. However, in the critical approach, the importance of the broader picture remains paramount as findings and insights are aimed at developing a critical awareness of the repressive nature of the social structure and dominant values of capitalism. This emphasis has been fundamental to the neo-Marxist Frankfurt School of social theorists. Theorists such as Habermas and Adorno have worked loosely within a Marxist tradition which they developed to generate new radical insights appropriate to advanced capitalism.

From this perspective:

1. Science and technology provide capitalism with efficient means of production and administration but the ends to which they are put are not seriously questioned. The culture of consumerism has had a dulling effect on critical awareness with the masses manipulated into a sterile contentment of low culture mass entertainment and technological gadgetry as an end in itself. The advance of the mass media has thus made ideological control all the more pervasive.

2. Positivist methodology claims that values of what 'should be' are not applicable to scientific procedures and that by applying a scientific approach to the social world it is adhering to principles of scientific neutrality. However, from the point of view of critical theorists this neutrality is deceptive. In fact, it accepts that what is should be and is therefore inherently conservative – it assists the perpetuation of existing arrangements of power distribution and social inequality.

3. As when Marx was writing, there is a need to enlighten oppressed groups through the insights of social theory and social research, but theory needs to be revised to accommodate advanced capitalism which now includes a diversity of oppressed groups. The role of social theory and research is to empower people through enhancing their critical awareness in the face of the pacifying influence of the mass media and the mentality of consumerism.

Feminist methodology and consciousness raising

Feminist approaches to research can also be viewed as a form of critical methodology. Up to the post war period, study of the experiences of women or women being active in the role of theorists or researchers figured little in sociology. For example, in studies of social mobility, the social class position of the household was invariably measured by the occupation of the male head of the household. This meant that females' social class was read off from that of males and reflected the subordinate position of women in society at the time. Such 'subordinate' activities as housework were also given little attention in sociology.

A rising consciousness amongst many women to challenge male domination throughout society accompanied the feminist movement of the late 1960s. This movement was also reflected in sociology through a growing interest in issues of gender inequality and identity. Whilst feminist sociologists have focussed on gender as the key category of social oppression and provided an alternative standpoint from which society can be viewed to that of 'malestream', they have also become increasingly aware of the extent to which such factors as social class, ethnicity, age, disability and sexuality comprise differences between women. But in particular, they have aimed to bring to the fore the once neglected voices of females and investigate areas of concern to women from their standpoint including housework, mothering, sexism, sexual harassment, violence against women, divorce, infertility and sweat shop labour.

Feminist sociologists tend to associate the structured and hierarchical positivist approaches to sociological research with male dominance in society and in the subject of sociology. In sociology, positivist approaches emphasise the importance of maintaining a detached and clinical relationship between researcher as expert and the passive subjects of the research who are treated like objects. For example, the formality and objectivity aspired to in traditional survey research reduces the respondent to the position of being just an object of data provision. For Ann Oakley, the supposed intellectual superiority of clinical rationality, objectivity, detachment and hierarchy in research closely corresponds to the values of traditional male culture (Oakley, cited in Lincoln and Denzin, 2003, p.251). This approach is justified by positivists in terms of the protection of the findings against the intrusion of subjective bias into research and in the interests of standardisation and replication. Viewed from the positivist and traditional male paradigm, 'getting involved with the people you interview is doubly bad: it jeopardises the hard-won status of sociology as a science and is indicative of a form of personal degeneracy' (Oakley, cited in Lincoln and Denzin, 2003, p.252).

Feminists have been strong to challenge this outlook. For example, Oakley has emphasised that the application of positivist methodology in sociology disempowers the subject and overrides opportunities for the feedback of insightful information and personal experiences which a more collaborative relationship in research would reveal. The use of interpretive methods, such as unstructured and in-depth interviewing, can improve the validity of information by establishing closeness and empathy between interviewer and interviewee, especially in the case of female interviewers interviewing female interviewees on topics of particular interest to female standpoints.

But this is not just a matter of male preference for positivist methods and feminist preference to use qualitative and ethnographic approaches, which itself is a vast oversimplification anyway. It is more to do with the way that methods are used. Feminists have developed their own approaches to using methods and conducting research and tend to argue that feminist methodology needs to go well beyond traditional methodological parameters. For Oakley, even the establishment of rapport with interviewees has been traditionally shaped and imposed by the interviewer. She argues that for research to not be exploitative, it is legitimate for the researcher to offer help, advice and friendship to participants to enhance a relationship of greater equality. This degree of give and take may help to overcome inhibitions and distortions to feedback introduced through more hierarchical approaches and participants can be consulted over the interpretation of the research data without feeling overwhelmed. Extending this process, a relationship of co-authorship may even be established whereby the validity of an interviewer's interpretations can be checked by revisiting their accounts and allowing the interviewee to revise them as appropriate.

Feminists often feel it legitimate to go beyond the stance of value neutrality and detachment expected in most traditional approaches to research. Although research is 'about' participants, feminists are usually keen to emphasise that the purpose of research is that it should be primarily 'for' them. Participants are not just objects who are unchanged by the interview process. Since all interaction influences the consciousness of participants, it can be seen as valid that participants in the research are encouraged through participation, along with readers of the research findings, in their intellectual liberation – a feature in common with critical sociology. With reference to her own research, Oakley puts it this way:

'I regarded sociological research as an essential way of giving the subjective situation of women greater visibility not only in sociology, but, more importantly, in society, than it has traditionally had. Interviewing women was, then, a strategy for documenting women's own accounts of their lives. What was important was not taken-for-granted sociological assumptions about the role of the interviewer but a new awareness of the interviewer as an instrument for promoting a sociology for women - that is, as a tool for making possible the articulated and recorded commentary of women on the very personal business of being female in a patriarchal capitalist society' (Oakley, cited in Lincoln and Denzin, 2003, p.253).

A good example of feminist methodology in practice is provided in the research of Roseneil into the life of women at Greenham Common who opposed the siting of cruise missiles at the air force base. The research methods employed included participant observation, in-depth interviewing and the analysis of documents, and much of it was retrospective. Roseneil was keen to document her feelings and experiences as a protester along with the other women. Identifying closely with the cause of the women, Roseneil argued that she should express her own values within the research against which the reader could judge her findings. She was keen to portray the women as active and from this micro research show connections with the issues of the broader women's movement (Devine & Heath, 1999, Ch9).

Feminist sociologists have frequently argued the merits of a uniquely feminine approach to research by which women can: 1) provide a view of reality from their own standpoint, interests and insights as an oppressed group which, in providing one truth amongst many, is as valid as that of any other group, 2) reveal feeling and intimacy in a more subjective approach to research which itself should be highly valued, and 3) raise the consciousness of women as an oppressed group for purposes of promoting social change.

Interestingly, some of the comments above refer to the existence of different gender related qualities which parallel common stereotyping. However, it is central to sociology that gender identity is largely socially formed and inequality is socially structured. Whilst not denying that different qualities and unique experiences exist based on sex and gender differences and that gender inequalities have shown themselves to be remarkably resilient, there is also evidence of a narrowing of gender identity differences and inequality. This would suggest the prospect of a growing area of common ground in the approaches of men and women in the study of society.

Postmodernist methodology – the end of social science

Many postmodernists claim that contemporary societies have so fundamentally changed compared to those of the modern era that conventional criteria and methods for establishing truth should now be rejected. They claim that established ideas of a knowable social structure and methods for gaining certain knowledge of it were part of the pattern of discourse of the modern 'metanarrative' (an all-embracing story of how society operates). In the modern era, characterised by the emergence of science and industry, conventional sociological research took place within the premise that methods and procedures can be applied to provide information by which certain knowledge about how society works can be gained. The social policy dimension of this approach is that such knowledge could then be applied to improve society.

Postmodernists emphasise that this view is part of an Enlightenment metanarrative which accompanied the period of industrial and scientific modernisation. This metanarrative placed faith in the capacity of science to promote social progress and emancipate humankind from slavery to old religious dogmas and superstitions. Sociology emerged within the modernisation process and its accompanying metanarrative. It is in this context that sociological positivism formed. In the positivist tradition, the idea of social engineering was related to the belief that scientific method would provide a reliable basis for establishing the truth through research and enable social intervention to remedy social ills such as poverty, misery and conflict. For postmodernists, the modern era has disappointed. Naïve faith in science and progress has been shattered by the events of the twentieth century.

Different writers that could loosely be called postmodern emphasise different key aspects of the postmodern condition. This variety includes an emphasis on post-industrialism, information society, post capitalism, postmodern capitalism, global media dominance, post-bureaucratic organisations and political revolutions ending communism etc. A common thread to them is that the postmodern environment exhibits, compared to modern society, a decline in social and moral unity and uniformity and a breakdown of rigid social structures. To claim that postmodern society is here or is emerging is to claim that a radically new social environment is unfolding. This environment is dominated by an electronic world of fleeting and diverse but all embracing media images which break down uniform identities of, for example, family life, social class and gender which were once prevalent in modern society. A radical postmodern position adopted by Baudrillard suggests that this media saturated world produces a 'hyperreality' in which media symbols, images and language are referenced by other media signs, symbols and language. These representations of reality thus become disconnected from the real world, the truth or underlying reality of which cannot now be known.

Given this environment, postmodernists are highly critical of conventional sociological research methods and claims to truth. They see conventional research as part of the old metanarrative of modernism which claims superiority for professional scientific knowledge. In postmodern societies, the modern matanarrative of truth based on rational thinking and scientific method collapses.

As truthful knowledge of social reality can no longer be achieved, it is no longer possible for sociological research to claim validity. Sociological research therefore loses its privileged status in claiming a superior understanding of society to that of any other explanation. Social science becomes just one of a number of competing narratives for understanding society and there is no way that it can rightfully claim privilege to a singular truth. Society is diverse, its condition is ephemeral and all knowledge is both tentative and relative. There is no longer any overriding criteria by which superiority for knowledge based on empirical research can be claimed.

Where then does this leave sociological research? Postmodernists often focus on the way that language is used to create the appearance of order and truth. They therefore argue that postmodern analysis should take the form of the scrutiny of texts written by others so that the techniques used to create the appearance of truth can be brought out into the open. In other words, research should take the form of textual analysis to reveal the justifications used for claims of truth by the author. This technique is referred to as the deconstruction of texts. Thus, when writers of sociological research claim validity for their findings, this is just one of a number of ways in which writers of texts claim legitimacy for their story.

A telling criticism of this postmodernist activity is raised by Mats Alvesson (2002) who regards it as both negative and parasitic, pointing out that if all social theorists were to engage in such a venture, the study of the social realm would degenerate into little more than a type of sociological literary analysis. Furthermore, Devine points out that this would lead to the need to deconstruct the texts produced by those deconstructing texts and so on endlessly. One could argue that there are surely more important and constructive concerns facing sociologists, such as attempting to understand the causes of war or poverty (regarding which for postmodernists such as Baudrillard we apparently cannot be sure about the nature of their existence) which can make the above preoccupation with textual scrutiny seem morally offensive.

In conclusion, there may well be validity to the claim that societies have entered a new era of social diversity and rapid change, but it should not be beyond the ingenuity of sociologists to respond with new techniques and approaches which would provide informed understanding of the social world as the basis for enlightened social intervention. This is the position adopted by Anthony Giddens who views the contemporary world as having reached a high modern as opposed to postmodern state.

Chapter 6
Sociology of Families and Households

Abstract

This chapter introduces the reader to some of the difficulties involved in attempting to adopt an impartial sociological approach to the study of family life. At the outset, the reader is alerted to the importance of reflecting on and examining personal experiences and values regarding 'the family' with the aim of enhancing awareness of any personal bias in this area and encouraging a broad overview of family diversity. It is emphasised that this overview needs to be guided by theoretical awareness and research findings. With regard to the application of founding theoretical perspectives and research into the social conditions of the post war decades, the author feels it appropriate to use the term 'the family', whereas reference is made to 'family life' to represent the greater diversity of lifestyles in more contemporary times.

Following the introduction of a number of key concepts, the founding sociological perspectives of functionalism and Marxism are utilised to provide general theoretical starting points and contrasting interpretations of the role of the nuclear family in modern society. A sketch of the broader social and historical context to changes in the family is also provided. Some well-established sociological research into the extended and the nuclear family is then reviewed and provided as a benchmark against which more contemporary patterns of family life can be later compared. Reference is made to feminist responses which highlight the disadvantages experienced by women within traditional family structures.

The reader is encouraged to appreciate that evidence can be assembled and looked at in different ways to provide different messages and some guidance on the interpretation of information is given.

Although also a founding perspective, it is suggested that symbolic interactionism offers greater flexibility and accommodation of analysis to more contemporary trends of growing diversity in family life than functionalism or Marxism can. Evidence of such growing diversity is then introduced in relation to the broader question of whether it can be best interpreted in terms of decline or change in family life.

Political and social policy preferences and interventions in response to changes in family life are referred to with reference to Conservative new right, New Labour, Conservative led coalition and Conservative government policy.

More contemporary sociological approaches emphasise that society has been undergoing fundamental changes which render the founding perspectives of functionalism and Marxism increasingly redundant for the purpose of explaining the contemporary pattern of family life diversity. These approaches include postmodernist and high modernist perspectives which raise issues of freedom, tolerance, and lifestyle and identity choice in the context of a rapidly changing society that is increasingly devoid of past structures and constraints. Common to these approaches is an emphasis on individualisation. Within the context of growing diversity, it is argued that viewing life in terms of life course rather than life cycle or family cycle has become more appropriate.

A further section looks at how personal identity, related to different stages in life, should be regarded as a social construction rather than a direct consequence of biological aging and that rather than universal it has been shaped variably throughout history and between societies.

It is also shown that a recent emphasis in researching family life has been to refocus on the definitions and perceptions of participants rather than the formality of family structures and organisation of roles. Indeed, it has been argued that it would be beneficial to shift the focus from 'the family' and even 'family life' to that of 'personal life'.

The sociological challenge

What guidance can be picked up from the previous chapters to prepare us to adopt a sociological approach to the study of households and families?

Firstly, it is important to pause and reflect on our personal experiences within our own home environment and be vigilant regarding any personal bias that these experiences may predispose us toward. Experiences in one's family of origin in particular are likely, through the profound effect of primary socialisation, to provide depth to a range of positive and negative outlooks that can colour our attitude toward family life generally. Given the highly personalised nature of family life, there may be emotive issues that we need to stand back from if we are to review this area as impartially as possible.

Secondly, one needs to be on one's guard against the bias of nostalgic reflection regarding family life, as for example may be encouraged by certain historical television documentaries. More generally, the view that there was once a more distant 'golden age' of family life that has been lost tends to overlook evidence which points to the severity of life for the majority of people in previous generations and centuries.

Thirdly, we should also be aware that personal experiences of life within our own family environments may not be very representative of the experiences of others. Whilst they can provide helpful insights, they will constitute a far too narrow and subjective basis of generalisation about family life for sociological purposes. There exists a wealth of research findings into family life which a sociologist should be prepared to delve into.

Fourthly, as sociologists, we should be cautious of explanations that rely heavily on human instincts or human nature to justify particular forms of family organisation as universally natural or superior. If the precise form of the family were determined by a narrow range of fixed human nature and instincts, we would expect to find 1) a high level of uniformity in family life throughout the world and 2) little scope for change. In fact, anthropologists have pointed to the diversity of family forms which have existed across the world and are embedded in different cultural belief systems and customs. Additionally, even in such a brief period of history as the last sixty years in Britain there is evidence of both substantial change and growing diversity in family life. Whilst the very being of society is dependant on instincts to procreate and provide care for the vulnerable young from a significant proportion of the population, there is great potential diversity of arrangements through which this is possible.

This leads to a fifth point. The very diversity of family life which now exists within contemporary western societies requires great care in the way that it is conceptualised. The 'nuclear family' may have once provided a powerful reference point as a social norm and majority institution. A sociology of 'the family' may have then been a more realistic conceptualisation. However, sociological vantage points and concepts have adapted to reflect the trend of recent decades toward increasing diversity of lifestyle options. Consequently, sociologists are now more likely to use less restrictive terms of reference such as 'families and households' 'primary groups' or even 'personal life' to study this diversity.

As a sixth point, whilst experiences within family environments may be very personal, direct and private, these environments are also situated within a broader social setting. As we have seen, C Wright Mills has argued that one needs to be able to apply the sociological imagination to think about the connection between the micro and the macro. In this case, both an understanding of experiences within and changes to family life and their connection to the broader social structure are important.

Having raised the point of the need for caution, how can one become better equipped as a sociologist to study families? For a start, sociological perspectives, such as those raised in chapter 3, and others, can be utilised to see what light they shed on family life. Furthermore, information obtained from research, at both a micro and a macro level, will provide more concrete content. Together, theory and research findings contribute a far broader range of insight into and information on family life than that which could be derived from personal experiences alone. However, it is important to remember that perspectives are touchstones and that theory must remain open to critical evaluation and evidence of social change.

It is particularly instructive in the study of family life to be aware that the moral values that provided a compass bearing for past generations may have impacted heavily on those who deviated from them. For example, having children out of wedlock was once heavily stigmatised. Such moral judgements have since become more broadly recognised as prejudices from a more contemporary vantage point as society has changed. It is important, but perhaps more difficult, to appreciate the likelihood that outlooks and ways regarding family life that tend to be taken for granted today will be looked back on likewise as based on prejudices by future generations. Developing this awareness can help us step back to recognise and question any taken for granted assumptions that we may have about family life.

Definition of main concepts

Sociologists need to be clear in defining the concepts that they use. It is particularly important in the study of family life to be aware of the social and historical context which has shaped these concepts and through their use helped to understand family life at the time. However, sociologists also need to engage in a reflective evaluation as to the enduring usefulness or otherwise of concepts fashioned in past social conditions and to be familiar with more contemporary ones. In this section, definition will be given to a range of traditional and contemporary concepts related to family life.

The term **monogamy** refers to the exclusivity of marriage of one person to one partner, traditionally of the opposite sex, at any point in time. This pattern, reinforced by cultural, Christian religious and social values and legal constraints, has been the traditional form of family life in western societies. Although monogamous marriage has remained a legal constraint, changes in social and cultural values have been paralleled by legislative changes which have enabled single sex monogamous civil ceremonies and marriage in a growing number of countries.

However, monogamy itself is not a universal family form. Within some non-western cultures, various forms of **polygamous** (marriage to more than one spouse simultaneously) familial arrangements are endorsed as perfectly natural. For example, in cultures of Muslim heritage, a man has traditionally been able to have up to four wives. However, in reality the expense involved has usually meant that this family form was only available to the more wealthy males and seen as a sign of social status.

In modern western societies, theory and research on 'the family' in the 1950s took place within the social context of the widespread existence of a standard family institution referred to as the **nuclear family**. This family type, strongly sanctified by religions and traditionally sanctioned within churches, comprised married parents of opposing sexes and their biological children, living together under the same roof. There would usually exist a recipe for separate but mutual responsibilities between husbands and wives which in effect provided an unequal power relationship through which husbands were the beneficiaries.

Research evidence has suggested that the spread of growing prosperity from the late 1950s was accompanied by a tendency for the family to establish a clear boundary between itself and the broader community. The term **privatised nuclear family** was used to refer to this phenomenon.

There is evidence of relatively high levels of conformity toward the nuclear family type in the post war decades. In the early 1960s, most children were raised within a nuclear family setting. Stigma acted as a powerful force to control deviations from this norm. For example, the pejorative term 'illegitimate' (and worse) was commonly applied to children born outside of marriage, strong moral pressures for a 'shotgun wedding' would often be applied on the partners in the case of pregnancy outside of marriage, and divorce tended to be morally condemned. However, there is evidence that role relationships were becoming less heavily prescribed.

Roles are the patterned activities that people engage in which involve them in relationships with others in other roles. They are usually prescribed by broadly recognised social guidelines, but can also sometimes leave scope for negotiation between participants. Role relationships within families generate reciprocal expectations regarding appropriate contributions by family members. Post war sociological research tended to take the nuclear family as given and focussed on studying, often via social surveys, role relationships within this family form. The term **conjugal roles** was used to refer to these relationships and the division of labour between partners within marriage. A distinction was be made between two different types of marital role relationship.

Segregated conjugal roles were relationships in which a clear distinction was made between the activities of husband and wife. The required roles followed traditional gender expectations: the husband was the sole or major wage earner, with the wife being responsible for the daily running of the household and the raising of the children. This is referred to as the breadwinner and homemaker model. These role distinctions were often themselves passed down the generations through socialisation and strongly maintained by social and moral pressures.

However, related to various broader social changes and, as research evidence suggested initially more commonly emerging within middle class households, **joint conjugal role** relationships were forming as alternative arrangements between couples. Such a role relationship took the form of a greater involvement of the husband in household chores and childcare and a degree of merging of domestic activities between husband and wife, with greater opportunity for the wife to enter employment.

The concept of the **symmetrical family** is very similar to, but can be distinguished from, that of joint conjugal roles. As applied by Young and

Willmott, the term 'symmetrical' places a lesser emphasis on the merging of roles. Although traditional assumptions loosely remained regarding the primary role responsibilities of husbands and wives, symmetry refers to greater role flexibility and a more equal participation in household chores and childrearing between husband and wife.

Extended families, whilst traditionally including the nuclear family unit, also encompassed a more extensive community of relations (established through marriage or blood relatives). Comprising a higher tier of generations and a broader span of relatives, extended families would potentially include members over three generations as well as uncles, aunts, nephews, nieces, and cousins. Extended family members would not necessarily all live in the same abode but traditionally resided in close proximity to allow ease of face-to-face contact and mutual help. Reciprocity was therefore an important expectation with different members exchanging different types of support. There is evidence that extended family life was once abundant in many stable working class communities, especially prior to the development of the welfare state. Indeed, the prevalence of an extended family mentality sometimes meant that non-relations were referred to as if family members, with, for example, their names prefixed by such terms as uncle or aunty. Sociologists refer to these members as **fictive kin**.

Extended families have not just been prevalent within working class communities. For example, they have been very important means of shoring up power amongst royalty and the aristocracy, whereas in contemporary Britain extended family life and significant parental pressures on choice of partner may remain important within Asian communities.

Although the term **kinship** has sometimes been applied to relationships within the extended family, it more strictly refers to people who feel related due to some real or imagined common descent traceable from an identified person. More traditional cultures were sometimes organised along kinship lines, with Scottish clans providing an example of this form of identity.

The term **role swap families** has been used in situations where conjugal roles remain largely segregated but where the wife becomes the main breadwinner and the husband's primary role involves domestic chores and childcare. Such arrangements are often practical responses to situations where the career opportunities and earning capacity of the wife are superior to those of the husband.

The ideal of **companionate marriage** has developed with the process of modernisation. Companionate marriage is not constrained by influences of parental choice or approval, economic imperatives or religious obligation, but is freely entered into by partners based on mutual love and affection. A rise in these marital ideals and expectations and a decline in external constraints holding a marriage together have often been interpreted as the context for rising divorce rates.

Reconstituted families are family units which come together following the break-up of previous family units. These family types have become an increasingly familiar part of the family landscape with an increase in divorce rates and relationship breakups followed by the establishment of new families. They include children from at least one of the previous marriages to whom new parents become step-parents and are more specifically referred to as **blended families** when children from both previous families are brought together in the reconstituted family.

The term **beanpole family** has been used to describe a family structure which is high generationally but narrow in breadth across each generation. This structure reflects relatively recent demographic changes. These changes relate to a combination of increased longevity leading to the possibility of four generation family relationships and smaller family units due to declining fertility rates, single parenthood and higher divorce rates. In this family structure, the vertical generational relationships of reciprocal help between members may become more important and those across the generations become narrower and less important. Within this structure, the term **sandwich generation** has been applied to those, mainly women, who become informal carers of both the aged and the young.

The 1980s was a decade which witnessed a significant upward trend in family units headed by a **single parent.** The single parent was usually the mother and the term was often applied pejoratively within the context of an increase in single parenthood that was the result of a non-married relationship and the consequence of positive choice or otherwise. A distinction is sometimes made between single parenthood arrived at by this route, and that from separation, divorce or the death of a partner, in which case the head of the family is referred to as a **lone parent**.

Families may reside within **households**. However, as a household comprises people living within a common residential unit and sharing facilities, these people do not necessarily constitute a family in the traditional sense. Conversely, circumstances of employment (eg. members of the armed forces on assignment), criminal conviction leading to imprisonment, or educational situation (youngsters away at boarding school or university) mean that not all families can necessarily be defined in terms of ongoing common residency.

Founding sociological perspectives on the family

Two contrasting theoretical perspectives on the family, functionalism and Marxism, will now be introduced. Each of these perspectives took the nuclear family and within it segregated conjugal roles as the standard family type. Each adopts a macro approach by which the form that the family takes is powerfully shaped by the characteristics of broader social structure. These theories place at least two challenging demands on the reader. The first is to understand the social and historical context within which the theories emerged. The second is to consider whether these theories can be adapted to adequately explain the diversity of contemporary family life and whether there are insights that can be salvaged from them.

Functionalism – the functional fit of the nuclear family

American functionalism, represented in particular by the towering influence of Talcott Parsons, was a highly influential perspective within sociology during the 1950s. Parsons identified the nuclear family, comprising a segregated conjugal role relationship between married a male and female, and their children, as a key family institution which fitted perfectly with the functional needs of modern industrial societies. How did it do so? According to Parsons, this family unit 1) synchronised perfectly with the efficiency needs of modern capitalist industrial society, 2) provided an environment for the upbringing of children as well moulded future citizens, and 3) provided the psychological benefit of an emotional haven and outlet for the parents.

Applied to any social institution, the term 'functions' refers to the positive contributions that it makes toward the well-being of society and consequently, functionalists claim, the lives of members of society. The family is regarded as a key social institution for functionalists because it is seen as transmitting quite uniformly society's core norms and values through successive generations, thereby promoting both social consensus and continuity. To explain how this process operates, Parsons (1951) placed a heavy emphasis on primary socialisation of the young which he argued is an essential function of family life. He maintained that at birth the mind of the baby starts as a socially blank slate. The child's mind gradually awakens to society's values, rules and norms through experiences within the nuclear family. These values, rules and norms become transmitted by the parents and internalised into the child's personality structure. As they are relatively uniform across society, this process is functional because it equips the young to fit into society and provides the basis for social harmony and stability.

For functionalists, it is a necessary prerequisite for a normal and healthy state of social stability that society only changes relatively gradually. This requires a high level of social reproduction (the continuation of social structures and values) from one generation to the next and for Parsons the family plays a vital role in this process. Thus, parents have been socialised within their families of origin into society's dominant values. As parents, in their family of procreation, they socialise their children likewise. This promotes a flow of social and cultural continuity and on-going social order and stability.

Parsons argued that the family unit benefits from internal role specialisation. In an increasingly competitive and impersonal social world, the nuclear family forms a protective privatised cocoon from which the male is best suited for the breadwinner role through which the family is financially supported, and the female is better equipped for childrearing and domestic responsibilities. Interestingly, despite Parson's emphasis on the impact of environmental influences and primary socialisation on the personality structure of the child, natural predispositions of the different sexes also enter the analysis. Parsons backed up this complementary role specialisation model with an emphasis on the apparently natural and inbuilt predispositions between the sexes. These took the form of male capacity for instrumental and rational thinking most suitable for the world of work, and female affective, expressive and emotional qualities, which are suited to a domestic and child rearing role and providing emotional support for the working husband.

Changes in the structure of the family were located within the context of long-term and broader social changes. This relates to the functionalist emphasis that the family is a social institution whose changes must synchronise with changes in the broader social structure. In terms of this social structure, pre-industrial society comprised a relatively closed social hierarchy, offering few opportunities for social mobility – ie. there was little movement up or down the social hierarchy between the generations. People's status in society was relatively ascribed, or fixed, at birth. Geographical mobility and industrial dynamism were limited and life tended to follow established traditions and agricultural routines. Little health, welfare or educational provision was available to the vast majority from outside of the family which had to take on much of these functions as best it could.

Within this social context, Parsons argued that the extended family was a logical adaptation. Ascribed status within the family, primarily determined by age and gender, was compatible with ascribed status within society. Nepotism – using one's social and occupational position to place relatives in employment – was commonplace and not dysfunctional (damaging to society) since it corresponded with the closed social hierarchy. Any boundaries between family life and the outside world were often quite permeable as communities were usually small scale, integrated and intrusive. People knew their place in within family, community and society.

For Parsons, the transition from pre-industrial to modern industrial society involved a fundamental change in the nature of the social hierarchy from one of inherited social status to a society in which social position had to be achieved on merit. In modern industrial society, there were far more opportunities for geographical and social mobility as an efficient social and economic system needs to more effectively utilise its range of available human resources. High levels of economic reward needed to be offered to those who demonstrated their individual ability and drive by competing successfully with others in a relatively open social structure. By such 'meritocratic' means, people become impartially allocated to appropriate occupational levels within the system.

What, according to Parsons, were the implications of these changes for the family? One is that the privatised or isolated nuclear family is a necessary adaptation to the needs of modern industrial societies and that the extended family is an incompatible institution. There is a fundamental inconsistency between ascribed positions within the extended family and achieved occupational status which would promote conflict within extended family structures. Nepotism would also be dysfunctional in a society where occupational standing needs to be allocated on individual merit rather than family connections. Also, by becoming more privatised, the nuclear family shears itself from the emotional and supportive bonds of the extended family network, enhancing its capacity for geographical and social mobility that dynamic modern society requires of its workforce.

In addition to socialising children into such core social values as the need to compete, to be enterprising and to respect private property, for Parsons a further key function of the privatised nuclear family is that it is ideally suited to provide for adult members - especially the male breadwinner - the possibility of retreat from the competitive demands and formality of the workplace, so as to provide replenishment within a haven of emotional security. Moreover, it caters for the therapeutic needs of adults to act out childish residues – affective, childlike behaviour which would not be acceptable in the outside adult world but which nevertheless needs release.

Functionalists argue that as society modernises, new institutions emerge to take on increasingly specialised functions. Functional specialisation accompanies 'structural differentiation' – the growing complexity of social structures. Through these changes, more efficient specialist institutions are producing goods and services and engaging in exchange relationships in a functionally integrated society. For Parsons, the family loses some of the functions that it performed in the pre-industrial world in this process. In modern industrial societies, it is no longer a significant unit of economic production or provider of education or welfare as specialist institutions external to the family have largely taken over these functions. In so doing, these institutions enable young family members to unlock their future opportunities from that which their family could alone provide for them and strive to achieve a place in society on merit. However, Parsons argues, this does not mean that as a consequence the nuclear family is a less important institution. It has adjusted to the needs of modern industrial society through developing male and female conjugal role specialisation, providing a privatised protective environment, and focussing on the key functions of the primary socialisation of children and the stabilisation of adult personalities.

Other writers in the functionalist tradition have included George Murdock and Ronald Fletcher. Whilst Parsons focussed essentially on the contemporary American family of the 1950s, Murdock studied the family across 250 societies and concluded that it was a universal institution because it catered for a number of essential social needs and functions. Thus, societies must reproduce their populations to survive, but the functionality of reproduction within families is that they provide a foundation for social order and stability through establishing a shared understanding of rules of sexual access and responsibility for the upbringing of children. Along with Parsons, Murdock emphasised the functional importance for social harmony of socialisation within the family (which he tended to refer to as the education function). Murdock also identified the economic function of the family in terms of complementary gender role specialisation, again similar to that proposed by Parsons.

Fletcher acknowledged that with the advent of modern capitalism, external institutions are catering for many of the functions, such as health, welfare and education, which in pre-industrial times were left largely to provision within the family. However, he argued that this has not weakened but assisted the family in the specialist support that these institutions provide. Furthermore, although the family has also largely lost its pre-industrial function of being the main unit of economic production, its economic function has been transferred to that of consumption and is thus the main target of consumer advertising.

Amongst the more obvious criticisms of the American functionalist model is the fact that it portrays an over simplified, over uniform and idealistic view of the family to support a theory of social harmony which justifies patriarchal power and largely ignores the darker side of family life, such as domestic violence and sexual abuse. Parson's model is therefore understandably a target for a range of feminist writers.

Through the emphasis placed on the pervasive effect of socialisation and its key role in social reproduction, one can understand from the functionalist perspective the continuity of dominant and shared social values (if they are or were that shared) over time. What is less clear is what drives social change, especially rapid change, in both society and the family.

Parson's answer is that the natural state of society is one of equilibrium – as a functioning system, society gravitates toward a state of balance. Significant social change disrupts this balance. Consequentially, various social institutions have to adapt and resynchronise with each other for a new state of equilibrium to be established. Thus, the driving economic innovations which were associated with the industrial revolutions had to be paralleled by changes in social values and institutions, including the family, for a new social balance to emerge.

However, the charge of excessive uniformity in the functionalist portrayal of the family would appear to be a strong one. Up to a point, some defence can be made in that this uniformity was arguably a more realistic snap shot of family life in the 1950s America that provided the context for Parson's theory. But could the greater diversity of family life that has since developed be accommodated within a theoretical framework that appears to be so wedded to the importance of shared values and family uniformity?

David Popenoe (Steel et al, 2012, pp.40-41), adopting a neo-functionalist perspective, argues that such diversity is problematic for society (rather than functionalism as a theoretical perspective) in that it is disruptive of social stability and that alternative arrangements to the nuclear family, especially those that marginalise the father, disadvantage children during their upbringing. He argues that a new standard family model needs to emerge that is appropriate for the contemporary age.

Marxism – the nuclear family as a support mechanism for capitalism

Marxist theory, like functionalism, in its classical form adopts a very traditional view of the family as headed by the male breadwinner and as a key institution of socialisation, social reproduction and support for the social system. However, this perspective fundamentally challenges functionalism on the nature of the system itself by emphasising its capitalist and exploitative nature. From a Marxist perspective, a society of achievement through individual merit – a meritocracy – which functionalists claim modern industrial societies to closely approximate, is incompatible with the capitalist form. Instead of equilibrium, synchronicity and social consensus, the fundamental social condition under capitalism is one of inbuilt class conflict. Instead of an open social hierarchy, it is argued that capitalism maintains a relatively closed class structure. This closed structure is one of economic inequality which is perpetuated across the generations by the inheritance of private property, or its absence, and the family is regarded as the main transmission belt of this form of social reproduction.

Arguing from a Marxist perspective, for his colleague Engels (1972), the institution of the monogamous nuclear family derived historically from the economic conditions that promoted the production of sufficient wealth to enable its unequal distribution to take the form of private ownership. This became the earliest basis for social class inequality. When private property became concentrated in the hands of males, its passage down the male line required, particularly amongst the most wealthy, the means by which legitimate inheritance by sons could be assured. According to Engels, the patriarchal monogamous nuclear family, which controlled women's sexual behaviour, was an institutional form that emerged in response to this economic necessity. The social reproduction emphasised by Marxists is therefore that of the social and economic inequalities of the class structure, with the patriarchal monogamous family evolving as a key institution of support. This analysis leads to the conclusion that the patriarchal nuclear family will remain a dominant institution as long as the capitalist system remains.

Marxists argue that the patriarchal family supports capitalism in various ways. As well as protecting the inheritable advantages of wealthy families, it locks those with few economic resources into a situation of being perpetually dependent on the need to supply their labour to earn an income. The owners of business constitute a capitalist class who rely on the supply of disciplined labour to enhance their profits. In return, workers are paid sufficiently low wages to reinforce their dependence on the need to work. The profits of one class are thus dependent on the exploitation of the labour of another class. The worker cannot escape exploitation within this system; with the pressing needs of a basic income and with family responsibilities he becomes tied to the workplace. The domestic support provided within the family by the housewife is essential for the maintenance of the productive worker. For this, the worker must provide economic support. However, the employer only pays the worker (in part) for the work that he has directly provided. Therefore, from the position of the employer, the female support role within the family for the worker's labour is a free one, or at least one that can be covered by a worker's wage that can be lower than if domestic work had to be paid for as a marketed service.

As an instrument of his employer's profit, the worker is treated as a commodity and is controlled as an efficient object in the productive process. The consequent experience for the worker is one of alienation – a feeling of powerlessness and meaninglessness in carrying out work which could otherwise be creatively rewarding. The worker is depersonalised and dominated for the purpose of maximising the production of value and level of exploitation which the provision of his labour makes possible. Within this context, the family is seen as acting as a safety valve against potential class conflict between employers and workers as other members of the family absorb aggression from the breadwinner which has been generated through negative experiences which often cannot find their outlet within the workplace.

Additionally, Marxists focus on the role of the family in terms of bringing up the next generation of exploitable labour, again at maintenance cost to the worker. Within the home, the young are socialised into submission to the authority of the father figure. This relationship works as a form of preparation for acceptance of the authority of future employers over workers, thus assisting in the social reproduction of class relationships. As a fall-back position, women constitute what Marxists refer to as a 'reserve army of labour' which can be taken up when beneficial to employers, for example during economic booms when workers might feel themselves to be in a stronger bargaining position, and more readily disposed of back into the family, for example during economic recessions.

Marx was confident that the stresses between classes that were built into capitalism could not be soaked up indefinitely and that this system would eventually self-destruct in class revolution. However, as capitalism has endured and the standard of living of workers has improved, other schools of Marxist thought have emerged which were less sure of this outcome. For example, neo-Marxist (modern revisionist) writers of the Frankfurt school, such as Herbert Marcuse, retained the basic Marxist analysis of class exploitation under capitalism, but recognised the growth in the seductive influence of the mass media. Marcuse argued that mass media advertising is often aimed at the family and encourages an appetite for domestic consumption by associating the acquisition of technological appliances with the image of freedom. The housewife is thus portrayed as free from heavy domestic drudgery if she has the latest domestic gadgetry. Acquiring a new fast car is also associated with the image of freedom. This enhances the demand for goods to help keep capitalism buoyant. But, more than this, it locks workers further into un-free, repressive and exploitative relations within the workplace to be able to afford these goods or keep up payments. From this neo-Marxist perspective, the attractions of consumerism distract workers from recognising the need for genuine freedom which can only be achieved through replacing capitalism with a social system in which the means of production are commonly owned and labour is not exploited for private profit. In other words, the view of 'freedom' often associated with conspicuous consumption is regarded from this neo-Marxist perspective as a 'false consciousness' that in fact binds workers more to capitalism and the workplace whilst enhancing its economic buoyancy.

A major criticism of the classical Marxist model is the economic determinism built into the theory – the view that the economic forces of capitalism are the key determinant of the form of all social institutions. Regarding the family, this leads to the view that only the monogamous and patriarchal nuclear family can adequately serve the needs of capitalism, despite evidence of diversity of family life between capitalist societies with different cultures and increasingly within societies that are capitalist.

Feminists such as Abbott and Wallace (1997, p.45) have been particularly critical of the fact that in focussing exclusively on class exploitation of male labour provided in the workplace, the classical Marxist position has not sufficiently recognised the value of domestic labour provided in the traditional housewife role and only attributed secondary importance to patriarchal domination and gender exploitation because it is seen as a consequence of class exploitation.

Clearly, functionalist and Marxist perspectives on the family are diametrically opposed. The former idealises the family as a haven of sanctuary within a competitive society of achievement, whilst the latter views it as a prop for an exploitative class system which offers the majority few opportunities. However, they both strongly emphasise the powerful constraining force of social structures and forces of socialisation working in uniform ways to mould individuals to society.

Family change from a broad social historical context

The theories that have just been reviewed place the form taken by the family within broad social and historical frameworks. Research by social historians has attempted to piece together evidence and identify patterns of change in family life. Ideally, this would provide the means by which the theories can be evaluated. However, there is some uncertainty regarding family life and how it has changed over the centuries, as the further one goes back, written details tend to provide some information on the lives of the literate and educated minority who were more likely to be found in the upper ranks of society, but little directly from the majority. The patterns that have emerged from research suggest a degree of consensus on the general findings but also point to a complex picture of change in the family and likely regional variability.

Life in medieval societies was for most experienced within a rural and agrarian setting. In Britain, most people lived out much of their lives within local communities which were well established social hierarchies in which there was little opportunity for social mobility. Research, for example by Shorter, has suggested that romantic attraction or expectations thereof played little part in choice of marriage partner or within married life itself. For the wealthy, marriage was more about consolidating wealth and power. In poorer households, it brought together members into an economic unit of production as the home was often also the workplace. Here, family members engaged in agricultural or handicraft activities with a degree of gendered work differentiation whilst young children were usually allocated housework tasks. In some cases, boys were apprenticed into other families to learn a trade and became part of that household. For landless agricultural workers (serfs), life was often brutal and harsh, limiting the possibility of the cultivation of romantic sensitivity. Moreover, serfs were bonded to their landlord who effectively owned them and had legitimate control over most aspects of their lives, including a final say on whom they may marry. Affection between partners may at best grow over time. For most, therefore, it is argued that both modern conceptions of romantic attraction as the basis for marriage and the separation of home from work would have made little sense.

To what extent does historical research square with the functionalist model which suggests that the extended family was prevalent in pre-industrial society and then declined as it did not fit the functional needs of more dynamic industrial capitalism?

Lawrence Stone studied family life in Britain during the period from about 1500 to 1800. His findings were based largely on the use of qualitative information such as that obtained from diaries, literature and family artefacts, adopting what Michael Anderson (Sclater, 2005, pp.38-40) has referred to as a 'sentiments' approach. Stone's findings can be summarised as follows:

1. At the beginning of this period, the smaller family unit often tended to be integrated into broader community and kinship ties. The unit was one of shared economic interest. It was hierarchical, male dominated, highly disciplinarian toward its younger members and unlikely to be a source of affectionate relationships between partners.

2. From about the 1550s, whilst remaining a patriarchal institution, there were signs of a growing separation of the nuclear family from more extended family and community ties and the emergence of more affectionate relationships within.

3. Between the middle of the seventeenth century and 1800, accompanying a rise in industrial activity, changing cultural values were emphasising a growing importance of individual autonomy and privacy. The nuclear family was becoming further isolated from the extended family and

community. Internally, it was becoming a growing source of romantic attachment and emotional warmth between partners and the separate status of children was becoming recognised. For Stone, this phase heralded the emergence of 'affective individualism' within a family type referred to as the 'closed domesticated nuclear family'.

According to Stone, there was also a social stratification element to these changes. In the early phase, the experience of romantic liaison tended to be limited to extra marital relationships between members of the upper social orders. By the middle phase, marriage through romantic attachment and family life within a more isolated nuclear family environment were becoming more common amongst the better off. By the end of the period in question, the experience of romantic choice of partners and a relatively closed nuclear family had percolated down the social hierarchy and become more characteristic of family life amongst the working class. This downward movement over time of progressive change in family life has been referred to by Young and Wilmott in their own research by the term 'stratified diffusion'.

Historical research into family life in England between 1564 and 1821 conducted by Peter Laslett (Sclater, 2005, pp.36-37) employed a broader demographic approach. This means that the focus was more on the data profiles of populations. Information from early periods relied heavily of parish records and census information was only available to cover the period from 1801. Laslett's findings also suggested that extended family life was not particularly common in the pre-industrial period, with only about 10% of families including kin beyond the nuclear and household sizes averaging about 4.75 persons. Given the time period covered by Laslett's research, which stretches from pre-industrial into industrial society, he concludes that the relative rarity of the extended family and commonality of the nuclear family in the pre-industrial period suggests much greater historical continuity in the form of family life between pre-industrial and early industrial society than was once thought.

Anderson (Sclater, 2005, pp.40-42) found that in the industrial textile town of Preston in 1851, 23% of households contained kin other than nuclear. Using a 'household economics' approach which involved studying documents relating to people's economic circumstances (for example records regarding employment, property ownership and family budgeting), Anderson argued that living as part of an extended family had become more of a pragmatic strategy for survival by this period than necessarily being a preferred way of life. David Starkey supported the drift of both Laslett's and Anderson's findings by arguing that the view of the prevalence of the extended family in pre-industrial society is a sentimental myth which is without historical substance and that the only time when it may have been more commonplace was during the very difficult times that many people experienced during early industrialisation.

Sociological research on the family in post war Britain has suggested that the extended family has undergone significant decline. When put together, all of this evidence seems to support a three stage model of the extended family rather than the two stages suggested by Parson's functionalist theory. In general outline, historical evidence would suggest the prevalence of the nuclear family, slowly withdrawing from its absorption into the local community, during pre-industrial times. The extended family (including within it the nuclear family) emerged mainly as a response to the hardships of life experienced by poorer sections of the population during the early phase of capitalism and remained a common feature within such populations well into the industrial period. It was giving way to the privatised nuclear family by around the middle of the twentieth century.

What accounts for these findings? Firstly, in pre-industrial society, life expectancy was relatively short, so it is likely that any three generational extended families would also be relatively short lived. Secondly, the common practice of primogeniture (the maintenance of property intact through its inheritance by the eldest son) meant that non-inheriting family members would have to make their own way in the world. In line with these findings, both the nuclear family and the work ethic could be argued to precede and assist industrialisation rather than adaptively emerge from or with it as the functionalist theory suggests.

What changes did industrialisation involve? Advances in science and technology, culminating in England in the late eighteenth century, brought about a revolution in the productive process. Workshops and factories were able to utilise powered machinery which could produce standardised goods more cheaply and efficiently than cottage industry workers in a domestic setting who largely relied on hand powered machinery were able to. Unable to compete, there was increasing pressure on cottage workers to seek employment in factories, bringing about massive population movements from the countryside to the towns – a process referred to as urbanisation.

Some of the important changes that industrialisation and urbanisation promoted regarding the family can be summarised as follows: 1) a redefinition of work as something external to the family where labour was sold to an employer in exchange for wages, 2) an increase in extended family living as a coping mechanism response to new hardships endured, and 3) the development of new segregated conjugal roles with the male becoming the chief breadwinner and the female taking on domestic chores. Taking each of these in turn:

1. The emergence of the factory system meant that labour had to be increasingly offered outside of the domestic setting to an employer who owned the new productive technology which required the concentration of waged workers in factories to maximise productivity. Seccombe (Sclater, 2005, pp.36-37) adds that as fewer families had any of their own means of cottage industry production to pass down the generations, this assisted the change from viewing marriage in property terms toward the importance of romantic attachment.

2. When workers moved to the towns, their accommodation would invariably be rented from a private landlord. Sometimes one family member, usually the father, would make the first move and acquire employment and accommodation. Employers often relied on workers to put in a word for other family members, signifying the retention of nepotism. These members would then follow and employers would come to take on whole families. This process encouraged the intensive occupation of meagre accommodation and the greater dividing up of the cost of rent. In such circumstances, extended family life offered some safeguard of mutual support to cover for situations of adversity such as ill health and unemployment at a time when little welfare provision was otherwise available.

3. From the 1830s, the consequence of the passage of the Factory Acts, restricting the employment of children in the harsh conditions of factory employment, was that young children and women tended to withdraw to the home, a location which was now viewed as a non-work environment. If women did work outside their own family, it was often as domestic workers, thus reinforcing their association with the domestic sphere.

To sum up, despite the complexity of the phenomena, the evidence from historical research suggests that the view that extended family life was more common in pre-industrial society is largely a myth. Functionalist theory which sees a transition from extended family to nuclear family as an adaptive adjustment to the transition from pre-industrial society to industrial society, does not seem to be supported by historical evidence, however neat the argument may be in theoretical terms. The nuclear family was more widespread in pre-industrial times than the theory suggested. The greater mobility that it allowed, along with the emerging cultural values of individualism and respect for privacy, may have actually provided an environment that was conducive to industrialisation. And following the Industrial Revolution in England, there is evidence that at least for a period of time in the nineteenth century, the extended family became a more, not less, common feature of the landscape, especially amongst the poor urban working class.

There are a number of reasons for a degree of caution over the evidence though. Care needs to be taken regarding the units of analysis that researchers use. For example, Laslett used evidence of household sizes averaging about 4.75 persons to indicate the relative rarity of the extended family in pre-industrial and early industrial England. However, it may be questioned whether 'household' is the most appropriate unit of measurement in this case. Post war studies such as Young and Willmott's (1974) mid 1950s research have revealed substantial evidence of extended family life when 'living in close proximity' was an alternative measure. Of course, there are also likely to be social class and regional variations in family life, as well as the fact that the findings regarding pre-industrial England may not apply to other pre-industrial countries. For example, evidence suggests that extended family life was more prevalent in some pre-industrial eastern European countries, thus possibly inhibiting their industrialisation.

Modernist sociological research:

1. The extended family

The extended family proved to be a durable arrangement in some working class communities well into the twentieth century. Whilst employment opportunities were stable and populations remained settled, work placement through nepotism was able to continue. Men often put in a word at work to find employment for their sons and other male relatives as, for example, in the case of acquiring work in the docks. Meanwhile, a key role for women was to provide the daily contacts of mutual support which comprised the extended family networks in the domestic setting and local community. Indeed, Young and Willmott still found such life to be quite common in working class communities of Bethnal Green in the mid-1950s, where local ties were further enhanced through the common practice of mothers ensuring that their daughters' names were put down early on local housing lists. However, broader forces of change were beginning to undermine the cohesion of the extended family in this and other localities. What were these changes?

One factor was the development of post war welfare state provision. This enabled people to fall back more on the impersonal help of the benefit and welfare system during times of need rather than feeling bound into the reciprocal obligations associated with extended family help.

Another change related to housing in the context of post war reconstruction. From the 1950s, families were being rehoused as new towns and new housing estates were built further out from slum areas such as in parts of the East End which were being demolished. Such rehousing usually led to the departure of the young nuclear family unit, attracted, as many interviewees in research conducted by Young and Willmott stated, by the prospects of a better environment for their children.

Industrial change, for example in the form of a decline in the availability of dock work in the East End, meant that younger family members could place less reliance on nepotism for finding work locally. Consequently, they sometimes needed to work or even move outside the area in which they had been brought up. And soon, the expansion of service sector employment and changing social attitudes toward female employment enabled more women to find work outside of the home, thus diluting their role at the hub of the extended family.

So, to what extent did the extended family continue to decline and family life retreat into the world of the isolated nuclear family? The evidence appears to be a little mixed. For example, Young and Willmott found that when young nuclear families were rehoused further out from the East End, wives' direct contact with extended family members declined significantly and they often experienced loneliness and isolation. However, in some cases, husbands retained employment in the locality of the original extended family and through their visiting of relatives whilst working in the area were able, to some extent, to perform the role of a link person in a continuing form of an extended family.

Broad based research conducted by the British Social Attitudes Survey (1995) more recently indicated that, when measured in terms of seeing a specified relative outside of the nuclear family at least once a week, the extended family remained more a feature of working class than middle class life, that women were still the main participants in maintaining contact, and that contact was more likely if there was a dependent child. Thus, in working class families with dependent children, 65% of mothers had 'regular' contact with a relative whereas only 33% of males in non-manual occupations and without children retained equivalent levels of contact.

Increased access to private transport enhanced the opportunities for regular face-to-face contact with relatives over greater geographical distances. Thus, Rosser and Harris (1965) found in their study of working class family life in Swansea that although extended family membership was more disbursed and day-to-day practical help more difficult to maintain, there remained strong affective bonds between members. Interestingly, a more recent large scale survey conducted in Swansea by Charles et al (2008) found the number of single person and small household units to have increased and households of three generations to have only remained within the Bangladeshi community.

Part of the reason for lower levels of face-to-face contact between middle class extended family relatives may have been related to greater dispersal as their occupations and careers tended to require higher levels of geographical mobility. Despite this, research evidence from Colin Bell (1968) in Swansea and Young and Willmott in the 1980s from a North London suburb suggests that there existed similar levels of positive concern within middle class families to maintain contact, even though it may be by such means as telephone and letter. Bell found that practical help by parents was often substantial when their sons and daughters were starting up new homes and families.

During the 1970s, the American researcher Litwak discovered that affective (feeling based) ties between extended family members remained strong despite sometimes substantial geographical separation, over which contact was often maintained through private transport, telephone and by letters. The family in this form he referred to as the 'modified extended family'.

In more recent times, the growth of the internet and new technological communication devices are surely enhancing opportunities for maintaining instant contact with relatives over vast distances. Assessing the survival of the extended family into the present day may therefore require taking into account the extent to which these new technological forms of communication are comparable with or an effective substitute for the help and support which once came from face–to–face contact with relatives living in close proximity.

We are now in a position to call further into question the functionalist account of the extended family. Historical evidence suggests that it was not a common part of the fabric of pre-industrial life, but became more prevalent during the early phase of industrialisation. And sociological research into post war society has shown that the extended family, along with the practice of nepotism, remained relatively vibrant in some communities. Even in contemporary society, it has shown some resilience, even if, as suggested above, in transformed form. The functionalist argument that the extended family is at odds with the needs of a modern dynamic economy should therefore alert us to the fact that if theoretical perspectives are to illuminate our understanding of society, we must apply them cautiously. We should not be blinded to alternative evidence just because it contradicts the self-contained logical consistency of a theory.

2. The nuclear family

As in post war functionalist theory, so in post war sociological research, the nuclear family was taken as the standard family form. The main focus of attention in research was initially on role relationships between husbands and wives and the designation of domestic activities within the nuclear family. Research carried out by Elizabeth Bott and Young and Willmott illustrates this well.

Bott's pioneering small scale study of families in London – 'The Family and Social Network', (1957) – generated some early insights into the social influences behind whether husbands and wives tended to engage in segregated or joint conjugal role relationships. She found there to be a connection between the type role relationship that existed between couples and the type of friendship network that they were connected to outside of the family. Her evidence suggested that segregated conjugal roles, in which clear demarcation existed between men's work and women's work, were more likely to be found in situations where each partner had established a closely knit friendship network outside of marriage; one in which many of the members knew each other (figure 1 below). This friendship and conjugal role pattern also tended to be more common in working class families. Joint conjugal roles, where there was more role overlap and common participation in domestic tasks, were more characteristic of middle class partners who had established dispersed friendship networks outside of the family, in which few members knew each other (figure 2 below).

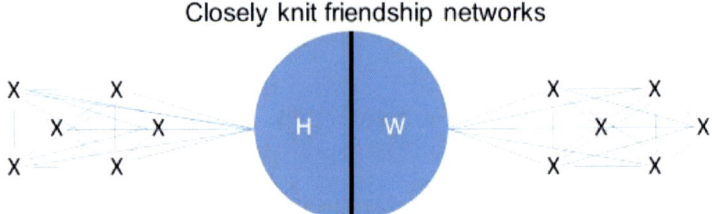

Figure 1 ## Segregated Conjugal Roles

Closely knit friendship networks

Husband and wife roles separate and complementary

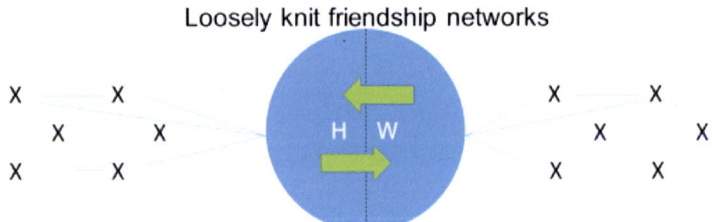

Figure 2 ## Joint Conjugal Roles

Loosely knit friendship networks

Husband and wife roles overlapping and more interchangeable

How could this relationship between type of friendship network and conjugal role relationships be explained? Bott argued that marriages were often superimposed onto pre-existing friendships. She speculated that the continuation of a pre-existing close knit friendship network after marriage draws partners into friendship activities outside the family and provides shared gender norms that reinforce gender stereotypes, emotional support and help. More loosely knit networks, by contrast, provided a less cohesive body of norms and degree of control over individuals and fewer opportunities for providing mutual assistance and emotional support amongst members. In this situation, couples had to turn to each other more for emotional fulfilment and achievement of tasks.

When Young and Willmott coined the term 'The Symmetrical Family' (1973), they were identifying a very similar pattern of role relationships to Bott's joint conjugal roles that they argued were becoming more prevalent within middle and working class families. However, they framed their explanation within the context of far larger scale research (a London survey of nearly 2,000 people) and a much broader historical time frame, the findings of which tended to correspond with the key changes identified in the earlier historical section of this chapter.

In their survey, Young and Willmott found evidence that contrasted with their previous documentation of traditional working class segregated conjugal roles and extended family communities. Their research showed that the nuclear family was becoming increasingly privatised and home centred and that the once clearly segregated conjugal roles within the family were blurring. The broader forces of change associated with this were growing levels of affluence and increasing opportunities for employment for women. As a result, husbands were becoming more engaged in housework chores and the home was becoming an environment for shared relaxation. However, although the model is suggestive of a more egalitarian and companionate relationship, the term symmetrical did not imply that identical tasks were being equally shared by the partners. Husbands would more likely engage in more DIY work whilst wives still spent a disproportionate amount of time in a childcare role. It was argued that these changes, which were regarded by Young and Willmott as evidence of social progress, indicated a convergence toward the pattern of role relationships that had earlier been more typical within middle class families as sections of the working class gained access to middle class levels of affluence. This dynamic was referred to as 'stratified diffusion'.

Again, evidence of trends toward joint conjugal role or symmetrical partner relationships is a departure from the family of the Parsonian functionalist model. However, such changes are not necessarily inconsistent with the functionalist perspective per se as they could be argued to represent an adaptation of nuclear family roles to broader social changes. Thus, as pressures of consumerism and changes toward a service orientated economy brought enhanced work opportunities to and put more pressures on women to gain employment, a change toward more egalitarian role relationships within the family can be interpreted as a necessary adaptation.

However, a contrary position to Young and Willmott's 'march of progress' interpretation has been adopted by those who refer to disadvantages, some new and increasing, experienced by women in terms of a 'dual burden' 'double exploitation' and even 'triple shift'. The concept of dual burden relates to the growing tendency for women to work outside the family, sometimes in a full-time capacity, yet be expected to retain many of their traditional domestic responsibilities. For Rapoport and Rapoport (1982), double exploitation refers to the continuing pressure that women are under to provide 'free' domestic labour whilst also pursuing work in which both career opportunities and pay are limited. And the term triple shift adds to the features of the dual burden the view that the management of the further emotional pressure that is placed on relationships under these circumstances falls disproportionately on the shoulders of women.

What did further research evidence reveal regarding these optimistic or pessimistic positions?

One area considered was that of the perception of equality or inequality of contribution to tasks within the household by partners themselves. A British Social Attitudes Survey of 1987 found differences in perception between men and women on the practice of gender equality in household task allocation within the family. 16% of men believed that household tasks were shared equally, but only 9% on women thought so. These different gender perceptions may well relate to different gender based starting points and expectations.

Whilst Young and Willmott were confident that their research findings indicated the emergence of more equal contributions to household work between male and female partners, the feminist Ann Oakley was much more cautious about their findings. She suggested that their optimism was undue since their starting point for purpose of comparison was that of segregated conjugal roles and that measurements were taken in such a way that even modest evidence of husbands' involvement in household tasks was taken as a sign of growing symmetry of contributions. Young and Willmott were therefore accused of 'over interpreting' their data. By contrast, Oakley's (1974) study of housework, conducted through in-depth interviewing of partners in 40 families in London, found more symmetry in the role relations of middle class parents than that of working class, but that even in the former symmetry was found to be minimal, with women maintaining primary responsibility for child rearing and housework.

Whilst not detracting from the importance of these findings, it should be recognised that R. Pahl's (1984) research found that conjugal role relationships can be effected by the stage reached in what was then regarded as the typical family life cycle. Greater symmetry or joint conjugal roles may be a more workable option for couples without children. However, if couples have children, it was found that the wife was more likely to give up employment when they were young. More segregated conjugal roles were likely to be associated with this phase in the family cycle. Later, as parenting responsibilities declined, the wife may re-enter the workplace and domestic roles and responsibilities would tend to become more equally allocated again. The important point here is that Oakley's findings, whilst providing a valuable insight into heavily gendered role allocation at the child rearing phase of the family life cycle, would not provide in itself a valid basis for any assumption that this pattern persists throughout the family life cycle. Any such assumption would be an over interpretation of the evidence.

Research by J. Gershuny (1983) found that even when they were engaged in paid employment, women still tended to spend more time on housework than men. However, other research that detailed time allocation, Gershuny (1992) showed that husbands committed more time to domestic work as wives increased their involvement in paid work. Moreover, between 1974 and 1987, husbands of wives in full-time employment doubled their involvement in cooking and cleaning activities. Wives, nevertheless, still tended to retain primary responsibility for housework. Gershuny concluded that such findings demonstrated that a process of 'lagged adaptation' was taking place. This meant that there was a delay in the adjustment of old ways and cultural values to the new economic situation of women increasing their participation in the workforce. It could also be argued, of course, that these changes could be burdensome on husbands who may themselves be caught between the pressures of traditional cultural values that emphasised sole breadwinner responsibility for the family and those by which he was expected to contribute far more to household tasks and childrearing. Such changes take time to resolve themselves and reveal new temporary adjustments.

From Sullivan's research (2000), it was found that as men worked fewer hours, their contribution to household work increased. However, it appears that there can be exceptions to this pattern since research findings by Morris (1990) showed that men who became unemployed but whose wives worked contributed little more to household chores than when they had worked. It appeared that in this case, both the experience of becoming unemployed and any participation in domestic work were regarded as a threat to their perceived masculinity.

Focussing on conjugal roles and task allocation alone within the family may tend to overlook other areas of potential gender inequality such as decision making and control of family finances. These dimensions are more to do with the use of power as viewed in a sociological sense – that is, the ability that some people have to exert control over others. Research conducted by Stephen Edgell (1980) found that although there was evidence of more participation by husbands in child rearing, males tended to predominate in making decisions which were defined by the couples as major and important, whilst females had responsibility for more routine and less important decisions.

Interestingly, research carried out by Jan Pahl (1993) discovered that although a variety of decision making arrangements existed between couples, husbands still tended to have more control over family finances and that both partners experienced highest levels of marital unhappiness in situations where husband's control was strong. However, research by Laurie and Gershuny (2000) which compared survey evidence from 1995 with that of 1991, did find a decline in the practice of husbands providing a housekeeping allowance to wives and greater equality in the making of major financial decisions.

Another area which has been researched covers a rather more subjective dimension – that of emotional input into relationships. Evidence from Duncombe and Marsden (1995) found that male partners were less likely to recognise the necessary extent of emotional input required to keep a relationship together and that women put in most of the work in this area and also took much of the strain.

In summary, this section of the chapter has concentrated on quite dated research that has tended to take the nuclear family as given and found that there has been some evidence of a modest growth in gender equality. Within this institution, both the evidence and its evaluation can vary significantly. Those who take a position of segregated conjugal roles as their starting point may find it easier to argue that substantial change has taken place, whereas many feminists, looking from the gender equality end of the spectrum, have maintained that the changes are modest and token and that new burdens have fallen on women. There is a broad range of research evidence which suggests the need for some caution regarding both the extent and inevitability of nuclear family life adaptation to modern society's apparent requirement for far greater gender equality. However, we will shortly consider evidence of a growing diversity of family types and personal relationships which makes research based exclusively on the nuclear family itself look very dated.

The family and gender inequality

The family is regarded as of crucial importance to feminists from a range of perspectives as it is here where gender socialisation, role allocation and the use of power to the benefit of males is regarded as so pronounced. But how did we get to this position historically?

Across much of pre-industrial British society, the key economic unit of production was often the family itself, within which various work roles were allocated. Although the male often held important powers and decision making, the output was usually recognised as the product of the work of all family members and women and the young had important roles to play.

We have seen that the Industrial Revolution brought about changes in the location of work, its definition and who were recognised as engaged in work. A fundamental consequence of the Industrial Revolution was to provide work in factories owned by others in places separated from the home. Whilst initially whole families were often taken on, legislative restrictions became placed on factory owners regarding the employment of women and children who became a less attractive employment proposition. This was the beginning of the retreat of women and children to the domestic environment. According to Abbott and Wallace (1997, p.142), these changes were already becoming well established in middle class households during the early nineteenth century and by the 1850s were being rapidly followed in working class family life. Whatever the contributions made by women there, the home was becoming redefined as a non-work environment and a unit of consumption rather than production.

This separation of male 'work' and female domestic responsibilities in the nuclear family unit headed by the male breadwinner led male workers, supported by trade unions, to press for a male wage level that was sufficient to support a family. Women were not in a position to make such claims since it was not they who 'worked' to support families. Women's withdrawal from participation in the workplace became supplemented by the view that this was the natural order of things.

Feminist perspectives on the family

Feminists have long challenged the male dominated nuclear family, portrayed as the natural order, as being an ideological construct. As an ideological construct, this image of the nuclear family protected the dominant interests of men whilst providing the appearance of also operating in the interests of subordinated women. After all, it was surely the true vocation of all women to be economically supported in the realisation of their natural and fulfilling role as child bearers and carers and providers of domestic and emotional support for husbands within the protective confines of the family.

However, anthropological studies which point to evidence of substantial diversity of family life throughout the different cultures of the world have suggested that the factual reality of this natural order view is unfounded. Furthermore, feminists such as Betty Friedan (1965) and Hannah Gavron (1966) have argued that the post war nuclear family did not just restrict the possibilities for women to gain their own economic income but in particular that the plight of the traditional housewife was virtually one of captivity in an environment of loneliness and domestic drudgery that undermined their potential for self-fulfilment.

Friedan and Gavron tend to be viewed as representing a liberal feminist perspective. This position does not oppose marriage and the family as such. Instead, the case is put for reforms that enable women to have equal access to and opportunities within the public sphere. Such reforms would include equal access to workplace, career and educational opportunities as well as support for maternity leave.

Liberal feminists have generally adopted a reformist positon which is relatively optimistic that by working through the system, social values, family structures and employment opportunities have and will continue to move in a progressive direction of liberation and equality of opportunity for women. Steps in this direction during the 1970s included trends toward more equal and flexible role allocation within the family and the passage of anti-discriminatory legislation in the workplace.

Marxist feminists, such as Margaret Benston, have adopted a far more sceptical position on the possibility that gender equality can be achieved by such means. From this perspective, it cannot be realised whilst the system remains capitalist since the oppression of women is intimately tied up with social class oppression. In essence, the subordination of women within both the public sphere and the family serves the needs of capitalism through providing a cheap reserve army of labour, cheap domestic labour and an outlet for male aggression within the family. The family is therefore a pillar of both class and gender exploitation.

For radical feminists, the oppression of women by men it so endemic throughout societies and human history that neither legislative reform nor even the overthrow of capitalism will provide a solution. Firestone traces patriarchal power to women's biological dependence on men and argues that genuine liberation would require technological advances such as test tube reproduction and social reforms that would enable women to live independently from men.

More recent interest has been shown in a development referred to as intersectional feminism, a pioneering figure in its development being Kimberle Crenshaw (1989). This approach is critical of much mainstream feminism as reflecting a white middle class female outlook. The key point is that women experience oppression in terms of different forms of disadvantage through which gender may be combined with ethnicity, social class, disability etc. which act as a matrix of oppression. The understanding of this oppression cannot be calculated by adding together the different dimensions of socially structured disadvantage but requires the study of their combined effects on the experiences of different individuals.

Feminist research into the family

Feminist researchers frequently argue the superiority of small scale qualitative research into family life to get close to how it is experienced by housewives and mothers. The findings have enabled some to challenge the claim by Young and Willmott (1973) that within the nuclear family more egalitarian and companionate relationships were emerging between husbands and wives.

As early as 1966, through using unstructured interviews, Gavron had found that against enhanced expectations of greater freedom in married life compared to that of their parent's generation, the experience for many young married women was one of feeling trapped in an existence of domestic chores and often experiencing negative psychological consequences.

Oakley's research in 1974 discovered that for many of the housewives that she interviewed, compared to the ideology of domestic bliss, housework and domestic life were found to be as unsatisfying and alienating an experience as that which is often found in industrial labour.

Such research findings, highlighting experiences of isolation and alienation experienced by women in traditional domestic roles, emphasise the point that experiences of family life are likely to be quite different for women than for men.

Nuclear family, still a cultural norm?

It could be countered that there has been a massive shift in the direction of diversity of family life and that present day feminists who aim their attack on the traditional nuclear family are fighting battles of the past. There is some need for caution regarding this assertion though.

Firstly, social surveys tend to show that public attitudes and values remain quite strongly in favour of the nuclear family, if less so amongst younger people.

Secondly, the main political parties have shown a clear preference for the nuclear family and have been somewhat reluctantly dragged along by social changes in the form of alternative lifestyles. For example, support for the nuclear family came powerfully from the Conservative new right governments of the 1980s and early 1990s. During this period, single parent families faced political stigmatisation and the Party came to launch a 'back to basics' campaign which provided strong moral sanction for the nuclear family. New Labour governments from 1997 to 2010 continued to view the nuclear family as fundamental to the promotion of social order but placed greater emphasis on the support role of state agencies and came to recognise that growing family diversity was a reality that they had to live with, for example passing legislation enabling same sex civil partnerships. Post 2010, the Conservative led coalition and the Conservative government attempted a delicate balancing act of supporting the traditional family institution whilst distancing themselves from past Conservative attacks on single parenthood and legislated to enable marriage between same sex couples.

Thirdly, what appear to be quite radical alternatives to the traditional nuclear family are not necessarily quite so much so. For example, although the numbers of couples cohabiting has substantially increased, these are now often stable relationships between couples whose roles may still sometimes closely correspond to those of the male breadwinner and female child carer in more traditional family units.

Symbolic interactionism – family as defined by participants

Positivist research tended to view 'the family' as conventionally defined and utilise official statistics and large scale surveys as the preferred method for obtaining information about it. As a perspective developed later into the modern period, interactionism may better equip the sociologist to approach the diversity and fluidity of contemporary family life than positivism and its associated perspective of functionalism. Interactionists emphasise that individuals participate in social situations where roles are chosen, negotiated, constructed and redefined by the participants' purposeful actions. Rather than functioning as a structured imposition on people's lives, for interactionists broader society, as the product of the wilful action of individuals, can be dynamic and diverse.

Interactionism also emphasises the importance of sociological researchers seeing society as through the eyes of social participants. Interactionists studying the family would therefore attempt to gain an understanding of any family life viewed as such by people themselves rather than working from pre-set definitions of what counts as a family. This approach enables the sociologist to adopt a neutral attitude toward family diversity. It emphasises, in contrast to positivist approaches, that sociologists should not base their knowledge entirely on the convenience of using social statistics on the family derived from official definitions of what it is. This number crunching loses sight of a broad diversity of relationships which are meaningful as families to participants. By adopting a micro approach, interactionists might certainly look at the experiences encountered by married couples as they negotiate married life and experience divorce (with marriage and divorce being the milestones provided in official data). However, they would also study those in other relationships which the participants define as a family and which may not form the basis of official statistics on the family, but which are equally worthy of study. In other words, sociologists should be guided in their research to try and understand all social life in ways meaningful to individuals or groups rather than the blinding convenience of easy to acquire social statistics based on conventional definitions. The sociologist who limits him or herself to the latter task risks the bias of making themselves an instrument of convention.

Symbolic interactionists are particularly interested in understanding the processes involved by which a family may identify insiders (members) and outsiders (non-members) and how processes on mutual adjustment between members take place over time. Of special interest may be the study of life in the early stages of partnerships or in newer family forms such as reconstituted families and same sex partnerships where participants have to navigate their way forward without necessarily having such clear role scripts provided for them as in the case of the conventional nuclear family. To understand the subtleties of symbolic communication, interactionists are likely to resort to the study of personal documents such as diaries and letters, time budgeting records, and use unstructured and in-depth interviewing to obtain qualitative information.

Studies adopting a broadly interpretive approach have provided fertile ground for developing new ways of looking at family life in a contemporary setting and there is some attraction of interactionist type approaches to feminist researchers. For example, Finch (2007) has utilised the concept of 'display' to explain that members of families engage in actions to constantly define and redefine their relationships within families and denote to others that the group that they are in is regarded as a family by them. Roseneil and Budgeon (2004) claim that what constitutes 'the family' is now far more contested and that friendship relationships are often becoming viewed more as family like, especially given the growing numbers of people living without partners.

'The family' – decline or change?

1. Divorce

Increase in divorce

One social change that has long been associated with the question of the decline of the family is that of rising divorce rates. Official statistics are available on petitions filed and divorces granted. Divorce statistics, currently compiled by HM Courts and Tribunal Services from information sent from the courts, are available through the Office for National Statistics which provides the main source of raw data utilised in the following sections. In a formal sense, this data is likely to be highly reliable, but, for sociological purposes, it needs to be interpreted within social contexts and may be more questionable in terms of its validity – how useful is it in measuring what it claims to measure in real life situations?

Statistics show that throughout the twentieth century there has been a substantial rise in divorce. This can be measured either in terms of simple aggregate totals or rates. Aggregates simply express the total number of divorces granted during a particular year. By contrast, divorce rates refer to the number of divorces per 1,000 of the married population per annum. Aggregate numbers are useful if interest is primarily in measuring the total magnitude of divorce. Thus, figures from *Social Trends* show, for example, that there were about 25,000 divorces granted in England and Wales in 1961, and that by 1986 the figure had reached approximately 154,000. If these figures were expressed in terms of rates, they would be 2.1 and 12.9 respectively – showing a greater than six-fold increase, which is roughly in line with the proportionate increase in the aggregate totals indicated above for this time period.

Rates may offer a more revealing measure when interest is in change over time. As they relate to a standard gauge of divorces per 1,000 of the married population, changes in rates may not always exactly mirror aggregate changes in the number of divorces. For example, compared to the 1993 peak in the total of divorces of 165,018 when the rate was 13.8, the 1994 total fell to 158,175, yet the rate increased to 14.2. How is this possible? It is because the rate per 1,000 relates to the total number of people married. If there are fewer people in total married, then the ratio of divorces to the numbers married can increase even if the total number of divorces declines (and of course the reverse is also true). In fact, there has been a general decline over recent decades in both the proportion and numbers of people getting married. For example, in 1971, over two thirds of the adult population were married. The figure has since fallen to about 50%.

Understanding statistics

Attempting to understand statistics in sociology can be quite baffling. The author suggests that one way of making the task easier is to invent a situation where the figures are much smaller and neatly rounded. For example, imagine a small town in which there are 2,000 married people. If in a given year there were 22 divorces, the rate would be 11 per 1,000 married people. However, if in another year there were only 1,000 married people, then the same aggregate of 22 divorces would represent a leap in the rate to 22. The same logic can be applied to the much larger figures outlined further above, and, of course, this type of exercise is worth inventing to assist the understanding of statistical information in other areas of sociological study.

Why an increase in divorce?

How can the historically high divorce rates of the late twentieth and early twenty first century be understood sociologically? To do so, one needs to look at various aspects of the social context.

One reason is that changes in divorce laws since the middle of the nineteenth century have gradually made divorce more easily accessible. Such reforms are referred to as 'enabling legislation'. The statistics show that as well as a general upward curve in the divorce rate, there is usually a jump in the figures following the passage of enabling legislation. This jump would include a number of divorces which would have been more difficult to actualise under previous legislative conditions.

However, enablement alone is insufficient to explain the very substantial increase in decisions to divorce, especially during the last four decades of the twentieth century. As the law changes, it usually reflects society's changing moral values which it puts into codified form. Therefore, more liberal divorce legislation has accompanied a decline in social stigma against divorce. But it is not necessarily the case that there is a clear cause and effect relationship whereby changing moral values bring about corresponding legal changes. The phenomena can also be viewed the other way around; the greater frequency of divorce which the legislation makes possible will have an impact on moral values by reducing the stigma against divorce which is becoming increasingly common, thus opening up possibilities when previously taboo. Changes in moral values and legislation can thus feed off each other.

This arguably still does not fully explain why more people decide to divorce. One explanation requires the application of historical understanding of the practical choices available to people, their expectations associated with marriage and the nature of marital bonds. Edward Shorter (1977) argued that in much of pre-industrial society, the family was a relatively uncaring environment, organised around the perpetuation of property or the domestic work unit. The economic necessity of the marriage remaining intact was often of prime importance. By contrast, following industrialisation, the workplace moving outside of the family reduced the extent to which ties were based on this form of economic necessity. Of further importance was a cultural change. As marriage became accompanied by higher expectations of romantic attachment and emotional fulfilment, these have become the more shaky mainstays of modern marriages. Such high expectations can be easily thwarted, often leaving little else to hold the marriage together.

Secularisation is a further dimension of social change which may be relevant to the long term rise in divorce rates. Secularisation is the assertion that the significance of religion in people's lives declines with the process of modernisation. This assertion will be reviewed in greater detail in the chapter on the Sociology of Religion – we cannot assume that it is a simple proven fact. However, from the point of view of the topic at hand, it can be argued that religion and the church may play a diminishing role in people's lives, when measured by the increase in marriages in register offices and other licensed premises compared to church weddings. The implications for divorce are that the sanctity of the church and the belief that a sacred promise has been made before an all seeing god (given at least the probability that overall a greater proportion of people who marry in church hold religious views) are more powerful sanctions making for a marriage to endure than a secular promise. Moreover, those who elect to have a church wedding may include a greater proportion of people with traditionalist attitudes toward married life in the first place. One would need to know more about the reasons why people marry in church or choose a secular setting and whether the choice has been freely available to them. For example, as divorce has increased and is frequently followed by remarriage, if any church retains a traditional attitude of not marrying divorcees, then more people may be pushed toward secular remarriage options.

Other social factors which coincide with the steep increase in divorce rates since the 1960s include, as well as higher marital expectations, a greater assertiveness of women which accompanied the political impact and cultural changes of women's liberation movement from the late 60s. Feminists in particular highlighted the issue of domestic violence, suffered mainly by women at the hands of men, and raised the profile of behaviour which should be no longer tolerated.

From about this time, women also gained more opportunities to become economically self-supporting through improved female employment opportunities accompanying the expansion of the service sector of the economy. As we have seen, despite increasing expectations of personal fulfilment in marriage (companionate expectations) these work 'opportunities' have involved some women in the stress of a dual burden if husbands' involvement in domestic chores remains minimal. Putting all this together, it should not be surprising to find that divorces filed by women rose to a proportion of about 70% of the total.

Despite historically high divorce rates by the late twentieth century, a majority of those who divorced remarried and statistics showed that their future marriage was also more prone to divorce. Indeed, over a third of marriages were a remarriage for at least one of the partners. Although people are living longer, the period of time over which marriages endured was decreasing. For example, figures for 1951, show that 10% of marriages ended in divorce within 25 years. By 1981, 10% led to divorce within 5 years (Sclater, 2005, p.74).

In 1970, the American writer Alvin Toffler argued that a trend was emerging in contemporary societies toward an accelerating pace of change and increasing human longevity in which the odds were increasingly stacked against couples developing along parallel paths and remaining together for life. He argued that a change in family life toward 'serial monogamy' – an emerging pattern of sequences of temporary marriages - was already under way. Toffler predicted that the traditional expectation of lifelong marriage would give way to the anticipation of relatively short lived marriage and further declining stigma against divorce. Couples would be increasingly confronted with key decisions when their paths diverged on whether to go their separate ways and find a more parallel path with another partner.

Older age groups and divorce

Divorce rates can be used to provide a comparative measure of proportions divorcing in different sections of society. For example, comparisons can be made between the rates for people of different ethnic groups, social class backgrounds, occupations and age groups. Regarding the latter, there is evidence to show that that divorce rates amongst the over 60s in England and Wales have recently been increasing despite evidence to show that overall rates have started to decrease. Between 1991 and 2011, the rate for men over 60 increased from 1.6 to 2.3 and for women from 1.2 to 1.6. A similar trend has been identified in the United States where divorce rates for those in their 20s and 30s have been declining whereas for the over 50s the rates are increasing. The National Centre for Family and Marriage Research at the Bowling Green State University has shown that whereas in 1990 1 in 10 divorces were from the over 50s category, by 2015 the proportion had risen to over 1 in 4.

A number of reasons have been put forward to explain this trend. One is that this time period will have included a greater proportion of women who have worked for substantial periods of their life and accumulated access to improved pensions. By acquiring greater financial independence, more women may feel that they can free themselves from unhappy marriages. Another relates to the demographic profile. People within this age group were married when marriage rates were higher and have since come to constitute a growing proportion of the married population. As they are living longer and healthier and active lives, they have a potentially longer period of unhappy marriage which they may not be prepared to, and given more liberal attitudes toward divorce, feel that they have to endure.

Decrease in divorce

Figures from the Office for National Statistics show that since the turn of the millennium, there is evidence of a decline in both totals and rates of divorce in England and Wales. During this period, the total peaked at 153,065 in 2003 and the rate peaked at 14 in 2004. There was subsequently a steady year by year decrease in both totals and rates through to 2009 when the figures stood at 113,949 and 10.5 respectively. This total was the lowest since 1974 and the rate the lowest since 1977. After 2009, and although the figures have oscillated, by 2015 the number of divorces stood at 101,055 and the rate at 8.5 (although there has subsequently been a small increase in both). A similar trend has also been identified in the United Stated. What possible explanations could there be for this more recent general reversal of the longer term upward trend in the divorce rate?

Why a decrease in divorce?

The theme of rising divorce rates and nuclear family decline has been so engrained in sociology that there so far has been little mention of or attempt to explain a more recent trend of decline in divorce rates in England and Wales (and the United States). A number of tentative explanations for the decline are here suggested.

Firstly, until recently, in England and Wales there has been a long term decline in the numbers of people marrying and despite recent occasional reversals this general trend has continued. It can therefore be argued that over time those who marry have become a smaller but harder core of those committed to marriage.

Secondly, the average age for first marriages is now much later. On average, both men and women marry seven years later than was the case 1971. What may work in favour of a decrease in divorce can be the greater maturity of those who marry. Furthermore, in the United States, delayed marriage accompanied with education to college degree level, often associated with greater economic security and the sharing of domestic duties, is related to lower divorce rates (Miller, 18/7/2018).

Thirdly, delayed marriage may sometimes follow a protracted period of cohabitation. With the growing acceptability of cohabitation, only those committed to marriage may feel it necessary to take that step. However, there is also evidence to suggest that prior cohabitation is associated with the increased chance of divorce!

Fourthly, immigration rates and cultural differences may play into the figures. Through immigration, a larger ethnic minority population includes a significant proportion of those who hold traditional cultural values regarding family honour, loyalty and commitments.

It is not clear how or whether there is a general relationship between economic hardship and divorce rates or if so whether this is overridden by other factors. For example, divorce rates were increasing around the time of the recessions of the early 1980s and 1990s but have been declining along with the long recession and period of austerity after 2008.

2. Growing family and household diversity

Although reference will in this section be made to general trends and the bigger picture through the use of official statistics, we will later see that recent sociological approaches to the study of family life are focussing more on understanding the meaning of its different forms from the points of view of the participants, indicating a more interpretive emphasis.

Reconstituted and blended families

As those who divorce often remarry, or when relationships breakup and new cohabiting partnerships form, if a child is involved the resulting outcome is 'reconstituted' family. When families bring together children from different families into a single home, the term 'blended families' is applied. Either type are likely to vary considerably in the extent to which they approximate a traditional nuclear family pattern or not. A major challenge, though, can be that of mutual adjustment between new family members. Children may find difficulty in adjusting to life with new siblings or feel that a stepparent is treating them unfairly compared to the way that they treat their own biological children. These stepfamilies can also pose the problem of the relative authority over children of step parents within the new family and biological parents outside who continue to exert an influence. The issue of access also requires past partners to work at establishing arrangements that work, although there is evidence of a tendency for biological fathers outside of a new unit to drift out of involvement.

When families break up and reconstituted / blended families are formed, there has been much dispute over the type of post-divorce arrangements that work in the best interests of children. Thery summarises two opposing positions (Cheal, 2002, p.64): the 'substitution model' and the 'durability model'. Substitution emphasises that the best way forward is in a clear break between ex-partners and the establishment of a new family unit as a stable environment for children in which the new spouse takes over full parental responsibilities from the external biological parent. By contrast, the durability model emphasises the importance of continuity in that the biological parent retains regular contact with their children in the new family unit. As a result, step and biological parental roles become differentiated. It is this latter approach which policy makers have generally come to prefer, in the belief, supported by some evidence, that continued contact from the biological parent (invariably father) will improve the support for and development of the child.

Upon the breakup of families, whether or not reconstituted families emerge, there is always the risk of 'parental alienation' where children are turned against one parent by the other. This parental behaviour has now come to be recognised as a form of child abuse.

A decrease in marriage

Statistics indicate that there has been a fall in the number of marriages in England and Wales in recent decades from an annual average of almost 400,000 between 1965 and 1975 to under 300,000 in 1993. By 2015, despite small annual fluctuations, the figure, which for comparative purposes refers to the marriages of partners of the opposite sex, had fallen further to 239,020. In the context of population increases, the trend in the rate of marriage remains that of a gradual fall. Civil wedding ceremonies are constituting an increasing proportion of the total, rising from 31% in 1964 to just over 50% in 1992 and 74% in 2015, a vast majority of which are now held in approved premises as opposed to register offices. If further allowance is made for the increasing divorce rates throughout the twentieth century, the tendency for divorcees to remarry, and the fact that the above marriage figures include an increasing number of second marriages or beyond, there is evidence to suggest that the population has been dividing into a declining proportion of people who are marrying, more of whom are divorcing and many remarrying, and a significantly increasing proportion who are not marrying. So what is the evidence of alternatives to marriage that are emerging?

Cohabitation

There is clear evidence in recent history of increased rates of cohabitation whereby couples live together and form a relationship outside of marriage. However, it is misleading to see cohabitation as just a relatively recent phenomena. From a longer historical perspective, despite powerful social taboos, pre-marital sex, cohabitation and transient relationships were not uncommon features of life amongst poorer sections of the working class in the eighteenth and nineteenth centuries.

From research conducted in the United Kingdom in the 1950s, approximately 5% of married women said that they had cohabited with their husband prior to marriage. Although not in strictly comparable form, the findings from General Household Surveys indicated that the percentage of women cohabiting doubled between 1981 and 1996 to 25% and that the average time period of cohabitation was significantly increasing. The figures also showed different cohabitation rates for different age groups and different rates for males and females within the same age group. The highest rate was for males in the age range of 30-34 where the figures exceeded 40%. It is, of course, possible that an element of this increase, especially when compared to the figure for the 1950s, may be due to people feeling freer to volunteer this type of information than in the past when such arrangements were more heavily stigmatised. Also, just because the rate of marriage has tended to decline and the figures for cohabitation have increased, the extent to which cohabitation is forming an alternative to marriage may be a little more questionable than these statistics alone suggest. This is because a) relatively high rates of divorce mean that more new couples need to await the completion of a divorce before they are able to remarry and may cohabit during this time and b) many cohabiting couples eventually marry.

Cohabitation itself subsumes a diversity of arrangements. These may range from short term relationships with little commitment to longer term relationships and the raising of children. Overall, though, a range of snapshot surveys for 2007 – the General Household Survey, the Labour Force Survey and the Annual Population Survey – together provide consistent evidence that there were approximately 2.25 million opposite sex couples in cohabiting relationships in England and Wales and that the proportion of never married amongst these was increasing. The Office for National Statistics has provided a figure of approximately 3.3 million relationships for the year 2016 and although future projections should always be treated with caution, most predictions suggest that the number of cohabiting couples will increase steadily in the coming decades. For example, according to *Population Trends* research, the figure is expected to rise to about 3.8 million couples by 2031.

Changing attitudes appear to correlate with these trends. A British Social Attitudes Survey of 2001 found that long term cohabitation was becoming accepted as relatively normal and that only just over 50% of those interviewed believed that people should marry before having a family, compared to almost 75% in 1989. Few, however, dismissed marriage which remained viewed as a viable lifestyle choice.

There is, of course, reason for some doubt over the precise accuracy of official figures on cohabitation. The issues can be raised of how officials on the one hand or the parties themselves on the other define a relationship, and the extent to which there may be incentives, such as claiming benefit, which are likely to encourage some people to hide cohabiting relationships from prying officials and others.

Single and lone parent families

Through to the 1950s, women who gave birth out of marriage faced a very powerful social environment of moral and religious condemnation. Sometimes, another female within the family may quietly take on the role of raising the child as if their own. In many cases, a pregnant unmarried female might have been sent to a hostel run by a religious charity where they would give birth and often have to give their child up for adoption. In other instances, single women resorted to having backstreet abortions.

Some women who gave birth 'out of wedlock' ended up in asylums for the psychologically 'neurotic' where they may come to spend many years. By contrast, lone parenthood resulting from the death of a parent was largely immune from such stigma.

By the 1960s, moral attitudes on such issues were beginning to relax and by 1972 single and lone parent households (usually female headed) in the United Kingdom constituted about 8% of all families with children. A significant increase took place during the 1980s, with the proportion of single and lone parent families reaching 15% in 1989-1990. More recent data from the Office for National Statistics has placed the figure (now referred to jointly by the less pejorative term as 'lone parents') for 2017 at approximately 2.8 million households, about 90% of which are headed by females. This can be seen in the context of a trend of modest increase from a figure of 2.4 million lone parent households in 1996 and the possible start of a downward trend from a high point of three million in 2015. There is, however, much that these statistics alone also hide.

Firstly, they are just a snapshot measurement in the course of people's lives. Many lone parents and their children will have lived in or come to live in married or cohabiting households for part of their lives.

Secondly, in reality the distinction between married or cohabiting and lone parent households may not always be quite as clear cut as definitions suggest. In some married households, the requirements of certain occupations such as travelling salespersons, involvement in the holiday business or members of the armed forces when away on service, can necessitate that a partner be frequently absent. In other cases, the partners may be separated or a partner might be in prison, whereas some lone parent households have frequent contact with or support from a partner.

Thirdly, when used in a broad generic sense, lone parenthood is a diverse category made up of changing proportions including a declining fraction of widowed and increasing proportions of divorced and never married lone parents. Situations may also vary significantly in terms of opportunities to work, support from other family members and friends and financial security available, but generally the never married lone parents are more likely to struggle on low income.

Providing a succinct historical overview, Robertson Elliot (1996, p.22) has extracted information from Social Trends to show that in 1960 about one birth out of every twenty was outside of marriage, whereas by the early 1990s the proportion had reached almost one in three. Of these, approximately a half were born into cohabiting relationships and a half born to lone mothers.

Singletons

The figures for those living alone (referred to as singletons) have shown a significant increase in recent decades. For example, in 1998, 12% of people lived in single person households compared to 3.9% in 1961 (a time during which living alone or remaining unmarried often cast doubts on the sexuality of a person). These comprised 12% of households in 1961 and 28% of households in 1998, since by definition they comprise the smallest household units. By 2008, singletons made up just over 30% of households, a proportion that increased slightly by 2017.

However, pausing here for a moment may alert us to some of the complexities behind these apparently straightforward figures. The routes to living alone are diverse and many who live alone do not do so through a positive decision of their own. This can particularly be the case for elderly people through the death of a partner. The singleton figures for those under retirement age may therefore be more indicative of positive choice. These comprised 4% of all households in 1961 and 12% in 1996-1997. By 2015, the aggregate number of singleton households in this age category stood at about four million, the majority being male, whilst in the older age group, with women living longer than men, the majority were female.

An increase in the proportions of singleton households may be related to an increase in divorce rates up to the early twenty first century and a tendency for people to marry later in life than they used to but it is also likely to both reflect and further promote the view that living alone is now far more socially acceptable. Young people are less likely now to go straight from their family of origin to family of destination or procreation but may instead leave home to set up their own home – if possible!

But how exactly are single person households defined? Take the example of a house divided into three separate flats, each let out to a student. Each flat may count as a single person household, but is this quite the same as people living alone in separate dwellings? What if each student in each flat shared common kitchen facilities and a television room? Do they still live alone and constitute single person households? Whether for definitional purposes they do or do not, presumably, qualitatively, their domestic lives would be quite different from those living in isolated and self-contained flats or separate dwellings. Furthermore, statistics only take a snapshot view of the domestic situation. Presumably, many of these students would return to families during vacation times, so to what extent have they 'left home'? Longer-term profiles would therefore more realistically show the varying domestic situations experienced than any snapshot measurement could.

As a word of caution, at the time of writing, increases in university debt, rising house prices and the difficulty of obtaining a mortgage appear to be associated with a rise in the proportion of young people aged 20 to 34 living at home with their parents. The figures show that numbers have plateaued between 2014 and 2016 at record levels of over 1 in 4 (1 in 3 males and 1 in 5 females) or 3.3 million in total.

Ethnic diversity

Another aspect of family diversity relates to the ethnic diversity of British society. The cultural identity and ways of different ethnic groups are acquired through socialisation into cultural traditions. These traditions may persist or change in the cultural environment of the host population.

When ethnic minorities migrated to Britain, their own cultural values and family structures were sometimes accentuated as a form of defence against the racism that they suffered from the host population. However, a substantial proportion of the ethnic minority population is now second or third generation. A key question at this point is whether life in British society has been narrowing the differences in family life between different ethnic minorities and white British people or whether ethnic traditions have been more resistant to change and thus contribute to another dimension of family diversity.

The complexity of differences both between and within ethnic groups regarding family life cannot be tackled here, only emphasised. As two quite contrasting examples, South Asian and Afro Caribbean family life will be briefly commented on. Generally, South Asian families have retained the highest marriage rates and low divorce rates and they tend to partake in extended family life where possible, including contacts with and visits to relatives in their country of descent. Sometimes parents still exert strong pressure toward arranged marriages, or at least accommodated marriage where they suggest prospective partners but allow the potential partners the final choice. A strong emphasis is often placed on maintaining traditional segregated conjugal roles and patriarchal power and family honour is especially directed at the behavioural expectations of females. One important difference between Pakistani and Indian families, though, is that in the former, the influence of Islamic religion is more likely to require a wife to remain within the household or family business to minimise contact with non-family males. Although single parenthood in both Indian and Pakistani families has significantly increased, this is from a very low base, and reaching about 5% remains well below that of the white British population.

By contrast, single parent families are much more common within West Indian communities, marriage rates are relatively low, divorce rates high and cohabitation, at a rate of about 10%, is not uncommon. However, research has also shown there to exist a diversity of Afro Caribbean family life in both country of descent and in Britain. This is partly economic based. Economically successful West Indians are more likely to follow a model of family life similar to the conventional British nuclear family. By contrast, common law families are more likely amongst the less economically successful. A third pattern identified is the female headed households in which males play a more peripheral role and the mother, usually working, relies on the help of female relatives or neighbours to run the family.

The question of whether cultural influences or situational circumstances of a more economic nature best explain family patterns of ethnic minority groups has been of much debate. If within the same ethnic minority culture, family structures vary according to economic factors and give rise to families similar to those of other ethnic groups in similar economic circumstances, it could be argued that situational circumstances shaped by socio-economic class may have at least as strong an influence on the way that people live as do ethnic cultures.

Whether the structure of family life of ethnic minorities is converging with that of family life of the host culture is a very complex matter and is likely to vary both between and within ethnic minority groups. However, it begs the question of convergence to what, given the diversity of family life that exists. On the one hand, second and third generation youngsters may have to delicately manoeuvre their behaviour between a family life in which parents hold traditional cultural values and the more permissive liberal ways of broader society, whilst parents may be keen for their part on safeguarding their cultural traditions from what they feel is a corrosive environment of 'anything goes'. Overall, the data from surveys and more in-depth research suggests both quite high levels of continuity in the different ethnic traditions and some diversity of family life within each of the ethnic minority groups. This would tend to add to the overall diversity of family life in Britain.

Same sex relationships

Although people can now be more open about gay and lesbian relationships, it is difficult to obtain any accurate measure of the changing extent of these relationships in society due to powerful past taboos. The greater moral uniformity of the post war decades placed very strong pressure on people with homosexual inclinations to either repress these tendencies, engage in clandestine relationships or face the risk of criminalisation or 'corrective therapy'. Only from 1967 did privately conducted homosexuality between consenting adults over the age of 21 cease to be a criminal offence (although not applied to the armed forces).

From the late twentieth century, people have been able to acquire legal recognition of same sex relationships in a growing number of countries, but moral values derived from church establishments have played an important role in this area. Initially, same sex partnerships were restricted to the status of 'civil partnerships' providing a distinction in legal terminology and status, based on religious sensitivities, from heterosexual marriage. Denmark pioneered same sex civil partnerships in 1989, to be followed by a number of other countries, including Britain in December 2005, and others since.

In Britain, the established position of the Church of England has been that the purpose of marriage is to fulfil God's purpose by promoting a committed and faithful relationship between a man and woman for the procreation of children. The term 'marriage' thus holds strong religious connotations and the state recognised this by initially limiting single sex partnerships to civil status and secular ceremony, officiated by a registrar at approved premises. However, in Britain the status of civil partnership does confer on partners legal equalities to that of married couples, for example in terms of taxes and benefits, protection against domestic violence and rules regarding migration and nationality.

Following the introduction of civil partnership legalisation, the figures for England and Wales quickly peaked at approximately 9,000 male and almost 6,000 female unions in 2006, demonstrating a surge effect of enabling legislation. The total figure for male and female civil partnerships subsequently levelled out at around 6,000 per annum between 2009 and 2013.

As not legally defined as 'marriage', breakups of these relationships were not referred to as divorce, but as 'dissolution'. However, the procedure follows a similar one to that of divorce whereby the partnership must have endured for at least a year and face irretrievable breakdown.

In late 2006, opposition between religious traditionalism and state reform on issues of sexuality and discrimination surfaced in Britain regarding the issue of adoption. It became possible for same sex couples to adopt in 2005. The Catholic Church, which runs a small number of adoption agencies in England and Wales, opposed the placement of children for adoption through its own agencies with same sex couples in civil partnerships which, in reference to religious scriptures, it did not recognise as equivalent to marriages which had to be a union of man and woman. The timing of this statement of opposition related to the then forthcoming 2007 Equalities Act (Sexual Orientation Regulations) which made it illegal to discriminate against anybody on the grounds of sexuality, including cases of adoption by same sex couples. In its response, the Catholic Church threatened to close its adoption agencies if it were forced to comply. Losing an appeal in 2010 for exclusion from the terms of the legislation, agencies have faced the prospect of loss of charitable status for non-compliance.

The Papacy, as the custodian of Catholic traditionalism, remains strongly opposed to same sex partnerships, and Pope Benedict XVI referred to homosexuality as an "intrinsic moral evil". More surprisingly, therefore, the third country to pass legislation enabling same sex marriage, following Holland in 2001, was Spain in 2005, a country where a substantial majority of the population still see themselves as Catholic. The Roman Catholic Church and many conservatives bitterly opposed the reforms of a socialist government, which also passed legislation to speed up the process by which couples could divorce.

The British Conservative led coalition government legislated to allow same sex partners access to full married status in England and Wales from the end of March 2014 (followed months later in Scotland). Weddings were made available through religious organisations that were willing to 'opt in' and conduct ceremonies. The Quakers were one such organisation that decided to 'opt in'. However, due to strong opposition from the Churches of England and Wales, the legislation provided a ban on conducting same sex marriages within these institutions.

With foreknowledge of this forthcoming legislation, there was a substantial fall in the number same sex couples opting for civil partnerships and in the year that followed the legislation over 50% of same sex marriages took the form of conversions from civil partnerships, a process which became a legal option during December 2014.

Whilst civil partnerships arc available in Northern Ireland, at the time of writing legislation enabling same sex marriage has not been enacted. Interestingly, the findings from a 2015 MORI poll in Northern Ireland found that 75% of those from a Catholic background supported reform as opposed to 57% of Protestants (Comie, 23/10/2017).

One feature of gay and lesbian relationships is that they are relatively free from the imposition of conventional male and female gender stereotypes. Hence, there is more scope for negotiation of roles which tend to be more egalitarian than in heterosexual relationships. This was indeed found to be the case in Gillian Dunne's (1999) study of lesbian households and Weeks et al (2004) add that there tends to be a more equal sharing of emotional work within same sex partnerships. However, the fact that domestic violence is a feature of some lesbian partnerships raises questions for radical feminists who relate it fundamentally to male power. Furthermore, data has consistently shown that the rate of dissolution of female civil partnerships as well as more recent data on divorces has run at about double the rate of that for males.

Legal recognition of same sex partnerships may be presented as a liberal reform put in place by the government as a response to demands for gay rights and an advance in social tolerance. However, it could also be argued that following decades of decline in marriage rates and evidence of substantial increases in numbers of cohabiting couples, this was more of a 'top down' initiative by a governments worried when people live their lives below the state radar. To take the point a little further, from a Foucaultian perspective civil partnerships and same sex marriage allow these relationships to become opened up to official recognition, providing the government with greater powers of surveillance over its population whilst also attempting to promote social stability by extending legal ties.

Changes in the law may not necessarily correspond with some people's privately held or publicly demonstrated traditional moral values. This may particularly, but not exclusively, apply to older generations whose socialisation was formative during an era of strongly heterosexual norms. Thus, some family members may decline to attend single sex weddings and some service providers, including jewellers and caterers, have been known to show disinterestedness.

In conclusion, the above sections illustrate the diverse forms which family and household life now takes in contemporary Britain. The reader is reminded that even within each of the family types referred to there will also be found diversity. This pattern of change is generally typical of family life in western cultures. A broader question still, in the context of globalisation and economic modernisation, is the extent to which cultural and family life in those non-western countries which have traditions of community orientation and loyalty to more extended family structures will converge with the western pattern and through growing affluence and the process of individualisation develop a pattern of greater family diversity and smaller family units.

Responses to changes in family life – sociology, politics and social policy

There have been a variety sociological interpretations and political and social policy responses to changes in family life. For example, one position adopted has been that despite evidence of lifestyle diversity, the nuclear family still remains the standard family form in contemporary British society. An alternative view sees the diversity of contemporary family life and evidence of high divorce rates (despite recent declines) as alarming indicators of the breakdown of the family and a sign of a broader social malaise. For yet others, evidence of growing diversity of lifestyle should be viewed positively as indicative of the emergence of a more pluralistic and tolerant society. These positions can be briefly elaborated as follows.

The first position was strongly argued by the sociologist Robert Chester during the mid-1980s. Much of his argument was based on the way that statistics on family life are viewed. On the issue of spiralling divorce rates, Chester argued that these increases represented a disruptive effect that was not too dissimilar to that resulting from marriage breakups through much higher mortality rates during the nineteenth century (Robertson Elliot, 1996, p.34). Increased cohabitation and declining marriage rates amongst the young during the 1980s were interpreted by Chester as a period of adjustment as the young were delaying the age at which they married. Cohabitation in the 1970s and 1980s tended to comprise more short term relationships which were often child free rather than a full alternative to or rejection of marriage. Moreover, although the number of single parent families was rising, it was argued that single parenthood was often either preceded or superseded by nuclear family life. Whilst in 1981, households with married parents and their children comprised only 32% of all households, being on average larger units, they included 49% of people. Additionally, since these figures were only a snapshot of family life, they did not show the fact that a majority of people lived in a nuclear family at some time in their life, even if this institution had changed somewhat with more women entering the workforce. For Chester, the nuclear family, or neo-nuclear with wives in employment, was thus still a popular majority institution. However, since his writings, figures have shown a significant decline in the traditional nuclear family whilst the numbers of those opting for an alternative, often long term, have continued to increase. Chester's argument therefore now appears to look rather dated.

The second position has been adopted by functionalists and particularly reflects the political ideology and social policy of new right British Conservative governments of the 1980s and 1990s. We have seen in a previous section that from a traditional functionalist position, the widespread nature of the traditional nuclear family was regarded as proof of its functional appropriateness to the needs of modern industrial society. As well as serving the economy, the nuclear family was part of a society unified around a dominant moral culture which promoted social stability and order. From this perspective, moral and family diversity tend to be viewed as dysfunctional and disruptive of social order.

In a similar vein, new right Conservatives, whilst liberals and supporters of free market policy in economics, felt that moral values were becoming too liberal in terms of tolerance of alternatives to the nuclear family. Singled out for particular concern was the increase during the 1980s in the number of never married single parents. It vexed the new right that what was viewed as irresponsible behaviour engaged in by a growing number of people often required state support and therefore the placing of an additional tax burden on others, including those who already supported conventional families.

Similar views were articulated by Charles Murray who, in the American context, associated the social problem of what he referred to as a growing 'underclass' with a high reliance of welfare. For Murray, single parent families were prominent within this underclass. He argued that their dependency on welfare and the absence of a working male parent to instil respect for authority and a work ethic, encouraged in their children a similar culture of dependency. The costs to society were a deterioration in social discipline and the penalty of higher taxation on working heads of households, conditions, it was argued, which could only be turned around by reducing, not increasing, welfare.

New right social policy in Britain, which intended to encourage traditional family roles and responsibilities, included the introduction of new child support arrangements and care in the community. Set up in 1993 to pursue absent parents, the Child Support Agency (later replaced under the New Labour Government in 2006 by the Child Maintenance Enforcement Agency) operated to assert traditional family financial responsibilities of the male provider for the female child carer by imposing financial contributions on absent parents. In so doing, it aimed to combine the purpose of enforcing moral responsibility with saving treasury expenditure, but could be a difficult arrangement for women who wanted to sever links with a previous partner.

Research (e.g. by Nissel and Bonnerjea, 1982) has shown that de-institutionalisation and the promotion of care in the community had the effect of placing an enhanced burden of care, especially for the aged and handicapped, on the shoulders of female relatives. From a feminist point of view, this was effectively an attempt to turn back the clock.

Running through the reforms of the 1990s was the Conservative prime minister John Major's moral message of 'back to basics', particularly regarding the traditions of family life. However, this became a hostage to fortune with publicity of the private lives of a number of Conservative MPs which fell short of this model and helped set the tone for the defeat of the Conservatives in the 1997 general election.

When New Labour came to power, the government continued to emphasise the importance of stable traditional nuclear family life to the maintenance of social order and the upbringing of responsible citizens. However, the reality of growing family diversity was also becoming acknowledged. New Labour's 'third way politics' (explained in the politics chapter) emphasised a new type of arrangement between state agencies and families in which it was the responsibility of families to provide for their own independence and state agencies to play a supporting but not controlling role in enabling them to do so. This included early intervention through the extension of pre-school education and the passing of legislation to provide possible parental leave for fathers to be with their families. Legislation allowing single sex civil partnerships was introduced, and whilst avoiding stigmatising single parents, the government were looking at ways to encourage them to return to work when their youngest child was twelve years of age rather than sixteen.

During their period in opposition, debates within the British Conservative Party regarding policy on the family ranged between those of traditionalists to modernisers. Traditionalists advocated strong support for marriage between heterosexual couples as the superior institution for the raising of children, if being somewhat more cautious in their condemnation of alternatives to this model. Those who saw themselves as modernisers opposed what they saw as the excesses of the new right and adopted a more tolerant stance toward the diversity of family life that had emerged.

The leadership of David Cameron broadly accepted the position of the modernisers and in opposition he had supported New Labour legislation on single sex civil partnerships. When the Conservatives returned to power as the senior partner with the Liberal Democrats in the 2010 coalition government, Cameron as Prime Minister was keen on cultivating his own nuclear family image and signifying a preference for the nuclear family institution, whilst signalling a break from past new right ideological hostility against single parents.

The 2010 Conservative Party manifesto aimed to provide financial incentives and reduce financial disincentives to encourage traditional family life. However, the reality of coalition government and the austerity programme that they pursued had other more marked impacts on family life. Opposition came from many of their own natural supporters to the withdrawal of child benefit to higher rate tax payers. Moreover, the imposition of a three year freeze on child benefit and cuts to child tax credits, whilst not having a beneficial effect for married couples, resulted in a substantial increase in child poverty experienced in households that were reliant on benefit. This was evidenced in terms of children going to school hungry and an increase in the number of people reliant on foodbanks.

On their reformist agenda, the government legislated, to some consternation within the Conservative Party, to allow same sex marriage to be officiated within religious denominations that were forthcoming, whilst providing an exclusion to the Church of England and Church of Wales. There therefore appeared to be a degree of convergence between the main political parties in the acceptance of social change in the direction of family diversity without either party fully embracing it.

Following the 2015 general election the Conservatives were elected to power, but in the 2017 election they lost their majority but retained power with the support of the Northern Irish Democratic Unionist Party. Key policy areas relevant to households and families in Northern Ireland included the DUP's opposition to same sex marriage and abortion rights. Throughout the UK, reforms have included the effects of transformation of the benefit system in the gradual rolling out of Universal Credit and modifications in housing policy that have attempted to provide more affordable starter homes for young first time buyers.

Briefly, Rhona Rapoport is representative of the third position identified above. This stance commends the diversity of family and lifestyle types which have come to characterise contemporary life in democratic societies. For Rapoport, tolerance of such diversity is seen as enhancing people's human rights to choose to live as they wish without condemnation.

Pause and reflection

Sociological theorists and the theories that they develop are arguably to a large extent prisoners of their times and social contexts. Thus, although both Marxist and functionalist perspectives may have revealed much about the family during past eras, they tend to be locked into a dated analysis of society and the family in which the traditional family form fits into a theory of the broader structure of the time. For example, Marxism traditionally saw segregated gender roles within the family as a vital prop to capitalism by providing both pressure outlets and support for productive male workers and the home as disciplining future generations of productive labour. Women formed a reserve and expendable army of cheap working class labour. Capitalism has however adapted and thrived despite evidence of a breakdown in segregated conjugal roles, a substantial advance in the diversity in family life and the integration of women, if not entirely on the basis of equality, across the workforce.

The emphasis placed by functionalism on the nuclear family tended to claim the superiority of a model of family life for which there was much greater social consensus at the height of the influence of this perspective in the 1950s. This indicates an inherent conservative predisposition in the functionalist perspective – it takes what is, argues that it therefore serves social needs or functions, and makes supporting justifications. Although the perspective should be able to anticipate and explain changes in the family as part of the mutual adjustment of institutions as society changes, functionalism has tended to remain associated with the 1950s model of the family. It is questionable whether it is possible to go far enough within this framework to explain the extent of change in family life and relationships in the contemporary context of globalisation and, arguably, new emergent conditions of postmodern or high modern society.

Ultimately, it is up to sociologists, through the scrutiny of theories and evidence, to come to their own decisions on the extent to which such theories can be accommodated to or retain applicability in the understanding of family life in contemporary times.

Symbolic interactionism was argued to be a more flexible perspective through which to understand the diversity of contemporary family life. However, as a micro perspective, it has far less to say about the broad social and historical changes which have accompanied this diversity. Some more contemporary approaches have attempted to explain diversity within this broader perspective.

Developments in sociological approaches to family life

A number of theorists are in broad agreement that society has in recent decades been changing fundamentally and that modernist explanations and concepts such as those utilised within Marxism and functionalism and post war research are no longer adequate for explaining contemporary society and family life. Two general theoretical approaches take the form of postmodernism and high modernism, although the distinction between these perspectives is not always clear cut.

Postmodernism – almost anything goes – no choice but to accept choice

For postmodernists, advanced societies have been undergoing a major transition from the modern to the postmodern social condition. Emerging in the latter decades of the twentieth century, a key feature of the postmodern environment is that the moral uniformities, social structures and social controls which were characteristic of the modern era have broken down in the face of accelerated and directionless social change. This change has led to a greater diversity in social and family life, allowing a massive scope of choice in terms of the way that people may decide to define and construct their own lifestyles and familial relationships. Such changes are usually viewed positively as liberating, against the backdrop of the modernist era when the nuclear family was the dominant institution of social and moral conformity in western societies in the post war era. According to postmodernists, certain assumptions were built into the modernist view, the key ones being:

1. That absolute truth based on scientific certainty could be established and that as a result, social progress could be assisted as rational analysis would enable informed social intervention and planned social

improvement. Regarding the family, this meant that social policy interventions could be orientated toward supporting the nuclear family.

2. That being the most technologically advanced, western societies held an image of the future for less developed societies. This view tended to assume that progress is unilinear – ie as less developed societies develop, they would converge with the ways of more advanced societies. Thus, the tendency toward the universality of the nuclear family could be argued.

Considering the first point, it is argued that a postmodern era has emerged in which there has been a breakdown of faith in the scientific certainties and uniform moral standards that were more typical of modern industrial societies. Postmodernists argue that the diversity of family life has become so advanced that there is no single moral consensus about a preferred family type and that policy interventions cannot and should not favour any particular family form. Moreover, the capacity for effective social intervention by the state has been overtaken by the speed of social change and the collapse of a sense of change in a progressive direction. Thus, governments have, perhaps reluctantly, had to accept that social policy has lost its grip in moulding family life toward a single preferred type. Lifestyle can be increasingly based on individual choice, so long as it does not transgress the like rights of others. A new level of tolerance has accompanied a massive increase in the diversity of types of family life and lifestyle variations.

Regarding the second point on convergence, it is clear that as well as an explosion of diversity within postmodern societies, there remains diversity between societies regarding family life which relate to cultural differences. And further challenging the first point raised above, through bringing into contact different cultures and belief systems, globalisation may be enhancing the process of family diversity within societies.

For writers such as Baudrillard, postmodern society is a world of fast communication and media images in which people are free to choose from an array of lifestyles and identities as they search for successful formulas for their lives in an ever changing social world. This is a world of high consumerism in which no single family form is able to establish a moral monopoly and no particular way of life or family form is universally recognised as superior to others.

Judith Stacey's research (Haralambos, 2013, pp.571-573) in the United States adopts a postmodernist stance in which she argues that high technology and globalisation have brought about rapid change and the need for flexibility in people's work lives which brings forth the need for adaptive changes in their personal and family lives. Her small scale study was conducted in the 1980s, and focussed on participants in the post-industrial economy of Silicon Valley, which, because of its technological advance, was argued to provide an image of family life in more developed postmodern conditions. Stacey discovered that participants were finding innovative ways of developing familial relationships to contend with uncertainty and change in their lives. She suggested that these practical responses were particularly embraced by those in working class occupations, thus questioning the march of progress assumption of 'stratified diffusion'; that the middle classes invariably set the trend of change which the working class follows.

In other research, Stacey found that gay and lesbian families were amongst the more reflective and creative in defining their own families which were less restricted to blood ties and more likely to include friends – a finding which has been supported by other research, such as that of Roseneil and Bubgeon (2004).

Postmodernists argue that bewildering choice and relativism in terms of truth and lifestyle are here to stay. There is no likelihood of a return to the predominance of the nuclear family or the emergence of a new single family form generally agreed to be the model to conform to and there is no detectable direction of change other than that of growing diversity of family and lifestyle. We have no choice but to accept choice.

High modernism and individualisation

There can be a very fine dividing line between views of the social condition adopted by more moderate postmodernists and sociologists who adopt a high modernist perspective. As in the case of postmodernists, those viewing the family from a high modern position emphasise that society has entered a new phase which is characterised by far greater social fluidity, diversity and individual choice compared to the relatively structured and stable world of post war modernism and the constraints of nuclear family life. However, unlike those who adopt a more extreme postmodernist position (eg. Baudrillard), high modernist writers do not maintain that modern society is being eclipsed by the transition to a postmodern world saturated by media images, dominated by fashion and experiencing a complete breakdown of past social structures and moral unity to the extent that it is beyond rational understanding and control. Instead, it is argued that modern society has entered a new phase of advanced modernism in which rational analysis of social change is possible if sociology develops new and sufficiently sophisticated theories and concepts. This means that, more difficult as it may be, it is possible to fashion social policy interventions to support family life in its diversity, but a further problem is the pressures that the state is up against in terms of financial constraints within an environment of competitive globalised capitalism.

Ulrich Beck distinguishes between 'first modernity', capitalist industrial society up to the 1960s, and contemporary 'second modernity', the latter being referred to as 'risk society'. Beck adopts a similar position to that of Giddens regarding the emergence of new risks in the context of social change and uncertainty. He relates a decline in traditional social constraints particularly to the advance of individualisation which accompanied first modernity and has reached a new level in second modernity. By the advance of individualisation, Beck means that the scope of choices facing individuals in the construction of their daily lives has massively increased. The thinning out of constraining social structures and identities of social class and gender stratification and the decline in traditional family life and communities means that people have had to take on the burden of navigating their own way in life whilst experiencing uncertainly and a feeling of lack of control in doing so. Their intimate relationships therefore become more important in an increasingly impersonal and insecure world in which people seek such relationships as a form of refuge. However, with the breakdown of a once more singular system of norms and a standard model of family life, the guidelines for these relationships must now also be fashioned more by the partners themselves. The advance of educational and career opportunities for women as part of this openness means that trying to make a relationship work can increasingly become a source of conflict based on new and differing expectations between partners. Beck's rather bleak outlook is that with the advance of individual freedom and opportunity, it becomes more difficult to establish a common ground of satisfaction and fulfilment in intimate relationships, which, in the search for security in a risk society, themselves become increasingly precious but precarious.

In a similar vein, Zygmunt Bauman views contemporary societies as having reached an advanced level of social fluidity and individualisation which leads to the experience of a heightened interplay between the inescapable advance of individual freedom and the search to establish a degree of security. Life has become uprooted from past traditions and structures and modern technology opens up broader networks of acquaintances but fewer lasting relationships. Bauman refers to this advanced stage of modernity as 'liquid modernity' in which intimate relationships are likely to be more transient.

Anthony Giddens conceptualises contemporary society to have advanced to a 'high modernist' stage of development. This stage is characterised by a change in the nature of people's commitment to intimate relationships which reflects a breakdown of social structures and personal commitments and ties that were more typical of modern society. From modern society has emerged a more fluid social condition in which individuals must continuously engage in a process of interpreting a rapidly changing environment (referred to as 'reflexivity') to make sense of the world and navigate their course in life.

In 'The Transformation of Intimacy' (1992) and 'Runaway World' (2002), Giddens puts forward a broad ranging model to explain changes in the nature of intimate relationships. According to this model, in pre-modern (traditional) societies, families were built around the economic imperative of property consolidation or operated as working units of economic production. For most, the severe conditions of life were not conducive to the development of romantic intimacy as the mainstay for attachment. High infant mortality rates meant that the social tradition of marriage for procreation was embedded in traditional culture and worked in harmony with the needs of nature.

A key feature of the modern industrial era was the application of reason to the aim of improvement, which promoted social change. Thus the hallmark of the modern period, compared to life in traditional society, was the emergence of a degree of 'reflexivity' – the need to weigh up and monitor traditions and institutions with the prospect of redesigning them to improve their effectiveness. This period, from the late eighteenth century, saw the appearance in the higher social orders, supported by the culture of the romantic novel, of romantic love as the basis for attraction and the binding of individuals in marriage. Increasingly, romantic attraction, the acceptance of the rituals of marriage and family bonds formed the basis of family tradition and stability across society in the modern era.

In contemporary or high modern societies, through scientific intervention and improved social conditions, populations have become self-sustaining at low reproduction rates. Consequently, these societies contrast to those of the past in that sex can become free from the need for and cultural emphasis on procreation, and advances in contraception have enabled people to acquire more choice on whether or not to have children. In this sense, for Giddens, intimate relationships exist at 'the end of nature'. The separation of sex from the imperative of reproduction enables key modernist and traditional assumptions on family life to undergo fundamental change.

Firstly, Giddens argues that relationships tend to become contingent. Rather than being constrained by the finality of having chosen the right person and pressures to remain together come what may, partners strive to achieve purer relationships, entered into on the basis of mutuality and free choice with the continuance of each being contingent on the emotional rewards and satisfactions derived. This marks a step change in reflexivity which reaches new levels as partners continually reflect on the purity of the relationship and whether or not to continue within it. Giddens refers to this as type of conditional relationship as 'confluent love'.

Secondly, a growing diversity of relationship types emerge. This diversity allows individuals greater choice in the construction of their self-identity and their search for genuine self-fulfilment, providing opportunities to experiment amongst these alternatives and shape their own lives. Many new forms of family require on-going reflexivity by partners as they are relatively free from the constraints of long established norms and individuals can construct relationships that work for them. As part of this diversity, the greater tolerance of same sex relationships is not just associated with more liberal attitudes and the breakdown of traditional family values but is a further logical consequence of the separation of sex and sexuality from procreation which the conditions of contemporary society enables.

Thirdly, in terms of the development of sociological concepts, sociologically it is now more appropriate to refer to 'coupling' and 'uncoupling' than to marriage and divorce. There are now higher levels of cohabitation and although the institution of marriage retains some popularity, Giddens views it as a 'shell institution' whose contents have changed, since decisions on whether to remain together are now more often based on individual choice in seeking a pure relationship. Marriage remains a possible ritual commitment and tradition which can help to stabilise a relationship, but this is now more a matter of free choice for couples. Although often still a traumatic experience, divorce or uncoupling now holds far less stigma than divorce used to and it is recognised as a relatively high possibility for those who enter into relationships. Marriage or coupling now introduces new risks into people's lives at a very personal level as many of these relationships will break up.

Fourthly, Giddens optimistically suggests that the advance of tolerance, freedom and individual agency promotes a greater equality in sexual relationships which mirrors political advances that are taking place in society and globally. There is a parallel between the advance of democratic political freedoms and personal relationships based on equality and mutual respect. The ways of democracy undermine the confines of tradition and embrace global cosmopolitanism – the contact between people from a diversity of cultural traditions in a climate of tolerance. There has been an increase in the number of cosmopolitan families as globalisation brings together people from different social, cultural and ethnic backgrounds. By contrast, fundamentalism is a reaction to increased social openness and an attempt to re-impose traditional certainties and constraints regarding gender inequalities. For Giddens, issues of gay rights, marriage and gender equality are at the centre of the battle between the democratic forces of cosmopolitan tolerance and the often religious based authoritarianism of fundamentalism which seeks refuge in moral certainty amidst global complexity and relativism which followers find intolerable.

In criticism of high modern views of the liberating effect of individualism on family life, Bottero (2005, pp. 122-124) identifies the argument that new forms of relationship have come to reflect changing wage level patterns in which a distinction between 'full wage' and 'contingent wage' employment needs to be made. The latter wage level would not enable the earner independent living, whereas through a full wage support of a family would be possible. Clearly, the traditional employment pattern would concentrate women in contingent wage and men in full wage employment, with women being dependent on the income of a male breadwinner. Although women have largely remained employed at contingent wage level, their greater access to the labour market has undermined the full wage (family wage) argument of males – a process further exacerbated for manual workers by economic reforms from the 1980s that have enhanced wage inequality and pushed more of these workers into a contingent wage status. In more such households, there is a new interdependence based on the necessity of both partners having to work for contingent wages which would not enable independent support for either.

From life cycle to life course and beyond

Life in traditional societies held much to ceremonies which took the form of 'rites of passage' that marked the transition to new stages in life which encompassed new responsibilities. These would often have been fixed by age, marking down the course of the future with a high level of predictability. Given the absence of dynamic change in such societies, old age often carried high social status and respect associated with acquired wisdom.

The transition to modern western industrial society has seen the emergence of finely graded age groupings. In the post-war decades, family life was strongly typified by the nuclear family and a standard family 'life cycle' seemed to be applicable as a realistic sequencing of life for many. Protected from work and provided with education, childhood within the nuclear family was a period of being cared for and controlled by parents. The emergence of youth culture amongst the later age group of adolescents during the 1950s and 1960s often resisted parental and social convention and with greater spending power led to youngsters acquiring more independence in both economic and identity terms. However, formal expectations of marriage and family life remained strong and given the relatively early age of marriage, the transition from nuclear family of origin to family of orientation with work and family responsibilities of adulthood was often very rapid. The concept of the 'life cycle' was related to the prevalence of the nuclear family and the view that nuclear family life goes through predictable cycles. Thus, after the child rearing stage, middle to late middle age often provided financial respite when children left home and retirement was associated with old age, declining income and purchasing power and increasing infirmity.

The life cycle view was a product of the period of modernism when the lives of people were encapsulated within social institutions and structures which prescribed for them expected pathways and stages. This was shown in research conducted by Neugarten et al (1965) who found a high level of agreement throughout American society as to the best age for women to marry (19-24) and men to have established a career (24-26) (Hunt, 2005, p.20). By the 1960s, sociologists had developed life cycle models of increasing sophistication.

However, it has been shown that the social uniformity upon which such models were based has given way to greater diversity of living. Consequently, it became highly questionable whether the concept of life cycle could any longer be meaningfully utilised. Instead, the concept of 'life course' has tended to replace the life cycle model in sociology. Although society still shapes our experiences, these experiences are that the community constraints and confining structures associated with the modern period have largely collapsed. Individuals are left with the burden of planning their course in life and identity choice with far greater freedom and with few obligatory rites of passage to steer them. Reflecting these broader social changes, the concept of life course looks at various trajectories of change that are accorded importance to social actors and does not so exclusively focus on standard family transitions (Morgan, 1996, pp.142–145). It offers a more flexible, open and subtle alternative to conceptualise directions taken in life through the agency of enhanced individual choice.

If postmodernists are correct, there is some optimism in the fact that even stages in the life course are becoming deconstructed, and thus even the concept of the life course, which suggests a number of likely life trajectories as opposed to a once common view of a universal cycle of stages, is losing its usefulness. Individuals are increasingly able to fashion their own identity. For example, people are living longer, may retire earlier or later, are in better health and are more active than the elderly of previous generations. As society is rapidly changing, older people tend to become out of touch and dependent as opposed to economically productive. Social status once associated with the wisdom of age has declined in the face of youth culture. On the other hand, pressure groups have emerged to represent the interests of older people and this age group are increasingly being targeted as consumers and voters. The traditional stereotypes of the elderly are thus being challenged and there is more freedom and variation in the construction of lifestyle and image for the elderly, whilst reproductive technologies have offered new possibilities of parenthood to infertile and gay and lesbian couples.

The social construction of age groups

This section will introduce some issues regarding cultural variability in the definition of age groups and identity. The stages in life which we tend to take for granted – infancy, childhood, adolescence, adulthood, elderliness and old age – are by no means fixed and universal categories. Different socially constructed divisions and meanings have existed in different cultures and periods of history and are still in a process of change.

An important starting point in the sociological study of age groups is to distinguish between the biological and the cultural. Clearly, human life is a biological process of growth from conception and birth through to maturity, followed by deterioration and eventually death. However, viewed sociologically, one can recognise the impact of environment on biology in at least two important ways.

Firstly, the social conditions of living, working and access to medical care and welfare impact on our biological condition. This impact can be measured in terms of infant mortality rates, health and longevity and shows significant variation between and within societies and throughout history.

Secondly, sociologists show how biological aging and sex differences are not just expressed directly but are strongly mediated through an environment of social and cultural meaning which provides socially constructed identities and self-perceptions. Although these identities vary historically and between different cultures, they are often justified as biologically determined and viewed as if they are natural and universal. For example, feminists point to the biological basis that Parsons claimed for segregated conjugal roles in the traditional nuclear family as an ideological construction using biological differences to justify the perpetuation of socially organised male privilege.

An area of growing interest in sociology has been the study of childhood as a socially defined, socially variable and historically relative concept. Research conducted by Aries (1973) showed that the contemporary western distinction between childhood and the stages leading up to adulthood, with the former distinguished as a time of vulnerability and absence of adult responsibility necessitating protection in the family, was alien within medieval society where from the age of about seven years 'youngsters' were seen as small adults, not children, and treated as such. Aries' research pointed to the fact that the notion of a more extended and protected childhood was a European development from the eighteenth century within the middle classes and later in the nineteenth century within the working class which accompanied the advance of protective legislation in the workplace and the development of state education.

Nevertheless, the harsh realities of life for the young amongst the poorer sections of many developing countries often require them to work as cheap labour to help support their families. Even within Britain, an estimate based on the 2001 Census calculated that 175,000 youngsters of school age face the reality of caring for parents (Steel, 2012, p.181). These youngsters often provide this support in a low profile capacity to avoid the risk of being taken into care themselves.

Functionalists such as Parsons viewed childhood as a formative process in which children are made into the stuff of future good citizens within the cocoon of a nurturing family unit. There is an absence within this perspective of seeing childhood from the perspectives of children themselves – they are just being shaped by social forces. Foucault's perspective on this protective and shaping process emphasises, by contrast, the negative aspects of surveillance and social control.

In recent years, sociologists have become more interested in understanding childhood as perceived from point of view of children rather than through parentally and socially imposed viewpoints and definitions. Research, such as that conducted by Mason and Tipper (Steel, 2012, p.175), has tended to use ethnographic methods in attempts to view families through the eyes of children. The findings point to the fact that children are often very active in the way that they construct their viewpoints of family life rather than being just the passive recipients of adult views and can come to define their family in ways that differ from that of adults. They may thus make their own subtle judgements and distinctions between members in reconstituted and blended families and have often been found to perceive their pets as part of the family.

Viewed sociologically, adolescence, although often commonly regarded as a biologically and psychologically situated stage in the maturation process, and thus assumed to be universal, is also a product of the cultural environment. In fact, adolescence is historically a relatively recent development of post war times during which adolescent identity emerged with the extension of education and growing affluence. As youngsters acquired more purchasing power and leisure time, advertisers and the media recognised a new source of profitability in music culture and fashion. This assisted the formation of adolescent subcultures with their own symbols, identity, norms and values.

Research into adolescent subculture has often focussed on deviance from and conflict with mainstream culture of the mature adult world, and thus, along with coverage in sections of the mass media, perhaps provided an exaggerated perception of these aspects of adolescence. Interestingly, from a feminist viewpoint, Abbott and Wallace (1997, p.124) cite McRobbie and Garber's comments that adolescent subcultures have been studied as a largely working class and virtually exclusively male phenomena. Feminists have emphasised that through the greater parental control and surveillance of adolescent girls and traditionally the magazine promotion of romanticism, female adolescent culture has found an important outlet and location in bedroom pinups and the adoration of pop star heroes.

The expansion of higher education in the 1970s, growing diversity of alternatives to the nuclear family and later marriage, have led to a more protracted period of adolescent lifestyle experimentation. However, Postman (1994) has argued that early exposure to the adult world of sex and violence through the means of modern technology and the more common experience of sex at a young age has led to the 'death of childhood' in the form of a loss of innocence.

Less has been written sociologically about the social construction of adulthood and the phenomenon of parenthood has been complicated by substantial changes in family life. One such change is the growth of lone parent families where the role of child rearing and economic support may need to be provided by the lone parent (usually female), sometimes assisted by persons external to that unit such as parents and ex-partners.

Regarding divorce or relationship breakups, children invariably again remain with the mother, either within a lone parent family or a reconstituted or blended family unit. An interesting point is made by Kathryn Beckett (Sclater, 2005, p.89) regarding fatherhood in this situation. She argues that commonly within the mother and father family unit, the mother mediates the relationship between the father and children. After the breakup of the family unit, the father will often be faced with the difficult task of trying to construct a new relationship with his children without the mediation of the mother. This could at least partly explain the tendency for fathers to slip out of involvement in their children's lives.

Another change has been a challenge to the traditional macho masculinity of the 'real man' by other images such as the 'new man' of the late 1980s and early 1990s. This social construction found currency in the media portrayal of stars such as David Beckham, in conveying a more domestically involved, non-sexist, well-groomed appearance and sensitive image which tallied with a more companionate type of relationship.

The aging process is often seen as a biological aspect of the life course in which people pass through socially recognised life stages. Feminists point out that these stages are often quite prescriptively applied to women in terms of their biology, and that although biologically rooted definitions could be applied to the aging process of males, this tends to be less the case. Since reproduction and certain images of beauty are viewed as central to the lives of females in contemporary western culture, older age holds particularly negative connotations for them. Since for males the productive process is viewed more as an economic one, their productivity can continue well beyond women's reproductive capability – although medical advances have again shown that this phase can be extended. In old age, women, who tend to live longer than men, often find themselves alone, lonely and undervalued and having to subsist on lower incomes due to at best limited occupational pensions to supplement their income from the state.

However, according to postmodernists, retirement is less automatically associated with the onset of poverty, declining health and the feeling of being cast onto the social scrap heap. Through improved health and longevity, there is more opportunity for elderly people to live active lives. Greater diversity and choice of lifestyle is available. New cosmetic appliances and technology, for example, are now able to assist older people to retain a more youthful appearance and combat the effects of biological ageing, thus enhancing control of their image and conceptions of self.

A subjective refocusing of personal relationships

Recent developments in sociology which focus on personal and intimate relationships have been taken up mainly by a number of sociologists who adopt a type of feminist interactionist approach to the study of family and personal life. From this perspective, for Jacqui Gabb, approaches to the study of family life which focus on relationships in terms of the structuring of obligations and responsibilities are not a good lens for appreciating the intimate relational world of family life. For this to be possible, Gabb (8/6/14, Abstract) argues the need to 'reframe the analytical lens'. This refocussing needs to put emotions and intimacy at the centre of the study of family life. Emotions and intimacy constitute the very glue of family relationships but are a dimension which has traditionally tended to be sanitized out of sociology as a too subjective area to be worthy of academic rigor.

For Gabb, small scale and qualitative research which includes autobiographical and anecdotal information and starts with feelings assists entry into this world of intimate reciprocity, allowing a 'dramatically different framework of thinking' (Gabb, 8/6/14, 3.7) to that which uses hard data to provide a patterned and structured picture of family life. This refocussing requires that 'we need to think more imaginatively if we are to capture the feelings and relational practices of intimacy that are in evidence all around us' (Gabb, 8/6/14, 8.3). She therefore argues in favour of the use of sociological methods which enable a qualitative insight into family life as experienced by the various participants. Information may be gleaned from conversation, observation and personal written documents etc.

Viewing family life in terms of the intimate experiences of family members takes us into dimensions of everyday experience that are usually screened out in more conventional analysis of family form and structure, one of which is the importance of cross species connections as part of the world of emotional experiences of family members. Taking a lead particularly from the viewpoint of children, pets are often seen as a part of the family, nurturing love and affection of family members. Family routines take pets into account and grief is experienced at their loss or death.

Parent and child relationships provide tactile pleasure at play times. Shared intimacy enables family relations to cut across broader cultural boundaries of generational and sexual distance and power relationships.

Even human relationships to objects play a role in family life. For example keepsake objects have personal and emotional meaning. Relating to such artefacts can provide a reawakening of past experiences and the sharing of stories, feelings and emotions between family members.

Carol Smart (2007) argues for a conceptual reworking of an area of sociology traditionally referred to as 'the family'. She argues that focussing on the family has led to a number of distortions and restrictions on our understanding of practices within families to fit the changes that grand theorists argue are taking place, often reflecting broadly held viewpoints and willingly taken up by policy makers but without a detailed and sensitive understanding which is only likely to be provided through micro and qualitative research.

Smart is critical of high modernist grand theorists such as Giddens, Beck and Beck-Gernsheim and Bauman who locate the contemporary family within the context of social change which she claims overemphasise the process of individualisation. They provide little supporting evidence of this extent of change, but would appear to be guilty of exaggerating a contrast between traditional family constraints and contemporary individual agency.

A conceptual shift from the traditional and grand theory focus on family life to the far more open and less exclusive vantage point of 'personal life' within and around the terrain of the family is claimed to provide a number of advantages.

One is that the direct study of personal life would avoid the excess of individualisation theorists in their emphasis on the autonomous individual by focussing on close relationships. Thus, Giddens theorises that with the advance of individualisation and reflexivity, the family has changed from a hierarchical institution to a more democratic and child centred one. Individualisation provides partners who are unhappy with relationships far more autonomy to walk out than would have been possible in the past. However, Smart argues that when the findings of qualitative research are analysed, this position can be shown to substantially overstate the capacity of people for individual autonomy and tends to overlook much of the darker nature of family relationships.

For example, if parents are in conflict, children are powerless to escape this situation. This powerlessness is related to their dependence and low status. In research, they are usually found to be reluctant to criticise their parents and in reality they have to find some way of managing a difficult situation from a position of relative powerlessness. If parents separate or divorce, the walking away is rarely as clean cut as Giddens suggests. Child care and contact arrangements may have to be arrived at. This need for continuing contact between parents can be a source of continuing conflict with damaging consequences to all parties. Memories of toxic relationships can be stirred under these circumstances and even more apparently straightforward breaks are rarely quite so.

In conclusion, Smart acknowledges that Giddens, Beck and Beck-Gernsheim and Bauman were correct in pointing out the moribund condition of the sociology of the family. However, she argues that the main problems with the alternative that they offered, the individualisation thesis, could be summed up as follows: firstly, they are 'free floating theorizations' (p.184) that lack empirical grounding. Secondly, they overemphasise individual agency and tend to lose sight of contexts of personal connectiveness. And thirdly, they are quite empty of the human content of personal life which can be revealed through qualitative research.

Smart argues that a 'personal life' approach breaks through the confines of an exclusive focus on the sociology of the family. She does not argue for throwing out the concept of the family altogether, but for refocussing on personal life in terms of the complexity of relationships and situations recognised from the point of view of the different perspectives, experiences and interpretations of the various participants, whether they would traditionally qualify as family members or not.

Chapter 7

Social Stratification

Abstract

Social stratification is defined as the hierarchical layering of society into different levels. Developing personal awareness of one's position in a social hierarchy and a range of associated experiences and opportunities may be a starting point for understanding social stratification. However, the reader is alerted to the fact that this would not be an appropriate point from which to make generalisations as a sociologist about the nature of stratification in society. This chapter will show that approaching the area sociologically requires a more detached and systematic approach. To assist in the preparation for this process, a number of key concepts are introduced.

It is important to gain a broad social and historical overview on stratification to help obtain perspective on and considered assessment of the degree of openness of the social structure in contemporary western societies or Britain more specifically. For this purpose, examples of the basic features of more closed stratification systems are introduced through reference to slavery, caste society, feudalism and apartheid.

Established theoretical approaches of functionalism, Marxism and Weber are introduced to help the reader develop an understanding of some of the founding concepts used and explanations of stratification dynamics. At this point, the reader is encouraged to ponder a number of questions raised regarding the viability of these perspectives.

Social class is a well established feature of stratification in sociology and the question of why and issues of how sociologists measure it and a number of problems that this entails are raised. This leads on to a consideration of some of the findings of social mobility studies. Logical scrutiny of the degree to which contemporary societies can be regarded as truly meritocratic – enabling position in the social hierarchy to be achieved through individual effort and ability alone – is undertaken.

Theories of change in the class structure comprise another section in this chapter and the theories of embourgeoisement, proletarianisation and decomposition are introduced. However, there are other dimensions to stratification in contemporary society than social class. In this chapter, gender, ethnicity and status are also considered, indicating the complex nature of social stratification. In approaching this subject, the reader is encouraged to recognise connections across different topic areas since, unlike the topic areas of sociology, the social world does not exist in clear cut compartments. Links are made from themes raised in this chapter to those in other chapters. For example, understanding gender stratification can be related to the impact on the family of industrialisation and in more recent history the expansion of the service sector. Evaluating the extent to which contemporary British society is meritocratic requires an understanding of issues of meritocracy in education.

Finally, more contemporary approaches to stratification are introduced in the form of postmodernism, high modernism and globalisation. These approaches raise the key issue of the high state of fluidity of contemporary society and raise fundamental questions regarding the continuing viability or otherwise of the more structured approaches of the founding theorists that were earlier introduced.

The sociological challenge

Social stratification presupposes the existence of a social hierarchy which is divided into layers, each comprising a distinct level. In a general sense, these layers or strata (stratum in the singular) are structured in terms of inequality in the social distribution of resources deemed within a society to be important. Such resources typically include wealth, income, knowledge, culture and lifestyle. Access to these resources will be socially structured, for example by legal title of property ownership, rules of inheritance, and strategies that some groups adopt to exclude access to valued resources by others. The typical shape of stratification systems is depicted as a pyramid structure, emphasising that as one ascends this structure greater concentrations of valued resources, usually accompanied by concentrations of political power, reside in the hands of fewer people.

If social stratification simply referred to social layering in terms of the unequal distribution of resources, a fundamental problem for the sociologist would be that of identifying the key points at which the boundaries between such layers exist. Two main criteria have often been emphasised to indicate the positioning of stratification boundaries. Firstly, the existence of a degree of shared values and common outlook amongst people which distinguish them from others can be a good guide to identifying stratification levels. Secondly, there would usually be far more upward and downward social mobility within these groups than between them.

Social stratification, though, is a very complex matter as: 1) it includes various dimensions such as social class, social status, gender and ethnicity, 2) there are complexities in measuring social stratification on any one of these dimensions which, 3) interact with each other within the context of, 4) society undergoing constant change.

The study of social stratification poses a number of problems. The most obvious one is the fact that the everyday usage the term social class can be vague and pejorative, often implying judgements of quality, such as a person 'having class'. Used in this sense, its meaning is in fact closer to 'status' as applied by sociologists. Issues of judgement in everyday definition also relate to gender and ethnicity.

Another problem may be the tendency to deride other societies and cultures from the viewpoint of the society to which we are accustomed. As analysts, it is important to guard against the block that this ethnocentricity puts on understanding and be prepared to ask, for example, how position in society tends to be justified to women in Islamic culture.

Furthermore, we may take for granted a certain view of the way that our own society is stratified. This may include the belief that equal opportunity for success is available to each individual by virtue of merit or that social class no longer exists. As sociologists, we need to be prepared to give careful consideration to evidence by which we can evaluate such taken for granted assumptions. It may be a sobering thought to appreciate that in the future, others may look back with incredulity at what we take for granted regarding the stratification of our society (especially given the sociological knowledge that we have) in a similar way to the way that we may view with amazement what was taken for granted in past societies.

At a personal level, we must always remain aware that our experiences from our own perceived position within the stratification system may bias the way that we view social stratification. Although personal experiences may be revealing to a limited extent, it is important to psychologically stand back and review theories and evidence regarding stratification from the more objective viewpoint of an analyst.

In Britain, sociologists have traditionally viewed social class as the major dimension of stratification. However, in recent decades they have been grappling to understand the changing and complex impact of the relationship between class and other dimensions of stratification such as status, gender, ethnicity, disability and age.

More recently, some sociologists have come to question whether even viewing society in terms of solid structures is any longer valid. They argue that rapid social change and complexity are so advanced that society should be viewed as in a state of constant fluidity. At best, this would mean that new sociological concepts need to be developed to grasp this reality. And it may be that society is now beyond the grasp of structured analysis?

Definition of main concepts

As Payne (2006, Ch.1) points out, social stratification is a specific form of **social division**. He refers to social divisions as structured divides that run through society and shape people's perceptions of commonality with like others and provide a basis for shared awareness of differences with other groups. People usually partake in many social divisions. For example, work colleagues in a dispute with management may feel a sense of common interest but may also otherwise feel divided, for example politically and recreationally, into different groups. **Social differentiation** refers to the ways in which societies undergo structural change in the direction of increasing complexity. The driving force of this growing difference is often the advance of economic modernisation which is accompanied by increasing occupational and work role specialization. The concept of **social stratification** adds to the idea of division and difference that of socially structured hierarchy, power and inequality.

In sociology, central to stratification, the term **social class** refers to a social category of people in terms of their similar economic situation. For example, Marx argued that ownership or non-ownership of the means of production was the key economic determinant of class divisions, separating a capitalist class of employers from a class of workers. He also distinguished further gradations at the bottom of each of these categories, referred to respectively as the petit bourgeoisie (small capitalist) and the lumpenproletariat (with some similarity to more recent references to an 'underclass').

More contemporary approaches, tending to derive from the tradition of Max Weber, measure social class by reference to occupational levels and categories of occupation distinguished in part by limited rates of social mobility between them. **Social mobility** refers to the extent of upward and downward movement experienced by individuals in the occupational hierarchy that takes place throughout society. It is usually measured in **intergenerational** terms, comparing the occupational level achieved by members of one generation with that of their parents. When one's position is **ascribed**, social mobility will be extremely low (in theory non-existent) since position in the social hierarchy is restricted to correspond to that of parents. By contrast, when social position is open to **individual achievement**, we expect to find relatively high levels of social mobility. However, even within quite open social structures, some groups may attempt to enhance social closure. This refers to strategies adopted to preserve exclusive access to valued resources, such as privileged education or professional organisations, by denying access to those beneath them in the social hierarchy. Examples of social closure are most apparent amongst the 'establishment' who, evidence shows, tend to utilise the top public schools and the 'old boy network' to enhance their children's access to elite professions.

Distinguishing social status from social class can be difficult. Indeed, the two concepts are often very closely connected. At this point, it will be emphasised that social status refers to the judgements made within a society regarding the prestige of a social group and its members. Social status is culturally defined by social values given to different ways of life, knowledge and possessions, and carries with it views of superiority or inferiority of different groups. Thus, although social class refers primarily to the economic dimension of occupational and income differences, occupations may also carry with them status connotations which relate to associated types and levels of education and skill and degrees of exclusiveness.

As in the case of social class, if status is ascribed, the social structure fixes people into the stratum of their birth for life. Such a stratification system is referred to as **closed**. Examples of societies with relatively closed social hierarchies include slave societies, feudal societies, caste society and apartheid, all of which will be reviewed shortly in this chapter.

By contrast, **achieved class** or status is associated with a more **open stratification** system which enables individuals to occupy positions in the social structure derived from personal characteristics, primarily effort and ability, whatever the status or class of their family background. Most contemporary western societies are recognised as relatively open stratification systems, although sociologists disagree over the exact extent to which they are so and the varied importance of social class and social status, as well as other features of stratification that may provide barriers to individual achievement.

These other dimensions of stratification include those of gender and ethnicity. **Patriarchy** is a term used to emphasise gender based stratification in which men have power over women. This may exhibit itself in the form of gender related concentrations of people in different employment spheres (horizontal segregation) and occupational hierarchical levels (vertical stratification), inheritance practices and domestic responsibilities. Values supporting such gender inequalities, often related to different presumed innate male and female qualities and capacities, are referred to as sexist, and to the extent to which they are viewed as distorting reality to justify male privilege would be referred to as **sexist ideology**.

Discriminatory practices against ethnic minorities are an important aspect of ethnic stratification. Such discrimination may be partly responsible for the concentration of particular ethnic groups in certain occupational spheres and levels as well as in residential areas. Attitudes which justify discrimination in terms of racially based notions of superiority and inferiority are referred to as racist, and, in a similar way to sexist views, can take the form of **racist ideology**.

The sociological concept of **life chances** refers to ways in which opportunities of access to quality of life and standard of living may be open or restricted according to the openness or closed-ness of the social structure and a person's position within it. There is a close correlation between life chances and the distribution of wealth and income in society which can provide access to different levels and qualities of education and healthcare. These inequalities in life chances may be more or less determined by family background in more or less closed stratification systems respectively. Thus, in comparing different societies or societies at different times in history, a key question to ask is to what extent are people's lives constrained by their inherited life chances to remain in the position in the social structure that they are born into or to what degree can they rise above them and create their own life chances? Ultimately, the effect of stratified life chances can be measured by such indices as socially patterned differences in health, life expectancy and infant mortality rates.

The concept of a **meritocracy** has often been applied to contemporary capitalist societies. According to this term, these societies are viewed as open stratification systems, enabling social mobility, both upward and downward, to reflect individual merit (effort and ability) alone. It is therefore a useful concept against which to measure the dynamics of such stratification systems.

Examples of closed stratification systems

History offers many examples of relatively closed systems of stratification in which life for the majority was often brutal and oppressive. However, even in the most oppressive societies, social hierarchies were supported by justifying ideas and values as well as by coercion. Viewed at a social and historical distance and with the knowledge that we now have, the ideological nature of these values may often seem clear. The following models extract the essential features of four different types of closed stratification system.

Slavery is a system of stratification most commonly associated with the early civilisations of the Greeks, Egyptians and Romans. Although in detail slavery exhibited different features between these societies in terms of its severity and responsibilities to the slave population, a characteristic common to them all was that there existed legally recognised and enforced social inequality through which slaves were owned as the property of others. Often taken through conquests, slaves would be put to a variety of tasks from heavy labour in mines or the building of monuments to teaching or even running estates. The main curb on the treatment of slaves by their owners might be their continuing effectiveness as productive labour. Control could include coercion in the form of the threat of physical punishment, or inducement of fear of offending the gods. There were usually hierarchical grades within the slave stratum and in some cases control may take the form of inducement through the possibility of slaves working to obtain freedom from slave status. Acquiring freedom (manumission) was sometimes possible for slaves in the Roman Empire who through hard work and personal loyalty could be freed, for example in the will of their owners. Others, when paid, could save up and purchase their freedom.

A more recent example of slavery is found in American history. During the slave trade, Africans were transported to the southern states and put to work on plantations. Their lives were highly regulated by their white masters. Slave status was reinforced by beliefs in black racial inferiority and the encouragement of the slave population to adopt Christian values of the virtue of humility. The institution of slavery was only formally abolished by constitutional amendment in 1865 following the defeat of the south in the American Civil War. However, it took a further century and the emergence of the Civil Rights Movement by the early 1960s for a fundamental challenge to remaining racial segregation and disadvantage to become effective.

Less dated examples of slavery can also be provided. One is the use by the Nazi regime of the forced labour of subjugated peoples and minorities during the Second World War. Another is the hidden pockets of slave labour which have been found to exist in contemporary societies such as Britain and France in the form of sex trafficking and debt bondage.

Caste stratification in its classic form was peculiar to traditional Indian society. In this society, a rigid form of stratification was sanctioned by the religious beliefs of Hinduism. The strata (varna) of this society were closed by rules limiting association with other varna and prescribing appropriate behaviour and rituals. Brahmin priests, as men of learning – and often also significant owners of land – formed the upper varna. Central to the Hindu teachings which the priesthood conveyed were the ideas of reincarnation and the relative purity of the different varna. The priestly caste were required to live the purest life, conduct religious ceremonies and administer the law. In descending order of purity followed the warrior, trader and labouring strata. Below them were placed the outcastes who engaged in the most degrading occupations. This hierarchy of prestige required the retention of caste purity through social separation to avoid contamination from inferiors, and thus comprised a closed status hierarchy.

Acceptance of this closed hierarchy was perpetuated by the belief in reincarnation – a concept referring to a continuing cycle of rebirth after the death of the physical body. Prospects for future life (dharma) were tied to conformity in the present life. To defy the codes of one's caste would lead to rebirth into a lower caste, whilst conformity could lead to rebirth into a higher caste. Fatalism in the here and now, conformity, and merit were all therefore intertwined and a closed stratification system was supported by the prospect of social mobility through reincarnation. Likewise, one's current position could be justified by one's supposed behaviour in a previous life (karma).

In **feudal** societies, life was essentially agrarian and lived out in local communities. Feudal life was typified by European societies during the early Middle Ages, but examples could be found further afield in, for example, Russia, Japan and China. In England, the key to power was land ownership, and this was concentrated in the hands of the two upper strata (estates), the nobility and the church. The third estate, or commoners, comprised mainly small landowning peasants, craft workers and landless serfs. The latter worked the land of the nobility and the church. As a form of taxation, they were required to give both produce and labour time to their landowners, and lived under inferior legal rights. Opportunities for social mobility were very limited as this section of the population were kept in perpetual servitude and legally recognised as bonded labour.

In this social system, deference (looking up and deferring to the superiority of those above) was expected by the upper orders to be shown from the lower estates. By tracing their family lineage back through many generations, the landed nobility were able to justify their superior status through claiming the inheritance of leadership qualities by appealing to the notion of superior 'social breeding' – a concept which harmonised well with the practice of animal breeding that was familiar in an agrarian society. In some cases, acquired wealth could be used to purchase social title (as it still can!) but in this case the key status feature of family lineage would be absent.

The social forces which would disturb this balance in the rural hierarchy would later emanate from a section of the population who resided more on the margins of the defining agrarian relationship – the more urban based traders, merchants and early industrialists.

Apartheid is sometimes viewed as a form of caste stratification. It refers specifically to a system instituted in South Africa shortly after the Second

World War and which lasted until 1992. Under this system, a white minority dominated non-white groups defined, in descending order, as mixed race or coloured, Asian, and black. Under this system, racial segregation was enforced in public places and black South Africans were forced to live in separate shantytown homelands. Given these segregated regions, members of a racial group would take care to avoid straying into a territory closed to them. Blacks who worked as domestics for whites would have to show an identification pass and often work at night. Even when working in the same occupations as white workers, the wages and conditions of employment of black workers were inferior. Infant mortality was far higher within the black than the white population. Political gatherings were banned and discontent ruthlessly put down by highly repressive methods of policing.

This system which kept blacks down was justified by reference to theories of racial types which had grown to prominence during the period of colonial expansion of the nineteenth century. Such theories maintained that different races contained different genetically inbuilt characteristics and that the white race had demonstrated its superiority of intelligence and determination over the blacks. In the hands of an apartheid regime, this reasoning could be used to justify the need for maintaining racial purity and making racial intermarriage taboo. The life chances of blacks could be kept vastly inferior to that of whites and this in turn could provide 'evidence' of black inferiority.

Although racial stratification was the defining feature of apartheid, other elements of stratification were discernible. For example, the white stratum mainly comprised groups of British, German and Dutch extraction, with the former at the top of society tending to control the economy, and the other groups often owning land. Whilst Indians and Asians were often less poverty stricken than blacks, race would remain a barrier to social mobility which application and the acquisition of money could not overcome. Within the black stratum, social divisions would take the form of tribal groupings, with Zulus tending to comprise the dominant group. Throughout all strata, patriarchal relationships tended to prevail with girls brought up to be good wives and domestic servants.

Founding sociological perspectives on social stratification

The coming sections will review three major founding perspectives on stratification – functionalist, Marxist, and Weberian. Each are macro perspectives, ie. they adopt a broad view of social structures. As established perspectives, they each analyse stratification in terms of social class dynamics, although not all do so exclusively.

Functionalism – modern capitalist societies and the realisation of an open social structure

It is often useful to consider the social and historical context in which social theory emerges to more fully appreciate its leaning. Functionalism is traceable back to the French social philosopher Auguste Comte who was developing his system of thinking in a period of French history following the Revolution of 1789. Comte regarded European societies at the height of feudalism, around the twelfth century, as stable and well established social hierarchies whose social order was sanctified by shared dogma in the religion of Catholicism. Following a long period of decline, the Revolution finally swept away the remnants of feudal society in France. The problem diagnosed by Comte in the post Revolution period was that of protracted social instability. The once socially integrating belief system of Catholicism had come under attack and the old social order had been overthrown but a new and stable order had not yet emerged. For Comte, the social ill of instability needed to be remedied.

Through Comte, functionalism emerged as a reaction to the socially destabilising effects of the French Revolution within a social climate of the desire to re-establish social order and stability. As such, the perspective emphasises the normality of stable social hierarchy. To underpin social stability, modern societies, just as much as traditional societies, need their own supporting value systems which members of society share and adhere to. Functionalism, as it has developed since the works of Comte, has remained true to this heritage.

Comte's ideas were built on from the late nineteenth century by the French sociologist Emile Durkheim. For Durkheim, modern industrial societies are like organisms which grow in size and complexity, promoting social differentiation (1964a). Technological advances extend the division of labour and promote an increasingly complex occupational structure. State education plays key functions in maintaining the social structure. It promotes the shared values necessary to build social consensus as well as the need for obedience to authority and conformity to rules. Education also helps to select and train people in the skills necessary to take up appropriate occupational roles and positions in the social hierarchy. People's acceptance of their position in this hierarchy has to be justified according to shared values appropriate to modern industrial society. This society requires the efficient utilisation of human talent. Both the process of educational and occupational selection and the prevailing social values that match these requirements are therefore those of a meritocracy – a society in which people's social position is achieved according to effort and ability and would be accepted as such.

A distinction between the feudal social order and that natural to modern industrial societies is clearly presented in the writings of the American functionalist Talcott Parsons. For Parsons, social hierarchies are a prerequisite (pre-requirement) of all stable societies but the basis upon which people acquire positions within social hierarchies varies with the type of society in question. Value systems must reflect this process by which people are positioned within the stratification system – values and processes of allocation must synchronise if order and stability are to be maintained.

So what were the main features of feudal society? Life was local centred and agrarian and custom and tradition predominated. Religious thinking prevailed. The social hierarchy was a relatively closed one. People married within their own stratum and the chance of movement out of the stratum of birth was for most highly unlikely. In this society of inherited privilege, social superiors expected shows of deference from those of lower social rank. The minimal social mobility that existed was likely to derive from sponsorship by a known patron. Parsons refers to this type of social relationship as 'particularistic' – opportunities for advancement were dependent on particular personal relationships in which favour may be bestowed by social superiors toward the less fortunate.

By contrast, modern industrial capitalist societies are large, impersonal, complex, integrated and interdependent social structures with a high division of labour. They are noted for their dynamism and efficiency. The materialistic motive force of the quest for maximising profit and waged income enhances competition between individuals. However, given this complex interdependence, conflict in any area of society can cause widespread disruption. It is therefore important that as well as striving for individual success and income maximisation, people accept their position within the stratification system as justly arrived at. For Parsons, American capitalism best typifies the appropriate value system around which social consensus and justification of one's position can be based in modern capitalist societies. These values include enterprise, competition, individual opportunity and achievement, self-support and materialistic aspiration.

The occupational hierarchy will need to consist of a highly differentiated hierarchy of income reward. This is because in modern complex societies the highest occupations place great demands on those who carry out these roles and who must have acquired sophisticated planning, managerial and organisational skills. Social efficiency requires that, at this and other levels of the occupational hierarchy, there is a close match between the ability and education and training of those who occupy roles and the demands of the occupational role. This being so, there will be maximum utilisation of human resources throughout the occupational structure and the resultant productivity levels will enable materialistic values and goals to be realised.

To effectively utilise the pool of talent in society, the social structure of modern industrial societies must be a highly open one. High levels of upward and downward social mobility will be likely as members of society are sifted for occupational roles which match their individual ability, education, training and effort. Compared to the allocation of social position by birthright or favour in traditional societies, occupational position must be acquired through individual competition according to impersonal and universally applicable performance criteria. Parsons refers to social relationships within this context as 'universalistic'. The shared values which correspond to this type of society are those of a meritocracy – a hierarchy of social inequalities in terms of social status, economic reward and power, which is justified by the widespread belief that whatever position an individual attains closely reflects their own abilities and efforts.

In the post war years, the American functionalists Davis and Moore focussed on the nature of this occupational structure by referring to it as a 'ladder of opportunity' (figure 1 overleaf). They argued that stratification is a feature of all societies, as it is a 'functional prerequisite' for the stability of societies to place people in different hierarchical roles. The form that this process of allocation takes in modern industrial society is that in an open and competitive social structure, society benefits from talented people moving up into demanding occupations in which they are more highly rewarded for conscientious application of their special abilities. For Davis and Moore, high income differentials across the occupational structure provide the motivating factor which enhances competition that the talented and hard-working win. They offer due return to talents in scarce supply in society and compensatory reward for the sacrifices made by individuals in extending their education and training (Crompton, 2008, p.13). Substantial income differentials in the context of an open stratification system are therefore viewed as functional; they are a socially beneficial driving force for the allocation of abilities. Such stratification systems and their accompanying value systems, functionalists argue, are not consciously devised and constructed. They are the naturally evolving outcome of the quest for efficiency maximisation between competing capitalist industrial societies.

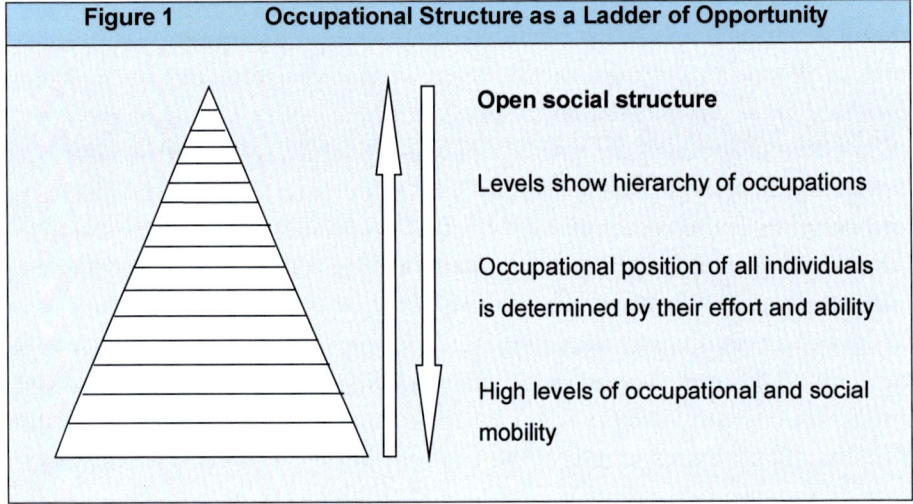

Figure 1	Occupational Structure as a Ladder of Opportunity

Open social structure

Levels show hierarchy of occupations

Occupational position of all individuals is determined by their effort and ability

High levels of occupational and social mobility

The functionalist view of these American theorists can be summarised as follows. The functional importance of substantial inequality of monetary reward in modern capitalist societies is dependent on 1) a broad consensus existing on the relative social importance of different occupational functions. This provides 2) the basis for a matching consensus on the different levels of reward that are appropriate for different occupational positions, 3) the allocation of people to, which is justified through belief in the working of an impartial selection process that matches talent to occupational position on the basis of equality of opportunity.

At this point, it may be beneficial to raise a number of questions that are critical of the functionalist perspective. The reader might pause and think through these questions and search for evidence that may support or undermine the criticisms.

1) Does not the emphasis on social consensus, order and hierarchy tend to

underplay the existence of conflict that exists between people of different social strata?

2) To what extent is the belief that society operates as a meritocracy shared throughout society or, alternatively, is it the wishful thinking or a self-congratulatory justification of a minority who may or may not owe their success entirely to individual merit?

3) Even if society is meritocratic, what degree of income differential is necessary between upper and lower level occupational levels to motivate individual competition and as it stands is it excessively high?

4) How have income differentials been changing over recent decades? If there is increasing stretch between the top and bottom of the social hierarchy, might this lead to a breakdown of consensus in the legitimacy of such a degree of inequality, leading to possible social instability? Tumin suggests that this may be so and that it would be dysfunctional.

For functionalists, the social system is viewed as naturally and beneficially self-adjusting. It is claimed that the functional importance of an occupation to society and the extent of the scarcity of skills required to carry out the tasks now corresponds to the position of the occupation in the occupational structure and the level of economic reward attached. However:

5) it could be asked to what extent there is a naturally adjusting free market system of labour which determines income differentials between different occupations. Alternatively, to what extent are these differentials partly the result of strategies of professional self-interest and the use of power that different groups are able to apply?

6) How can the relative functional importance to society of occupations be assessed objectively when they are so different? If there is no way of doing so, does not the concept of functional importance just collapse into a justification of the prevailing inequalities in the occupational hierarchy and reward structure?

7) It may be that meritocratic values are broadly shared, but this may be no guarantee that rewards will match public perceptions of fairness. For example, the public may express strong criticism of massive severance

payments given to certain public figures to terminate their employment as a result of poor performance or incompetence.

8) Regarding the virtues of meritocratic social systems, it is argued that substantial income differentials provide the incentive for the application of talent as a means for the talented to achieve social mobility. In terms of enterprise values, claims of openness of the stratification system and the extent of income differentials, America is one of the highest placed capitalist industrialised societies. Yet research has shown (Jantti et al, 2006) that compared to the Nordic countries of Denmark, Finland, Norway and Sweden, where income differentials are less stretched, America, followed by Britain, have shown the lowest levels of earnings mobility between the generations. It would appear that there is great disparity between values and perceptions of opportunity, if these are broadly shared, and reality in these societies where income differences are more stretched.

The reader may be able to add other questions to this list to reflect on. One further question to be raised at present is a very fundamental one which will figure elsewhere in this chapter and in the chapter on education.

9) Meritocracy refers to having equal opportunity to compete for unequal monetary reward, status and power in a stratified occupational hierarchy. But how can the very stratification system that is meant to separate out talent, motivate individuals and create a level playing field of competition work as envisaged when inequalities produced in one generation become unequal life chances which impact right from the start of life by providing unequal the opportunities of next generation?

Marxism – capitalism remains a class stratified social structure

Marxist theorists strongly dispute the meritocratic nature of modern capitalist societies. For Marxists, capitalist societies are highly stratified in terms of class division. Moreover, this division is one of class opposition, which Marx, whose works spanned the early 1840s to the early 1880s, argued would eventually lead to open conflict that would destroy capitalism.

Marx applied the term 'class' more broadly than most sociologists who relate it specifically to occupational categories in modern industrial societies. He maintained that class stratification, shaped by economic factors, has existed throughout much of human history. Once early societies had settled and developed rudimentary means of production, they were able to produce more wealth than was necessary for the basic subsistence of the community. The surplus above subsistence enabled inequalities of wealth to emerge. These inequalities over time became institutionalised and transmitted down the generations through the recognition of private property rights, laws of inheritance and private ownership of the means of production. Through their consolidation of wealth, those who owned the means of production acquired the power of a ruling class and were able to utilise the labour which others had to provide in return for an income sufficient to keep them in a state of subsistence.

Throughout history, the technological means of production have developed, accompanied by the emergence of new classes who own them. Marx argued that conflicts in which aspiring ruling classes owning modernised means of production challenge established ruling classes have been the motive force of social change. Successful challenges result in new ruling classes replacing old ones as societies move by revolution through a series of different social and stratification systems.

Marx, then, developed a theory which attempted to explain dynamic social change driven by class conflict throughout history. Viewed broadly, this change took the form of social evolution occasionally punctuated by revolutionary breaks in which one system and ruling class was replaced by another. It placed ownership of the means of production at the centre of an analysis of class conflict and social change. The key social relationship in stratified societies is between those who own the means of production and those who own only their labour power. Just to subsist, the latter are compelled to supply their labour to the service of the former. For Marx, political power, broadly defined as the ability of some to impose their will over others, derives from economic power. Thus, through the concentration of their economic and political power, the owners of the means of production constitute the ruling class and those whose labour they utilise comprise the subject class. The power of the ruling class enables them to engage in an unequal exchange relationship with the subject class in which the latter do not receive full remuneration for the labour that they contribute to the creation of value in the productive process. Marx refers to this shortfall as class exploitation. The extraction of this value excess (surplus value) from the labour of others is the means by which resources become further accumulated in the hands of a minority and the means of production expanded and advanced. It is also the basis of class conflict between the ruling and subject class.

How can this broad sweeping theory be applied to the stratification of modern capitalist societies and how did these societies emerge? Marxism offers an explanation of how capitalist societies grew out of medieval feudal societies. In feudal societies, the main means of production were land, animals, agricultural buildings, machinery powered by natural forces and the use of hand implements. Most production derived from the land and the greatest concentrations of wealth took the form of concentrations of land ownership. Serfs were agricultural workers who toiled the land but did not own it. The key class relationship was thus between major landowners (the various ranks of the nobility and the church) and the serfs who worked the land and lived in a state of perpetual subsistence, bonded to landowners who extracted economic surpluses from their labour.

Although landowner and serf was the defining class relationship of feudalism, many other gradations and occupation existed. Some peasants were small landholders who worked their own land. Craft workers made goods for the market. Others were occupied in trade, commerce and rudimentary forms of industry. It was amongst these latter groups, involved in forms of enterprise and risk taking, that moneyed wealth was gradually accumulating.

This increasing wealth accumulated by the owners of early industrial means of production was assisted by the competitive drive to apply advances in science and technology to make the productive process more efficient. Capital assets put into economic activity to enhance the creation of value provided, in part, income for workers, but also income to early capitalists, and, by reinvesting in the business, provided the opportunity for the further growth of capital. The key advance was the development of powered machinery and the factory system which massively increased production and drew a rapid influx of workers from rural and agricultural pursuits into industrial employment in expanding towns. The consequent expansion of industrial wealth by employers provided them with the political power to challenge the social dominance of the old landed elite, enabled the transfer of class power to a new entrepreneurial (risk taking and private business owning) elite, and marked the transition from the remnants of feudalism to early capitalism. This was a revolutionary break from the past, for example in the form of the Industrial Revolution in Britain. Put simply, it replaced feudal ruling and subject classes with capitalist ruling and subject classes. In this system, new relations of production emerged between the new social classes. Contractual relations of employment between business owning employers (forming a capitalist class) and waged employees (forming a working class) replaced a feudal class relationship of labour bonded to landowner. These relationships structured new divisions of conflicting class interest, as indicated in figure 2 below.

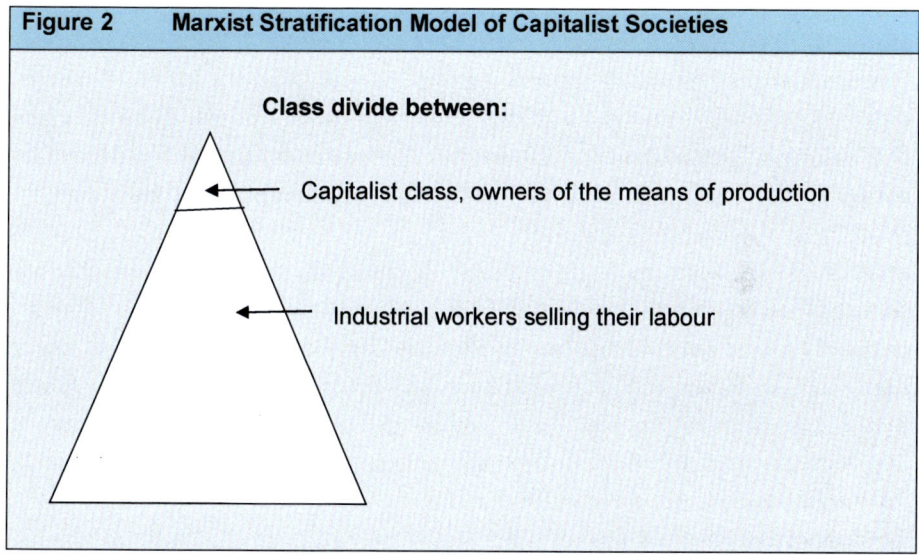

Figure 2   Marxist Stratification Model of Capitalist Societies

Class divide between:

Capitalist class, owners of the means of production

Industrial workers selling their labour

For Marx, although all class societies by definition contain opposing class interests, open class conflict is usually averted. To understand how this is possible, the superstructure and infrastructure need to be defined and their relationship explained.

In Marxist theory, dominant social institutions and ideas are referred to as the superstructure, whilst the economy and the class divisions and stresses that it generates are referred to as the economic infrastructure (see the diagram in chapter 15). The function of the superstructure is to contain and dissipate class conflict which is generated by exploitation that takes place within the infrastructure. For example, the police and the courts, imposing the law of the land, and at times even the military, can control outward expressions of social discontent.

However, from a Marxist perspective, that discontent can often itself be averted if the subject class are not consciously aware of their true plight. For this to be the case, the way that reality is conveyed is through ideological distortion. Ideology is a natural phenomena in the maintenance of all class divided societies. It provides a plausible and systematically distorted social image which is skewed to reflect the vantage point of a powerful ruling class. It is therefore ruling class ideology. Under capitalism, existing social arrangements are justified as the inevitable consequence of free market forces, providing freedom of contract and a fair wage for labour supplied. The outcome of such ideological distortion is to encourage the acceptance, conformity and application of the subject class and hide the reality of their exploitation. Internalisation, through socialisation, of an ideologically distorted view of society leads to a 'false consciousness' in the subject class. For example, the institution of private property is upheld by dominant social values and enforced by the law of the land, protecting rightful owners of property from theft. There is widespread public awareness that theft is a criminal offence and detailed statistics are available on such crimes. However, from a Marxist perspective there is one form of crime which is continuous but hidden by dominant values – class based theft by employers of a proportion of the value created by workers in the production process. Ideological distortion hides this reality of exploitation through the concept of rightful profit to the employer.

From a Marxist perspective, the economy structures the objective reality of opposition of class interests by which we can define a working class as a 'class in itself'. However, conflict of class interests will not lead to class conflict if the situation is not apprehended as such by the working class as a consequence of the distorting effect of ruling class ideology.

Marx claimed that he had demonstrated the objective forces that would lead to class conflict and ultimately revolution, but such an outcome was dependent on a leap in the consciousness of the subject class. He argued that there are powerful tendencies within free enterprise capitalism which would bring this about. Capitalists must compete with each other to sell their goods and services in the market to make a profit and ultimately to survive. They therefore have to constantly innovate to increase efficiency of production through introducing new technology and reducing their labour costs. Those who are successful will have instituted efficient procedures and kept wages low. Thus, although workers under capitalism are better off than serfs under feudalism, the wealth of their employers has increased even more through combining the labour of workers with highly efficient means of production. Through this tendency for wealth to polarise, Marx concluded that the rift existing between the classes is likely to become more evident.

Moreover, the low purchasing power resulting from depressed wages leads to decreased demand in relation to increased productivity, periodic economic depression and mass unemployment, further pushing wages down. Marx argued that it is at such times of inevitable economic malfunction that ruling class ideology becomes vulnerable. The reality of conflict of class interests is more likely to be seen through by workers whom capitalism has concentrated in large numbers in factories and urban communities. Under these conditions, a common class consciousness can emerge between workers. Should this transpire, the objective reality of conflict of class interests built into capitalism becomes subjectively evident across the working class.

False consciousness gives way to class consciousness, providing the means by which the subject class recognise their objective condition of being an exploited class and become a 'class for themselves'. The solution of class revolution becomes clear; the majority class need to rise up against the minority class and take the means of production into common ownership. By such means, according to Marx, a communist society would replace capitalism. Since the means of production would be taken into common ownership, this society would by definition be a classless society.

It is clear that within this perspective, social classes are not just descriptions of different levels of socially structured economic inequality. They are explained within a theory that views them, dependent on the varied interpretations of Marxist theory, as potential or inevitable categories of organised social action that provide a motive force for social transformation. A number of questions can be raised with regard to Marx's theory. The reader may like to pause and reflect upon those raised here and to consider others.

1. One issue is the charge of reductionism. This term refers to the simplification of something which in reality is far more complex by reducing it to basic categories of analysis. In the case of Marxism, social stratification and conflict becomes reduced to that between classes and social class becomes reduced to people's relationship to the means of production. As a consequence, both Marx's view of classes and of social conflict can be criticised as being too mechanical and simplistic. This criticism will become more evident when Max Weber's approach to social stratification is introduced.

2. Another matter relates to the question of the potentiality or inevitability of revolutionary social transformation. Even if Marx was correct about

the economic forces at work within capitalism, is it possible to predict with certainty that economic inequalities will trigger a mass revolutionary response? If so and Marxism is a scientific theory, at what point does this take place? Marx was somewhat ambiguous on these points and this has led to different interpretations of Marxism.

Capitalist societies have weathered numerous recessions and depressions since Marx developed his theory, but the advanced societies have not succumbed to proletarian revolution. Indeed, capitalism may be more entrenched at the beginning of the twenty first century than ever before. Can the absence of the predicted revolution be answered within a Marxist framework, as for example Frankfurt School neo-Marxist theorists have attempted, or does it require a rejection of the theory?

3. Marx developed his analysis of capitalism against the backdrop of a free enterprise system which emerged in England by the mid-nineteenth century. This raises certain questions regarding the contemporary relevance of Marxist theory. For example, at the time that Marx was writing, under entrepreneurial capitalism, private enterprises were often owned and run by individuals, partnerships or families who made the key decisions and took the profits or faced the losses.

There was arguably a clearly defined capitalist class who owned the means of production outright. But is this now the main form that capitalism takes? The expansion of corporate enterprises through mass shareholding in the twentieth century, typically into very large and complex organisations, has required highly trained managerial employees and professionals to take charge of much of the decision making process.

Control has thus arguably been wrested from owners (now usually external shareholders interested in how their investments perform) and, as proposed by those who believe that there has been a 'managerial revolution', managers may not be driven by the same ruthless profit maximising motives as the entrepreneurs of earlier capitalism.

Moreover, as controllers of workers but nevertheless employees of the organisation, people in these managerial occupations may, in Marxist terms, experience a contradictory class position. Class is further complicated by a massive expansion in the number of lower ranking white collar employees and middle ranking professionals, all of whom Marx would classify as working class but who may adopt a more middle class consciousness.

4. As suggested above, large corporations have arguably not just seen control pass from entrepreneurs to professional managers, but a further important issue relates to the question of just who now owns the means of production? The development of joint stock companies over the last century and a half has enabled millions of people to become shareholders. As such, whilst most of these people need to work for a living, they would also be, according to the Marxist model, through their share investments, part owners of the means of production and therefore have a foot in each of the opposing classes as defined by Marx. They would occupy a dual class position which is likely to affect their orientation toward capitalism. The issues raised in points 3 and 4 will be taken up later in this chapter with reference to decomposition theory.

5. Is it not the case that these various changes in capitalism, combined with the development of welfare state security and improved standards of living, would suggest, contrary to Marx's predictions of radicalised workers and class revolution, the emergence of a new form of capitalism; one with which a large middling stratum of de-radicalised workers will tend to identify as at least tolerable or even working in their interests?

Weber – class, status and party

Like Marx, Weber provided a conflict theory of stratification. He agreed with Marx that social class derives from economic factors. However, by contrast, Weber maintained that stratification is not exclusively reducible to economic social class, but includes social status and political party dimensions. Whilst recognising that Marx's conceptualisation of class may be applicable in certain social and historical conditions, Weber argued that Marx was wrong to 1) relate social class formation exclusively to the means of production 2) view class conflict as the primary driving force of social change and 3) not sufficiently recognise the significance of other forms of stratification such as social status.

Weber was critical of the strong tendency in Marxist theory toward economic determinism; the view that the nature of social relationships, the state of belief systems and the possibilities for collective action are determined by forces originating in the economy. For Weber, the relationship between the economic structure, belief systems and action was seen to be more open and contingent.

Social class as occupational categories in a competitive labour market

Weber, whose writings straddled the late nineteenth and early twentieth centuries, related social class in capitalist societies to the position of occupations in the competitive labour market which requires different skills and qualities from workers. In return, workers receive different levels of remuneration, security, work conditions and perks. A person's marketability in the employment market will effect, amongst other things, their income level and the goods and services that they have access to. Social classes are formed and can be analysed in terms of the clustering of occupations that are alike in the skills required and rewards offered which makes them distinguishable from other occupational groups. Weber recognised that within particular social classes, people will experience similar life chances and opportunities.

Social groups do not necessarily relate to a competitive labour market passively but often actively struggle to maximise their returns. They may adopt strategies and use power in an attempt to control the labour market. Sometimes, the threat of or actual use of collective action can be the strategy applied in the attempt to maximise rewards or improve terms and conditions of employment. This approach has traditionally been more typical of those employed in manual working occupations. Another strategy can be that of restricting entry into an occupation compared to the demand for services, thus creating a degree of labour scarcity as a means to bolstering rewards. As Parry and Parry (1976) show, this approach has been effectively applied by a number of professional organisations. Workers are therefore not necessarily as powerless under capitalism as the Marxist model suggests, and neither do they act within a perfectly free market. For Weber, opportunities and rewards can be partly influenced by purposeful action.

Weber identified a tendency toward the growth of large bureaucratic organisations as a key feature of modernisation, a process that he referred to as bureaucratisation. A bureaucracy is a formal organisational power hierarchy, primarily comprised of white collar employees, with a top down authority structure referred to as a chain of command, clear rules and precisely designated employment roles and responsibilities, providing a framework for the rational organisation and application of labour. Whilst often associated with the public sector, Weber argued that its superior formal efficiency would lead to it becoming the predominant form of organisation throughout society. The process of bureaucratisation gives rise to an expansion of white collar occupations and classes around the middle of the stratification system. Weber therefore disputed the Marxist analysis of tendencies of capitalism to polarise society into two opposing social classes. By contrast, he contended that the class system was fracturing into a more complex hierarchy. This, along with the subjective independent mindedness of actors, reduced the likelihood of the emergence of a mass working class consciousness as a vehicle for the destruction of capitalism through mass class based revolution.

A Weberian approach to the study of occupational classes recognises that the labour market divides people into different economic worlds with regard to income and job security levels. This means that people in some sections of the labour market may be particularly vulnerable. Research by Warren (2015) based on the findings of large scale surveys, and adopting a Weberian framework, analysed the impact of the 2008-2009 recession on workers in Britain on labour contracts; predominantly hourly paid manual workers. The findings challenge the common perception that this was a recession that particularly hit the middle classes.

Unemployment increased, but those on labour contracts had been particularly vulnerable to underemployment through work time reduction. The research reported on subjective measures of the experience of underemployment and the consequent feeling of insecurity and hardship. It was found that for work time employees, the experience of financial difficulties correlated with wanting to work more hours, with both phenomena well above pre-recession levels. Underemployed work time employees experienced an increase in not being able to afford a holiday – this taken as the best general index of family hardship. The greater vulnerability to the loss of hours and its consequences on work time (mainly manual) workers meant that the impact of the recession on such vulnerable sections of workers was particularly severe.

Social status as lifestyle attributes

Weber also analysed stratification in terms of social status, which is analytically distinguishable from class. However, both conceptually and in the real world there is often a complex symbiotic interrelationship between them. Weber distinguished status stratification from the economic dimension of occupational class by defining it in terms of cultural judgements of social prestige. Essentially, status judgements relate to lifestyle which includes types of leisure activity, patterns of consumption and the symbolic meaning of goods acquired, and involvement in community activities. A status group comprises people who share a similar type of lifestyle which is viewed by themselves and to varying degrees others in terms of superior or inferior levels of prestige. At a personal level, status may be associated with one's social standing and reputation.

The complexity of class and status stratification

Building on Weber's analysis, what are some of the stratification complexities that can be derived from the studying the interplay of class and status?

1. Occupations, as a measure of social class, may also attribute cultural status levels through employment. This is because occupations themselves may be perceived in status terms. Thus, a person working as a hospital consultant is likely to be attributed higher status than hospital cleaner. These judgements may relate to differences in educational background, skill level and income associated with the occupations. Furthermore, the range of lifestyles available to people such different occupations is itself likely to be strongly influenced by different income levels as well as social contacts and tastes.

2. On the other hand, status stratification may impact on or even override class stratification through restricting occupational access. Its impact has been particularly prevalent in traditional societies and closed stratification systems. For example, in the traditional Indian caste system, impenetrable social status barriers were also barriers which restricted social access to a limited range of occupations. And the ascribed social status of racial inferiority consigned black South Africans in the apartheid era to lowly occupations with poor pay and conditions of employment. In such closed stratification systems, social status can be seen as strongly and consistently impacting on class by restricting the occupational opportunities of people of designated status groups. However, even within the relatively open stratification systems of most contemporary societies, status stereotypes regarding a person's speech code, gender or ethnicity, may influence opportunities for access to occupations positively or negatively.

3. In comparatively open stratification systems, status mobility may be acquired through the use of economic assets derived from class mobility,

but it may take time. Culture, in the form of taste and manners, is an important dimension of status judgements. People who have become well off financially but are seen to lack etiquette may be judged as brash in status terms by others, even if the latter are less well-off economically. For example, during the nineteenth century, some who still claimed high status by virtue of the more aristocratic notion of established wealth and cultured upbringing, looked down in status terms on the economically upwardly mobile who had achieved new wealth through business enterprise and viewed them as 'Philistines' who lacked cultural refinement. The response of the moneyed businessman so looked down on was sometimes to use their new made wealth to enhance the status prospects of their children by sending them to public school to gain the appropriate cultural attributes (Wiener, 1981, Ch.2).

4. A person's position in social status terms may be quite separate from their social class position, especially within relatively open stratification systems. For example, status can be derived from living in a particular residential area. Although a residential area may tend to attract residents from similar occupational groups and levels of income – ie similar classes in Weber's terms – there is unlikely to be a hard and fast correlation between the status of a neighbourhood and the occupational class of all residents. Alternatively, within the same occupational category (social class), status distinctions may be made between people with different types of educational background and cultural tastes. Viewed either way, when this autonomy of class and status leads to individuals occupying substantially different positions on each of the scales, the term 'class and status dissonance' is used.

5. Irrespective of class, social status itself can be a complex phenomenon in which individuals may project an image of status inconsistency. For example, a person living in a poor housing area and driving a top of the range expensive car may convey a confused image of status ambiguity in the minds of others.

6. In contemporary societies, social relationships, especially in large towns and cities, are likely to be of a more impersonal nature than in small traditional communities. The quicker pace of life is likely to lead to people engaging in quite fleeting acquaintances. In the more open social structure

which contemporary urbanised societies arguably exhibit, a person's social status may be judged by the external show of possessions in the form of status symbols that hold well recognised stereotypical meaning rather than others' close personal knowledge of the individual. There may therefore be more room for personal manipulation of status by the acquisition of widely recognised symbols of prestige, even if acquired through means of the availability of credit and indebtedness.

7. Even in relatively open stratification systems, social status can play a part in gaining or restricting access to key institutions. The universities in Britain tend to be themselves status ranked with the traditional institutions of Oxford and Cambridge at the top of both the league table and the university status hierarchy. But how does one gain entry to the higher status universities? Clearly, ability is a prerequisite but statistics suggest that prior access to independent sector education, which normally requires the advantages of parental capacity to pay fees, also appears to be a significant factor. There is hence arguably a degree of social closure in access to the elite universities and consequently some of the higher occupations which recruit from them, a matter which will be later reviewed in the context of elite theory.

8. Although attributes of social status may be broadly recognised across society, worthiness of status is sometimes contested. For example, opposed generational interpretations may be made of the status worthiness of those made famous through celebrity culture, and within schools, the status of a youngster within a subculture is likely be quite different from their status within the school culture which they may deride.

9. Challenges may also emerge to the derivation of status from occupational position (class) and authority in the work place. For example, within a college or university, managerial positions may earn a higher income and hold more decision making power than those of lecturers. In occupational terms, managers are likely to rank higher, but what about their social status? Whilst lecturers are required to accept managerial authority within the organisational structure, they may try to enhance their own sense of relative status through emphasising the symbolic worth of their superior academic qualifications and even deriding managers as non-academic mercenaries.

Party and the political dimension of stratification

'Party' was a further dimension of stratification for Weber which adds complication to the stratification picture. As used by Weber, the term needs to be distinguished from its more familiar and restricted application to political parties. For Weber, party relates to socially patterned differences in the ability to impose power over others. Party stratification would therefore be strongly etched on the stratification system of societies where political elites are able to impose authoritarian rule over the masses.

In more open and pluralistic societies, party brings together people with shared interests and aims and can therefore include common identification with mass political parties or pressure groups in contestation for power and influence. The important point is that people's party identification may or may not correlate closely with their social class or status. For example, in the case of a trade union which is fighting for the interests of a particular section of workers, party identification and class stratification are likely to be closely associated. However, party can also bring together people from different class and status groups who intend to pursue shared aims, even if the aims are pursued for different reasons.

Opposition groups to new road building schemes can illustrate this point. Such groups have been known to bring together major local landowners and other local residents, concerned primarily with issues of quality of life and property prices, and geographically mobile members of new environmental pressure groups that advocate direct action. These people are likely to be highly distinguishable in terms of class and status differences. They may often have little time for each other. Yet, in terms of their shared aim of halting a road building scheme, there have been examples of local residents providing meals and washing facilities to support direct action environmental protesters.

In conclusion, Weber's approach to stratification suggests weaknesses in both functionalist and Marxist stratification models. For example, the remuneration of groups within the occupational structure might not simply reflect the functional importance of an occupation or the workings of the free market as functionalists maintain. Instead, in the struggle over access to resources, it may derive from strategies pursued by occupational groups, such as control of entry into a profession, to enhance the market position and income of their members. And as well as the effect of economic inequalities on the life chances of people, status distinctions and social connections may also provide impediments to equality of opportunity for individuals to arrive at merited positions on the occupational ladder.

Weber's analysis leads to the view that stratification is a highly complex and multidimensional phenomena. There are many possible combinations of position in class, status and party terms that people occupy, as well as making decisions to form shifting alliances with others as they engage in the pursuit of their varied interests. For Weber, attempts by Marxists to reduce an analysis of stratification to that of class and of class to the means of production, both lacks subtlety and distorts reality.

Social stratification – traditional sociological issues

1. How to measure social class

When analysing stratification in industrial societies, sociological theorists have focussed primarily on social class and status. Measuring social class requires the translation of theoretical concepts into key measurable indicators of the concept and the one that is overwhelmingly selected is occupation. Social classes are then viewed in terms of occupational categories, a procedure referred to as the 'employment aggregate approach' (Crompton, 2008, p.50). However, there are disputes over the theoretical basis upon which such measuring devices can best be constructed and applied.

Most social surveys, whatever their focal interest, will attempt to measure respondents' social class. This is because class has been shown to be an important influence across a broad range of social phenomena and thus often anticipated to be an explanatory factor in an equally broad range of research findings.

A major area of interest in studies of stratification in modern industrial societies has been the measurement of social mobility – the amount and range of movement of people throughout society up and down the social hierarchy. If the extent of social mobility could be quantified, evidence would be provided of the degree of openness of modern social structures as potential meritocracies. But how can social mobility be reliably measured? The conventional means has been for sociologists or government officials to construct occupational scales which bracket occupations into a hierarchy of categories, usually referred to as social classes. Such scales can be used in research as standardised measuring devices by which can be quantified the frequency and range of movement of people up and down the social structure. Measurement may either be taken across the working lives of a cohort or generation of individuals (referred to as intragenerational social mobility) or more commonly by comparing the occupational levels achieved by one generation with those of their parents (referred to as intergenerational social mobility).

Reflecting the male breadwinner assumptions of the time, traditionally, when occupational scales were used, only the occupations of males were recognised in the measurement. Thus, within a household, all members were deemed to be of the same occupational class which was presumed to be derived from the male head of household. If married females or daughters still living at home were questioned in social survey research, which they often were not, their social class position was read off from their husband's or father's occupation. This practice was subsequently strongly criticised by feminists as typical of patriarchal society and occupational scales now tend measure the occupational position of women as important in its own right.

Constructing occupational scales poses a number of problems. For example, what criteria should be used for grouping occupations into categories and deciding on the number and the positioning of cut off points of class divisions? Should the organising criteria be based primarily on level of income, work skill, social prestige, power in the workplace, etc. associated with an occupation, or a combination of these? If the latter, what is an appropriate formula for that combination? These matters remain open to dispute. And whichever emphasis is given, there remains the problem of locating all occupations in a society into their appropriate groupings within the scale. It is not surprising, then, that a number of different occupational scales have been devised.

In the construction of a social class scale, it is debatable whether the social prestige of occupations should provide the organising criteria since prestige is the key criteria of social status. However, it could be argued that this is an academic distinction and that in the real world class and status do overlap in the status of occupations. Scales which conflate the two concepts should therefore more realistically be referred to as 'socio economic scales'.

Further, although occupational scales are intended to be used as standardised measuring devices, they are likely to require occasional restructuring. This may happen for two main reasons. One is to do with changes in the underlying criteria for organising the scale, for example from occupational status to work skill based criteria, leading to a change in the way that occupations are classified. Scales are also likely to require restructuring to reflect changes in the social and occupational structure, especially in the form of major 'occupational transitions' such as from a predominantly manufacturing to a service economy. Social change thus introduces the conundrum that whilst scales must avoid becoming antiquated, updating and restructuring can interfere with their basis for making standardised comparisons in measurements over time.

A brief review of a number of occupational scales will now be undertaken. The first scale to be applied in Britain, the Registrar General's scale, was devised by a social statistician for the government's statistical department in 1913 and used from 1921. It originally comprised five occupational categories – two of which contained predominantly white collar occupations (upper and lower professional) and three predominantly blue collar occupations (skilled manual, semi-skilled manual and unskilled manual). To reflect a subsequent expansion in white collar clerical occupations, the scale was reconstructed in 1971 as a six class scale by the addition of a further largely white collar division below the other two predominantly white collar categories. The organising principle of occupations on the scale up to this time was the rather subjective and status based criteria of their 'standing within the community'. However, from 1981, the scale was reorganised by grouping occupational categories in terms of different levels of work skill. The scale has been criticised by sociologists for its conceptual confusion and lack of theoretical underpinning and it has been superseded by other scales.

The fact that the Registrar General's occupational scale was originally constructed by a government social statistician begs the question of whether there may be a more organic way of tying in a scale to the phenomena which it is intended to measure. A key approach to achieving this has been to conduct social surveys which ask respondents to rank occupations in accordance to specified criteria and basing a scale on their responses. Using this method of construction, Hope and Goldthorpe (1974) were able to devise a scale which ranked occupations in terms of their 'perceived social desirability' and North and Hatt in the United States (1947), constructed a scale which positioned occupations via their 'social standing' (Crompton, 2008, p.55).

For many sociologists, there remain two main problems with the scales that have been identified above. One is a matter of conceptual confusion over whether they are measuring social class or social status or a rather confused and subjective mixture of both. The other point is that they are largely descriptive – they lack a foundation in sociological theory to guide their formulation of social classes and, particularly for Marxists, the nature of relationships between them.

Approaches to scale construction which take their lead from sociological theory have rested mainly on Weberian and sometimes Marxist foundations of social class formation. Scales that are linked closely to Weberian theory will emphasise that the construction of class categories should reflect the life chances and marketable skills associated with each occupation. An early Weberian based approach by Goldthorpe (1972) also included the criteria of authority in the workplace that an occupation gave. Thus, occupations were classified in terms of 1) levels of pay and other material rewards, job security and career prospects, and associated life chances and 2) degree of power and authority and control and autonomy experienced by the worker in the workplace. These combined criteria were applied to guide decisions in the construction of the scale with regard to the number of class categories in society and the positioning of cut off points between the classes was guided by evidence from previous research which showed social mobility pinch points.

Goldthorpe's original scale, utilised in the Oxford Mobility Studies, comprised seven occupational categories. These were bracketed into three main social classes. The term 'service class' was used to apply to the two occupational categories of higher and lower professions respectively. Higher professional occupations included managers in large companies and amongst lower professionals were included high grade technicians. An 'intermediate class' comprised the three occupational categories: routine clerical work, small business proprietors and self-employed, and lower grade technicians and supervisors. Finally, a 'working class' consisted of two occupational categories – skilled manual work, and semi and unskilled manual work.

From this starting point, Goldthorpe's scale has gone through a number of revisions but remained essentially framed by Weberian theory. A more recent adaptation of the scale has changed the organising criteria to that of 'employment relations' and developed eight occupational categories through the subdivision of routine non-manual occupations into higher and lower grade categories. This clearly recognises the expansion of lower grade routine office work and takes on board criticisms by feminists that when such work is undertaken by females it is often in the form of a dead end job rather than, as more typically for males, a temporary point in a longer term career structure. Consequently, the routine clerical work category needed to be reallocated a position on the scale below that of skilled manual occupations but above semi-skilled and unskilled manual occupations. Now recognising the gendered aspect of occupational stratification, female routine office workers would tend to be placed in this new category seven on the eight category scale.

Strongly influenced by Goldthorpe's revised scale and constructed by Lockwood and Rose, the Office of National Statistics developed the National Statistics Socio Economic Scale in 1998 (the NS-SEC scale, see table 1 below). The theoretical basis has remained largely Weberian in origin with the positioning of occupations determined by a combination of labour market criteria (income, security and advancement prospects) and work situation (position in the workplace system of authority). On this scale the traditional distinction between white and blue collar occupational categories which had invariably tended to place the former above the latter, has been discarded and replaced by positioning in terms of degrees of work routinization. A category 'never worked and long term unemployed' has also been introduced at the bottom of the scale. Furthermore, the positioning of the household on this scale is now identified through the occupational position of the highest earner, irrespective of whether they are male or female.

Table 1	NS-SEC Social Class / Occupational Scale	
Weberian based on market criteria and work situation		
Social Classes	**Occupational Groups**	**% GB Pop. 2002**
Advantaged	1a Large employers and higher managerial	10
	1b Higher professionals	
Intermediate	2 Lower managerial and professional	22
	3 Intermediate	13
	4 Small employers	8
	5 Lower supervisory and technical	10
Subordinate	6 Semi-routine	18
	7 Routine	15
	8 Never worked or long term unemployed	5

Occupational scales may be useful tools in the hands of positivist inclined researchers as when used in social surveys they provide quantifiable data. This would be particularly useful for measuring the frequency of social mobility, a topic area turned to in the next section of this text. However, as valid measuring devices for social class (can we be sure that they are measuring what they claim to measure), these scales do have certain weaknesses.

Firstly, they tend to neglect consideration of perception of class community amongst people. Constructing categories of like occupations, however refined the classificatory exercise may be, says nothing about whether a sense of class community exists amongst people within those grouped occupations or that any subjective experience of class that they may hold corresponds to the categories on the scale.

Secondly, occupational scales correspond quite closely to a hierarchy of income. However, the wealth held by people who work at similar occupational levels (for example share and property ownership) is not taken into account and differences can be substantial and important.

Thirdly, preoccupation with social class and status has led sociologists to traditionally overlook the importance of gender and ethnicity to stratification. Only in more recent years have attempts been made to develop scales which reveal more about gendered and ethnic aspects of stratification.

Fourthly, there are many theories about the way that the class structure is fundamentally changing in contemporary society. One theory had been that we are all becoming middle class whilst another suggests that the class structure is completely breaking down. In response to the latter position, the construction of continuous occupational scales without division into class categories, such as the Cambridge scale, has been proposed. To construct such scales and to enhance their validity, surveys are carried out in which people are requested to locate occupations against one another.

Fifthly, whether occupational stratification even remains a significant aspect of life in contemporary society is an issue which will be addressed in more detail toward the end of the chapter, particularly with reference to postmodernism.

An attempt to break away from an occupational category based approach to measuring social class has been developed by Savage et al. working in conjunction with the BBC. Through evidence from a large web based survey (of over 16,000 participants) and a smaller survey sample from which were conducted face to face interviews (of over 1,000 participants), the Great British Class Survey constructed a seven class scale. The scale is organised in terms of Bourdieu's concepts of economic capital (here defined as household income, savings and house price), social capital (here defined as status and number of social contacts) and cultural capital (here with a cultural interest in classical music, museums etc. defined as 'highbrow' and visiting social network sites and watching sport etc. defined as 'emerging' capital) as the organising criteria. The resultant scale is summarised as follows in table 2.

Table 2	Great British Class Survey Scale			
Based on Bourdeau's concept of economic, social and cultural capital				
Social Classes	Capital Characteristics			% of GB Survey
	Economic	Social	Cultural	Sample Pop. 2013
Elite	Very high	High	Very high highbrow	6
Established middle class	High	High	High highbrow and emerging	25
Technical middle class	High	Very high	Moderate	6
New affluent workers	Moderately good	Moderately low	Moderate highbrow and good emerging	15
Traditional working class	Moderately poor	Low	Low highbrow and emerging	14
Emergent service workers	Moderately poor	Moderate	Low highbrow and high emerging	19
Precariat	Poor	Lowest	Lowest	15

Adapted from Savage et al, 2013

The authors claim that by classifying classes in terms of the forms of capital, they are offering a more sophisticated and multidimensional approach which is more relevant to contemporary British society in which the middle and working class divisions that are characteristic of traditional occupation based scales are becoming less relevant. This also enables the scale to break away from prevailing white and blue collar distinctions. Furthermore, as the social structure has become more stretched, it is argued that the scale beneficially identifies an elite at the top end and a 'precariat' (those whose situation is precarious) at the foot of society, a distinction which traditional occupational scales have failed to make.

Marxists dispute the theoretical basis upon which neo-Weberian scales are constructed, arguing that they say little about the power relationships which exist between capital and labour. For example, Braverman (1974) emphasised that, despite the various divisions of occupational categories that such scales divide the population into, in capitalist societies there remains a single majority working class, defined by the necessity to sell its labour, and a capitalist employing class. Braverman acknowledged that the development of capitalism in the twentieth century has given rise to an intermediate class who are marginal to the other two. This class comprises upper managerial positions, the occupants of which, despite their reliance on a salary, are well paid to do the bidding of their employers with whom they largely see eye to eye. However, Marxists generally maintain that conventional scales misleadingly construct separate class categories within the working class, wrongly base these divisions on labour market criteria and are largely unable to pay recognition to the existence of a small but powerful capitalist class who are occupation-less in terms of the criteria used.

Erik Olin Wright, adopting a Marxist framework, eventually developed a more elaborate scale of twelve finely graded occupational categories (Crompton, 2008, pp.56-59). Exploitation is the key organising feature of the scale. The primary division is therefore between owners of the means of production and employees. Further divisions are then made in terms of the number of employees businesses employ, and amongst employees, scarcity of skills and relation to authority. The scale ultimately divides owners of the means of production into three categories and employees into nine.

The problem that this scale presents for Marxists is that the traditional two class model now looks over simplistic and outmoded in relation to the complex structure of contemporary capitalism. Furthermore, irrespective of one's theoretical persuasion, through its complexity the scale has proved difficult to operationalise (apply in research).

Scambler (2016) argues that despite the transition underway from the 1980s to global financial capitalism, the fundamentals identified by

Marx remain intact, with political leaders now led by financiers and chief executive officers of transnational companies rather than industrialists. Criticising commonly used socio economic scales that provide a hierarchical classification of occupational categories, Scambler argues that they lack what Marx emphasises as central to social class formation: 'a social relation between social groups with different positions in the economy' (Scambler, 2016, p.9). Indeed, given greater polarisation in wealth and income, he maintains that a Marxist view of social class has even greater contemporary explanatory power. The reality also is though that class has a declining significance in people's subjective identity formation in contemporary financial capitalism.

Whilst financiers and CEOs amass largely unaccountable oligarchical power, they do not appear on conventional scales. For Scambler, a Marxist scale needs to rectify such deficiencies. Scambler's proposed scale (see table 3 below), which he refers to as neo-Marxist, is essentially constructed as follows:

Category A comprises those who constitute a global capitalist class who are able to exert their will over and through national political elites. This global dimension is absent on traditional occupational scales. Below them, category B is the new middle class of professional supporters of financial capitalism including managers, accountants and lawyers, paid for their co-operative services. Category C is referred to as the old middle class and is made up of supporting and lower level independent professionals. Category D, the main section of the working class, ranges from supervisory down to unskilled workers, and category E, also working class, are referred to as 'Displaced Workers' who have rarely or never worked.

At the very top, capitalist monopolists are referred to as 'players' who set the rules. Below them, and descending as far down as the top end of class D, (for example foremen), are beneficiaries rewarded for supporting and co-opting in roles.

Importantly, Scambler, unlike the Great British Class survey scale, does not locate a 'precariat' exclusively in the bottom stratum alone. Instead, as an endemic feature of global financial capitalism, the 'precariat' condition applies to positions up to middle managerial roles in category B.

Table 3	Scambler's scale	
Based on Marxist theory applied to contemporary financial capitalism		
Category	Social class	GB pop% estimates
A Capitalist executive	1 Capital monopolists 2 Capital auxiliaries 3 Capital sleepers	1
B New middle class	4 Insider higher managers 5 Outsider higher managers 6 Middle managers 7 Capital aspirers	24
C Old middle class	8 Insider professionals 9 Outsider professionals 10 Semi-professionals	15
D Working class	11 Insider workers 12 Outsider white collar workers 13 Outsider blue collar workers 14 Outsider semi and unskilled workers	45
E Working class	Displaced workers – never worked and long term unemployed	15

Adapted from Scambler, 2016

In summary, although different theoretical bases have been used, the development over time of scales as social class measuring devices reveals much about the changing occupational and class structure. Over a century ago, when the Registrar General's scale was first developed, its majority of manual working class categories reflected a predominantly manufacturing economy. Following the post war expansion of the service sector, the Goldthorpe scale comprised only two strictly manual occupations out of seven occupational categories.

Recognising the expansion of routinized white collar work, the NS-SEC scale developed semi-routine and routine categories of employment near the bottom of the scale, irrespective of whether the occupations were white or blue collar. Echoing the growing impact of neoliberal global capitalism, the Great British Class Survey Scale charted a stretched social hierarchy with a precariat rooted at the bottom and the Scrambler scale traced this condition from the bottom of five categories up to half way up class two.

A rather different approach to measuring stratification is adopted in the form of geodemographics (Crompton, 2008, p.54). Used mainly by commercial companies for marketing purposes, this type of scale combines measures of economic class and social and cultural status in identifying different types of neighbourhood, for example as affluent middle class or deprived working class, through the use of postal codes. Clearly, such scales would need to be regularly updated to accommodate housing developments and changes in fashion regarding areas of residence.

2. Measuring social mobility

Before reviewing some research findings and issues regarding social mobility, the reader may find it beneficial to consider the meaning of social mobility at an individual level. We have seen that occupational level is regarded as the single best rough and ready measure of a person's social class or position in a social hierarchy. The question to ask regarding 'intergenerational' social mobility is how does an individual's occupational level compare to that of their parent's (traditionally male's to father's)? If measured on an occupational scale, has there been upward or downward mobility and to what extent, or has the position remained about the same? This must, of course, only be a starting point to help envisage the meaning of intergenerational social mobility throughout society. Individual perceptions of the openness or closed nature of the social structure may reflect one's personal experiences, but such perceptions do not provide evidence of broader social patterns. Sociologists attempt to reliably measure patterns of social mobility across society. This is achieved through the statistical analysis of measurements taken from a sample of the population. Using the measuring device of occupational scales, the openness or fluidity of a social structure can be calculated in terms of overall movement between social classes. Such a measure is of 'absolute' social mobility levels.

Since the Second World War, a number of social mobility studies have been conducted in Britain and other countries. Some studies have made comparisons of mobility rates between societies. Comparisons can also be made between measures taken at different times to attempt to establish whether levels and patterns of social mobility are changing. Whether between societies or over time, such comparisons are referred to as measures of 'relative' social mobility and would require answers to the following questions. Are mobility measures greater or lesser in comparisons made between societies or over time? Also, what are the relative chances of social mobility at different points in the social structure? Allowance for changes in occupational structures would need to be factored into the calculations.

The statistical information from social mobility studies can be conveniently summarised in table form. Tables, as illustrated below, comprise a grid of data that quantifies the amount and range of social mobility at different levels of the occupational structure. In this case, reflecting the times, information on father's and son's (the horizontal and vertical dimensions respectively) occupational level is summarised.

The following table (table 4 below) compacts the findings of the Goldthorpe research into occupational mobility in England and Wales in 1972 (Cited in Abercrombie & Warde, 2006, p.135). The information is here compiled in the form of an 'outflow' table. This means that the table takes as its base or starting point the father's occupational level and from this is measured the percentage of sons from each of the father's occupational backgrounds who end up in each of the various occupational categories themselves.

Table 4		David Goldthorpe, Oxford Mobility Study, England and Wales								
Outflow Table										
		Son's Occupational Category, 1972								
		1	2	3	4	5	6	7	Fathers in sample	
									No.	%
Father's	1	**45.2**	18.9	11.5	7.7	4.8	5.4	6.5	688	7.3
	2	29.1	**23.1**	11.9	7.0	9.6	10.6	8.7	554	5.9
Occupational	3	18.4	15.7	**12.8**	7.8	12.8	15.6	16.9	694	7.3
	4	12.6	11.4	8.0	**24.8**	8.7	14.4	20.5	1329	14.1
Category	5	14.2	13.6	10.1	7.7	**15.7**	21.2	17.6	1082	11.5
	6	7.8	8.8	8.3	6.6	12.3	**30.4**	25.9	2594	27.5
	7	6.5	7.8	8.2	6.6	12.5	23.5	**34.9**	2493	24.6

In Goldthorpe's research, an early version of his seven occupational category scale, as referred to in the previous section, has been used. In the table, the 1-7 category column on the left refers to the father's occupational background. The figures in each box running across each row indicate the percentages of their sons who ended up in each of the seven column headed occupational categories. Toward the end of each row is given the total number of fathers in the sample in each occupational category and these figures are converted into percentages to indicate the relative size of each category in the father's generation.

Although dated, it can provide a useful resource for social mobility table reading. If we look at the figure of 11.5% in column three of the top row, this means that 11.5% of sons from occupational category one background (their father's occupation) were downwardly mobile into category three occupations. The 6.5% figure at the bottom of the first column shows that 6.5% of sons from occupational background seven were upwardly mobile into the occupational group one category. The same approach can be applied to any figure on the table and it is worth pausing to work through a number of the figures to familiarise oneself with reading such tables.

To interpret the table requires a broader view and an element of judgement. We will start with some simplified observations which will later need to be qualified. One approach would be to assess how far the pattern of evidence suggested that society was removed from a completely closed stratification system. If the stratification system were completely closed, the bold figures in the diagonal from top left toward bottom right would all read 100% and all other cells would contain 0%, showing that all sons worked at the same occupational level as their fathers. This is clearly not the case – some intergenerational social mobility is clearly evident. However, the highest figures do fall on or near to the diagonal. These figures further indicate that the highest levels of self-recruitment come from category one and category seven occupational backgrounds and that those from group three backgrounds are the most occupationally mobile. Overall, there is therefore evidence of relative closure at the top and bottom of the occupational structure, more openness around the middle, and only limited long range social mobility.

Another approach would be to compare the research evidence with the expected distribution of figures within a completely open social structure. In such an open structure, the figures would be more evenly spread across the rows and certainly much higher toward the corners opposite the diagonal, indicating higher levels of long range social mobility. Significant impediments to total openness can be judged from the research figures which show that whilst 45.2% of males from category one backgrounds are found in category one occupations, only 6.5% appear in category seven employment (which is also a much larger occupational category) and 34.9% from level seven backgrounds are in level seven occupations whilst only 6.5% achieve level one occupations (a smaller category though).

In relative terms, compared to the findings of a study previously conducted by Glass et al in 1949, there is some evidence of higher levels of long range social mobility. Although the findings are not strictly comparable as different occupational scales were used (Glass used the Hall – Jones scale), the earlier research, based on a smaller sample, showed that only 1.5% of males from category one backgrounds were found in category seven occupations and 0% from category seven backgrounds achieved level one occupational status.

Other studies of relative social mobility have attempted to make international comparisons. Pioneering work in this area was conducted by Lipset and Bednix (1959) and somewhat more recent research has been carried out by Erikson and Goldthorpe (1993). Whilst recognising the problem of standardisation of data in such research (differences in occupational structures make the use of standardised occupational scales for direct comparison impossible), these studies provided comparisons of nine and twelve industrial countries respectively. They found that a very similar profile of moderate social mobility pertained to all of the societies. The one main exception for Lipset and Bendix was the limited upward social mobility from lower occupational backgrounds in Italy which related at the time to a less developed economy and a larger agricultural sector.

Although social mobility studies were not available at the time, perceptive observers of mid-nineteenth century America such as Alexis de Tocqueville were impressed by the apparent degree of openness of the social structure and the opportunities available for social mobility. In this regard, America was viewed as exceptional. If this observation was valid, more recent research has questioned whether it remains so. Although Blau and Duncan (1967) characterised the United States as a society of high social mobility, they also evidenced a high degree of self-recruitment into some of the upper occupational categories.

More recent research by Jantti et al (2006), in comparing occupational mobility between the United States, the United Kingdom and four Nordic countries (Denmark, Finland, Norway and Sweden) has found that, as in the case of previously reported findings, there is a generally higher level of intergenerational social mobility in the Nordic countries than in the United States (the UK often appears in an intermediate position). The research indicates that in the country (USA) with the most stretched occupational hierarchy in terms of income differentiation, compared to the other countries, the sons of the lowest earning groups are relatively more likely to remain in the lowest earning category and the sons from the highest earning occupational backgrounds are relatively less likely to experience long distance downward mobility. This would appear to raise questions regarding the justification of high income differentials as an incentive for the competition that is necessary for a meritocratic society – as proposed in functionalist theory and the politics of the political right.

3. Analysing society in terms of meritocracy

The case for the existence of meritocracy

There is a close link between an open social structure and a meritocracy. Since a meritocracy is a society that enables individuals to reach occupational positions entirely in terms of their own efforts and abilities, its existence presupposes an open social structure. But we will see that the two are not exactly the same thing. Research statistics on social mobility through the occupational structure suggest the existence of a partially open social structure in Britain. Interpreting this degree of openness, especially in terms of meritocratic opportunity, is fraught with difficulties.

It can be argued that a society that appears to exhibit a degree of social closure may still be highly meritocratic. How can this apparent contradiction be reconciled? It has been suggested that social mobility levels that on the surface fall short of the very high mobility levels that one would expect to accompany a meritocracy may be the consequence of social class related differences in levels of intelligence and (or) effort. In this case, it is argued that those of higher occupational background have inherited higher levels of innate intelligence and acquire more aspirational values and those of lower occupational background, lower levels of each. If this were the case, it could be claimed that society offers equal opportunities to all, but that social mobility levels short of those otherwise expected in a meritocracy can be explained in terms of these differences in levels of ability, aspiration and effort related to class background.

A strong advocate of this type of explanation is Peter Saunders. His arguments derive from a Conservative new right perspective. This position offers a strong defence of the liberal democratic institutions and individual freedoms of capitalist societies. It is emphasised that the dynamism of such societies is enhanced by substantial inequalities of occupational income, which promotes individual competition. A highly differentiated occupational reward structure with large disparities between top and bottom is therefore the motivator for individual success. As the main criteria for success are effort and ability, success does not just benefit individuals exhibiting these qualities, but by appropriately placing people in suitable occupations it enhances living standards for all through the efficient utilisation of human resources. A highly differentiated income structure can thus be legitimised, as can the accumulation of private wealth based on individual achievement.

Saunders argues that class linked differences in innate individual ability and also effort go a long way toward explaining the differences in occupational achievement levels of people from different social class backgrounds. And whilst he acknowledges that modern Britain is not perfectly meritocratic, his research also indicates that ability is closely associated with occupational destination. Where differences in ability alone cannot sufficiently explain variations in level of occupational achievement, then differences in individual aspiration and motivation, related so social background, also have an important impact.

Arguments against the existence of a meritocracy

In considering these arguments, there are a number of reasons to be cautions or critical of Saunders' position. Firstly, the proposition that there are inherited ability differences that derive from social class background requires examination. The importance of educational opportunity and achievement to meritocracy is established in chapter 8 on education. In that chapter, it is argued that evidence of class related differences in inherited ability are not compelling. Any ability differences will therefore have very limited effect on explaining levels of continuity in stratification position from parents to children. Instead, it is argued that the way that intelligence and educational performance are assessed reflect class related differences to the advantage of the middle classes. The educational system is further bent toward the middle classes through the extra help that parents are often able to make available to their children to enhance their prospects of academic success. Such a class based influence built into education will have consequences for both educational and occupational achievement to the extent that occupational position is related to educational achievement.

Furthermore, if levels of aspiration, motivation and individual effort are related to social class, the argument can be taken in different directions. If those of manual working class background tend to hold more restricted horizons and fatalistic attitudes in terms of their occupational destination, on the one hand it can be argued, as did Hyman, that these will act as self-imposed barriers to success in a society which offers meritocratic opportunities which will be passed by at this level. In this case, the fault is claimed to lie in the adoption of negative values, not in impediments to social mobility in the social structure. On the other hand, from his research into a group of working class lads, Willis suggested the explanation that in their lesser effort to succeed at school and aspire to higher level occupations than their fathers, they made a realistic assessment of the limited opportunities available to them within a society which was far from open and meritocratic. In other words, the lack of aspiration was more a consequence of the realization that society is not meritocratic.

A number of other reasons to be cautious in claiming British society to be highly meritocratic can be made. One of these is to do with changes that take place within the occupational structure itself. The size and makeup of occupational classes changes over time. For example, during the post war decades there was a period of rapid expansion in professional occupations. However, the fertility rate of the middle class was lower than that of the working class. Over this period, it was difficult for expanding professional occupations to sufficiently recruit from the young of the middle classes alone to fill all posts. Under these conditions, even in a partially closed social structure there would need to be some upward social mobility as the numbers of children born in the different social classes is not mirroring the needs of a changing occupational structure to have positions filled. Goldthorpe's research covering this period indicated greater levels of upward than downward mobility and more long range social mobility compared to the previous findings of the Glass research. This particular pattern of social mobility enabled more people of manual working class background to gain access to middle class occupations without threatening to displace many from middle class backgrounds on merit. It is therefore doubtful whether such opportunities for upward mobility should be equated with a meritocracy. They are likely to be highly contingent on the conditions identified which did not threaten the advantage of middle class occupational self-recruitment. A measure of social fluidity which more closely represents that of meritocratic mobility would therefore need to extract changing social class sizes and different fertility rates from the calculations.

The expansion of the 'middle classes' during the latter part of twentieth century has been more toward the bottom end in the form of relatively low paid and low skilled office work. As the more professional levels have gone through their main period of expansion, pressures for upward mobility to that of the professional middle classes are now likely to meet with their resistance. As the structure above the middle classes narrows and is arguably more closed, there is little opportunity for their upward mobility. Upward mobility into the middle classes from below would therefore spell displacement of more children of the professional middle classes downward. Consequently, the concept of a meritocracy is likely to be less appealing to the middle classes who will want to defend their position against the threat of downward mobility.

Within this context, evidence from a report by the Social Mobility and Child Poverty Commission (2015) identifies barriers that the middle classes are able to put in place to protect their children from downward social mobility on merit, thus restricting meritocratic upward social mobility from below. These barriers, referred to as the 'glass floor', are a result of a number of advantages that the middle classes possess, including the ability to seek out the best schools in the state system, the provision of access to independent education and private tutors, offering a supportive home learning environment including enhanced parental help with academic work, the provision of confidence coaching and the utilisation of social networks to support their children. Unsurprisingly, recent social mobility studies have indicated a decline in upward mobility into the middle classes and the report evidence shows that there is a greater likelihood of less able children from middle class backgrounds entering more highly paid occupations than more able children from working class backgrounds.

A further problem for the meritocracy thesis is that whilst a totally open social structure is a prerequisite for a meritocracy, a high level of social mobility is not in itself sufficient proof of mobility through meritocratic means – that of fair and legitimate competition based on individual effort and ability. Levels of social mobility derived from marriage into wealth or through criminal activity would hardly equate with the normally accepted means of meritocratic success.

Another issue regards a weakness of general occupational scales in that they lack the precision to measure social mobility levels at the very pinnacle of society. For example, in Goldthorpe's sample, the top occupational category on the scale comprised 7.3% of fathers' occupations and by implication the size of that category in the population during the father's generation. This class had grown slightly is size by the time of the son's generation. However, a researcher's focus of interest may be in measuring social mobility into the 'elite'. In occupational terms, this category will include such professions as ambassadors, senior judges, high ranking officers in the armed forces, members of parliament (especially the Cabinet), high ranking civil servants, and directors of major industrial, banking and insurance companies. This group borders onto a propertied upper class and in total comprises well under 1% of the adult population. Occupational scales will not include the propertied upper classes and lacking a separate elite stratum will not be sensitive enough to measure social mobility across this point. Moreover, in general social mobility studies, very few participants from this elite category per 1,000 in a representative sample of the population are likely to be included. There will therefore be insufficient participants for statistical purposes to measure levels of social mobility around elite occupations.

An alternative approach could be to select a sample of people comprising entirely those in elite occupations. Such groups, however, tend to be wary of the enquiries of prying sociologists. The study of this stratum therefore needs to be approached from another angle. One way of going about this is to obtain a measure of the percentages of people in elite professions who have attended the most exclusive public schools and compare these figures with those of people in other occupations or for the rest of the population at large. In fact, there exists massive disparities showing that those in elite occupations are far more likely to have attended exclusive public schools, providing strong evidence of non-meritocratic elite self-recruitment.

According to Peter Saunders, 'a meritocracy is like a race where everybody lines up together at the start' (Saunders, 1990, p.44). Assuming that this is a close account of the basis of opportunity in society appears to be a remarkably superficial view. Even if competition for occupation and income level is largely determined by ability and effort, this does not explain how the resulting accumulation of wealth and its inheritance squares with a meritocratic society. The distribution of wealth is even more unequal than that of income. Saunders defends the legitimacy to pass on legally acquired wealth down the generations. However, the problem here is that even if wealth in one generation is entirely achieved by merit, through right of disposal to descendants, it, and the advantages that it provides, would then not remain acquired by meritocratic means to that and to subsequent generations.

Another way of approaching these issues is to imagine the creation of a capitalist society as a meritocracy from a social blank slate. For the first generation, all would start, as Saunders suggests, on an equal footing to compete for occupations in terms of ability and effort. Assuming the motivation for competition to be a substantial inequality of income reward associated with different levels of occupation and assuming the existence of a system of private property and inheritance, it is quite obvious that the meritocracy would be undermined in the following generation through the inheritance of different life chance starting points based purely on accident of birth, offering some the advantages deriving from their parent's achievements and others the disadvantages of their parent's lack of achievement. These advantages and disadvantages can include access to different study conditions and educational privileges, and differences in nutrition, health and access to levels of healthcare. Such factors are often interrelated. It is well documented that the physical and health condition of those of manual working class background is generally inferior to those of middle class background. Individual competition for academic achievement and occupational status will not be taking place on a level playing field.

The above reservations have related primarily to social class. In terms of class stratification, although contemporary Britain (and like western democracies) is a relatively meritocratic society by very broad historical comparisons, evidence and arguments show it to be substantially short of being a pure meritocracy. However, there is also an ideological dimension which may colour assessment of this area. Functionalists and supporters of the political right find meritocracy to be compatible with capitalism. In fact, they tend to utilise the concept of meritocracy to justify massive inequality of income as a motivator for competition and the achievement of social mobility. However, it has already been demonstrated (Jantti et al, 2006) that when international comparisons of occupational mobility rates have been made, there is evidence that the USA, which ranks amongst the highest in income differentials, demonstrates relatively low levels of long range social mobility and relatively high levels of occupational closure at the top and the bottom. The values and justifications of meritocracy are therefore not born out by evidence of its existence. Critics from the political left tend to question the need for such vast income differentials and are likely to be more cautious of the extent to which modern capitalist societies are meritocratic. Moreover, as suggested earlier, it could be argued that there is a logical contradiction between the institutions of capitalism itself and meritocracy.

Negative aspects of meritocracy

Even if a meritocratic social structure were to come into existence, might there be any negative consequences? Michael Young, in the seminal work 'The Rise of the Meritocracy' (1958), argued that there might. Hennessy (2014), in summarising Young's thinking, highlights two important areas of concern:

> Firstly, in a society which prioritises achievement through intellect, those who achieved higher social positions by this means might adopt a lack of compassion or even contempt toward the non-achievers for whom the system has offered opportunities and who have therefore been 'proved' to fail on merit.

> Secondly, the loss of talent within the working class due to the reallocation of ability on merit into the higher social classes would deprive the working class of talented leadership from within to help promote its own interests.

Meritocracy, concluding comments

Assessing the extent to which contemporary society shapes up as meritocratic can only be more comprehensively evaluated when other dimensions of stratification such as gender and ethnicity are also considered and questions raised regarding the continuing existence of institutions of privilege and status that perpetuate birthright. Our political leaders are often keen to appeal to the concept of Britain as a meritocratic society but less keen on engaging in or encouraging others to engage in joined up thinking to really scrutinise this area. Pursuing this logical analysis too far may raise awkward questions which point to the incompatibility of some of our social institutions, from which many political elites and their children have been beneficiaries, with the realisation of a meritocracy. Indeed, following such an analysis, the reader, at a personal level, may have come to feel more or less comfortable with the idea of meritocracy in principle or practice. However, as a sociologist, the aim should be to enlighten, not obscure. An attempt must be made to step back and assess society in terms of a comparison with the logical outcome of the application of such concepts as meritocracy.

Class stratification – changing but how?

Linked to the areas of dispute between the founding theoretical perspectives on stratification (functionalist, Marxist and Weberian) are a number of interpretations of how the class structure in the second half of the twentieth century has been changing. One such interpretation was the 'embourgeoisement' (becoming middle class) thesis. This thesis was rooted in the experience of virtually full employment and growing affluence of the late 1950s and early 1960s and was associated with such writers as Jessie Bernard and Ferdinand Zweig. Zweig's research, for example, suggested that within this context more affluent manual workers were looking to maximise their income within the system rather than to change it. Viewed broadly, as a consequence of economic modernisation, traditional working class occupations, such as dock work, mining and agricultural work, were undergoing long-term decline.

However, a new type of blue-collar employment on modern production lines was expanding and enabling workers to earn incomes increasingly comparable to those of the white collar middle classes. In the resultant mass consumer society, affluent blue collar workers were gaining unprecedented access to consumer goods and holidays and as a consequence were apparently adopting an attitude to their work, a lifestyle, status and even political views which were once regarded as more exclusively typical of those in middle class occupations. The traditional working class was therefore argued to be in decline both in terms of size and class consciousness, whilst the middle class, now comprising a growing proportion of affluent blue collar workers, was expanding, as illustrated in figure 3 below.

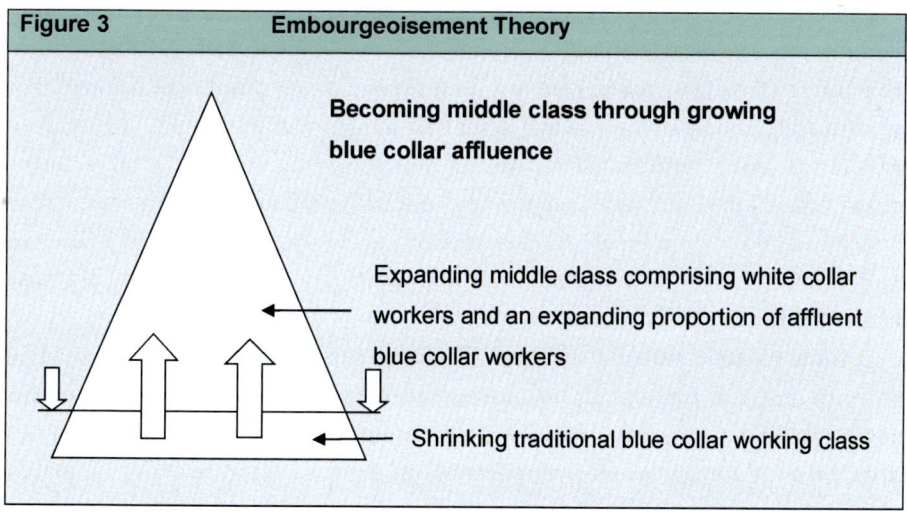

Figure 3   Embourgeoisement Theory

Becoming middle class through growing blue collar affluence

Expanding middle class comprising white collar workers and an expanding proportion of affluent blue collar workers

Shrinking traditional blue collar working class

There are clear theoretical implications of this interpretation of change. One is that Marx's analysis of the essence of class conflict to capitalism and his predictions of class polarisation, enhanced working class consciousness and political radicalism, were fundamentally mistaken. According to proponents of embourgeoisement, Marxist analysis looked increasingly dated and redundant as capitalism became able to transcend class conflict and evolve toward a largely single middle class society. This emphasis on 'middleclassness' as a basis for shared values and social integration would instead align embourgeoisement with the consensus theory of functionalism.

It has been well established that the embourgeoisement interpretation was undermined by research conducted by Goldthorpe and Lockwood during the early to mid 1960s. Their research focussed on a sample of affluent blue-collar workers in the Luton area and found that they were neither traditional working class nor had they become middle class. This conclusion can be viewed on various dimensions. For example, the research found that although their work provided access to income levels more characteristic of workers in white collar occupations, they did not expect nor experience a degree of job satisfaction or close identity with the firm that was more typical of white collar workers. Instead, the affluent workers held a practical and instrumental attitude toward their work as a means to maximising their pay. They were relatively isolated from one another through working from fixed production line work stations which allowed little opportunity for the development of a workplace collective community. Any collectivism therefore tended to be of an instrumental nature, through commonly emphasising the importance of trade unions to bargain for higher wages rather than to change society.

The affluent workers' view of the social structure did not tend to follow a more traditional industrial working class ideological class conflict model characterised in the imagery of 'us versus them'. Nor did it take the form of an attitude of deference toward social superiors within a rightful hierarchy which had been traditionally more common amongst agricultural workers. However, it also did not regard the social structure through the more typically middle class image of a ladder of career opportunity and a prestige hierarchy. Instead, the affluent workers viewed the social hierarchy in terms of economic class divisions.

In their lifestyle outside of work, the affluent workers tended to adopt a consumerist and privatised, home centred life. They were frequently owner occupiers. This and the spread of their neighbourhoods did not facilitate the type of working class community relationships that were more typical of non-owned tightly packed terraced housing layouts. However, privatisation also extended to them not seeking to befriend white collar workers.

The affluent workers were not deserting the Labour Party for the Conservatives, the party of high preference rates of the middle class, as the embourgeoisement thesis would suggest. In line with their orientation toward trade unions, the attitude of the affluent workers toward political parties was one of practical or instrumental as opposed to ideological commitment. At the time, their support for Labour was numerically high but was based on the calculation of a Labour government being of practical benefit to them rather than out of any deeply held working class convictions.

In conclusion, it was found that the affluent manual workers experienced a more privatised life than traditional industrial workers both in the workplace and in their neighbourhoods and the collectivism that they experienced towards trade unions and voting Labour was more instrumental than ideological. From Goldthorpe and Lockwood's research, they were seen to be a modernising section of the working class. Such findings point to a more differentiated stratification system implied in Weber's perspective.

A rival interpretation, from a Marxist perspective, suggested that very different dynamics of change were taking place in the class structure. This explanation contended that a process of 'proletarianisation' was taking place. Marx had argued that the logic of capitalism drove businesses, in the struggle to survive and maximize profits, to innovate and introduce new technology, expand in size and cheapen the cost of labour. As a result, social polarisation would take place between a small number of increasingly wealthy surviving capitalists and a mass of impoverished workers, resulting in a potential for growing consciousness of their position by both camps.

Working within this theoretical perspective, Harry Braverman (1974) maintained that despite absolute improvements in standard of living and the expansion of white-collar occupations, a mass working class still existed. Importantly, technological advance by no means guaranteed an upgrading of work skills. By contrast, it was argued that through the advance of mechanisation in the workplace, many blue-collar occupations had undergone a process of 'deskilling'.

Braverman pointed out that from the early decades of the twentieth century, small workshops employing highly skilled craft workers were being replaced by larger businesses introducing repetitive production line work systems, employing low skilled workers following narrowly designed job specifications in large factories turning out mass produced standardised goods. Workplaces became increasingly organised around 'scientific management' techniques developed by the efficiency expert Frederick Taylor. Taylor argued that, rather than workers passing on their skills, it was the responsibility of management to design systems of production in which the most efficient mechanical job procedures could be systematically combined to maximise the productivity of shop floor workers. This meant designing and imposing highly repetitive work processes in which jobs were drained of skill content, were easy to learn and workers easy to replace, and which enabled employees to reach maximum efficiency very quickly. If management 'equipped' workers with these 'skills', workforce motivation and efficiency could be manipulated through a material reward system of piece rate payments that were related to productivity levels. Under such conditions, Braverman argued, production line workers, such as those working on car assembly lines, commonly experienced, compared to their predecessors, a loss of skill level and personal autonomy and a heightened experience of alienation in the workplace.

As a contemporary example, one might consider the design of work systems in fast food outlets as archetypical of the efficiency of scientific management systems.

Of particular importance to Braverman was the view that deskilling of work and workers was also becoming an increasingly common feature of white collar employment. During the mid-nineteenth century, office clerks comprised less than 1% of the labour force in Britain. They usually worked in very small offices, had much contact with their employer, were significantly better paid than most manual workers, were required to have a high level of education or training for their time, experienced relative job security and high status and did not join trade unions. However, the twentieth century witnessed the development of larger businesses and the growth of white collar employment in increasingly large and mechanised offices. This was becoming an environment of highly supervised and low skilled office work which offered workers little autonomy and responsibility and few promotion prospects.

Call centres might be considered as a contemporary example of such a form of deskilled white collar work.

The proletarianisation thesis maintained that under modern capitalism there exists a mass working class which is identified by a common experience in the workplace. That experience is one of declining skill levels, autonomy and responsibility, increasing supervision and a heightened experience of alienation - processes common to a mass of relatively lowly paid blue-collar and white-collar workers, all with poor promotion prospects. Consequently, from a Marxist perspective, it is a false consciousness for this growing body of deskilled white-collar workers to distinguish themselves as middle class and separate from working class blue-collar workers just because they work in a white collar capacity, and occupational scales which make this distinction are themselves faulty measuring devices.

Figure 4 below illustrates the key features of the proletarianisation theory.

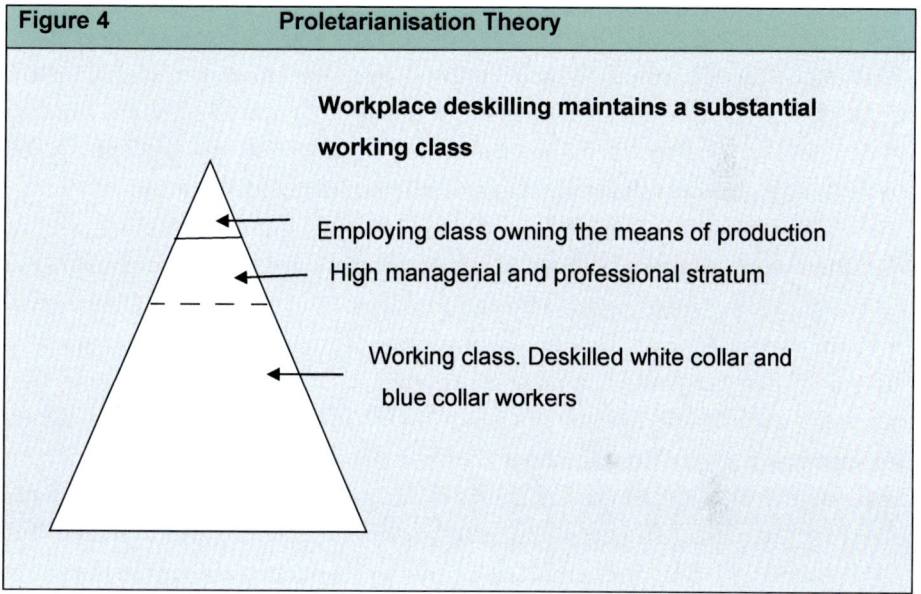

Figure 4	Proletarianisation Theory

Workplace deskilling maintains a substantial working class

Employing class owning the means of production
High managerial and professional stratum

Working class. Deskilled white collar and blue collar workers

Research evidence regarding this theory is mixed. In the 1950s, Lockwood claimed that much white collar work had retained employment privileges and status superiority over blue collar work and in 1980 Stewart et al pointed to the retention of superior promotion prospects for many white collar workers. However, research by Crompton and Jones (1984) did find, in the automated offices that they studied, evidence of enhanced supervision and experience of alienation as well as restricted promotion prospects. Perhaps the uptake of trade union membership by white collar workers can be taken as an index of their deskilled employment situation.

Of the various criticisms of Marxist interpretations of the class structure, one of the most challenging has been the 'decomposition' thesis which was associated with Ralf Dahrendorf (1959). Dahrendorf argued that rather than the class structure of modern capitalist societies polarising and crystallising into two clearly opposed class camps as Marx had predicted, it was in fact breaking down or decomposing throughout.

During the early phase of capitalism in the first half of the nineteenth century, most businesses were privately owned and run by individuals, partnerships or families. In this form of capitalism, power, authority, ownership and decision making were typically consolidated in the hands of a social class of entrepreneurs, who personally benefited from profits made and were accountable for losses. This stratum comprised Marx's capitalist class. However, from the later nineteenth century, the predominant type of private enterprise was shifting in the direction of the joint stock company. This was a development which enabled the size of businesses to grow through accessing capital from a large number of external share-holding investors. For Dahrendorf, the emergence of the joint stock company led to a fundamental change at the top of the stratification system.

The implications of this change were radical, but Dahrendorf argued that the consequences had been inaccurately portrayed by James Burnham's account of a 'managerial revolution'. For Burnham, the managerial revolution was essentially a revolution from above. As businesses grew in size, Burnham argued that power had passed wholesale from those who privately owned the means of production, the entrepreneurs, to expert managers who were now in control of the productive forces. In Burnham's analysis, this still left capitalism with two homogeneous and opposed social classes: now managers and workers rather than capitalists and workers.

By contrast, Dahrendorf emphasised that the separation of ownership from control that emerged with joint stock companies led to a duality at the top of society. Those providing the capital were now investors in stocks and shares. They were not directly involved in the internal running of the company and their main concern was in the performance of their investment. Those running the company were trained and salaried managers, highly skilled employees who did not own the company. This separation of ownership and control, functions which were once consolidated in the hands of the entrepreneur, into two groups with somewhat different interests, Dahrendorf equated to a process of decomposition from a once single class. As he put it 'The roles of owner and manager, originally combined in the position of the capitalist, have been separated and distributed over two positions, those of stockholder and executive' (Dahrendorf, 1959, p.44). Furthermore, referring to executives, Dahrendorf maintained that 'this new ruling group of industry bears little resemblance to the old "full capitalists"' (Dahrendorf, 1959, p.43).

We could add that from this perspective, through the privatisations of nationalised industries in Britain from the 1980s, the social base of share ownership had been broadened, enabling more of the working population to also become part investors in and legally part owners of private enterprise. Thus, a significant proportion of the public, as investors in private enterprise, were becoming, in Marxist terminology, technically part owners of the means of production. The problem posed for classical Marxist class analysis of capitalism is clear. For Marx, capitalist and proletarian classes were distinct, exclusive and homogeneous groups with opposed interests. However, most share owning investors today would also be in paid employment and therefore, according to Marx, also usually proletarian. For Dahrendorf, the class dividing line between capital and labour was decomposing.

Dahrendorf also argued that a decomposition of the working class was taking place. Central to Marx's thesis was that capitalism brought about a growing commonality amongst manual workers through the spread of deskilling. Dahrendorf acknowledged that this was a valid analysis of the consequences of the extension of the division of labour during nineteenth century industrial modernization. However, the twentieth century had witnessed a growing differentiation amongst manual workers which equated to the decomposition of the working class. In a complex occupational structure, the blue-collar 'working class' was fragmenting into a number of occupational strata comprising a growing proportion of skilled, a relatively static proportion of semi-skilled and a declining proportion of unskilled workers, each with different interests to protect and different levels of social status. Dahrendorf documented this decomposition in the following way:

> 'we find a plurality of status and skill groups whose interests often diverge. Demands of the skilled for security may injure the semiskilled; wage claims of the semiskilled may raise objections by the skilled; and any interest on the part of the unskilled is bound to set their more highly skilled fellow workmen worrying about differentials' (Dahrendorf, 1959, p.51).

Since Dahrendorf first published his thesis, more blue-collar workers have become owner-occupiers of their homes and achieved comparative prosperity, arguably introducing further distinctions within 'the working class'. According to this analysis, the 'working class' have been breaking down as a discrete stratum and experiencing a decline in common class consciousness.

Regarding the 'middle classes' (notice the plural), Dahrendorf argued that they consist of an extremely disparate social category. They comprise, for example, clerical employees through to supervisors and executives in a broad range of occupations. Employment may be in the state or the private sector. Some of the middle classes are engaged in a self-employed capacity. The middle classes, which were 'born decomposed', have expanded throughout the twentieth century. Moreover, the top occupations within this category, such as members of parliament, shade into the elite whereas at the bottom end, there is little distinction between, for example, some engineers and skilled manual workers.

The stratification changes argued in Dahrendorf's decomposition theory are illustrated in figures 5 – 7 below.

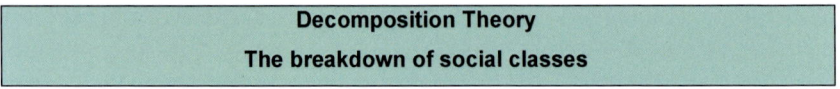

Decomposition Theory

The breakdown of social classes

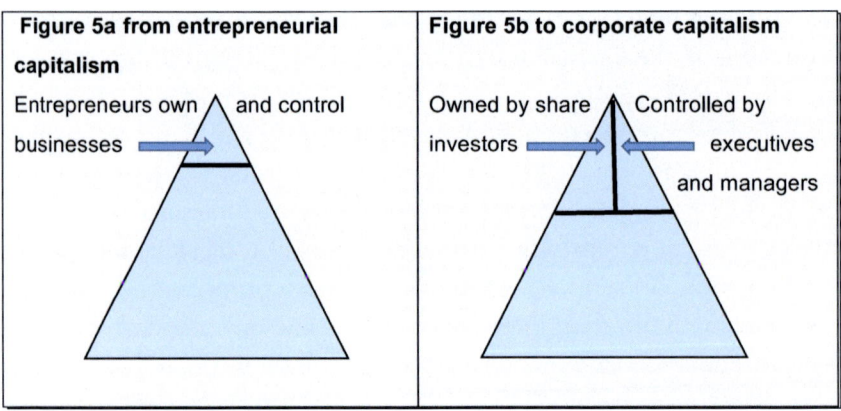

Figure 5a from entrepreneurial capitalism

Entrepreneurs own and control businesses

Figure 5b to corporate capitalism

Owned by share investors Controlled by executives and managers

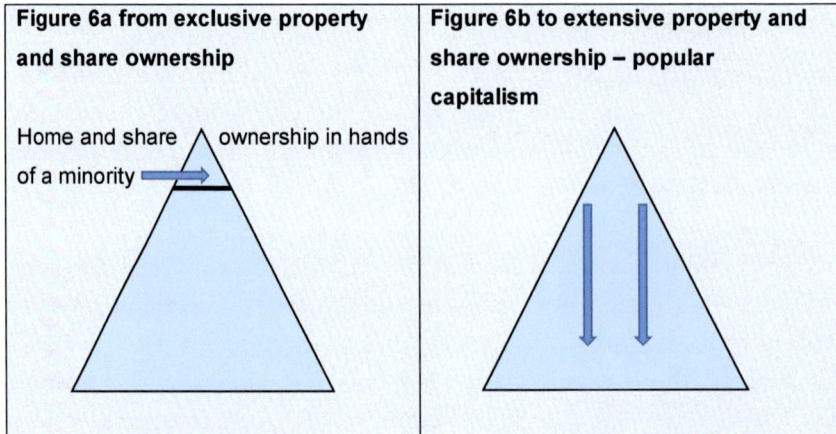

Figure 6a from exclusive property and share ownership

Home and share ownership in hands of a minority

Figure 6b to extensive property and share ownership – popular capitalism

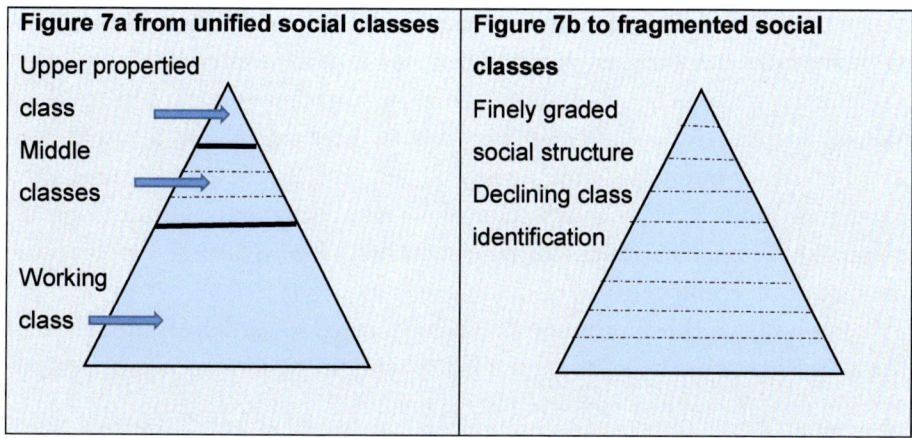

Figure 7a from unified social classes

Upper propertied class

Middle classes

Working class

Figure 7b to fragmented social classes

Finely graded social structure

Declining class identification

Dahrendorf's model suggests that, contrary to Marx's predictions, contemporary capitalism has progressed to a more open social structure, differentiated by finely graded occupational levels, status groups and interest distinctions. Class conflict between two opposing classes has given way to rivalry between numerous sectional interests and individual competition. A wider variety of people feel that they have a stake in the system as power has percolated down to shareholders, and more socially and organizationally accountable executives and managers have replaced entrepreneurs. Compared to its mid-nineteenth century form, capitalism has thus become more tamed and socially inclusive.

Such features of twentieth century capitalism identified by Dahrendorf as challenging the contemporary relevance of the Marxist model were actively promoted through new right policies of privatisation that spread shareholding and home ownership in Britain to more people than ever before during the 1980s and early 90s and heralded the advance of 'popular capitalism'. Through a greater proportion of the population becoming 'capitalised', they could more readily identify with the capitalist system.

Images of the social hierarchy and class structure

Images that people hold of the social structure are not just individual or random views but can be related to their perceived individual or collective position in a social hierarchy and the cultural influences of particular periods in history.

Based on extensive readings on community life, David Lockwood developed a typology of social structure imagery adopted by traditional workers and related to distinctive occupational spheres. Those who worked in heavy industry, such as ship building, dock work and coal mining, were likely to hold an image typical of 'proletarian traditionalists'. This outlook viewed society as class divided between us and them; fellow workers as a collective community with opposing interests to employers and their managers. Trade unions, to which workers were often strongly ideologically committed, were regarded as an important basis for organised opposition to the power of employers.

Agricultural workers, although also being located toward the bottom end of the social structure, by contrast tended to work in smaller and more isolated groups and developed closer working relationships with their employers. Consequently, they were more likely to hold a deferential view toward their employers. Not too dissimilar to that expected of agricultural labourers in feudal society, this comprised knowing one's place at the bottom of a social order which was seen as a rightfully graded hierarchy.

By the 1960s, each of these occupational sectors were in decline and an alternative outlook tended to exist amongst those employed in the expanding middle class white collared occupations. This viewed the social structure as akin to that of a career structure; one in which status could be enhanced through climbing the structure through aspiration and individual application. Embourgeoisement theorists had claimed that the dynamics of occupational change and the spread of affluence would enhance this view of the social structure at the expense of the previous two.

Cannadine (2000) has adopted a more cultural explanation of social structure imagery. He has argued that over the last three centuries in Britain, three main cultural images have provided alternative touchstones through which social inequalities have been envisaged. Each of these provide oversimplified models of the social structure. Cannadine has argued that often more than the social structure itself radically changing, the way that it is viewed, by giving primacy to one of these models, changes.

The alternative models are as follows:

1. Society as a natural and justifiable seamless hierarchy. This tends to provide a traditional, backward looking view.

2. Society as a three layered structure, projects an image of how it is claimed that society is from the virtuous vantage point of a respectable middle stratum.

3. A two strata oppositional model, emphasising class conflict, and portraying society as it might or should be.

For Cannadine, politicians are key figures in influencing cultural change in public perception regarding the persuasiveness of one of these models. In so doing, they provide the language and the categories through which they encourage people to envisage the social structure and their own identity with a virtuous place within it.

During the post war decades, the two class model imagery was one which held some sway amongst academics and within broader society. Thatcher provides the example of a leader who saw it as her messianic duty to change the social vision by eradicating social class dialogue and encouraging the adoption, particularly by winning round 'respectable' working people, of an outlook from the centre of a three level model that promoted the virtues of middle class enterprise. In this respect, as well as fundamentally opposing the collectivism of the two class model, Thatcher, although inegalitarian, was at odds with the old condescending establishment who identified with the seamless hierarchy model.

A fundamental reorientation of the imagery of the social structure from the vantage point of the middle was a cultural change, which, with varying emphasis, was continued by Thatcher's successor John Major and the New Labour prime minister Tony Blair. For Cannadine, it is a far more open question, especially given the extent of economic inequality and educational privilege, as to whether we have moved toward a classless society or been persuaded to accept that imagery.

Gender stratification – continuity and change

The existence of a sexual division of labour in society is sometimes justified by reference to biological differences which are said to form the basis of differences in emotional and intellectual qualities between men and women suiting them for different social roles. This division of labour has often disadvantaged women in terms of access to income and wealth and occupational and life opportunities compared to men. Although linked to biological sex differences, the term gender refers to socially constructed and modifiable identity. Looked at sociologically, there is significant scope for gender identity and gender roles to change as society and its institutions, culture and values change. The justification of fixed gender roles can therefore be viewed as ideological support for the continuance of male privilege and power over females – referred to as the exercise of 'patriarchal power'.

Throughout the post war decades, the primary stratification focus in sociology tended to be on social class and to some extent social status. However, as the women's movement gathered pace during the late 1960s and early 1970s, the issue of gender stratification was brought to the forefront. In this section, whilst the writer will focus on gender stratification, the reader is alerted to the view that simply challenging or attempting to substitute the primary or singular importance of class stratification with an equally singular emphasis on gender stratification is regarded as too simplistic. The issue of gender stratification is fact a highly complex one, taking on board issues of socialisation and interacting with other dimensions of stratification including social class, ethnicity and age. This will be briefly touched on at the end of this section. For the moment, the writer will outline some of the social changes associated with gender stratification and come to focus particularly on the stratification related issue of occupational opportunity.

Employment and educational opportunity, as well as family relationships, are key dimensions of gender stratification. How these have changed can be viewed in historical terms and the following comments can be related to the relevant content of chapters in this text on the family and education.

In pre-industrial Britain, quite a high proportion of economic production took place within domestic settings, combining work and family relationships. Although productive domestic work was often divided along gender lines, later notions of male (working) breadwinner and female (non-working) housewife were little recognised. Housework was likely to have been allocated to children.

Gender role segregation took on a new and pronounced form following the Industrial Revolution. As the productive process moved outside of the home and into the factory, work was becoming redefined in terms of this external setting in which workers were employed in large numbers in the pay of an employer. Initially, whole families would often be taken on. However, by the 1830s, the passage of a number of Factory Acts offered children increasing protection from harsh factory conditions by imposing age and working time restrictions on their employment. During the following decade, legislation was passed placing regulations on the employment of female labour. Consequently, by the middle of the nineteenth century, the number of women working in factories was declining and their lives were becoming situated within the home. Here, they engaged in domestic activities and childcare in an environment which was no longer regarded as a place of work. This gender based reconfiguration and the redefinition of work is sometimes referred to as the rise of private or 'domestic patriarchy', supported by the ideology of domesticity in which the 'natural' caring and serving qualities of females suited them to a domestic role and dependence on the male wage earner. For their part, male workers often exhibited opposition to the employment of women as a threat to their employment security and their justification of the need for a 'family wage'.

Throughout the nineteenth century, entry into many professions was either closed to women or their employment was restricted, as in teaching or health care, to low level roles. The main employment available for working class women was that which reflected their perceived natural role: that of domestic service. According to Charles Booth, as many as 400,000 people, 85% of whom were women, were employed in domestic service in London alone in the late nineteenth century.

During the first half of the twentieth century, patterns of employment for women fluctuated greatly. Two world wars required the mass mobilisation of women into the workforce, where they often engaged in heavy-duty work to support the war effort. However, at the end of each conflict it was expected that they would return to their domestic duties so that men, if they returned, could 'rightfully' reclaim the jobs that it was emphasised had only been temporarily vacated to women.

After the Second World War, larger numbers of women resisted pressures to leave their jobs, but were often faced with male hostility and powerful government propaganda to resume their portrayed primary domestic role. However, from the 1960s economic change in the form of the growth of service sector employment (including white collar support work and a range of customer service occupations), enabled more women to enter the workforce, which nevertheless remained heavily gender segmented and stratified, restricting the scope of work available, levels of pay and promotion prospects on offer to women.

Against this backdrop, and following the success of the civil rights movement in combatting racial discrimination in the United States, emerged the challenge of the women's movement. By the early 1970s, some of its theoretical advocates took up a radical stance. Radical feminists, such as Firestone and Millett, viewed patriarchal power as endemic throughout society and universally prevalent. For Firestone, such prevalence derived from biological sex differences by which women giving birth and during childrearing become dependent on men. Gender stratification was thus viewed as more fundamental than social class stratification; it predated social class which only tends to emerge at the point of social development when societies become productive enough to generate significant inequalities in the distribution of wealth. This view of gender stratification can be referred to as a form of biological reductionism (gender stratification can be ultimately reduced to biological differences) or biological determinism (gender stratification is determined by biological differences). From this vantage point, the technological advance of the pill, in allowing female control of contraception, was regarded as having liberating potential.

Nevertheless, for radical feminists, male dominance exhibits itself throughout society and in ways as varied as inequalities of power within workplace hierarchies to violence within the family. It is the latter institution which is seen as the main perpetrator of patriarchal power and radical feminists have often argued that it needs to be abolished if women are to be more fully liberated.

By contrast, following Betty Friedan's influential 1963 work 'The Feminine Mystique', the focus of liberal feminism was that women could only achieve self-fulfilment through their liberation from ties to domestic drudgery through acquiring equal access to educational and employment opportunities. Liberal feminists adopted a more reformist approach in advocating that equality of gender opportunity can be achieved by working within the system for cumulative piecemeal reforms, particularly of a legislative nature, and including supporting institutions such as creches. In Britain, legislative reform through the democratic process assisted advances toward equal pay and opportunities from the early 1970s.

This strand of feminism came to hold some appeal to middle class careerist women in the context of an invigorated enterprise culture which accompanied new right governments during the 1980s and 1990s. The growth of the service sector had enabled more women to enter the workforce and gain a degree of financial independence and in conjunction with the liberalisation of divorce law had made it possible for more women to escape unhappy marriages. Family roles were becoming more flexible, educational materials less sexist and educational opportunity for females was significantly advancing. Liberal feminists were therefore more confident that such gradual changes across a broad front were leading toward a society of equal opportunities for women.

However, of particular concern to feminists from this period has been the implications of care in the community policy which was promoted in Britain from the 1980s. Research has shown that much of the caring takes place within family settings and that the burden falls excessively on females. The costs involved in taking on this burden can be substantial. For example, as well as loss of earnings, carers lose out on making extra pension contributions, thus restricting their income later in life. They are also likely to have missed out on retraining and promotion prospects and may find it difficult to return to work or when they do, face demotion. On top of these career and economic penalties, carers risk suffering anxiety and isolation which can affect their health and well-being.

There is also evidence that growing economic and social polarisation during the 1980s and 1990s had a greater impact on females than males. Whilst, particularly from the 1980s, the number of lone, usually female, parents living in poverty was increasing, a growing number of women, although remaining minorities, were entering higher professional and managerial positions, some in dual career professional households. Improved entry by women to these higher occupational positions may be set to continue as significantly more females are entering higher education than males, although there remains evidence that females often need to be better qualified than males to enter equivalent occupational levels.

By the turn of the twenty first century, the workforce in Britain (and other western societies) shows that women have been narrowing the gap between themselves and men regarding proportions in employment. When scrutinised more closely, there is evidence of both continuing gender inequality and of change in terms of patterns of sectoral concentration and occupational level. A number of issues can be raised.

Firstly, in Britain women remain more highly concentrated in routine clerical level occupations than men. As a result, they tend to experience a different pattern of social mobility to that of men. Marshall et al indicated in the 1988 Essex Mobility Study that women were both more upwardly and downwardly mobile from a variety of occupational backgrounds as they tended to converge in the routine clerical occupational stratum. Moreover, these jobs were more likely to remain dead end occupations for females than males who tended to use routine clerical employment as a temporary career stepping stone.

Much debate has taken place as to whether routine office work, as Braverman had argued, has become deskilled. If it has, and if through these jobs women achieve fewer promotion prospects, then it is possible, as Stanworth has argued, that women have disproportionately experienced the effect of proletarianisation. In contrast to this interpretation, Marshall has provided evidence that routine clerical workers have retained greater autonomy in the workplace than manual workers (Marshall, 1993, p.120).

Secondly, whilst there has been a significant convergence in employment rates between men and women since the 1970s, such that by 2013 76% of men and 67% women of working age were in employment, far more women than men work part-time (about 42% as opposed to 12% according to 2013 Office for National Statistics figures) or under flexible working conditions which can include zero hours contracts, providing employers with access to a highly flexible supply of on call low waged labour for minimal layout of training cost or sick pay. This may be of advantage of both employers and to women with domestic commitments, but such employment is usually in what Piore has referred to as the 'secondary' sector of a dual labour market, marked by relatively low wages, poor employment prospects and employee insecurity. Traditionally, there have been proportionately more males employed in the 'primary' sector of the labour market, comprising relatively secure employment and good career prospects. However, there are signs that the primary market has been hit somewhat during the period of austerity following the 2008 – 2009 recession.

Thirdly, there remains a pattern of gendered horizontal segmentation in employment; that is, patterns of gendered separation into different occupational spheres. There remain marked concentrations of women working in catering, cleaning, selling, education, welfare and health, and men in construction, extractive industries, the armed forces, the police and security services, and science and technology, with the segmentation often supported by gendered occupational cultures. Abbott (Payne ed., 2006, Ch. 3) thus refers to the existence a gendered 'glass wall'. However, there has also been evidence of a thinning of these gendered cultures and some convergence in employment patterns as females have been entering more traditional male preserves, such as the police and armed forces, and, vice versa males entering such occupations as nursing, suggesting that the glass wall is showing signs of breaking down.

Fourthly, despite a growing number of exceptions, evidence remains of significant gender differences in access to the higher occupational levels. Gender therefore remains a substantial element of vertical differentiation within the stratification hierarchy. As a general rule, there is a correlation between the higher levels of pay and status as one ascends occupational hierarchies and a declining proportion of women employed at these levels. Certain occupations in which women have not progressed far, despite evidence of occasional successes, include entry into the upper echelons of the legal profession and the police. Even in those occupations where women are more concentrated, such as in teaching and social work, they are particularly predominant at the lower levels and participate in declining proportions at the higher managerial and professional levels. In occupations in which males are concentrated, women are usually quite a rarity at the higher levels, revealing the limited opportunities that are available as a result of the combined effect of horizontal segmentation and vertical stratification.

Fifthly, given the professed meritocratic culture of the business world, it is worth briefly putting the spotlight on women's progress into its upper echelons. In this area, Cranfield University's School of Management has, from 1998, commissioned research and annual reports on the issue of female representation on the boards of directors of major FTSE companies. General findings of the report for 2019, authored by Vinnicombe et al (20/1/2020), and here focussing on FTSE 100 businesses, showed that female representation had impressively increased from 6.7% to 32.1% between 1998 and 2019. Also, more women were holding multiple directorships and chairing committees.

The 2019 report however provided reservations, particularly regarding access to the more powerful executive director positions. Women occupying these posts comprised only 8.6% of the total in 2015 and this figure had only increased to 10.9% in 2019. Furthermore, the length of tenure in these posts showed marked gender differences. In 2003, females held executive directorships on average for 2.9 years compared to that of 5.2 years for males. Whilst by 2019 females' tenure increased to 3.3 years, the tenure of males showed a greater proportionate increase to 6.6 years. Such figures have suggested that women in these positions may experience a 'glass cliff' and have been related to questions about their symbolic value, box ticking to achieve targets, and corporate culture.

Evidence has also been provided of a significant gender pay gap at board level. For the top ten FTSE businesses regarding the proportion of women on the board, their earnings were on average 15.7% less than that of men, whilst for those who were ranked in the bottom ten, the gap was 22.6%.

Taking a more 'intersectional' approach, black, Asian and minority groups comprised 11% of females on boards of directors in 2019, or 3% of directors overall. Little evidence was provided on women directors' social class background. As an indicator of previous independent education, it was noted that 11% had an Oxbridge education, but no comparison was provided to that of males nor data on women directors from manual working class backgrounds.

Despite the passage of legislation through the British Parliament during the first half of the 1970s with the purpose of to combatting discrimination in the workplace and promoting equal pay, as well as the impact of more recent EU legislation, women are still paid lower hourly rates than men, work shorter hours, are more likely to be in part-time employment, obtain lower pay for equivalent qualifications, and are more likely to be employed in the insecure secondary labour market. Even when comparing the hourly rates of males and females each working full-time, females still only earn about 80% of male levels of pay. Some clarification is required here however. This calculation includes overtime work, which is often paid at a higher rate than work during a flat working week. When paid overtime, partaken more by men, is taken out of the equation, women in Britain in the early twenty first century earn about 90% of male levels of pay. The remaining 10% difference is partly the result of men tending to occupy more senior positions, but experts have not been able to calculate how much of this 10% may still be due to the illegal practice of paying females less than males for carrying out the same type of work.

In 2018, this issue gained renewed prominence by highly publicised cases of pay differences between male and female editors and programme presenters at the BBC and the introduction of the legal requirement that all but relatively small companies must publish data on their gender pay gap.

Clear evidence remains of different aspects of employment inequality between the genders, but there have been significant changes which have narrowed the gap in opportunities between males and females. Recent evidence points in the direction of some convergence in the form of a growing similarity in spread of occupations that men and women are employed in and similar social mobility rates. Moreover, when women take time out of work to have children, they are now more likely to re-enter career streams, whereas more men are faced with career breaks due to redundancy and some are able to avail themselves of paternity leave. The glass ceiling may therefore be starting to break down.

It is important, however, to remember that gender stratification intersects with class, age and ethnic stratification etc. Originating in a criticism of mainstream 1960s and 1970s feminism, 'intersectional feminists' such as Kimberlé Crenshaw, who first used the phrase in 1989, have been keen to point out the white, middle class vantage point adopted by most feminists. She argued that this viewpoint could not necessarily be generalised to the experiences of black women. As well as ethnicity, intersectional feminists have come to argue that age and disability aspects of stratification intersect with gender in ways that cannot be assumed to be an arithmetic aggregate of them all, but will manifest themselves differently in different people.

Measuring gender stratification – a case for individual assignment?

We have seen that sociologists such as Goldthorpe traditionally measured the stratification position of the family unit by deriving it from the occupational position of the presumed male head of the household. Powerful social expectations during the post war decades supporting the housewife role meant that if women did work, their opportunities were restricted, employment was often recognised as temporary and their earnings were seen more as a supplement to the family income. As the husband's commitment to employment, as breadwinner, was usually the greater, it could be argued that his employment position in the occupational structure should be taken as the benchmark for the social class of the family unit. At a time when gender stratification was marked but more accepted, this dimension of stratification tended to be overlooked by sociologists focussing primarily on class stratification deriving from male occupation.

Women have since entered the labour force in far greater numbers and in diverse circumstances. Whilst many rely on a 'component wage' which is hardly sufficient to support themselves independently, more are now self-supporting and independent through employment and others make significant or major contributions to a family income or are the sole supporters of a family. It is therefore often felt to be unrealistic to measure the position of women in the stratification system in terms of the occupation of males assumed to be heads of households. Recognising some validity to these criticisms, use of the Goldthorpe scale now measures a woman's occupation as determining the class of the household if her occupation is the highest.

However, women's progress in the occupational sphere has been mixed. Despite evidence of the liberation of women from domestic patriarchy, there remains evidence, despite advances here also, of significant vertical and horizontal segregation patterns in male and female employment, invariably working to the detriment of the females. Consequently, measuring the social class position of females in terms of the occupation, where it is possible, of a male partner, would hide these differences and the degree of gender based occupational stratification that still exists – a point raised by Abbott and Wallace (1997).

Alternative approaches to the measurement of the social class position of females have been developed which either allocate position in terms of occupation on an individual basis (for example Michelle Stanworth and Arber et al) or, if the household remains the unit of classification, take female employment into account (for example Heath and Britten). However, various complications and difficulties arise. In the case of families or partnerships, if both partners work, they might hold similar level occupations. In such cases, there would appear to be little problem or difference in measuring social class individually or jointly. But there may be a problem of comparability between families. Would it be realistic to accord the same stratification position to a partnership where only one partner works but at the same occupational level as another with both working?

Furthermore, if within a partnership both partners work but hold employment at different occupational levels, is it appropriate to allocate each to a different social class or to refer to the unit as a cross-class unit or to take an average position? Alternatively, is it more viable, as in the revised use of the Goldthorpe scale, to just take the highest occupational position in a partnership, whether that of the male or the female, and read the social class of the partnership off from that designation? As well as being important regarding the issue of gender and social class allocation, answers to such questions also have implications for the measurement of intergenerational social mobility, the findings of which will be skewed by the base point used for comparison between the generations.

Because social class is indexed by occupation, radical feminists are likely to maintain that measuring stratification by occupation, however it is approached, may indicate little more than that class and occupation are also gendered. This does not bring out other aspects which, they argue, make gender stratification primary to and more fundamental than class, in particular the oppression of females by males in a broad range of social relationships and the existence of sexist attitudes, etc.

Differentiating race and ethnicity

The view that the human race can be divided into racially distinct categories defined by physical characteristics, especially skin colour, denoting different biologically inbuilt characteristics and capacities, developed in European thinking as white Europeans colonised different parts of the world. During the nineteenth century, this notion of racial types was commonly linked to evolutionary theory, in which, compared to the dominant white race, other races were regarded as relatively backward. Racial theory gained further prominence and the kudos of science in the early twentieth century with the emergence of the eugenics movement. However, the scientific basis behind the view of innate and fixed racially distinctive characteristics has to a very large extent been subsequently discredited.

In place of race, sociologists apply the term ethnicity to different cultural groups. Ethnicity is explained in terms of environmental as opposed to biological differences. Different ethnic identities are formed through people's socialisation into distinctive cultural traditions, religions, languages, and perceptions of ancestry. Viewing people in terms of their ethnicity avoids misleadingly attributing fixed and inbuilt racial traits to categories of appearance difference and also emphasises cultural distinctions within otherwise crudely designated racial groups, distinguishing for example Irish or Italian whites or Indian or Pakistani 'Asians'. And then, of course, one should be careful not to stereotype people in terms of their ethnic culture either, but to cautiously use the latter as a backdrop to understanding people's outlooks, behaviour and experiences.

However, viewed sociologically, the problem does not finish with the intellectual defeat of the concept of race. A key sociological question is why, despite the discrediting of the assumptions behind racial types, race, racism and ethnic intolerance still constitute a 'common sense' for some people within society? Explanations have varied in their emphasis between cultural and economic factors.

Post war immigration

Although there have been population movements into Britain throughout history, mainly in the form of invasions or as a result of those escaping religious or racial persecution abroad, it was only after the Second World

War that black ethnic minorities were entering the country in significant numbers.

Post war reconstruction created a situation of low unemployment and as some of the white population were experiencing upward mobility, labour shortages existed in areas of unskilled manual employment. Against this backdrop, the British Nationality Act of 1948 offered relatively open access and rights of permanent settlement for citizens of Commonwealth countries and recruitment drives were launched abroad. From the late 1940s to the early 1960s, the main flow of immigration came from the Caribbean. Employment of members of this ethnic group was particularly focussed in relatively poorly paid and unskilled or semi-skilled work in public transport and also in the National Health Service.

By the mid-1960s, more black Africans were entering Britain, as well as immigrants from India and Pakistan. Following this period, Bangladeshi immigration peaked during the early1980s. Again, employment was often taken up at an unskilled or semi-skilled level and Indian, Pakistani and Bangladeshi ethnic groups tended to be concentrated more in the textile work occupations and engineering. Very few ethnic minority workers acquired employment in managerial positions during these decades and so constituted a growing proportion of the working class.

Tensions, both cultural and economic, often arose between the indigenous and immigrant populations. As clearly identifiable groups, immigrant workers brought with them what were perceived by sections of the white British population as alien beliefs and ways of living. They were also often perceived as competing for and taking jobs from the white population. The response of the 'host' population was therefore often unwelcoming and resentment could surface in the form of racism and hostility, as in the case of the first race riots in Notting Hill in 1958.

Traditional models and theories of ethnic stratification

How could the stratification position of recently arrived immigrants be understood sociologically and what would the future hold? Different stratification models, especially with reference to black immigrants, were developed to attempt to explain the dynamics of this situation, two of which have been frequently cited: the immigrant – host model and the white racism model.

The immigrant – host model, also referred to as the assimilation model, was pioneered by the Chicago School sociologist Robert Park to explain the integration of European immigrants into American society in the early decades of the twentieth century (Bottero, 2005, p.93). The model holds many of the characteristics of functionalist theory. It is a position which has tended to find favour with the political right and contains at least the implicit ethnocentric assumption of the superiority of the host culture over that of the immigrants.

This model starts from the position that before the arrival of immigrants, the host society shares a common national identity, culture and consensus of values and that there exists a stable stratification hierarchy. New immigrants are initially perceived as strangers due to their cultural distinctiveness and are likely to be concentrated in occupations toward the bottom of the occupational structure. When the host population experiences an influx of people unfamiliar in their appearance and ways, the response is often one of ignorance, suspicion and hostility which can take the form of racism. At this stage, contact can lead to conflict and animosities are likely to have a destabilising effect on society. However, Park argues that in time, an accommodating truce will emerge as a prelude to the full assimilation of migrants into – ie adjustment toward and integration into - the culture of the host society. Consequently, hostility, racism and discrimination decline as the culture of minorities melts into that of the dominant culture. This cultural homogeneity forms the basis for a new social stability in which the once disadvantaged minorities who faced racism and discrimination become integrated across the social structure and can take up their social and occupational position more on merit.

In Britain, Sheila Patterson applied the assimilation model to the study of first generation post war West Indian immigrant minorities. Although they shared class disadvantage with some of the white population, due to their cultural distinctiveness and perceived threat in the form of competition for jobs, they often experienced hostility in the form of racism and discrimination which separated them from whites. For this first generation, Patterson found that conflict was giving way to accommodation but that the stage of assimilation had not been reached. According to this model, only resistance to full assimilation on the part of ethnic minorities through the retention of their cultural traditions and separateness would continue to make them subject to racial discrimination and stratification. In this event, there is a clear issue of blame; the problem is seen to be largely of their own making.

This model suggests that racist hostility and racial discrimination are likely to be a relatively short term malady and temporary deviation from a normal state of social consensus. However, given evidence of persisting levels of separation and disadvantage experienced by black ethnic minorities compared to that of white minorities, it does not seem to have had good predictive value.

An alternative interpretation of the dynamics involved is that it is the persistence of racism (values) and racial discrimination (action) from the white population which keeps black ethnic minorities separate from white society in a largely disadvantaged position toward the foot of society. If we are to attribute blame, then we are to look here instead.

This analysis is sometimes taken in the direction of a Marxist critique of capitalism which analyses ethnic stratification as class and economic based in its origin. Ethnic stratification, racism and discrimination, however major an experience, are analysed as a bi-product of economic class stratification. Ethnic and racial subordination are status distinctions which can introduce animosities and cleavages within social classes. In this respect, working class racism against working class ethnic minorities is regarded as a form of false consciousness which is divisive in its effects. Like sexism, it divides and weakens a common economic class. From this perspective, ethnic minorities often provide (as do women) a cheap and competitive supply of labour. Sections of the white working class are therefore vulnerable to media generated hostility toward immigrants who are scapegoated as the cause of their insecurity through competing for their jobs as cheaper labour and threatening their way of life. The policies of far right political parties can hold some appeal within these sections of the population.

From a Marxist position, although many ethnic minority people are through their employment position part of a broad working class, it is the false consciousness of white racism which excludes them from the white working class and helps to keep them at the base of society. From the vantage point of this theory, because racism and racial discrimination are viewed as a consequence of the class structure under capitalism, it is endemic and there is little room for optimism in effective assimilation of ethnic minorities under capitalism.

A more Weberian approach to understanding the stratification position of many ethnic minorities has been adopted by Rex and Tomlinson. This position is distinguished from the Marxist model in that ethnic disadvantage is not just regarded as a bi-product of class stratification, but, in the struggle that different groups have for access to resources, ethnic minorities are seen as often experiencing multiple disadvantages compared to whites. Occupationally, they are more likely to be concentrated in the secondary labour market of less skilled, more casualised and less secure employment than the white male population. They are often also concentrated in deprived inner city areas where co-existence alongside the white working class can lead to fractious relationships. They suffer lower social status due to racist discrimination and resentment and are likely to search for status within their own groups, thus enhancing their social and political marginality. Through a combination of class, status and power disadvantage, it can be argued that a significant proportion of ethnic minorities, along with other minorities, take their own distinctive position at the base of society.

The concept of an 'underclass' came to prominence during the 1980s against the political backdrop of neoliberal thinking in the United States and new right politics in Britain. In America, Charles Murray applied the term particularly to inner city black ghetto areas where it was argued that moral, cultural and intellectual deficiency were associated with high levels of dependency, criminality and lack of aspiration. Arguing that an aspirational and meritocratic society essentially existed, the focus of attention on the problem could be shifted from the effects of discrimination. Instead, it was argued that more generous welfare intervention that had been intended to alleviate poverty had encouraged the formation of an underclass by enabling people to live in irresponsible dependency combined with other unofficial sources of income. For Murray, the key to tackling underclass lifestyle was in fact to reduce welfare support. As a result, some would be liberated from a life of dependency and illegality to that of aspiration and self-support for their own and society's benefit, whilst others should be allowed to rightfully fail.

Although with less specific focus on ethnicity, a similar line was taken in Britain by new right thinkers such as Peter Saunders, who again argued that a broadly meritocratic social structure existed but that some sections of the population wanted nothing of it. Comprising disproportionately high numbers of Afro-Caribbean ethnic minorities and an increasing number of 'single' parents, these groups were characterised by negative and fatalistic values associated with a culture of poverty and the lack of a desire to assimilate into mainstream society. This underclass was analysed in status terms as inferior as they did not adopt the aspirational values of the majority and would be looked down upon as a drain on the wealth created by others.

Of course, one could argue that such groups can find themselves excluded from mainstream society, in part at least, through stigmatisation from those who view them in underclass terms and by anti-meritocratic discriminatory practices. Moreover, it tended to be supporters of the free market policies (the new right in Britain and neoliberals in the United States) which enhanced economic polarisation in these countries who were keen to blame the victims for their supposed deficiencies.

Ethnicity and occupational profile – diversity remains

From the early 1960s, and particularly with economic slowdown during the 1970s and the recession of the early 1980s, legislation was passed in Britain which effectively placed increasing restriction on non-white immigration. These restrictions were followed by a tightening of asylum regulation as more people wanting to enter the country, including economic migrants, were pursuing this alternative channel. With a stemming of immigration, a growing proportion of the black and Asian ethnic minority groups comprise second generation British citizens with some third generation.

Evidence on the occupational profiles of ethnic minority groups compared to the white British population and with each other provides an important gauge of their stratification position. Compared to their predecessors, what is the more contemporary pattern of ethnic minority participation in the occupational structure? Valuable information has been provided by the Labour Force Surveys.

The term 'employment rate' refers to the proportion of people in employment as a percentage of the total working age population. This rate can then be used to compare the employment rates for different ethnic minority groups to that of the entire working age population or to the white British population. The resulting measure of difference is referred to as the 'ethnic employment rate gap'. Data for 2016 has shown that whilst the employment rate in Britain as a whole was 74% (from 73% in 2004) and for white British and white other categories 75% and 80% respectively, the Pakistani and Bangladeshi ethnic group indicated the lowest participation rate at 54% (from 44% in 2004), with non-white ethnic groups as a whole showing a participation rate rising to 64%.

For those in employment, figures have shown that when ethnic minorities are taken together, differences in the occupational profile compared to that of the white British are very small. The same applies regarding aggregate gender figures. However, when the information for individual ethnic groups is studied, the picture is a very complex one of distinctive profiles which can only be touched on here.

For males, evidence of concentration in general occupational sectors has indicated some continuity with past patterns of employment. For example, Pakistanis have remained highly represented in manufacturing, Bangladeshis and Chinese in hotel and catering, Afro Caribbeans in transport and communications and Indians in transport and communications and manufacturing.

However, in terms of occupational level, Chinese and Indian males have entered professional, managerial and technical occupations in larger proportions than whites but the proportion of Bangladeshis employed at these levels has remained substantially lower than that of whites. In the largely manual, partly skilled and unskilled occupations, Indians are represented in about the same proportion as whites but the percentages for Bangladeshis and black Caribbean groups remain substantially higher. These profiles bear some relationship to the relative levels of educational achievement between ethnic minority groups, although recent substantial improvements in the educational performance of Bangladeshis would suggest the possibility of filtration through to higher occupational achievement.

Gender employment rate gaps can be related ethnic groups. Labour Force Survey figures for 2016 have shown that for Britain as a whole, 69% of women and 79% of men were in employment. Under the rather unsatisfactory classification of 'black', women's labour force participation has been relatively high amongst ethnic minority groups at 64% and the gender rate gap relatively low with 71% of men in employment. Whilst relatively high proportions of Pakistani and Bangladeshi women are employed in partly skilled and unskilled occupations, Bangladeshi women have the lowest rate of participation in employment outside the family. This reflects traditional family life and the values of Islamic culture and is a reminder that the study of stratification should also look at different patterns of family life and the distribution of power and resources within families. It also alerts us to be aware of the effect of cultural barriers as well as discrimination in gendered employment opportunities. Thus, employment participation rates for Asian Pakistani and Bangladeshi women at 35% showed the largest gender gap with the participation rate for men standing at 72%, figures which provide a fascinating comparison with the Asian Indian respective rates of 64% and 81%.

For females, compared to whites, the figures indicate that significantly larger proportions of Chinese are employed in professional, managerial and technical occupations, but that smaller proportions of Pakistanis and Bangladeshis are employed in these groups. A smaller share of Chinese than white women work in the partly skilled and unskilled occupations, whereas a substantially higher proportion of black African women are employed at this level.

In partly skilled and unskilled occupations, figures for female participation rates are consistently higher than for males with the exception of black Caribbean workers that show slightly higher proportions of males than females employed in these categories. A fuller understanding would necessitate more detail on the actual occupations that males and females worked in.

Across the range of ethnic groups as a whole, women tend to hold lower occupational positions than men. The biggest gender difference in professional, managerial and technical occupations is amongst Indians. However, some groups provide exceptions. For example, there are higher proportions of women than men from black Caribbean, other black and black mixed groups working in these occupational categories.

Overall, a degree of gendered occupational stratification is evident across white and a range of ethnic minority groups. Moreover, evidence suggests that ethnic minority females are generally less differentiated in terms of income and occupational level from white females than is the case in comparing ethnic minority and white males. For some feminists, despite variations between the ethnic groups, this is taken as evidence of the overriding significance of gender stratification. As women are generally more concentrated toward the lower end of the occupational structure than men, there is less room for occupational and income differentiation between females in the different ethnic groups.

On a positive note, the occupational restructuring accompanying economic modernisation from the 1980s drew in ethnic minorities in such a way as to narrow the occupational profile differences between themselves and white British workers. Overall, their distribution across the occupational structure showed signs of convergence with that of white workers, loosely suggesting that a degree of assimilation based improved opportunity has occurred. However, there remain greater differences between specific ethnic minority groups than between ethnic minorities as a whole and the white population in terms of both stratification level and differentiation into different types of occupation.

In terms of comparative intergenerational occupational improvement levels, the general evidence of ethnic minority achievement compared to that of the white British population appears to be positive but again in detail remains mixed. That is, from relatively disadvantaged positions, second generation ethnic minorities have tended to improve their occupational position more than that of British whites (Dustmann et al, 30/8/2018).

However, there are reasons to remain cautious in interpreting the data.

Firstly, figures of occupational distribution within general category levels only reveal part of the picture. For example, evidence of more ethnic minority men now employed at the professional, managerial and technical level tends to hide the fact that relatively high proportions of minorities work in more precarious positions of self-employment.

Secondly, disparity of earnings and expenditure still exist between the different ethnic groups and the white population. For example, Bangladeshis, the later arriving of the ethnic groups, comprise the most economically disadvantaged, with poverty reflecting both lower rates of employment and occupational and wage level.

Thirdly, research conducted by Dustmann et al showed that in 2009, compared to British born whites, British born ethnic minorities earned on average 4.8% more, with the figure for ethnic minority males at -2.7% and for females at +13.3%. However, these figures alone were found to be misleading. This was because, firstly, ethnic minorities tended to be between four and five times more highly concentrated in London where wage levels and costs of living are relatively high, and secondly, the educational performance of ethnic minorities has overall improved more rapidly compared to whites when measured in terms of their comparative improvement over the course of their education or their improvement compared to previous generations. Indians and Chinese tended to outperform whites, and Bangladeshis, once amongst the most educationally disadvantaged, have rapidly improved their performance. Dustmann et al concluded that when controlling for educational performance and regional allocation, British born white and ethnic minority females earned about the same but that the wages for ethnic minority males were approximately 16% lower than for white males.

Fourthly, account should also be taken of hours worked, conditions of employment and treatment in the workplace, job insecurity and risk of unemployment, on all of which there is some evidence of ethnic disadvantage. For example, ethnic minorities have traditionally been concentrated in less secure employment. Thus, during the recession of the 1980s which hit manufacturing very hard, Pakistanis, Bangladeshis and Afro Caribbeans became unemployed at about twice the rate of whites. When employment picked up, it was also at a quicker rate for these groups than for white workers. This pattern of effect on ethnic minorities has been referred to as 'hyper-cyclical'. Nevertheless, evidence suggests that male black ethnic minorities still experience about double the rate of unemployment to that of British whites.

Racial discrimination – grounds for optimism?

What evidence is available on racial discrimination practiced by employers and to what extent is the situation changing? To measure behaviour in such an emotive and sensitive area, the use of covert (concealed) methods may be necessary. Such an approach was adopted in research conducted by D.J. Smith and published in 1977. In this research, applications were submitted from applicants of white and ethnic minority background with matched work histories and qualifications for a range of blue collar and white collar jobs, with names making ethnic differences evident. Employers' responses to blue collar applicants indicated a tenfold preference of whites to blacks, and in the case of applicants for white collar jobs, those with names indicating Asian or West Indian background were 30% less likely to be even offered an interview than white applicants.

To what extent are ethnic minorities still disadvantaged by racial discrimination? In small scale covert research employing hidden recording devices, journalists in a BBC documentary (Black and White) visited the Bristol area in an attempt to measure racial discrimination, especially by employers and landlords. Taped and filmed evidence of racial discrimination was evident in this area. When the journalists followed up advertisements for jobs and accommodation, that which was unavailable when the black applicant turned up sometimes became available when the white applicant appeared later.

Another approach to the question of racial discrimination has been to conduct self-report surveys. National surveys conducted by the Policy Studies Institute have asked ethnic minorities about their experiences of racial discrimination. There was evidence here of differences between ethnic groups in their perception of being victims of racial discrimination. Measurements taken in the 1980s and 1990s revealed a consistent pattern that about 25% of West Indians perceived that racial discrimination had led to them being refused a job. The figures for Asians were substantially lower. Of course, the problem with such research is that the findings are based on subjective judgements and can be difficult to interpret. Whilst complacency should be avoided, it is at least an ironic possibility that the high figures of perceived discrimination may be partly the product of more enlightened times in which a greater sensitivity to being the victims of discrimination is felt.

New anxieties

More recently, issues of ethnicity have again returned to the theme of immigration. New concerns and hostilities have been raised in the media regarding suspected bogus asylum seekers who are in fact economic migrants, and levels of illegal immigration. Furthermore, as the European Union expanded eastwards to include countries such as Poland, Czechoslovakia and Hungary in 2004 and Bulgaria and Romania in 2007, a shortage of skills in the building and construction trade in particular, but also the attraction of vacancies for unskilled labour in areas such as agriculture, has attracted workers from these countries, especially Poland, to Britain.

Compared to patterns of previous Commonwealth migration, these migrants are more likely to be in Britain temporarily, referred to as 'pendulum migrants' who work to return home with savings. Nonetheless, as documented in the 2008 BBC 2 series 'White Season', the concentration of these workers in such towns as Peterborough has often been accompanied by hostility from locals. Within this cultural climate, the use of cheap overseas labour even sparked a rash of wildcat strikes in power stations and oil refineries in January and February of 2009 when an oil company owned by the French company Total employed, through an Italian firm, Italian and Portuguese workers to carry out maintenance work.

Subsequently, immigration had become such a focal political issue that it was a major factor in the 2016 referendum result for the UK to exit the European Union.

Contemporary sociological thinking on social stratification

The decline of social class?

Social class has previously been defined as primarily based on economic differences. Class stratification therefore to a large extent reflects the distribution of wealth and income in society. In a class stratified society, stratification primarily takes the form of different occupationally grouped strata within each of which people experience similar levels of income, as well as life chances and experiences and a degree of consciousness or subjective awareness of their distinctiveness from people in other social classes.

Social stratification by economic class was a well-established feature of modern societies and a predominant theme in the sociological tradition. Class societies, offering prospects of social mobility but also imposing barriers to it, represent a position in stratification terms somewhere in between the extremes of highly closed and highly open social hierarchies. However, much sociological debate has emerged over the continuing prevalence of social class in the way that contemporary societies are stratified. Doubts over the salience of class stratification have taken various forms. From the late 1960s, both gender and ethnic stratification have gained greater attention and sociologists have come to realise the complex and sometimes unpredictable ways in which class and gender and ethnic status interact.

Moreover, a pattern of evidence suggesting the declining significance of social class has been emerging. For example, we have seen that Dahrendorf argued that social classes were decomposing or breaking up and Crewe has indicated the declining importance of social class as an influence on voting behaviour.

The growing importance of social status?

Social status has been defined in terms of values and judgements regarding ways of life that people aspire to and the acquisition of possessions of symbolic status significance, all of which accord individuals and groups levels of social prestige. Although we have seen that occupations themselves can be viewed in status terms, the link between social status and economics may relate more to what people do with their money than the occupation by which they have earned it. How people attribute symbols of status to the objects of possession and how owners of these objects derive status from them can be evident by the experience of changes in treatment on the road by other drivers that a person may experience with a significant change in the status type of car driven! Some sociologists, particularly amongst postmodernists and high modernists, argue that, in affluent consumer societies, social status is replacing social class as the predominant form of social stratification. From a broad historical perspective, the social structures of contemporary societies are seen to be relatively open. The objects and lifestyles of status aspiration can change rapidly with fashion, thus giving status a high potential fluidity. In such a more open society, people are likely to feel free to aspire to status symbols of success and reinvent their lifestyles and self-image rather than being resigned to accepting their inherited occupational class position or the traditional status ascriptions associated with gender or ethnicity. The importance of status awareness in a more open social structure may mean that it is eclipsing that which class consciousness played in a more heavily class stratified society. In relatively open status societies, people tend to compare themselves to others and base their sense of self-worth on the signs of status achievement that they can project. Thus, from a once more class based community in a more uniform local authority housing estate, one can sometimes witness the personalisation of homes that have been privately acquired as a statement of individuality and status. More generally, this heightened status awareness and comparison with others can lead to new psychological anxieties associated with what Alain de Botton has referred to as 'status anxiety'.

Postmodernism – the demise of social class

Postmodernist writers tend to adopt the farthest position in claiming demise of social class. Their broad view of history distinguishes three phases: traditional, modern and postmodern. In traditional or pre-industrial society, a person's possessions, rights and appropriate behaviour were heavily prescribed by their inherited position in the stratification system. Indeed, attempting to take on the ways of those higher in the social structure risked the charge of 'personation' – the non-legitimate copying of social 'betters'. As the old structure broke down and modern industrial societies emerged, enhanced occupational mobility opportunities led to competition for objects as confirmation of new status by new moneyed classes. The social structure nevertheless remained heavily stratified, now by new class relations, as strongly emphasised in the works of Marx.

Now, postmodernists claim, a new type of society has emerged in which, in contrast to traditional and modern societies, heavy structural constraints on people's lives have broken down. Through the capacity of advanced societies to generate growing affluence, objects have become less desired in terms of subsistence need or purely functional use and more in terms of the status image of their owner that they convey. In the conquest of necessity, it is not economic relationships within the system of production which determines people's position in a social structure, but the freedom of acquisition of possessions as status symbols which enables the individual to have much greater control over the construction of their social identity. Image related to consumption increasingly governs perceived social status and liberates individuals from the constraints of old class stratification systems. People are viewed much less in terms of what they do and much more in terms of their lifestyle image. It is therefore the symbols associated with products and lifestyles that are desired by consumers and changing fashions fuel insatiable desire. The old class structure of the modern period becomes replaced by a more free-floating, superficial and ephemeral world of fashions in relation to which individuals have a high degree of freedom available for 'self-assembly'.

Postmodernists tend to emphasise the positive aspect of these apparent changes. Such a position is adopted by Pakulski and Waters who argue that in postmodern society the structuring effect of and concern with social class has collapsed. This is because the productive capacity of a contemporary society of abundance has made the old social class battles driven by economic necessity redundant. The achievement of economic security has led to a society preoccupied with the acquisition of products and the leading of lifestyles more for the images that they convey in a highly consumerist and media saturated world. Economic security enables people to choose products and lifestyles more freely and independently of occupation. As a result, social status becomes increasingly decoupled from social class, and even for people with similar income levels, status based on lifestyle choice – cultural differences – distinguish them as they freely shape their lifestyles. In postmodern society, stratification boundaries rooted in social class have collapsed as abundance has enabled symbolic meaning to become independent from and ascendant over past economic constraints. Indeed, it is increasingly possible for those living on modest incomes to aspire to higher status than others better off by adopting prestigious lifestyle choices, especially with the easy availability of credit.

The values, lifestyles and fashions associated with social status are ever changing. Furthermore, individuals are much freer to change their personal lifestyle choices than they would have been to change their social class. Social stratification therefore enters a new level of fluidity in which, in contrast to old homogeneous class structures and gender and ethnic status stratification, status becomes more individualised as individuals partake in a variety of status groups. For Pakulski and Waters, social stratification in the postmodern world is a pick and mix 'status bazaar'.

The implications of this position are profound for stratification analysis. It would mean that society can no longer be understood in terms of socially structured economic inequality which once provided constraints that shaped identity and behaviour and enabled society to be amenable to causal analysis. Toward the advanced stage of the modern period, the social structure and its analysis was complicated by class decomposition. Further, the mutually cross cutting effects of class, status, gender and ethnicity with the unpredictability of their effect on individuals was recognised by intersectional theorists. At the postmodern phase, even this complex structure gives way to social fluidity. Culture and image increasingly prevail and because of the highly fluid form that they take and the enhanced capacity of individuals to create and recreate their own identity, society is seen as no longer amenable to causal analysis. Postmodern society therefore renders the possibility of social scientific understanding redundant and with it social policy intervention to tackle economic inequality futile. And one could add that this fatalistic outlook provided a convenient accompaniment to the neoliberal reforms which, from the 1980s, had a polarising effect on the distribution of wealth and income.

Furlong et al (2006) have however challenged the view that that structural analysis is no longer viable. They argue that the process of individualisation provides an appearance of fluidity which renders structural influences, that are still subtly operative, more difficult to detect than was the case in a society where clear stratification divides were visible with regard to educational and employment profiles.

Based on a nine year longitudinal study of over 1,000 youngsters living in the west of Scotland, the authors have identified patterns in the life profiles of groups of youngsters. They distinguish between 'linear' and 'non-linear' routes from school into education or work. Linear paths are those that lead in a clear direction, whereas non-linear routes wander and change direction. Past routes of youngsters from different social class backgrounds tended to be quite different but each relatively linear. By contrast, contemporary pathways show more non-linear profiles. Postmodernists would tend to interpret this as evidence of greater social fluidity and enhanced individual choice biographies. However, Furlong et al found that these non-linear pathway profiles provide less advantaged progress into careers and are more characteristic of those from more disadvantaged social and educational backgrounds. By contrast, linear routes, more characteristic of those from more privileged backgrounds, provide greater career opportunities. It is therefore concluded that despite seeming to indicate enhanced individual choice, non-linear routes provide evidence of socially structured disadvantage. Rather than viewing these important years in the lives of youngsters in terms of fluidity and choice, it is argued that the concept of 'structured individualism' is a more appropriate concept for interpreting the evidence.

High modernism / late modernism – the individualisation of risk

Although the analysis of high modernists often highlights similar features of contemporary society to that of postmodernists from whose analysis it is sometimes difficult to distinguish, for high or late modernists, the new phase that advanced societies have entered represents the high point of the modern era rather than an entirely new era of a postmodern society. In claiming this, they challenge the postmodernist view that scientific understanding of contemporary society is impossible. Instead, they argue that the theory and concepts of classical sociology are becoming unfit for purpose in a rapidly changing world which is feeling as if it is out of control. To regain a grip on understanding society as the basis for enlightened intervention, sociology requires a new toolkit of theories and concepts that are relevant to the contemporary age.

In the works of writers such as Anthony Giddens and Ulrich Beck, the hallmark of high modern or late modern societies respectively is the emergence of new types and levels of risk. In modern society, the need to create wealth and conquer poverty were the key aims of science and technology. For Beck, in this context the unequal distribution of limited resources and risks in life prioritised social class in people's experience. By contrast, late modern society is characterised by the fact that material need has been largely met. Despite the fact that inequalities of class societies remain, new risks, which are the consequences of development, have emerged. These risks include nuclear hazards, environmental damage and possible global economic meltdown. The geographically widespread nature of such risks means that people right across societies are vulnerable to their effects, against which wealth can only offer limited protection. Exposure to risk therefore becomes more equalised. As they operate across and tend to dissolve both class and national boundaries, the way that risks are experienced becomes more individualised. For example, in the face of rapid technological change, people need to prepare for frequent retraining and career change. Innovation and the risk of unemployment no longer hit manual workers hardest but tend to spread their impact more equally across the lives of service sector workers in an increasingly service sector type society. In such a risk society, individuals are left equally free of career structures and class constraints to navigate their own way reflexively (always having to reflect and weigh up options and adapt) through life.

For Beck, class analysis is of very little relevance in understanding this new reality. Continuing to use such concepts equates to the application of 'zombie categories' which have remained more alive in sociology than are useful in the study of a changed social world.

Zygmunt Bauman refers to the transition from solid modernity to liquid modernity. The phase of solid modernity was one in which occupation and production provided a structured sense of security in a class stratified society. This stage of modernity has given way to a consumerist society in which, through security of productive output, status is achieved through freedom of consumption. This status freedom places new burdens on individuals to constantly weave their own status patterns without workable traditional recipes to fall back on.

Bottero (2005, pp.246-247) has criticised of both postmodernist and high modernist positions with regard to the issue of the demise of social class. It is argued that individual freedom (for good or ill) to adopt a chosen lifestyle or construct a status image is not distributed equally to people across all levels of economic income. Indeed, it is suggested that writers from these perspectives emphasise lifestyle choice from the position of the middle classes which gives them more choice because of their class position – thus substantiating the view that social class remains an important feature of society.

Globalisation and liquid modernity – the polarisation of mobility, the domination of capital and the detachment of the individual

Theorists disagree on the impact of globalisation on social stratification. The most optimistic position is adopted in the neoliberal approach of Ohmae who sees in globalisation evidence of movement toward a borderless global economy. For Ohmae, this is a world of mobile capital and free enterprise capitalism. Governments most go with the grain of change and work to promote such open global economies by which in the long run all will benefit as consumers in their choice of goods and services available.

Not all writers on globalisation are so optimistic or likely to downplay the importance of social divisions. For Zygmunt Bauman, despite his analysis of the burden of status freedom, globalisation accentuates differences in mobility chances which fall along class lines. This has led to increased social polarisation which works to the detriment of workers.

In modern societies (as explained in Marxist theory), in social and work hierarchies, employers and workers had relatively fixed positions and relationships. Social class and industrial relations included direct conflict and settlement, with both sides locked into mutual dependence. At this 'solid modernity' stage, the potential for disruption by organised workers introduced the threat of uncertainty which business managers and owners had to take account of.

Bauman argues that in contemporary conditions of global capitalism, wealth has polarised and has been accompanied by a polarisation of mobility chances. Given the greatly enhanced mobility of capital and information made possible through the cyberspace of contemporary global technology, 'liquid modernity' has enhanced the threat of disengagement of capital from local rooting and has become an uncertainty to workers who remain relatively geographically rooted. For Bauman, mobility, wealth and power polarisation now fundamentally disadvantages workers and 'frees' them from the possibility of effective collective response to the interests of capital due to the constant threat of the withdrawal of employment opportunities which highly mobile capital presents (Gane, 2004, pp.25-27).

In liquid modern societies, individuals thus become detached from effective collective action and forced into a freedom of taking responsibility for their self-determination in situations of transience and uncertainty. This environment leads to increasing social polarisation as geographically mobile global elites become disengaged from the masses who, dependent on providing their labour for income, are relatively tied to their localities and left to struggle with this new 'freedom'.

Postmodernism celebrated the emergence of positive individual freedom to choose identity and transcend class ties. For Bauman, given the economic inequalities of liquid modern societies, only elites really have this privilege. The freedom that workers now find themselves placed in is not the positive freedom of the old entrepreneurial middle class. For many, the experience is primarily of the negative aspect of freedom – the freedom of being cut adrift, like it or not, from the confines of a secure class structure. We therefore need to address the issue of not just liberation from, but raise the question of liberation to. Individualisation in the contemporary context means de-identification and the perpetual burden of uncertainty and striving for identity (for many of the poor throughout the world, not even this negative freedom is available). This leads to new conflicts in the form of 'recognition wars' in which people attempt to impose both their own identity and force identities onto others. A key resource here is use of PRs, spin doctors and access to the mass media. Furthermore, growing insecurity can lead people to the search for culprits and populist government responses in the form of toughness on crime and immigration.

Chapter 8
Sociology of Education

Abstract

This chapter begins by alerting the reader to the fact that a sociological approach to education cannot be based on generalising from one's personal educational experiences. Some key concepts relevant to the sociology of education are then explained. To transcend the personal view, various theoretical perspectives are introduced – functionalist, Marxist, Weberian and interactionist, and at the end of the chapter postmodernist and high modernist – to offer a range of explanations of the relationship between education and broader society.

At a more empirical (evidential or factual) level, social, historical and political factors are reviewed to help provide a contextual understanding of the influences behind educational developments in England. This historical dimension is then carried forward into a review of post war educational policy.

Issues of genetic inheritance versus social environment regarding intelligence and educational achievement are raised. These issues are firstly related to social class where the perennial issue of different levels of educational achievement associated with social class background is introduced. The validity of explanations in terms of inherited differences in intelligence levels related to social classes is strongly contested and a number of established sociological explanations which identify a range of environmental influences are provided.

Similarly, in the case of gender, the viewpoint of different intellectual capacities, here based on biological sex differences, to explain different achievement rates between the genders, is challenged from an environmental viewpoint. In distinction to biological sex differences, it is emphasised that gender identity and opportunity are a product of the social environment. Changes in this environment are touched on regarding women's liberation. Later, evidence is provided which shows a remarkable advance in the educational performance of females.

Next, regarding ethnicity, geneticist arguments regarding the educational performance levels of different 'races' based on supposed inherited intelligence differences are strongly countered. The scientific validity of the concept of race to explain evidence of different levels of academic achievement is shown to be discredited. Instead, the environmental concept of the influence of different ethnic cultures is utilised. The reality of prejudice based on racist beliefs and the stereotyping of different ethnic groups is also part of an environment of influences on performance. As in the case with gender, evidence is provided that the educational performance of different ethnic minority groups has been rapidly improving alongside social change, thus contesting the view of different fixed intellectual capacities being innate to different races.

Developments in education policy are sketched to explain a change from a post war political consensus on the social democratic model and the social engineering of education to promote a more just society. It is shown that this change takes the general form of a greater emphasis on a market driven approach which has been followed by governments of the Conservative new right, New Labour and the Conservative led coalition and the Conservative government. Education policy is then put in the broader context of a global neoliberal turn.

Statistics on educational achievement and the associated issues of educational standards and the worth of qualifications are presented and discussed with reference to 'grade inflation' 'grade deflation' and 'credential inflation'.

As an exercise in applying the sociological imagination, the concept of meritocracy in society and education is explained. The reader is guided through some of the issues by which one may arrive at assessments of the degree to which the English education system is meritocratic.

The question of the complexity of our educational system and the issue of diversity and choice are finally related to theories of postmodernism and high modernism.

The sociological challenge

The British educational 'system' is complex and diverse. Patterns of provision vary from one locality or region to another and there are national differences in provision between England and Scotland. This issue of complexity and choice can be understood within the historical context of political and social policy changes and will be reviewed later.

The challenge that first needs to be addressed is to recognise that our attitudes toward education generally, and different types of school and the process of selection in particular, are likely to reflect our own educational experiences. These experiences and attitudes may run deep. Do we have a liking or disliking for grammar schools? Do we sympathise with or condemn the aims non-selective education? Do we feel that faith schools are superior for promoting moral discipline or do they divide youngsters and communities? Do we admire the apparent excellence of independent education or do we view it in terms of providing unfair advantage for a fortunate minority? Whatever they are, our personal judgements and their implications in terms of our broader view of educational provision are likely to be influenced by our personal experiences. This may make it difficult to engage in impartial analysis of the educational system. Yet, as sociologists, we must be vigilant against the bias of our own experiences. How can we attempt to achieve this?

We need to raise our awareness of potential bias by stepping back and examining our own experiences and attitudes. By so doing, we can become better prepared to study and evaluate sociological theories, explanations and evidence regarding education in a more open minded way. Theories offer frameworks to make sense of educational processes and classroom experiences as well as encouraging us to look at educational systems within social, political and even global contexts. We can apply sociological concepts systematically and analyse to what conclusions they take us. We can also review research findings. As a result, our own views on education may be refined or even fundamentally changed. We should not fear this possibility, but recognise it as the reward of engaging in sociological thinking.

It would also be wise to step back and consider what the aims of education are, could be or should be. For example, to what extent should education tend to prioritise the acquisition of employment related skills or focus more on learning for its own sake or for personal growth and development. Furthermore, to what extent should, or could, education have a role to play in shaping a fair and just society? What would this be and how could it best be achieved? How can educational resources be best allocated and to what extent should private enterprise become involved? These may at present be more questions of personal value, but will be touched on or addressed sociologically throughout the chapter.

Definition of main concepts

There has been much debate over the decades regarding the criteria for pupil entry to schools and school internal organisation. The term **selective education** is normally applied to schools whose intake is based on measured academic ability. This approach was most universally used within the English state system in the post war era when children in a majority of local authorities were allocated to a type of secondary school at the age of 11 based on their performance in standardised tests. Academic selection can also be on an institution by institution basis, as was the case with a number of grant maintained schools that were introduced from the 1980s. However, selection can also take other forms. For example, some schools select in terms of gender, perhaps along with ability as in the case of a number of grammar schools. For others religious belief is a factor and some select by parental ability to pay and others by a mixture of ability to pay and academic selection.

Non-selective education advanced with the comprehensivisation of secondary education in England from the 1960s. The purpose of state comprehensives was to educate pupils of all abilities from within entire catchment areas within a single institution. In tune with the comprehensive ethos was the teaching of **mixed ability** classes. However, most comprehensives **streamed** classes according to ability. This meant that pupils were placed in classes of tiered academic levels which they remained in together for all subjects taught. A more finely tuned form of academic ability separation takes the form of **subject setting**. Where this is used, pupils are placed in different level classes on a subject by subject basis, although this approach is usually applied only to a limited range of subjects. **Banding** is an approach that has been used to try and structure a balanced intake across the ability range within a school and between schools.

Viewed formally, education is often seen in terms of achievement levels, evidence of which is provided in the form of official statistics of performance at key stages and the acquisition of qualifications. A preoccupation with acquiring formally recognised qualifications can be related to **credentialism** – an increasing tendency for the requirement of certificated qualifications as a prerequisite for entry to a broader range of occupations. This process is in part associated with the transition to a high tech economy and a largely white collar workforce.

But how are we able to judge the standard of qualifications, especially if it is suspected that they change over time? One concern about the standard of academic qualifications is expressed in the suspicion that **grade inflation** has taken place. This is the belief that continuously improving evidence of educational performance, as for example shown in grade achievements in GCSEs and at A Level between the 1980s and early twenty first century, are illusory in the sense that they are the result of a softening of standards. More recently, governments that have been persuaded by this argument have attempted to put in place measures that toughen up qualifications and better distinguish levels of achievement, especially at the top end. They have attempted to counter grade inflation with **grade deflation**.

Although the employment market now calls for greater certification, the expansion of education and acquisition of qualifications, especially at higher education level, has led to a flooding of the job market with highly qualified people in search of work. **Credential inflation** can be a consequence of this situation whereby the market power of qualifications declines because the number of qualified applicants runs substantially ahead of the supply of jobs for which applicants are competing. The outcome of credential inflation is a tendency for people to need to acquire ever higher qualifications compared to their predecessors just to stand still in the job market.

Marketisation refers to a process whereby public sector organisations are reorganised so as to mimic the competitive market of the private enterprise sector. This process has been particularly apparent in educational reforms in Britain which were under way from the 1980s. These reforms introduced a greater variety of school types and public access to educational performance data with the intention of enhancing competition between schools and opening up consumer choice as a means to driving up standards.

One way to look at education sociologically, and which will provide a link to the first theory of education in this chapter (functionalism) is to identify a number of **functions** that education performs. The concept 'functions of education' refers to ways in which education works to provide various benefits for society, or is functional for society. For functionalists, these functions tend to be viewed as universal requirements – in one form or another they are necessary for the well-being of all social systems.

Through the **economic function**, education imparts appropriate work related skills and knowledge and also behavioural guidelines and values which enable individuals to perform effectively in employment situations and support themselves and their families. An emphasis on this function would incline educational provision in the direction of apprenticeship, vocational and professional type training. The prosperity of businesses, economic productivity and ultimately social prosperity are dependent on the effective operation of this function with education viewed in terms of resources invested related to improved economic output.

The processes through which the system selects people for different types and levels of education are referred to as the **selective function**. This function is closely connected to the economic function since selection in education feeds through to different employment roles and positions in the occupational and social structure. If in the education system pupils are selected through competition to achieve and progress academically entirely in terms of their own abilities and effort, sociologists refer to the existence of opportunities for **contest mobility.** In a society of such educational opportunity, functionalists emphasise that the education system would synchronise with and service an open occupational and social structure in which the allocation of all people to positions is based on individual merit. Such a society is referred to as a **meritocracy**.

Education is also an important vehicle for the **transmission of culture**. Culture used in this sense refers to society's traditions, values and identity which are communicated through language and symbols. Subjects which may particularly lend themselves to this function include history (taught in the image of a society), literature (the selection of a culture's greatest works) and religious studies (particularly the traditions of a dominant religion). Core values, such as tolerance and mutual respect, are likely to be imparted across the board, and whilst society changes over time, functionalists emphasise that through the transmission of culture function education helps society to achieve both continuity and cohesion by conveying a shared cultural identity from one generation to the next.

Social order is promoted through the **social control function**. Through imposing rules and regulations and the expectation of respect for authority within educational institutions, education lays the groundwork for a society of law-abiding citizens. For functionalists, this is vitally important because however effectively the other functions are preformed, society is likely to be damaged by high levels of disorder if within education (and the family) the young are not adequately socialised into accepting a certain level of compliance.

The officially stated content of subjects is referred to as the **formal curriculum**. Teaching, learning and assessment are guided and constrained by course curriculum. However, hidden curriculum processes and influences may also be taking place alongside the delivery of the formal curriculum. As an example of the impact of the **hidden curriculum**, an issue highlighted by feminists has been the effect of gender stereotyping. This can work in a variety of ways. School timetabling of subjects based on gender stereotyping of 'natural' male or female subjects or activities, can make it difficult for males or females to take certain subject combinations. The content of academic materials may instil more than just learning. It can affect pupil's choice of subjects or how they relate to them along gendered lines by conveying positive or negative gender messages or particular learning styles. Teachers or careers advisors may think in terms of gender stereotypes when advising students on their choice of courses and careers. These processes can affect pupil's experiences, opportunities, self-perception and levels of achievement. Bringing them to view has initiated much educational reform.

Acquiring an overview of the functions of education should help to make it clear that the above functional distinctions that have been made are somewhat artificial; the functions have been divided up for academic purposes to help clarify processes and assist analysis. In the real world, these functions intermingle. For example, the impact of them all can be identified in the economic sphere. The economic function of education, viewed in a restricted sense, provides the economy with variously educated and skilled workers. But the way that the selective function works has an important bearing on the matching of individual abilities and skills to the requirements of occupational roles. A key question is the extent to which academic selection separates out individuals in terms of merit and what type of educational system can best enhance this. Again, the cultural values conveyed through education may be more or less favourable to the formation of attitudes, such as commitment, application, competition and enterprise that are conducive to the needs of the workplace. And social control, in nurturing certain levels of self-discipline as well as obedience to authority and the structuring of the school day according to timetables, can be viewed as preparation for individual responsibility and the acceptance of authority and structured routines by the individual within work institutions. Clearly, recognising the combined effect of functions in this way helps to identify the significance of the hidden curriculum in educational processes.

Viewing education as a system which is functionally connected to the social system enables one to analyse types of social policy interventions that may influence the functional effectiveness of education for the overall benefit of society. Ultimately, the implementation of education policy from this viewpoint is a political matter in balancing and prioritising particular educational functions.

Founding sociological perspectives on education

Functionalism and Marxism provide major founding perspectives on education. They are both macro theories – they locate an understanding of how education operates within their own analyses of the broader social orders and systems. However, these perspectives differ fundamentally in their view of the nature of the broader social framework and therefore the role of education in society. For functionalists, education, like the family, is a vital element of the social bedrock. It should contribute toward the maintenance of an efficient and stable society. To do so effectively, the way that it operates must synchronise with the needs and key characteristics of the broader social structure. Therefore, as society changes, so must the education system. Locating an understanding of education within this holistic approach of functionalism alerts us to the priority of firstly gaining an overview of the key features of the society within which it operates and how it changes. Only then can sense be made of the changing nature of educational provision.

Functionalism – education and the changing social order

a) Education in pre-modern society – upholding a closed social order

When adopting a broad historical vantage point, functionalists point to the relatively closed structure of social hierarchies in pre-modern or traditional societies (at their height in Europe under feudalism before and during the Middle Ages). This means that there were few opportunities for people to rise above their place of family origin in the social order. Their social status was 'ascribed' and the position of the privileged was supported by ideas of respect for family lineage and birthright. The sons of the wealthy were the main beneficiaries of formal education through having virtually exclusive access to private tutors and elite higher educational institutions. Their formal studies included traditional subjects – for example theology, philosophy, law, and Latin – which, if they did not live off the inheritance of an estate, prepared them for entry into elite professions such as the church, the law or government office. Through their privileged access to education, they would also develop the etiquette, manners and leadership qualities appropriate to their social rank.

The commercial classes may have had the monetary means to purchase a different form of education for their sons. The type of education would very likely have been relevant to commerce, placing an emphasis on such practical areas of study as trade, commercial law, arithmetic and accountancy, thus providing preparation for entry into commercially related activities.

The sons of artisans may have been versed in craft skills through working with their fathers or being apprenticed to another family. For the vast majority of peasants and labourers, there was little or no provision of formal education and the church would have been a key institution for the conveyance of moral messages. In the virtual absence of formal education, children would have helped parents in their work from an early age. Whilst occasionally a wealthy benefactor may assist in enabling a child of lowly social background receive an education, such assistance was in the gift of the patron. It was a personal favour and certainly not an established right. This type of personal relationship is referred to by Talcott Parsons as 'particularistic' – it was particular to the personal inclinations of the benefactor.

To sum up, in traditional society, the way that the selective function of education worked closely synchronised with and helped to perpetuate a relatively closed social hierarchy. The position of parents within the social structure largely determined access or otherwise to and type of education received by their sons and largely denied to their daughters. Education, or lack of it, itself served to perpetuate privilege or disadvantage from generation to generation and access to education bore little relationship to selection by individual talent, much of which therefore remained unfulfilled.

b) Education in modern society – servicing a meritocratic social order

Functionalists argue that, by contrast, modern industrial societies develop highly open social hierarchies and require a well educated and highly trained workforce. New technology necessitates that more people are prepared for higher levels of work skills. The development of new and more specialised occupations leads to highly differentiated occupational structures. To prosper in a dynamic and more integrated world of industrial competition, modern industrial societies need to utilise their human resources far more effectively than did pre-modern societies. Consequently, the allocation of people to occupations must take place according to their assessed individual ability rather than by birthright. Educational provision has to adapt to these broader social changes. To do this, it must become universally available in institutions external to the family and offer opportunities for achievement and success based on individual merit. In so doing, it can act as an intermediary between the family (a closed social hierarchy) and society (an open social hierarchy) and liberate individuals from a form of educational provision which once only reflected what family background could provide. By such means, education offers opportunities for occupational and social mobility. In modern industrial societies, the selective function in education adapts to synchronise with the needs of a more open social structure and meritocratic society. This is particularly the emphasis of the American functionalist Parsons who referred to education as being provided as a matter of right and selection by individual competition within the context of impersonal and impartial standards as 'universalistic' – rules regarding educational assessment and opportunity are applied impartially and formally to all.

However, Emile Durkhiem, writing around the turn of the twentieth century, was acutely aware that excessive individual competition could be socially disruptive. For Durkheim, modern society has to balance individual achievement through meritocratic opportunity with the need to maintain social order and stability. Compared to pre-industrial societies, where people were expected to know their fixed place in the social order, a more competitive and meritocratic system could increase individual discontent and social disharmony if it promoted an excessive preoccupation with the self, unrealistically raised individual expectations and stimulated unbounded ambition. To rein in the socially damaging effects of excessive individualism, Durkheim emphasised that society needed also to impose constraints and remind individuals that they also have obligations to society.

To this effect, schools effectively were seen to work like society in miniature, moulding and preparing future citizens. As well as encouraging individual competition between pupils, Durkheim argued that educational institutions must impose order and a sense of obligation by the individual to the school as a collectivity. Schooling should therefore nurture in each individual a sense of pride in and identification with its body of members and the school institution. It must demand obedience to rules and regulations and the acceptance of the school hierarchy. Schools promote social cohesion amongst their pupils through developing their own collective rituals (school assemblies and award ceremonies) and a sense of respect for their symbols (the school uniform, badge and mottos). These rituals and symbols, in tying the individual to the collectivity, find their functional equivalent in society in the form of nationalistic sentiments and reverence for such powerful symbols as national flags and anthems, each of which bind a society together.

Talcott Parsons agreed with Durkheim regarding the importance of education in the promotion of shared values and a sense of moral community and national identity. We can see this within American education in the prominence given to allegiance to the Constitution and the national flag. However, in developing functionalist theory in a more individualistic and competitive enterprise culture context than his French predecessor, Parsons placed greater emphasis on education as promoting competition in a social system with an occupational hierarchy which is highly differentiated in levels of monetary reward. It was important that members of society shared meritocratic values and that society itself was seen to be meritocratic. Parsons maintained that although American society placed a greater emphasis on the individual, it is the shared nature of these values of enterprise and fair individual competition that would provide the bond which held society together as people accepted their position within the social order as the rightful outcome of this fair competition.

For both Durkheim and Parsons, the development of educational institutions in modern industrial societies enables individuals to separate their achievement and ultimately their social destination from that of their parents. Furthermore, schooling provides a bridging role between the personalised world and established hierarchy of family life and the formal requirements of adult society. The intermediate institution of the school performs the key function of moulding individuals to the needs of broader society from a young age and over a protracted period of time. These needs include the acquisition of skills and values of competitiveness required in the occupational sphere. They also include the need for a common moral education which imparts shared values, moral standards and the need for engagement in co-operative behaviour. The school is therefore also a crucial institution in the development of individual self-restraint through the use of authority and discipline.

A key criticism of the functionalist perspective is that it an almost exclusively top down approach which looks at education in systemic terms and individuals as being shaped and constrained by functional forces and the needs of society. It therefore tends to lose sight of the capacity that people have for making their own choices and takes little account of individual autonomy and education for self-fulfilment. The question of the intrinsic worth of education for the development of the individual becomes buried below a focus on the needs of moulding individuals to society.

A more specific focus upon the link between economic incentives in the occupational structure and academic competition was drawn by Davis and Moore in 1945. They argued that society's occupational hierarchy represented an income differentiated ladder of opportunity, with educational achievement through merit providing an important key to occupational success. Education instilled the values of competition and achievement and provided a proving ground for future occupational success and financial reward by preparing those of proven ability for the most demanding, functionally important and highly paid occupations, and others accordingly throughout the occupational structure.

How convincing is this metaphor that the education system provides one big ladder of opportunity for all to compete to climb by their individual efforts and abilities alone? To pursue the metaphor, perhaps a more realistic view would be that overall education comprises various ladders which provide different barriers to overcome and different opportunities for ascent. In access to and ascent up these different ladders, the effect of family background is not negligible. Furthermore, one who manages by effort and ability to ascend high up a ladder with many obstacles may find that at the top there are doors to certain occupations that are virtually closed which other ladders give enhanced access to.

Marxism – education in capitalist society perpetuates the appearance of a meritocratic society

The Marxist perspective on education provides a radical alternative to that of functionalism. We have seen that functionalists emphasise the functional importance of equality of opportunity within education to a harmonious, integrated, efficient and meritocratic modern industrial society from which all to some extent ultimately benefit through social stability and enhanced performance of the social and economic system. By contrast, Marxists locate educational provision within capitalist societies which by their very nature, it is argued, cannot be meritocratic. From this perspective, capitalist society is inevitably divided by economic and social class inequalities which, to the benefit of a powerful minority, are strongly perpetuated from one generation to the next. In this sense, Marxists argue that, despite appearances to the contrary, capitalist societies are not as different from the relatively closed social structures of pre-modern societies as functionalist accounts maintain. They challenge the view that education under capitalism can ever select impartially to educate individuals according to assessed ability and then match them to appropriate occupations and levels of reward.

From a classical Marxist position, class is determined by people's relationship to the means of production. Viewed this way, education primarily assists those who own the means of production and benefit from the labour of others. Various insights have been developed from this general perspective by neo (more contemporary) Marxists. One is that education primarily assists the process of social control in the workplace. It achieves this through promoting the acceptance of authority within educational institutions and oversupplying the labour market in terms of the credentials or skills required. This empowers employers in their selection of those seeking work. From this perspective, Braverman (1974) has argued that capitalism has, in fact, brought about deskilling in the workplace as advances in the division of labour narrow down the required performance of more jobs to that of highly repetitive processes, make labour more easily controlled, and increasingly reduce it to the experience of a meaningless activity. From this Marxist slant, the real economic function of education is not to enlighten but to ensure that workers are sufficiently prepared to be able to operate in a disciplined and efficient manner in the workplace, accepting authority and boredom and acquiring sufficient skills to effectively enhance their own exploitation.

The impression of equal opportunity within education and throughout life, conveyed, for example by media focus on a statistically very small number of high profile cases of rapid social ascent, helps to legitimise the extreme economic inequalities that exist under capitalism. The importance of this appearance is that it encourages people to believe that through education and within society individual competition has a fair competitive basis. This both encourages personal application and, for those who fail, the tendency to view their failure in terms of personal inadequacy. Viewed in Mills' terms, the social issue of restricted opportunity for the many becomes hidden in the personal trouble of the perceived inadequacy of those with ability but without economic or cultural resources and who fail to progress. From a Marxist perspective, the overwhelming reality of the selective function of education under capitalism is in fact that it cannot provide the reality of equality of opportunity, only the illusion. Instead, it reproduces through family background from one generation to the next social class differences in life chances and opportunity which substantially distort individual educational and occupational outcomes away from the pattern expected in a meritocracy.

Whilst Braverman focussed on deskilling, other theorists writing within a general Marxist framework have analysed education in relation to a more differentiated workforce and social class background (eg. working class and middle class) within what Marx would have more broadly referred to as the proletariat. Along these lines, Bowles and Gintis (1976) developed their 'correspondence theory', arguing that there is a correspondence between organisation and the authority structure within the education system and the requirements of capitalism for appropriately skilled and disciplined workers. In this top down model, the needs of capitalism shape the education system and the education shapes future workers.

Bowles and Gintis argued that whilst the formal curriculum emphasises that education is about the development of thinking capacity and the acquisition of knowledge, through the hidden curriculum pupils are required to follow rules and regulations in preparation for the types of authority relationships that await them in the workplace. Different occupational and employment roles require the provision of a range of skills and the education system differentiates pupils by largely policing those in the lower grades, providing an experience which corresponds with the discipline that they will be expected to work under in the workplace, and allowing more autonomy to the higher achievers who are likely to progress to employment roles which require more autonomous application.

Through their research on senior pupils in a New York high school, Bowles and Gintis (1976) claimed to further show that the process of educational and occupational differentiation relates back to social class background. They found that when compared, pupils of average measured I.Q. showed great variation in their achievement of qualifications and levels of occupational access. Additionally, level of qualifications obtained did not correlate closely with occupational levels achieved. Those of high I.Q. did tend to achieve higher qualifications than others, but the researchers argue that I.Q. could be developed with length of stay in education which itself was related more to enhanced educational opportunities deriving from a more privileged social background.

Overall, Bowles and Gintis argued that differences in social class background had a substantial effect on time spent in education, the development of measured I.Q., qualifications gained and occupational success. Social class background therefore showed a higher correlation with educational achievement and occupational outcome than did individual ability. They concluded that rather than education performing a meritocratic selective process for the allocation of students to future occupational roles, social stratification, in terms of the impact of student's family background, tended to impose a non-meritocratic and class based selective process on educational performance and occupational outcome. Education only appears to select according to individual ability through the example of a relatively small minority of those from working class backgrounds who against the odds excel educationally and occupationally. However, for capitalism to benefit, it is crucially important for a sense of fairness and motivation that this appearance is maintained. In reality, the key function of education in capitalist society is to help perpetuate the false consciousness of meritocracy within education and society to justify massive economic inequality, whilst in reality social class privilege and disadvantage tends to be passed down the generations.

Pierre Bourdieu has offered a more cultural based explanation of education under capitalism from a Marxist perspective. He has argued that dominant social classes are able to impose their culture into the education system as the legitimate medium for success or failure. The culture of the higher social classes tends to be more highbrow, whereas that of the working class is more allied to pop culture. For Bourdieu, there is nothing academically superior in the former, but it reflects the yardstick for assessment which derives from class power.

Furthermore, for Bourdieu culture is not just about academic criteria but also relates to such matters as appropriate behaviour, manners, etiquette, speech, dress sense and taste. This whole cultural environment within educational institutions is referred to by Bourdieu as the 'habitus', meaning that it is an environmental habitat to which some pupils begin more adjusted than others. Since the formation of a person's cultural attributes is acquired during early socialisation within the family, children enter school with different class cultural advantages (middle class cultural capital) or disadvantages (working class cultural deficit) in an educational system where the culture of the dominant social classes comprises the environment and the worthy measure of success.

Cultural capital can be acquired through the extension of formal education. However, those entering education with cultural capital are more likely to extend this capital, as comfort within the habitus of the school will more likely enhance the prospects of extending their stay, which their parents are often better placed with 'economic capital' to prolong. These parents may also be more able to provide tutoring themselves or pay for private tutors.

By contrast, those lacking cultural capital in the first place have to attempt to adjust to the school cultural environment as well achieving academically if they are to be successful in education. The outcome is to minimise the chances of working class pupils' educational success and access to the higher occupations as they are more likely to underachieve in terms of poor academic performance and to drop out of education earlier compared to their middle class counterparts.

The purpose of exams, from Bourdieu's perspective, is to offer the appearance of fairness and merit, since all students who sit them know that they take the same exams at the same time and under the same examination conditions. However, given the effect of different class cultures on educational and exam performance, certification formally legitimises relative upper and middle class success and working class failure. From this viewpoint, the transmission of culture in education does not, as functionalists maintain, take the form of a neutral national cultural consensus for the objective and meritocratic assessment of performance. Instead, it is class based, and its real function resides in maintaining social class privileges and disadvantages across the generations.

Allied with the advantages of cultural capital are the influences of 'economic capital' and 'social capital'. All three often cluster together or where they do not are to some extent transferrable. Thus, from a social background comfortable in economic resources but which lacks cultural capital, parental economic resources can be used to gain access for pupils to more exclusive institutions such as independent schools which assist in the acquisition of cultural capital, whilst the success that it assists through the currency of academic qualifications may later become transferred through occupational success into economic capital. Social capital refers to the resource of having access to networks of social contacts and the ability, enhanced through shared cultural capital, to utilise these networks to children's advantage and the exclusion of others. For Bourdieu, children of working class background tend to be disadvantaged through their lack of access to all of these forms of capital.

Weber – education as an arena of struggle

For Weber, different social groups, including but not restricted to social classes, compete to shape and obtain access to institutions as valued resources. Education is no exception. At the extreme, powerful groups will attempt to maintain a degree of social closure and exclusivity by denying access to other groups to the most valued educational institutions. Within this context, it could be argued that despite the expansion of and reforms to the state education system, powerful elites have managed to retain for their children the benefits of exclusive access to the top public schools in preparation for their entry into the elite professions, whereas throughout much of the state system, there has been increasing pressure in the direction of narrowing the education of the majority toward occupational training through the influence of business. When using the state system, the middle classes have managed to gain disproportionate access to the more academically competitive and highly performing institutions such as the prestigious grant maintained schools when they existed and now the few remaining grammar schools. There are powerful arguments that through marketisation of the system, the middle classes have enhanced their access to the better performing schools through their knowledge of working the system and marginalised many of the poor and ethnic minorities to using poorly performing local schools.

Symbolic Interactionism – labelling and self-agency

The interactionist perspective opposes both Marxist and functionalist accounts of educational systems as being too deterministic. By this it is meant that these macro theories emphasise the determining effect of broader social structures and educational systems on educational outcomes of individuals and pay little attention to the micro level of classroom situations as environments that are more autonomous from these broader forces and are highly important in their own right. Rather than focussing on social systems, symbolic interactionists explain pupil behaviour and performance at the level of processes that take place within the social settings of classrooms. They look at how pupils' self-concepts (self-images) are influenced in these situations and usually focus on the effect that this has on their performance.

As explained in chapter 3, Mead, from a symbolic interactionist perspective, claimed that self-identity is not something which is biologically pre-determined but is the result of interaction with others. The self is shaped through the ability to see oneself by taking the viewpoint adopted by others of oneself. This capacity for socially generated self-consciousness is referred to as a process of 'representation'. However, the construction of self-image is not just a passive social product. Learning how to convey a public image enables the individual to also work the social environment. The self is therefore socially shaped but not socially determined. There is therefore the potential from this perspective for explaining educational processes as exchanges in the form of fluid social encounters involving the negotiation of meaning and identity.

In educational research, interactionists have often focussed on the impact of labelling by teachers on student self-concept and performance. Imposing a label refers to making a judgement, often with either positive or negative connotations, and acting toward another on the basis of that judgement. Labelling may rest on stereotyping which enables a short cut to be taken in 'understanding' the individual by placing him or her within pre-existing categories. When teachers make judgements of pupils and communicate these to them, these judgements may be based on a range of criteria such the stream that the pupil is placed in, their appearance, use of language, manners, application, conformity and the teacher's past experience of siblings or assessment of parents etc. These criteria and judgements may have little bearing on the ability of the individual student. However, when held and communicated, even subconsciously and unintentionally, they can strongly affect the self-image of the pupil, positively or negatively, and may develop responses that confirm the correctness of original label by virtue of the effects of its application.

Studying the effect of labelling imposed by teachers has been the main area of interest in interactionist research. From this approach, research has often provided findings which have been critical of the selective process of the old tripartite system of academic selection based around the 11+ and streaming or setting in schools, all of which can affect teacher stereotyping and labelling and for a significant number of pupils dampen down their aspirations and influence underachievement.

Streaming has also been related to pupil membership of school cultures, with pupils in higher streams likely to engage in the conformist culture of the school and those in lower streams adopting counter cultural values. The effect of involvement in these different cultures on behaviour and academic performance has been studied by sociologists such as David Hargreaves and Colin Lacey.

Moreover, although focussing primarily on classroom interaction, interactionist studies have often found a conspicuous relationship between academic streaming and social class, with those of working class background overrepresented in the lower streams and pupils of middle class background in higher streams. Such findings thus can be related back to the broader issue of social class background and equality of opportunity.

Given the emphasis on the impact of teacher labelling on student self-concept and performance, an interactionist approach has sometimes not been able to avoid falling into its own determinism since pupil performance is often seen as socially determined by the judgements and actions of teachers. This is because the teacher – pupil relationship is not an equal one due to the authority that the teacher has over the pupil. However, this outcome is not always necessarily the case as pupils are not powerless and may develop a range of responses, individual or collective, to manipulate labelling or negate its possible consequences. In research conducted by Margaret Fuller (1984) for example, black girls in a London comprehensive school were found to have strongly resisted negative stereotyping which they were determined to prove wrong by their application to their studies. This resistance enhanced their educational success.

From an interactionist perspective, it should be able to fruitfully analyse the generation of self-image through student to student interaction and the ability of pupils to manipulate teacher's perceptions of them in the first place.

Schooling in England – change, in social and historical context

In pre-industrial England, sons of the wealthy landed classes had access to an elitist and traditional style of education and daughters were sometimes tutored in social airs and graces. The sons of the commercial classes were likely to have been equipped with a more commercial and practical type education. The education of children of manual workers and agricultural labourers would largely comprise the direct acquisition of work based skills and worldly wisdom through assisting their parents in their occupations from an early age. Most females were denied access to education, save the possibility of that provided by religious orders.

A complex mixture of fortuitous factors lay behind the Industrial Revolution which was apace in England by the late eighteenth century. The development of practical and scientific education in dissenting academies during the eighteenth century, to which we will shortly return, was part of the complex picture of influences. However, throughout much of the nineteenth century, as industrialisation developed, educational provision showed only limited advance and on an ad hoc basis with minimal state involvement. Some continental countries that had industrialised later than England were introducing state organised educational systems before England. For example, by the mid nineteenth century, Germany and Holland were developing systems of elementary education. Given the apparent connection between industrial modernisation and the need for a more highly skilled workforce and the seeming emergence of a more meritocratic society, why was state education in England relatively slow to develop?

To begin to answer this question requires going beyond education systems and looking at cultural values, religion and social class dynamics. A strong culture of *laissez faire* (self support through individual enterprise and hard work) prevailed in England through the middle decades of the nineteenth century. This was a value system which particularly appealed to the successful industrial middle classes. England was the first country to industrialise and the process had therefore not been state planned. The benefits of non-intervention had apparently proved themselves. The rising entrepreneurial (risk taking owners of private enterprise) classes thus associated freedom and prosperity with the values of individualism and private enterprise. Individual success and freedom was associated with freedom from state interference.

This view was also linked to the preservation of religious freedoms. The industrial middle classes had a long tradition of religious beliefs which dissented from the Church of England. Consequently, they sometimes sent their sons to dissenting academies of their own religious persuasion (for example Quaker) where they would gain a more scientific and practical education. Since they paid for their own children's education, many felt entitled to resist also paying for state education of working class children through higher taxation. Furthermore, many feared that state sponsored education would interfere with their freedom of religious persuasion through the imposition of the state religion of the Church of England. Indeed, the Anti-State-Church Association was a nonconformist pressure group set up to resist the state funding of education for this reason. It was also feared by some employers that a more educated working class may push up their labour costs and further that, in their defence of a highly ordered society, these people may forget their social station.

There were therefore powerful forces of cultural, religious, economic and social class self-interest which help to explain why the introduction of state education was delayed in this country. How, then, can the advance of state education later in the nineteenth century be explained? A number of factors coincide quite closely with the timing of the introduction and extension of universal elementary education dating from Forster's Education Act of 1870.

1) To explain the first factor, an analytical distinction needs to be made between social class and social status. Social class is to do with social levels or strata identified in terms of a hierarchy of occupational bands and income levels, whereas status refers to social groupings who share a common culture in terms of taste, manners and lifestyle from which they derive a certain level of social prestige. The latter decades of the nineteenth century witnessed a decline in the values of laissez faire enterprise culture. The reasons for this are complicated, but one thesis (Wiener, 1981) argues that an important factor in this decline was the greater use of public schools by the entrepreneurial classes. Commonly viewed as uncultured Philistines by those of more traditional elite status groups, many businessmen sought a more gentlemanly status for their sons. This could be achieved by utilising their economic resources to send their sons to public schools. However, it was in this elitist environment of classical education that they became ingratiated into a culture of disdain for industry.

2) England's waning economic performance during the second half of the nineteenth century, partly explained by the above culture change, meant that other countries were closing the lead in economic modernisation that England had once established. These later developers appeared to have benefited from the provision of universal elementary education. The economic function of universal education in the context of international competition was therefore apparent to governments.

3) There also existed a fear that, by being left to their own devices and setting up discussion and reading groups, the working classes were beginning to educate themselves and in so doing often gaining access to politically subversive ideas. This situation could get out of control. To counteract it, the state could promote the social control function by imposing a form of education which provided the indoctrinating experience of rote learning and 'safe' god fearing religious messages for the masses.

Despite legislative reforms in 1876 and 1880 which required compulsory full-time school attendance for children up to the age of 10, elementary education and a rote style of learning was all that was available to most pupils without parental means, whatever their abilities. And despite educational reforms early in the twentieth century which offered a proportion of free grammar school places to able children of working class background, access to secondary education at the age of 11 remained largely on a fee paying basis up to the end of the Second World War. This meant that even though the minimum school leaving age had been gradually raised to 14 by 1918, most pupils who did not have parents of means had to remain in elementary school through to the end of their education.

Educational reforms followed both the First and Second World Wars. Each time, the low level of education of war recruits had been identified. Additionally, wartime promises of reform in a range of policy areas including education were made to either circumvent the risk of political radicalism (First World War) or to raise wartime morale (Second World War).

Education policy – post war social democratic approach and social engineering

Social policy refers to government interventions which steer social change and provide a framework within which to influence behaviour. It is guided by political ideology which provides a set of values and an image of an ideal society as a compass bearing on an improved future from the viewpoint of that ideology (note the more restricted use of the term ideology in party politics and social policy compared to its use in the Marxist perspective).

Politics during the post Second World War period was dominated by Labour and Conservative governments. Generally speaking, Labour favoured more state control, interventionist and redistributive policies, whereas the Conservatives looked more to the free market. Nevertheless, the policy reforms introduced by each party in government can be seen as based on a 'collectivist consensus' which emerged during the war and remained relatively intact for at least two decades afterwards. This consensus between the main political parties and across much of society favoured state intervention to protect the vulnerable whilst enhancing opportunities for the able irrespective of their social background. Such intervention aimed to engineer social justice from the education system to broader society and has been referred to as the social democratic approach.

Against the backdrop of this consensus, reforms to the system of state schooling in England contained in the Butler Act were implemented by the post-war Labour government in 1946. Resources for the state sector were to be provided through public funding and delivered through the local authorities. The reforms included both the extension of the minimum school leaving age to 15 and the transition from primary to some form of secondary schooling at the age of 11 for all children within the state system, along with the abolition of fees for access to state secondary education. With the barrier of parental inability to pay fees removed and the introduction of standardised intelligence testing in the form of the 11+ exam, it was expected that this system would enhance the modern selective function to channel pupils with different levels of ability into different types of state secondary school. The reforms were therefore expected to extend pupils' equality of opportunity to demonstrate their inequality of ability irrespective of social background, and then to educate them accordingly. These were therefore meritocratic principles (although the independent fee paying sector, which runs counter to this logic, remained in place) which when applied in the selective process of the 11+ test for entry into the new largely tripartite system of secondary moderns, technical schools and grammar schools, were expected to show significantly improved access for able working class children to the academically challenging grammar schools. It was further expected that the incentive to achieve educationally through selection for access to occupations on merit would promote social mobility and assist overall economic performance through more effective utilisation of talent.

Levels of social mobility were increasing through the post war decades, a phenomena which coincided with the bedding in of selective education reforms. It would therefore be tempting to jump to the conclusion that the grammar schools were working effectively as a vehicle for social mobility. However, rather than a causal factor, it can be persuasively argued that increased upward social mobility over this period was necessitated through changes in the broader occupational structure in relation to the different reproduction rates within the working and middle classes. With the expansion of professional occupations and the lower reproduction rate of the middle classes, a powerful social dynamic was in place whereby greater numbers of those from manual backgrounds were needed to fill these vacancies without significantly threatening downward displacement of children from middle class backgrounds. Therefore, it would seem that grammar schools were more of a coincidental factor in this process. This view is born out by a substantial body of sociological theory and research.

Research from the 1950s indicated that there was, in fact, little improvement compared to the pre-war years in the access of children from working class backgrounds to grammar schools, proportionate to those from middle class backgrounds. One of the criticisms of the tripartite system was therefore that selection still led to a degree of social class segregation in the schools attended. Children of the middle classes were far more likely to attend the academically challenging grammar schools whereas those of working class background tended to enter secondary moderns which provided a more concrete education and restricted educational and occupational opportunities. Secondary moderns, attended by a majority of pupils, also came to be viewed as schools for those who had 'failed' the 11+ test, thus also arguably dampening aspirations.

The reforms of the Butler Act had been premised on the view that individual differences in intellectual ability were innate, fixed and scientifically measurable. Furthermore, the presumed precision and infallibility of intelligence testing to provide a once and for all measure of ability and allocate pupils to different schools accordingly has since been much questioned. Sociologists do not tend to deny the existence or importance of differences in innate abilities. For example, even with the greatest educational and social support only very few people could reach the academic level of a professorship. However, they emphasise that 1) environmental factors can substantially enhance or retard the development of intellectual capacities, and therefore 2) a once and for all test at the age of 11 overemphasises the fixity of innate abilities and 3) such testing does not provide a neutral and precise means of measuring intellectual ability. It is therefore not surprising that research in the 1950s by Yates and Pidgeon indicated that approximately 70,000 children a year were wrongly allocated to their schools at the secondary stage.

During the 1960s, political party divergence opened up with the Labour Party supporting non-selective education through comprehensivisation and the Conservatives more intent on retaining the tripartite selective system. For Labour, comprehensive schools, which would take in pupils across the entire ability range and from a diversity of occupational backgrounds within their catchment area, linked in with the idea of the promotion of a modern classless society. Labour governments required local authorities to draw up plans to introduce comprehensives and through the establishment of Educational Priority Areas extra resources were targeted to deprived localities.

Research, for example by Benn and Chitty (1996) and Glennester and Low (1980), has shown that in comparison to performance within the tripartite system, comprehensive schooling (which has various models) has tended to improve the exam performance of those assessed as of average ability and below without detrimental effect on the performance of the most able. Furthermore, McPherson and Willms found in the 1980s that in Scotland comprehensive schooling had reduced the differential effect of social class on educational attainment.

Yet even with the growth of comprehensive education, which invariably continued the process of academic streaming, social class differences in achievement levels tended to remain remarkably resistant. It was therefore the case that rather than being able to engineer social justice through the education system, broader social inequalities had a social injustice invading effect into the education system. There would seem to be much in the title of Bernstein's article (1970) that 'education cannot compensate for society'.

Education and social stratification

Education in the post war decades can be contextualised within a heavily stratified society. This next section touches on sociological explanations at the time of the effect of social stratification on education. Whilst these explanations need to be understood in their social and historical context, the reader should be able to critically reflect on their enduring relevance or otherwise to the contemporary world.

1. Social class – the seemingly impenetrable barrier to equal opportunity in educational achievement

Much post war educational research focussed on the issue of working class access to grammar schools and social class related levels of academic achievement. Given the meritocratic reasoning behind the post-war reforms, research tended to focus on establishing whether pupils of working class background were the main beneficiaries as may have been anticipated. In fact, much evidence confirmed that class related differences in terms of access and achievement remained relatively unchanged. For example, research conducted by J.W.B. Douglas (The Home and the School, 1964) compared the GCE O level (the main exam sat by 16 year olds at the time) performance of students of similar high measured ability but different social class backgrounds and found that performance levels declined in correlation with descending social class background. A far greater proportion of able lower working class pupils were also leaving school at the minimum departure age of 15.

Later research carried out by Halsey, Heath and Ridge (1980) found that, in terms of school leaving age, qualifications obtained, and entrance to university, the performance of youngsters from all social class backgrounds had improved when pre-war and post-war cohorts were compared. However, in terms of their relative underperformance, the position of children of working class background remained largely unchanged. Their chances of entering grammar school were three times less than that of children from professional and managerial backgrounds – a proportion little different from pre-war figures.

What were the main approaches to explaining these persisting social class related differences in levels of educational success? At a very general level, a distinction can be made between explanations that emphasise differences in natural or innate abilities and others which refer to the predominant influence of environmental factors. The first approach tends to be more prevalent within psychology. For those adopting this position, such as Herrnstein and Murray in the United States, the relationship between social class background and level of educational achievement is seen as largely the result of social class differences in inherited intelligence levels. As far as this genetic inheritance argument goes, the data may appear to fit the interpretation. It would also enable evidence of limited levels of social mobility to square with the view that society is nevertheless meritocratic, in that there exists equality of opportunity, but that working class children inherit lower levels of innate ability which tend to keep them in their class of origin.

There are a number of major problems with this interpretation. Firstly, it may be questioned whether it is possible to measure innate intelligence levels that have not already been influenced by environmental factors. Secondly, even if working class parents are less intelligent than middle class parents whose occupations may demand higher intellectual qualities, there is no evidence from laws of heredity that from this starting point these same intelligence levels will be directly inherited by the next generation. Laws of heredity suggest that differences in innate intelligence are more likely to be randomly distributed throughout the social structure. Thirdly, the inheritance argument tends to be further undermined by a large body of evidence showing different levels of educational performance related to social class background when comparing children of similar measured ability. Fourthly, it is highly questionable whether testing for intelligence only measures intelligence levels. For example, practice can often improve test performance but access to the opportunities for practice, as well as guidance and support, is likely to be a socially constructed inequality.

Whilst not denying the existence of innate differences in intellectual ability (nature), sociological explanations attribute far more importance to environmental factors (nurture) in influencing the development of ability and opportunities for educational achievement. One broad category of explanations emphasises the impact of differences in social class cultural environments. Culture, in the sociological sense, refers to shared usage of language, values and understandings.

Class cultural explanations

An early explanation of the persistence of social class differences in levels of educational achievement which emphasised cultural factors was developed by Basil Bernstein (from 1961). Bernstein identified the importance of different class related use of language, referred to as 'linguistic codes'. He argued that speech codes developed in working class families tended to be of a 'restricted' type. By this, Bernstein meant that communication is likely to take place through the use of descriptive vocabulary. Grammatical form is often incomplete because it assumes that others have a shared knowledge of the particular circumstances to which it relates. In correcting children, parents are more likely to issue imperatives along the lines of 'don't do that or else…'. By contrast, within middle class families, 'elaborated' speech codes are more likely to be used. This form of communication is more grammatically rounded, there is greater use of abstract concepts and more detailed explanations are provided. In correcting children, parents are more likely to explain 'you should not do that because…'

Before even attending school, children are socialised within the family environment into the linguistic code of their social class as a way of communicating. As the mode of communication used by teachers within schools tends to conform to the elaborated speech code, working class children are at a social class disadvantage in getting onto the frequency of communication and expressing themselves in a way that is deemed to be appropriate in that context. It could also be added that intelligence testing tends to rely on pupils showing that they can deal with abstract concepts, that more working class pupils tended to fail their 11+, and that secondary modern schools were designed as appropriate for children who thought in more concrete terms, thus being heavily populated by children of working class parents.

Bernstein also related achievement to pedagogy, the influence of which works in the same direction to that of linguistic codes. School pedagogy refers to the creation of curriculum and educational processes designed to enable the learner to learn. It includes rules of the education and learning environment. Bernstein argued that within schools there is an explicit and implicit pedagogy. The explicit pedagogy, in the form of rules of the learning environment that are clearly communicated, tends to be visible to all pupils. By contrast, the implicit pedagogy rests on the assumption that pupils understand implied expectations of the learning environment and how they should conduct themselves. Bernstein argued that this dimension of the school pedagogy tends to be picked up on by pupils of middle class background as something familiar, but that it remains more hidden to those of working class background. Although this relates little to their abilities, it is the criteria by which they are judged and can significantly influence their performance.

As identified in a previous section, Pierre Bourdieu offered a cultural explanation of working class relative educational failure through lack of cultural (as well as economic and social) capital. The reader may have recognised some similarities between Bourdieu's ideas and those of Bernstein. However, Bourdieu's concept of cultural capital is broader than that of Bernstein's linguistic codes and pedagogy and he also adopts an explicitly neo-Marxist analysis in which the power of the dominant social classes to impose their culture as the means of assessment disadvantages the working class. For the child of working class background to be academically successful, as well as competing academically they face the added burden of having to adjust to an unfamiliar cultural environment. From Bourdieu's position, it is unlikely that such educational disadvantage can be easily overcome, even with the best of intentions, whilst society remains divided into economically dominant and subordinate classes.

A quite different approach which emphasised a cultural dimension to educational achievement was adopted by Herbert Hyman (1967). In a study of a range of research findings in the United States, Hyman explained educational achievement differences mainly through the effect of different class cultural values. He argued that the cultural values of the lower social classes tended to place less emphasis on personal achievement than those of the middle class. He maintained that they also place less value on striving for upward occupational mobility and educational achievement. Their values are more fatalistic. Children from these backgrounds become socialised into these fatalistic cultural values which do not prepare them well for success in education.

Although Hyman acknowledged that these values are in part a realistic reflection of the lesser opportunity that society offers the poor and the working class, the greater emphasis in his analysis is that it is the negative value system of these groups which is the barrier to their success within a society of opportunity. The key to combating the problem is therefore instilling, particularly through education, values of individual competitiveness into pupils from more deprived backgrounds at the youngest age possible to counteract the culture of negativity and help them to reach their educational and occupational potential.

A further type of cultural explanation, developed by Barry Sugarman (1970), related educational achievement to time horizons and time horizons to parental occupations. Sugarman argued that working class and middle class occupations tended to promote different time perspectives. The career structure of middle class occupations meant that planning for the future and making sacrifices now – referred to as 'deferred gratification' – would be recognised to pay off in the long run. By contrast, most manual working class occupations did not tend to have a long-term career structure but instead a wage structure that peaked quite early in life and related more to physical fitness. The outlook associated with these occupations was likely to be a present time orientation which generated a 'live for today' approach to life. These different outlooks could influence children's orientation to education, which for success required individual application and deferred gratification.

Research by Paul Willis (1977) is unusual in that it was conducted at a micro level within a broader Marxist framework of analysis. As a result, he came to some rather different conclusions than many sociologists who work within the Marxist framework tend to. In his small scale study of 12 'lads' of working class background, he found that their response to a school environment, which they experienced as alienating, was to develop a counter culture in which they avoided school work, played up, and ridiculed others whom they viewed as conformist swats. Whilst the 'lads' valued the superiority of street wisdom and quick wit, they also knew how far to bend the rules. According to Willis, they realistically anticipated their working class occupational destinations and so did not value academic conformity and achievement. Consequently, they became confirmed through their failure at school in their expected occupations.

Willis also studied the 'lads' when they entered the workplace. He found that the school had not been successful in inducing conformity to rules and application to work. Indeed, their school counter culture had prepared them with a type of pre-vocational experience in preparation for a workplace in which quick wit and manipulation of the rules were part of the shop floor culture in coping with tedium. In this way, working class culture and restricted horizons were actively reproduced. The lads did not feel that they were either just down beaten failures at school or suppressed in the workplace.

Home environment and parental interest

Other explanations of differential achievement related to social class place less emphasis on class cultural values. One such is Douglas' (1964) research, which has already been referred to. Douglas identified parental attention to children in the pre-school home environment and interest in their children's education at school as particularly important to children's educational achievement. It was claimed, through measuring parents' school visits, that the middle classes expressed a greater interest in their children's educational progress.

This way of measuring parental interest has been contentious. However, Douglas also related educational success to other class connected phenomena such as the child's health, the size of the family, study and living conditions, and the quality of the school, all of which can count against the working class child. There was therefore a mixture of cultural and material social class factors affecting pupil's achievement.

Class structure and rational decision making

For Raymond Boudon (1974), position in the class structure is more important than aspects of class culture in explaining class differences in educational attainment. Given their different class background starting points, Boudon argued that it would be misleading to suggest that working class youngsters with horizons for working class occupations hold more fatalistic values than middle class youngsters aiming for middle class occupations.

He emphasised that educational systems offer various potential educational pathways and exit points, and argued that pupils engage in a rational process of costs and benefits analysis, which is partly but not exclusively economic, in making their educational decisions. The different class backdrops to these decisions means that pupils of different social class backgrounds may well come to different but equally rational decisions regarding their educational options. For example, the transition from school or college to higher education is a potential exit point where decisions have to be made. The prospect for a pupil of working class background of embarking on a higher education course which could lead to a profession may entail a distancing, both geographically and socially, from family and friends and the need to adjust to a new cultural environment and social circles. Since such a decision may not carry much support from family and friends who may not share these horizons, potential costs may have the off-putting appearance of outweighing benefits. By contrast, in considering pursuing the same pathway, the pupil from a middle class background may assess that the benefits outweigh the costs as their family expects and supports further study and friends make similar decisions. For Boudon, both decisions may be equally rational and made by individuals, but they take place against the backdrop of the class structure which they then ultimately feed back into.

Class, stereotyping and streaming

Nell Keddie (1973) applied an interactionist approach to the study of streaming in a comprehensive school. Although the research was focussed at a micro level, it raised broader questions regarding stereotyping and the relationship between streaming and social class. Keddie found that, in a school that adopted streaming but also ran a course that was not meant to be taught in a streaming based differentiated way, teachers still gave pupils from different streams differential access to course knowledge. 'A' stream pupils were viewed as academically able and easy to work with and so were given access to abstract curriculum knowledge. 'C' stream pupils were regarded as less able and seen as more difficult to work with because they tended to think in a concrete way. They were likely to speak up if their concrete experiences contradicted the teacher's subject knowledge. When this happened, their contributions tended to be dismissed. Keddie thus found that schooling tended to reward the ability of the predominantly middle class 'A' stream students to conform to the requirements of the curriculum and penalise the more critical contributions of the predominantly working class 'C' stream students.

The above explanations comprise just a limited selection from a body of well established sociological research and explanations into social class differences in educational achievement. Given the variety of influences identified, it is hardly surprising that substantial class related achievement differences have remained so persistent despite reforms to the education system which would seem to be designed to enhance equality of opportunity to succeed. At first glance, explanations in terms of the inheritance of social class differences in intelligence levels could appear to fit the facts of the connection between social class and educational achievement levels. However, sociologists focus more on the effect of the social distribution of influences and opportunities for personal development and achievement to explain the same facts. The above explanations suggest, from a sociological viewpoint, that it is more the impact of different class related life chances on educational performance that is transmitted across the generations than genetic differences in levels of intelligence.

2. Gender – changing social and educational horizons

Sex differences between males and females are biological differences that have been imposed by nature. By distinction, the term 'gender' refers to socially constructed differences in identity related to sex differences rather than the view that such identity differences are biologically predetermined. Being socially constructed, they vary from society to society and can change over time. As in the study of social class, sociology adopts a mainly environmental or nurture emphasis in explaining differences in educational achievement in gender terms. Within the framework of a broad historical outlook, gender roles and opportunities for many women in the western world changed quite rapidly and dramatically following the women's liberation movement of the late 1960s and early 1970s. It is more than a coincidence that in subsequent decades the performance of females in education has dramatically improved compared to that of males. This pace of change in social liberation and educational performance is far too great to be explained in terms of evolution in inbuilt intellectual capacity.

Educational research in England has long established that girls have tended to perform better than boys up to about the middle stage of secondary school. Their performance then often declined relative to boys, they were less likely to study traditional male subjects than boys and were also less likely to stay on at school. This reality could be explained in terms of a combination of socially constructed gender expectations and discriminatory practices.

During the post-war decades, the expectations for many girls were that a future housewife role required little consideration of occupational striving and the necessity for gaining educational qualifications. These social expectations were often reproduced across a range of educational and general reading materials, appearing most prescriptively in the *Housekeeping Monthly* magazine of 1955 which explained how in being a good housewife a woman should run the home, serve her husband and know her place. Even in the early 1970s, Sue Sharpe found that the girls in her London based research saw their futures mainly in terms of marriage and domesticity and gave aiming for a career little consideration (however, as many of the girls were of working class background, the possible combined effect of class and gender on their outlook cannot be discounted).

Discriminatory practices in education up to this time included gender quotas which were operated by some local authorities. Given the superior performance of girls at the 11+ stage, a number of authorities would raise the pass mark for girls compared to that for boys so as to level out the proportions of males and females entering grammar schools. At the margins, therefore, boys with a slightly lower mark than girls may have obtained grammar school places that girls were denied.

Females had also experienced widespread prejudice and discrimination in the workplace. Women who took on 'men's jobs', despite evidence that women had capably performed such work as part of the war effort, often faced extreme hostility. More generally, they were often denied promotion, offered lower rates of pay to men, and in some occupations were even expected to give up their work if they married, on the assumption that they would be 'kept' by their husband.

Early feminist writers such as Betty Friedan (1965) were challenging the restriction on their self-fulfilment that the traditional housewife role was argued to impose on so many women. By 1970, the emergence of feminist consciousness in a number of western societies focussed on challenging female disadvantage in a broad range of social contexts. One area of attention was that of traditional sexual stereotyping, which related to presumed fixed and innate differences in abilities and predispositions between females and males, casting females as natural carers and males as their providers. From at least one strand of feminist thinking (radical feminism), views which emphasised these apparently immutable differences were in fact male ideology – the ideas supported social arrangements through which males exercised power over females throughout society.

Studies focussing on the impact of socialisation in the formation of gender identity held liberating potential, since, if its effect was shown to be substantial, reform of the social environment and socialisation could bring about reformed gender identity. Research conducted during the 1970s and 1980s paid greater attention to the impact of early gender socialisation within the family and playgroups through the different treatment of boys and girls and different toys they were given to play with. School reading and teaching materials also came under greater scrutiny. For example, content analysis of stories in school books by researchers such as Glenys Lobban (1974) often revealed that gender stereotypes of male adventurousness and female domesticity were present. Such practices and materials were now exposed to more critical scrutiny.

A further issue was that subjects themselves were often gender stereotyped along the lines of maths and sciences being natural male subjects, whilst humanities and domestic science were regarded as natural female subjects. Traditional gender related subject choices were then sometimes reinforced by stereotypical assumptions built into school timetabling and often supported by teacher guidance. Researchers were also studying ways in which some subject texts were written which assumed one gender or the other to be the natural audience. And observational studies found widespread evidence of male dominance in classroom participation.

Reflecting the climate of growing awareness and criticism of gender inequality, the Sex Discrimination Act was passed in 1975. One consequence of this legislation was that the practice of operating different 11+ pass levels for boys and girls became illegal. Other social changes would encourage significant improvements in the educational performance of females. One was the perception of enhanced employment opportunities for women. This was associated with the expansion of service sector employment and examples set by some highly successful female role models in business and politics. A social and political climate of enhanced enterprise culture values during the 1980s emphasised the individual striving of career women, a position with some common ground in liberal feminism as opposed to earlier more collectivist feminist protests. At the same time, rapidly rising divorce rates arguably placed greater importance on females to recognise the need to be able to prepare for financial independence.

These changes may be seen as constituting the backdrop of both enhanced opportunities and motivations for substantial progress in female educational performance and participation which will be outlined later. Francis (2000, Ch.1) alerts us to the little recognised fact that even in the 1970s more girls were achieving five O Level passes than boys and that the speed and extent to which the gender gap that has since opened up in favour of girls at this level can be exaggerated. Nevertheless, a substantial improvement in top grade performance and university entrance levels over a short historical time period provides a powerful argument against those who maintain that fundamentally different intellectual capacities are built into the nature of males and females which prescribe different opportunities and roles in life.

3. Ethnicity – early period educational performance levels and general explanations

The Swann Report (1985) identified, despite improvements over the preceding ten years, that Afro Caribbeans were the ethnic group with the poorest record of educational performance. By contrast, 'Asian' (the ethnic categories used more recently have become more refined) pupils' performance was comparable to that of whites, even though they were often from lower occupational background. Evidence provided by the Department of Education and Skills tended to substantiate the findings of the Swann Report. Figures for 1989 that measure achievement in terms of passing at least 5 GCESs at grade C and above showed a 30% achievement rate for whites, 29% for 'Asians' (no figures for separate national classifications were provided) and 18% for 'blacks' (including Afro Caribbeans, but again there were no figures for separate national classifications). By 1992, data from the Youth Cohort Study of 16 year olds showed the achievement level of whites to have improved to 37%, of Asians to 33% and 'blacks' to 23%. It is interesting to note that within the Asian category, more detailed classification became available which showed Indian achievement at 38%, 'other Asian' (including Chinese) at 46% and Bangladeshis (a minority who tended to arrive in England later) at only 14%.

The aim of this section is to provide a brief overview of a range of explanations from this period that have been used to account for differences in the educational performance of ethnic minority groups in England. In a later section, we will review evidence of more contemporary levels of academic achievement by ethnic group, touching on some explanations of the progress since made.

Intelligence and the concept of race

What explanations have been provided to account for such a variation in achievement levels? One type of approach has attempted to explain the differences as being due to variation in inherited intellectual capacity between different 'races' that were defined in terms of skin colour and other physical features. This type of explanation can be traced back to colonial days when the view of different racial characteristics was used to explain and justify the dominance of white Europeans over other races, as well as the practice of slavery. An early exponent of the racial approach was the nineteenth century French aristocrat Joseph Gobineau, who essentially argued that the different races of white, black and yellow skin colour had different genetically inbuilt attributes. He claimed that the capacity of the white race to establish civilisations was because of its superior qualities of intelligence and organizational capacity, and that intermixing with other races would lead to the degeneration of these qualities. Similar reasoning has been applied in the twentieth century to support the institution of South African apartheid, Nazi persecutions and discrimination against blacks in the American southern states.

More recent geneticist arguments have attempted to add a gloss of scientific respectability to this position by comparing the findings of IQ testing of different racial groups. For example, in America, Arthur Jensen (1969) pointed to evidence that IQ scores for black Americans were about 15 points below that of whites. Herrnstein and Murray (1994), based on a summary of a broad range of studies, provided similar findings and concluded that IQ test differences were substantially influenced by genetic inheritance. These writers, along with H.J. Eysenck, maintained that about

60% of the measured IQ difference was the result of genetic differences between the races.

Charles Murray, with particular reference to the United States, also related the view that certain groups are intellectually inferior to what he referred to as an underclass, containing a high proportion of ethnic minorities who were trapped in poverty. He provided partly social and partly genetic explanations to account for this, each of which provided support for social policy that would limit or reduce welfare expenditure. The social component of his explanation was that prolonged reliance on welfare benefit encouraged an attitude of fatalism and a 'dependency culture' system of values which, when passed on to the next generation, curbed their capacity for self-help. However, the perpetuation of poverty was also seen as deriving from the inheritance of lower levels of intelligence within this stratum. Thus, attempting to tackle poverty through enhanced spending on education and welfare would be at best a worthless investment and at worst counterproductive.

Analysed sociologically, the argument that there are fixed differences in the innate intellectual capacities of different races is highly contestable. Various reasons have been put forward to explain why the validity of IQ tests (their ability to test what they claim to test – innate intelligence) can be questioned. A key issue raised is that the tests were usually initially standardised on a white middle class population. They are therefore not a neutral measuring device but are culturally biased and as such arguably depress the measured performance of other ethnic cultural groups. Moreover, regarding the middle class bias built into the standardisation, it must be remembered that a greater proportion of members of most ethnic minority groups occupied lower social class positions. And why is that? To what extent is this due to a lack of ability or the practice of discrimination? There is evidence to suggest, certainly during the time period that we are looking at here, that the latter has played a very significant part.

Educational achievement and the concept of ethnicity

At this point, it needs to be emphasised that sociologists tend to strongly contest the very use of the term 'race' as a useful concept and make a similar distinction between race and ethnicity to that of sex and gender. Just as gender refers to the impact of socially constructed identities over biological differences between the sexes, so ethnicity refers to the social impact of different customs, histories, and traditions over differences of appearance referred to as race. By emphasising the influence of social factors rather than innate characteristics, it becomes apparent that improvement can come through changes in the environment – for example from social reform. Furthermore, such crude racial categories as 'Asian' can be avoided, and the more subtle concept of ethnicity can be applied to help understand the differences in the educational performance of, for example, Pakistani, Indian and Bangladeshi ethnic minorities in England.

Even if we provisionally accept the view that I.Q. testing provides a neutral and scientific measurement of innate ability, new problems arise for the geneticists. One problem is that I.Q scores appear to be improving by about 3% per decade. How is this possible? It would appear to be far too fast as a measure of evolutionary change. Moreover, in the United States, the I.Q scores of black Americans improved at a faster rate than that of whites during a time frame which follows the civil rights reforms. This would seem to suggest that what black Americans had previously 'inherited' and has at least since been partly lifted, was the overwhelming effect of racial discrimination and disadvantage on their 'ability' to do themselves justice. In the case of social class, we have previously explained differences in attainment levels in terms of a broad range of environmental influences. The same would appear to be the case regarding gender and ethnicity, providing optimism with regard to progress that these groups have made.

More contemporary evidence with regard to gender and ethnicity will be presented later to show that in England significant educational improvements in terms of the achievement of qualifications have been made by females, who have come to outperform males in all ethnic groups, and that certain ethnic minorities (Indian and Chinese) are significantly outperforming whites. Those ethnic groups who started well behind (for example Bangladeshis) have either substantially closed the performance gap with or even overtaken the performance of white pupils.

Given the number of ethnic minority groups and the variations in level of educational performance, a thorough understanding of the social influences on educational performance would require an extremely complex comparative analysis to tease out the relevant influential factors in each case. This is further complicated by the fact that even though evidence is available for more specifically identified ethnic cultures, each of these can be internally diverse and can change. Indeed, dismissing race and emphasising the influence of ethnic culture, McKenzie (2001, p.157) rightly warns that one needs to be cautious to avoid substituting a simplistic approach of ethnic absolutism for that of the discredited racial absolutism to explain differences in levels of educational achievement. Here, there is only room for the less ambitious task of sketching some general explanations.

Ethnic minorities have tended to face disadvantaged material circumstances compared to whites. However, the groups vary in the extent of these disadvantages and their capacity to resist the impact on educational performance. For example, Bangladeshis remain amongst the most economically disadvantaged of the ethnic groups, yet the performance of their children has improved remarkably over the last twenty years, suggesting major adaptation of second and third generation of this minority to the host culture. When family poverty is measured in terms of eligibility for free school meals, its negative effect tends to be less dramatic on the performance of any of the ethnic minority groups than on whites. Of course, the proportions of families where children are entitled to free school meals will vary between the ethnic groups, yet for Bangladeshis where we would expect eligibility to be high, those within this group who are eligible for free school meals perform almost as well as those who are not. Such evidence suggests the remarkable resilience in educational performance of this group to economic deprivation.

Although essentially dismissing 'race' as a valid approach to understanding educational performance differences, sociologists have to deal with the reality that racial prejudice and discrimination still exist, if now more covertly, and have consequences. Evidence of racial discrimination is provided elsewhere in this text. At present, it is reasonable to argue that its effect has been to over represent some ethnic minority groups (Afro Caribbean in particular and Indian less so) in poorly paid manual occupations and high levels of deprivation with little chance of improvement. The poorer school performance of Afro Caribbeans could therefore be partly explained by their disproportionate concentration in poverty and working class occupations. Indeed, the Swan Report referred to the impact of deprivation, resulting from discrimination in both employment and housing, on educational performance, research conducted by Eggleston found that the fathers of 87% of Afro Caribbean children were employed in manual occupations (1986), and Smith and Tomlinson (1989) have argued that social class more strongly relates to educational attainment levels than ethnicity does. However, to more accurately measure the impact of ethnicity itself on educational performance, one would need to control on class by comparing the performance of pupils of different ethnic groups but of the same social class backgrounds.

Another approach to understanding levels of educational performance relates to the family life of ethnic minority groups. For example, Afro Caribbean families have traditionally comprised far higher proportions of lone parent female headed families than any other ethnic group. Evidence has indicated that more generally pupils from lone parent families perform less well educationally. Common explanations for the poor performance of children from lone parent family backgrounds have often pointed to a negative effect of the absence of a male breadwinner role model and authority figure. Poorer educational performance associated with this family type can be itself at least in part influenced by teacher stereotypes shaped by these common explanations. This is likely to have impacted more heavily on Afro Caribbeans when associated by teachers with a casual attitude to learning and indiscipline in the classroom; apparently substantiated by high levels of school expulsion recorded for this group.

Explanations of poor educational performance may also be couched in terms of ethnic subcultural values. Two such approaches will be mentioned here with one tending to attribute blame to ethnic minorities and the other not. The first explanation looks to place the blame on negative or anti-educational values argued to be held by an ethnic group and has in the past sometimes been used to explain the poor educational performance of Afro Caribbean boys. Similar explanations have been used regarding the poor performance levels of white working class boys who are members of deviant school subcultures.

The second type of explanation, taking a lead from the ideas of Bourdieu, looks at poor achievement in terms of cultural deficit. In this explanation, the education system is shaped by the ability of the middle and upper classes to impose their culture as the framework by which assessment and achievement is measured. Thus, just as the working class may be disadvantaged by a lack of middle and upper class cultural assets, so ethnic minorities may experience ethnic cultural disadvantage. Even though parents within these groups may be just as highly motivated as any others for their children to do well at school, they may lack the cultural assets to be able to help as much. Even so, the parental response is not necessarily a passive one, as witnessed by examples of the setting up of Saturday schools by ethnic groups to improve the performance of their children.

More explanations can be found by focussing on aspects of the school environment. For example, one may question the extent to which the high level of exclusion of Afro Caribbean boys from school is simply a measure of particularly challenging behaviour of this group, often explained in terms of lack of a father figure in the family, or is at least to some extent a consequence of negative labelling by teachers based on this very stereotype, whereby similar behaviour by pupils from other ethnic groups that teachers hold a more favourable stereotype of is less likely to lead to expulsion. This interpretation is supported by the research of Wright (1992) who found that in the primary schools that she studied, Afro Caribbean boys tended to be singled out for disciplinary treatment when similar behavioural conduct by white boys did not lead to similar levels of disciplinary response.

Negative stereotyping of Afro Caribbeans by teachers was found in the Swann Report of 1985. Research conducted by the Runnymead Trust (1997) discovered that teachers often used negative stereotypes in the way that they related to ethnic minority students, and research by Connolly (1998) found that at the primary school level teachers differentiated their judgements of Afro Caribbean and Asian pupils in negative and more positive terms respectively in relation to their general stereotypes and views of the supposedly different family life of these ethnic groups. Clearly, teachers' treatment of students based on ethnic stereotyping can lead to a self-fulfilling prophecy in the performance of pupils. However, research findings by Fuller (1984), Mac an Ghaill (1988) and Mirza (1992) into the performance of black ethnic minority girls offers a cautionary reminder that groups may resist negative stereotyping and perform well. Whilst the girls exhibited a defiant attitude toward their learning experience, unlike the white working class boys in Willis' research they did not adopt an anti-learning culture and in recognizing the practical importance of obtaining qualifications worked hard to achieve them.

The Swann Report also found that Afro Caribbean pupils experienced high levels of placement in schools for the 'educationally subnormal'. It highlighted the inappropriateness of this provision when in the many cases the difficulty was more to do with the language used rather than innate backwardness, and that youngsters could be better supported through other specialist provision which took this into account. Furthermore, the view that linguistic variations from standard English are necessarily intellectually inferior can itself be highly questioned.

The school environment and curriculum may be experienced as alienating, especially to recent migrants, if it provides little or no consideration of their cultural heritage. This ethnocentrism, linked to the immigrant / host viewpoint and emphasis on assimilation, can lead to a disconnection of pupils from the educational process through the excessive emphasis on British culture in such subjects as English literature and history. Ethnic minorities can feel alienated if the implication is that their cultural background is worthless.

Developments in educational policy

We have seen that during the post-war years up to the 1960s, there existed between Labour and Conservative governments a degree of consensus on the importance of extending state education in such a way as to enhance meritocratic opportunity. The socialist tinge in Labour ideology emphasised the importance of enhancing equality of opportunity by which more children of working class parents may through educational achievement experience social mobility. The Conservatives, tending at the time to adopt a 'one nation' approach, placed greater emphasis on competition and the incentives of inequality of outcome, but conceded to attempts to improve equality of opportunity in the interests of social harmony and stability. These differing emphases became clearer in the dispute over the retention of the selective tripartite system, generally supported by the Conservatives, and the promotion of comprehensive education by Labour governments. However, both parties tended to share the view that state intervention in education was an important part of a broader process of social engineering guided by an ethic of social justice and thus subscribed to what we have previously referred to as a social democratic approach to education.

1. Conservative new right (neoliberal) policy – the promotion of diversity and choice

In the context of Britain's waning economic performance, debate from the mid 1970s was increasingly focussing on the appropriateness of educational provision to cater for the needs of employers and the broader economy. This issue was raised to prominence in 1976 by the Labour Prime Minister James Callaghan in his Ruskin College speech. In sociological terms, concern across the political spectrum was emerging about the effectiveness of the education system in performing its economic function. This was compounded by a period of growing labour unrest which culminated in the widespread industrial disputes that marked the 'winter of discontent' during 1978 – 1979 that brought down the Labour government.

When the Conservative government came to power in 1979, they were intent on reforming education with the aim of improving the country's economic efficiency and competitiveness and re-imposing social order within an increasingly challenging global environment. A greater emphasis was placed on vocational training and education with, for example, the introduction of the Youth Training Scheme which was aimed at providing work related skills for school leavers, and NVQs to provide occupationally related training and qualifications. Significantly, their general approach to educational reform signalled a break from the social democratic model pursued by previous Labour and Conservative governments. The issue of enhancing social justice by promoting equality of educational opportunity, particularly with reference to social class background, tended to be downgraded, with greater concern being placed on raising overall standards. From a new right perspective, it was argued that this could best be achieved by 'marketising' the education system - introducing reforms into the public sector to create a competitive environment similar to that of the private sector and in which individual schools would be run like competing businesses to attract consumers.

The old tripartite versus comprehensive battle was becoming eclipsed by a policy of promoting greater diversity of schools and enhancing (parental) choice or preference. As things stood, selective education was allowed to continue in those, mainly Conservative, areas that had retained grammar schools. Many local authorities were in the process of converting to comprehensive provision, whereas in some localities grammar schools coexisted alongside 'comprehensives' which were therefore strictly speaking not comprehensives at all for their catchment area. Most schools were coeducational, but some had single sex intake. Faith schools, partly funded by churches, offered further options in many local authorities.

New right reforms extended this diversity. City technology colleges, funded by both central government and business and specialising in science, technology and business subjects, were established in a small number of urban localities. Schools could also elect to become 'grant maintained'. These schools 'opted out' of local authority finance and control, were funded directly from the government, and were run autonomously by boards of school governors that included parents. Some introduced highly selective intake procedures, whilst others did not. The government also introduced the Assisted Places Scheme. This provided means tested support for able children of poorer families to enter independent schools and thus further supported that sector.

Alongside this growing diversity of provision, uniformity of assessment within the state sector was enhanced through the introduction of the national curriculum and periodic standardised testing. This uniformity formed the foundation of publicly accessible information on academic achievement. On the basis of standardised information compiled in the form of published league tables, it was intended that schools would have to become more publicly accountable for their performance and that parents would be able to make enlightened decisions on the best schools for their children to attend. Schools needed to be more competitive as intake quotas were no longer guaranteed and funding followed their ability to attract pupils. All of this meant that schools had to become better at marketing themselves within a competitive environment.

Another element of educational diversity remained in the independent school sector. Independent schools, as privately run charitable organisations, rely heavily on parental payment of fees for their children to attend. Within this sector, the more exclusive and prestigious schools are referred to as public schools. At secondary level, public schools usually have an entry age of 13, which coincides with completing private preparatory school, and pupils are required to have passed the common entrance exam. Many public schools offer boarding facilities and a number have retained single sex intake.

A degree of power was taken away from the teaching profession and local authorities (the providers of education) and the system was more centralised through the introduction of the national curriculum, standardised testing and Ofsted inspections. On the other hand, power was diffused down to consumers of education, particularly parents in the case of school children, through their greater involvement in choice of school, opportunity to vote for a school to be transferred to grant maintained status, and involvement on boards of school governors. However, an opening up of the selection process to parental choice arguably also enhanced a process of covert selection by social advantage whereby some parents with greater economic, social and cultural capital were more able to get far more for their children from the choices available than those without.

So did new right reforms improve educational standards? There is clear evidence if one takes GCSE and A Level grades as the benchmark that performances have improved year after year through to the early twenty first century. However, two important questions will be raised at present. Firstly, because the market test is set in terms of qualifications and grades, there are pressures to 'teach to tests'. Therefore, improvements in results may be gained by retreat to a narrowed experience of education by pupils. Secondly, improvement in grades may in part be a consequence of 'grade inflation' – the view that the standards by which grades can be achieved become watered down over time.

2. New Labour policy – no return to the social democratic model

When New Labour came to power in 1997, they were faced with an increasingly fluid globalised world market where inward investment needed to be attracted. It was argued that to successfully compete in this global market, the state had a key role to play in providing the infrastructure and skilled workforce that was necessary to attract business investment. A 'magnet economy' had to be created in which, through the expansion of education and training, businesses would be prepared to invest and offer high wages to highly skilled workers. In effect, forces of globalisation were encouraging a more instrumentalist educational culture by which could be detected an increased emphasis on education taking the form of training for vocational utility.

In many respects, Labour followed the neoliberal reforms of the new right era. They were as determined as the Conservatives had been to promote diversity and competition within education and to impose a demanding inspection regime, all to promote high educational standards. In fact, the passage of their reforms sometimes relied on Conservative support in Parliament. Although admissions within the state secondary system became largely non-selective, in contrast to the policy of previous Labour regimes the government did not actively promote the abolition of the remaining grammar schools but left decisions as to their future to local democratic processes. Whilst grant maintained schools reverted back to local authority funding, with most becoming foundation schools, their governing boards retained a high level of decision making autonomy from local authorities. City technology colleges that were established by the new right joined the ranks of city academies, set up by New Labour to improve educational performance in a number of deprived and underachieving inner city areas by replacing comprehensives. City academies were run as self-governing trusts, which were partly supported by private funding and expertise. Specialist schools, allowed to select up to 10% of their pupils in terms of their specialist ability, were set up with such varied emphases as sports, modern languages, technology and the arts. Comprehensives, once favoured by Labour, were encouraged to become specialist schools and the formation of new faith schools had government support.

The Labour government required all new schools to operate as self-governing trusts, organisations partly supported by charitable foundation partners and run by their own boards of governors. In the long run, all state secondary schools were expected to become either specialist schools or academy trusts. Overall, local diversity and autonomy, market competition, parental choice, and the driving up of standards, measured by examination performance, remained central features of government policy on education.

New Labour even took the use of private finance within the state education system further than the Conservative new right had. Private finance was used to help re-equip schools with the latest technology and even provide capital for building new schools. In the case of the latter, the taxpaying electorate was saved the burden of the up-front payment for the provision, but interest rates were to be paid by governments over a contracted period of time.

Other reforms held somewhat more social democratic credentials. Pre-school and nursery provision were substantially expanded, Education Action Zones were established to inject more funding from government and private enterprise into inner city areas of deprivation and poor educational performance, and financial support of up to £30 a week for students from poorer backgrounds and aged 16 to 19 was introduced through the Education Maintenance Allowance. Also, resources from the winding up of the Assisted Places Scheme were redirected toward reducing the size of primary school classes.

Two issues will be raised at this point. Firstly, Brown and Lauder (1996, in Ball ed. 2004) have suggested that New Labour's broad economic approach places too much faith in the superior magnetic attraction of the home economy to achieve inward investment. It is argued that other countries within a competitive global environment, some with lower labour costs, will be pursuing similar policies and will likewise be developing their infrastructure and human resources to attract inward investment. Thus, whilst the government may be able to enhance people's employability through boosting education and training, it may not be within their control to deliver close to full employment of the educated and trained.

Secondly, although examination performance continued to improve under Labour's watch, there were far less impressive findings in terms of social justice. Commenting on a 2006 Organisation for Economic Co-operation and Development survey which looked at literacy and numeracy skills in

29 member countries, Green and Unwin found that in England the impact of social background on educational performance was the fifth most severe (Chitty, 2009, p.250). Chitty went on to comment that 'for all of the political rhetoric about raising educational standards and furthering opportunity, English schools do more to lock in intergenerational inequality than to promote social mobility' (Chitty, 2009, P.250).

3. Coalition and Conservative policy – adding to diversity?

With the election of a coalition government headed by the Conservatives in 2010, the market competition approach to education very much remained in place. The government strongly pushed toward far more schools becoming academies, with the aim that most new schools would be of this type. However, in distinction to the policy under New Labour of using academies to improve educational performance in deprived and underperforming areas, under the Conservatives schools that have achieved outstanding performance could be fast tracked to academy status and in some cases poorly performing schools have been forced to make the transition.

To further the mix of schools, a new type was introduced in the form of 'free schools'. Like academies, these schools are run independently of local authorities and are intended to strongly reflect local needs. Free schools can be set up by parents, community groups, charities or teachers. Through the utilisation of buildings that can be converted to schools, these schools have provided a cost saving advantage on building at a time of budget cuts. As in the case of academies, free schools do not necessarily need to employ fully qualified teachers or heads, they are not required to abide by national terms of pay and conditions of employment, they allow greater freedom of teaching styles and curriculum and do not have to adhere to nutritional standards guidelines in the provision of meals.

There have been some high profile cases of free schools failing to reach acceptable standards, linked to inadequate teaching and leadership, even leading to cases of closure. As some free schools are faith schools, they have also been criticised, along with other faith schools, as promoting segregation. In some cases, schools have failed Ofsted inspections following claims that Islamification has led to a narrowing of the syllabus and differentiation in the teaching of boys and girls according to Islamic strictures. Furthermore, some free schools have been established in areas where there already exists a surplus of local authority school places, with many of these schools already performing at good to outstanding levels. A strong case can therefore be made that in such areas available resources are being wasted.

Overall, the government's preference for academies and free schools has been criticised for eroding national terms and conditions of employment and pay levels, further fragmenting the educational 'system' in England, and its propensity for segregating children along religious and social class lines.

The Education Maintenance Allowance, introduced by Labour to support students from poorer backgrounds, was replaced by a more restricted and tightly targeted fund. However, the introduction of the Pupil Premium retargeted funds to schools dependent on the numbers of pupils that claim free school meals.

When Teresa May took over as leader of the Conservative Party and Prime Minister in 2016, she made great play of building a meritocratic society. Allied with this was resuscitated the view that grammar schools promote social mobility, and so the expansion of grammar school provision was put out as a straw in the wind. Whilst likely to appeal to some sections of popular opinion, it is at least highly questionable in terms of past sociological evidence whether such expansion can further the stated objectives.

The issue of faith schools has again been raised as proposals are being drafted for the removal of the cap of 50% selection on the grounds of religious faith for free schools that are oversubscribed. Critics argue that such a change is likely to further segregate pupils along religious lines.

In higher education, tuition fees that universities can charge have had their ceiling raised to £9,250 as from 2017. Although overall this does not appear to have had a detrimental effect on higher education applications from students of poorer backgrounds, there is evidence that they are tending to choose institutions closer to home and with lower fees. This may include enrolling on HE vocational courses provided at local FE institutions.

Global context of educational policy – the emergence and dominance of neoliberalism

The state as provider approach to the delivery of education not only failed to engineer the desired degree of social justice in terms of equality of opportunity and meritocratic based social mobility, but was also often seen as associated with the poor performance of economies throughout the 1960s and 1970s. During this time, a number of think tanks were developing ideas to fundamentally reform public sector institutions from the perspective that they must respond to and enhance the economic competitiveness of free market knowledge economies. As documented in section 1 above, in Britain these reforms were positively taken up by a Conservative new right government that came to power in 1979. Like reforms were embraced by a number of governments, particularly those of the United States and Australia, in pursuit of free market policies of the political right from the 1980s and 1990s.

A key role in steering this direction of reforms was adopted by international development and funding organisations such as the World Bank, the Organisation for Economic Co-operation and Development (OECD) and the United Nations Educational, Scientific and Cultural Organisation (UNESCO). As Rizvi documents (Lauder, H. et al (ed), 2006), the ideological outlook of the OECD prior to the 1990s tended to strike a balance between more state interventionist European social democratic / social justice models and an American free market neoliberal policy emphasis. Their programmes could also be shaped to some extent by the national agendas of recipient countries. However, the American neoliberal economic efficiency view came to prevail during the 1990s with the OECD becoming prescriptive regarding this outlook on globalisation. The OECD and other international organisations have increasingly tied financial support for education to a neoliberal approach that requires free market reforms, measures efficiency and provides internationally comparative data on educational performance. Consequently, the view of relating educational provision to combatting social class disadvantage has virtually disappeared off the agenda.

How can neoliberal educational reforms be best conceptualised? Governments have to reshape educational institutions so that they must operate within and respond to competitive market pressures. This means that the state plays a shrinking role, retreating from direct involvement in overall planning and provision to a newly formed but hardened role of enforcing market accountability. The performance of institutions has to be measured and monitored with precision through the provision of performance data according to standardised criteria. This top down drive for accountability, efficiency and value for money is referred to by Ward (2014) as 'decentralized centralization'. The post 2008 global recession has intensified the impact of neoliberal reforms to maximise returns on resources restricted by spending cuts.

A key aim of neoliberal reforms is to tie knowledge production to the needs of markets. The consequence will be both greater accountability to the wishes of individual consumers of education and a closer link to the needs of free enterprise economies. Whilst arguably resting more comfortably with governments of the liberal right, the rhetoric and policies of governments throughout much of the world on educational policy has tended to converge on neoliberal ground. This has enabled long term entrenchment of policy changes to take effect.

The wishes of consumers of education and the needs of the economy come together in the drive for more effective self-capitalisation of labour. In other words, a key aim of institutional reforms has been to encourage individuals to regard education as an ongoing source of personal investment in the knowledge and skills that are required from workers to continually adjust to the dynamic economies of 'fast capitalism'. The purpose of education within the neoliberal perspective, as viewed, prescribed and imposed by the OECD, is to service free enterprise economies within a competitive global world with a flexible and efficient source of labour. For Rizvi, this means that the effect of education on individuals in the marketised approach is to produce 'the self-capitalising, flexible, neoliberal subject' (Lauder, H. et al (ed), 2006, p.259). And as Ward (2014) emphasises, central to this model is the need to change public sector institutions in the direction of free markets to such a fundamental extent that over time people's outlook, fundamental sense of being and behaviour become attuned to the needs of the free market as the only conceivable way of life. Clearly, education provides a profound learning context for this new outlook.

Developments in education

1. An emphasis on examination performance:

Measuring performance

Education can have many purposes, including that of nurturing personal development and shaping a responsible citizenship. However, preoccupation has often focussed on academic performance which is conventionally viewed as synonymous with the achievement grades and certificates. This allows ease of statistical measurement of performance across the student population and the establishment of trends of change. In a more personalised way, examination performance is annually symbolised in the media by students receiving their (usually high grade!) results.

Such statistics provide the appearance of factual data on achievement levels that positivist minded sociologists might prefer to work with. However, there are various reasons why caution is necessary in their use. Firstly, in the case of GCSEs, changes in the grading system are well advanced and should be complete by the summer of 2020. The old system that ranged achievement from A* down to G grades is being replaced by a more finely graded system of 9 down to 1 which is intended to be more sensitive to measuring overall stretch of performance, especially toward the top end of the scale. Whilst under the old grading system the pass grade was established at C, originally, in the context of a government attempting to toughen up qualifications which it was believed had softened as a result of grade inflation, the intention was to set the new pass level at the more challenging grade 5 which was pitched as equivalent to the top end of a C grade and the bottom end of a B. The consequence of this would have been a likely decrease in pass rates and difficulty in comparing performance at the point of transition between the systems. It was subsequently decided that the achievement of a grade 4 would be regarded as a 'standard pass' and grade 5 designated a 'strong pass'.

Secondly, one needs to be aware of the different way in which measurements are taken. These can lead to slightly different conclusions. For example, if we were considering performance at GCSE level, some statistics will be in the form of the percentage of students who have achieved a recognised pass grade or above in at least five subjects, whereas an alternative measurement may simply relate to the proportion of passes and above in relation to the total number of subjects sat. Other measurements may focus on the proportion of top grades achieved. Data may or may not include other equivalent level qualifications. Even with awareness of factors such as these, it is important to establish whether the statistics refer to just England or the UK. In the latter case, figures for Northern Ireland and Wales would be included but it would need to be clear whether or not figures for Scottish equivalent qualifications were. Moreover, the most up to date information that is provided after results are released is usually provisional and may require revision in the future due to the outcome of appeals.

Norm to criterion referenced assessment and the question of grade inflation

The issue of grade inflation needs to be put in the context of a change from norm to criterion referenced assessment. Norm referencing relates individual performance to the performance of others. Thus, from 1963,

GCE A Levels were essentially norm graded, a process by which the marked work would be allocated according to fixed proportions within different grade bands. For example, the top 10% of work, whatever the marks were in a particular year, would be awarded an A grade pass and the next 15% a B and so on. In total, only the top 70% would pass. The main argument in favour of this approach was that since the intelligence distribution across all entrants was believed to follow the same consistent spread from year to year, then this system would compensate for those years in which the exams might be more or less difficult. However, it would not be well suited to measure whether performance against fixed standards was improving or deteriorating.

Related to this latter criticism, from 1987, assessment was shifted to criterion referencing. In distinction to norm referencing, criterion referencing assesses the performance of each individual against specific performance criteria, a change that would eliminate fixed band proportions and arguably provide a more realistic basis from which to measure changes in performance. Thus, for more than two subsequent decades, the proportion of pupils achieving in the different grade bands significantly changed. By 2011, A grades accounted for about 27% of results and overall passes rose above 95%. Such changes led to growing criticisms that, given a fixed distribution of intelligence spread across the population, the improved figures could only have been achieved through a softening of assessment and a decline in the standard of the grading categories. Hence, it was argued that grade inflation was providing the appearance of improved academic performance which was in fact the result of the watering down of standards.

The aim at present is to convey a sense of what the statistics show at face value, bearing in mind that for the time period concerned reference has to be made to the old grading system.

One of the most remarkable trends in the data has been the opening up of a gender gap in GCSE and A level performance as the attainment of girls improved more rapidly than that of boys. Since the replacement of the GCE with the GCSE qualification in 1988, the performance of girls had moved ahead of boys in each year up to 2002 with the exception of 2001. As a result, the overall GCSE United Kingdom (excluding Scotland) figures for August 2002 showed that 62.4% of girls' entries achieved a grade C pass or above compared to 53.4% for boys. At the top end, 5.9% of girls' entries achieved an A* grade compared to 4.1% for boys. Likewise, at A level, girls were consistently outperforming boys in overall pass rates. What changed was an overhauling of the achievement of boys at the level of A grade passes. During the early 1990s, boys slightly outperformed girls in the achievement of top grades. However, in August 2002, 21.9% of girls' entries achieved an A grade pass compared to 19.3% of boys'. This represented a threefold increase in their lead compared with 2001 figures.

On a subject by subject basis, girls during this period extended their lead in performance in those areas where they have more traditionally outperformed boys (in the arts and humanities) and were increasing their participation and often moving ahead of boys in most of the traditional male subject areas (in science subjects). This advance was arguably assisted by the impact of the national curriculum, which required all students to study sciences, and the use of less gender biased texts.

In the light of the above figures, attention came to increasingly focus on the problem of relative male underachievement which was been usually explained in terms of laddish culture and behaviour, especially amongst those from poorer backgrounds who most underperformed. On the other hand, it was suggested that a greater proportion of coursework assessment favoured females who tend to be more methodical in their application to their studies and better in the presentation of their work.

The performance figures for girls and boys for 2006 and 2007 indicated that the gap opened up by girls over boys was closing. Thus, at GCSE level in 2006, the achievement gap in A* and A grades narrowed compared to 2005 by 0.5%, but still remained at 7.7%. This gap narrowed by a further 0.2% by 2007 and the A* to C grade performance gap narrowed by 0.6% between 2006 and 2007. At A level, between 2005 and 2007, boys closed the gap on girls slightly in the achievement of A-E passes, but between 2005 and 2006, girls had increased their lead over boys in achieving A grade passes.

One explanation for this modest and brief reversal of the previous trend is that a number of schools had selected more adventure and action based texts for study which boys tended to find more appealing – an interesting reversal of past feminist crusades to make texts more female friendly at a time before the opening of a substantial gender gap in favour of girls.

However, data for 2013 showed that in aggregate GCSE A* and A grades, girls still excelled over boys by over 7% and within the range of A* to C grade passes their performance was superior by over 8%. There did though remain a very pronounced gendered pattern of subject preference. For example, at A level data showed that boys comprised 80% of physics and over 60% of maths entries, as well as significant majorities in economics and computing, whereas girls strongly outnumberd boys in pursuing English, psychology, biology and art.

The performance of ethnic minority pupils generally improved more rapidly than that of white students. This was sometimes from a relatively low base of achievement. For example, in GCSE grades A*-C, the performance of black Caribbean students improved by approximately 6% over the two years leading up to 2006 to reach 41.7% and black Africans by 5% to 48.3%. At the higher end, the figure for Chinese students improved in the year up to 2006 by 6.8% to reach 74.2%.

Certain ethnic minority groups had achieved superior performance to that of whites for some time, and most other groups were at least closing the performance gap. When figures are broken down in terms of ethnicity, gender, and living in poverty, the poorest performers were white boys from poor backgrounds. Research conducted by Cassen and Kingdom (2007) for the Joseph Rowntree Foundation found that 62% of white boys who take free school meals appeared in the bottom 10% of performers in education (18/6/2014, p.14), a figure far higher than for equally poor Afro-Carribeans. The research identified an anti-education culture amongst classmates and at home a poor learning environment and limited language communication as part of the problem.

Regarding the performance of ethnic minority groups, the Statistical First Release figures for England use a slightly different measurement in terms of achieving at least 5 GCESs at C and above, including within the definition English and maths or International GCSEs. By this measure, Chinese pupils still performed the best, exceeding the national average by 17.6% in 2012, (20/11/2013) but given their very high performances in previous years, their lead over the national average had decreased by 4.1% compared to that of 2008. Other notable points were that the performance of Indian pupils was not far behind that of the Chinese and that Banglsadeshi pupils had improved their performance to such an extent that they had risen from below the national average in 2008 to above it in 2012. Afro Caribbean performance improved between these dates, but remained the lowest of the ethnic minorities.

Ethnic minorities have a comparatively high likelihood of entering higher education, although to date have remained conspicuously thin on the ground in the most elite universities. Of particular interest here is the fact that despite relatively poor school performance and high levels of exclusion of Afro Caribbean males, their entry rate to higher education studies is higher than that of white males. Some light can be shed on this by small scale research carried out by Wright (2013) on Afro Caribbean youngsters in London and Nottingham. Wright found that supported by the social capital of their communities, they were able to construct a 'turnaround narrative' which enabled them to show a determination to change that resisted failure and adversity.

Data on traveller communities has shown extremely low performance levels and only slight improvement. An issue here can be the disconnection which is often evident between these communities and schools. Research conducted by Flecha & Soler (2013) suggested that stereotypes of travellers as uninterested in education, which themselves contribute to keeping them on the margins of the system and creating distrust in teachers by parents, need to be challenged, since it is these stereotypes which promote marginalisation and exclusion. In their case study research conducted at a primary school in Spain, they found that Roma's value education but their distrust has often put them off. Adopting a more inclusive approach to overcome distrust improved the attendance, equality of opportunity and performance of Roma children.

During the early twenty first century, the general trend in examination performance continued to be an upward one. Dramatic jumps in the figures took place between 2001 and 2002 when the number of students fast tracking to take GCSE exams at the age of 15 or under more than doubled and A level passes (grades A-E) showed the largest annual increase, climbing from 89.8% to 94.3% of all entries. By 2006, A-C grade passes at GCSE reached 62.4% of all entries and the number of A* and A grades increased by 0.7% on the previous year's figure to 19.1%. The figures for 2007 had further improved to 63.3% and 19.5% respectively, whilst the proportion of fast tracked students (fifteen year olds or under), had reached 14% of all entries. The 2006 A level figures for A-E grade passes reached 96.6%, and A grades achieved improved by 1.3% on the figure for the previous year to reach 24.1%. By 2007, A-E passes improved further to 96.9% and the proportion of A grades awarded increased by a further 1.2% to reach 25.3%. By comparison, the A Level A grade figure for independent schools rose from 41.3% of entries in 2002 to 47.9% in 2006 and remained almost unchanged at 47.8% in 2007. Interestingly, it is from within this sector of the education system that the highest proportion of appeals are lodged.

We can now return to the question of what we are we to make of this data which on the surface indicates a continuous improvement in standards of performance from the mid-1980s through to the early twenty first century? Much debate had emerged over the question of standards and the problem is that approaching this issue is difficult to reduce to a purely technical matter. It is quite likely that enhanced competition within the system had improved the focus and effort put in by both teachers and students. Amongst the greatest increases in performance were amongst a range of ethnic minority groups. These were likely to be real improvements that reflected the assimilation of these groups over the generations. It is also the case that that given their concern about league table placing, schools became more cautious in their selection of pupils for exam entry. Additionally, the introduction of AS levels would have enhanced the process of filtering through self-selection. By taking AS levels after one year, students were able to make decisions on which subjects they would drop and which they would continue to study through to A level. The fact that the largest annual increase in A level performance coincided with a 6% drop in entrants following the introduction of AS levels appears to offer confirmation of these effects of self-selection.

However, opposing arguments were forthcoming that statistics that show such remarkable upward trends can only come from an erosion of qualification standards. Those who adopted this view tended to maintain that innate ability follows a standard distribution curve for the population as a whole and that it does not significantly advance over time. Thus, it is argued that the evidence suggesting annual improvements in success bears little relationship to 'real' improvements in performance. This position often lies behind the criticisms of those who identify with the political right. Ruth Lea, of the Institute of Directors, argued that grade inflation – the watering down of performance required to achieve higher grades and give a statistically misleading suggestion of improvement – was an unfortunate reality.

But how might this happen? Ironically, the finger of blame can be pointed at competition, which is meant to drive up standards. Whilst schools have to compete for league table places, exam boards are also in competition for exam entries. In this toxic mix, schools tend to search for 'softer' exam boards that they think will maximise their success rates and exam boards compete to oblige.

It is arguably difficult, with advances in technology for accessing information and presenting work, to directly compare the performance of students over time and it is quite possible that both grade inflation was taking place and, through more effective teaching and learning, student performance was improving.

During and after the summer of 2003, a number of universities expressed concern regarding problems of differentiating student performance. As more students were passing A levels with top grades, concern was raised over the growing difficulty of using these grades to separate out the most able students. Students themselves were increasingly finding that top grades were no guarantee of gaining access to popular and competitive courses and the most prestigious universities. As a consequence, more universities started to set their own entrance exams and looked to alternatives to A levels which they felt would better differentiate levels of student ability and performance.

Within schools, one response was an increasing uptake of the more demanding Advanced Extension Award which replaced special level papers from 2002. This exam, aimed at the top 10% of A level students, required the demonstration of a deeper level of subject understanding. Universities occasionally made the Advanced Extension Award part of an offer. The government also became involved in piloting a toughening of A level questions with the aim of introducing more challenging A levels from September 2008. The changes introduced included a movement away from structured exam questions and the requirement of more extended answers, as well as an A* grade for those who achieve 90% or above in their final exams. In measuring differentiation at the top end of achievement, the introduction of the A* grade from 2010 led to the virtual withdrawal of the Advanced Extension Award.

A further development was an increasing take up in schools of the International Baccalaureate Diploma which combines core and optional elements into a broad education. This offered highly differentiated outcomes ranging from certificates in individual subjects for those who do not pass the diploma overall to a top end of achievement equivalent in UCAS points to that of six grade A A levels. A leading examining board also piloted a baccalaureate type qualification which added to three A levels a paper in general studies, critical thinking or citizenship and a piece of extended essay or project work.

An enhanced measure of GCSE performance and preferable foundation in choice of subjects for progression on to A levels and university was proposed by the Russell Group of top universities. This would constitute achievement in terms of an English Baccalaureate combination of GCSE subjects (the EBacc, not to be confused with the later ill-fated English Baccalaureate Certificate, the EBC, that was meant to replace GCSEs). From 2010, this more demanding measure of success originally required grade C performance or above in a core of the following subjects: English language, mathematics, history or geography, two science subjects and a modern language. Data for 2010 showed that significantly fewer students eligible for free school meals took the Baccalaureate combination than those not eligible (8% as opposed to 24%) and of those entered, a smaller proportion were successful (4% as opposed to 17%).

Achievement in the university sector has also been scrutinised with regard to the debate over grade inflation. Statistics show that in the award of degree categories, as in the case of A Levels, there has been a clustering of achievement toward the top end. For example, by 2012 – 2013, 70% of university degrees were awarded at first or upper second class honours grades compared to a figure of about a third in 1970.

Arguments pointing to grade inflation have suggested that competitive pressure for position in league tables has led to a softening of assessment standards and that financial incentives to increase intake has compromised quality of entrants.

Counterarguments, that real improvements in academic performance have taken place refer to greater student diligence within the context of a more competitive job market and improved teaching techniques and educational technology. Another issue, emphasised for example in research carried out by Johnes and Soo (2017) at the University of Lancaster, is that improved level of degrees awarded is related to better prepared students at the intake stage as indicated by higher A Level grade performance. Thus, more traditional universities that ask for higher entry grades are able to offer a higher proportion of high degree grades based on the quality of their intake without compromising standards.

However, research by Sonner (2000) in the United States found that increasing use of university lecturers employed on short term contracts could lead to grade inflation. The insecurity of their employment provided extra pressures to create a good impression with students. An important consequence of this was a tendency for these 'adjunct' lecturers to award higher grades to student than their established counterparts.

An emphasis on grade deflation

As indicated above, pre-2010, New Labour governments had attempted to provide more challenging measures of educational achievement. Following the general election of 2010, a coalition government was formed with the

Conservatives as the senior partner. Michael Gove, as Secretary of State for Education, clearly took on board the message of the grade inflation camp. His aspiration to return more fully to traditional 'O' level type exams was blocked by the Liberal Democrat coalition partners. Gove conceded that his intention to replace GCSEs with an English Baccalaureate Certificate (EBC) was a step too far, at least in the time span envisaged, but already more students were choosing subjects which led to the English Baccalaureate structure of GCSE subject choices (EBacc) and which included less internal assessment and a greater emphasis on final exams. The proportion of students choosing these subjects increased from 22% in 2010 to 48% in 2012 and the government subsequently set a target of 90% by 2025. Whilst the trend toward EBacc subject choices reversed a decline in the number of students studying history, geography and modern languages at GCSE level, critics pointed to a constriction of choice which had a detrimental effect on the number of pupils following the arts.

In 2011, against the backdrop of a climate of scepticism regarding the academic value of GCSE and A level qualifications, Ofqual, a regulative body previously set up to oversee standards of pre-university qualifications in England, advised the A Level exam boards to peg the awarding of A grades to no more than the top 27% of achievers. This signalled the introduction of a more mixed criterion and normative approach tied up with a political ambition of countering grade inflation with measures of grade deflation. Various changes were subsequently introduced with the aim of toughening up standards, include the following:

1. In terms of curriculum and learning, a more facts based approach to reciting 'correct' information was adopted. Opponents have criticised this change as narrowing the experience of education toward that of memory recall at the expense of considering alternative viewpoints and encouraging critical thinking.

2. There was a substantial increase between 2012 and 2013 in the entry of under 16s (by 39%) for GCSE exams and a smaller (9%) increase of post 16 entries, both groups of which perform significantly more poorly than 16 year olds at grades C and above and in achieving the highest grades.

3. Following the highly publicised shifting of the grade boundaries in English Language between January and June 2012, with the outcome

of increasing the difficulty of passing at grade C, there was a significant increase in multiple exam entries for the same subject, as for example in GCSE English and International GCSE English, as schools attempted to protect their position in league tables. This practice was not confined to the subject of English.

4. Science GCSE subjects were toughened up between 2012 and 2013. This led to a collapse in entry, with fewer than half the number of 16 year olds that entered in 2012 put in in 2013. C and above grades for 16 year olds fell in all of the sciences (but not in mathematics), the greatest fall coming in science from 64.7% to 47.9%, whilst in physics, chemistry and biology the increase in the numbers of under 16s performing more poorly than 16 year olds in was between two and threefold.

5. GCSEs were reoriented away from coursework assessment and toward assessment of performance in final exams. One anticipated consequence of this was the likelihood of a narrowing of the achievement gap between boys and girls.

6. The GCSE grading system is changing, with the transition in all subjects expected to be completed by the summer of 2020. The grading categories have been extended to nine, with grade 9 being the highest achievement level and 1 being the lowest. The purpose behind this new grading system was to toughen up the criteria for passing and increase the achievement stretch. When originally set, the grade 5 pass level was positioned to correspond to the top third of a grade C pass and the bottom third of a grade B pass under the old system, with expectations that this would reduce passes by about 20%. This stern measure was later compromised with grade 4 classified as a standard pass and grade 5 a strong pass. At the top end of the scale, a grade nine is approximately equivalent to the top half of achievers of the old A* grade.

7. The AS and A Level system has been changed. Whereas AS Levels previously could be used to contribute toward A Level outcomes, the qualifications have now become decoupled with the former constituting one year courses that stand alone and do not contribute toward A Level results, whilst A Levels stand alone as two year courses.

8. Access to Higher Education examining boards have introduced grading to their units at pass, merit and distinction and capped achievements in some of their units, particularly at the introductory stage of the course, at pass level.

The changes referred to above aimed to put into reverse the contended effects of grade inflation and were starting to come into effect between 2012 and 2013. Provisional data published by the Joint Council for Qualifications (28/11/2013) indicated that, in terms of all entries for GCSEs (still using the A* – G grading system), for 2013 there was a drop in achievement across the United Kingdom (England, Wales and Northern Ireland) of C and above grades from 69.4% to 68.1% and A and A* grades from 22.4% to 21.3% compared to 2012. Further, the 2012 results for A and A* grades were down on those of 2011.

Results have remained remarkably consistent from this point. In subjects still graded within the A* - G grading system, for the years between 2013 and 2018, combined A* and A grade achievement figures were 21.3%, 21.3%, 21.2%, 20.5%, 21.3% and 21.7%. In 2018, A* to C passes were at 66.9%, a little up from the previous year. Data shows that when comparisons were made in 2018 with courses that had switched to the 9 – 1 grading system, 7% of achievements were at A* with only 4.3% at grade 9. Across the pass grades of 9 – 4, the performance figures were identical to the A* - G courses at 66.9%. Had the earlier decision to pitch the pass boundary at grade 5 and above been followed through, the aggregate pass figure would have only been 50.3%.

In the case of GCSE mathematics, students are entered for exams at different levels. Decisions are made within educational institutions on setting. Cautiously made decisions to minimise risk of pupil failure can ultimately lead to large numbers of pupils entered for lower tiered exams where top grades cannot be achieved.

The standard measure of deprivation that is frequently used in educational studies is that of eligibility for free school meals. By this measure, the performance gap between those eligible and those not, with reference to achieving at least 5 GCSEs at C or above, narrowed from 26.7% in 2008 to 16.5% in 2012. However, the definition of this category had been broadened from 2012. Previously, it comprised those pupils who were eligible for free school meals in the spring census. In 2012, the measure was changed to include all pupils who had been eligible for free school meals at any time during the previous six years. One might expect that broadening the category in this way may by itself have had the effect of reducing the measured difference in performance between those eligible for free school meals and those that are not. Nonetheless, the performance gap had consistently narrowed in the years before the classification change.

Of pupils classified as having special educational needs, the poorest performing group were those having behavioural, emotional and social difficulties. Those with visual impairment were amongst the highest performing groups, but their performance was substantially below the national average.

Provisional data on A level results for the United Kingdom for 2013 supplied by the Joint Council for Qualifications (28/11/2014) showed that 7.6% of all entries achieved A*, 26.3% A* or A, and 98.1% a pass. Compared to grades in previous years, the overall pass figure was up by just 0.1% on the figure for 2012. However, the figures for the combined two A grade categories showed a second year of decline, the respective figures being 27% in 2011, 26.6% for 2012 and 26.3% in 2013. Generally, there has since been a stabilisation and in some cases a decline in the proportions of higher grade achievements in recent years. For example, the proportions achieving highest A level grades declined slightly for the 5th year in a row leading up to 2016. Whilst the number of A level entrants had decreased between 2015 – 2016, those pursuing more vocational qualifications such as applied general and technical level courses significantly increased, with a major proportion of the latter taken up in the further education college sector.

Broken down by gender, girls performed better at A Level than boys in the A* and A categories (26.7% as opposed to 25.9%) in 2013, but compared to the previous year the gap was closing as male performance was only down by 0.1%, whereas that of females declined by 0.5%. Girls used to outperform boys at A* level, but during 2012 and 2013 boys outperformed girls at this level, the figures for 2013 being 7.9% and 7.4% respectively. When broken down into subjects, boys' A* performance was most ahead in maths, with a 3.3% lead over girls. However, girls' performance was ahead of boys in English.

Regarding changes in subject choices, the influence of the GCSE English Baccalaureate as an indication of university subject preferences appeared to have filtered through to A level to increase student take up in mathematics, the sciences and geography, but not in languages which tended to be down on the previous year. As with GCSE, the best A level performance was in

Northern Ireland, where, for example, 30.7% of students achieved A* and A grades.

The phasing in of A Level reforms has seen a decoupling of A levels from AS levels and a movement away from coursework to final exams. The consequence for AS Levels, which can no longer contribute toward A Level achievements, has been a rapid decline in entrants from 281,600 in 2015 to 64,810 in 2018.

Despite the reforming of A Levels, most of the changes in grade achievement levels have been very modest, with Ofqual emphasising the overall stability of the transition. 2018 A level results showed very little change from those of 2017 and a small fall from 2012 in the % of A*-A grades. However, in 2018, boys edged ahead of girls in these top grade categories for the second year in a row, reversing a lengthy period of superior performance at the top by girls.

The overall pass level at 97.6%, down slightly from the previous year, was in line with figures going back over a decade, and continuity was also shown in the outperformance of English pupils by those in Northern Ireland. For example, in achieving A* to C grade passes, the figures were 76.8% and 85% respectively.

With reference to subject areas, traditional gender preferences remained quite pronounced with about 80% of English Literature pupils being girls whilst 88% of computing pupils and 78% of those taking physics were boys. However, in each of these latter two subjects, small proportionate increases in the numbers of girl pupils were evident.

One change regarding the offer of university places in 2018 was a massive increase of 40% in the number of unconditional offers made as universities competed for intakes in the context of a demographic dip in the number of 18 year olds in the population. This seems to have had little overall downward impact pupils' grade achievements.

We have seen that the coalition government bought into the argument that grade inflation has watered down educational standards and has responded with attempts to toughen up on the criteria for achievement. However, an alternative interpretation to this toughening up has been proposed by Allen (19/6/2014). This questions whether globalisation has brought about the highly skilled and well paid jobs that were expected, suggesting instead that relatively low skilled, low paid and casualised work has been created. Employment opportunities for the young have been particularly hard hit and opportunities for social mobility have gone into decline. As a result, particularly with the expansion of higher education, very many youngsters have found themselves overqualified for the work that is available, or unemployed. From Allen's vantage point, the drive to toughen up educational standards, ostensibly for the purpose of tackling grade inflation, is interpreted as an attempt to limit aspirations and levels of educational achievement in order to establish a closer correspondence between education and limited employment opportunities. However, the evidence so far suggests that the downward pressure on achievement levels has been very modest.

2. Types of illiteracy

There may be marked generational differences regarding definitions of literacy. Older generations may view youngsters who are more familiar with using the latest technology as less literate through the use of abbreviated forms of expression which accompany the use of new technology, for example in the form of commonly accepted standards of communication by e mail or on social media.

On the other hand, young generations have been brought up amidst new technology and introduced to relevant technological skills from a young age at school. They are often far more familiar and comfortable with using this technology throughout their everyday lives than older generations. The latter might well appear to them to be technologically quite illiterate; a type of 'new illiteracy'.

3. The expansion of higher education

Higher education in the UK has witnessed massive expansion in terms of student numbers since the early 1960s. For example, during 1962-1963, approximately 216,000 students were in full-time higher education. By 2017-2018, the figure had risen to approximately 1,845,000 (Bolton (b) 26/32019) with just over a third of all 18 to 19 year olds entering higher education studies. However, despite this expansion, a social class background remained a persistent factor in entry rates. For example, in 1991-1992, when 23% of 18 to 19 year olds were entering full-time higher education, 55% from professional background gained access whilst from unskilled manual background only 6% went on to higher education. By 2001-2002, these figures had risen to 79% and 15% respectively. Figures for 2017-2018 indicate that, measured in terms of past eligibility for free school meals, the most underrepresented group in accessing higher education by the age of 19 was white British boys, with a rate of just 12% (Bolton (b) 26/3/2019).

When one looks at entry to higher education in terms of gender, there has been a remarkable increase in female participation rates. In 1960, with women only comprising about a third of a small undergraduate population, just 5,575 women obtained degrees compared to 16,851 men. By 1992-1993, more women were entering university than men and by 2011, 197,565 degrees were awarded to women compared to 153,235 to men (Bolton (a) 26/3/2019). Data for 2018 higher education entry by the age of 19 shows a figure of 38% of women compared to 28% of men (Bolton (a) 26/3/2019).

The pressures of global economic competition have been a key driving force in the expansion of higher education, a phenomena which is particularly evident in most rapidly developing countries. The increase in student numbers and the provision of new technology places massive pressures on the cost of the provision of education. However, as capital investment becomes more globally mobile, there is competitive pressure between governments to reduce the taxation level on corporations to encourage inward investment. For example, the British government reduced corporation tax to 19% from the tax year of 2017 – 2018 compared to the 28% rate that was in place when the coalition government came to office in 2010. It plans a further reduction to 18% for 2020, making Britain's rate one of the lowest amongst G20 economies. With resistance to increases in income tax (especially in relatively low tax tolerant societies such as the United States and Britain) as political parties compete for votes at elections, the burden of increased educational costs is squeezed in the direction of private sector sponsorship and input from students and their families.

Student finance has changed over the decades to accommodate these pressures. Up to the mid 1990s, students in higher education were supported by local authority grants. These grants were means tested in that parental income was taken into account. Students whose parents were on modest incomes would receive the full grant, whereas those whose parents earned higher salaries would have their grants reduced by an assessed amount of parental contribution. Higher education fees were also paid by local authorities. By the late 1990s, grants had been phased out and replaced by low interest loans and charges for fees were introduced. The latter initially were paid up front, but repayment has since been deferred alongside loans until a certain level of income is obtained through employment.

From the start of the 2006 academic year, top up fees were introduced. This allowed universities to increase fees from the old flat rate of £1,100 per year to up to £3,000 per year. Most universities imposed the full increase. At the time it looked as if the cost may have had a detrimental effect since the number of students enrolled fell by 3.6% compared to 2005. However, closer scrutiny suggested that the decreased numbers for 2006 followed a surge in entry in 2005 as many students who would have otherwise taken a gap year, knowing of the proposed future fee increase, went straight to university to avoid paying the higher fees which a delay would incur. This interpretation is born out by the 6.4% increase in applicants to British universities for 2007. At this point in time, 221,523 applicants were female and 173,784 were male. Unsurprisingly, subjects which attracted the greatest increase in applicants were vocational subjects such as business and administration (a 25% increase) which offer the prospects of a quicker clearing of student debt. Such financial pressures therefore encouraged students to choose courses most obviously linked to the economic function of education.

From September 2012, the government raised the fee ceiling to £9,000. Early evidence suggests that applications to British universities by British students have significantly dropped since 2012, perhaps by over 10%, arguably due to the combined effect of the substantial fee increases and the deep and protracted recession. The ceiling for 2017 was raised to £9,250, has remained so for 2018 and is planned to remain at this level for 2019.

The problem of credential inflation

Despite this post 2012 dip in higher education applications and a degree of downward pressure on A level and GCSE grades, it remains the case that given the number and level of qualifications being achieved across the education system, their value in a labour market swamped with qualifications has tended to decline and more or higher level qualifications are required for particular jobs than was the case in the past. This phenomena is referred to by the term 'credential inflation' and means that individuals are under pressure to obtain more qualifications to just stand still in the labour market. At the same time, to pay for this expansion in provision, a greater financial burden is passed from governments, keen to limit public expenditure, down to individuals and families. It total, this is arguably a recipe for growing dissatisfaction amongst a younger generation whose academic endeavours face an enhanced risk of dislocation between employment expectations and work available.

4. Meritocracy – advance or retreat?

The concept 'meritocracy' has been previously introduced and refers to a society in which achievement is based on individual effort and ability alone. As well as being central to the debate between major theoretical perspectives, this is a term which has been applied positively by politicians to our educational system. As an exercise in sociological thinking, we should now be able to apply this concept systematically to scrutinise educational opportunity. The following points would appear to be salient:

1. In terms of educational achievement at GCSE and A level, entry to higher education and success in higher grade degree passes, it would appear that there have been significant advances toward a more meritocratic educational system for females. However, there is more doubt, as argued in chapter 7, about the extent to which this translates sufficiently into equal opportunity with males for occupational success.

2. Regarding the enhancement of market forces in the school system, a key issue is that of social class differences in utilising the system. In an increasingly diverse system, there is strong evidence suggesting that middle class parents understand it better, know how to get the best from it, and are better able to prepare their children for success, for example through paying for private tutors. Working class parents are more likely to accept sending their children to a local school which may include poorly performing schools in run down areas. Therefore, if parents are given greater choice in the schools attended by their children, this would appear to enhance class related differences in children's educational opportunity, promote a degree of social class separation and suggest a retreat from meritocracy as family background life chances play a greater role in differentiating educational access once again. This is not necessarily a reflection of more negative attitudes toward education by working class parents, but rather supports the argument of Phillip Brown that marketization spells a retreat from meritocracy (selection in terms of how the child is able to perform) to that of 'parentocracy' (selection in terms of what the parent is able to do to assist the child).

3. The massive expansion in higher education numbers up to 2012 may at first glance appear to further meritocracy within education as more people are offered the opportunity to pursue their studies at this level. However, increasing access may not advance meritocracy when to do so a new funding system has had to be introduced in the form of the replacement of student grants with loans, coupled with substantial increases in the level of fees. The loan system introduces financial hardships and pressures which are unlikely to be experienced uniformly across the social classes. Those from poorer backgrounds who are considering entering higher education may be faced with a painful costs / benefits analysis in which the calculation of future debt, with less likelihood of parental financial support, could be of overriding importance and off-putting. However, recent university application figures show that, although remaining a significantly lower proportion than those of middle class background, the proportion of applicants from poorer backgrounds has held up. How can this be explained?

Small scale research conducted by Clark et al (2015) into high achievers from disadvantaged backgrounds has argued that the marketization of higher education and the introduction of loans, at the heart of neoliberal policy, has been accompanied by a cultural normalisation of debt. It is argued that higher education applicants from poorer backgrounds have therefore not been put off as much as might otherwise be expected, but that their orientation to the process has changed. The authors explain this change in the outlook and strategy of students from within the framework of Beck's risk society.

Clark et al found that rather than a deterrent, a marketised system and increased fees provides new challenges for forward navigation through harder work and an attitude of meritocratic individualism which tends to screen out concern with socially structured disadvantages associated with poorer backgrounds. Given the higher stakes which higher fees have brought about, important amongst key choices made by these students were a variety of rational choice preferences in terms of: 1) favouring high status universities which were seen as providing a better return in terms of employment opportunities to pay off debt incurred, 2) choosing vocationally relevant courses as safe routes in terms of career outcome and 3) the strategy of living at home whilst studying and / or working part-time during studies. These reflexive biographical choices are not always compatible and can bring their own disadvantages. For example, living at home may reduce the opportunities of acquiring valuable social capital which can come with the contacts built up by living away from home. Also, the greater financial pressure that these students are likely to be under to combine paid work with study is likely to undermine any possible level playing field of academic achievement.

This last point is supported by research conducted in 2005 by the Higher Education Funding Council for England. It was found that students from poor and ethnic minority backgrounds were under greater pressure to work during term time. Figures showed that about 30% of these students worked for twenty hours a week or more. Many felt under pressure to skip lectures and give in poor work. Evidence indicated that students who devoted fifteen hours a week or more to work had only a 62% chance of achieving a first class or upper second class honours degree compared to those who were able to devote their time fully to their studies. Furthermore, there was evidence that students of working class background who completed their studies were likely to end up with bigger debts. It could therefore be argued that although the grant based system could only support a smaller HE intake, and in that sense was more elitist, it operated more meritocratically in that it enabled a more level playing field of academic competition.

It should be added that the higher education sector is not an undifferentiated one. The higher status universities invariably charge fees at the top level. At the end of the day, given the academic, financial and cultural barriers of entry to elite universities for those of poorer background, it is hardly surprising that, other than for the very most able, even if they enter higher education it is more likely to be at a lower status university closer to home and possibly charging lower fees or even a vocational HE course run at a local FE institution.

4. Part of educational diversity has been the retention of the independent sector. At the pinnacle of this sector reside the prestigious public schools, entry to which is in large part based on social connections and parental ability to pay high fees. These schools offer enhanced access to elite universities and the exclusive higher echelons of the top professions. Whilst politicians of the major political parties have frequently been keen to refer positively to meritocracy, they usually prefer to remain silent on this vestige of privilege which flies in the face of meritocracy. It may be suspected that this omission is an attempt to discourage citizens from engaging in joined up thinking in this area (providing an example of Lukes' second face of power). By

contrast, sociology encourages us to think systematically and follow where logic leads us when applying such concepts to our educational system. In so doing, assertions by politicians about meritocracy in education may turn out to look superficial and unconvincing.

Contemporary sociological perspectives on education

Postmodernism – the liberating potential of education

According to postmodernists such as Lyotard, contemporary societies are entering a stage which is very different from past traditional and modern societies. A hallmark of traditional pre-modern society was the predominance of religious dogma and superstition. Religion provided an all embracing metanarrative which claimed to provide a single truth and education reflected this. However, during the eighteenth century, Enlightenment thinking, in the form of scientific and rational criticism, undermined religious dogma and promised the realisation of intellectual liberty and human progress through applying rational thinking to social intervention. The development of modern education as a self-evident good was the product of this Enlightenment optimism of the modern period.

Postmodernists argue that the promise of science has disappointed as modern society substituted one claim to a single truth, the metanarrative of religion, by another, the metanarrative of rational analysis and the methods of science. In terms of application, it has failed. Thus we have seen that education policy in the post war era was aimed at engineering an educational system which improved social justice by opening up life chances and social mobility opportunities to those from less privileged backgrounds. However, we have also seen that 1) social class related differences in educational achievement remained quite obstinately entrenched and that 2), as explained in chapter 7, the modest improvements in social mobility experienced by the time that children of the post war generation entered the work place were more to do with changes in the occupational structure than rationally engineered educational reform.

Moreover, postmodernists claim that rational and scientific thinking itself became repressive by imposing its logic and methods on society and education as the only criteria of truth. It is also argued that compulsory attendance within educational institutions has been used to shape and control populations. For example, within the English state system central control was enhanced through the introduction of the national curriculum and Ofsted inspections, and a strong emphasis has been placed on skill acquisition as opposed to other possible purposes of education. Postmodernists argue that with the emergence of contemporary postmodern conditions of social and cultural diversity, faith in a single and indispensable foundation for certain knowledge will collapse and along with it the modernist metanarrative.

For postmodernists, contemporary societies entering the postmodern era become increasingly pluralistic and comprise diverse cultural and consumer interests. Education must reflect this by moving away from belief in the absolute truth of science and rational thinking and the imposition of a standardised system. Education under postmodern conditions needs to become diverse in provision and relativistic, questioning the ascendancy of any single approach to education and the idea of a single absolute truth. Rather than moulding, controlling and shaping individuals, education should be a diverse resource that can be utilised by people to cater for their disparate and changing needs. Whether pursued to further lifestyle image, out of general interest, for personal fulfilment, to acquire work related skills, or for any other reason, there should be no single standard against which any of these purposes can be deemed universally superior.

For proponents Usher and Edwards, postmodernism challenges the favoured status to work related skills and the emphasis placed by governments that education should be organised primarily along such lines. Contemporary educational provision needs to be part of a society of growing variety of choice and lifestyle as it becomes increasingly utilised by individuals who - as in the case of other products they consume – may use it to seek status and convey an image. There is nothing intrinsically superior in formal classroom teaching and learning in which the teacher is the lecturer and fount of all knowledge. Instead, the teacher should be the guider and facilitator of student learning in which, assisted by advanced technology, a broader range of approaches and settings are becoming available. For postmodernists, only by such varied and flexible provision and a relativistic view of knowledge itself can education become truly liberating.

High modernism – education for adaptation

One of the leading high modernist theorists is Anthony Giddens. For Giddens, rational thinking associated with the Enlightenment is viewed in a more positive way than by postmodernists. The high modernist view is that in contemporary society science and rational thinking can still demonstrate superiority over other forms of knowledge. It is still the basis for understanding society and guiding progress, albeit under more challenging conditions of social complexity, globalisation and rapid technological change.

High modernists view education in the context of rapidly changing high tech knowledge economies. In this context, constant updating of work skills is a vital element of education as societies compete to attract inward investment in a globally competitive market. Governments need to play an active role in encouraging individuals to update their skills through retraining. Individuals cannot expect to complete their education at a fixed point in life but must be prepared to engage in lifelong learning.

Britain's New Labour governments tended to follow this line in promoting a more flexible culture of education in globally competitive conditions. People were encouraged to embrace advances in technology and constantly update their work skills, benefiting themselves, their families and the economy. New computer technology both required the mastery of new skills and enabled learning to occur in a diversity of settings, including workplace training, education and training in people's own homes through an expansion of distance learning made possible by the internet, and the development of outreach centres in local communities.

These challenges offer both opportunities and introduce strains and burdens into people's lives as they struggle to respond to a rapidly changing world and risk getting left behind. In addition to preparing people for work related skills, a key purpose of education must be to equip members of society with the skills to adopt a reflexive approach to life, a requirement against which the more recent government emphasis on a return to factual learning seems to be somewhat at odds.

Chapter 9

Power and Politics

Abstract

There are various levels at which it is possible to view politics. One, often adopted by the general public, is that which focuses on political parties, governments and elections. Sociologically, this is a relatively restricted view. In this chapter, the reader is encouraged to adopt a broader and more systematic approach to politics. This will be based on tracing the workings of power in social relationships. Definitions of power and other central concepts in the sociology of politics are introduced to assist the reader in that analysis.

A range of established sociological perspectives on power and politics, particularly with regard to representative democracies, are reviewed. These comprise functionalism, Marxism, the approach of Weber, elite theory, pluralism and second wave feminism. Each of these theories apply sociological definitions of power systematically to social relationships. They offer differing analyses of the sources and distribution of power in liberal democracies, who holds power and to whose benefit it is used.

In a further section, a review is undertaken of a range of sociological perspectives on the scope and impact of the state in liberal democracies.

A more restricted outlook on politics is adopted in the sections on voting behaviour. However, the approach remains sociological in the sense that attempts to understand voting behaviour are related to social influences and broader social changes. The question of the decline in the influence of social class on voting behaviour and the consideration of alternative influences is of central importance in this section. This is followed by a section in which the political impact of voting is contended by briefly contrasting analyses from Marxist and pluralist perspectives.

The study of politics in a more contemporary light requires an understanding of the ways in which globalisation is reshaping the political world. Some alternative interpretations of the effect of globalisation on the political landscape are considered. Globalisation is related to postmodern and high modern approaches. These perspectives point to fundamental changes taking place in society and raise challenging questions for both a sociological understanding of contemporary politics and, regarding high modernism, the guidance that sociology can give for the fashioning of political institutions appropriate for the current age.

Reference is made to the emergence of new social movements and how they can be related to the influence of globalisation. The work of Castells is introduced to explain how in an era where political elites have succumbed to powerful financial interests, widening accessibility to internet networking has provided new opportunities for mobilisation of participatory protest. However, it is shown that Foucault's approach puts emphasis on the potential for surveillance and political control.

Postmodernists are shown to argue that politics of the modern era of state engineering and class and ideological conflict is over. The postmodern world is characterised as one in which political power is fragmented and politics reduced to the manipulation of symbols in a world of illusion.

The idea of 'power decay' is explained in the writings of Niam as associated with a decline in the power of outmoded political and corporate power hierarchies. For strong political decision making power to be reacquired, it is argued that political institutions need to be transformed from hierarchical to networked structures.

An attempt is made to draw connections between Giddens' approach to high modernism, his transformationist position on globalisation, and his advocacy of 'third way' politics which provided an underpinning for New Labour. A sketch is then provided of the reasoning behind the civic Conservatism of the post 2010 period.

A brief outline of the development of the European Union and the UK's changing relationship toward it is sketched. The chapter concludes with a review of Brexit in the UK as an example of populist politics versus the political establishment. The outcome of the referendum vote to leave the European Union is examined in terms of the social characteristics of voters, some of the domestic political consequences of this outcome at the time of writing are outlined, and a brief evaluation of Brexit through the lens of some classical sociological perspectives is made.

The sociological challenge

Politics is commonly seen to be about political parties and the actions of governments. Viewed at this level, attention focuses on the policies and ideological positions of political parties, general election campaigns and outcomes and Parliamentary processes. The media often reinforce this viewpoint. Furthermore, the tabloid press in particular tend to focus on the deeds of politicians in their professional capacities and their private lives, both personalising and trivialising politics. Viewing politics at this level alone, our involvement is likely to be limited to participation in general elections when the aforementioned preoccupations become heightened.

Otherwise, we are often preoccupied with the day to day issues and problems of our immediate personal world. We may not consider these matters to be of a political nature and, as C. Wright Mills has maintained, we may tend to individualise problems rather than link them to broader public issues.

The study of politics in sociology requires us to break away from the vantage points identified above. In sociology, the study of politics is about the concentration, distribution and exercise of power at different levels within society, between societies and globally. Looked at sociologically, power, briefly defined, is to do with the capacity that some people have to exert their will over others. This concept of power can apply to any social situation. Following this view of power, a focus on political parties, the formal institutions of government, and political personalities, can be seen as too restricted and may hide more about politics than it reveals. Instead, a sociological view can reveal the power, and therefore political nature, of organised groups such as trade unions or the capital of employers. Power can be exerted through military or paramilitary means. Playground bullying can be viewed as political as can the use of patriarchal (male over female) power in a variety of contexts. Even the language that people use in everyday social encounters to negotiate with others and attempt to persuade them or impose their meanings and viewpoints can be seen as political.

The tendency to individualise the relationships and problems of our personal lives is likely to blind us to their connections to broader social and power structures. Intimate relationships can be regarded as political in terms of the above definition of politics, even if we often do not see them as such. Furthermore, we should be prepared to recognise that the political influences acting on even our most immediate social world do not necessarily stop even at the recognised borders of nations! Decisions made by people at great geographical distance from us to move investment and businesses between countries can affect people's employment opportunities, standards of living, capacity to take political action, quality of life and relationships within families. Migration can bring about a range of new relationships and responses between ethnic groups and cultures within a society. The fact that political issues can be global in origin takes us into the area of global political responses in terms of transnational pressure groups such as Greenpeace and supra-national governmental organisations like the European Union.

The difficulty that we may face in trying to adopt a sociological view of politics can be in putting more conventional and limited preconceptions about its nature and scope to one side. We will need to understand the precise use of sociological concepts and how applying them systematically may open up new vantage points on the origin and distribution of power. In so doing, it will become apparent that politics surrounds our daily lives. We may even gain insights which suggest why it is convenient to certain others that our view of politics should remain restricted.

Definition of main concepts

Establishing a clear meaning and use of key concepts is a necessary platform for developing a sociological approach to politics. So how does sociology approach politics? Politics is to do with the use of **power**. Power can be defined as the capacity that individuals or groups have to exert their will over others in social encounters. The inclination or capacity for resistance will depend on other features of the power relationship. If power is exerted in the form of **coercion**, it is experienced as an oppressive force exerted, from the viewpoint of the oppressed, without effective justification. In such situations, those with power are likely to be opposed by the oppressed should opportunities arise. However, if those exerting power are able to justify their use of it to others, they are able to claim **authority**. As the exercise of authority is backed up by justification, it is likely to realise a degree of willing compliance form those over whom it is exerted. In this case, the use of power is recognised as **legitimate**.

The term **ideology** has more than one application. More conventionally in politics, ideology is related to the different value systems that distinguish the political parties. These value systems provide particular interpretations of the world and offer ideal images of beneficial directions of social change.

Appealing as much to emotions as the intellect, party ideology is important to attract voter and activist identification to the cause.

But the concept of ideology is also used in sociology in a more all-embracing way. In Marxist theory, it refers to beliefs and images that provide a systematic distortion of reality with the consequence of obscuring the truth of that reality – in this case, the reality of class exploitation. Religion and the mass media in particular assist in this process. When ideological distortion is embraced by a subject class, they are said to experience a state of **false consciousness**.

We can now distinguish between this big use of the concept of ideology and the term **propaganda**. Used in its Marxist sense, ideological distortion is naturally generated by the systemic inequality of capitalism. Propaganda, however, is the conscious manipulation of the world view of the relatively powerless by the powerful with the purpose of serving their vested interests.

Ideology provides the justifications by which authority gains its legitimacy. For the neo-Marxist Gramsci, the concept of **hegemony** was developed to explain the domination of one group over another. For Gramsci, ideology, dominant political institutions and economic forces may work in a complementary way to powerfully support ruling class power and project a distorted view of the prevailing institutions of capitalism as natural and beneficial to all. However, ideology, false consciousness and hegemonic dominance are unlikely to be total. When peoples' direct experiences contradict dominant ideologies, **counter ideologies** and **counter hegemonic resistance struggles** may emerge.

Legitimacy may not always be easily maintained. If the behaviour of authorities falls conspicuously short of the values and standards by which it is justified, as, for example, if political corruption becomes evident, the authority of those in power, or even the entire social and political system, may face a loss of legitimacy. This can prove to be a fertile ground for the spread of counter ideologies and opposition movements. Under such circumstances, a government may be faced with a breakdown of social order and resort to coercive methods in an attempt to retain control.

Nations of the world are bounded territories governed by **states**. Institutions of the state include the government, regulatory apparatus such as the civil service, the armed forces, the legal system, welfare and educational institutions and local authorities. We will later see that some theorists would define the state even more broadly than this. States hold **sovereign** power over national territories in their exclusive right to make and apply laws, guarantee citizens' rights and impose the rule of law. **Citizenship** denotes individual rights held by and duties required of members of a society, but states hold a monopoly of the legitimate use of force within their territory and establish compliance through the courts, the police or the military.

In reality, states in contemporary societies have found it beneficial to relinquish some sovereignty to **supra-state** bodies such as the European Union for the economic benefit of trade arrangements, political allegiance, and helping to tackle a range of problems and risks such as international crime and terrorism which in a globalised world do not stop at national boundaries.

Societies involve conflicts of interest. How these conflicts are managed by government will vary with the type of political institutions that are in place. In **authoritarian** states, power is imposed oppressively to limit the rights and freedoms of the subject population. If elections take place, it is effectively with the purpose of legitimising single party rule.

In **representative democracies**, the population in the form of the electorate can periodically choose its government from rival political parties. Whilst the precise nature of political institutions and electoral systems varies from society to society, success in the electoral process gives government a **mandate** (the authority to act on behalf of the electorate) to introduce policies deriving from the manifesto that it was elected on for a term of office without the need to regularly re-consult the electorate.

The matter of legitimacy is however not always straightforward in the real world. Governments in representative democracies legitimise their policies and actions through acquiring power by democratic means and as such hold authority. However, consider the situation whereby through popular vote a government came to power pledged to nationalise certain industries. Whilst it would derive legitimacy and authority to do so from the electorate, implementing nationalisation could be viewed as a coercive act by representatives of private industry and therefore non-legitimate. The problem here would be a conflict of legitimacy based on the will of the electorate as opposed to the legitimacy of the ownership of private enterprise in a capitalist society.

The term **fully participatory (or direct) democracy** is reserved for systems in which those whom any decisions will effect must be consulted and allowed their input into the decision making process. Although arguably an unworkable form of democracy in complex modern societies, examples of participatory democracy on a smaller scale include Israeli kibbutzim communities as originally constituted in the post war years and businesses run as workers co-operatives.

By contrast, a **bureaucracy** is an organisational hierarchy in which power flows downwards and operatives carry out their allocated work tasks in a formalised and impersonal way. For Weber, bureaucracy was the epitome of organisational efficiency but has since come to be associated more with inefficiency.

The use of power may not be as transparent as these introductory definitions suggest. Various **faces of power** have been identified by Steven Lukes. At the most obvious level, its first face, a measure of power may simply be the ability some people have to impose decisions on others. However, a second face of power can include the capacity that some groups have to avoid the raising of certain issues in the first place, thus precluding political debate and decisions in these areas. Lack of debate over the privileges of public schools may be an example of the use of this type of power. Furthermore, in its third face, power can even involve the capacity that some people have to persuade others to make or accept decisions which could otherwise be shown to be against their best interests. The abandonment by many workers of trade unions in Britain during the 1980s could be regarded as an example of the use of this face of power.

Founding sociological perspectives on power and politics

Sociological theory applied to politics attempts to address a variety of complex problems. Classical perspectives offer differing analyses of the origin and distribution of power in society, how it can best be measured, who holds it, and how they use it. These perspectives differ over the extent to which social relations are viewed as essentially harmonious or rooted in conflict, what the basis of harmony or conflict is, and where lines of conflict are likely to occur. They also attempt to address such fundamental questions as the relationship between people's position in the social structure and their political consciousness and political action.

Despite essential differences between the classical perspectives, key features which they have in common are 1) the view that societies are highly structured and can be analysed in structural terms and 2) the tendency to view societies as if they are bounded entities. It will later be shown that more contemporary approaches increasingly question the validity of these positions and, in some cases, even the degree to which political awareness still exists.

Functionalism – representative democracy and the use of power in the collective interest

The founding social context of functionalism can be traced back to the aftermath of the French Revolution of 1789 and the writings of Auguste Comte which dated from the 1820s. Developed by Comte as a reaction to the social instabilities in France following the Revolution, functionalism has retained an emphasis on gradual change, social order, hierarchy and stability as being both the natural and desirable social condition. Societies are seen as like systems or organisms. Although tending to self-regulate toward equilibrium, they can experience rapid and disturbing changes. For Comte, the forces of change of the French Revolution were rapid and fundamental in sweeping aside the institutions of feudalism, but left social disarray in their wake. A new social and political order needed to be established, and Comte argued that this could be assisted by rational social analysis.

Following in this French tradition, Durkheim maintained that a key practical aim of scientific sociology should be to assist in the fashioning of new social institutions to replace those that had been swept away with feudalism, for the purpose of assisting modern democratic societies to adjust to a new state of social stability.

Talcott Parsons developed the functionalist perspective within the modern American context. For Parsons, modern industrial societies are viewed as complex and highly differentiated social structures. For their efficient operation, and in contrast to traditional societies, positions of command must be allocated in terms of individual ability and expertise rather than through birthright. Modern capitalist society should operate as a meritocracy and to synchronise with this reality the values of a meritocracy would provide the most appropriate basis for social consensus. To motivate individual competition, a highly differentiated reward structure of occupations is necessary. Against the background of individual aspiration and materialistic values, high on the list of shared social goals by which governments can be judged is the enhancement of material living standards.

The institutions of representative democracy allow judgement of government to be expressed by the populace in the form of an electorate. Access to universal suffrage and choice between competing political parties enables the population to grant power on trust to the government to mirror collective sentiments and pursue shared social goals. The winning party, legitimised through the electoral process to pursue common goals, will have to face future elections at which its performance will be again judged by the electorate. Their consent, if necessary, can be withdrawn and power transferred to an alternative political party whose programme better expresses the will of the electorate. This process ensures a relatively smooth transfer of power.

As a consensus theory, functionalism focuses on the power 'of' society – led by government – measured in terms of its capacity for achieving common goals. The power of society can therefore grow with technological development, improved efficiency and minimal social conflict. From this healthy social condition, it is argued that members of society generally will benefit.

Marxism – representative democracy hiding the power of the capitalist class

A weakness of functionalism is clearly its inability to explain persisting levels of conflict and instability in capitalist societies. Most other sociological perspectives, and particularly Marxism, pay more attention than functionalists to divisions and conflicting interests within society. However, the works of Marx and Engels are so extensive that different emphases have been detected in different works and varied interpretations of the 'inevitability' of revolution and role of the state have been proposed by those who follow in the footsteps of Marx.

The basic Marxist position is that social relations are fundamentally shaped by economic factors that structure society into social classes. For Marx, political power derives from the ownership of economic resources – especially the means of production. Power is firmly located in the employment relationship between employer and employee and this is a social class relationship. Ultimately, political power is as concentrated or distributed as is the ownership of the means of production. Under capitalism, economic and political power is concentrated in the hands of a minority capitalist class whose wealth depends on the employment of workers. Marx viewed this relationship as one of class exploitation and conflict of interest in which 1) an employing class are able to politically exploit workers' weakness of having to offer their labour to earn a living, 2) providing the power to economically exploit – short change workers compared to the value that their labour input into the productive process creates.

However, productivity and the wealth it creates can only be fully effective if workers are both industrious and compliant. It is in the interests of employers that this is so. Since conflict of class interests is built into the capitalist system, how can such compliance be brought about?

From a Marxist perspective, conflict of class interests is generated in the economic sphere. Marxists refer to this domain as the infrastructure. This conflict is managed by the dominant institutions and ideas of capitalist society, together referred to as the superstructure. The institutions are primarily those of state control. The key controlling institutions of the state, such as the legal system, the police and the military, can suppress resistance by coercive means if necessary. However, these institutions of control are vested in legitimacy and authority by appearing to represent the common good rather than, Marxists claim, primarily serving ruling class interests.

This takes the analysis on to another level of control. The willing compliance of the subject class is most effectively furthered by the existence of a systematically distorted image of society that permeates society. Referred to as ideology, its effect is to perpetuate the continuity of the system by inducing in the subject class a false consciousness that their real interests are bound up in it. Ideological distortion is a natural feature of stratified systems rather than originating as a conscious construct by one social class for the manipulation of another. However, as the main beneficiaries of the system, a capitalist class will hold a natural affinity to this world view which they will be keen to maintain.

For Marx, religion and the political institutions and values of liberal democracies comprised a potent means of such control. Religion softens the pain of suffering by holding out an illusion of hope in the form of paradise in an afterlife to those who live a good life of compliant application. The political institutions of liberal democracies claim to offer freedom of choice and the prospect of meaningful political change through the ballot box. Marxists have since come to focus more on the controlling impact of education and the mass media, and some even the family, in restricting consciousness. All of these institutions and the values that they enshrine are seen to play a political role in the broad sense of the term as defined earlier in this chapter – the capacity that some people (in this case a dominant social class) have to exert their will over others. Against this backdrop, the focus here will be on what Marxists view as the real political significance of the political institutions as more narrowly defined – political parties, general elections and the policies and actions of elected governments.

The political institutions of capitalist representative democracies convey an image of accountability of political leaders to an electorate. Government, and the political system itself, are legitimised through giving citizens access to an electoral system in which they are free to choose between rival political parties by casting their vote at elections.

From a Marxist perspective, such legitimacy is based upon illusion and serves the purpose of ideological control. The primary purpose of the political institutions of capitalist liberal democracies is to maintain the smooth working of the capitalist system. Reducing politics to the outcome of an aggregate of individual voting decisions for the transfer of power assists this process. This is because whichever party wins an election has to govern through the state apparatus and within the constraints of the capitalist system. Therefore, the appearance of significant choice between political parties turns out to be quite narrow when they enter government. For example, it could be argued that changes in policy when New Labour replaced the Conservatives as the party of government in Britain from 1997 were not great and that the replacement of a discredited government by a fresh government with a strong electoral mandate was beneficial to British capitalism.

As power in capitalist societies actually originates through ownership of the means of production, the view that it rests with democratically elected governments fosters the illusion that the electorate has significant political power in its capacity to change governments and provides the government with its necessary legitimacy in the eyes of the electorate. From a Marxist perspective, whatever debate and acrimony takes place within Parliament, it is essentially a talking shop which restricts the image of politics to that of elected government and through the appearance of representation emasculates more radical and direct political action. Despite the veneer of democratic choice, government is effectively little more than through a single party state, as whichever party governs will need to be more attuned to the power and interests of the 'hidden rulers' than that of the electorate.

For Marx, genuine democracy would need to be more fully participatory. This would require the diffusion of political power. However, as political power derives from economic power, its diffusion could only come from acquisition of the means of production into common ownership. As the capitalist class were unlikely to give up wealth and power without a struggle, meaningful democracy was only likely to be achieved through the revolutionary overthrow the capitalist class and the entire capitalist system.

There are, however, different Marxist interpretations regarding the degree to which such a revolution is inevitable. A straightforward economic determinist view emphasises that 1) economic polarisation between working and capitalist classes is built into capitalism and 2) this is exacerbated during periods of inevitable economic depression. These economic forces are likely to act as a trigger for the emergence of class consciousness which is a prerequisite for revolution. According to this interpretation, revolution is the outcome of powerful social and economic forces with actors following the roles in an historical script.

Writing early in the twentieth century, Antonio Gramsci picked out a different emphasis from Marx's works. He argued that the state governed through the use of both coercive force and ideological control and referred to the complimentary dominance of economic and political institutions and ruling class values as hegemonic control. However, for Gramsci there will always be political challenges to ruling class dominance. This is because worker's direct experience often contradicts the picture given by the dominant ideology and opens up alternative insights. Timely concession will therefore need to be made to the subject class to maintain its compliance, providing them room for political manoeuvre. Moreover, awareness of this contradiction offers an opening through which class consciousness could emerge, providing space for the actions of radical political parties, trade unions and intellectuals to foster class consciousness, challenge ruling class hegemony and engage workers in direct political action. The ruling class will always have to battle to close down such situations.

Box 1: Seminal hegemonic moments

Some events provide a momentary insight into the authorities' use of power. One such event was the widespread coverage given to the verdict of the coroner's court investigation into the Hillsborough Stadium tragedy.

On 15 April 1989, as a result of a massive crush in the Hillsborough football stadium at Sheffield, 96 football fans lost their lives and over 760 were injured. At the time, the police authorities blamed the fans for the tragedy and some sections of the tabloid press, but most notably the *Sun*, vilified the fans as urinating drunkards acting like animals and attacking the police who were trying to save fans' lives. Those present knew that far from the 'truth' which the *Sun* claimed, this was a massive distortion of the events.

> Twenty seven years later, on 26 April 2016, following a two year inquest, the verdict of the coroner's court was that the 96 fans had been 'unlawfully killed'. It was found that the police had lost control of the situation and that their actions and inactions had caused or contributed to the situation. In an attempt to cover up their own blame, police sources had lied, claiming that drunken fans had forced a gate open that led to the crush, and smeared the behaviour of the fans.
>
> The widespread publicity of the momentous verdict provided one of those momentary glimpses into press manipulation, corruption, abuse of power and incompetence, and there were suggestions that the South Yorkshire Police would not have put out their account without political cover. Such insight into the activities of the authorities the author would like to refer to as providing a 'seminal hegemonic moment'. For the authorities, these openings require rapid closure. The church assisted this process in leading a vigil outside the town hall the following day and in a news interview a fan revealed the classic default position that it was now up to the authorities how to take the matter forward.

At the centre of the state apparatus in capitalist societies are senior politicians and civil servants, the upper echelons of the military, the legal profession and the established church. The exact relationship between the state and the capitalist class is open to some debate within Marxist theory. An instrumentalist interpretation, advocated by Ralph Miliband (1973), emphasises that the key positions of state are manned by a privileged group, at least in part comprising those directly representing powerful business interests, all of whom tend to share a common elite background and outlook. Since the power and views of a capitalist class prevail and capitalist interests predominate, the state is effectively headed by a ruling class rather than an elite (for an alternative perspective, see the elite theory section).

An opposing Marxist interpretation is provided by the structuralist theorists Louis Althusser and Nicos Poulantzas (Poulantzas, in Blackburn ed. 1972). Here, in contrast to Milband's position, the social background and motives of state officials are of little importance. The structural position of the state imposes on officials service to the interests of capitalism, regardless of their social class background. A degree of autonomy between the ruling capitalist class and the governing political class is necessary for the more effective regulation of the system. This distancing allows the state to occasionally act against particular capitalist interests (for example through passing anti-monopoly legislation or acting against rogue elements) or offer timely concessions to the working class (for example through welfare reforms), thus enhancing its capacity to promote the long-term interests of the capitalist system. It can rise above any factionalism within the capitalist class which would be damaging if they directly governed. Furthermore, the appearance of the state as acting neutrally and for the benefit of all is a fiction that can be more effectively conveyed.

For all of its valuable insights into power and control in capitalist societies, the Marxist perspective, developed around the middle of the nineteenth century, has faced a number of fundamental challenges in recent decades. Firstly, when communist societies did emerge in the twentieth century, they took the form of repressive single party states, run by party elites, not the fully democratic societies that Marx predicted would eventually emerge. Secondly, the collapse of Eastern Block communist systems between 1989 –1991 has led to the virtual global spread of capitalism – a historical trend (outcome?) operating in reverse to Marx's predictions. Thirdly, within capitalist societies, economic class as the key configuration of political divisions has arguably evaporated rather than advanced. For example, in Britain although economic inequality has grown since the 1980s under both Conservative and New Labour governments, class consciousness appears to have declined and more fractured interest group politics advanced. Fourthly, it is a new challenge for Marxists to show how their perspective can be applied to a modern service and information economy as opposed to the industrial capitalism of Marx's day.

Weber – representative democracy and bureaucratic accountability

As explained in the social stratification chapter, for Weber social conflict is not essentially reducible to class conflict. Modern liberal democratic societies are arenas of conflict between status groups and interest groups as well as classes, all of which are likely to defend or attempt to enhance their power. In societies that are representative democracies, as in societies with other formal political systems, those who hold power usually attempt to retain it at the expense of others. To understand how power is legitimised to enable rulers to claim authority, Weber emphasised that legitimacy must be understood in the context of prevailing cultural values and belief systems. Weber developed 'ideal types' to assist this understanding. Ideal types are intellectual models which highlight the essential features of a society. Their purpose is to assist in the understanding of highly complex social phenomena and to classify different types of society. However, Weber's typology of authority types was not just a static classificatory system but part of a theory of social change. The essential types of authority that Weber identified were traditional, rational-legal and charismatic.

Traditional authority is prevalent in pre-industrial, particularly feudal societies, and societies earlier in history. In feudal societies, life is largely tied to agriculture and the routines of the seasons. It is lived out in small communities which comprise well established hierarchies with people experiencing little geographical or social mobility. Religion and custom prevail in people's thinking and actions. Tradition – the justification of present ways through reference to things having always been that way – tends to be accepted in its own right. In such a society, leadership is a privilege of inheritance. Obedience to one's 'social betters' is often justified by recourse to such ideas as superior social breeding – the notion that demonstration of a family lineage of leadership denotes the inheritance of leadership qualities. The credibility of authority justified in this way can be related to social settings where people are familiar with livestock breeding.

For Weber, the advance of rational thinking, science and technology undermines tradition. This process, referred to as rationalisation, promotes the quest for efficiency and the need for change. These forces prepare the way for industrial capitalism which eventually comes to develop large scale and impersonal organisational structures. Life becomes more freed from the traditions and routines of nature and agriculture and is dominated by the man-made routines and formal relationships within factories and offices, the latter, according to Weber increasingly taking the form of impersonal bureaucracies – rationally designed institutional machinery to maximise efficiency in the achievement of goals. In such a society, authority in the workplace is justified by achievement and merit. Selection is a formal process in a system of rules and laws that require people to impersonally compete for occupational position. The formation of government through a system of representative democracy takes place through political party competition within the formal rules of a democratic framework for election to office. Weber referred to this type of authority, framed by standardised and formal procedures, as rational-legal.

Use of authority is not intrinsic to the person but derives from one's position within the organizational hierarchy. Although increasingly challenged by more recent organisational theorists, Weber maintained that bureaucracy would spread throughout society as it is the most efficient form of social organisation. This efficiency stems from the way that formal selection matches skills with position, the top down imposition of authority through the machinery of a tiered formal organisational structure, and the conformity of functionaries to orders, rules and regulations. Weber argued that competition between organisations and the drive for efficiency inclines modern complex industrial societies to become bureaucratised throughout both public and private sectors.

Weber harboured grave concerns for the human condition in such bureaucratised social conditions in which slavish adherence within the workplace (and outside) to rules and regulations would reduce individuals to the position of being like cogs in a machine. Furthermore, with the growth of a far reaching modern sophisticated state apparatus, Weber was concerned that democratic accountability would become choked as decision making and power fall into the hands of un-elected bureaucrats and experts, and that the political participation of citizens may decline. Could anything check these consequences of the relentless march of bureaucratisation?

Weber maintained that capitalist liberal democracies offered more potential of some resistance to this process than socialist systems would. Firstly, contrary to Marx, Weber argued that the state was not simply an instrument of the capitalist class but the product of a lengthy process of rationalization and bureaucratisation. The owners of capital may thus be in a position to offer some resistance to state bureaucrats. Secondly, a well-established multi-party representative democracy in which civil servants are accountable to politicians, who themselves are accountable to the electorate, may help to restrain the power of unelected officials.

For Weber, to overthrow capitalism and representative democracy by revolution and take the means of production into public ownership would not lead to the fully participatory democracy that Marx had predicted, but its antithesis in the form of top down bureaucratic regulation. This is because, contrary to Marx, power does not flow exclusively from ownership of the means of production but can be concentrated in the means of state administration. State ownership of the means of production would thus concentrate bureaucratic and economic centralisation of power. Consequently, a revolution in which the means of production become

426

commonly owned would lead to a single party state of party bureaucrats with little check, in the absence of private capital and electorate choice of political party, on the advance of bureaucracy and the concentration of power within an unaccountable state apparatus.

Charismatic authority, Weber's third type, differs from both traditional and rational-legal authority in that it claims legitimacy through the perceived exceptional qualities (real or otherwise) of an individual leader in the subjective consciousness of devoted followers. Viewed historically and sociologically, such leaders are most likely to come to power during times of social crisis when significant sections of the population are more primed or susceptible to follow a person who is believed to have mystical qualities or intuitive genius to address their plight. This type of political authority is the least rational and political decisions are likely to be justified through belief in the special insight of the leader. It is therefore often the most mercurial use of authority. Leaders are likely to engender strong emotional identification from followers, almost a hypnotic charm, and often adopt an authoritarian leadership style. Napoleon and (after Weber wrote) Stalin and Hitler each exemplify this type of rule arising from social crisis. However, charismatic authority, which may break out from predominantly traditional or rational-legal settings, is usually relatively short lived. Given its emotional intensity and personal nature, charismatic authority is by definition difficult to institutionalize and is likely to lapse with the fall of the leader.

Of course, in the real world, authority is likely to exhibit a mixture of these ingredients. For example, in contemporary Britain, authority may be predominantly exercised within the framework of rational – legal legitimacy, but the institution of a constitutional monarchy and the performance of traditional state ceremonial occasions enshrines a degree of traditional legitimacy. Furthermore, the crisis of the 1978 – 1979 'Winter of Discontent' brought a charismatic response in the leadership style of Thatcher.

Classical elite theory – representative democracy, fine as long as it does not amount to much!

Classical elite theorists, developing their ideas during the late nineteenth and early twentieth centuries, also strongly contested Marxist theory. They agreed with Marxism only at the most general level – that power in society is concentrated in the hands of a small minority who attempt to retain exclusive access and control. However, for classical elite theorists, rule by a small superior minority is regarded as a necessary and inevitable feature of all societies. That minority will comprise those who occupy key positions in society and especially the state, including senior politicians, civil servants, ambassadors, judges, religious leaders and high ranking military officials. It could include owners of private business and top financiers, but not exclusively, and there is no reason why power should specially emanate from ownership of the means of production. In their criticism of the economic determinism of the Marxist model, classical elite theorists argue that Marxists pay insufficient recognition to the political and cultural sphere as a source of power. The identification of rulers as an elite rather than a ruling class emphasises this key point. By contrast, for Marxists, as we have seen, even though elites rather than capitalists may man the state, the influence of the capitalist class, openly or behind the scenes, on these elites is so substantial that it is justified to refer to a state ruling class.

Classical elite theorists argue that a feature of societies throughout history is that their populations are divided into elites and masses. For Vilfredo Pareto, this universal feature relates to the social distribution of personal or psychological qualities. Following his distant predecessor Niccolo Macchiavelli, Pareto distinguished two main types of leadership quality: stealth and cunning, and the ability to take decisive action. Pareto argued that people with these leadership capabilities will always be in short supply in any population. The majority, lacking the qualities necessary for political leadership, will need to be and even prefer to be led by others. Indeed, Pareto went as far as claiming that the masses were by and large deficient in the capacity for rational thinking and that elites can intelligently best manipulate the masses by appealing to their instincts, sentiments and emotions. On this basis, elite rule is inevitable and democratic accountability of elites to the masses is far from being equated with progress.

Members of an elite often act as a cohesive group to protect their interests and privileges. Denial of access by other groups is common as circulation takes place within elites who interchange between privileged positions and are able to pass privileged access to elite positions down the generations. There can arise, however, threats to elite dominance. Pareto recognised that the style of elite rule must be suited to the social needs of the time. As social circumstances change, elites must either adapt so as to enable themselves to retain political control or they are likely to face a challenge from other aspiring elites, counter-elites, more suited to rule in these conditions. Such a challenge may take the form of a military coup or a revolution, which if successful brings about a circulation of entire elites with counter-elites assuming power. Moreover, although the masses are considered to be generally lacking in leadership qualities, an elite that becomes too socially closed off risks becoming decadent, out of touch and vulnerable to challenge. Some degree of social mobility of the able few from the masses, who must in the process adjust to the needs of elite rule and culture, may therefore be desirable so as to replenish an elite and deny the masses potentially capable leadership, thus enhancing the longevity of the elite.

Pareto's analysis of the distribution of power was similar to that of Gaetano Mosca, to whom he owed unacknowledged intellectual debt. However, Mosca did recognise that the qualities of elites may be acquired more through inherited social advantage than superior innate qualities. He also appreciated that elites that govern within the institutions of representative democracy can serve the general interest, especially if not drawn exclusively from privileged backgrounds. Mosca further recognised the importance of a growing sub-elite organisational stratum comprising, for example, managers, engineers and intellectuals, who contributed to the effective governance of modern society. However, both theorists held the view that the masses were generally unworthy of exercising power and should be excluded from doing so. And, even further, for Pareto in particular, it is in the best interests of society that in a representative democracy elites can use their political abilities to effectively manipulate the masses into believing that they are being consulted rather than meaningfully consulting them.

Robert Michels, in his work 'Political Parties' (1911), reached a similar position to that of Pareto and Mosca but built his analysis on society's organisational requirements. Like Weber, he argued that bureaucracy, a top down form of organisation, was necessary for any large organisation or modern society to operate efficiently. Hierarchical organisation inevitably leads to rule by the few – otherwise known as 'oligarchy'. Michels argued that representative democracy is the only form of democracy which is feasible for the efficient political organisation of large populations. In this form of democracy, electorates are only occasionally consulted and political leaders govern for the vast majority of time on their behalf. It is impossible for populations to be regularly involved in the decision making process (a situation akin to fully participatory democracy). Instead, full-time bureaucrats and political leaders are required to take key decisions and implement policy on an ongoing basis. For Michels, a disillusioned ex-Marxist, however radically democratic the policies of a party may have been when in opposition, once established into power, they have to govern. To govern efficiently, regular consultation with the masses is not possible. The consequent tendency is then for political leaders to become disengaged, acquire privileges and in time develop a vested interest in protecting their own position more than representing the populace who may have bought them to power. The assumption of power even by radical parties therefore ultimately equates to elite rule. Even in representative democracies, oligarchical structures headed by relatively unaccountable elites are inevitable – a process for which Michels coined the phrase the 'iron law of oligarchy'.

From the classical elite theory perspective, Marxism is not the scientific theory of social change that it claims to be, but just a utopian ideology. As an ideology, it is a system of thinking which distorts reality and can itself be used by an aspiring counter-elite to engender the support of the masses against a ruling elite. Marxism is utopian because the fully participatory democracy that it promises for the future cannot be realised. Any revolutionary party that gains power will need to govern a modern and complex society. In such a society, fully participatory democracy, if attempted, would lead to massive inefficiency associated with the necessity for regular consultation of the populace. To tackle this, direct leadership would need to be asserted. Thus, even out of communist revolution, a new oligarchical structure must emerge with leaders becoming increasingly detached from the lives of the led. A revolutionary party, in gaining power, gives rise to a new elite which will protect its power and privileges by controlling the masses through both coercive means and myth or ideology rather than the impossible reality of communist fully participatory democracy.

If Michels is correct, in the interests of efficiency, fully participatory democracy is an unworkable type of political system, and even representative democracy will amount to little in terms of meaningful consultation. Governments in representative democracies, of course, have to periodically face the electorate. Whether a particular change of government is a change of elite or a change within an elite is a matter of analysis. However, oligarchical structures will remain in place.

Applying Michels' analysis to contemporary politics, the detachment of leaders from the led which oligarchical structures brings can become particularly evident when governments that have been in power for a long time display a growing tendency, when facing the potential accountability of media questions, to not have ministers available for comment.

Other sociologists have taken elite theory in a more radical direction. From this position, elite rule is recognised but not regarded as preferable or inevitable. Instead, it is lamentable that many modern societies that masquerade as democracies can be better understood as being controlled by elites who are by and large un-elected. An early exponent of this position was C. Wright Mills who argued in the 1950s that America was dominated by a single and largely unaccountable power elite comprising a network of personal contacts and occupational exchanges across the upper reaches of business corporations, the military and the governmental apparatus.

More contemporary sociologists use insights from elite theory to raise a number of points. There are certain key occupations in society, positions at the top of which confer great power, status and privilege to people in these positions and include the armed forces, the church, the legal profession, the civil service, government and large business corporations. The top occupational positions within these institutions tend to be held by people of similar privileged social and educational background. These people often know each other and share a similar elitist social outlook and membership of exclusive clubs. There is much movement across the top of the occupational structure. For example, business leaders may move into top governmental positions or vice versa and individual politicians may hold interlocking directorships (be directors of a number of companies). All of this takes place across what John Scott calls a 'web of connections' at the top of society.

Great power resides in the hands of senior civil servants who invariably will have an Oxbridge or public school background. Many operations of the state take place behind closed doors and most institutions are not directly accountable to the public. Allegations of abuses involving elites are often historical, and the destruction or 'loss' of potentially incriminating documents may look suspiciously self-protective. If public pressure leads to the setting up of an inquiry, the government sets the framework and appoints a figure from the elite as head. Further, it has been argued that, through consumerism and growing affluence, general populations have become depoliticised and politically apathetic.

Amongst the political elite, the evidence available suggests there to be a modest long-term decline in the proportion of MPs with a public school educational background, but that substantial differences remain between the main political parties. For example, figures provided by

Bilton et al (1985) indicated that in 1966, 76.6% of Conservative MPs in Parliament came from a public school background as opposed to 19.5% of Labour MPs. At the pinnacle of government power, it was found that in the 1963 Conservative cabinet, 63.6% of members had attended one of the top six public schools, and the figure for the Labour cabinet for 1967 was 15.8%.

Research by Criddle indicated that in 2001 the proportions of MPs with public school background had declined to 64% of Conservatives and 17% of New Labour members. Two out of 412 Labour MPs had attended Eton whereas 14 out of 166 Conservative MPs had. However, New Labour achieved a large majority in the 2001 general election.

Following the 2010 general election and the formation of a Conservative headed coalition government, 19 out of 306 Conservative MPs had been educated at Eton alone and 62% of the coalition cabinet and 54% of Conservative MPs (compared to 7% of the general population) had been privately educated. Information provided by the Sutton Trust (23/5/2018) indicates that following the 2015 and 2017 general elections, the respective figures for privately educated Conservative MPs were 48% and 45% and for Labour 16% and 15%. With such marked differences in privileged educational background between the parties, the overall proportion of privately and top public school educated MPs and cabinet members is likely to fluctuate with a change of government, sometimes bucking the more modest long-term downward trend.

Regarding their previous occupations, information from the House of Commons Library (23/5/2018) shows that following the 2015 general election, 44% of Conservative MPs were from a business background compared to 11% of Labour MPs (both percentages up from the previous election). MPs of manual worker background comprised 1% of Conservatives and 7% of Labour, totalling 3% overall (a decline from 4% following the previous election).

Within the occupational category of professions, Conservative MPs in the 2015 intake were more likely to have come from what would be regarded as elite professions. For example, 8% had been barristers and 4% were from the armed forces. These figures compare to 4% and 0% respectively for Labour MPs, whereas university, college or school teaching backgrounds comprised only 2% of Conservative MPs compared to 8% of Labour MPs.

Pluralism – representative democracy as a balancing of diverse interests

Classical pluralism, which has strong roots in American political theory of the 1960s, adopts a position which is strongly critical of the power concentration models of both Marxist and elite theory perspectives. By contrast, it adopts a self-congratulatory view of the virtues of modern liberal democratic political systems as dispersing power down to individuals and across to numerous competing interest groups. This structure Dahl refers to as 'ployarchy' (many hierarchies). It is the hallmark of a healthy and vibrant liberal democracy that a broad variety of interests can be fed into the political process and, through contest and compromise, interest groups can, to a greater of lesser extent, influence the political decision making process and government policy. It is up to citizens to actively pursue their interests in this political arena and government to act as an 'honest broker' between the parties and guardian ensuring that participation takes place according to the rules of the political game. It must then have the power to implement policies which are the outcome of this democratic process.

From this perspective, representative democracies are complex societies which comprise a broad spectrum of interests. Individuals have their own range of interests which they may want to register into the political decision making process. People are free to voice and pursue their interests through pressure group activity and can come together to do so with other individuals who agree on specific issues. In the competitive process of influencing political decisions, all interests can have an input, although the involvement and influence of groups will vary over time and according to the issues contested. As new issues evolve in society, new pressure groups will emerge along with new configurations in the dispute of interests.

For pluralists, it is possible to empirically test this model by studying which groups are involved in the political arena, the processes taking place in their engagement, the outcome of these processes and the degree to which the interests of different parties have prevailed. In support of this model, Dahl (1961) used empirical evidence from his study of New Haven politics to show that across a range of issues the decisions arrived at gave no single interest group a monopoly of influence and that group influence varied from issue to issue.

The pluralist model points to three key areas in which the populace are able to exert political influence in liberal democracies; at elections, through pressure groups and as consumers. Taking each of these in turn:

1) A cornerstone of representative democracy is the competition between political parties by which, at elections, voters periodically hold governments and local authorities accountable. Political parties offer viable options to a universal electorate, allowing them to have their say in the formation of government. To attract the support of voters, political parties must keep a careful eye on the state of popular opinion. To this end, voter opinion surveys are regularly conducted and parties may need to change their policies or political position in their bid to retain or acquire power. The power of the vote therefore gives the electorate the power to shape policy and to replace political parties in government. Thus, from a pluralist position, in contrast to a Marxist interpretation, it was not the constraints of the capitalist system which forced the British Labour Party to 'modernise' between 1983 and 1997 and acquire office, but the opinion of the electorate which they had to satisfy to gain their adherence.

2) Pluralists emphasise that whilst voters are free to vote for a party which most closely reflects their range of interests, pressure groups enable people to fine tune their influence on decision makers regarding more specific issues and on an ongoing basis. Government is therefore not just about becoming elected, but responding to the pressure of different organised interests and seeking compromise. By such means, in representative democracies the process of democratic accountability is a more continuous process than the periodic contesting of elections.

Where, then, do the boundaries of legitimate pressure group activity lie? Traditional pluralists tend to have in mind a model of pressure groups as hierarchical organisations whose representatives engage in regular contact with local and central government decision makers. These organisations have been referred to by Wyn Grant (1995) as 'insider' or conventional pressure groups. In Britain, such groups may include the Confederation of British Industry, The British Medical Association, Age Concern and the Automobile Association. Their representatives have meetings with government officials, often behind the scenes, and they operate within the law and the established rules of the political game. Their influence can also be extended by the fact that the government relies on them for information and expertise in helping to shape policy in their specific areas.

Other types of pressure group may employ the tactic of rapid response and direct action and operate on the margins of or outside the law. Their actions are likely to make these 'outsider' groups (Grant, 1995) to the political establishment. Within this category would be included the Animal Liberation Front, Fathers for Justice, and some environmental pressure groups. Against such groups, the traditional pluralist position is that state power may need to be rallied to ensure that the law is not subverted and, in the extreme, the very institutions which safeguard the freedoms of law abiding individuals are not threatened.

3) A further type of political influence open to people is the use of their consumer spending power. Contrary to Marxism, which emphasises the relative powerlessness of the employee, pluralism focuses on the power of the consumer. Classical pluralists argue that in a system of private enterprise and competition in the pursuit of profit, businesses must respond to consumer demand in order to flourish or even survive. As well as the need to satisfy customers with particular goods and services, businesses, along with political regimes, will be concerned about their ethical image since if viewed as disreputable they may face concerted action in the form of consumer boycotts. Consumer action against the apartheid regime in South Africa during the 1980s and more recent boycotting of foodstuffs from genetically modified crops (if known!) offer good examples of the potential impact of such movements combining consumer and pressure group influences.

How does pluralism compare to the other political theories introduced in this chapter? Like functionalism, the pluralist perspective recognizes the importance of commonly agreed values. However, for pluralists these are more of a backdrop to social diversity and particular conflicts of interest which can be pursued within the agreed rules of the political game. The closest approximation to the common interest comes as a result of compromise within this conflict through which no single sectional interest can consistently prevail.

Contrary to the Marxist model, the interests of private enterprise (if such a uniformity of interests exists) are not seen as holding a monopoly of power and the ability to continuously shape political decisions in their favour, but are checked by various other interest groups. Neither is there an undifferentiated working class whose class forms the main basis for united political action, since in complex contemporary societies divisions of interest break up the formation of any significant cross cutting common class interest.

Unlike classical elite theory, classical pluralism does not maintain that liberal democracies are or should be governed by a single ruling elite, nor does it emphasise the inferiority and manipulated compliance of the masses. Power is diffused down to an enlightened and active citizenship and can be effectively mobilised.

Elite pluralism or fragmented elites?

Pluralism, a particularly influential political theory in the United States from the 1960s, provides, indeed, a highly self-congratulatory view positing the widespread distribution of power in capitalist liberal democracies. But just how accurate is this model? A number of questions, including the following, have been frequently raised. Are all sections of society adequately represented? Are some groups substantially over-represented in the power that they can exert in relation to their numerical composition? Are pressure groups themselves always internally democratic? Answers to such questions have led some writers such as J. K. Galbraith toward a refocusing of pluralism in the direction of elite pluralism (sometimes referred to as neo-pluralism) (Heywood, 1999, pp.78-79). Although retaining the pluralist perspective as a touchstone, advocates of this modified position acknowledge that some groups in society, in particular large business interests, are likely to have a disproportionate influence on political decisions, especially in the economic sphere. On the other hand, the needs of other sections of society, such as the homeless, tend to get overlooked. It is also often now emphasised that there has been a degree of reconfiguration of pressure group activity away from a focus on national governments, as political problems and the means of tackling them have become more globalised. Furthermore, as hierarchical organisations, conventional pressure groups are often not very open to democratic influence by members from within but are effectively run and represented to government by their own elites. Overall, power may not therefore be as evenly spread, aimed at national government, or as diffused down to active participants as classical pluralism once maintained. From this modified perspective, liberal democracies are sometimes referred to by elite pluralists as 'deformed polyarchies'.

From the other end of the scale, there have also been criticisms of and modifications to the classical elite theory position. The idea of 'fragmented elites', adopted by Ian Budge et al, argues that rather than a single cohesive elite acting with a unified purpose and sense of direction, there exists different interests which elite factions strive to pursue. The interests of business elites may diverge with that of government elites, for example over taxation and anti-monopoly legislation. The elite of the judiciary can come into conflict with government elites over sentencing policy. There may even be fragmentation within each of these elite factions. For example, it is doubtful, other than at a very general level, whether there exists a single business community interest between elites in manufacturing, agriculture, banking and retailing, and within government career civil servants may have different interests to politicians whilst different spending departments often have to compete for limited resources. However, although fragmented, from the above perspective these elites may share a similar general background and outlook and often experience little popular control.

Taking into account these variations, elite theory and pluralist positions can be represented as follows:

Table 1	Continuum of Elite Theory and Pluralist Perspectives		
Classical Elite	**Fragmented Elite**	**Elite Pluralism**	**Classical Pluralism**
Single ruling elite exists with a shared interest. This is necessary, beneficial and inevitable. Masses need to be led and should not have power.	Elites rule, but not as a single cohesive group. Despite similar background and outlook, there are divisions of interest.	Popular participation in interest groups may be limited as leaders represent interests. Some groups have disproportionate power.	Diversity of pressure groups involves members in active and effective participation in pursuit of their interests. Influence of groups varies with issues.

Modernism and second wave feminist politics

The approaches to politics so far have been gender blind, but the myopia of the modernist period reflected the traditional assumptions that the world outside the family was the man's world. In this section, we will focus on second wave feminism – ie that which followed on from the earlier key aspiration of first wave feminism for women to acquire the vote. The focus of second wave feminism was on broader social and political issues regarding equal opportunities (liberal feminism) and the challenging of patriarchal power (radical feminism) which reflected and provided intellectual and consciousness raising stimulus during the period of the women's movement that peaked in the late 1960s and early 1970s.

A pioneer intellectual of post war feminism was the French feminist Simone de Beauvoir. In her work 'The Second Sex' (1949), de Beauvoir described a situation in which women tended to accept the security of a domestic environment and dependence on a husband as powerfully sanctioned by traditional cultural values that prescribed for women a life of domesticity as an image of natural femininity. De Beauvoir was keen to point out that this image of femininity was socially manufactured rather than an essential condition of womanhood and that changing social conditions (particularly technological advance and contraception) were providing the opportunity of a new historic freedom of choice for women.

However, the main difficulty facing women in acquiring this freedom was the need to overcome the conventional view of womanhood which presented liberation as an 'unbearable freedom' compared to the certainty of domestic security. For de Beauvoir, following Sartre, not grasping responsibility for one's fate but resting on the security of convention was an act of 'bad faith' (Bryson, 2003, pp.130-131) – a form of self-deception whereby freedom of action is denied in the comfort of obeying powerful forces of convention.

In America and across western societies during the 1950s, a culture which conveyed to women that their natural source of fulfilment was through their domestic role was powerfully supported by the advertising industry and in women's magazines and educational materials. Governments were also keen to support the traditional family as the bastion of social order. However, by the early 1960s in the United States, the black civil rights movement was challenging racial discrimination and more women were coming to question their own limited rights and opportunities. The cultural climate had thus become more receptive to feminist thinking when Betty Friedan wrote The

Feminine Mystique in 1963 which reflected, articulated and augmented these feelings of the time.

For Friedan, women's domestic confinement was unfulfilling. Further, for many it was also psychologically damaging, but many women suffered in ignorance of the extent of widespread suffering due to their very confinement. Friedan argued that, as for men, women could only experience true fulfilment through acquiring full access to life in mainstream society. In particular, this meant equal access to and opportunities within educational and workplace institutions.

In her critique of female domesticity, Friedan was laying down the foundations of liberal feminism which emphasised the need for equal opportunities within the system through legislative reform.

By the late 1960s, a more radical form of feminism was emerging, an important social background to this being the ongoing sexism experienced by women engaged in civil rights politics. Radical feminists such as Firestone and Millet viewed men's oppression of women as both the most fundamental and universal form of oppression. They placed the concept of 'patriarchal power' at the centre of their analysis, arguing that the political control of women by men patterned itself throughout society and could not be overcome by tinkering with the system. Instead, a more partisan view of women's experience required a more overtly political challenge in the form of a sisterhood of collective action against male dominance.

For Marxist feminists, sexism and the subordination of women are regarded as a product of the class structure under capitalism. In supporting the traditional family unit, whilst male workers have pressed for a 'family wage', women provide cheap domestic support for the maintenance of the breadwinner which in aggregate benefits the interests of employers and the capitalist economy. If women do work, they are also of benefit to capitalism by providing a more flexible and lower paid component of the workforce. Moreover, Phillips and Taylor (1986) (Bryson, 2003, p.208) have argued that men have been able to pass the brunt of deskilling that is built into the dynamics of capitalism on to women.

Society and the state

A general definition of the state can usefully be taken from Max Weber who defined it in terms of a community of persons with the capacity to impose power through authority or coercion over a given territory. To quote Weber, the 'state is a human community that (successfully) claims the monopoly of the legitimate use of physical force within a given territory' comprising 'a relation of men dominating men, a relation supported by means of legitimate (i.e. considered to be legitimate) violence' (Gerth & Mills, 1977, p.78). Ultimately, state power can be exerted through the institutional use of force.

The nation state is viewed to hold sovereignty over its territory – that is, the right to pass laws and enact policy within a geographical boundary, recognized by international law and supported by powerful national symbols. It will also confer to members of society as citizens certain duties and rights.

The state uses its powers through various institutions at its disposal, but how may we more specifically define the scope of the state? There are more or less obvious components to it, depending on the breadth of definition applied. Even a relatively narrow and formal definition of the state would include the institutions of political parties and government, the civil service, the legal and judicial system, the armed forces, the police, the apparatus of local government, the National Health Service, the state education system and a variety of regulatory bodies such as, in Britain, the Health and Safety Executive and Ofsted. These institutions both regulate and protect the lives of citizens.

Some social theorists view the institutions of the state more inclusively. For example, the Marxist Poulantzas also includes in the state the mass media and even the family as these form part of the means of ideological control.

In the various sociological perspectives on power and politics covered in this chapter, it can be noted that the state is viewed as deeply rooted within the broader social context. For most of these perspectives, this engenders a 'society focussed' view of the state which relates it to surrounding social forces rather than a 'state focussed' approach which emphasises its power and influence on society as an entity in its own right.

For functionalists, the state can be seen as a rational directing power, utilising the ability of experts appointed on merit to intervene in society to promote social order and integration for the common well-being. It therefore performs the key function of engineering the smooth functioning of society. To this rational dimension can be added the importance of a more emotional aspect of state ceremonies and rituals which convey to individuals, through powerful state symbolism, a collective consciousness and feeling of national identity. These latter issues will also be picked up on in the chapter on religion.

By contrast, as a basic recipe, Marxists view the state in capitalist societies as shaped by relationships of class power and representing the interests of an economically dominant ruling class. There is, however, some debate within Marxist circles as to the extent to which the state is simply a direct instrument of the ruling class (an instrumentalist view) or whether it has to act more autonomously. We have seen that an instrumentalist position was adopted by Ralph Miliband who regards the state as run by an elite but controlled by a capitalist class. The capitalist class is therefore a thoroughly ruling class.

However, Poulantzas has adopted the position that for the benefit of the long term continuity of the capitalist system, the state must avoid such direct class control which would simply reproduce in the state any divisions which exist within the capitalist class. From this Marxist perspective, greater autonomy from the capitalist class enables the state to both act as a more cohesive representative of capitalist class interests and to offer concessions when necessary to the subject class. For example, from this position and that of Gramsci, if the capitalist class ruled too directly through the state, it is questionable whether the welfare state would have developed to the extent that it has. However, the welfare state could be seen as the worthwhile ransom price that needs to be paid for social harmony and the longevity of capitalism itself, especially if the main beneficiaries of welfare state provisions are also the main financial contributors. A degree of state autonomy thus enables the state to institute reforms that help to perpetuate the system from which the capitalist class are the prime beneficiaries and to save them from themselves.

For Weber, the growth of the nation state is part of a more general process of bureaucratisation in which social relationships become increasingly formalized. However, his approach tends to be a more state centred one than others in this section since it focusses on the rational decisions and actions of actors within the machinery of state and how these are imposed on the population through the bureaucratic apparatus.

In contrast to Marxists, elite theorists view the state as a separate political entity from the economy. It is an oligarchical instrument of rule headed by a privileged minority ruling primarily in the interests of an established elite and manipulating the masses through the facade of democracy. State oligarchical structures are inevitable, even if one elite should replace another.

Pluralists tend to view the state in liberal democracies as a relatively light handed entity in terms of the limited imposition of institutional power. It acts as the arbiter of competing interests, all comprising the means by which political decisions are arrived at through a broad process of democratic participation and compromise. It then implements the outcomes of the decisions arrived at within the rules of the game. Neo-pluralists, such as Galbraith, have developed the pluralist model in a way which recognises the distorting effect of corporate power on this decision making process.

Another variant of pluralism is the post war corporatist state model in which government brings representatives of the interests of labour and capital into the social and economic planning process to seek their co-operation and agreement to compromise their aspirations in the interest of social harmony and economic stability. Such an approach was last attempted in Britain through the Labour government's 'social contract' of the mid-1970s.

Noam Chomsky locates the American state as both an instrument of powerful economic interests and a powerful economic and military entity in its own right. As such, he provides a scathing condemnation of America's democratic credentials.

For Chomsky, American politics in recent decades has been dominated by a neoliberal free market philosophy. Powerful supporters of this approach argue that free enterprise capitalism and free trade for all enhances democratic freedom and the standard of living throughout the world. However, Chomsky argues that in reality American social policy is shaped by and caters for the needs of large corporate interests and the rich. Democratic accountability is thus undermined as policies which may benefit the majority, such as welfare reform, are blocked as the taxation necessary to implement them clashes with the economic self-interest of the rich and powerful who provide the funding that is necessary for political campaigns. The policy difference between the major political parties is therefore negligible. Furthermore, the media tends to restrict the scope for political discussion and stifle genuine debate through generating a climate of fear of political enemies of America. The United States is therefore not democratic even in the rather restricted sense of the pluralist model.

Further, despite claiming to be the advocate of democracy throughout the world, America's priority is always the self-interested one of maintaining its political and economic power. To do so, it has intervened to subvert the outcome of democratic elections which are viewed as a threat to its interests (for example, the CIA assisted overthrow of the Marxist sympathetic and democratically elected Allende government in Chile and its replacement by the Pinochet military junta who favoured free market reforms) and supported undemocratic regimes by which America benefits (for example in oil rich Saudi Arabia).

In terms of international trade, the principles of free trade are also distorted through economic self-interest. For example, poorer countries find that loans from the World Bank and the IMF invariably have strings attached that require them to open up their economies to free trade from which wealthier countries such as the United States are the main beneficiaries, whilst in America agricultural subsidies are used to protect their own farming interests.

Society rooted approaches to the state are not the only focus which has been adopted. An alternative position regards the state as a powerful and separate entity in its own right with the capacity to shape society according to its own goals, if necessary against resistance. This position is well exemplified in the works of Theda Skocpol. In her analysis of the French, Chinese and Russian Revolutions, she argues that the key animating force of change may appear to have been the revolutionary movements, but more decisive was the incapacity of those who had commanded the state to rise to the challenge of changing international conditions. The success or otherwise of revolutions is related to the strategic strength of the state, the international circumstances in which it is operating and its capacity to respond based on the choices taken by rulers. We might further illustrate this with the example of Japanese modernization. Japan managed to avoid revolution because the elites, learning from the example of western destabilisation of China, restricted western intrusions and forced reform from above through state directed modernization during the late nineteenth century.

Whatever the differences between the theories of the state so far examined, there is at least agreement that it is a sovereign entity governing a nation. We will later see that this basic assumption has been increasingly called into question, especially through the impact of globalisation.

The vote – more an index of power than power itself?

Universal franchise – the extension of the vote to all people over a certain age bar limited prescribed sections of the population – is a fundamental feature of contemporary representative democracies. Having access to the vote opens up a degree of choice and provides some political power to the electorate; just how much choice and power is open to debate and is an issue which is disputed from various theoretical perspectives such as those introduced above. Moreover, viewed sociologically, power, as previously defined, is potentially an element of all social relationships. Prior to the study of voting behaviour, it is therefore important to appreciate that the acquisition of universal suffrage can itself be placed in the context of political struggles between groups within society for a say in the formation of governments. In this context, the restriction or extension of the vote itself provides a barometer of changing power relationships within society.

Groups that have used their power to acquire access to the vote have sometimes attempted to exclude its extension to others. By so doing, they try to promote social closure. In Britain in the early 1830s, the extension of the vote to a broader section of male property owners reflected the growing social power of the middle classes following the Industrial Revolution. At the time, the exclusion of non-property owners was justified on the ideological basis that a more open social structure had emerged in which property acquisition by the self made man was proof of industriousness and the capacity to make sound judgements. Property ownership was therefore argued to demonstrate proven worthiness of the capacity to make sound political judgements and the criteria of deservedness for access to the vote.

At various times and in different societies, other ideological justifications, including those based on racism and sexism, have been used by some groups to exclude other sections of the population from acquiring full access to the vote. Thus, although universal suffrage is the hallmark of modern liberal democracies, it has been fought for by chartists, suffragists, supporters of civil rights, and anti-apartheid movements, etc.

In Britain, through legislative reforms responding to the growing organisation and power of the industrial working class and the suffrage stage of the women's movement, all males over 21 had gained access to the vote in 1918, and females, on an equal basis to males, in 1928. Legislation passed in 1969 brought the minimum voting age down to 18 and there has also more recently been talk of a possible further reduction to the age of 16.

Sociological approach to voting behaviour

Academic sociology is parcelled into different topic areas to assist in the focus of analysis. Politics, and more specifically voting behaviour, is part of this process of academic specialisation. However, the real social world is interconnected. To reflect this, sociologists need to be able to make interconnections within their subject. Hence, to understand voting behaviour sociologically requires a sociological understanding of surrounding social conditions and changes within which evidence of patterns of voting behaviour can be interpreted. The reader is therefore encouraged to relate an understanding of voting behaviour to sociological analysis in other chapters, especially the one on social stratification.

A post war baseline – voting behaviour and social class

During the post war years and up to the early 1970s, voting in Britain appeared to exhibit quite a stable pattern. Voters tended to retain loyalty to their chosen political party from one general election to another. Swings in party support between elections were modest. The beneficiaries of this stability were the Labour and Conservative Parties, who between them regularly obtained over 80% of the vote and took their turns in government.

Prior to the early 1970s, social class appeared to be the influence of overriding importance that provided an anchorage point for people's political outlook and voting (Pulzer, 1967). Explanations of this stability tend to emphasise the long term and cumulative effect on people of political socialisation within a relatively stable social structure, referred to by Coxall et al (2003, p.101) as 'primacy' factors. Partisan identification refers to a high level of voter commitment and loyalty to a particular party, often based on commitment to a set of ideological values and the pursuit of a cause. Partisanship therefore often entails a high degree of emotional commitment from the voter, who may not necessarily have a detailed knowledge of issues and policy across the political parties. Class alignment emphasised a link between a person's social class and the tendency to vote for a party which is perceived to represent that class interest. Seen as combined, these influences are referred to as partisan class alignment. In a stable class structure, with limited opportunities for geographical and social mobility, the impact of family socialisation and class identification – reinforced, according to Butler and Stokes (1969), by the type of neighbourhood lived in, school attended and work environment – provided a class differentiated pattern of socialisation which produced a strong predisposition toward class based voting behaviour. According to this explanation, a strong bond existed between being manual working class and voting for the Labour Party and being white collar middle class and voting for the Conservatives. Social class provided the best single indicator and predictor of voting behaviour.

The impact of working class community life on political consciousness and voting behaviour was picked up on by Parkin (1967). Parkin argued that the dominant ideological culture of the state and the privileged and wealthy social orders is more attuned to the political outlook of the Conservative Party. If the impact of this dominant culture were all embracing, working class support for the Conservatives would be high. However, the characteristics of working class communities and socialisation, as suggested by Butler and Stokes, provided a degree of insulation from the impact of the dominant political culture and provided support for an oppositional culture with a degree of class consciousness and support for Labour as the party of the working class.

Detailed evidence to support partisan and class alignment was not abundant in the post war years, since sophisticated electoral surveys in the form of exit polls only date from 1964. However, supporting circumstantial evidence was strong. This included low levels of net voter volatility between elections, comparatively high electoral turnout of around 75%, and the dominance in politics of two major parties, Labour and the Conservatives, reflecting a society of two main social classes, the working and middle classes.

However, evidence also indicated that a significant proportion of voters in each class did not conform to the dominant voting pattern. For example, research conducted by Ivor Crewe (1983) established that in the 1959 general election approximately 1/5 of non-manual workers voted Labour and about 1/3 of manual workers voted Conservative. An important concern during the 1960s and 1970s was therefore to explain the reasons behind these levels of 'deviant voting' or 'class defection'. Some of these explanations are briefly summarised below.

Firstly, social classes are not uniform blocks; different occupational sectors exist within social classes which may encourage different political outlooks. Within the working class, Goldthorpe and Lockwood argued that agricultural labourers and coal miners tended to adopt opposing political attitudes which were based on their differing views of the social structure. Such differences were related to distinctive occupational and community influences. For example, the dangers of coal mining required high levels of co-operation between workers who also lived in tightly knit community networks around the pits. This life encouraged a view of the social structure as divided between 'us (the workers) and them (the bosses)' – a view which promoted strong identification toward the Labour Party, that had grown out of the trade union movement, as the party of the working class. By contrast, agricultural workers, who worked and lived in smaller scattered groups and communities and had more regular contact with their employers, were more likely to view the social hierarchy as a justifiable order. Associated traditional attitudes of deference to social superiors would incline many of these workers toward voting Conservative as the party of natural leaders.

Secondly, there is the question of how social class is defined and measured and who is defining and measuring it. If people are designated to a social class by sociologists through the use of traditional occupational scales alone, their own subjective interpretations of their social class position are being ignored. Butler and Stokes found that where people's subjective judgement of their social class did not agree with that allocated to them by researchers, there was a higher tendency for them to be deviant voters in terms of sociologists' class definitions, whereas if their subjective views correlated with sociologists' definition of their class they were very likely to be class conformist in their voting. Personal perception of their class was therefore of some importance to a person's voting decisions and when taken into account could help to explain levels of so called deviant voting.

Thirdly, voters experiencing cross class social mobility may, through the continuing effect of earlier political socialisation, remain loyal to the party of their class of origin, thus becoming deviant voters in their class of destination. The upwardly mobile may therefore remain loyal to Labour – as discovered by Goldthorpe and Lockwood in the case of the sons of affluent blue collar workers who became white collar workers. Likewise, those downwardly mobile from the middle to working class may retain adherence to the Conservative Party.

Fourthly, although the impact of social class was arguably very powerful, other social factors can cut across and to some extent break up its overriding influence. For example, Anthony Heath has shown that within the working class, private home owners were more likely to vote Conservative than council house occupants.

Another cross cutting influence is that of religion. In England, Catholics have traditionally tended to vote Labour whereas those who identify with the Church of England (the religion of the establishment) are more likely to vote Conservative (seeing it as the party of the establishment). For example, Heath found in 1992 that of middle class voters who identified with the Church of England, 72% voted Conservative, whereas only 47% of middle class voters who held no religious beliefs voted Conservative. Moreover, the intensity of the impact of religion is likely to vary alongside levels of religious identification in different parts of the country.

Locality, gender, ethnicity and age all show some influence on voting behaviour. They therefore also provide potential for breaking up the single influence of social class.

However, even during the 1960s, there was evidence emerging of a changing relationship between the electorate and the political parties that they supported. For example, Goldthorpe and Lockwood (1969) found that although 80% of affluent blue collar workers in their research had voted Labour at the 1959 general election, their identification was based less on strong party loyalty and an ideological commitment than was thought to traditionally be the case for working class Labour voters. Although these affluent voters still tended to see themselves as working class, their greater affluence and home centeredness encouraged a more isolated lifestyle and instrumental attitude toward trade unions and political parties, support for which became more contingent on the furtherance of their standard of living. As affluent workers comprised an expanding section of the working class, there was a possibility of potential desertion from voting Labour by a growing section of blue collar workers in the future if Labour failed to deliver.

Some similarity to the above trend but with reference to the nature of attachment to voting Conservative was argued by McKenzie and Silver (1972). Goldthorpe and Lockwood, and long before them Walter Bagehot, had argued that a substantial proportion of Conservative support, including that from working class voters, was based on a deferential social outlook toward those perceived as natural superiors. However, McKenzie and Silver argued that the deferential outlook was declining whilst of increasing importance in voting Conservative was a 'secular' outlook which focussed more on party policy and assessed the practical implications for a voter's standard of living.

From the mid 1950s, a number of changes were affecting working class community life. These included: the start of a long term decline in employment in traditional industries such as steel working, shipbuilding, and dock work, followed by a later dramatic decline in coal mining, and with this a decline in the possibility of working class nepotism (finding jobs for relatives); geographical movement required with the demolition of slums and re-housing or the search for new types of work; and some improvement in opportunities for social mobility. In these developments can be seen the undermining of community life and a thinning out of the boundaries of class formation which were likely to diminish the impact of social class on working class social and political outlook and voting behaviour.

Whatever direct influence social class was likely to retain on voting behaviour, if, as Dahrendorf has argued, class decomposition was taking place, it should be expected that likewise a pattern of decomposition in voting behaviour would follow. This and the decline of the traditional working class already signalled long-term problems for the Labour Party it if relied on appealing to the traditional working class voter.

The decline of social class based voting?

Signs of how these underlying social changes were having a significant effect on voting behaviour were first observed in the February 1974 general election. In this election, the Liberal vote increased substantially to 19.3% from a 1951 low of 2.6% and a level of still only 7.5% in the 1970 election. This increase was at the expense of the combined Labour and Conservative vote which fell from 89.4% in the 1970 election to 74.9% in February 1974 (and this later declined to 65% in the 2010 election). After falling back a little in the 1979 election, the 'Liberal' vote surged again in 1983 when the Liberal SDP Alliance polled 25.4% of the vote; only about 2% behind the Labour vote. This decline in the two party monopoly, at least as far as proportion of the vote is concerned, suggested a significant move away from the two party partisan identification and class alignment model of voting behaviour. Of much debate since has been the question of how fundamental this change has become and what other social factors may be emerging to influence voting behaviour at the expense of social class.

Of some significance to the debate has not just been the increase in the 'Liberal' vote (the parties of the Liberal SDP Alliance merged in 1988 and eventually settled on the new name of Liberal Democrats), but also the nature of its support. Until well into the 1990s, the Liberal Democrats had retained the Liberal tradition of being fairly centrally positioned on the left to right political scale between the Labour and Conservative Parties respectively. Their supporters have been amongst the most fickle section of the electorate, with only a minority remaining loyal over two consecutive elections. Instability in voting behaviour, although not only concentrated here, appears to have become an increasing feature of British general elections. There was also clear evidence of a significant decline in voter turnout in general elections around the turn of the millennium: 77.7% in 1992, 71.4% in 1997, just below 60% in 2001, just above 60% in 2005. This trend would appear to offer evidence of declining partisan identification by the electorate. However, since then, a modest upward trend has been established with a turnout of 65.1% in 2010, 66.2% in 2015 and 68.7% in 2017.

It is against the backdrop of such evidence that arguments over dealignment in terms of both party loyalty and class identification have emerged. An early advocate of the interpretation that a fundamental dealignment was taking place in voting behaviour was Ivor Crewe who headed the British Election Studies of 1974 and 1979. He argued that voting was becoming less based on feelings of loyalty toward a particular political party – a process referred to as partisan dealignment. An effective way to measure this is to look at the strength with which voters identify with political parties. To this end, research conducted by Crewe and Thompson found that whilst 44% of voters identified very strongly with a political party in 1964, this figure had fallen to 16% by 1997, and later, according to Saunders et al, to 9% in 2005.

Furthermore, evidence suggested that social class, based on occupation, was becoming a poorer indicator of voting behaviour – suggesting that class dealignment was also taking place. General election figures provided by Saunders show that during the1960s, Labour and the Conservatives held steady class based monopolies of the vote at the expense of the Liberals. The Liberals then made some inroads in 1974. Over the four elections between 1979 and 1992, Labour were the main casualties of dealignment with the Conservatives regularly polling between 35 and 36% of the manual workers' vote. However, in 1997, dealignment worked against the Conservatives with Labour becoming New Labour and capturing 40% of the non-manual vote.

Anthony Heath (who also headed a number of the British Election Studies) had been initially more sceptical of the long-term impact of dealignment. He acknowledged that there was research evidence indicating a decline in partisan voting, but cast doubt on the extent and lasting effect of class dealignment. He argued that much depends on how social class is defined. Heath made more specific distinctions than between middle class and working class and when focussing on the voting behaviour of powerless blue collar workers, found an unchanging pattern of support for Labour through the 1960s and into the 1980s. Overall, for Heath, changing patterns of voting behaviour were tending to reflect changes in the class structure itself with a declining size of the working class disadvantaging Labour.

However, Heath argued that growing inequality under the Conservatives could reverse any class dealignment and lead to the re-emergence of class as the major social factor in voting behaviour.

It is very doubtful, however, whether a process of realignment has transpired. As inequality was increasing under the Conservatives, class consciousness may have been simultaneously declining. A more individualistic culture had been promoted by the new right. Many blue collar workers were turning away from trade unions who (still strongly associated with the Labour Party) were blighted with unpopularity following the 'winter of discontent', and were looking toward the potential individual benefits from Conservative reforms such as the promotion of home ownership. There is therefore not necessarily a straightforward causal relationship between occupation and economic factors and class consciousness. Furthermore, an important component of New Labour's landslide election victory in 1997 was a substantial shift toward Labour support from sections of the middle class, whilst in their defeat in the 2010 election, it appears that it was amongst skilled manual workers that a major desertion from Labour took place.

Could patterns of voting behaviour still be explained in primacy terms? Could they be better explained by reference to an overriding social factor other than social class? Dunleavy and Husbands (1985) thought so in their sectoral politics model. Central to this explanation is the view that a closer fit with voting behaviour than social class division appears in the division between the public and private sector. This model predicted that the more that people were involved in the public sector in their employment position, consumer capacity and housing situation, the more likely they were to vote Labour whatever their occupational class, whereas the more they were implicated in the private sector, the greater likelihood that they would vote Conservative, again largely irrespective of social class. In terms of consumer capacity and use of services, important areas of the pubic and private divide would include housing, educational provision, health provision and pensions. This model suggested a shift from class to status as a major influence on voting behaviour. And given the changing balance in favour of private commodity and service as opposed to state provision and the declining numbers employed in the public sector during the 1980s, each brought about by Conservative reforms, it is clear that if this analysis is correct, the Conservatives were building a substantial social basis of long term support that Labour would need to respond to.

Another possibility is that no single primacy (long term) or structural factor can any longer adequately explain voting behaviour, but that a fluid combination of influences may be coming into play. Religion, region and neighbourhood, age, gender and ethnicity all show some impact on voting behaviour. However, it may be suspected that higher levels of volatility are associated with the impact of more short-term influences. These have been referred to as 'recency' influences (Coxall et al, 2003, p.105) and tend to be associated with a more instrumental and individualised approach to voting in which individuals reflect on political issues and make rational decisions based on the calculated impact of policy on their personal well being, especially on their standard of living, in contrast to necessarily following class, family and community traditions. Amongst these influences may be leadership image, the econometric or 'feel good' factor and the impact of the mass media. Indeed, as the latter enables the electorate to acquire up to date intelligence on the state of the parties through the findings of opinion polls, effective tactical voting (usually taking the form of switching to a party which has a perceived better chance of defeating a disliked party than voting for one's party of first choice in a constituency) becomes more of a possibility. This arguably both presupposes and promotes a decline in partisan voting and further assists volatility.

Leadership image arguably played an increasing profile in the British 2010 general election as for the first time televised debates between the leaders of the three major parties were held. Extensive polling suggested that, following the first debate on 15 April, Liberal Democrat support surged from about 20% to 30%, at the expense of Conservative and, to a slightly lesser extent, Labour support (House of Commons Library, 12/8/2013, p.69). This was by far the most marked opinion shift of the campaign and, according to an Ipsos MORI poll, 60% of respondents claimed that the debates were an important factor in influencing who they would vote for (House of Commons Library, 12/8/2013, p.73).

A further aspect of voting behaviour relates to the ideological and policy positioning of the political parties themselves. For example, in the 1983 general election, there was clear polarisation between the Labour Party and the Conservatives both ideologically and on a range of issues including privatisation and nuclear disarmament. The Conservatives won the election and attracted the vote of 35% of voters in manual occupations. The wide gap in the middle of the political spectrum enabled the Liberal / SDP Alliance to occupy a position from which their percentage of the vote peaked. Labour had since become rebranded as 'New labour' and in distancing itself from its historical connections with trade unions and the imagery of being the party of the working class, and accepting many of the Conservative reforms, had moved into the political middle ground. In doing so, New Labour successfully managed to broaden its appeal across society to the extent that in the 1997 general election it obtained about 40% of the middle class vote.

A narrowing of party positions around the centre of the political scale is likely to make it more difficult for voters to make clear cut ideological distinctions between the parties. It has been argued that they will therefore be more likely to base their vote on judgements of how they think that the different political parties will tackle particular issues that they deem to be important, a phenomena referred to as 'issue salience'. Of high priority, but not necessarily determining election outcomes, is the electorate's assessment of a party in managing the economy and raising standards of living. This was clearly an important factor in the 2010 election which took place in the wake of the banking crisis and economic recession, with polls conducted by the British Election Study showing that the Conservatives had a substantial lead over Labour in the electorate's views of who could best manage the economic situation going forward.

However, politics arguably remains as much about the manipulation of subjective perception by political parties and the ideological filtering of information as it is about debate over objective facts. As things stood in the spring of 2014, the Conservative led coalition government were able to provide the electorate with evidence of sustained economic recovery whereas Labour questioned who the main beneficiaries of this recovery were. The appeal of the arguments put forward was still likely to relate to people's position in the social structure, the ideological filtering of the messages and the degree to which they remain committed to a particular party.

The impact of voting, Marxism versus pluralism

The classical sociological perspectives differ in their evaluation of the political impact that the electorate can have in shaping policy and bringing about political change. This should be quite apparent in a comparison of classical pluralist and Marxist perspectives on the sources and distribution of power in capitalist democracies. For Marxists, the electorate can only appear to have significant say in the complexion of government in capitalist societies, but for the main beneficiaries of capitalism it is important that this appearance is kept up. In reality, much of the power to influence policy is concentrated in the hands of a capitalist class and serves the interests of capital.

The pluralist model, by contrast, has been argued to effectively explain the impact of recency influences and instrumental attitudes toward voting. This model, put forward for example by Himmelweit (1985), suggests that social class and party ideology have little impact on the decision making of voters because they adopt a pragmatic consumer based approach to voting. They shop around and rationally compare the benefit to themselves of the policies on offer in a similar way to that in which they choose from a range of products before deciding on a purchase (or not) when casting their vote (or not). Political parties must compete in packaging their policies to attract the votes of political consumers who are thus able to shape party policy.

This approach explains the preoccupation that political parties have for conducting political opinion polls in search of policy proposals that will promote their appeal to the broadest audience of voters. It also suggests that in the competition to do so, the range of political party options will tend to narrow and usually seek support on the centre ground of politics. Thus, just as the Labour Party had to reposition itself from its left of the spectrum position in the early 1980s toward the centre of the spectrum under New Labour to win the 1997 general election, the Conservatives were successful in the 2010 election, becoming the main party in a coalition government with the Liberal Democrats, by repositioning themselves, compared to the 1980s, in a more moderately right position and promoting a more caring and consensual image nurtured under the leadership of David Cameron.

Despite modest increases in voter turnout in recent general elections, a growing concern amongst the political parties has been that a substantial proportion of the electorate do not appear to be buying into party politics. It is with this concern in mind that various alternatives to people having to turn out to the voting booth, such as the expansion of postal, electronic and telephone voting, are being considered. In the next section, it will be suggested that the process of globalisation appears to be having a significant effect on national and electoral politics.

From regulated toward deregulated capitalism

The role of the state in the post war period related to the rational planning of the economy and the exercise of sovereign political power within the prescribed territorial area of the nation. This role was exemplified in the Keynesian model of judicious government intervention to regulate the economy and protect members of society from the ravages of mass unemployment which had been suffered during the interwar years. An underlying assumption of this model was that such interventions can be effective within the territorial confines of the nation state. The virtual abandonment of the Keynesian approach in the UK was underway from the mid-1970s.

When the new right Conservative government came to power from 1979, a period of industrial strife and poor economic performance that they inherited was laid at the door of excessive government interventionism through Keynesian and corporatist consensus approaches. It was argued that through competition for the popular vote, pressures were built into the system toward pledges to the electorate for more government intervention. This had led to government overload and governments had become overstretched in their regulatory role. Excessive intervention, especially in economic matters, arguably brought inefficiency.

Upon their election, the political response of the Conservative new right was to move society in a deregulatory free market direction, diminishing the interventionist role of the state and the size of the public sector through privatisations, marketisation and the contracting out of in-house services – changes largely taken on board by the incoming New Labour government when it came to power in 1997. These developments, and subsequent ones, need to be placed in the broader context of globalising forces.

Globalisation and changing configurations of power

Globalisation is a complex set of processes, the extent and impact of which, as well as advocated responses, have been hotly debated. What most analysts would agree is that fundamental changes have taken place in the global environment which are having a profound effect on the role of the state and democratic politics.

Processes of globalisation can be overviewed in terms of the emergence of networks of information, economic relations and political and cultural processes that cut across national boundaries. There is little doubt that these processes have extended their range, speed of operation and mobility with the advance of high tech global capitalism. Satellite, internet, and mobile phone technology allow instantaneous communication of information around the world. Masses of information can be exchanged. Social protest movements can more easily communicate and operate rapidly across national boundaries. Global financial movements can instantly take place based on access to the latest financial market intelligence. Businesses can more readily move their production between countries to take advantage of cheaper labour and / or more profitable activity. As nations have become increasingly enmeshed in this maelstrom of activity, governmental processes have had to adapt. But how?

A number of issues and questions, including the following, can be raised with reference to globalisation and politics. Just how fundamental and wide ranging is the impact of globalisation? What are the benefits and risks involved? What are its consequences for national governments? Are they losing power to forces of global capitalism and if so how and to what extent? How may globalisation be changing the activities of the nation state and national democratic politics? What political responses are emerging to globalisation, and what new types of political institutions may be necessary? Are governments able to retain a monopoly in the use of power in their prescribed territories? And to what extent is it necessary, or possible, for national governments to beneficially reconfigure their use of power by a degree of its devolution downwards to regional and local levels and by passing some sovereignty upwards to supra-state organisations? Such questions are being debated across a range of positions adopted on globalisation.

One position identified by Held (2000a & b) is labelled 'traditionalist'. This emphasises that despite evidence of extensive internationalisation, globalisation is something different and its impact has been overstated. According to this view, whilst states have had to adapt to changing international conditions, they remain strong and powerful political entities. Alternatively, it has been argued that the forces of globalisation are profound and irresistible, fundamentally weakening the power of the state. This position is sometimes referred to as 'hyperglobalist', with advocates usually adopting a positive and optimistic view of the benefits of global free enterprise, especially for consumers. Whilst agreeing with the profound effect of global capitalism, others take a far more pessimistic interpretation which emphasises the ravages brought by large corporations for the primary benefit of a transnational capitalist class. In between the traditionalist and globalist positions lies the 'transformationist' position. Transformationists agree that profound forces of globalisation are at work and contend that they bring both benefits and risks. Advocates of this stance tend to be cautiously optimistic. For transformationists, although difficult, it is possible and necessary to steer the globalisation process through utilising various levels of governance from the local through to a global level, working with national governments so as to enhance benefits and minimise risks which are emerging in a globalising world.

Hirst and Thompson are proponents of the traditionalist position, tending to adopt the 'state as container' view of politics, which maintains that control of national boundaries remains relatively intact and nation states retain strong control within their territory and remain very powerful units of political influence in the world. Whilst major corporations hold significant power, Hirst and Thompson argue that a distinction needs to be made between multinational businesses (with their headquarters fixed in one country and operations in other countries) and transnational businesses (which can move between countries much more freely). They claim that multinationals provide an index of internationalisation but that only transnationals are truly global organisations and these do not predominate. Hirst and Thompson also use economic data to argue that the differences in levels of international trade proportionate to GDP in the contemporary world and that which existed in previous conditions of colonialism around the turn of the twentieth century are not that great. International trade was then well advanced and national economies have not since become integrated into a single global economy, as the impact of truly transnational corporations has been limited. Instead, they are integrated into an international economy, with some divisions into trading blocks, and where multinationals with headquarters in nations where they are subject to control are the key business organisations.

This position now tends to be a minority one. Most analysts recognise that modern technology has compressed time, sped up the pace of change and reduced the barriers of distance. Finance, financial institutions and high tech industry, a growing element of advanced economies, create 'light economies' in which productive forces are much more mobile than those of traditional manufacturing and extractive industries. Immediacy of access to information is part of the new global environment. As communication is global and instantaneous, events happening in different parts of the world and communicated globally are received in countries at their own local time. At the cultural level, long gone seem the days (the early 1980s) when most people in Britain had access to only three television channels, each of which went off the air late at night, with the BBC airing the national anthem.

The effects of globalisation are arguably both various and penetrating. Change and innovation are vital to the survival of businesses in a competitive global environment. National governments are likely to find it increasingly difficult to operate as bounded sovereign entities in the face of interconnected world financial markets, business investment decisions and flows of information. Faced with these dynamics, workers have had to become more prepared to retrain or relocate and national governments have needed to support this process, as well as keeping down rates of corporation tax, if they are to attract and retain inward investment. As countries open up to attract investment from overseas, they tend to also be open to the threat of its potential withdrawal.

Kenichi Ohmae adopts a hyperglobalist position and argues that the forces of free enterprise global capitalism are both irresistible and beneficial. Left to itself in a free market globalised world, he argues that business finds the most advantageous places for the production and distribution of goods and services. According to Ohmae, such freely operating globalised business and trade enhances overall prosperity and should therefore be embraced. In complete opposition to the 'state as container' view, Ohmae maintains that national governments should tend to shed their functions of economic regulation as the forces of economic globalisation bring about a 'borderless world'. Attempts to erect national trade barriers or introduce protectionist subsidies would distort the beneficial effect of the global free market and thus be backward looking and counterproductive. By contrast, the natural role of government in a capitalist globalised world is to promote conditions of flexibility and free markets for both businesses and workers, and their main interventionist role should be to provide adequate infrastructure and well educated and trained employees. In a global free enterprise and free trade world, it is argued that power becomes increasingly transferred to consumers who benefit from diversity, choice and competitive prices. From this perspective, there would be little role for supra-national governance apart from guaranteeing a framework for the operation of global free trade and enterprise.

Ohmae claims a further benefit of globalisation to be a reduced risk of war between nations. This is because as the capital of businesses becomes increasingly global, wars between nations would destroy abroad the resources of home based businesses.

However, critics have suggested that Ohmae's position is reminiscent of the ideological arguments adopted by mid-nineteenth century liberal economists on the civilising and wealth creating benefits of free trade. As such, it attempts to justify those processes which primarily benefit a few by emphasising that the benefits are widespread.

The availability of cheap goods and services may be attractive to consumers. However, such goods and services often originate from countries where cheap labour is available. Given the relatively high mobility of capital compared to labour, in a competitive global free for all it may be very difficult for many workers to resist pressures toward a deterioration in their terms and conditions of employment when they face the possibility of unemployment that can come from the threat of businesses to move capital investment to lower wage economies. Governments that try to restrict the mobility of capital investment are likely to find it difficult to attract inward investment in the first place and traditional trade union action to protect wages and conditions of employment is likely to be ineffective or even counterproductive as businesses are more freely able to utilise cheap labour that is available in developing countries.

Leslie Sklair adopts an opposing stance on the nature of free enterprise global capitalism to that of Ohmae. He takes evidence of the growth of transnational corporations as an index of globalisation. Sklair argues that the driving force for expansion of these organisations is a transnational capitalist class whose primary aim is maximisation of shareholder profit. It is not the consumer with whom power lies under global capitalism but, via the spread of cheaply available mass media throughout the world and the indoctrination of people into the ideology of consumerism, the real beneficiaries are the corporations and their shareholders. Otherwise, the effects of global capitalism are largely negative in two interconnected areas. Firstly, it is claimed that this form of globalisation brings about growing inequality between and within nations, and secondly that it is ecologically destructive. Driven by rampant consumerism and the quest for profits, transnational corporations hold little concern for the sustainability of resources or the needs of indigenous populations – issues which have become of focal importance as pressure groups have forced environmental concern up the political agenda.

The transformationist position on globalisation tends to be aligned with high modernist sociological analysis and Held and McGrew favour this perspective. From this position, in the context of an increasingly complex and quickly changing world where events can have long range impacts, it is argued that the forces of globalisation need to be politically steered to minimise new and potentially widespread associated risks and maximise beneficial outcomes. To do so, national governments need to become reconfigured to work with supra-national political and organisational bodies, non-governmental organisations and local political bodies, thereby trading a degree of sovereign power to enhance overall political purchase. This is part of a complex and changing world of democratic politics which may raise questions about the capacity of national governments to reflect the will of their electorates, lead to a disconnection between citizens and political establishments, and increase political activity through 'new social movements'.

New social movements

Whilst there is some disagreement on the extent to which the issues and strategies of 'new social movements' are strictly 'new', the main hallmark of these movements is their capacity to organise and engage people in rapid and often direct action protests with remarkable speed and often on an international scale.

Direct action protests are not themselves new; witness the 1932 mass trespass in the Peak District to acquire access rights for walking the countryside and the Jarrow March of unemployed workers in 1936 during the Great Depression. However, from the late 1960s direct action protests in terms of growing scale and global impact were really making their mark. A new generation, socialised into a society of relative prosperity following the post war austerity, were seizing on issues of liberation and identity in protest movements for civil rights and women's rights and in opposition to the Vietnam War. These types of protest movement were arguably a stepping stone to the new type.

New means of communication, for example in the form of satellite communication and the internet, have extended the range and immediacy with which large sections of the population can receive information about events throughout the world. Such communications technology, especially the internet, mobile phones and social media, provide the scope and speed of global and immediate interactivity between people to engage in instant communications networks that enable the sharing of information and the mobilisation of action. The outcome has been an array of global protest movements including those on environmental issues, against hunger and starvation, against global capitalism generally and against the Gulf war and the Iraq war. And even protests which are more locally focussed, as, for example, those opposing the expansion of particular airports or road building programs, often take their lead from issues of global relevance such as damage to the environment.

The mass media has also been instrumental in assisting the organisation of online petitions. The potential speed by which a response can be mobilised is illustrated in a petition initiated in May 2014 which received over 100,000 signatures to pressure the American authorities to resume their search for the crew of a yacht that capsized in the mid-Atlantic within about 48 hours of their decision to call off the search.

How do these movements contrast with the more conventional politics of the industrial age? Evidence suggests that labour movements emerged and declined alongside the era of industrial capitalism. This era witnessed the growth of trade unions, established to protect the interests of industrial workers, and it was from the trade union movement in Britain that the Labour Party was established to represent workers' interests in Parliament. Labour became the party of significant sections of the working class at a time when voting was often both partisan and class aligned. Social and political divisions were shaped by battles for resources and the achievement of material security in a relatively class conscious society. Political engagement was thus often allied with industrial and class struggles and was channelled largely through the formal organisations of trade unions, employers' associations and national political parties.

We have seen strong arguments and some supporting evidence elsewhere that the class attachments of the past have become of less significance in rallying contemporary voters. Furthermore, a period of declining turnout rates in national elections was argued to be indicative of growing apathy or disillusionment in UK national politics. One reason for this could have been the lack of range available to voters during a period when the battle for the mass vote tended to narrow the position of the political parties toward occupancy of the centre ground. For example, in the UK, from the late 1980s through to the early twenty first century, Labour and then the Conservatives moderated their positions in an attempt to maximise their appeal to the mass electorate. However, this can mean that parties find it difficult to establish clear policy and ideological battle lines and increasing proportions of the electorate come to feel that there is little clear choice available to them. The repositioning of the Labour Party in Britain was particularly instructive. Once adopting a position sufficiently to the political left to advocate an alternative model to free enterprise capitalism, in New Labour it became by the late twentieth century far more attuned to the interests of business and global capitalism. Those opposing these forces might well have felt attracted to becoming politically involved outside of party politics to make their mark.

New political infrastructure of supra-national organisations emerged in a globalising world. These included the Common Market and in its expanded and more politically integrated form the European Union, various regional trading blocks, the United Nations, the International Monetary Fund and the World Bank. Agreements have been made between governments to act to tackle issues such as global warming by restricting greenhouse gas emissions and, following near global recession, in 2010 the Basle III agreement on monetary control over international banks. States have therefore had to surrender a degree of national sovereignty for the common good in the face of global problems. The view that conventional national politics cannot offer solutions to problems of global scale, along with the perception of the erosion of national sovereignty and thus also the declining impact of the electorate on the policies of national government may also in part explain a political reconfiguration process which has seen more people turn to the politics of new social movements.

In an age of relative affluence and social class decline in western democracies, the political agenda moved more toward ethical global issues and new arenas of protest. New social movements have emerged which broadened both the view of politics and the types of political involvement. Protest has become less exclusively organised through established political hierarchies but can take place through wide ranging networks. The protest movements themselves have often enshrined anti-bureaucratic and anti-hierarchical values and sometimes broad alliances of groups under such general umbrellas as anti-globalisation and anti-capitalism have formed. Peace movements, environmental protection movements and protests against rampant capitalism have taken the form of global social movement responses, famously coinciding with international forums of politicians established to reach agreement on global issues but which appear to protestors to be protecting the vested interests which are part of the problem. Widespread access to communications technology has therefore arguably enhanced and enlivened the democratic process and as well as extending communication, globalisation has extended opportunities for geographical mobility.

Direct action has included protests outside the World Trade Organization meeting in Seattle in 1999 in which groups on a wide range of issues, including participants from various countries and adopting a variety of strategies, protested under the general umbrella of opposition to global capitalism. It was the direct action of some in the form of damage to property which grabbed the news headlines globally. Anti-Iraq war demonstrations in cities throughout the world, culminating around the 15th–16th February 2003, provide an example of the mobilization potential of new social movements with the largest gathering in Rome estimated to have attracted about three million people.

Yet despite their global nature, how new social movement protests play themselves out in different countries can remain quite variable. This suggests that there can remain a significant degree of national framing to political responses. For example, research by Koopmans (Porta (ed) 2009) into protests against the Gulf War in January 1991 compared the protest movements in Germany, France and the Netherlands. Despite global transmission of sanitised and standardised images as a result of military censorship, Koopmans found vastly different levels and types of protest in the three countries which he related to different political opportunity structures and cultural and historical interpretive frameworks.

Castells: networked society and new social movements

Manuel Castells has been a major contributor to the understanding of new protest movements in a networked world. He sees the emergence of information networking as providing a new arena of conflict between oppressors and oppressed, replacing the old social class opposition of industrial capitalism.

In the competition for inward investment under conditions of fluid global capitalism, Castells argues that governments have fallen under the power of financial institutions and elites at the expense, in democratic societies, of representing the interests of their electorates who have no party to champion the welfare state and protect workers' rights. In this context, other avenues of political protest have emerged.

Castells (2012) argues that advanced technological communication in the form of widening accessibility to the internet has significantly changed the politics of protest. It has enhanced the prospects of participatory democracy to challenge the injustices of dictatorships and pseudo democracies within which the priority of government has been to protect powerful banking and financial interests. Against such backdrops, widespread feelings of grievance can become viral through cyber space and unleash protest movements which come to occupy urban space, as witnessed by demonstrations in the early twenty first century.

One basis of widely felt grievance and injustice has been the sufferings of peoples in the Arab world at the mercy of globally rising food prices and suppression by dictatorial regimes. Castells has shown that in those societies where the internet has been most intensively taken up, cyber space networking provided populations with a sphere of autonomy within which to share grievances to organise protest movements which bring people out onto the streets to occupy symbolically important public spaces.

Beginning with protests that brought down the dictator of Tunisia, Ben Ali, and powerful imagery of protests in Egypt against Mubarak, protest movements were buoyed up and spread rapidly throughout the Arab world in early 2011. Internet communication played a major role in this process. However, post Castells' 2012 work, the situation in Syria offers a salutary warning that when faced by a determined dictator backed by a power attempting to extend its geopolitical influence, the outcome of protest movements can never be assured.

In the 'democratic' west, the social base of protest was generated by massively growing inequality of income over a number of decades between the top 1% and the rest of society (Castells, 2012, p.157) and the crisis of financial capitalism which hit home from 2008. It was clear that the main personal beneficiaries in the financial world were also those responsible for stoking up the crisis. In many countries, these individuals were allowed to escape conviction whilst governments placed emphasis on propping up financial institutions with the money of taxpayers, the vast majority of whom were victims of the crisis. There was a growing perception of injustice and the view that politicians and formal democratic institutions had fallen under the power of financial interests. 'Democracy' had for many people showed itself to be pseudo democracy, with politicians, political parties and the formal channels of 'democratic' politics losing legitimacy.

The first responses of protest were in Iceland where the stock market crash, bank debt and financial crisis were viewed by many as related to a democracy that had been corrupted by the subordination of political parties to powerful financial interests. Protests ensued in which one of the demands was for a new constitution. The legitimacy crisis led to the election of a new government which instituted legal action against leading financial figures and the former prime minister, avoided a drastic austerity response to the situation, and involved social networks in the drafting of a new constitution.

The protests and subsequent reforms in Iceland helped pave the way for protest movements to emerge in other 'democratic' western countries. In Spain, the response of the government to the financial crisis was to protect the self-interest of politicians and bankers whilst imposing deep spending cuts on the population. Calls to the streets (ignored by the political parties and the traditional media) spread across the internet. This new medium, an autonomous network of leaderless communication, was able to circumvent the media block and the hierarchical politics of the conventional party system. Public squares in a number of Spanish cities became quickly occupied and provided an opportunity for debating a range of social and political issues that the political parties were attempting to ignore.

The communication space provided by the internet helped to initiate the occupation of physical public space (referred to by Castells as a cyber and urban space hybrid) and was further used by the protestors to disseminate images of urban protest to a broader audience who could be rallied to support the occupation at key times when the authorities attempted to disband them through the use of force. Most importantly, Castells has argued that the consequence of the protests was to effect the culture and consciousness of the broader population to fundamentally question the political institutions of what was increasingly recognised as a 'pseudo democracy'. Furthermore, through the use of on line communication and participation in popular assemblies, the workability of horizontal networking and participatory democracy as an alternative to hierarchical political structures and bureaucracies was demonstrated. The internet played a key role for protestors, who did not share a clear ideology or single blueprint for reform, to engage in the process of direct democracy. They were prefiguring the type of democratic process of decision making which Castells argued might recapture in society more broadly in the future a democracy responsive to the input of the people rather than primarily representing the interests of a financial and political elite.

The Occupy Wall Street movement in the United States was a movement in which protestors occupying urban spaces were pursuing a wide range of grievances. Whatever the specific aims of individuals, there was a more common cause in the pursuit of reacquiring meaningful involvement in democratic decision making which they felt had been taken away from them by combined powerful political and financial interests. The protestors were not necessarily against capitalism as such, but the destructive form that financial capitalism had taken.

The practice of participatory democracy through the use of gatherings was thus both an attempt to influence political change and also experience the very type of democracy which it was felt had been lost.

However, one could also speculate that in open societies, social media such as Facebook provide unprecedented opportunities for surveillance authorities to monitor the thinking of millions of citizens as they are encouraged to share with others what is on their mind.

Foucault – the power of discourse

For Foucault, the term 'discourse' refers to ways of thinking and talking that relate to the use of power. The advance of the Enlightenment promoted the discourse of science – the view that science and rational thinking can be used to ameliorate the social condition. This Enlightenment discourse heralded new approaches to the problem of social control in the form of a transition from punishment of offenders through the imposition of bodily pain, to confinement, treatment and surveillance. From the perspective of the Enlightenment discourse, this was viewed as an advance in humanitarianism.

Foucault challenged this interpretation. Instead, he argued, the Enlightenment discourse helped to shape an acceptance of control by scientific professionals in the treatment of those who do not conform to moral norms. Experts grade and classify behaviour and refine appropriate punishment or treatment for non-conformity. As with the panopticon prison design where the threat of observation is always present in the mind of the prisoner, the general trend has been toward a 'carceral society' of rationally regulated thinking and behaviour in which the state and various social institutions have developed the capacity to oversee populations as a means of imposing discipline and control. Indeed, self-reflection on the possibility of surveillance makes self-control all the more effective, but, Foucault argues, through the capacity that people have for evasion, control is never total.

Consider, for example, the surveillance threat of possible inspection at any time which is designed to control the performance of teachers. Although acting as a powerful constraint on performance and behaviour, like people in other situations where control is imposed through the constant threat of surveillance, teachers are not helpless in employing tactics of resistance or evasion and at the right time taking a sudden step change in performance.

Discourse brings deviance into being. For example, homosexuality was once regarded as sinful behaviour in the context of religious discourse. As such, it was either suppressed or perhaps owned up to in the privacy of the confessional. It subsequently became seen as a deviance and illness in need of scientific treatment to suppress and cure, continuing similar moral judgements but now through the control of scientific jargon and professionals. From a Foucaultian viewpoint, on the one hand liberalisation of the law and the more recent availability of gay civil ceremonies and marriages appear to be libertarian and humanitarian reforms resulting from challenges to the dominant discourse of sexual deviance. However, one could also argue that reforms have enabled greater surveillance of sexual preference by making the choices available more open and thus more visible to the state.

According to Foucault, prior to the Enlightenment, the mad were viewed as relatively harmless and left to go about their lives unhindered. Foucault argues that the advance of the discourse of reason accompanying the Enlightenment brought into sharp relief the danger of madness and the need for confinement, control and treatment to bring the person to reason. The development of the sciences of treatment, especially psychiatry, in a sense create deviances for purposes of intervention, institutionalisation and control. They claim a truth in their scientific diagnosis, but the claim to scientific truth is in reality more a claim to the control of deviance. For Foucault, treatment of the mad does not represent the commonly accepted advance in humanitarianism, but is part of a broader surveillance society of regulation and discipline across a range of institutions in which people become the objects of power in the form of scientific discourse.

Niam – the end of power?

Niam (2014) identifies an era of state and private sector bureaucracy as peaking during the middle decades of the twentieth century. Large centralised hierarchical organisations wielded considerable power in politics and business and were able to erect virtually unassailable barriers to access to rivals. For many, this hierarchical view remains the way in which power is viewed. However, for Niam, from the late twentieth century, social changes were undermining the capacity of large scale top down organisations to project and protect their power. These changes Niam summed up in the form of three revolutions: more, mobility and mentality.

By more, Niam is referring to a vastly expanding global population, with, it is argued, more people lifted out of extreme poverty, improved literacy and educational access, improved health and life expectancy and a rapidly expanding global middle class, especially amongst many developing country's growing young populations. This is having an impact in raising expectations.

Mobility refers to greater movement of people within and between societies. Internally, developing countries in particular, such as China and India, have seen massive population movements from rural locations to urban centres and an expansion of the more mobile middle classes. Migration levels have also increased, for example as more people aspire to and have the opportunity to escape relative deprivation, and cultural transfers move between developed and developing countries. More people travel for professional meetings and new technology has enabled information to be rapidly exchanged across national borders at great distance with immediacy. Niam argues that various aspects of mobility make national borders more porous and increase the difficulty for governments to exert power over audiences that are no longer such captive populations.

Mentality focusses on changes in people's outlooks and expectations. Improvements in people's lives opens up discontent with traditional expectations and institutions, especially amongst more youthful sections of the population. This might include challenging traditional family values on matters such as divorce and opposing political authoritarianism. A rise in material and opportunity expectations by a growing proportion of people without commensurate job opportunities enhances political activity against governments that have not delivered, making populations increasingly difficult to control.

These revolutions, Niam argues, challenge traditional barriers that have held the use of power intact within large bureaucratic organisations that have controlled people and are shown to be unfit and unresponsive to new needs and expectations. People become politically disconnected. Large top down political and other organisations are shown to lack the capacity to respond to the revolutions. Power is assailed as global media are able to expose political corruption and abuses of power along with the increased ability of those with raised expectations to organise into responsive networks of direct political action. In business, as in politics, large organisational power ebbs as it is assailed by versatile challenges by 'micropowers' from all directions. The outcome is that power has become fragmented, eroded and easier to both acquire and lose, with big governmental power facing loss of trust and growing ineffectiveness.

For Niam, there is the need to re-establish governmental power. However, this is reliant on the restoration of trust in government. Time is ripe for a new 'disruptive innovation' in politics as significant as past innovations associated with Greek democracy and the French Revolution (2014, p.243). New political institutions of a more networked and less hierarchical form that are fit for the twenty first century are needed to regain the political trust that is necessary to combat the decay of power and enable much needed stronger political decision making.

Postmodernism – the illusion of politics

The effects of globalisation, especially with reference to the media, are an integral part of postmodern theory. For postmodernists, the positive connotation of modernity associated with the eighteenth century Enlightenment was the idea of progressive human liberation from control by fear and superstition through the application of science and rational thinking. Faith in the application of science to society brought the prospect of social improvement through social engineering. However, for Bauman, this metanarrative (all-embracing system of beliefs) became associated in the twentieth century with the political metanarratives and collectivist ideologies of fascism and communism which were adopted by totalitarian regimes through which states controlled their populations through fear and repression. In Britain, the post war creation of the welfare state was seen by Bauman as another example from the modern period of the state attempting to engineer policy based on a single set of ideals.

Thus, in modern society, the state intervened into the personal sphere to deliver universal policies. Intervention was guided by political metanarratives such as social democracy, liberalism or Marxism and faith in the application of science. Metanarratives provided people with ontological security – a feeling of the comfort of certainty – which also related to social structures that provided fixed identify and lifetime projects.

Postmodernists maintain that the crisis that confronted modernity was the abject failure of social engineering shaped by political metanarratives to deliver the progress that it promised. With this failure collapsed the modernist metanarrative and from it postmodern society, devoid of an overarching metanarrative, and experiencing a fragmentation of state power, was emerging. Arguably, the watershed of this change in Britain and the United States was the emergence of the political right anti-collectivist politics during the 1980s when the promise of improvement for the poor through social engineering gave way to policy of general improvement through opening up free market forces. The failure of social engineering was dramatically evidenced in the collapse of the Eastern Block regimes from the late 1980s. For Bauman, in the postmodern global environment, collective projects and actions collapse and the state retreats from being a focal point of both power and political protest. The politics of control by or fear of the state give way to a new type of fear that people experience in having to make choices in situations of massively enhanced individual autonomy.

Those who argue that a postmodern condition has emerged emphasise that belief in singular moral codes and universal truths has collapsed, as has social structuring and identity in terms of class, gender and ethnicity. Within this context, ontological security has to be continuously sought and reinventing one's personal identity becomes an essential skill.

Postmodern societies are media, information and high tech societies. The condition of the cultural environment is thus seen as coming to play a more important role in life than economic factors. In such societies, according to Lyotard, knowledge loses its monopoly as an all embracing truth, used by the state to engineer social control. Instead, people apply knowledge for its usefulness in a society of diverse interests. Through this relativistic and pragmatic use of knowledge, power becomes dispersed down from the state to various pressure groups and businesses who use information to advance their different interests.

The postmodern world is one of social fragmentation and fluidity, one in which metanarratives will not form useful guides to thinking and organising one's life. Participatory democracy loses its vitality as life has become individualised. Fewer people participate in conventional politics and civic activities; politics has become personalised and perhaps trivialised as an activity of individual status aspiration and, especially for the younger generation, more often takes on the form of direct action new social movements of post material politics focussing on ethical issues.

Baudrillard takes the postmodernist position further and argues that in a media dominated society, politics recedes to the manipulation of symbols to convey political messages which have no necessary connection to any underlying political events. As political messages rely on endlessly back referenced media images, neither truth nor authentic reality can be substantiated and politics collapses into the realm of illusion.

Ulrich Beck – second modernity, risk society and a new democratic politics

For many founding social theorists of the nineteenth and early twentieth centuries, the advance of rational thinking, science and technology held the potential for social betterment through control of the social and physical environment. Regarding the contemporary stage of modernisation, Ulrich Beck, like Anthony Giddens, has recognised the precariousness of rational intervention and our capacity for control. Neither of these writers, however, adopt the view of many postmodernists that society has reached a stage where rational intervention for social betterment is a forlorn quest.

Beck delineates three key social historical stages: 1) pre-modern, 2) first, simple modern and 3) second, reflexive modern.

1. Pre-modern societies preceded the political, industrial and social revolutions of the eighteenth and nineteenth centuries. In these societies, communities lived closer to nature and many of the risks in life were related to that attachment.

2. First modernity opposed tradition with science and rationality. This 'simple modern' stage is the classical industrial society, organised around the principle of the production and distribution of goods and structured into a hierarchy of social classes. Accompanying this degree of technological intervention and the associated faith in progress, new risks that emerged such as pollution and insanitary living conditions, were viewed as undesirable side effects.

This period witnessed the advance of formal political rights. During this stage, business tended to be regarded as a non-political private sphere in which enhancement of the standard of living and progress which it brought protected it from criticism regarding its negative consequences.

However, Beck goes on the state that 'just as modernization dissolved the structure of feudal society in the nineteenth century and produced the industrial society, modernisation today is dissolving industrial society and another modernity is coming into being' (Beck,1992, p.10). This is the second modern, reflexive, risk society.

3. Second (contemporary) modern society introduces new insecurities into people's lives. The breakdown of constraining but supporting social structures and the advance of individualism has transpired at the same time that the effects of scientific and technological advance have increased the risks that are consequent on their growing capacity for intervention in society and nature. This has raised the production of risk to a position of primacy over production itself. The key task is now managing the risks created but, Beck argues, this cannot be achieved within the circle of science alone that created them. Consequently, a fundamental change in politics is required.

People working within scientific specialisms act as technical experts working in detached laboratory type conditions. A cultural environment of 'scientism' (the belief in the unassailability of science) accompanied the first modernisation stage in which scientific expertise had frequently overpowered critical public feedback by imposing unreflexive scientific boundaries on public debate. However, frenetic changes in the 'techno-economic system' during the latter decades of the twentieth century led to growing political challenges as the risk consequences of the techno-economic system were enhanced and the protective trust in progress became undermined. For Beck, new political engagement requires genuine reflexive public input into political decision making in the application of science and technology. New social movements, such as green politics, have emerged to refocus politics into this previously non-political area. Industry had thus had to increasingly work within a new political and moral framework where the consequences of its interventions can be checked and monitored.

High modernism – transformationism and political power

Unlike most postmodernists, high modernists argue that the modernist task of rational understanding as the basis for social intervention should not be abandoned. They tend to adopt what Held refers to as a transformationist approach toward globalisation and acknowledge that global processes are intruding into national politics. However, unlike hyperglobalists, this does not mean that state power is in substantial decline. Transformationists argue that governments can and have to respond to the impact of globalisation through reconfiguring their power and legitimacy alongside that of other institutions by steering the process at appropriate levels. For transformationists, this means that national governments must be prepared to share some sovereignty with international (for example the United Nations), transnational (for example the European Union) and sub-state organisations (for example non-governmental organisations, often carrying out humanitarian work).

Like Beck, Anthony Giddens draws attention to new levels of manufactured risk that are a product of technological advances, including those which were aimed to control other risks. Manufactured risks are often of global magnitude and include environmental damage, the consequences of global warming, reliance on internet computer systems which are vulnerable to computer virus and cyberattacks, possible economic destabilisation through rapid and vast currency movements, polarisation of rich and poor nations, and international crime and terrorism.

Giddens points out that in mature democracies people appeared to be losing faith in the capacity or will of national governments to tackle global problems as intrusive global forces cut across domestic democratic politics. In Britain, for example, a steady decline in voter turnout during early twentieth century general elections may have reflected a growing lack of confidence that national government has the political purchase on events in a globalised world that it once had.

On the other hand, there is evidence of increasing involvement, especially by young people, in global pressure groups on issues such as world trade, poverty and the environment. These movements are usually less hierarchical than more traditional pressure groups and utilise modern technology for people to communicate and organise quickly, sometimes at a global level. Against high tech new social movement networks, government, which tends to operate top down, can be slow-footed.

For high modernists, new appropriate institutions, guided by contemporary theory, need to be developed to help obtain political purchase on events in the face of new global risks. It is argued that we cannot be resigned to the intellectual anarchy of the postmodernists and the economic anarchy of the global free marketers. Instead, guided by the insights of a transformationist and high modernist analysis, political institutions need to be refashioned and sufficiently sophisticated to respond to new challenges in a rapidly changing world. This relates particularly to the need to develop supra-national institutions which can operate to combat global problems and risks more effectively than states can individually.

What practical guidance can theory provide to improve governance in a globalising world? In *Runaway World* (2002), Giddens argues that democratic political institutions are the only ones that can be sufficiently equipped to respond to a dynamic global environment. Democracy therefore needs to be enhanced. For Giddens, improved responsiveness to people and processes requires a deepening of democracy. He emphasises the following dimensions:

1. Democratic institutions need to be devolved below state level to regions, localities and pressure groups which national governments should work closely with.

2. The expansion of voluntary and self-help groups requires the nurturing of a civic culture of responsibility. Free market reforms are not enough. They can damage the social fabric by leaving a void between the individual and the state, as experienced in the rapid reforms introduced in Russia following the collapse of the Soviet Union.

3. The development of a range of democratic institutions above the state are essential to cope with global matters. Of those mentioned earlier, international organisations, such as the United Nations, have limited power over the sovereignty of state members. In the case of transnational organisations such as the European Union, member states pool a degree of their sovereignty to engage more effectively at a transnational level. In organisations of the former type, it may be beneficial for member states to cede more sovereignty, whilst regarding the European Union, a case is put for its greater democratisation.

Deficiencies of supra-national organisations

A number of criticisms have been frequently made against supra-national organisations. Some organisations, such as the World Bank and the World Trade Organisation, were set up ostensibly to promote the development of poor countries. A strong criticism is that grants, loans and debt cancellation usually have attached to them the requirement of liberal market reforms which arguably have often worsened the life of the poor in the recipient countries.

A related criticism is that wealthy nations are the main beneficiaries of free trade, yet they have the power to oppose free trade agreements when it suits them. An example here is the deadlock faced in free trade negotiations following the 2001 World Trade Organisation meeting on such sticking points as the refusal of the United States to relinquish payment of subsidies to its farmers.

Both the World Trade Organisation and the G8, which represents the world's leading eight industrial nations, have often been perceived as being only concerned with the interests of powerful capitalist nations. As a result, the meetings of both organisations have encountered massive protests, the most notorious being at the WTO meeting in Seattle in 1999. A related issue is that these organisations are also sometimes seen as out of step with issues of concern to their own populations. For example, at the 2006 G8 meeting at St. Petersberg, attention was focussed on co-operation on energy and combating global terrorism, whilst opinion polls conducted amongst people in the member states indicated that they wanted issues of global poverty, human rights and combating infectious diseases discussed.

Some supra-national organisations, such as the United Nations, lack binding controls over member states. For example, although the UN General Assembly can pass resolutions, these are not legally binding and cannot override national sovereignty. Furthermore, national sovereignty again prevails vis-à-vis the UN International Court of Justice in relation to which only about a third of member states, notably excluding the United States, accept its jurisdiction.

Against the backdrop of such criticisms, several pointers toward institutional reform of supra-national organisations have been suggested by J. Lloyd in *'The Protest Ethic'* (2001). Firstly, he argues that global institutions need to be framed on a broadly agreed global ethical basis without appearing to be an imposition of the west. Secondly, it is likely that new and more powerful supra-national organisations and agreements will need to be established to form a binding obligation between nations if some of the most pressing global problems are to be tackled. Thirdly, institutions need to be established in a form which is more responsive to challenges than traditional bureaucratic hierarchies are. Fourthly, these institutions must not be too remote but need to be in touch with issues of concern to citizens. Fifthly, governments will often find it beneficial to set up cross-national organisations sharing surveillance and intelligence to deal with problems such as the global dimension of criminal activity and terrorism.

A link between high modernism, transformationism and third way politics

Anthony Giddens offered a broad analytic basis for New Labour politics and has been open in his intellectual association with 'the third way' approach in the text of that title (2000). Applied in the context of British politics, he argued that the politics of the traditional Labour left and the old new right Conservatives were increasingly inappropriate approaches for an age of global capitalism. By demonstrating the intellectual foundations of third way politics, Giddens argued that the radical nature of this centre ground position would become clearer.

The collectivist politics of the old left regarded the motives and actions of private enterprise as suspect and in need of regulation. The traditional left distrusted the free market as a means of allocating goods and services. Instead, faith was put in state bureaucratic centralisation, in economic planning and in the nationalisation of strategic industries. Egalitarianism was to be promoted through redistributive taxation and welfare services delivered through the public sector. Top down planning was imposed to control the anarchic features of free enterprise capitalism. Politics following this model was adopted by the post war Labour government and, the author of this text would add, more reluctantly by post war Conservative governments.

The economic failures of the 1970s led to a resurgence of free enterprise thinking and the coming to power of the new right Conservatives in 1979. State regulation and an over bloated public sector were blamed for the economic sclerosis and social breakdown of the 1970s. The response of the new right was to cut down bureaucracy, pursue privatisation and reinvigorate the free market. With successive election victories in 1983, 1987 and 1992, anti-collectivist policies were followed.

Giddens argued that the fluidity and interconnectedness of the new global world had rendered both positions inappropriate. On the one hand, the central control and planning approach of the old left was too top down and not responsive enough to the needs of quickly changing modern global markets. The suspicion of and restrictions on private enterprise were not necessarily well founded and would be counterproductive to investment and employment in a global environment of mobile capital. On the other hand, it was argued that relinquishing social responsibilities and allowing free market forces to rule would very dangerous to social and economic stability in the fluid conditions of global capitalism.

So what was the alternative? For Giddens, capitalist markets cannot be banned or overregulated. At one extreme, the collapse of the old Eastern Block command economies showed that such central planning cannot cope with the pressures of global capitalism. At the other extreme, however, left to their own devices, free markets will wreak havoc. Giddens suggested that markets need to be improved by intelligence led governmental action working alongside responsive institutions both above and below the state to improve the workings of the free market and offer safeguards against its negative effects. World economies had become so integrated that the impact of financial crises could be swift, major and extensive. This did not mean turning away from global capitalism but establishing institutions for both surveillance and rapid response.

Man's impact on the environment is bringing global changes to which technology often provides solutions. Thus, waste is now increasingly becoming a resource and the knowledge economy produces more with less resources. However, the increasingly global nature of risk does mean that globally agreed political responses with teeth and based on science need to foster ecological responsibility in both producers and consumers.

New Labour – a radical centre ground?

There was much debate over the policies and ideology of New Labour. Had it betrayed the values and goals of the old Labour Party? Was it bereft of ideological guiding principles and preoccupied with pragmatic decision making? Was it little different from new right Conservatism but with a limited added social dimension? In this section, a brief account of New Labour policy and its intellectual basis will be offered.

The 'third way' tag and official re-branding of Labour as New Labour emphasised a break from the old ideologies of the post war political left (collectivism) and the 1980s to 1997 new right approach to conservatism (anti-collectivism). Respectively, these ideological positions prioritised the state and public sector or the deregulated private sector as superior models for organising society. Unlike the new right, New Labour retained the view that there is such a thing as the common good, but just what this common good is and how it can best be achieved marked New Labour off from traditional Labour.

Given the high tech nature of the contemporary economy, the break up of the old class structure and the decline of class politics, New Labour had not put itself forward exclusively as a party of the working class. Rather, it had managed to broaden its appeal to attract electoral support from people across a range of occupations.

Reform of the public services was central to Labour's modernisation agenda and exemplified its third way approach. It was argued that whilst the goal of providing good quality public services remained, the means of achieving this needed to be more flexible. The old model of state provided and top down planned public service provision was argued to be insufficiently responsive to user needs and fluid market conditions. By contrast, the new right emphasis on the free market, privatisation and contracting out had arguably damaged public services. New Labour's position was less ideologically fundamentalist than either of these approaches. It relied on breaking down boundaries and the ideological divide between public sector provision and private sector provision. It acknowledged that in a number of cases, the resources for public services could be maximised by public and private partnership arrangements. The exact configuration for the provision of different public service projects would be a matter of analysis in each case.

New right reforms had placed emphasis on the individual and tended to neglect 'society'. A criticism of this emphasis was that a social void tended to be left between the state and an atomised free market. This also left a moral void which New Labour argued needed to be filled through more intermediate level institutions such as voluntary groups helping to bind civil society and encourage people in their civic responsibilities.

For New Labour, it was the role of government to help create the conditions for both businesses and workers to adapt to global change. Given the enhanced challenges of global competition, the government attempted to work with the grain of capitalism by promoting a flexible labour market underpinned by retraining to encourage economic competitiveness and inward investment. This was referred to as the creation of a 'magnet economy' of skilled labour in which the government attempted to combine the economic competitiveness of a market economy with social justice goals of fairness through such safeguards as the minimum wage.

On the question of opportunity, New Labour attempted to enhance opportunity of the many by maximising opportunities for participation in work to those who may otherwise have been excluded (for example the unskilled and single parents). In doing so, it balanced the left derived principle of rights with the right orientated principle of obligations. This meant that the government provided schemes, including retraining and child care, to help people to become self-supporting, but emphasised that it is their responsibility to take advantage of such opportunities.

On the question of equality, New Labour dismissed the conception of equality of outcome as a relic of old Labour which would be completely inappropriate in a market driven global capitalist world. Instead, equality should be seen primarily in terms of opportunity. There were problems here however, which tended to get side stepped. For example, Giddens pointed out that the diverse outcomes of equality of opportunity for one generation can lead to inequality of opportunity for the next generation. Little was said by Giddens or New Labour on whether or how this can be countered. Furthermore, society had itself, by some measures, become increasingly unequal in the distribution of income, not just during the period of new right government but also during the time that New Labour was in power. In this context, the Labour government was remarkably quiet on the issue of executive and director pay packages and massive city bonuses, all of which were way above the settlements that lower paid workers had to accept.

It could be argued that those who opposed the third way and criticise it as an amorphous compromise with no real compass bearing tended to do so if they were rooted in the old left or right ideological opposition and models of the past. For Giddens, by abandoning these trenchant and redundant positions, it could be appreciated that politics of the third way had a dynamic cutting edge necessary for coming to terms with and managing the challenges of globalisation where past approaches would fail.

Civic Conservatism

New Labour was defeated in the 2010 General Election and replaced in government by a Conservative led coalition with the Liberal Democrats. David Cameron had been leader of the Conservative Party since 2005 and had engaged in a process of modernizing the Party image and ideology. This process was influenced by a number of important factors. Firstly, Cameron wanted to develop an alternative form of conservatism to the free market model of the new right and to distance the modern Conservative Party from its past reputation as the 'nasty party' of greed and heartless individualism and move in the direction of a more caring image. Secondly, he needed to retain Conservative opposition to the tendency for growing state intervention which had taken place under New Labour. Thirdly, he had inherited an economic crisis which had to be managed following the global banking crisis. Fourthly, his party had to find sufficient common ground for working with their Liberal Democrat junior partners in a coalition government.

Much of the intellectual basis for Cameron's new conservatism is traceable back to the work of David Willetts in the mid-1990s. Willetts developed the idea of civic conservatism. This approach looked to involve people in various voluntary and local groups to help deliver some of the services of the state. It was argued that (despite talk of greater civic involvement) the growth of the state under New Labour had undermined people's sense of civic responsibility. Civic conservatism maintained that by transferring some of the burden on the state to civic organisations, citizen involvement and community integration would be enhanced. This anti-state strand of new conservatism opposed what was viewed as New Labour's state centralized approach and to that extent worked with the anti-collectivist heritage of new right conservatism. However, there was also a more communal element to civic conservatism which picked up on traditional conservative values of promoting local communities to help bond individuals to society and combat the destructive effect on community life of the excessive individualism associated with the free market approach of the new right. It was argued that civic responsibility must be promoted by encouraging people to become involved in local civic organisations which stand in between the state and the individual to deliver services. This approach thus claimed to expand society (hence Cameron's reference to the 'big society') not through the power of the state but through displacing downwards to communities some state activities.

Local civic groups could include residents associations, church groups, political parties, pressure groups, new social movements and numerous charitable organisations and self-help groups. A good example of civic group involvement stemming directly from government policy was the introduction of free schools. Although taxpayer funded, these institutions are set up locally by such participants as parents, teachers or religious groups and operate independently from local authorities.

Given the government's priority of deficit reduction through the austerity of sending cuts and rebalancing the economy in the direction of public to private sector, economic policy does not appear that dissimilar to policy once pursued by the new right. Critics may therefore suspect that the notion of the 'big society' provides a cloak of respectability to cutting back state expenditure.

From Common Market to European Union

In 1957, following the Treaty of Rome, the European Economic Community, or 'Common Market', an internal free trading group of six western European nations protected by a common external tariff barrier, was formed. After a previously failed applications for entry during the 1960s, the UK successfully negotiated membership for the start of 1973 under the Conservative Prime Minister Edward Heath. Although attracted by the economic advantages of trading block membership, other sentiments for joining amongst many of this generation of politicians were the background of two world wars and the hope of bringing nations together to avoid such conflicts in the future.

The Labour Party at this time was split on the issue of membership. Whilst some MPs were in favour of membership, others were opposed, either on the grounds that it would erode national sovereignty, or, from some on the left of the Party, that the EEC was a 'rich man's club'. Following their rise to power in 1974, the Labour government headed by Harold Wilson held a referendum in 1975 on 'continuing membership', with the official party line for remaining supported by Wilson and a significant majority of mass media coverage. The outcome of the referendum was a clear 67% in favour of remaining, although splits were still evident within the Labour Party.

During the 1980s, the EEC and the UK were beginning to move in different directions. The EEC was becoming more politically integrationist and socially interventionist, and in this form became the European Union in 1993. However, the Conservative new right government under Margaret Thatcher had been introducing a vigorous program of free market reforms. Relations were becoming strained as the precedence of European law over UK law was regarded by many, especially on the political right, as a dangerous infringement of national sovereignty and democratic accountability of the UK government to its electorate. For Thatcher, EEC social interventionism risked the encroachment of 'socialism through the back door' (*Speech to Conservative Party Conference*, 1988, 4/6/2019).

Reflecting these concerns, the Referendum Party, a single issue party, was established in 1994 under the leadership of James Goldsmith. Its key message was that the political elites of both mainstream parties were selling out the UK's national sovereignty to a bureaucratic European Union super state. Goldsmith argued that time was running out to reverse this process and issued a patriotic clarion call to 'battle for Britain' and for a referendum on EU membership.

Meanwhile, John Major, who had replaced Thatcher as Conservative leader and Prime Minister in 1990, was battling with a Eurosceptic group of MPs toward the right of the Conservative Party who held a hostile stance toward the EU. In 1995, to try and put to rest these divisions, Major resigned his Party leadership and challenged his opponents within the Party to 'put up or shut up'. Major duly won an endorsement of his leadership, but rancour within the Party continued.

The general election of 1997 saw Tony Blair's New Labour enter power. The Referendum Party managed only 2.6% of the vote and Blair's government embraced the EU. The intellectual presence behind New Labour's political and social policy was Anthony Giddens. Whilst recognising the need for greater democratic accountability of EU institutions, Giddens' transformationist position argued the need for shared sovereignty and steered globalisation and provided the intellectual backdrop for a pro-EU stance. Anti-EU sentiment appeared to have abated.

Revolt against the political establishment?

New Labour lost power in 2010 to a Conservative led coalition government under David Cameron. Although the minority Liberal Democrats were strongly pro-EU, the government adopted a more sceptical approach, especially on the general matter of closer union, as well as the issues of benefit rights to migrants and regulatory burdens on businesses.

For the electorate, the impact of the government's austerity programme and the issue of migration were becoming key concerns. An early sign of change from 'politics as normal' was strongly signalled in the 2014 European elections. These elections demonstrated an upsurge in anti-political establishment feeling across much of the EU, filtered through the varied national consciousness of different countries. In a number of countries, including the UK and France, the upsurge came from the nationalist political right. In the UK, the UK Independence Party acquired the largest vote count and through the operation of a proportional representation system also the largest number of MEPs, the main casualties being the Conservatives and Liberal Democrats (Vote 2014, 30/5/2018). However, in Greece, where suffering from austerity had been particularly severe, the challenge came from the political left.

The background to UKIP's rise had been analysed by Ford and Goodwin (2014). It had often been thought from its positioning toward the rightward end of the political scale that increasing support for UKIP would come predominantly from those who identified with the right wing of the Conservative Party, and as disaffected middle class Conservative voters found an alternative, more authentic, home in UKIP. However, an alternative position was that UKIP had been successful in attracting working class voters from Labour. Ford and Goodwin recognised the importance of this position, but argued that there were only partial truths in each interpretation and that over time, in varying amounts, UKIP had benefited by taking votes from each party.

Based on their findings from the British Election Study and interviews with UKIP insiders, Ford and Goodwin argued that the social profile of UKIP voters tended to particularly comprise a working class, lesser educated, white, male and older section of the population. These were the older blue collar workers who felt 'left behind' through the process of de-industrialisation and the expansion of a young, educated and more cosmopolitan middle class. They were traditionalists who did not feel at home in the contemporary world and felt neglected by the political establishment, whether Conservative of Labour, who were equally seen to have ignored them.

The decline in the turnout of the manual working class in the general elections of the early twenty first century indicated this alienation from the main parties. The authors argued that this had created a pool of discontent which found attraction in an avowedly anti-establishment party, UKIP, that reflected their concerns and world view. Whilst the above documented social profile of UKIP support had remained quite stable, the drift toward them from the major parties had fluctuated over time as discontent tended to be stronger from those who had previously voted for the party that come to power. Thus, during the New Labour years, UKIP benefited more from voters who turned their back on Labour and during the Conservative coalition period from 2010, a greater proportion of voters abandoned the Conservatives for UKIP than left Labour. Furthermore, the traditional 'non-establishment' party of the Liberal Democrats, who were strongly in favour of the UK working within the EU, had now entered power and as a result suffered major damage to their image as an alternative and to their popularity.

UKIP, under the charismatic leadership of Nigel Farage, offered to the left behind a more traditional world view regarding national sovereignty and immigration control. UKIP's alternative was attractive to this social base in that it blamed the liberal elite political establishment of both Labour and the Conservative governments for their damaging cosmopolitanism and for failing to address the alienation of the left behind in ignoring their concerns on these matters.

The 2015 general election produced narrow majority for the Conservatives – one that was not predicted by the polls which had underestimated the Conservative vote and overestimated the Labour vote. The Liberal Democrats were a major casualty at this election, having been judged by sections of the electorate to have reneged some key manifesto pledges when joining the 2010 coalition government. The Labour Party lost heavily in Scotland to the Scottish National Party and although UKIP came third with 12.6% of the vote (approximately four million votes), through the first past the post electoral system had only one MP.

Recognising concerns within the country and within his own party over UK European Union membership, Cameron had pledged before the election, to enhance the chances of his Party's success, to hold an in / out straight majority referendum, and set to work to renegotiate the terms of UK membership in the hope of delivering a vote to remain.

In his negotiations with the EU, Cameron claimed to have delivered a deal which protected the UK's special status within the EU. In particular, on the issue of national sovereignty, an opt-out agreement to protect the UK from the drive for closer union was successfully negotiated. In other areas of negotiation, which included benefits for EU migrants, the safeguarding of multiple currencies and a recognition of the need to reduce the regulatory burden on businesses, some government concession were made (Landale, 1/6/2018).

The promised EU referendum took place on 23 June 2016 and on a 72.2% turnout 51.9% of the electorate voted for the UK to leave the EU and 48.1% to remain in. House of Commons Library data (30/5/2018) indicated that within the constituent UK countries, England and Wales had voted to leave and Scotland and Northern Ireland to remain, with significant regional variations within each country. Evidence showed that localities with strong UKIP support in the European elections unsurprisingly closely correlated with high levels of leave voting. However, there appeared to be no significant relationship between leave voting and Conservative or Labour supporters at this stage.

Voting patterns showed correlations with the following social characteristics:

1. Areas with higher proportions of people of immigrant background produced lower leave votes.
2. Remain voting tended to correlate with young age groups (18 – 29), graduate educated and professional and managerial occupational grades, whilst non-graduates and those in social scale grade C2DE manual occupations, casual workers, the unemployed and pensioners tended to vote leave.
3. Rural locations tended to be associated with leave voting, whereas, although very mixed and only weakly related, there was a slight tendency toward voting remain in urban areas.

In studying the role of the mass media in the referendum outcome, Berry (4/6/2019) argued that there had been significant short term and more powerful long term influences toward Euroscepticism. In the short term, he found that the leave campaign had been very effective in their repetition of short and simple messages such as 'take back control' which resonated with the insecure. Leave had also been very effective in social media targeting. The remain campaign, split between Labour and Conservative remainers, was unable to convey an equally simple narrative on benefits of staying and the mass media overall included more coverage of leave content.

Over the longer term, Berry argued that there had been a powerful cumulative media effect of hostility toward the EU, mainly from a number of the high circulation tabloid newspapers. Imagery included immigrants 'sponging' off the welfare state, 'bleeding' the NHS dry, and engaging in high rates of criminality. Immigration became a lightening rod for broader discontents which could be turned against the EU who required free movement of nationals between member states.

Recognising a disengagement of voters from the Labour Party, MPs such as Frank Field were looking for ways to reengage their support and developed a position referred to as 'blue Labour' (Geary & Pabst ed., 2015). Field, along with Maurice Glasman and John Milbank, argued that the advance of free market economic liberalism had atomised society. Whilst particularly associated with new right conservatism, New Labour had advanced a top down, target driven technocracy and a global open market approach. It was argued that the consequences had been that the wealthy had benefited from the free flow of labour within the EU through access to an enhanced pool of cheap labour which drove up company profits and top salaries whilst for many workers their wages were driven down. Unsurprisingly, working class voters in particular had been abandoning the main parties, with significant numbers turning to UKIP.

Blue Labour proponents argued for a post-liberal moral revival that challenged both materialistic individualism and mechanistic bureaucratisation. Taking guidance from the romantic and conservative traditions within the nineteenth century socialist movement, a key emphasis was the need to resuscitate local community life to reintegrate individuals into the social and political sphere so as to better respond to their wishes. Institutions which would assist this process could include professional associations, company profit sharing schemes and the protection of local libraries and hospitals etc. Furthermore, protecting a sense of national identity and community meant enhancing national boundary maintenance. Blue Labour thus emphasised the importance of greater control of immigration and labour movement.

In arguing for the above reforms, those who identified with blue Labour would surely have looked at the success of UKIP in the European referendum and concluded 'we warned you'.

The term 'galloping populism' has been used in relation to the rise in support for mainly far right nationalist political parties as vehicles of protest against the political establishment over much of Europe (and the USA). The main catalyst was the long post 2008 economic downturn and the refugee crisis of 2015. On these matters, political elites were criticised for not protecting the interests of poorer and more vulnerable sections of the population and the political right were quick to use the politics of fear in the populist protest. The continuation of the populist rebellion was witnessed in the 2018 Italian elections through the success of the right wing Five Star and League parties, gaining much support from the poorer regions of southern Italy and the young seeking work in a situation of high unemployment rates.

The election of Donald Trump to the White House in November 2016 can also be seen as an anti-political establishment vote, gaining powerful support from white male Americans voters in old declining industrial areas. Trump's pitch was patriotic, charismatic and authoritarian – he offered simple fixes to make America great again and blamed establishment politicians for letting the American people down on such key issues as immigration and trade.

As popularised by Trump, an important angle of attack on the political establishment was the accusation of media bias and 'fake news' in their favour. Yet Hayden (*Andrew Marr Show*, 20 May, 2018), ex CIA Director, referred to the existence of a 'post truth society', exploited by Trump, whose policy he argued was detached from objective reality and based on feeling, emotion, instinct and intuition.

In the UK, David Cameron resigned shortly after the European referendum delivered a leave result, to be replaced by Teresa May as Prime Minister. With the outsider Jeremy Corbyn taking over the leadership of the Labour Party, May set a June 2017 general election in the hope of increasing her majority. The result, however, was a hung parliament, with the Conservatives reliant on the support of the Democratic Unionist Party in Northern Ireland to form a small working majority.

Interesting features of this election included:

- A dramatic collapse of the UKIP vote from 12.6% to 1.8% following the leave victory in the referendum.
- A significant fall in the SNP vote which led to the loss of 21 seats.
- A further small increase in voter turnout to 68.7%, building on increases over the previous three elections from a low point of 59.4% in 2001.

Prior to 2017, anti-political establishment voting had been turning voters away from both the Conservative and Labour parties. With the issue of Brexit apparently resolved, the 2017 election witnessed a return to the binary politics of the past with the combined Conservative and Labour vote amounting to 82.3% of the votes cast – the highest combined share since 1970. This alone did not suggest a return to partisan class alignment voting though. Indeed, compared to the 2015 election, Labour increased its share of the middle class vote whilst the Conservatives increased their share of the working class vote, and it says nothing of strength of commitment.

The main preoccupation of the May led government was to negotiate with EU representatives the terms for the UK leaving the EU on the planned date of 29 March 2019. However, having reached an agreement, this was found impossible to get through the House of Commons, being heavily rejected on three separate votes through opposition from Labour, the DUP and a number of May's own MPs, mainly Brexiteers who felt that the deal arrived at did not sufficiently honour the referendum vote.

Meanwhile, massive street marches and an on line petition were organised by anti-Brexiteers for a people's vote or for the revoking of Article 50 through which the UK was to leave the EU. Both Labour and the Conservatives faced defections by remain MPs, initially forming a new party which became named

Change UK. The parliamentary stalemate led to the granting of an extension to withdrawal by the EU to October 31st, requiring UK elections to the European Parliament to be held on 23 May. The outcome of this election was a victory for Farage's new Brexit Party and a much improved turnout for the pro-EU Liberal Democrats with both Labour and the Conservatives haemorrhaging votes. Following a disastrous showing for the Conservatives in the local elections earlier in the month, May's position had become untenable and she was forced to stand down as Party leader on 7 June, precipitating a leadership contest. The victor, Boris Johnson, now promised to leave the EU on October 31st, 'do or die', with or without a deal.

With this deadline also missed, a new deal had nevertheless been negotiated. In the subsequent general election set for December 2019, the Conservatives under Johnson achieved a majority of 80 seats. This enabled him to push the deal comfortably through parliament later that month along with the promise to leave the EU by the end of January, which duly transpired.

What was the background to the Conservative's election victory?

Labour had pitched its message at the young and university educated, traditional working class communities and the cosmopolitan middle classes. The problem was that the cosmopolitan middle classes and the young university educated were often facing different ways to traditional working class communities over the issue of Brexit. Labour thus needed to take the focus off Brexit.

By contrast, the Conservatives, with their clear mantra of 'get Brexit done', put themselves forward as a pro-Brexit Party and in so doing were assisted by the decision of the Brexit Party to not stand candidates in constituencies previously won by a Conservative candidate. Furthermore, it is interesting to note that the Sky News channel were consistently referring to the forthcoming general election as the 'Brexit election'.

Given their need to satisfy diverse sections of the electorate, the Labour Party were unable to match the Conservative's Brexit mantra with an effective alternative. In the event, the Conservative Party moved from a hung parliament position in the 2017 election to having a majority of 80 in 2019.

What does the basic turnout data reveal? The *House of Commons Library Briefing Paper, General Election 2019: results and analysis* (accessed 10/2/2020) provides a substantial basis of data.

At 67.3%, the turnout was similar to recent elections – about 1.5% down on that of 2017. Of this, the combined Labour and Conservative vote had declined from 82.3% in 2017 to 76%, with the avowedly remain Liberal Democrats taking a larger percentage than in the previous election. Labour's vote had declined by almost 8%.

What patterns and influences lie behind the election outcome? The following points regarding Brexit would appear to be salient:

1. Compared to the 2017 general election, Labour's vote took a big fall in a number of previously solid Labour seats. For example, in the north east their vote fell by 12.9% whilst the Conservative's rose by 3.8% and the Brexit Party achieved its highest proportion at 8.1%. The Brexit influence here was undermining Labour solidarity even within traditionally loyal working class communities.

2. Analysing the 2016 referendum data in terms of constituency boundaries, it is remarkable that of the 58 constituencies that switched to the Conservatives in 2019, 55 had voted leave in 2016. Of all the seats won by the Liberal Democrats, all but one had voted remain.

3. Voting in the 2016 referendum was clearly a strong aligning factor in the subsequent general elections. A YouGov poll calculated that of those who voted leave in 2016, 65% went on to vote Conservative in 2017 and 74% did so in 2019. The figures of leave voters for Labour in the two elections were 24% and 14% respectively. For remain voters, 25% voted Conservative in 2017 and 19% in 2019. The figures for Labour were respectively 55% and 45% and for the Liberal Democrats 12% and 21%

Information on the social characteristics of voters can be gleaned from Ipsos MORI and YouGov polls which in total gathered information from 68,000 voters.

1. On the issue of social class, it would appear that evidence would continue to confirm the dealignment thesis. Using the six occupational category National Readership Survey scale favoured by IpsosMORI, support in 2019 for Labour fell in all groups compared to that of 2017, whilst for the Conservatives it increased in all but the highest group and the Conservatives held a lead over Labour across all groups.

2. Age was found to be an important factor. Whilst Labour led the Conservatives by 43% in the 18-24 year old group, the Conservatives led Labour by 47% in the 65 and over group, with the tilting point from Labour to the Conservatives being around the age of 39. However, when the younger vote was broken down more carefully, it was found that education

cut strongly across age to the extent that in 'student seats' (identified as comprising an over 10% student proportion of the electorate), 55 of the 77 seats were won by Labour but in other seats with young electorates comprising less than 4% students, 26 out of 35 went to the Conservatives.

3. Overall, the YouGov poll suggested that gender had little effect on voting behaviour but that there were marked differences in the 18–24 age range group with evidence suggesting that 46% of males voted Labour as opposed to 65% of females and 28% of males voted for the Conservatives whilst only 15% of females did so.

4. The support for Labour was clearly most solid across ethnic minority groups. According to the IpsosMORI poll, 64% of voters defined as black and ethnic minority voted for the Labour Party and 20% the Conservatives, whereas 29% of white voters voted Labour and 48% Conservative.

Brexit viewed from classic sociological perspectives

The aim of this short section is to briefly highlight some insights that the lenses of different sociological perspectives that were identified earlier in this chapter can provide on the phenomena of Brexit.

From a pluralist perspective, enlightened public opinion is formed through the free and open contestation of ideas and differences of opinion within the framework of liberal democratic institutions. Through such means, people's opinions over whether or not the UK should leave the EU were formed and the referendum enabled a political decision to be arrived at based on the aggregate measurement of these opinions by those who voted, thus constituting a straightforward exercise in democracy with power residing in the hands of the electorate. This, however, tells us little about power involved in the political decision to hold the referendum in the first place or the power of the media in the formation of popular opinion. Furthermore, pluralists also argue that democracy is an ongoing process involving the activity of protest or pressure groups. Given the closeness of the vote, deep and ongoing rifts around this major issue proved to be highly problematic to the implementation of the referendum outcome.

Functionalists adopt a similar perspective on voting as the testing popular opinion to that of pluralists. However, they place less emphasis on democratic societies as arenas of conflict for the resolution of disputes. Instead, they view such societies holistically as like integrated organisms in which gradual social change in shared values and institutions is beneficial to maintaining social stability. The function of elections is to enable the smooth transition of political power to take place peacefully and legitimately for this purpose. From a functionalist perspective, the protracted period of acrimony and social dissensus resulting from the referendum would be regarded as a condition of social malaise. Furthermore, since the UK entered the EEC in 1973, its institutions had gradually attuned themselves to synchronise with those of the EEC as it also evolved into the EU. Withdrawal was therefore likely to involve dysfunctionalities within the UK and also the EU, the extent of which is likely to depend on the suddenness of the break and the type of arrangements that can be agreed.

Each of these interpretations would be countered from a Marxist perspective in which attention would be focussed on the capacity of those with the power to shape popular opinion to their own interests. For Marxists, political power derives from economic power. In capitalist societies, those who own the means of production of ideas, ie. the mass media, are part of a broader class of primary beneficiaries of the system who will promote more broadly opinions and outlooks that assist their quest for profit maximisation. From this class viewpoint, the growing social dimension and regulations of the EU that were designed to offer workers minimal protection become perceived as constituting a threat to maximum profitability. The media provided a powerful means of shaping popular opinion and the long term drip drip effect of anti-EU rhetoric, especially through some of the mass circulation tabloid newspapers, helped shape popular opinion to support leave. The actual effect of withdrawal would leave workers, many of whom voted for it, especially if the outcome were no agreement, more vulnerable to the insecurities of the free market forces of capitalism. From this perspective, workers have been vulnerable to what Lukes has referred to as the third face of power.

Insights from a Weberian perspective would point to certain historical social conditions that formed behind the referendum outcome. The conditions in question were the effects of years of austerity on suffering populations. Under such conditions, people can become vulnerable to a more emotional appeal to the solution of their problems and find attraction in charismatic leaders. Within this context, Nigel Farage was able to rally discontent, often within an impoverished social base, in a nationalistic crusade against the EU. Feeling that they had little to lose, these sections of the population could be vulnerable to powerful emotive messages such as 'taking back control' over more dire warnings from economic experts which could then be dressed up as 'project fear'. This demonstrates that people's outlooks will not always prioritise arguments of economic rationality in shaping their actions and social change.

For elite theorists, Brexit can be regarded, in the contest for power to influence the masses, as a battle ground between established and contending elites (Fuller, 14/10/2019). Here, the established elites in the UK and the EU were likely to look to maintain the social stability of the status quo as a means of safeguarding their own elite status. They would therefore tend to prefer the UK to remain within the EU. However, other aspiring elite factions recognised their self-interest in acquiring power through the destabilising effect of whipping up anti-establishment feeling amongst the masses. Support for leave that came from sections of society that may be particularly vulnerable to the consequences of leaving the EU became buried below anti-establishment sentiment, but in the power game between elites, any negative consequences for the masses are only regarded as collateral damage.

Chapter 10
Sociology of Religion

Abstract

The study of religion offers one of the most testing challenges of the need for the sociologist to suspend personal beliefs so as to approach the study of the subject area dispassionately. Sociology does not attempt to answer questions about the existence of a god or gods but analyses religions as belief systems and their influence within society. To do so, the reader will need to be prepared to consider different and unfamiliar ways of defining religion, some of which go well beyond religion as conventionally defined.

Some of the key terminology utilised in the sociology of religion is explained, along with classification systems of religious organisations. This is followed by a study of the role of religion in society from the vantage point of the modern founding sociological perspectives of functionalism, Marxism, Weber's social action theory and phenomenology.

The question of secularisation is addressed. Secularisation is defined as the assertion of the declining importance of religion and is related to the process of modernisation. The secularisation debate is introduced as strongly influenced by Enlightenment thinking which pitted rational scientific reasoning against religious belief systems, an influence which fed strongly into the thinking of the founding sociological theorists. Various dimensions on which religiosity can be viewed and measured are considered, along with the reliability and validity of the data. The question of whether the relative vibrancy of religion in America can be treated as an exception to strong secularising trends European societies is raised.

Contemporary disputes within the church in terms of tradition versus reform reflect debates within society. Those touched on here will be the issues of gender equality (the ordination of women priests) and sexuality (the ordination of gay priests).

The issue of secularisation is returned to with reference to the question of a possible resurgence of religion. This is approached in different ways. One way of viewing the possible revitalisation of religion is through considering new approaches to its study. Those introduced here, located mainly in an American context of religious diversity, new religious movements and free market competition, are rational choice theory and resource mobilisation theory. It is questioned whether these approaches may now be forming a credible new paradigm to challenge the traditional Eurocentric view of secularisation.

Another approach focusses on the emergence of fundamentalist movements, especially within the context of globalisation. Relevant here is Huntington's thesis that following the collapse of the ideological conflict of the post war cold war era, world religious civilisations have emerged as reconfigured global clash points.

From a more European context, postmodernist and high modernist theoretical perspectives on religion are finally considered. Postmodern theory characterises contemporary society in terms of diversity of belief systems which consumers are free to choose from and move between as lifestyle options. This may be more accommodating than founding theory to recognising the persistence of religion. For high modernists such as Giddens, a world of diversity, rapid change, and uncertainty holds both the prospect of religious diversity and tolerance, and the risk of attraction to the certainty of religious fundamentalism as a source of potential conflict.

The sociological challenge

Religion, as conventionally understood, entails belief systems that explain the world or universe as governed by forces beyond human comprehension. For the believer, adherence to a system of religious belief is essentially an article of faith. Resulting insight and experience are likely to be profound and the belief system will provide guidelines for ethical behaviour.

In its approach to the study of religion, it is not the task of sociology to speculate about the existence or otherwise of supernatural realms and powerful entities or to enter into theological disputes. This is the province of theology and philosophy. The framework for sociology is to relate the existence of religious beliefs and practices to their social base. Attention will therefore be focussed on questions such as: what is it about people living in society that gives rise to religion? How may it influence people's social behaviour? What effect does religion have on the social condition? Is religion declining or increasing in society, how can we know, and what are the social causes and consequences of such changes?

Take for example the matter of measuring the extent of religion in society. We will later see that this is a highly complex academic matter. However, in terms of personal orientation toward the issue, people's beliefs may predispose them toward viewing evidence differently or disagreeing on what even counts as evidence. For example, the prospect of a decline in religious belief may elicit from a person holding strong religious beliefs the tendency to dismiss supporting evidence or if acknowledge it lament a presumed associated decline in moral standards. Alternatively, to an atheist, such evidence may be welcomed as indicating progress from the grip of dogma and superstition. Atheism, though, is just as much a belief system as are religions. The challenge for the sociologist is to step back and attempt to suspend judgements which may flow from their own belief systems.

Sociologically, religions are viewed as systems of belief which relate to human needs and social purposes. Sociologists are thus interested in studying religion as providing systems of meaning which sanctify moral values and guide social behaviour. A socially focussed approach can lead to an expansiveness in the definition of religion beyond traditional ones that we may as everyday citizens be more familiar with. This is because belief systems that are not conventionally viewed as religions, for example political ideologies, may be argued to perform similar personal needs and social functions to those of traditional religions. These belief systems have been referred to in sociology as 'quasi religions', providing a broadening of the definition of religion which one who adheres to traditional religious beliefs may find difficult to accept. But, as in the case of power and politics, so in the study of religion, sociological inquiry requires the capacity to hold in check everyday viewpoints which may constrain analysis.

Neither is it the role of sociology to compare the plausibility of different systems of religious belief. If sociologists are to compare religions, it is in terms of their impact on behaviour and society. From this vantage point, key questions include the following: to what extent do religions tend to promote social harmony or conflict? In what ways do they primarily support tradition or help bring about social change? What opportunities do their organisations offer or deny to different social groups such as men and women? What is the relationship between religion and politics in terms of controlling people's lives? How do different religious organisations relate to the state?

A further issue relates to disagreements over the extent to which science can lay claim to a different and superior way of establishing the truth to that of religion. This can lead, within sociology, to the need to be prepared to examine certain assumptions about the nature and practice of science.

Religious belief systems relate closely to cultural belief systems. This raises the question of ethnocentricity. Socialisation into a particular religious tradition through family, community or broader cultural influences may incline the believer to view the religions of other cultures as strange or incredible, bizarre or inferior, compared to what they are familiar with. But it is a salutary lesson to remember that this outlook is likely to be reciprocated – a similar orientation is likely to be applied by those of other religious and cultural traditions to their and our beliefs. The sociologist must be prepared to step back from adopting an ethnocentric stance and partisanship and examine religious belief systems relativistically as part of different social and cultural contexts and the different ways of life that they sanction.

A problem which is quite acute in the sociology of religion relates to the use of certain terminology. In their classification of types of religious organisation, sociologists have traditionally employed the terms sect and cult to smaller religious groups. To many people, these terms as applied in everyday life carry highly negative and stereotypical connotations from which it may be difficult to insulate their use in sociology. Sects and cults have often been viewed with suspicion and hostility and held in low status as deviant communities. It is therefore particularly important that sociologists are able to adopt maximum value neutrality in the use of such terminology. Indeed, in the face of invasive pejorative connotations, sociologists seem to be abandoning reference to the terms sect and cult in preference for the more neutral alternative of 'new religious movements'.

Definition of main concepts

A **belief system** comprises an integrated and self-contained set of ideas. It provides the basis for a community of believers to share a common understanding of the world. The interconnection of ideas can make belief systems self-reinforcing and resistant to criticism or even change. Ultimately, belief systems rely on followers retaining faith in the basic ideas, principles and values upon which the system is based. Religions are classic cases of belief systems, but there is debate in sociology as to how different they are to other systems of thinking, in particular that to which they are often contrasted; the sciences.

Defining **religion** is highly problematic. Definitional attempts have varied in the importance that they attach to such different aspects as institutions, rituals, beliefs, sacred texts, and the existence and influence of supernatural beings. For example, it has been suggested that a universally applicable feature of all religions is their claim that supernatural beings have a governing effect over events on earth. This definition derives from the work of Ronald Robertson. Anthony Giddens regards the universal features of religion to include the existence of sacred symbols which elicit a feeling of reverence from a believer; engagement in ritual activities by a community of believers; and places separated from everyday activities in which ceremonies can take place. In so doing, Giddens adopts a definition of religion close to that of Durkheim.

Disputes within sociology regarding the pervasiveness of religion in society and its effects are partly related to the application of such different definitions. Some definitions can be criticised as being too exclusive – being rather narrow, they would exclude some belief systems which others would argue to be religions. Robertson's definition of religion, for example, would exclude Confucianism on the grounds that it lacks belief in a supernatural being. By contrast, other definitions may be so broad and inclusive that they could include as religions some belief systems which many would discount. For example, if religion includes any system of beliefs through which followers acquire an answer to ultimate questions of life, as emphasised by phenomenologists, it may be possible to include Marxism, for all of its atheistic pronouncements, as a religion.

A distinction can be made between substantive and functional definitions of religion (Davie, 2013, pp.19-20). A **substantive definition** views religion in terms of what it is. The focus here is on the particular beliefs and practices with regard to the supernatural that are adopted by different religions and the effect this has on behaviour. Although he did not define religion, it will become apparent that Weber tended to adopt this approach.

By contrast, a **functionalist** definition of religion emphasises its social utility, moving the focus from what religion is to what is does for society. In this case, the focus is a broader one as belief systems which perform religious functions without necessarily making reference to a supernatural realm can be included. This approach is exemplified in the works of Durkheim.

An alternative approach to the problem of definition tends to derive from those who would adopt an **interactionist** perspective. Since a key aim is to be able to see the world as through the eyes of those being studied, then religion has to be taken as how those others define it.

It is important to be aware in this topic area of the variable scope of definitions applied by different sociologists, especially as it may be suspected that definitions employed, the types of evidence sought and the way in which that evidence is interpreted may be used to provide support for desired conclusions. In such a potentially emotive area, normally expected procedures of objectivity and neutrality may be vulnerable.

A further issue is that it is not always easy to distinguish whether certain beliefs or activities should be referred to as religion or magic. To help distinguish between these terms, an emphasis tends to be placed on religion as relating to matters of general public wellbeing and the engagement in ritual by a community of believers in the hope of promoting these ends. In usually recognising the existence of supernatural powers or beings, the attitude of believers is likely to be one of conciliation and humility toward these powers in the hope that benign intervention will bring beneficial outcomes.

By contrast, **magic** tends to be practiced in small groups or by individuals. According to Goode, magic comprises beliefs and practices in which supernatural forces can be harnessed in a more instrumental and manipulative way to bring about specific desired outcomes for the individual. For Malinowski, magic is pre-scientific in the sense that it is likely to be turned to in cultures where scientific understanding of and technological intervention in life are too limited as a means of effecting desired outcomes. In this context, magic can include the belief that occult forces can be manipulated by a specialist, such as a magician, to cast a spell on certain others, often to perform harm. Voodoo or vengeance magic would provide good examples of such beliefs and practices. If a cult claims to be able to call up supernatural powers, offered in service to individual customers, as in the case of spiritualism, this practice could according to the above definition be classified as magic rather than religion. The fact that it often isn't highlights some of the definitional problems which abound in this area of study.

Magic may also include the belief in fortune telling or individual acts of ritual which are thought to bring good luck. The rituals that some sports people engage in, in the hope of continuing their sporting success, may, although seemingly trivial, be examples of magical superstition. Likewise, a student may place a lucky charm object on their desk when facing the uncertainty and importance in life's fortunes when sitting an exam. The evolutionary anthropologist E.B Tylor referred to the continuing existence of such rituals and beliefs in the contemporary context as 'survivals'; they survive, somewhat out of context, into the modern scientific age as a relic of more primitive times where their original purpose can be more clearly apprehended.

Distinguishing between religion and magic is therefore not always a clear-cut matter and can be fraught with the problem of pejorative judgement.

An enduring debate in sociology surrounds the question of **secularisation**. Secularisation is the view that the process of modernisation brings with it a decline in the significance of religion. Its advance is often related to the progress of scientific knowledge, industrialisation and urbanisation which are accompanied by rational explanation of and control over the world. It is argued that the advance of rational thinking inclines behaviour toward formality, efficiency and change, which, along with the application of logical scrutiny, undermines tradition and religious beliefs. This suggests that science and religion are opposed ways of thinking and are inversely related – the more there is of one, the less there is of the other. The key European sociological theorists who established the foundations of the discipline during the modern period were writing against the backdrop of the Enlightenment and were convinced that forces of secularisation were powerfully at work. They tended to adopt a linear view of social change which placed secularising European societies at the front of the queue of social progress, showing the path that less advanced nations would take in the future.

A number of more contemporary theorists have however become far more cautious of the view that religion is in terminal decline. Indeed, some, particularly in the United States, have argued that from the latter decades of the twentieth century religion has become revitalised – positing in effect a **desecularisation** thesis. These issues will form a substantial part of this chapter.

Classification of religious organisations

As well as in the form of belief systems and ritual, religion can be studied sociologically in terms of organisations which can be classified into types. The approach traditionally used classifies religious organisations as churches, denominations or sects. At present, these organisations will be defined but the shortcomings of this classification system should be noted. Firstly, it is a western derived typology which may make little sense if it were attempted to be applied to religion in non-western societies. Secondly, the classification of specific religious organisations in terms of this typology may not be clear cut. Thirdly, confusion can arise when these and other terms are used loosely in everyday contexts and applied inconsistently by sociologists. Fourthly, definition and classification should only be a starting point for assisting analysis, not an end in itself.

A church is a large and formal religious organisation, run by a hierarchy of professional theological specialists and support staff. Church 'membership' is inclusive; it is open and loose in the sense that people are seen to be born into an established church which they are free to opt out of if they so decide. Membership is conducive to full participation in mainstream social life and church teachings have a close connection to society's dominant culture. A church will therefore need to balance the extent to which it adapts to changes in the values and culture of society with moral guidance based on adherence to traditional teachings.

An established church is usually closely allied to the politics of the state and claims a monopoly religious position. In England, for example, Westminster Abbey sits adjacent to the Houses of Parliament, high dignitaries of the Church of England (Anglican Church) are involved in state ceremonies and bishops sit in the House of Lords. Being part of the political establishment, the Anglican Church tends to be closely identified with by the upper echelons of society. Like the Conservative Party (the Anglican Church has been referred to as the Conservative Party at prayer) it nevertheless relies on support from all levels of society and particular bishops have at times spoken out against governments on such issues as homelessness and poverty. This evidence of a degree of autonomy between church and state and declining church attendance rates are sometimes regarded as demonstrating that it is developing some denominational like characteristics.

Although the Catholic Church in England has the characteristics of a church rather than a denomination, it is not here the established church as it is in a number of other countries. It provides a good example of how a church can impose sanctions on the behaviour of its members through the possible withdrawal of sacraments as in the case of refusing to marry divorcees.

The concept of a denomination was developed by the theological writer Niebuhr. Denominations form part of a pluralistic culture that recognises the legitimacy of a number of religious organisations. They have been particularly noted as a feature of the American religious landscape in which constitutionally there can be no single dominant religious establishment that claims monopoly representation and acquires privileges from the state.

Denominational religion is conducive to a free market consumer society in which people may switch between denominations as a form of free choice. It is an intermediate level of religious organisation between that of church and sect, and takes the form of a relatively open institution which one nevertheless joins out of choice rather than assumption and may appeal to those dissatisfied with a mainstream church. The organisation is more likely than a church to use lay preachers and allow a more fervent style of preaching. It will be more removed from close identification with state policies than a church and is likely to find less support from the upper classes. A denomination does not tend to place restrictions on members' full participation in mainstream society but may be a little more particular in providing its guidance to followers on its expectations regarding a good way of life. It is also likely that its places of worship will comprise smaller and simpler buildings than those of the established church. As in the case of nineteenth century Methodism, a denomination may grow out of a smaller and more radical group, a sect, which had originally broken away from an established church but over time 'cooled down' in fervour, compromised its strictures, developed a hierarchical structure and grown.

The term sect was used by Weber to denote small religious groups who adhere to an intensive body of beliefs and forming religious communities which usually originate as dissenting breakaway groups that have become dissatisfied with what they perceive as the laxity of churches which they condemn as having compromised their teachings. They therefore often claim to uphold pure religious beliefs to which they expect from their followers close adherence. Sects are likely to put in place strict entry requirements for membership and a close monitoring of demanding lifestyles. They will attract larger proportions of people who oppose the state and the ways and values of mainstream society than other religious groups. This type of religious organisation therefore faces a high risk of being viewed as deviant or worse by those whom adhere to mainstream culture, religions and lifestyles. To uphold their differences, sects may sometimes erect protective barriers between their group and broader society in the form of geographical distance, distinctive ways of behaving or speaking, and distinctive dress.

Methodism at the time of the Wesleys in the eighteenth century was a fiery religious sect and the Quakers during the time of the Restoration of the monarchy in the seventeenth century adopted a defensive sect posture to separate themselves from the more politically radical levellers. Both sects have since developed in the direction of denominations by growing in size and 'cooling down'.

Membership of sects can be highly exclusive and may require of the potential entrant proof of a conversion experience, the undergoing of initiation ceremonies and the expectation of a deep level of commitment. Members may therefore claim the exclusivity of being part of the initiated and superior few. The relatively small size of sects means that a prescribed way of life can often be closely monitored. Authority and control is not likely to work through a bureaucratic hierarchy but more likely through a charismatic leader.

In common usage, the terms sect and cult are often confused. Unfortunately, even within sociology one can find definitional and classificatory inconsistencies in the use of these terms. Both are small scale organisations, but sects are usually more intensively organised. Both may be regarded as holding beliefs and practices that deviate from mainstream values and ways, but sects tend to require a greater demarcation against and withdrawal from the mainstream than cults. The term cult has been used by Roy Wallis to define a sect like but less inclusive religious organisation which may not form a cohesive community with a collective place of worship or have a clearly established membership count. For Stark and Bainbridge, the distinguishing feature of cults is that their ideas are either created anew or refashioned from imported traditions, often resulting in eclectic belief systems. Differentiated in the above terms, Heaven's Gate would tend to be classified as a sect and Transcendental Meditation, a derivative of Hindu religious beliefs, would be recognised as a cult.

However, there do seem to be some differences in terminology between predominantly British and American classifications of sects and cults. For example, the Americans Stark and Bainbridge include in their definition of cults a diversity of belief systems and degrees of organisational intensity, ranging from a token interest and involvement to that of living within a total institution dominated by a powerful personality requiring close adhesion to prescribed beliefs and subject to precise behavioural controls. Accordingly, they have provided a typology which subdivides religious cults (Hunt, 2002, pp.143-144). In this classification scheme, an audience cult would include deviant mystical belief systems such as astrology where the 'follower' may be showing little more than an inquisitive interest. At the other end of the scale, Heaven's Gate could be classified as a cult movement which required intensive commitment and sacrifice from its clearly prescribed members. In between these extremes they located client cults which offer services, such as the technique of Dianetics provided by Scientology, to help people make adjustments to cope with the difficulties of contemporary life. This type is therefore compatible with successful life within mainstream society. It closely resembles what will shortly be defined as Wallis' world affirming new religious movements and would seem well adapted to the needs of a consumer society.

Millenarian movements are religious groups which anticipate fundamental world change through supernatural intervention and are sometimes referred to as revolutionary religions. Such intervention invariably offers salvation to followers and punishment to others who are seen as corrupt. Millenarian movements therefore can appeal to people who have been marginalized in mainstream society and who feel oppressed or have experienced painful personal circumstances or social change. These religions may predict a specific date of reckoning or read into signs foretelling apocalyptic events. However, Chomsky argues that for their teachings to be attractive to followers, the prophesied events need to be within their lifetime. These groups usually take the form of sects or cults, although more mainstream religions may also include millenarian dimensions. The Jehovah's Witnesses, usually regarded as a sect, provide an example of a millenarian movement.

It is not surprising that many sociologists have decided to stop using the terms cult and sect which are laced in everyday language with sinister meaning and even in sociology are susceptible to inconsistent usage. Instead, the more neutral sounding term new religious movements has grown in common usage. The term refers to a diversity of small-scale alternatives to established religion which usually originate in cults. These movements often take the form of more loosely organised cults. Moreover, the term 'new' can imply the decline in support for traditional religious organisations and the emergence of novel alternatives within a more pluralistic environment, much in the same way as new social movements may indicate a turning away from conventional party politics.

A classificatory scheme for new religious movements has been devised by the British sociologist Roy Wallis. The basis of the classification is the movement's relationship with mainstream society. He identifies world rejecting religions (similar to Stark and Bainbridge's cult movements) as those which are highly critical of the beliefs and ways of broader society. Such movements usually establish a clear psychological and sometimes spatial divide between themselves and conventional society through their own intensive community life and may be referred to as introversionist. Members are likely to have turned their back, at least temporarily, on the outside world and may be expected to renounce contact with broader society, including their family, and undergo a process of conversion to the strict theological dogma and life of the movement. This can include the giving up of past identity, giving over possessions to the movement, acquiring new names and wearing uniforms. In such extreme and rare cases as the Heaven's Gate movement (see box 1), intense control of group members combined with millenarian beliefs has led to mass suicides.

It is through examples of groups at this extreme end of the scale that the labels cult or sect have generated public hostility. Yet the conventional wisdom that cult and sect members are disproportionately drawn from poor backgrounds and are passive and brainwashed victims is not born out by broader evidence.

Box 1: Heaven's Gate
A case study of a world rejecting new religious movement

Leaders
Heaven's Gate was a world rejecting religious community. It was established by Marshall Applewhite and Bonnie Nettles in 1975. Within the group, Applewhite took the name of 'Do' and Nettles the name of 'Ti'. When Ti died, Do became the exclusive group leader.

Claims
Do claimed that he had been sent to earth on a mission from the 'next level', as had Jesus, to save souls. The purpose was to save those who could be saved from base human ways, since the day of reckoning was at hand when those who adhered to such base ways would be 'recycled'.

Belief system and opportunity
The belief system was explained through a gardening analogy. Do explained that from the level above human, occasional contact with humans was made. On such occasions, souls from the level above human enter pre-prepared human bodies. Do and Ti were themselves incarnated into human bodies to spread the message – an identical process and purpose to that of Jesus 2000 years ago.

At the time of contact, only some individuals receive souls. This gives them an initial capacity for growth to a higher level, but only under the guidance of the incarnated representative, Do. Do's purpose was to nurture souls, taking followers on a difficult path of renouncing base human ways, a path which only some would be able to follow.

According to Do, each 2000 years, base humans, like weeds, are 'spaded under' and a new cycle of human existence starts. The purpose of the human body in this is to grow souls. Those who are able to follow the rigors of working toward this new level of knowledge and consciousness will ascend to the next level on the day of reckoning. This point in time is immanent and joining the group offers a window of opportunity.

Lifestyle

The community took the form of a highly controlled total institution in which salvation could only be possible through following the tutorship of Do. All members were given new names. Since the next level to which members were aspiring to graduate was sexless, within the group sex was banned and sexual thoughts had to be guarded against as forms of base human ways. Females had their hair cropped, unisex clothing was worn and some males were castrated. The higher level was able to add to its members through the process of metamorphosis which members were being guided to achieve. Any slippage toward sexuality had to be admitted.

A list of regulations prescribed behaviour in great detail. Exact recipes and procedures had to be followed in the cooking of meals. Occasional fasting was required to cleanse the body. Even the process of shaving had to follow specific instructions. Members were watched over by 'check partners'.

Since Do was convinced that the group were being watched by the authorities, he devised deception techniques. The community were often on the move, and where they were established, only a limited number of members were allowed outside the building in an attempt to deceive the authorities as to the size of the group.

Behind such controls there was always the threat that the movement offered members their last chance of salvation, to which Do was the only one who held the key.

Science

The imagery of science took numerous forms. It was claimed that Do and Ti had arrived on earth in UFOs. A group member explained that to rise to the next level of consciousness was just like reprogramming a human computer brain with next level knowledge. Web sites were frequently used to propagate the cult's message. The appearance of the Hale-Bopp comet was taken by Do as a sign from Ti that a spaceship was arriving to evacuate the group who would be saved from the spading under process. Even the costumes that group members wore on the goodbye video had space insignia on them.

Evacuation
On 22 March, 1997, in preparation for evacuation, the 39 group members took their own lives, mainly through the ingestion of pain killer mixed in apple sauce. The scene of the mass suicide showed the bodies laid out in a highly organised fashion in an attitude of serene countenance.

By contrast, world affirming religions focus on developing the spiritual powers of individuals to cope within society. Techniques for coping are aimed at enabling individuals to achieve their full potential. These religions therefore enable followers to positively embrace mainstream society rather than turn away from or against it. They tend to be far less intrusive into lives of followers than are world rejecting religions and may not even require participation in a place of collective worship. World affirming religions usually actively market themselves, sell their services and seek widespread participation. This type therefore tends to coincide with Stark and Bainbridge's category of client cults. Clients may include high profile celebrity figures, as in the case of the attraction of the Beatles to Transcendental Meditation (a derivative from eastern religions) and Tom Cruise to Scientology, as they offer means of achieving peace of mind and the capacity to cope within a world of stress through the use of a technique. Given their therapeutic dimension, world affirming religions can come into conflict with mainstream psychiatry, as has been the case of the practice of Dianetics within the Scientology movement.

World accommodating religions can be distinguished from each of the above types in that they are neither driven by alienation from broader society nor the enhancement of success within it. Instead, the attitude toward the ways of the world tends to be one of indifference. World accommodating religions may become established through process of breakaway from churches or denominations in the quest for religious and spiritual purity which it is believed the parent organisation has compromised. They therefore tend to to have the characteristics of sects as earlier defined and are likely to focus on improving the inner spiritual life of followers through participation in collective worship, but otherwise make little imposition into the everyday lives of their followers.

An example of a world accommodating religion is Neo-Pentecostalism which is an American Christian revivalist denomination that emphasises the importance of the personal experience of closeness to God, direct spiritual experience rather than dogmatic adherence to religious strictures, and the instilling of such experience in others through lively participation at religious meetings. Another is the Atherius Society which combines influences from Christian and eastern religions with the belief in contact from extra-terrestrial intelligences.

Founding sociological perspectives on religion

Functionalism – the social utility of religion

Functionalism is a theory of social utility. In the case of religion, it therefore focuses on how religion benefits society or promotes social well being. This perspective adopts a holistic approach; religion is seen as giving sanction to a single body of values that provide constrains on individual behaviour, thereby integrating society.

Early functionalist approaches to religion were heavily influenced by the social destabilisation of the French Revolution of 1789. Auguste Comte, writing between the 1820s and 1850s, was pained by what he saw as the anarchy of the times, but believed that a new stable social order was on the horizon. From Comte's theoretical perspective, the condition of society is largely determined by the prevailing condition of knowledge about society. Comte emphasised that the Catholic Church was a powerful force for social stability through the Middle Ages because Catholicism was a coherent doctrine that bound the individual to society in a series of religiously sanctioned duties which provided a singular body of powerful moral constraints on behaviour. However, throughout the eighteenth century, Enlightenment writers were attacking the dogmatic teachings of the Catholic Church with rational, scientific and atheistic critiques. This period of intellectual criticism advanced ideas of individual rights as opposed to religious based social duties. According to Comte, this intellectual attack on the integrated belief system of Catholicism undermined the religious consensus which had upheld the old social order of feudalism, and helped to precipitate the French Revolution which was followed by a protracted period of intellectual and moral anarchy and social destabilisation.

Comte argued that the re-establishment of a stable social order required a new and positive coherent social doctrine to bind people to society. He maintained that as knowledge progresses, theology can no longer do this job. Science must replace religion in this constructive role. In this future 'positivist' society, experts would use social science to analyse and organise society and science would operate as a new integrating body of beliefs for the populace as religion once had.

In his later works, Comte came to change his position and argue that although intellectually theology had become surpassed and positive social science would guide the political process, religion still had a vital function to play in promoting altruistic feeling that was necessary to emotionally attach individuals to society. The most appropriate form of this religion would have a secular focus. For Comte, the 'religion of humanity', celebrating the greatest individuals throughout human history, would perform this role.

Following in the tradition of Comte, Durkheim's functionalist approach views religion in terms of its social utility. However, he maintained that as societies evolve and grow in size and complexity, the essence of religion from a sociological viewpoint becomes increasingly difficult to disentangle. For Durkheim, establishing the essential functional utility of religion suggested that the difference between belief systems themselves (a substantive approach) was not of great importance. He argued that to understand the fundamental nature of religion, it needed to be studied in its most primitive but still existing form. For this purpose, his study of Australian Aboriginal clan society provided the information upon which Durkheim based his universal theory of religion in his 1912 work The Elementary Forms of the Religious Life (1976).

In Aboriginal society, clans were social groups which claimed a common ancestry. However, clans were made up of smaller social units called bands in which people lived out their daily lives. Much of these lives were devoted to everyday and mundane activities, referred to by Durkheim as the 'profane'. Each clan was distinguished by its symbol which took the form of a specific natural feature such as a plant or animal. These distinguishing symbols appeared on totems and held imagined special powers, demanding respect and veneration from clan members and acting as rallying points for bands to come together and participate in collective ritual and worship. When engaging in collective ritual in the presence of the totem, individuals often experienced religious ecstasy and felt themselves to be in contact with a superior force. This is the realm of the 'sacred', much elevated above the profane world of everyday life. Durkheim wanted to rationally examine what the source and social function of these activities and experiences was.

He argued that the purpose of religion is to assert the primacy of a powerful sense of group being - the collective consciousness - over individual self-interest, for the benefit of society. This requires symbols representing the group to be perceived as having sacred significance. As such, individual consciousness and conscience are impressed through the experience of ritual participation within the group with respect for the community whose codes of conduct are given sacred sanction. In primitive societies, with a low division of labour and much common experience, the capacity for the collective consciousness to overwhelm the individual was immense – hence the feeling of awe in the presence of a powerful entity.

What fundamental truth about religion did Durkheim claim that this analysis revealed? He argued that religion must have some substance given its universality. But that substance is not the same as that imagined by those who engage in collective worship. For Durkheim, religion acts as a unifying social force. All that can be rationally established is that when worshipping what they experienced as supernatural forces and the superior power of a deity, group members are in effect worshipping the personification of the superior force of society imposing itself over the self-interest of individual members. This is the essential function of religion.

Sociologically, the question of the truth or otherwise of people's religious beliefs is of little importance. From this perspective, individual conscience, often vested in religious feelings, is in fact a social product. Through the socialising experience of group participation, focussed upon powerful sacred symbols, the individual internalises the sacred nature of social guidelines demarcating acceptable and non-acceptable behaviour. Durkheim emphasised that this function is particularly important in modern industrial societies in which greater size and enhanced individual differences brought about by an extended division of labour required the effect of powerful integrating forces of the collective consciousness to act against the potentially socially damaging impact of excessive individualism.

From the study of religion in primitive social groups, Durkheim claimed to have identified a universal and indispensable function of religion, equally applicable therefore to religion in the contemporary world. What, then, if the advance of rational thinking undermines faith in the supernatural? Adherence to religion thus defined must surely decline with damaging consequences for social integration. Durkheim's answer was that a religious type function is indispensable to any society.

'There is something eternal in religion which is destined to survive all the particular symbols in which religious thought has successively enveloped itself. There can be no society which does not feel the need of upholding and reaffirming at regular intervals the collective sentiments and the collective ideas which make its unity and its personality. Now this moral remaking cannot be achieved except by the means of reunions, assemblies and meetings where the individuals, being closely united to one another, reaffirm in common their common sentiments; hence some ceremonies which do not differ from regular religious ceremonies, either in their object, the results which they produce, or the processes employed to attain these results' (Durkheim, 1976, p.427).

As secularisation takes place in the sense that belief in the form of worshipping a god declines, new belief systems with their powerful symbols of allegiance are necessary to keep the collective consciousness alive. For Durkheim, faith based on reason must have humanity as its object.

From a Durkheimian perspective, nationalistic and patriotic belief systems hold a religious type significance. We can extrapolate that symbols associated with these belief systems, in the form of national flags and anthems, are kept alive in the minds of individuals through such occasions of collective focus as political and state ceremonies and national sporting events which reawaken common feelings of shared national identity. These belief systems and occasions have been subsequently referred to as 'quasi religious' – they are not religions in the conventional sense of the term but perform a similar and indispensable social function. A functional definition of religion, focussing on what it does, is thus a very broad and inclusive one.

As for Comte and Durkheim, Parsons' functionalist approach to religion emphasises its positive attributes and necessity in promoting social order. Religion provides a sacred source for beliefs and meanings and an umbrella for shared social values and norms. These constitute specific guidelines and recipes for behaviour which are shared by a community and are given ultimate religious sanction. However, for Parsons, rather than becoming secularised, traditional religion would endure.

Firstly, this is because in life there will always remain the necessity to support individuals and bring communities together in the face of unforeseen events, misfortune and injustice. Religion is uniquely placed to sooth, help in coping and motivate where rational responses alone are inadequate.

Secondly, religion has itself been purified in this role through the advance of structural differentiation. This refers to a general process whereby as societies grow and modernise, new institutions develop to perform increasingly specialised social functions. Old institutions, which once provided a broad range of functions, lose some of these functions. Religious institutions are no exception. They have had to disengage from many areas of life that they were once involved in, such as being the main provider of education and welfare, as other institutions have taken over. Parsons argues that this enables religious institutions to concentrate on their key function of furnishing the profound meaning systems that individuals require and providing a sacred aspect to shared social values. In America, despite its religious denominationalism, its culture and values are Christian, and often more specifically Protestant in their origin, hence the capacity for the creation of a general value consensus. Furthermore, even in the phenomena of the counter culture of love from the late 1960s, Parsons detected the revival of religious values not dissimilar to those of early Christianity.

Parsons' functionalist theory of religion, more than Durkheim's, combines a recognition of individual with social needs. As well as promoting shared values and norms, religion's capacity for serving profound individual needs contributes toward the maintenance of social harmony.

Marxism – religion and ideological distortion

From a Marxist perspective, social ideas, institutions and people's consciousness are powerfully shaped by economic forces. The most important economic forces in this process are the means of production – the means through which production takes place. When these are privately owned, a system of dominance by a minority class of owners inevitably exists. Such social systems where wealth is concentrated in the hands of a powerful economic minority naturally generate ideas that explain social reality in a systematically distorted way. Marx used the concept of ideology to refer to this systematic distortion. The effect of ideological distortion is to shape the consciousness of members of society in such a way as to protect the system and induce the compliance of the subject class. For Marx, religious beliefs and institutions are strongly implicated in this process and invariably act as a highly conservative force. Under capitalism, they encourage amongst an exploited class an attitude of application to work and acceptance of its position in the class structure, whilst obscuring the very existence of exploitation. This shaping of ideas by economic forces is referred to by the term 'economic determinism', the extent of which is a matter of some dispute amongst Marxists.

Important to understanding religion from a Marxist perspective is Marx's use of the concept of alienation and its origin in the form of economic arrangements within which labour takes place. Work is regarded as a potentially creative and satisfying process through which human potential can be fully realised. However, under capitalism, the worker becomes an object in the production process, his labour power used for the profit of others. In this class relationship, the worker experiences powerlessness, meaninglessness and lack of fulfilment – a dehumanising experience of being an appendage to a machine and working under the discipline of the factory work regime (Marx, 1973, p.74).

This for Marx is alienation. Under these conditions, religion provides an attractive and safe 'compensatory fantasy' (McIntosh, in Matthewman ed., 2007, p.279) that fills the meaning vacuum. For exploited workers, it offers solace to a hard life, without revealing its true social origin, and may even portray hardship as a test of faith. Religion is therefore a natural phenomena of social and economic orders of exploitation that require illusion for the system to remain intact. It then becomes distorted and utilised by those in power to assist in the process of social control.

A number of points can be raised to illustrate these rather abstract ideas. For example, Christianity provides the image of paradise in an afterlife that awaits the righteous or eternal suffering for the wicked. Some austere sects, such as puritans, have even elevated worldly suffering to a virtue. Religions that contain a strong millenarian dimension, such as the Jehovah's Witnesses, prophesy that the wrongs of the world will be put right by future supernatural intervention, thus the need to wait and prepare rather than to politically challenge them.

From a Marxist perspective, religion provides belief systems of supernatural mystery that has the effect of stupefying the believer. It distracts the attention of the exploited from the socially created situation of their exploitation and the need or possibility of improving life in this world through direct political action. Under capitalism, an important role of Marxist political activists is therefore to strip away the illusions of religion to expose the 'real' nature of capitalism, making a progressive challenge to the system possible.

Notions of an incomprehensible 'divine providence' directing social change draw a veil of mystery over what Marx argued were the real laws of social change. He argued that the latter could only be understood scientifically by adopting a materialist view of history. From this viewpoint, the driving force for change can be found very much on earth in the development and ownership of the means of production and the resulting class relationships. It is through the understanding of these laws of social change that mature and responsible political action can hasten the end of capitalism.

Religious authorities have often sided with the political forces of order and repression. When religion teaches that human nature is essentially sinful or wicked, it provides a backdrop against which political repression can be justified as necessary for the maintenance of social order. By contrast, Marxism adopts a view derived from the Enlightenment that the condition of human nature is in fact not fixed, but is a product of the social environment. Wicked behaviour, referred to by religions as 'sinfulness', is itself a product of the social conditions of oppression and exploitation rather than a fixed characteristic of human nature. From a classical Marxist perspective, it is only by recognising and eradicating the social and economic conditions (of capitalism) that give rise to this behaviour that a new social order of communism can be realised a) which human nature can beneficially adjust to and b) will provide the conditions in a classless society for the redundancy and withering away of religion.

To sum up, Marxists agree with functionalists that religion tends to integrate society, but thereafter their analyses are diametrically opposed. Whilst Comte argued that the driving force for social change and economic development was the progress of systems of thinking, Marx argued that systems of thinking are shaped or even determined by the type of economic system. Whilst functionalists relate religion to the necessary promotion of social integration for the benefit of all, Marxists view the source of religion as exploitative social systems that benefit only a minority. Whilst Durkheim related religion to the positive integrative function of promoting the collective consciousness, Marx referred to the containing effect on potential class conflict of religion through promoting false consciousness. Both perspectives explain forces of secularisation. For Marx, religion can become redundant, but only with the advent of communism, whereas Durkheim argued that 'religion' will always be of functional social necessity, even though the form it takes is likely to become increasingly secular. Consequently, from this perspective, even atheistic communist societies, such as the old Soviet

Union, would require their own totems (as in the statues of leaders), flags, anthems and celebrations which integrate society, and a communist belief system, all of which perform the task of a quasi religion.

Weber – religion and western capitalism

Weber's social action theory examines the complex interplay between the motives and actions of individuals and broader belief systems and social structures. He emphasised that individual action could only be understood with reference to people's motives. Therefore, although sociology uses broad categories to understand the framing of social action, the springboard for action is in the individual's subjective consciousness. However, to understand individual's motives for action, the broader meaning systems that they relate to and how individuals interpreted them must be studied. Amongst the most potent of meaning systems for orientating action can be systems of religious belief. But for Weber, in contrast to Marx, systems of meaning are not necessarily just the product of economic systems. Cultural meaning systems can have their own dynamics and effect on social action independently of and even influentially over the economic world. Weber was therefore countering what he believed to be the excessive economic determinism and materialism in Marxist theory.

Of special interest to Weber was the relationship between religion and social change. As a result of comparative and historical studies of world religions, Weber felt that he was able to demonstrate that a relationship existed between religious belief systems and the propensity for social and economic modernisation or relative stagnation. In particular, he was interested in explaining why England was the first country in the world to industrialise and what shaped the value system of western capitalism. Through comparative analysis of world religions, he believed that he had identified a key influence (but not a singular cause) in the form of a religious ethic which was more strongly present in England prior to the transition to modern rational capitalism than in most other countries. This, as he argued in his 1905 work The Protestant Ethic and the Spirit of Capitalism (1978), was seventeenth century Calvinism, an ascetic protestant belief system similar to that of puritanism, which came to instil in believers a powerful work ethic.

To fully appreciate Weber's explanation, it is important to attempt to make a psychological leap to a time in history when religious beliefs may have profoundly affected in many people a deep sense of self and shaped their actions. Calvinism was preached by the charismatic John Calvin in the sixteenth century as a salvationist religion. For Calvinists, only an 'elect' few are chosen by God to enter heaven. Although this choice was seen as predetermined and fixed by God, individuals were left not knowing whether they were one of the elect. Weber argued that this created in the mind of the believer a great tension, which he referred to as 'salvation anxiety'. Anxiety drove believers to attempt to psychologically resolve the following tensions. Actions on earth could not change individual predestination. Yet believers questioned whether God could have predestined an elect who disobeyed his commandments. They thought it to be likely that he would have chosen those who live by his commandments. From this position, for the Calvinist believer, following a religiously sanctioned upright life of sober dedication was a necessity. But by what observable and measurable sign could one take that God had chosen them as worthy? The answer arrived at was that God favours the elect with material prosperity. In a logically contradictory but psychologically satisfying way, this now put the answer to the question of predestination in the hands of the believer. A life of asceticism (industriousness and single minded systematic application to hard work and a simple life of moral rectitude) guided the believer in the resolution of salvation anxiety; the resultant achievement of economic worldly success was not primarily driven be greed but the search for a token or sign of one's worthiness to enter heaven.

Weber argued that there was a conspicuous similarity between this religious work ethic, which channelled salvation anxiety into application, and the values of what later became western capitalism – the one was conducive but not singularly causal to the emergence of the other. Driven by their religious beliefs and anxieties, many ascetic Protestants were industrious and enterprising in their values and behaviour in a pre-capitalist age. Calvinism was therefore a religious belief system originating in pre-capitalist society which promoted action in the believer that would be conducive to capitalist modernisation. Worldly success could be measured in terms of profit derived from individual application and the rational organisation of the labour of others. Profit maximisation required abstinence from luxury or squandering one's hard worked for gain. To the believer, time and money should not be wasted on idle pursuits, but profit should be relentlessly ploughed back into one's business. Calvinist salvation religion was therefore a powerful driving force for believers to live a simple, dedicated and industrious lifestyle. Furthermore, it tended to promote rational and innovative decision making at the expense of following tradition for its own sake since profit maximisation required careful calculation of the comparative returns from different courses of action and necessitated the development of rational accountancy.

A number of important points emerge from this perspective:

1. Weber was able to show that a religious belief system was an important factor in the process of modernisation along the lines of western capitalism. Ascetic protestant beliefs sanctioned dedicated action and domination of the environment as a route to economic success and salvation. But individual believers had no necessary consciousness or intention that their actions would bring about the structures of modern rational capitalism.

2. By contrast, eastern religions were more contemplative. They tended to emphasise in the believer the importance of escapism to spiritual experience, contemplation and harmony with the environment. These eastern societies, many of which were once scientifically and technologically advanced compared to the west, did not in this religious and cultural environment tend to generate an internal dynamic of capitalist modernisation. Furthermore, the predominant religious belief systems of China and India (Confucianism and Hinduism respectively) promoted amongst social elites a literary culture of disdain for economic activity. Ascetic Protestantism did not contain these barriers to the development of modern rational capitalism.

3. Comparing western societies, the prominence of Catholicism in a society was not conducive to early capitalist modernisation. Catholicism did not readily provide an ascetic based work ethic. The church conveyed an image of splendour and luxury, fostering the view that it was acceptable to idle one's time in comfort from any money made. Moreover, Catholicism offered an outlet to the continuous anxiety regarding individual salvation experienced by the Calvinist that was absent in ascetic Protestantism - its use of the confessional by which the believer could acquire forgiveness for straying from the straight and narrow. Ascetic Protestantism was also more of the 'real world' than monastic, as in the case of Catholicism.

4. Although indicating their great potential influence, Weber did not regard religious belief systems as a single determinant of social change or

stagnation. Maintaining a multifactoral view of change, Weber recognised that religious belief systems would be one of a number of factors of varying importance in different societies at different times in history. For example, another favourable factor contributing to the creation of industrial wealth in England was that as part of an island, less wealth creation was diverted to supporting standing armies than was necessary in a number of European countries that shared borders with potential enemies. For Weber, capitalist modernisation was influenced by a contingent mixture of circumstances, an important one of which was the presence of an ascetic protestant belief system.

5. For Marx, the economic arrangements of capitalism preceded and largely determined the form that religion took, the latter invariably acting back on society as a conservative social force. Weber challenged this economic determinism and materialist approach to religion. In his study of the emergence of capitalism in England, he argued that religious beliefs that were conducive to capitalism tended to precede the economic arrangements of capitalism and promoted the dynamic action which helped to bring it about. But Weber did not challenge the materialism of Marxism with a similarly one-sided idealist account which would emphasise that ideas always determine economic matters. For Weber, the question of causality was always open to detailed analysis. He also recognised that the different positions that people occupy in the social structure may incline them toward different religions beliefs.

6. Weber proposed a powerful theory of secularisation. He argued that over time Calvinism proved to be a religious ethic that undermined religion itself. The rationality and quest for profit maximisation that Calvinism helped set in train, even though driven by the quest for salvation, had focussed action on this-worldly business endeavour. Over time, the values and organisation of modern capitalism that had been set in motion were able to become self-sustaining, enabling rational action to increasingly become a secular orientated end in itself rather than a means to an end in an afterlife. Thus, in time, the cultural belief system of the work ethic remained, but the religious roots of its origin withered. The forces of modernisation which Calvinism helped to unleash were creating an increasingly spiritless and disenchanted world which was dominated by the achievements of scientific and rational thinking and formal and efficient bureaucratic organisations at the expense

of the mysteries of more religious and magical belief systems. Ascetic Protestants had made their own decisions to constrain their lives to relentless work. Without the purposeful intention of bringing it about, Weber argues that the rational and bureaucratic structures of emergent western capitalism have become external impositions from which there is now no escape.

Phenomenology – religion and ontological security

Phenomenological approaches to religion focus on its crucial importance in the construction of meaning. The meaning systems provided by religions are seen to be of the most profound importance as they relate to ultimate questions regarding the meaning of life itself.

A leading exponent of this phenomenological perspective is Peter Berger. In similar vein to Durkheim, Berger recognised in religion the powerful impact of the sacred in commanding awe and respect as a socially constructive feature of religion. For Durkheim, religion is intrinsic to the existence of social formations. But for Berger, the existence of religion has an existential basis in the human condition; it provides a 'sacred canopy' of protection against meaninglessness, which he referred to as the terror of chaos, to which we would be vulnerable in its absence. Religion provides individuals with 'ontological security' – the comfort of universal meaning.

Central to the phenomenological perspective is the distinction between the human and animal condition. Unlike animals, human behaviour is not highly pre-ordered by its biological makeup. However, human intelligence includes the capacity and need to impose meaning on the world. Society is the product of this active creation of shared meaning and provides the civilising influence of the ordering of behaviour.

Berger (1969, Ch.1) identified the main components of this process as externalisation, objectification and internalisation. Externalisation refers to the projection of meaning onto reality. The communication of shared meaning and understanding provides a social environment of belief systems and institutions. These come to take on an independence of their own and become experienced as if they were an external objective reality – the process of objectification. Reacting back on its human creators, this shared social world becomes internalised into the subjective consciousness of individuals. As a result, the actions of individuals take place within the constraints of society as a human product. The creation of meaning and the imposition of order thus act as a shield against social anarchy and in particular the terror of intellectual chaos that would otherwise be experienced by the lack of biological ordering of behaviour and the quest for meaning which is part of the human condition.

Within society, through shared meaning, humans rise above the rest of nature. The capacity to ask ultimate questions about life requires answers to which, Berger argues, only religion can provide a satisfactory meaning system. It plays a key strategic part in maintaining social and intellectual order. This is because it offers an ultimate legitimisation of social meanings and institutions by providing sacred sanction and locating them within a cosmic frame of reference. Religion assists human activity to operate within humanly constructed social constraints which nevertheless appear to have an inevitability of their own and provide a necessary framework of security.

Berger, in his early works, argued that the protection of the sacred canopy required the dominance of a single religion within society to provide the comfort of a single universe of meaning. The discomfort of contemporary life is that with the emergence of a plurality of religions, the plausibility of the scared canopy becomes undermined by questions arising from the choice between alternative religious belief systems or none at all. Secularisation detrimentally sets in, and alternative meaning systems cannot adequately fill the meaning void.

Secularisation – an introduction and overview

In sociology, the term 'secularisation' refers to the assertion that religion is being undermined by forces of modernisation. Key features of the modernisation process include the advance of scientific and rational thinking and their application to understanding an increasing range of phenomena, the development of technology and industry, the process of urbanisation, and the enhanced capacity of humankind to predict and control its environment.

A paradigm, as defined by Thomas Kuhn, refers to the theoretical orthodoxy, viewpoint and set of practices which exist within a scientific community, making it self-sustaining until an accumulation of anomalous evidence can lead to a paradigm shift. Up to the 1970s, in the sociology of religion, secularisation provided a predominant paradigm. Disputes tended to focus on issues of measurement and meaning of evidence, with those disputing secularisation in the minority.

Davie (2013) points out that the background to this paradigm was a very European one which took the form of a powerful theoretical tradition that emphasised the modernising forces of rationalisation, with the secularisation thesis being supported by various measures of religious decline, including falling church attendances within the major churches. Davie, however, suggests that an alternative paradigm has emerged more recently in the United States which challenges the secularisation thesis. Within this American paradigm, rationality takes the form of rational choice amongst a diversity of religions and is applied to explain religious revitalisation. Davie suggests that in recent decades this paradigm is eclipsing the European centred secularisation paradigm. Both paradigms will be reviewed in this chapter.

Measuring the extent of religion in society is a complex matter. Its dimensions range across religious behaviour, belief and belonging and important sources of evidence include the official statistics from religious organisations and social surveys. Key themes include the measurement and interpretation of institutional participation levels, ascertaining the extent and intensity of religious belief, evaluating the degree of church disengagement from societal provisions and functions and, particularly important regarding the different European and American paradigms, interpreting the impact of the advance of religious pluralism.

A European paradigm – progressive secularisation and seeming victory for the rationalists

Developing from the climate of the eighteenth century European Enlightenment, a rationalist tradition emerged which viewed science as a progressive force toward the establishment of truth in the face of religious obscurantism, dogma, and superstition. Through theory, prediction, observation, measurement and testing, rationalists argued that science provided a superior means of achieving certain and grounded knowledge compared to religion that is based on superstition and revelation. The advance of the rationalist attack on religion opened up a 'great divide' between religious beliefs and scientific method.

Viewed in this way, science and religion are incompatible and completely opposed ways of thinking. They can also be seen as essentially inversely related – the more there is of one, the less there is of the other. Therefore, as science, which employs logical method and fact based explanations, provides demonstrable knowledge to explain a growing area of reality, its progress, it is argued, tends to erode understanding derived from religious faith. As Steve Bruce has put it, as the spread of science and technology advances, it enhances the ability of humankind to exert increasing prediction and control over the world and reduces the need to resort to supernatural explanations of events or to appeal to supernatural forces for benign intervention.

Rationalism and the Enlightenment were a powerful influence on the emergence of European sociological thinking in the nineteenth century. Advances in the physical sciences held the prospect and kudos of the extension and application of science to the understanding and improvement of society. This was the aim of positivism – the understanding of society through observation, measurement and the rational analysis of data. Such understanding could assist judicious intervention in society in the form of social engineering. The most influential founding social theorists adopted a rationalistic approach to the study of society. Their personal convictions tended to be atheistic or agnostic and their theories claimed to show that social forces were leading to a decline in theological belief systems. The works of these thinkers provided a powerful impetus for secularisation theory in sociology for a number of decades thereafter.

Secularisation tended to be viewed in unilinear (single line) terms, suggesting that there is a trajectory of social change in the direction of the progress of scientific and rational thinking, setting in motion a cumulative decline in religion, which all societies in time would tend to follow. Rooted in European thinking, this approach suggested that modern secularising European societies held a future image for the 'less advanced' societies. Sociologists such as David Martin, who challenged the secularisation thesis, tended to do so from a phenomenological perspective from which they adopted a more cautious interpretation of the meaning of the evidence. Martin, along with Larry Shiner, also raised the issue of the varied and imprecise use of the term 'secularisation' within sociology.

Behavioural indicators of religion

One way in which sociologists attempt to measure the extent of religion in society is through the dimension of religiously related behaviour. This approach can often be linked to the positivist tradition of looking for hard observational type evidence. An obvious source of such evidence is the availability of organisational statistics showing the extent of public involvement in religious institutions. Those who work in the positivist tradition tend to regard this evidence as reliable (that it is standardised and accurate) and valid (that it measures what it claims to measure – religiosity) evidence by which to gauge the extensiveness of religion in society. For purpose of analysis, official statistics, particularly on church and denominational attendance, are readily available. In Britain, the sources of statistics on church attendance in a range of Christian 'churches' go back to the 1851 Census on Religion (completed by responsible church ministers on the Sunday of the census) and include more recent periodic Church Censuses. This data can be studied to establish trends of change over time.

Overall, these statistics indicate a long-term decline in regular Sunday attendance from a crude estimate of almost 40% of adults in 1851 to now little over 6% by the early twenty first century. Using regular Sunday attendance provides measurement with a degree of historical standardisation. However, given that work and leisure activities are now commonplace on Sundays (itself possible evidence of secularisation), a more contemporary measure of weekly church attendance on any day of the week would seem to be justified. But even by this measure, the figures for the late twentieth century were only closer to 8% of adults, although according to Brierley they indicate a levelling out during the early twenty first century from a long term period of decline. There is evidence of a significantly higher level of just occasional attendance, such as at seasonal church ceremonies, than weekly attendance figures.

Regarding attendance rates amongst those who in Britain identify with a Christian religious organisation, two major surveys have enabled time lines of attendance rates to be drawn to supplement official statistics. These are the British Election Study and the British Social Attitudes Survey. Defining regular church attendance now as at least once a month and excluding special occasions, data shows that at just under 20%, Anglican attendance has flat lined for at least the last four decades. By contrast, Church attendance rates of Catholics have shown a fall from about 70% in the mid-1960s to about 40% by 2012. The trend in attendance levels of those who identify with other Christian churches tends to fall in between those of Anglican and Catholic churches and has therefore shown a gradual decline. According to the British Social Attitudes Survey, there has been a large increase between 1983 and 2012 in the proportions of non-attenders across all groups, usually at the expense of infrequent attendance which shows declining figures (Clements, 2015).

According to official statistics, the numbers of baptisms, confirmations, church weddings and burials have significantly declined throughout the twentieth century. For example, marriages in the Church of England comprised 56% of all marriages in England and Wales in 1929 and fell to 37% in 1973. Following the extension of the availability of civil marriages to approved premises other than register offices, by 2012 total church marriages fell to about 30% of all marriages and marriages in approved premised rapidly increased to 85% of civil marriages.

On the surface, these figures would appear to offer compelling evidence to support the secularisation thesis. There are variations and some exceptions within this general trend though. Firstly, when looked at regionally, in Northern Ireland, figures on attendance (and membership) held up remarkably well for a period of time. Over 70% of the adult population were members of Anglican, Roman Catholic or Presbyterian churches in 1995, with total membership figures slightly up from those of 1980. There has, however, since been a significant decrease in church attendance and membership rates.

Secondly, whilst attendances have declined amongst the main Christian churches and denominations (the latter including Methodists and Baptists), some Christian religious organisations have shown a significant expansion in their membership. Survey figures provided by Brierley show that The Church of Jesus Christ of the Latter-day Saints (the Mormons) and the Jehovah's Witnesses have shown a growth in their membership by around 70% between 1980 and 2010, a trend which has since continued. These are organisations with global followings and have shown themselves to be highly effective in resource mobilisation to recruit new members. The smaller Church of Scientology has seen its membership approximately quadruple over this time period. However, the membership in total of these and other small but growing Christian churches still remains very much a minority one.

Thirdly, the phenomena of 'new religious movements' must be taken into account. There have been definitional problems regarding this category, but at present the term will be applied to a diversity of small contemporary religious groups which may otherwise have been referred to as sects and in particular cults. New religious movements often eclectically utilise ideas from a diversity of sources including eastern and pagan religions. They are usually very loosely organised and often require little formal commitment from their followers. Therefore, precise statistical evidence on 'membership' or participation (attendance would often not be an applicable term as there may not be formal church gatherings) is largely lacking. Whilst probably becoming an increasing feature of contemporary societies, many movements are relatively short lived and it will later be shown that the interpretation of their significance in contemporary society is a highly contested one.

Overall, the figures indicate a decline in religion if religion is measured in terms of church attendance. However, they also indicate a changing balance in which the monopoly of the main Christian churches has given some ground to a greater diversity of religions. This partly reflects the growing ethnic diversity of Britain's population composition but may also be evidence of a more general process of religious fracturing which is taking place with the emergence of smaller denominations and new religious movements. This would appear to be reflected in Brierley's (2014) research (Evangelical Alliance, 28/7/2018) on the opening and closing of church buildings which between 2008 and 2013 showed a net figure of -324 for the Church of England and + 1,899 for smaller denominations. The case made for secularisation therefore is not just about attendance numbers but also has to take account of evidence of divergent patterns of change and greater religious pluralism and what this means.

So far, we have taken official church attendance and survey statistics at face value. However, the reliability and the validity of these statistics can be brought into question, with the following points being particularly pertinent.

There are questions about the reliability of data on church attendance rates that is collected from surveys. There are two main points here. People completing a survey may not accurately recall the frequency or otherwise of their attendance at church. They may forget some of their attendances, thus underrepresenting the true frequency. However, the main distortion would appear to be an exaggeration of claimed attendance when compared to the figures recorded by head counts in churches. For example, according to Hadaway et al (Davie, 2013, p.82), although surveys measured that about 40% of Americans attended church regularly, head counts of actual attendance showed this to be a significantly inflated figure and that the discrepancy between claimed attendance and actual attendance was as high as a two to one ratio. This would appear to be a common phenomenon which also applies to Britain. Although the following measurements are not strictly comparable, British Social Attitude Survey figures for 2014 show 13.1% of the sample claiming to attend church once a week or more, whilst according to information compiled from church Sunday census points

(Humanists UK, 27/07/2018), the figure is closer to 6% and down from 11.1% in 1980.

As well as church attendance figures derived from surveys being likely to exaggerate the extent of churchgoing compared to attendance figures provided by the institutions, even the institutional figures may be subject to upward distortion for vested interests in attempts to keep churches with declining congregations open. Furthermore the purpose for attendance can vary. For example, Humanists UK (27/07/2018) refers to Church of England research which has revealed a conspicuous association between local oversubscribed Church of England Schools and high church attendance which suggests that some parents are attending to gain their children a place in an Anglican school.

Different churches or religions also vary in the importance that they attach to regular institutional participation. For example, in its emphasis on church hierarchy and ritual and sacraments, the Catholic Church arguably places greater importance on communal attendance than the more liberal protestant tradition of the Anglican Church. Further, given the growing diversity of religious life, it is important to consider both the different emphases on attendance and what membership actually means between the different religions. Does attendance and membership therefore really provide a comparable statistical basis of measurement between the different religions, especially given the unknown extent of interest in new religious movement adherents?

Religion as belonging

Religious belonging can be defined in different ways. One measure is that of membership as defined by religious organisations. However, for purposes of measurement, this raises the issue of reliability since different churches construct their statistics on different membership criteria. For example, the Catholic Church traditionally defines its membership as those who have been baptised into the Church whereas for the Church of England membership figures can be taken from its electoral roll or those who attend Easter Day Communion. By such formal measurements, Anglican membership in the UK has shown a steady decline to about 2% on the population by the early decades of the twenty first century.

An alternative and more inclusive measure of belonging can be taken from survey measurements of those who 'identify' with particular religions. On this count, both the British Election Study and the British Social Attitudes Survey point to a significant decline in Anglican identification, the latter survey for example providing figures of about 40% for 1983 and 16% for 2014. By contrast, the proportions of those identifying as Catholic have remained relatively stable at 9.6% and 8.7% respectively, although we have seen that Catholic attendance rates have witnessed a sharp fall from a comparatively high position (Clements, 2015). According to the survey, 6% of the population said that they belong to non-Christian religions.

Membership in the United Kingdom of world religions other than Christian has shown a variable pattern of change but an overall sizeable increase, in this case of over 70% between 1980 and 1995. The most significant increase has been amongst Muslims and Sikhs, together roughly doubling their membership during this period. Since then, followers of the Muslim faith have shown the greatest rise. In terms of the more general measure of percentage of the population, estimates from 2011 Census figures put followers of non-Christian religions at just under 8% of the population. However, attendance and membership figures for these religions tend to be a higher proportion of followers than those of the main Christian religions.

Measuring religion in terms of belief

Another source of quantitative measure of religiosity is through the use of social surveys of the extent and certainty of religious belief. Surveys regularly indicate that religious belief is far more widespread than implied by measurements of institutional involvement and is sometimes referred to as believing without belonging. For example, a 1991 British Social Attitudes Survey found that 62% of respondents could be classified within three religious belief categories ranging from having no doubt about the existence of god to believing at some times but not others.

Whilst such surveys may offer a challenge to the validity of measuring religious belief through church attendance rates, even these relatively high figures may support rather than undermine the secularisation thesis when taken from a number of surveys over time. Thus, comparing survey findings from the late 1950s, Steve Bruce found that there was evidence of a decline in religious belief.

This trend has appeared to continue as the Social Attitudes Survey of 1998 found that only 58% of respondents fell into the same categories of believers as identified above in the 1991 survey. Moreover, the decline was concentrated in the two strongest belief categories. In fact, in the strongest category – having no doubts about the existence of God – figures have shown a gradual decline in Anglican, Catholic and other Christian categories, with the figure amongst Anglicans being the lowest by 2008 at 17.5% (Clements, 2015). In similar vein, a 2014 Survation poll found that 8% of the sample claimed to be very religious, whereas a You Gov poll in the same year put the figure at only 3% (Humanists UK, 27/07/2018).

Surveys have also shown a clear relationship between belief and age. For example, the British Social Attitudes Survey of 2017 found that for 2016, 71% 18 – 24 year olds in its sample professed to hold no religious beliefs. It is only when one gets into the more elderly age groups that surveys now show that those who hold religious beliefs are in the majority.

Nevertheless, there still remains a discrepancy between the level of church attendance rates and the more widespread extent of religious belief, albeit with different levels of belief or certainty that has been measured in social surveys. With this in mind, an argument which cautions the extent of secularisation is the view that church religion still has much following but that religious 'participation' is taking a more privatised form. Bradley, for example, points to the high figures for television audiences watching religious services from their homes. These people, many of whom do not attend church, are expressing an interest in religious matters. For Bellah, pursuing religion as a more private activity allows greater freedom of choice and thus provides a strong index of genuine belief.

However, there are problems with this interpretation. One criticism is that if religious belief is being pursued more privately, it is difficult to be sure of its nature. And a further point, raised by Wilson, is to do with Bellah's preferred definition of religiosity. If people are becoming privatized believers, belief is arguably becoming separated from belonging, which for Wilson is further evidence of secularisation as religion retreats to the private sphere and in so doing becomes deficient in its socially integrating role.

There is also a more profound question which relates to the choice of the social survey as a research methodology. For Wilson, it is no coincidence that those challenging secularisation use social surveys of religious belief to provide evidence of its greater extent and to question the validity of declining church attendance rates as a measure of secularisation. Surveys of belief might record much higher measurements of belief than attendance rates suggest, but they use a methodology which just provides an aggregate measurement of individual belief, devoid of measuring what Wilson argues are the key dimensions of religion – those of participation and community.

Religious pluralism and secularisation

For Wilson, a staunch supporter of the secularisation thesis, religion is defined simply in terms of 'invocation of the supernatural', thereby defining out from consideration belief systems which others might regard as functional equivalents to religion in which belief in the supernatural is absent - referred to as quasi religions. Wilson views the characteristics of a religious society in traditional terms, arguably assisting the ease with which his case for secularisation can be made. His view of a religious society is one of common participation in which religion is rooted in communities. Belief must be complemented with belonging and at societal level a religious society shares one predominant faith which provides social stability and unquestioning authority. From this point of view, declining participation rates within the major churches and denominations provides clear evidence of secularisation. The decline of local communities through the process of urbanisation and heightened levels of geographical and social mobility undermines the continuity of religious beliefs across the generations. And the expansion of a diversity of new religious movements is regarded as evidence that religion has fractured into a scattering of minority cult pursuits which require little commitment, and sects, which suggests that religion is becoming consigned to the margins of mainstream secular society. He argues that a plurality of religions undermines the capacity of religion overall to provide the basis for a single moral order. Moreover, the point is raised that as well as the relative superficiality of many new religions, the question of which religion to choose raises the further question of whether to choose religion at all, thus further assisting the process of secularisation.

We have seen that from a phenomenological position, Peter Berger has argued in his early works that in their everyday lives, people need an ordered sense of reality which requires meaning systems that provide them with the certainty required for ontological security and action. Berger adopted a holistic view of religious meaning systems and looked negatively on the fracturing of world views in an increasingly pluralistic world as evidence of secularisation, doubting whether they can provide the ontological security that a single and dominant religious world view can.

However, the phenomenologist Thomas Luckmann adopted a broader definition of religion than Berger has. For Luckmann, a sense of ontological security can come from within a diversity of meaning systems such as political ideology, support for a football team or following a particular genre of pop music. Whether or not meaning systems derive from religion as conventionally defined, it is argued that they still perform a necessary and similar purpose to that of religion in enabling people to make sense of the world.

Others, particularly from an American context, have argued that religious pluralism is compatible with a religious society. For example, the American Andrew Greeley has pointed out that as some sects in particular and denominations to some extent require a higher level of commitment, intensity of belief and degree of sacrifice from their members than is usually required from churches, religious pluralism may be deepening and reviving religion – a process which he refers to as resacrilisation. Furthermore, it should be noted that religiosity, measured in terms of attendance rates, is relatively high in the United States – the most religiously pluralistic society - compared to other western societies.

Secularisation – a longer term perspective

Wilson appears to offer convincing evidence of secularisation. Like Weber, he closely aligns secularisation to the process of rationalisation but Wilson gives greater emphasis to the influence of scientific advance than to ascetic Protestant sects such as the Calvinists. However, others have argued that some caution may be necessary in assessing the extent of its advance.

One such British sociologist is David Martin. As a phenomenologist, Martin has emphasised that establishing the extent of religious belief is more important than measuring action, and questions the assumption that belief necessarily correlates highly with institutional participation and non-belief with non-participation. From this position, Martin has argued that the relatively high rates of church attendance recorded in the nineteenth century were partly attributable to the quest to show social status which attendance gave people at this time. Attendance rates were particularly high amongst the middle classes and some sections of the working class who wanted to portray a superior image of themselves to that of other workers. As a greater proportion of people were attending church for such secular motives, Martin argues that the validity of the church attendance figures as a measure of genuine religious belief must be questioned. Consequently, the extent of secularisation since this period derived simply from a decline in the figures may be exaggerated due to the misleadingly high historical reference point that they provide.

In taking an even longer range historical view, it can be argued that a strong case for secularisation can be made by contrasting the Middle Ages as a 'golden era' of religion in terms of strong religious cultures and communities and high rates of participation against the 'take it or leave it' religious culture and low participation rates in much of Britain today. However, the validity of this interpretation can be questioned since the image of a past golden religious age has been questioned as being no more than an unsubstantiated caricature. In this vein, Larry Shiner has questioned exactly when and where this golden age was and suggests that firm evidence for its existence is lacking. Moreover, for K. V. Thomas, views of the pervasiveness of religion during the sixteenth and seventeenth centuries are excessively influenced by an image left by elites of the time with regard to established religions and tell us little about the beliefs of the general population. Indeed, McIntosh (Matthewman ed. 2007, p.284) provides evidence from historical recodes which suggests that behaviour in church was often far from pious. Furthermore, at the contemporary end of the historical spectrum, greater credence has been given to the importance of religion which is more likely to be freely chosen rather than externally imposed with the expectation of outward expressions of faith as Martin argues was likely to have been the case in the Middle Ages.

Looking beyond the question of church membership and attendance, there is little dispute that, over the long term, the involvement of the church in different areas of British social life has declined. This process is sometimes referred to in terms of the 'disengagement' of the church from broader society. In this sense, compared to its deeply embedded involvement in European societies during the Middle Ages, the church in contemporary society has retreated from involvement in many areas of daily life, including politics (where although it still retains important state ceremonial roles, in Britain the Anglican Church has occasionally expressed criticism of the social consequences of government policy), health care, the provision of welfare for the poor, education, and as a major patron of the arts. Taking education and the arts as examples, for largely illiterate populations, church services performed an important role in moral educational, with stained glass religious artistic imagery providing visual aid to the religious message. The modern state has taken over as the main provider or organiser of each of the above services. This process has arguably been accompanied by a degree of separation of church from the state, a cooling of relations between these institutions and a growing secular influence in these service areas.

General agreement on the process of disengagement has been met with alternative interpretations regarding the implications for secularisation. For Wilson, this retreat of the church from its rooting in social life provides further evidence of religious decline through its marginalisation from everyday life. For Steve Bruce, secular state provision in people's lives has expanded and church provision has declined. The secular state has grown in power and largely side lined the church from the process of political decision making and thus the influence of the church and religion in society has waned.

By contrast, David Martin argues that the distancing of church from state may have assisted the cause of religion. This is because in the Middle Ages, the church could be more easily corrupted by its involvement in politics. Detachment from politics has enabled the church to specialise in becoming the source of more purely religious ethics and enhanced its social status.

The disputes over secularisation covered in this section have shown that despite much supporting evidence, the issue has not been entirely clear cut. More contemporary theory and evidence will be introduced that raises the issue of a possible revitalisation of religion. As a stepping stone to this position, the question of American exceptionalism needs to be raised.

American exceptionalism?

Survey evidence indicates that 'church' attendance rates in the United States are as high as about 40%, and even if, as Hadaway et al claim, actual attendance rates may be only half this figure, they are significantly higher than in Britain and Europe. According to Finke, church membership in the United States increased from about a third of the population in 1850 to two thirds in 1980. More precise figures from the 'Yearbook of American Churches', show that church membership between 1940 and 1957 increased from 49% of the population to 61%.

This evidence would appear to fundamentally contradict expectations deriving from the secularisation thesis. Since secularisation is supposed to be intimately connected to the forces of modernisation, why were these membership figures increasing at the same time that American was modernising and how is it that the most industrially and technologically advanced nation shows such a high measure of religiosity in terms of church attendance rates compared to Britain and other European societies? Based on this data, is America more religious than European countries? If so, from the viewpoint of the European paradigm and the strong emphasis on secularisation, the question arises as to whether religion in America should be regarded as a special case.

One early attempt to explain of this phenomena was provided by Will Herberg. According to Herberg (1956), in essence, religious institutions adapted to change more effectively and took on a more secular emphasis in the United States, and so, compared to the retention of old medieval dogmas and beliefs inherited in European churches, were able to retain greater plausibility in attracting followers. Moreover, America experienced high levels of immigration up to the mid-1920s. Settlers faced with an unfamiliar environment adopted high levels of religious participation for two complementary reasons. Firstly, continuing or taking up religious participation within their ethnic communities provided a sense of ethnic tradition and continuity in a new land, and secondly, participation corresponded with church going as a requirement of being a good American citizen which they were keen to show. Herberg argued that the pressure of this necessity declined in the second generation of immigrants but re-emerged in the third generation (corresponding with the time period of the membership figures cited above) in the form of a search to re-establish cultural identity. The reasons for the pursuit of religion were therefore strongly influenced by secular purposes. By contrast, the medieval heritage of the European churches created a plausibility gap between their teachings and the needs of a secular orientated population whose adherence it was losing.

An American paradigm – the revitalisation of religion

Altogether new approaches to the study of religion have emerged in the United States which have fundamentally challenged the underlying assumptions of the secularisation thesis. Contemporary western societies have become highly consumerist and diverse, arguably none more so than the United States. Whilst even in Europe, the secularisation thesis has come under increasing attack from postmodern or high modern theoretical approaches, in the American context rational choice theory, pioneered by Stark and Bainbridge has provided the dominant challenge.

Rational choice theory (Aldridge, 2013, pp.73-75, Hunt, 2002, pp.32-36) places religion within the broader context of a free market environment of supply and demand for goods and services. America is a highly pluralistic society and plurality applies to religion in a society where, in contrast to European societies, constitutionally there can be no established church. Rational choice theory retains the idea of the advance of rationality, but applies it to a society of diversity of religious supply to satisfy demand. For Stark and Bainbridge, any decline in religion is not part of a relentless linear downward process but the downward phase of a longer term cycle within which we are now entering an upward phase of religious rejuvenation and reinvigoration. This particularly applies to the United States, but there may be some impediments to the process in European societies.

Why is there an ongoing demand for religion? Rational choice theory locates religion within rewards and costs analysis. Rewards are desirable outcomes which individuals crave but which carry costs in their realisation. Such rewards can include wealth, status, good health and the quest for immortality. The simplest positive choice is in deciding to pursue rewards where it is calculated that the benefits outweigh the costs incurred in their achievement. However, some rewards, though highly desirable, may be very distant, difficult or uncertain in their realisation, or not achievable at all. Moreover, the costs or sacrifices made in their pursuit may seem too high for the choice to be made. This is why religion satisfies a perennial need; it provides 'compensators' in such situations. Compensators are surrogate rewards for those desired rewards that may not be achievable in this world (classically relating to life after death) or painfully costly in their pursuit. Religion is regarded as uniquely placed to fill this role as compensator. The prospect of eternal and blissful life after death is a reward that relies on faith rather than proof. Religion is the only type of belief system which can provide powerful enough compensation for the costs incurred (ie the demands made on the life of the believer) to achieve such ultimate rewards, providing faith for motivation and answering ultimate questions which science and ideological belief systems cannot fulfil. Only some form of supernatural belief in an afterlife can satisfy the quest for immortality.

Stark and Bainbridge argue that a perennial quest for compensators follows from the psychological needs of individuals to pursue challenging rewards and answer ultimate questions. Compensators therefore provide a response to the psychological need for a belief system that acts as a prop in doing so. Different types of religious belief system offer different types of compensator. For example, audience cults are only likely to provide relatively weak compensators, whereas those of cult movements are stronger and will be quite all embracing. Choosing between religious belief systems and their compensators may be a rational one, but the belief systems themselves must include reference to the supernatural.

From the position of rational choice theory, national churches are regarded as like any other nationalised monopolies in that through state support and privileges, they are likely to lose their competitive vibrancy. By contrast, religious denominations, sects and cults are organisations that compete to satisfy the needs of religious consumers and provide a competitive market of free choice through this diversity of religious belief systems. Indeed, rational business like decisions are made within competing religious organisations to adapt their message in the battle for market share. Religious organisations within this environment are thus vibrant and through free consumer choice religion becomes resurgent. This 'new voluntarism' makes religion stronger, not weaker as suggested by Wilson. In the free market of the United States, religions adapt to satisfy individual requirements, compared to the less responsive state religions in European societies which, as a consequence, despite latent belief and need, lose support. Furthermore, from this viewpoint, whatever the religious participation rates were in the European Middle Ages, this period cannot be viewed as a golden age of religion since often participation was not willingly chosen but instead the result of powerful social impositions.

Religion, which provides supernatural belief of reward in an afterlife, offers the ultimate compensation for hardships experienced in this life. Religion will therefore prevail and it is only a question of the forms that it takes. Any tendencies toward secularisation will be self-limiting and religions which neglect the supernatural will decline as they cannot provide adequate compensators for rewards that are very distant and difficult to achieve. From this viewpoint, rather than dismissing new religious movements as superficial phenomena in a largely secularised world, they are seen as part of a vibrant religious revival. As a free market in religion, America is regarded by Stark and Bainbridge to be a truly vibrant religious society.

A number of criticisms have nevertheless been made of rational choice theory. For example, Stark and Bainbridge can be criticised for the psychological reductionism in their theory. If the explanation of social phenomena is reduced to psychological need, then external influences such as marketing and manipulation tend to get overlooked. It can be argued that the role of tradition and emotion which can be important in decisions of religious faith is virtually ignored. A further point raised by Davie (2013, pp.87-88), is that given European history where churches are seen as public utilities rather than competing businesses, a greater supply of religious choice may not necessarily stimulate demand. Instead, as suggested by Gill, the consequence can be an oversupply, smaller congregations, disillusionment and decline. Bruce suggests that the rational choice between religions presupposes the fact that society is essentially rational at the expense of religion in the first place, whilst Wilson goes on to suggest that the high participation rates in the United States belie the secular and shallow nature of religion as mainly providing a choice of recipes for good citizenship. And a further criticism of new religious movements is that theological guidance seen as deriving from divine inspiration is being replaced by religion as a type of plaything in the pursuit of gratification and this worldly experience.

Resource mobilisation theory is another approach to religion with strong American roots. The emphasis here is how in the free market religious organisations effectively use resources as a means of survival and grow by supplying and stimulating demand. This approach has been adapted from pioneering work by Tilly et al. originally into new social movements. Like other organisations in a competitive environment, religious organisations must work hard for their success by maximising the utilisation of the resources at their disposal to win and retain adherents by adopting rational organisational strategies. These resources will include leadership skills and effective organisation, the support of activists, effectiveness in fund raising and capacity to adjust to a changing broader social environment. This framework has been used to explain the remarkable success of such movements as the Unification Church (or Moonies) in America, the Church of Jesus Christ of Latter-day Saints (the Mormons) and the Jehovah's Witnesses.

In summary, the processes and features of modernisation identified by the founding sociological theorists emphasised the importance of the spread of rational thinking and science, and the associated belief in the certainty of its explanations and solutions. A highly secularised, rational and scientific society, variously interpreted in terms of a range of positive and negative characteristics, would be the end point of historical progress. However, the implication that modernisation necessarily leads to religious decline has become increasingly disputed. In American sociology, rational choice theory has provided a prominent explanation of how in a pluralistic free market system religion may be resurgent.

Religion: tradition and reform – gender and sexuality

Contemporary society has witnessed reform toward gender equality, for example in the workplace, improved educational opportunity and achievement levels for females, and changing roles within the domestic sphere. Compared to these advances, there is substantial evidence available to support the view that religion is an essentially conservative force which perpetuates traditional gender inequalities. In most religions, male figures or symbolism have come to predominate. Within most religious institutional hierarchies, women have traditionally been excluded from power by being confined to low level positions. Moreover, religion has often supported the subordinate position of women to men in the family and in society. The major religions may therefore be seen as reflecting and legitimising male power throughout societies across much of the world.

In recent decades, though, in Britain opposition between liberals and traditionalists on the question of the ordination of women has arisen within the Anglican Church. From the late 1980s, the Church sanctioned the opportunity for women to become deaconesses and later opened up access to the higher level of the priesthood. The response of a number of male and female traditionalists was to convert to the Catholic Church which had remained staunch in its opposition to such reforms. Many traditionalists remained within the Anglican Church, but for others reform appeared slow, as demonstrated by the acrimony which resulted from the failure of the passage of a measure to allow women to become bishops to gain the necessary two thirds majorities in all three Houses of the Church Synod in 2012. A new vote in July 2014 resulted in the necessary majorities throughout the Synod for women to have access to the post of bishop – with arbitration available within parishes that object, and within a year six women bishops had been appointed.

On the issue of sexuality, homosexuality had (with age and certain occupational exceptions) ceased to be a criminal offence in Britain following legislation passed in 1967, and from December 2005 secular ceremonies allowed same sex couples to enter into civil partnerships. Legislation has since been passed allowing same sex partners to achieve married status within religious organisations that are prepared to officiate, but the legislation formally excludes this option within the Churches of England and Wales.

An issue which has ignited much feeling and debate within the Anglican Church has been that of the ordination of gay priests. In England, Jeffrey

John, a priest who admitted to having a past gay relationship, stood down from his appointment as Bishop of Reading as a result of much opposition from within the church, and the ordination of a practicing gay priest in the United States was the focus of much attention in the Anglican Church throughout the world. Opponents have been forthright in quoting from the scriptures, whereas supporters have looked to the need for change and tolerance in promoting a feeling of inclusivity for all members of the Church.

More recently (2016), a number of gay clergy have defied the Church line and married their partners and there are calls for Church blessings to be available for married same sex parishioners.

Secularisation revisited

Up to the 1970s, secularisation was a predominant theme within British sociology. Debate was largely waged on methodological grounds as to how best measure religion, with sceptics of secularisation struggling to put persuasive counter arguments. However, during the late twentieth and early twenty first centuries, the religious landscape has changed significantly in ways which are challenging the once pervasive case for the relentless march of secularisation. Two important themes will be picked up on in this section: a) the growth of new religious movements and b) within a global context, issue of fundamentalism and the re-emergence of civilisation consciousness.

a) New religious movements

There appears to be a growing interest in alternative religions in western liberal democracies within the context of an increasingly free market environment. Combining Wallis' and Stark and Bainbridge's classification, world affirming / client and world accommodating / audience sects and cults are well suited to this market environment and are prospering.

Comprising a very mixed bag, new religious movements can be defined as having the following distinguishing characteristics. Firstly, they are not just new in the sense of being relatively contemporary (post Second World War), but that they are usually quite original or they select ideas from religions of other times or cultures which are interpreted and recombined in novel ways. Secondly, especially regarding the types identified above, and in contrast to world rejecting / cult / sect movements, organisation and membership are often relatively loose, unstructured and non-hierarchical, and membership turnover is usually high. Thirdly, although cults and sects are minority movements, they vary significantly in size and some have international following. However, in many cases an exact measure of membership is difficult to establish. Fourthly, the values of some new religious movements may provide common ground with new social movements. A good example of this would be that of New Age religion which, on environmental issues, may hold much in common with environmental protest groups and although the latter are primarily political they may also be viewed as quasi-religious movements.

Sociological explanations for the attractiveness of new religious movements have been varied and include the following.

1. One approach is specific to the conditions of the late 1960s and early 1970s, especially in America, which arguably provided fertile ground for the emergence of counter cultural values and new religious movements. These conditions can be documented as a reactive response to the experience of bureaucratisation, spiritless materialism and the Vietnam War, growing escapism to drug taking culture and an increase in the activities of missionaries promoting eastern religions.

2. Alternatively, Glock (Furseth & Repstad, 2010, p.148) explains attraction in terms of the experience of deprivation. Deprivation may here be viewed economically but could also be seen in terms of other dimensions such as not feeling valued. In these cases, some cults or sects may provide an answer in denigrating material aspiration and enhancing the self-esteem of the member.

3. If a search for fellowship amidst the decline of community in the contemporary urban world and the need to find meaning and identity in a world that is experienced as cold, impersonal and bureaucratic may turn people to religion, why may they not turn to the more established churches? Stark and Bainbridge argue that in a rapidly changing world, more established religions have left gaps in the market that new movements are better suited to fill.

New religious movements have often had to contend with hostile public reaction, (especially within societies less familiar with religious pluralism) viewing them in a common stereotypical way as authoritarian total institutions, led by charismatic personalities who brainwash vulnerable individuals to become mindless followers. In reality, the broader evidence available suggests that very few groups, more likely to be of the world rejecting type (see earlier information on the Heaven's Gate group), conform to this caricature. Even within this type, Eileen Barker demonstrated in her study of the Unification Church that such perceptions that had been applied to this movement were not well founded. She found that, as in the case of most new religious movements, followers of tended to be young, well-educated and of middle class background. Rather than being passive victims, they often made active decisions to experiment with an alternative way of life and rather than becoming manipulated, brainwashed coerced and hooked in, made as active decisions to leave as they did to enter the group.

Richardson (1993) suggests that hostility toward and misperception of new religious movements can stem from a number of vested interests. For example, sections of the mass media have an interest in focussing on any group that can provide sensational stories to maximise their newspaper sales or television viewers. In cases where family breakdown has preceded members joining a religious sect, family members may be keen on moving the focus of attention away from family problems and on to the persuasive techniques of the movement to explain what has happened. And professionals may have a vested interest in providing therapeutic deprogramming help for the indoctrinated that leave the sect.

But what are the consequences of public hostility to minority religious groups? In his study of the Scientology movement in Britain (a world affirming / client cult), Wallis (1993) applied the deviance amplification model – an approach which has been effectively used by labelling theorists to study the dynamics involved between the general public, who feel themselves to be custodians of moral good, and groups labelled as deviant. For Wallis, the initial public reaction to the Scientology movement was one of hostility, framed by the perception of their deviation from conventional social norms. Social hostility generated a siege mentality within the movement and led to enmity toward its detractors. This response was taken by the press as evidence to confirm that the initial hostile public assessment was correct. The mass media constructed and projected to the public a negative stereotypical image of the movement and a moral crusade which induced a public panic reaction against the movement emerged. In Britain, this ultimately led to legal and governmental denunciations of the movement and the refusal to recognise it as a religion or provide charitable status.

When debating secularisation, those who retain a traditional view of religion, which provides a specific definition of what religion 'is', invariably including reference to the supernatural, and are likely to find evidence of secularisation in the process of modernisation. Much depends on how far one is prepared to broaden out the definition of religion. For example, traditional definitions that refer to the supernatural will probably not enable one to classify certain UFO cults in which salvation to believers is promised through messages sent by superior beings as religions. However, the potential for a more broadly embracing recognition of religion is usually substantially enhanced by those who apply a functional approach which defines religion not in terms of what it 'is' but in terms of what it 'does' – for example, it provides a body of sacred beliefs that tie people into a community of shared values. Definitions of this type are more likely to recognise the continuance of religious functions in new quasi-religious forms, possibly even comprising secular belief systems. These may have their own spiritual dimension such as health fads and environmentalism, or in the case of supporters of football clubs revered club symbols, tradition, ritual, collective gatherings and the worship of footballing icons. Perhaps the issue has become more one of change in the form of a fracturing of single world views, growing pluralism of belief systems and diversity of choice than secularisation (although some convinced secularists would equate these very changes with secularisation!), since sociologically it could be argued that in the case of quasi or secular religions the social functions and psychological needs of religion are still being met.

Summarising the growth of religious diversity, Davie (2013) raises two important points. The first is that what was once regarded from a European secularisation perspective as 'American exceptionalism' is no longer exceptional. The second point, which follows on from this, is that a paradigm shift may be under way in sociology from the dominance of secularisation toward rational choice theory and the recognition of religious revitalisation.

b) From ideology to religion

The collapse of the atheistic regimes of the Eastern Block communist states dates from the late 1980s. In many of these states, the Catholic or Orthodox Church had been highly influential in pre-communist times. During the decades of communist rule, religion had been largely driven underground by the state. However, as these regimes came under challenge from reform movements during the 1980s, churches were often allying themselves with the forces of change. A good example of this was the growing prominence of the Catholic Church in Poland during the growth of the free trade union movement 'Solidarity'. As communist regimes collapsed, many societies witnessed a revived influence of Catholic or Orthodox religions.

These changes offer a significant challenge to the secularisation thesis, but the extent of religious revival, or desecularisation, is difficult to ascertain. This is because although religion revived openly, there remains uncertainty about the extent to which religious belief and practice were secretly maintained by people under the old communist regimes. However, the re-emergence of religion can be interpreted as providing support for the phenomenological viewpoint of Berger who argued that only religion can adequately respond to the need for ontological security which is part of the human condition, thus making the revival of religion always a distinct possibility.

A further change of great magnitude has been the rise of religious 'fundamentalism'. This term is fraught with both definitional problems and emotional overtones. It has been questioned whether it provides an equally valid description of the reassertion of traditions when applied to different religions and in different settings and sometimes the less pejorative term of 'neo-traditionalism' is preferred. However, for Bruce, fundamentalism is a valid concept which includes the following components. Fundamentalist approaches to religion emphasise the importance of referring to a source of beliefs which is claimed to be free from error, for the purpose of supplying strict moral guidelines for behaviour. The social significance of tradition as opposed to changes which are regarded as compromising is therefore asserted. These changes may have negatively affected the social status of those to whom fundamentalism is more likely to appeal and an image of presumed past pure religious conditions is held up as something to return to. Yet despite strong opposition to the eroding effects of modernism, fundamentalist movements are not usually averse to the use of modern technology by which to communicate their message. Thus defined, evidence of resurgent fundamentalism poses a major challenge to exponents of secularisation.

The phenomenon of religious fundamentalism has been explained in terms of crisis theory. Explanations under this heading view the appeal of fundamentalism as a response to various aspects of modernisation as crisis.

Fundamentalism has therefore provided, in response, a coping mechanism. For example, the rise of Christian right fundamentalism in some parts of the United States during the 1970s and 1980s can be viewed in the social context of a reaction by the so called 'moral majority' to the growing permissiveness of the late 1960s. American Christian fundamentalists believed that Christian teachings had liberalised too far and in so doing compromised from correct and non-negotiable moral and religious strictures deriving from a literal interpretation of the Bible. The issues that they raised shared some common ground with the political right which came to prominence in the United States (and in Britain) during the 1980s – in particular, the need to return to such basics as the sanctity of family life and sexual restraint outside of marriage. The measures that more extreme factions have been prepared to take have included direct action in the form of threats and extreme violence against practitioners at abortion clinics. Other fringe groups organised themselves as militias in preparation for the coming collapse in the social order – a type of apocalyptic vision of the future.

The actual impact of Christian fundamentalism on mainstream culture in the United States is quite debatable though. For example, for Bruce, the prominence that it acquired is out of proportion to its geographically and numerically restricted appeal and the attention that it caused should be seen as a measure of the largely secular background against which it so clearly stood out.

In Britain, religiously inspired resistance in the 1960s and 70s to the permissive society took a relatively mild form. For example, it emerged in the moral pressure group the National Viewers and Listeners Association which was influential in having films with what was argued to be content offensive to Christian religion banned and sex shops closed down. During the new right governments of 1980s and early 1990s, 'back to basics' was formally more a political than religious campaign, especially aimed at supporting traditional family life. However, more recently, controversy has been sparked by the inclusion of creationist teaching, applying literal interpretations of the Bible to explain creation, in a small number of mainly independent Christian schools. Although hardly fundamentalist, New Labour policy encouraged the establishment of faith schools, even though they require more liberal entrance criteria on religious grounds than some religious organisations would prefer. Under the Conservative led coalition government and subsequent Conservative government, a number of free schools have been opened, some promoting Islamic and other religions of non-western tradition. In some instances, schools have been put under the spotlight for their alleged application of hard line Islamic principles.

The rise of Islamic fundamentalism can be viewed as an attempt to return to literal and uncompromising teachings from the Koran in the broader historical context of the perceived corruption of an Islamic culture that has been in retreat from the influence of westernisation – especially the United States – and Christianity. A momentous example of this religious and cultural re-purification process was the Iranian Revolution of 1979 which overthrew the modernising and pro-Western Shah of Iran. The emerging state was effectively a theocracy – a society ruled by religious clerics in strict accordance with religious strictures. The rule of the Taliban in Afghanistan between 1996 and 2001 provides another example of rule by those claiming adherence to fundamental Islamic principles. Such societies in the grip of resurgent Islamic fundamentalism have been strongly resistant to the political institutions of contemporary western democracies.

The impact of Islamic fundamentalism was brought home most dramatically by the 11 September 2001 attack on the twin towers in the United States. These events, the reasons behind them and the response of the west would seem to indicate the opening up of global fault lines between Christian and Islamic civilisation and a heightening of religious awareness at a global level following the collapse of the communist empire and the ending of ideological opposition between the capitalist west and the communist east. Reversion from political to religious opposition on such a scale could be taken as strong evidence of desecularisation.

Religion, globalisation and civilisation consciousness

There is much debate about the exact nature and impact of globalisation, but to many the world can now be less effectively understood in terms of nation states as relatively closed territorial units with distinct boundaries. Countries are becoming increasingly intertwined as economic, technological, political and cultural forces operate across national boundaries. The technology of the internet enables a new level of the communication and access of religious ideas across the world. Thus, at any location, the potential for choice is greatly enhanced and religions can become more freed from geographical grounding – a process referred to as 'deterritorialisation'. It is possible that, through growing contact between people of different societies and cultures, a greater understanding and tolerance of diversity can emerge. Both Giddens and Beck consider this optimistic possibility, to which Giddens applies the term 'global cosmopolitanism'.

However, it is also possible that globalisation may bring about intolerance and new conflicts. For example, the growth of global capitalism can lead to western (particularly American) values, culture and ways infiltrating and being perceived as imposing themselves on the cultural traditions of the societies that they are seen as 'invading'. Although non-military, such an invasion may nevertheless be experienced as a pervasive attack on cultural traditions. In response, in some cases a rise in nationalism and religious fundamentalism can result. Thus, we have seen that the 1979 Iranian Revolution can be viewed as a response against western cultural and political influence brought about by the reforms of the Shah of Iran. The response took the form of a resurgent Islam which initially took a strongly fundamentalist form.

For Samuel Huntington (2002), by the late twentieth century religion had become renascent within the global context of the emergence of 'civilisation consciousness'. Civilisation refers to the broadest level of cultural identification and religion tends to be the single most important culturally defining characteristic of civilisations. The rise of western civilisation was the rise of Christian civilisation. By the early twentieth century, this civilisation reached its peak of global dominance. Subsequently, powerful ideologies were becoming a driving force of political conflict between states, forcing new rifts and alignments during the Second World War (involving the ideologies of fascism, communism and liberal democracy) and the cold war standoff between the capitalist west and the communist east.

Huntington argues that people naturally search for identity and meaning which defines themselves and others. This is particularly so in a rapidly changing and urbanising world. With the collapse of Eastern Block communism and cold war animosities shaping people's views of the world, cultural, civilizational and religious identities which had remained suppressed during a period of ideological conflict were released and reinvigorated to play this role by filling the vacuum left. Civilisation consciousness has emerged to shape new fault lines of potential conflict throughout the world.

According to Huntington, the latter decades of the twentieth century have seen a global pattern of social and economic modernisation within the context of a religious renaissance. Rather than the modernisation of Islam in the Islamic world, we have seen the Islamization of modernisation, with fundamentalism playing its role in cultural resurgence. Huntington thus provides a more singularly culturalist theory of social change than did Weber – a position from which he has been criticised.

More materialistic arguments deny that culture and religion are the primary force at work in global conflicts. For example, Karen Armstrong views Islamic fundamentalism as a reaction to forces of rapid social and economic modernisation experienced in a number of Muslim countries. She has argued that these strains tend to undermine moderate religious traditions and give rise to fundamentalism - a response which blames the west (often especially the USA) as the cause of changes which it reacts against. Hatred of America by radical groups derives from its perceived arrogance as a superpower and supporter of the main beneficiaries of change – the corrupt feudal oil rich dynasties, which they oppose. In this context, terrorist sacrifices against America and the west can come to be raised to that of religious duty, with the global mass media offering these groups the impact of a global theatre for sensational actions.

Huntington was challenged by Alam (26/3/2019) for making sweeping cultural and religious generalisations when the regions which he identified as bound by a common religious culture and civilisation, such as the Islamic world, are often fractured with their own national and geopolitical disputes and ambitions. Elsewhere, (27/3/2019 and 2008), Alam was highly critical of the primacy that Huntington gave to cultural and religious distinctions as precipitating fault line clashes throughout the world, citing evidence to indicate that there was a greater likelihood of conflict between states within civilisations than of different civilisations. For Alam, conflicts are primarily over economic interests and global inequalities which the clash of civilisations thesis acts as an ideology to hide.

Contemporary European sociological perspectives on religion

In European sociological thinking, high modernism and postmodernism have perhaps had more impact so far than rational choice theory as providing theoretical contexts within which to understand contemporary religion. Both offer frameworks of caution against a secularisation thesis which was so closely bound to the changes associated with European modernisation and the period of modernity. At a general level, both perspectives place religion within the context of contemporary societies in which the individual is seen as set free from the social constraints and intellectual certainties of the modern period. In contemporary society, monopolistic church institutions and optimism in the ability of science to claim a monopoly of truth and control the world for human benefit are argued to be giving way to a growing diversity of belief systems, including religions and quasi religions. Against this general backdrop, there is dispute between proponents of high modernist and postmodernist positions as to the exact nature of life in contemporary society and how fundamental this change from the modern period has been.

Postmodernism – religious and cultural diversity

For postmodernists, in postmodern society individuals are free from the imposition of traditional or modern metanarratives (all encompassing belief systems) which once offered all-embracing truths as well as guidelines for and constraints on behaviour. Dominant religious metanarratives in traditional society (for example, feudal society of the early Middle Ages) engulfed thinking in religious dogma and superstition which provided an essentially non-optional belief system for moral guidance.

The modern period (scientific, industrial and urban) witnessed the emergence of a new metanarrative of rational and scientific truth which promised liberation from the constraints of religion and the guidance of behaviour through rational intellect, but which imposed its own certainties and, in Weber's terminology, an iron cage of rational thinking. This is the context of secularisation theory.

It is argued that what is distinct about the postmodern world is the collapse of all metanarratives and with it a collapse in the perception that there are single universal truths, religious or scientific. Individuals are therefore set free to search for intellectual and moral guidance through a diversity of belief systems and lifestyles, offering bewildering choice in a market in which they are the consumer. Change is relentless and choice of beliefs may take more the form of fashion or status statements as people freely move through different belief systems and lifestyles. In such a society, culture is fragmented and a diversity of new types of religion will emerge as recipes for living which will replace the discredited metanarrative of rational and scientific certainty of the modern period. Religion will thus tend to lose its role as the conveyer of tradition, a situation which traditional churches will find it difficult to adapt to.

There is arguably some evidence to support this process of fragmentation in the form of a growing diversity of 'new religions'. Such religions may appeal to those turning away from institutional religion in a search for greater spiritual meaning in more intimate settings. They may also be chosen as fashion accessories and status symbols, something which has been referred to as 'spirituality shopping'. In Britain, although in aggregate new religions appear to have a minimal following, this following may be increasing, especially if quasi religions are also included. Overall, such belief systems offer evidence of growing diversity and choice in religious beliefs as adherence to mainstream Christian church religions appears to be declining. As David Lyon argues (Flanagan & Jupp ed., 1999, Ch1), freed from the grasp of metanarratives, people still require some form of more micro level narratives by which they can choose to orient their lives and even frequently change.

In his postmodernist writings, Zygmunt Bauman claims that advanced contemporary societies have reached a stage which is fundamentally different from modern scientific and rational societies. For Bauman, the modern metanarrative had enabled individuals to evade moral responsibility in their choice of action through the justification of rationally and institutionally framed behaviour to achieve ends. This had led to many of the disasters of the modern era.

Individuals in the postmodern world have to act more autonomously. They have to seek 'self-determination' and 'self-construction' in a social world without single clearly prescribed models for behaviour. People have to relate to a rapidly changing environment 'reflexively' – they have to engage in constant self-reflection and self-evaluation, processes which enhance moral self-awareness. Consequently, ethical debate becomes heightened and religious type agencies specialising in moral values may gain attractiveness. Ultimately, the diversity of availability places choice and moral responsibility in the hands of the individual.

High modernism – religion and responses to reflexivity

Anthony Giddens prefers to refer to contemporary societies as having entered a high modern stage. Unlike postmodernists, who view society as collapsing into a state of moral and intellectual relativism, Giddens argues that rational criteria can still be applied to distinguish between the viability of different intellectual and belief systems to assist in enlightened social intervention. However, high modern societies face new challenges in applying rational understanding in an increasingly complex and rapidly changing globalised world. Although society is still driven by rational calculation, the application of scientific advances generates unanticipated and sometimes unwelcome consequences, creating a new environment of manufactured risks which raises unprecedented challenges. These include the consequences of global warming or the possibility of economic meltdown.

It is this rapidly changing world of new risks and uncertainties that individuals have to navigate through. They have lost their anchorage in local communities which reinforced social positions, identity and beliefs. This breakdown of traditional social constraints offers unparalleled opportunities for individual self-construction. Faced with diversity and choice of ways of life and belief systems, individuals have to relate to life reflexively – they need to constantly examine their beliefs and life strategies in an ever changing environment in which the risks from action need to be factored in as best as possible. One's life becomes a project of self-creation for which one is responsible. The search for their own belief systems to escape the experience of meaninglessness becomes a continuous and daunting task in which this liberation can be troubling.

In traditional societies, religion provided relatively fixed belief systems and moral imperatives within quite closed social structures. The transition to modern societies undermined pervasive religion and promoted secularisation with the advance of logical thought and the testing of truth through empirical observation. However, Giddens argues that the personal doubt and insecurity which is the product of high modernism leads to a resurgence of religion, for example in new and diverse forms or more dangerous fundamentalist varieties.

In 'Runaway World' (2002), Giddens expresses concern that against the experience of openness in a high modern risk society, some people will feel the need to retreat to tradition as far as turning to religious fundamentalism. He argues that the security of tradition that fundamentalism provides takes the form of certainty and intolerance, pitched against a world of rationalism and uncertainty. Furthermore, what many manufactured risks associated with high modernism and globalisation have in common is their cataclysmic nature. As such imagery is also common to religions, the experience that the world is running out of control can encourage responses in the form of religious revivalism.

Chapter 11

Sociology of the Media

Abstract

The media is defined as all forms communication between people that take place through technologically mediated symbols. The mass media is sometimes viewed as having a direct and controlling effect on people's beliefs and behaviour. This type of position will be considered, challenged, and more nuanced approaches introduced. Alternatively, people may consider themselves to be relatively immune to the influence of the media which is seen largely as a source of entertainment and information. This position will also be questioned. Viewed sociologically, it will be emphasised that both a culture of consumerism and political messaging may be entwined in the conveyance of entertainment and information in subtle ways that we may not be aware of but that shape our view of the world.

A number of concepts that are key to this topic area are introduced, followed by a review of some founding sociological perspectives on the media: those of liberal theory, functionalism, Marxism and neo-Marxism, pluralism, elite theory and symbolic interactionism.

The issue of ownership and control of the media is considered in the context of various forms of corporate growth and related to the power of media corporations and their owners.

Media content, its selection and presentation, is shaped by incentives and outlooks of those working within corporations, especially magnate owners, editors and journalists. These people work within the broader context of a competitive market. This topic area considers influences on the content of the media through regulatory control, political influence and the need to appeal to advertisers and the public. An analysis of the agenda setting capacity of the media to the public is undertaken, as well as issues of newsworthiness and presentation of media content.

Regarding media content, a section looks at how this may be measured by considering content analysis and semiotic approaches. However, in the following section, the reader is alerted to the fact that measurement of content, even if manipulative intent is shown, should not necessarily be equated with direct and predictable effects on audiences. In this section, a number of models of media effect are considered, some of which do emphasise the potential for mass manipulation whilst others regard the public as more active and resilient via-a-vis the influence of the media.

The topic of public service and commercial broadcasting is introduced, along with the question of the fate of public service broadcasting within a more competitive and deregulated market.

Up to this point, much of the chapter content refers to traditional or mass media. However, the following section takes account of the emergence of 'new media' in relation to the technological developments of digitisation and the internet, paving the way for social media. The question of the extent to which new media challenges the traditional mass media, as well as optimistic and pessimistic interpretations of its impact, are considered.

Media content can shape representations of people, for example in terms of the portrayal of characteristics of gender and ethnicity. A section in this chapter considers the form that these representations have taken and how they have changed along with broader social change.

Social and cultural implications of the globalisation of the media touched on in this chapter include its effect on the perception of time and space, the implications of mass and social media for democratic public debate and arguments regarding media imperialism.

The chapter concludes by identifying postmodern and high modern explanations of the highly mediated reality of contemporary society. Those who argue the society is entering a postmodern stage relate the media to the breakdown of social structures and the emergence a bewildering diversity of meaning and the freedom of identity formation in a world in which illusion becomes the new reality. High modernists, whilst acknowledging the growing necessity for individuals to constantly reappraise their self-identity under social conditions of fluidity and uncertainty, argue that the media can play an important role in helping them to navigate this process.

The sociological challenge

Humans have the capacity to attribute meaning to symbols as a means of communication. This communication may operate at a face-to-face level where it takes place through the direct exchange of linguistic sounds that are part of a culture of commonly understood meaning. Likewise, experience of events may be direct through our personal participation or observation.

The development of the media refers to the means by which communication of meaning can be released from face-to-face interaction and the necessity for direct participation in or observation of events. This may be through written texts. The capacity to mass produce texts and the spread of mass basic education enabled the advance of this form of mass media – essentially, a one way flow in the written communication of meaning in a standardised form.

Through the technological inventions of the telegraph, telephone, radio and television, media were developed by which communication became possible without the need for the physical transportation of the medium itself. As devices for reception became commonly available, the capacity for mass media communication massively increased. The development of satellite and internet communication and powerful appliances for receiving and sending information have advanced communication through media even more in people's lives. A vast proportion of what we know about the world is now received by such means rather than face-to-face communication or direct experience. What are the implications of this?

We might realistically refer to our social environment as being media information saturated. The world that we 'know' is an immensely complex place and the information available to us now is of global proportions. Most of what we see and believe about the world is now mediated to us through the imagery of media, with no alternative direct means of testing its veracity. This reliance gives the media huge potential in shaping our consciousness.

There are, however, two simplistic and somewhat contradictory but commonly held views regarding the impact of the media (especially mass media) that we need to guard against. The first is that the media has a direct and controlling effect on people through, for example, exposure to media violence 'causing' violence, or by people being easily manipulated by others on mass to think in a particular way through their exposure to the mass media. Alternative academic approaches to the question of media effects tend to regard these views as misleading and over simplistic.

The second view is that as individuals it is easy to feel that it is only others, 'the masses', who may be susceptible to this degree of media impact or manipulation and that we are somehow immune to its influence. Yet, to others who also adopt this viewpoint, it is us who become seen as part of that manipulated mass and they are felt to be immune. We should therefore question both the manipulation of the masses view and that of the immunity of the individual.

From these introductory comments, a number of points can be raised:

1. It is important to recognise that we may each be complicit in making ourselves prisoners of our world views through the comfort derived from actively selecting mass media output or social media acquaintances that we know are likely to confirm our views. Yet however true this may be, it raises a broader question of the diversity of media output that is available within which such choices are made. The very view that all viewpoints are catered for is itself a media construct which may not stand up to scrutiny.

2. Media content can entertain, inform or advertise etc., but it is important to appreciate that these categories are not mutually exclusive. What can appear to simply be entertainment may also be advertising and subtly influencing our views on life and our values. Its influence may be political in a broad sense of the term by conveying the view that certain institutions and ways of thinking are natural and justifiable by the omission of other alternatives.

3. Although we live in a media engulfed world, as sociologists we need to take a step back to study it as impartially as possible. For example, like the everyday citizen, the sociologist of the media will be studying its content. However, for the sociologist, the posture is likely to be a different, more detached one. Rather than becoming absorbed in the topic material as an end in itself, the sociologist may look for evidence of manipulation techniques employed in the use of language and presentation of materials, whilst also being aware that individuals are not necessarily passive in their reception of this information.

4. Stepping back to study the media, it is worth returning to the comments in the first paragraph of this section. Compared to the ability to base our own interpretations of the world on our direct experiences, we need to appreciate the extent to which representations of the world are media saturated.

Despite this, media content comprises only an infinitesimally small amount of the goings on in the world. The selection of mass media content and the way that it is presented is the outcome of institutionally organised processes in the manufacture of the messages, and that this may be political not just in obvious terms of bias (Lukes' first face of power), but in focusing the agenda of legitimate public debate to the exclusion of alternative topics and viewpoints (Lukes' second face of power).

Definition of main concepts

The term **mass media** was once singularly applied to media communication. The focus at the time was restricted to the media that were available. This might now referred to as the **traditional media**, essentially comprising the distribution of printed sources such as newspapers, books and magazines, and electronic communications via radio and television, all in the form of standardised communication of information flowing from producers to mass audiences as recipients of the content.

An important distinction can be made, at least conceptually, between situational reality and mediated reality. **Situational reality** is that experienced by people directly, as, for example, when people interact face to face with neighbours or with colleagues in the workplace. **Mediated reality** refers to images of reality conveyed through such symbolic means as text, pictures and sounds conveyed through a medium of communication. This may take an immediate interactive form, as in the case of a telephone conversation, a delayed interactive form, as transpires through social media, or non-interactive form, as is primarily the case with traditional mass media. Regarding the mass media in particular, receivers of communication may be people who have or who often have not had direct experience with the specific reality depicted. The understanding of this depicted reality may be a very different one between people in these two different situations.

This leads to the question of **media effects.** Mediated reality can only comprise a very small selection of a highly complex reality. It is the end process of a manufactured product in which people such as journalists and editors make decisions on what to include and exclude and how to present the content. **Audiences** are the recipients of this content. The potential for distortion or bias in the material and the possibility of manipulation of audiences may be substantial. However, there is in fact much dispute over the potential for such audience manipulation. Some postmodernists have argued that society is now becoming so **media saturated** that situational reality has effectively collapsed into mediated reality.

Mass media output is the product of media organisations. Some media organisations have been very successful in growing in size into very large businesses or corporations through mergers or takeovers. The forms that this may take can vary, and a simple classification frequently used distinguishes between the following types of organisational growth. **Horizontal integration** is a process of the coming together of similar media organisations. For example, as one newspaper company may take over another newspaper business or a publisher may take over another publisher.

By contrast, **vertical integration** is a form of integration whereby a business acquires ownership of other businesses in the same industry but operating at an earlier or later stage in the productive process. An example here would be a newspaper company acquiring a papermaking company and or a chain of newspaper outlets.

Through a process of **diversification**, a media company may spread their involvement into a broad range of media activities and even venture into non-media enterprises such as hotel or leisure centre chains.

The term **'tabloids'** or **'red tops'** has traditionally been applied to newspapers that compete for mass circulation. To maximise their sales, publishers of tabloids must be careful not to pitch the message above the heads of their readers. Consequently, in the competitive media industry, especially regarding battles for newspaper sales, the term **tabloidisation** has been used to suggest that there are pressures to 'dumb down' the quality of content and communication toward that of the tabloids in battles for audiences.

Infotainment, a term coined by Franklin, has been used to suggest that news content has become shaped and dumbed down by competitive pressures to gain advertising revenue and public attention through a preoccupation with the lives of celebrities and lightweight issues of public interest at the expense of coverage of more serious matters.

Stereotyping refers to the application of catchall categories to sections of the population that are deemed to share common characteristics. Use of stereotypes is more common in the tabloid press as it enables shorthand communication of the assumed characteristics of those who fall into the category. By such means, benefit claimants have for example been disparagingly labelled as 'social security scroungers' and immigrants as 'aliens'.

The term **scapegoating** refers to the channelling of blame for a problematic situation onto those who were not its cause. Sections of the tabloid press have often been criticised for scapegoating vulnerable groups such as immigrants and refugees as the cause of social ills. This focusses attention away from a more nuanced consideration of other possible causes.

One way in which the focus of public attention may be influenced is through the **agenda setting** capacity of the media. Agenda setting refers to the tendency across the media to pick up on common themes for public discussion through inclusion or exclusion of issues for attention. The mass media was traditionally viewed as a powerful force its ability to set the public agenda.

The **public sphere** is a concept used by Habermas in relation to democratic political involvement. It is an area outside of private life that provides space for rational debate and discussion through which public opinion can be rooted. Habermas has argued that with the development of capitalism, the power of the mass media has damaged the public sphere and democratic politics through its capacity to dominate public opinion.

Technological developments in the form of the internet and social media, along with the devices through which they can be accessed and contributed to, have vastly increased the content, speed, interconnectivity and geographical range of media output. These developments, referred to as **new media**, have enabled individualised media input by, for example, citizen journalists.

New media has arguably introduced a far more active ingredient into the media sphere whereby issues circulating through social media can become viral and challenge the preferred agenda of those who have traditionally held sway over mass media output. On the other hand, **social media** may often pick up on themes already established in the more traditional media, as well as encouraging a preoccupation in trivia. An important question to consider is the extent to which traditional and new media work as alternatives or in a complementary way and the degree to which the media as a whole has changed as a result.

Founding sociological perspectives on the media

Liberal theory – media freedom assists the advancement of truth

In classical liberal theory, a positive link between the media and individual freedoms was established. It was argued that the free press promotes accountability of authorities to public scrutiny, and thus serves the public interest. This position draws on the eighteenth century Enlightenment tradition within which writers were applying rational scrutiny to question traditional belief systems and social structures, sometimes in the face of censorship which they opposed.

In England, John Stuart Mill, writing around the middle decades of the nineteenth century, argued that the great virtue of freedom of the press is that it promotes unrestricted discussion. For Mill, this had the general benefit of augmenting progression toward the truth and the virtue of encouraging scrutiny of and possible modification of individuals' own views in this direction. Challenges to the intellectual obstacles of dogma and sectarianism and a closer approximation to the truth would emerge within an environment of unfettered contesting of views and opinions amongst engaged individuals (Barlow & Mills, 2009, Ch.4).

The optimism of this model may now seem rather naïve. In an era of corporate capitalism, the power of contemporary media corporations to shape public arguments and opinions would seem to be immense, with the risk of 'truth' being at best selective and at worst a casualty.

Functionalism – the media promotes moral and social consensus

Also writing before the radio and television era, Durkheim had little to say on the role of the mass media in society. However, some important points can be deduced from the perspective that he developed.

Functionalism is a holistic theory which adopts a consensus view of society. Viewed as whole entities, societies are seen as comprising systems of interlocking institutions. Individuals are integrated into society through socialisation into a body of broadly agreed norms, values and moral codes which are synchronised with and backed up by legal sanction. A key function of the institutions of the mass media is to reflect society's norms, values and moral codes back onto society, thus promoting a binding effect between its individual members and assisting in the promotion of social consensus and stability which is regarded as a healthy social condition.

Durkheim acknowledged, however, that the advance of freedom and diversity within modern liberal societies may blur the boundaries between morally acceptable and unacceptable behaviour, to the potential detriment of social cohesion. Furthermore, he maintained that society can never be eradicated of crime and deviance. Thus, although 'crime…consists of an act that offends certain very strong collective sentiments…crime is normal because a society exempt from it is utterly impossible' (Durkheim, 1964b, p.67). Just what did Durkheim mean by this and how is it relevant to the role of the mass media?

Durkheim argued that in modern societies moral consensus can only be maintained through the criminality of some who transgress this consensus and are held up as a reminder of where the boundaries between morally acceptable and unacceptable behaviour lie. From this, it can be argued that the mass media play an important functional role in a) identifying and calling out behaviour which is regarded by the moral majority as criminal or deviant, b) enlisting a moral response to transgressions, and c) showing to the public the penalties for criminal or deviant behaviour. In so doing, the mass media rallies support for the norms and values that have been infringed and helps to maintain moral consensus for the benefit of broader social cohesion.

In addition to this predominant function, Lazarsfeld and Merton (1948) identified a status conferring function of the media; individuals who appear in the media are likely to gain enhanced social status. However, it is also likely that a degree of pre-existing social status will enhance the likelihood of a person's media appearance in the first place.

McQuail (2000, cited in Long & Wall, 2009, pp.244-245), itemised further functions of the media in terms of the uses and gratifications that it can provide for individuals, including escapism from the travails of everyday life through the provision of fantasy and entertainment.

Working within a functionalist framework, Robert Merton was also interested in developing the concept of 'dysfunctionality'. A 'dysfunction' refers to a negative function – something which is damaging to individuals and especially the social fabric. Applied to the mass media, Lazarsfeld and Merton identified a 'narcotizing dysfunction' whereby passivity can result from excessive preoccupation with the media.

Marxism – the media promotes ruling class ideology

Like Durkheim, Marx had little directly to say on the role of the mass media in modern society, the defining characteristics of which he identified as free enterprise capitalist. However, there are clear leads that have been taken up within the Marxist framework. In contrast to a functionalist perspective on the media with its emphasis on its positive role in social consensus building, Marxism locates the mass media within a social structure divided into social classes that hold opposing interests. Economics is at the heart of classical Marxist analysis. Under capitalism, the economically dominant owners of private enterprise form a capitalist ruling class. The owners of private media companies are part of that capitalist class. They own the means of production of ideas, giving them the capacity to project an image of society that is natural from their class position which legitimises the system within which they are primary beneficiaries into the minds of workers, who, Marx claims, have structurally opposed class interests.

It is at this point important to distinguish between the concepts of propaganda and ideology. The use of the mass media to produce and convey propaganda messages is viewed as the conscious manipulation of the world view of the relatively powerless by the powerful with the purpose of serving the latter's vested interests. However, Marx was more interested in the way that an image of society as being a natural hierarchy tends to be systematically generated within capitalist systems. This systematically distorted image is what Marx meant in his use of the concept ideology. As Long and Wall (2009, p.285) put it with reference to the social generation of ideology, 'there is a dynamic mechanism at work within power structures, by which they become self-justifying and 'natural' to a point where they are unquestionable. The mass media largely reflects this ideological realm'. Its effect on the shaping of (false) consciousness is therefore regarded as immense.

However, occasional economic malfunctions built into capitalism can become trigger points for working class mass discontent that can have a liberating effect from the grip of false consciousness, enabling them to see through ideological distortion and recognise that their true interests lie in overthrowing capitalism. Thus, both the capacity for class domination and the possibility of a revolutionary response are analysed as largely determined by economic factors, making classical Marxist theory vulnerable to the charge of economic determinism.

Neo-Marxism – cultural and political effects of the media

The failure of communist revolution to be sparked in situations of economic malfunctioning in advanced capitalist societies during the twentieth century led to revisions of Marxist theory that placed less emphasis on the determining effect of the economy on society and more emphasis on the importance of the cultural realm within which ideology is situated. Here, brief reference will be made to two such approaches, that of the Frankfurt School and Gramsci's theory of hegemony.

The Frankfurt School of neo-Marxism emerged in Germany during the 1920s. Led by Max Horkheimer and Theodor Adorno, a pessimistic view from within a Marxist perspective was developed regarding the possibility of workers resisting dominant ideological conditioning and political propagandist broadcasting through the radio that they witnessed in the rise to power of Hitler's Nazi Party.

Fleeing to the United States, their account of the effect of the mass media under a liberal form of capitalism was equally pessimistic. Here, they viewed the mass media as playing a key role in the trivialisation and de-politicisation of culture in the form of rampant consumerism as an end in itself.

The German theorist Jurgen Habermas developed a more contemporary Frankfurt School position on the role of the mass media and the relative passivity of the masses under capitalism. Habermas analysed the historical development of the public sphere and the emergence of the mass media as the destroyer of meaningful democracy with the advance of capitalism. During the seventeenth and eighteenth centuries, coffee houses, salons and literary, philosophical and scientific debating societies, as well as small circulation periodicals, provided a space for vibrant public debate; a public sphere intermediate to the state and the family through which public opinion was autonomously generated by process of rational discussion. That, in theory at least, anyone could potentially participate through the force of their arguments and irrespective of their social status made this a relatively open and democratic process of opinion formation. However, the commercialisation of the mass media since the nineteenth century became so powerful that it captured the public sphere from above, leading to its collapse as vehicle for democratic opinion making from below. This marked a transition from a public sphere of political debate to a public sphere of mass consumers, dominated by the interests of a small class through the mass media to win their public approval. For Habermas, politically all that was left was a type of phantom public sphere.

The question arises, can the public sphere be rejuvenated and democracy regained under capitalism? On this point, Habermas was less pessimistic than his Frankfurt School predecessors, particularly in his later works where he saw some hope of a developing public sphere through a greater plurality of groups raising issues at a transnational level regarding, for example, poverty, human rights and environmental issues.

Applying Habermas' ideas to the emergence of social media, a key question to consider is whether it will tend to challenge or reinforce the dominant institutions of capitalism and their supporting ideology. Even if it is effective in rejuvenating public sphere democratic engagement, could it then become colonised by powerful private enterprise and political interests that play such a dominant role in opinion formation and are able to frame discussion from above within a narrow range of acceptable viewpoints?

Antonio Gramsci's revision of Marxism was written in conditions of prison confinement under the fascist regime of Mussolini. Gramsci's departure from more economic determinist variants of Marxism is encapsulated in his theory of hegemony. Hegemony refers to the need to rule by consent and not force alone. For ruling class hegemony to be effective, it must constantly work at persuading those governed that prevailing social conditions are legitimate. Ideological distortion of reality and false consciousness of the subject class play a significant role in this.

However, they can never be total. Although advantaged by their control of media institutions, ruling class ideological dominance of working class consciousness can never be complete. This is because a) the conditions that workers live under will always provide them with glimpses of an alternative consciousness for developing counter hegemonic ideas, for example through the radical press, that can guide resistance, and b) social conditions are constantly changing, providing openings whereby consent to the rule of the ruling class can be challenged. Therefore, the ruling classes have to remain vigilant to the possibility of making timely concessions and retreats to hold on to their dominant position, whilst the working class need to develop a coherent alternative hegemonic vision if they are to do more than fight battles of attrition.

Pluralism – the media reflects social diversity

Pluralist theory, as developed by American writers such as Robert Dahl and Herbert Gans, reached its peak of popularity during the 1960s and 1970s.

Advocates of this perspective lauded the virtues of capitalist representative democratic systems within which political and business powers were seen to be held accountable to citizens as an electorate, through pressure groups, and as consumers. This social and political theory provided the context for an account of the role of the mass media as responsive to rather than manipulative of public opinion.

According to this perspective, audiences, as consumers, are in the driving seat. To understand the role of the media in democratic free enterprise societies, of which America was regarded as at the forefront, a starting point is the recognition of a diversity of interests and opinions held by citizens. As audiences and consumers, citizens subscribe to media output by freely choosing that which reflects their viewpoints and preferences. Under the competitive conditions of free enterprise capitalism, media organisations have to seek out the opinions and interests of the public, or the section of it to which they are aiming their appeal, to satisfy the needs of media consumers in order to maximise their profitability. The overall balance of media output is thus attuned to meet the diverse needs of the public.

In contrast to the early Frankfurt School writers, the public are not viewed as a passive and manipulable mass audience but are active in their selection and interpretation of mass media output. Attempts to systematically manipulate audiences would go against the grain of pre-existing public opinion and result in a decline in media market share. Moreover, any audience demands that were not catered for would leave a potentially profitable opening for a new media organisation to exploit.

From this perspective, the range of media output is broad and diverse, reflecting the breadth and diversity of public opinions and interests. If hard left newspaper and magazine circulation is very small, this is not seen as a consequence of mass manipulation of the public against its stance, but simply the result of limited popularity of these views in the first place. At the end of the day, the profile of overall media output would be shaped by the requirement to satisfy the diversity of consumer needs through the economic incentives of the free market.

Elite theory – the power of the media in mass society

A number of sociologists in the classical tradition, notably Durkheim, Weber, Simmel and Tonnies, commented on the 'loss of community' that was claimed to have accompanied the advance of the industrial society from the latter half of the nineteenth century, only to be replaced by more superficial associations between people in the industrialised and urbanised world.

The elite theorist C. Wright Mills (1956) documented like changes in public life from a condition of thriving primary groups, referred to as 'communities of publics', to a 'society of masses'. Communities of publics involve direct discussion amongst participants in the process of opinion formation, providing a degree of democratic autonomy from elite control. In theory, the media can enhance this process. However, elite unease regarding this public autonomy furnished the need to control and manipulate the public. The means to do so was provided by the technological advance of the mass media. Its increasing dominance was paralleled by a decline in 'communities of publics', the outcome being a mass society of individuals whom are vulnerable to mass media manipulation. According to Mills, the decline in community led, particularly in 1950s America, to a fragmented mass society within which individuals had become increasingly dominated and controlled by elites who had at their disposal an ever more sophisticated mass media in the hands of large institutions (Barlow & Mills, 2009, Ch.12). Mills' elite theory of the role of the media therefore strongly challenged the democratic accountability model put forward by pluralists.

The social fragmentation has meant that the grounding of our understanding of the world through direct communal experience is being replaced by knowledge mediated through mass media stereotypes to the extent that people need a media provided framework to trust their own experiences. This takes us back to Mills' discussion of personal troubles and public issues. The mass media avoids providing vantage points whereby the troubles experienced directly in people's personal worlds can be connected to the broader social structure and related public issues, thus undermining the potential form autonomous collective political action. The institutions of democracy may remain, but elite control of public life through an invasive mass media depoliticises the outlook of the fragmented masses and limits their horizons to the desire for commodities. For Mills, real democracy can only be reasserted if the public are able to regain control of opinion formation and the capacity to connect personal troubles to broader public issues and act to influence social conditions according to the insights obtained.

Symbolic Interactionism – media generated 'moral panics'

The focus of symbolic interactionist theory in its founders such as Mead and Cooley has been on the study of the ways in which meaning is exchanged at the micro level and its effect on self-image creation. Within this perspective, Howard Becker later showed how groups can be defined as deviant through others having the capacity to successfully label their actions as outside of acceptable social norms. Sociologists working within this perspective have particularly studied the effects of labelling on the behaviour of those labelled. Becker, however, had little to say about the role of the media in this process.

Through the advance of media technology, symbolic communication at a face to face level has been powerfully supplemented by the mediated reality of a range of mass and social media communication. Regarding the mass media, those working within a symbolic interactionist perspective have broadened their vantage point to study the dynamics involved whereby the media play a key moral crusading role in identifying the actions of some groups as a threat to social values that are broadly held dear.

Pioneering research within this perspective has been conducted by Jock Young and Stanley Cohen. Young's research was of a media fuelled crime wave panic regarding marihuana users in the Notting Hill area in the 1960s. Young found that through media highlighting and exaggerating the deviant lifestyle of the users, subsequent intervention by the authorities alienated the deviant community and enhanced a hippy culture identity.

In a classic study of the emergence of the mods and rockers phenomena in the 1960s, Stanley Cohen explained the mass media's role in 'deviance amplification'. Cohen identified the broader 1960s social backdrop as one of an emergent youth culture questioning of authority of an older generation. This social condition was one of vulnerability to the emergence of 'moral panics'. As Cohen stated (1973, p.9), it is particularly at such times that

> 'a condition, episode, person or group of persons emerges to become defined as a threat to societal values and interests; its nature is presented in a stylised and stereotypical fashion by the mass media; the moral barricades are manned by editors, bishops, politicians and other right-thinking people.'

For Cohen, the tabloid media played a key role in sensationalising an initially limited level of youth violence on an Easter bank holiday in Clacton in 1964.

Working with 'respectable' public opinion and led by 'moral entrepreneurs', these reports helped to generate a moral panic imagery of youths on the rampage. This set in motion a process of 'deviance amplification' whereby:

1. Two opposing deviant group identities of mods (motorbike riders) and rockers (scooter riders), each with their own identifiable clothing, formed.
2. The publicity helped recruit more disaffected youths into the groups.
3. The media predicted forthcoming bank holiday clashes at seaside resorts.
4. The presence of the media at these locations at the predicted times to report on events, along with the police and curious onlookers, provided a stage upon which ritual conflicts would be acted out on for years to come.

From the point of view of this perspective, and without denying a degree of violence which was initially present, one might question whether, had an alternative major event captured the news headlines during the skirmishes at Clacton over the 1964 Easter bank holiday period, this particular phenomena would have even materialised.

This perspective, within a broader neo-Marxist framework, was utilised by Stuart Hall to provide insight into the role of the mass media in the social construction of a 'mugging' panic during the early 1970s in which young black males became the folk devils.

Corporate ownership, media power and the issue of control

The pattern of media ownership is particularly important because as a source of information the media can have a powerful influence on shaping public perceptions and debates. In totalitarian political systems, the mass media is completely state controlled and used as a direct instrument of government. Striking examples from twentieth century history have been provided in Nazi Germany and the Soviet Union. In the latter, the function of the state owned mass media was to communicate to the people a cohesive and positive world view that conformed to official communist doctrine and denigrated capitalist societies. At its height, the system relied on the capacity to screen out sources of information from western capitalist ideological opponents that might challenge this world view.

By contrast, as applauded by supporters of liberal and pluralist theories, the virtues of privately owned media in capitalist liberal democracies are that a broad range of public outlooks and interests are catered for. This section will look at patterns of media ownership, primarily within the liberal democracy of the UK. The key issue touched on will be that of forms of media corporate growth and, implicitly and explicitly, the challenge that this might pose to the viability of the pluralist model.

Private enterprise under free enterprise conditions is driven in large part by the quest for profit maximisation and corporate security. This can generate tendencies toward oligopoly – the market being dominated by a small number of large corporations. One motivation that can bring this about can be the economic advantage of economies of scale whereby bulk ordering and production can lower unit costs compared to those of competitors. The media industry is no exception. Particularly through the process of mergers and takeovers, media corporations have been seen to grow rapidly. A politically promoted climate of deregulation has been beneficial to enabling media empires to grow in a number of ways.

(Laughey, 2007, pp.134-138) refers to a classification system of media company growth that was developed by Murdock and Golding in the 1970s which identified dynamics of concentration and diversification in media mergers and takeovers. This system, with one small refinement, can be summarised as follows.

The simplest form of media business integration can be referred to as horizontal. In this process, media companies merge with or take over companies of the same type. Thus, newspaper publishers may acquire ownership and control of more newspaper titles, as did Rupert Murdoch in his acquisition of the quality newspapers the *Times* and *Sunday Times* in 1981 to add to his News UK (formerly News International) holding of the tabloid newspaper the *Sun*.

Alternatively, growth through vertical integration can take place when businesses expand upwards or downwards in the media production process. As an example, corporations that produce newspapers may take over paper supplier companies further down the production chain and / or supply outlets further up the chain to increase their control over the flow of supplies and availability of outlets for their product. Vertical integration in the film industry can be illustrated by 20th Century Fox and Warner Brothers Entertainment in the United States who, as well as producing films, own film studios and chains of cinemas.

Before moving on to Murdock and Golding's classification of diversification, a strategy of lateral expansion can be identified. By these means, corporations engage in cross media diversification but within the broad media industry. For example, Murdoch's News Corporation acquired extensive holdings throughout the world in a range of media, including terrestrial, cable and satellite television, newspapers and magazines, film studios and book publication.

Full diversification, in Murdock and Golding's sense, takes a broader form whereby media organisations branch out into different activities altogether, as in the case of Virgin diversifying from its early media base in record production to other media ventures such as radio, mobile phones and publishing, and beyond media to other business interests including airlines, railway franchises and banking.

Apart from economies of scale and control over supplies and outlets, what other corporate benefits can be derived from expansions? One is that of crossover benefits. Corporations that own a diversity of media products can benefit from cross advertising. Murdoch's News Corporation was able to adopt this strategy by, for example, advertising its satellite television in its newspapers. This process can run quite broadly in highly diversified corporations.

Another type of crossover benefit is that of cross subsidisation. During 1997 and 1998, the then News International was able to slash the price of the *Times* at a loss to the paper and to the detriment of its competitors through the profits made from its parent corporation, News Corporation (Street, 2001, p.128). By such means, large corporations can damage or eliminate competition and the massive investment involved to enter the market can form a barrier to the diversity that could be provided by new entrants.

The strategy behind a high level of full diversification is usually that of enhancing corporate security by spreading risk in the context of changing market conditions.

But what are the consequences of such corporate growth for the consumer of the media? The *UK Media Ownership Report*, commissioned by the Media Reform Coalition (6/2/2019), have documented what they regard to be an unhealthy degree of concentration of media ownership, exemplified, for example, in the following facts:

1. 71% of national newspaper circulation derives from just three newspaper corporations: News UK, Daily Mail and General Trust, and Trinity Mirror,

and when online readers are included five companies command 81% of market share. These concentrations, it is claimed, are creating a 'democratic deficit'.

2. 80% of local newspapers are owned by just six regional newspaper organisations, resulting in a lack of focus on local community news, producing what is referred to as 'news deserts'.

3. Just two conglomerates control almost 40% local analogue radio licences and two thirds of commercial digital radio stations.

The fact that media output is concentrated into the hands of a small number very large and powerful corporations is a process that is sometimes less obvious when businesses taken over retain their original name. However, a quick glance at the opening titles of films or the pyramid structure in the publishing business will give some idea of the extent of this coming together. A key area of concern is regarding the extent to which such organisations use the media to promote their own corporate interests and those of their tycoon owners ahead of serving the public. The issue of ownership, control and size is therefore an important one because it is intimately bound up with power and influence.

Power and influence is often caricatured in the personal interests of media tycoons themselves. The issue of the power of media magnates and their ability to manipulate public opinion would appear to rest on a number of factors. One is that of growing media corporate size. Another is the extent to which owners are able to impose control on editorial policy and from there on down to the output of journalists. These professionals, whose backgrounds tend to be middle class, through careful selection can often be found to share the vantage point of owners, and when necessary, close control over editorial policy and newspaper content has been demonstrated in the interventions of proprietors such as Rupert Murdoch. From the output and distribution stage, power and influence is then a matter of how effective the message is in shaping or manipulating public opinion.

Given the growing concentration of media ownership, a further issue regarding the power of media magnates is the weight that they can put behind their support for political parties that share their world view, especially for non-intervention and media self-regulation as heralded in the 'freedom of the press'. In such circumstances, a symbiotic relationship of reciprocal benefit can exist in the form of mutual support between media magnates and their profit driven business interests and political parties favouring deregulation. Murdoch's support for Thatcher and Regan during the 1980s provides a good example of this shared interest. Both Murdoch and Thatcher opposed the power of trade unions and in their own ways took them on.

Taken even further, the coming together of media business and direct political interest in a single person can be seen in the way that in Italy Silvio Berlusconi use his power of media ownership to support non-interventionist policies and help acquire his own victory as Prime Minister.

The power of the individual agency of media magnates to advance their own business and political interests is therefore plain to see. However, Street (2001, Ch.6) argues that a more rounded understanding of the use of media power should be judiciously framed within the context of both wilful agency and environmental constraint. The main constraining external forces on the media include:

1. Government regulation of the media. Although the purpose of anti-monopoly legislation is generally to limit the market share and dominance of corporations, Kuhn (2007, p.91), has commented that 'there is no maximum statutory ceiling on newspaper ownership in Britain'. Mergers or takeovers may be referred to the scrutiny of the Monopolies and Mergers Commission. However, as Kuhn points out, there have been a number of cases where the takeover of newspapers, for example News International's acquisition of the *Times*, the *Sunday Times* and *Today* during the 1980s, were given the go ahead by the Secretary of State without reference to the Monopolies and Mergers Commission. In the example provided, the reason given was that the papers were not going concerns and could only be sustained by such means.

In terms of commercial television broadcasting, a number of corporate consolidations took place during the 1990s when merger rules had been relaxed. Regarding cross media (lateral) ownership, under changes introduced following the 2003 Communications Act, if a company owns more than 20% of newspaper circulation, it must not own in excess of 20% of an independent television service, with the regulatory agency Ofcom providing the key oversight role.

2. Advertisers and consumers. Commercial media is often highly reliant on income from advertising. The interests of advertisers will therefore need to be taken into account when decisions on content are made. But what of the power of consumers? Pluralists are keen to point out that control over private media enterprise is exercised through the power of consumer choice. However, this assumes that there exists significant diversity of media providers and outlooks in the first place to choose between, something which takeovers and concentration may limit. The appearance of diversity of output through the retention of previous titles or corporate names may be somewhat illusory when consumer choice is restricted to that of a small number of giant corporate providers.

Selection and presentation of media content

The world comprises a massive amount of information potential from which decisions are made on what is presented in the media and how it is presented. The selection of media content and its presentation make it far from a pure and representative mirror image of the world 'out there'. That content, produced within organisational structures, is the manufactured outcome of decisions and pressures regarding what not to include, as well as what to include and how to communicate the content. The owners of media corporations, the editors that they employ and journalists working on stories are key actors in the decision making process. However, they are not entirely free and autonomous agents. Their decision making takes place within their own media institutions and a broader environment of social structures and constraints, one that they may be able to influence through the media itself.

From the 1980s, the broad business environment in the UK was moving in the direction of a deregulated competitive free market. These changes have affected organisations throughout society, including the media. Private media corporations have had to compete for audiences and with a public sector provider in the form of the BBC for ratings. Within media organisations and their location within this broader environment, how is media content selected and presented?

Our first port of call is to consider the various influences working on journalists. As Street (2001, Ch.7) points out, journalists' professional training emphasises the ideal of autonomous and objective observation and reporting. However, an alternative view is that subjectivity of personal agendas and biases are likely to intrude into their work. According to this model, journalistic integrity can be maintained through the honest acknowledgement of individual prejudices and is further supported by the assumption that across the breadth of the media biases are randomly distributed and will balance each other out. However, there are two highly questionable assumptions built into this view. The first assumes that there is no systematic bias in the social background and outlook of journalists and the second that within both institutional and external pressures, they are able to work with autonomy. These assumptions have been challenged in the previous section.

Furthermore, within a highly competitive institutional environment, deadlines and formats can have a constricting effect on media content. For example, journalists working in highly pressurised situations with large workloads and tight schedules may feel pressured into obtaining readymade information from official sources such as the police and political parties. A consequence of this is that content and viewpoints are likely to be influenced by the outlook of the officialdom from which they originated.

Political parties attempt to manage the output of the media to suit their own purposes. This can be seen quite acutely in the run up to general elections when the parties battle to gain media prominence for the issues and angles on them that are likely to suit their purposes in influencing the agenda of debate and winning over sections of the electorate. Likewise, governments will try to control media output in their favour through the use of 'spin doctors' to shape the message to go out in the form that suites them. New Labour gained notoriety for this process when in power from 1997.

This leads on to the more broadly political question of agenda setting. Agenda setting, as introduced by McCombs and Shaw, refers to the capacity of the media as a whole to focus public attention on certain issues by the coverage that it provides. In so doing, it may be seen as shaping the range of public thinking toward the views of advertisers, newspaper owners, editors and journalists. The continuing political importance of newspapers in agenda setting across the media can be illustrated by the prominence they are given in television politics programmes such as the *Andrew Marr Show*.

Despite their apparent diversity, a range of newspapers and television stations usually pick up on common news themes and may access their information from similar sources such as the Reuters news agency. Consequently, a limited range of issues is likely to gain prominence across the breadth of media coverage. This may be enhanced through intensity of repetition and the prominence given to issues in the format of the communication through, for example, front page or top of the news status. Once themes are established, they can come to form interpretative frameworks of reference for seeing the world, and may even play an important part in constructing what neo-Marxists refer to as a broader hegemonic and controlling view.

As well as or even through preoccupation with particular themes and issues, the media may tend to leave certain areas off the agenda. Decisions on inclusion and exclusion are an important part of the media's 'gatekeeping' role. Agenda setting therefore can be related to both Lukes' first and second faces of power; the power to focus the public agenda and to preclude certain areas of discussion. As Laughey (2007, Ch.2) suggests, a topic of major importance in sociology is an analysis of the interests that agenda setting serves.

Agenda setting can be impacted by corporate dominance. Thus, the three media corporate giants in Britain who provide 71% of newspaper circulation are powerful forces in setting the agenda for the rest of the media, as is the fact that most commercial radio stations rely for their news content on Sky which is controlled by Murdoch's News UK.

Another influence of content and style is the quest for newsworthiness. Stories which are dramatic, lend themselves to graphic and simplistic portrayal, and can be located within a background of a managed common consensus are particularly favoured features of the tabloid press content. For example, violent crime can be easily visualised, understood in its physical form, generate strong moral feelings in response regarding the law and punishment, and shape public perception of crime itself. White collar or corporate crime are likely to figure less prominently in such newspapers as they do not lend themselves to such simplistic, direct and dramatic imagery and the events are likely to be of a more distant and technical nature.

Sometimes, events are of such major proportions that they are able to impose themselves across the media to the extent of side lining content which through a variety of the above influences otherwise might have appeared. The outcome of the UK European Union Referendum which dominated news in the UK on 24 June 2016 and has again done so in the run up to withdrawal deadlines provides one such example. The terrorist attack on the twin towers in New York on 11 September 2001 monopolised global media coverage to such an extent that in an e mail a Labour government advisor, Jo Moore, suggested that this was a 'good day to bury bad news' – ie slip it out without public notice.

Although closely related to selection, presentation focuses more on the finished product. The composition of targeted audiences is an important factor in shaping presentation which includes use of language, graphics and positioning of articles.

The positioning of selected content will reflect the importance that they are given by the media outlet. Within the traditional tabloids, largely headlined and sensationalised front page billing both denotes the importance attributed to the news item and attempt to grab the attention of the reader. Decisions on the positioning of articles in terms of proximity may be based on attempts to manipulate the reader. For example, an article on 'benefit scroungers' placed in close proximity to one raising concerns over immigration levels could lead readers to form a link and interpretation which neither article placed independently might suggest.

In the mass circulation battle, tabloid newspapers often resort to sensationalist and emotive content, big headlines and graphic pictures in an attempt to maximise their readership in an intellectually non-challenging way. There is a tendency to use stereotypes as convenient communication shortcuts that avoid the need for detailed and sophisticated analysis. Content is likely to take the form of 'infotainment' – easy to digest information which is shaped to entertain.

Particularly important for quality newspapers as a source of income, given their smaller circulation, is to attract revenue from advertisers whilst maximising sales to audiences targeted with known characteristics and views. This provides advertisers with a bridge to their desired audiences and a degree of power to shape decisions on specific content, with editors being conscious of avoiding stories that may be in the public interest but that could damage their advertisers. Indeed, some advertisers have been known to require forward copies of newspapers to check for this purpose.

However, there is also a broader point to be made here. Advertisers are more likely to be attracted to media that provide an environment of lifestyle issues over that of the political probing and revelations from investigative journalism. Being aware of this, those with power within media corporations are likely to structure the organisation to allocate resources accordingly. It has thus been contended (Street, 2001, p.157) that within this environment Andrew Neil, when editor of the *Sunday Times*, introduced restructuring that reduced investigative journalism at the newspaper.

Despite their professional ethics of objectivity and autonomy, the influences enumerated above provide a framework within which the activities of journalists are embedded. Furthermore, their predominantly middle class background is likely to influence their shaping of media content in the direction of a prevailing moral consensus. As employees within an organisation, this may work in the same direction as the known preferences of editors and owners toward a status quo view of the world. The degree to which journalists operate with true autonomy would therefore be comfortably circumscribed.

The power that media ownership brings enables the owners of media organisations to influence output according to their social and economic position and political outlook. If, as Herman and Chomsky (1994) suggest, the media as powerful corporations serve the interests of themselves and other large and powerful corporations which coincide with the interests of political elites and advertisers in support of the political and economic institutions of the capitalist system through which they are the main beneficiaries, a dominant elite viewpoint is likely to be formed in the selection and presentation of content across the media.

In conclusion to this section, the content of the media is likely to affect the way that people view themselves and the social world, the extent of which will be discussed in a later section. This may be particularly the case when there is a long term cumulative effect on issues such as immigration. Given the power that comes with concentrations in media ownership and changes in the broader environment toward free market conditions and a light touch regulative framework, there has been a tendency for the content and tone of media output to move away from investigative journalism and toward human interest and lifestyle type content. The consequence of this is likely to be to move the focus away from the analysis of serious individual problems and how they may be linked to major issues of public interest that would encourage the nurturing of the sociological imagination.

The analysis of media content

But how is media content studied and measured? One approach is genre theory. In this approach, the media is divided into different genre such as comedy or news etc. with the realisation that the content of each genre is structured according to its own rules. This then forms an appropriate framework for analysis.

Studying media content and meaning is often approached through the method of content analysis. Through this method, research may focus on measuring media representation in the social construction of, for example, gender, ethnic, social class, age and disability characteristics or the extent of media coverage of violence. This is undertaken through quantified measurement of the incidence of certain words, phrases and / or images that relate to the phenomena in question. If a number of researchers using the same measuring frame come up with identical measures, this approach can be regarded as highly reliable. Moreover, the quantified information taken at different times can be used to establish trends of change in media content.

However, there are searching questions that can be raised about this approach. One is that it is too easy to assume that the measured content will have a predictable and standardised effect on what might be misleadingly assumed to be a relatively passive and susceptible audience. This will shortly be questioned in the section on media effects. Another area of concern is that this form of measurement is rather mechanical and lacks subtlety through the attribution of literal meaning to signs. For Barthes, this only takes us as far as recognising 'denotative' meaning.

An alternative approach to the study of media content, originating in ideas developed by de Saussure, is taken in semiology. This approach is arguably more sophisticated and interpretative than the literal and surface measurement of media content that tends to be adopted in content analysis. Instead, it attempts to probe subtle, underlying and more hidden meanings that reside within linguistic or non-linguistic symbols of communication referred to as 'texts'. Decoding these meanings in referred to by Barthes as extracting 'connotative' meaning (Norgrove, in Matthewman et al ed., 2007, Ch.17); that of identifying associated meanings that the signs convey to audiences without literally having to say so. This approach is more likely to uncover hidden ideological messages and forms of communication which have the potential for manipulating an audience in such a way that they may be unaware of it. By using a semiotic approach to reveal these hidden meanings, it becomes possible to see through to the intended or unintended subtle meanings of the communication.

The Glasgow Media Studies Group have conducted numerous studies of media content with the aim of revealing bias and manipulation. For example, regarding television news coverage of industrial disputes, it was found that the imagery of workers on a picket line was likely to convey a negative image of them compared to a more authoritative image of managers situated within offices.

Fiske and Hartley (Trowler, 1996, p.45) found that in news coverage of riots or in picketing during industrial disputes, filming often took place from behind police lines, thus conveying an image of professionals working under pressure in the face of unruly mobs, a message with deep political meaning.

The assumption behind this type of analysis was often that of the direct influence of the meaning of the message, as revealed in research, on the consciousness of audiences. Although more subtle than straightforward content analysis, this approach assumed that the audience will be influenced by the message according to the meaning revealed by the analyst, even if subconsciously. This assumption will shortly be associated with the mass manipulation model. It will also be shown that subsequent approaches to media effects placed more emphasis on studying the different interpretive frameworks that audiences use to enable different decodings of the same communication to take place.

Media effects – from mass manipulation to entertainment?

The effects of the media on the knowledge, attitudes, opinions, feelings and behaviour of audiences has been a matter of contention. Much can be made of the omnipotence of the media in the contemporary world – it seems to invade almost every area of our conscious existence and may appear to have the potential to powerfully shape the way that we see the world. However, it is one of a number of influences which shape people's outlook, others of which include people's position within the social structure and their direct impersonal relationships, contacts and encounters. These various influences may have short or longer term effects, may be complementary or contradictory, and may inhibit or assist the reception of particular messages. Audiences may be more or less sophisticated in their relationship to the media and adopt more passive or active responses toward it.

Variants of manipulation effects of the media

A useful starting point would be to consider the view that the media has massive controlling power over the thoughts and behaviour of audiences that are relatively passive and easy to manipulate. This is referred to as the 'mass manipulation' or 'hypodermic syringe' model (see figure 1), the latter term providing a metaphor for the capacity of the mass media to inject ideas directly into the minds of susceptible audiences who are rendered into a state of narcotised passivity.

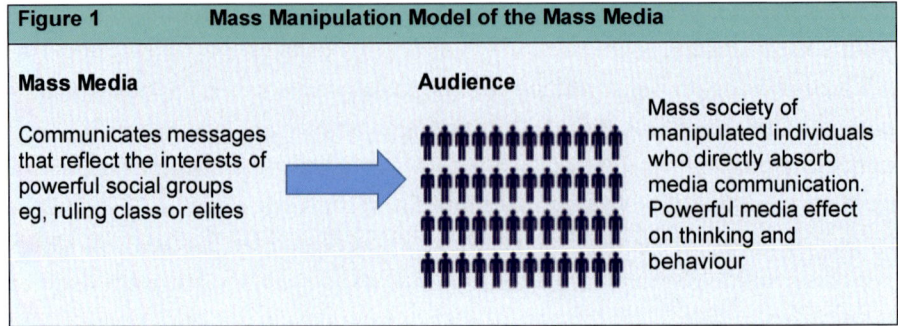

One strand of this position can be found in classical Marxist theory. For Marx, the capitalist economic and social structure works for the benefit of a dominant minority capitalist class who are reliant on the acquiescence of a majority working class. Given, from this perspective, the diametrically opposed interests of the capitalist and working classes, capitalist societies must generate ideological belief systems that systematically distort reality for the system to endure. During his lifetime, Marx regarded religious belief systems as providing powerful forms of ideological distortion. However, with the advance of the mass media in the twentieth century, Marxists have come to recognise it as one of the main ideological support mechanisms of capitalism. From this perspective, the mass media becomes a powerful force, instilling a false consciousness into the working class to keep them suppressed by gaining their acquiescence.

Marx retained faith in the capacity of workers to resist the effect of ideological control when they experienced the inevitable harsh reality of economic crisis that capitalism was doomed to throw up. However, under such economic conditions during the 1920s and 1930s and the absence of revolution in the advanced capitalist economies, early Frankfurt School neo-Marxists, in particular Adorno and Horkheimer, analysed within a broad Marxist framework the pervasive capacity of the cultural realm and the role of the mass media to perpetuate capitalism indefinitely. In so doing, they moved away from the economic determinist view still adhered to by more orthodox Marxists. These theorists applied their analysis to two very different variants of capitalism.

The first was to that of their homeland, Germany, which during the 1930s had become a Nazi dominated totalitarian state in which the mass media was used as a powerful instrument of state political propaganda to control the masses.

In emigrating to the United States, they applied their critical theory to a different variant of capitalism; that of a liberal democratic society of capitalist free enterprise. It was there that they witnessed a culture industry of mass produced superficial entertainment, driven by the profit motive and delivered to the masses by the mass media. As Long and Wall (2009, p.306) explain, for these theorists, the key features of the culture industry were, as with other forms of production, the standardisation of output. It was a profit making production line, which, whilst providing the guise of choice and diversity, through the application of successful formulae, for example in popular music, dumbed down the level of culture to that of the mass consumer market.

Frivolous and superficial entertainment supplied a cathartic need of audiences for temporary and unchallenging escape from the frustrations and routines of work, whilst discouraging critical thinking of the forces behind their frustrations. And the long term effects of exposure to this cultural environment were the creation of an unimaginative and conformist consciousness amongst the masses that would offer little resistance to the power structures of capitalism. These theorists were elitist in their derision of mass culture and pessimistic that the masses would ever be able to see their interests beyond its trivia.

For Althusser, a structural Marxist, the mass media under capitalism form part of a powerful ideological state apparatus. Working alongside the institutions of schooling, politics and the church, they are able to impose a false consciousness that is so all embracing that their controlling function cannot be seen. Taken to this degree, it would appear that the prospects for overcoming ideological control are remote.

Neo-Marxists influenced by Gramsci, who adopt a hegemonic approach, recognise that the embrace and effects of ruling class ideology are never total and that there will always be latitude for counter ideologies to emerge. Research guided by this perspective, variously referred to as a cultural hegemony or cultural effects view, has been conducted by the Glasgow University Media Group. Their early research, focussing on news coverage of industrial disputes from the mid-1970s, adopted semiotic studies of media content which revealed the communication of subtle biases in favour of employers. Analysis of the textual content revealed that journalists tended to employ language that demonstrated a pro-establishment world view and imagery content communicated in television news reports. It was found that, despite claims to neutrality, interview imagery depicted management in situations of authoritativeness (suit, office and textbooks) and workers as irresponsible (scruffily dressed, standing near a burning brazier). Whatever the rights or wrongs of the conflict, it was argued that these images would tend to reflect the interests of management and employers. An implicit assumption of the researchers at this time was that the communication would be quite universally received by audiences in this way.

This assumption was qualified in their later research. For example, during the miner's strike of 1984–1985, although ideologically biased content against the miners was found, evidence showed that this bias was more likely to be resisted by those who had personal experience of the dispute whilst accepted by those who did not. It was therefore recognised that variations in personal experience can be important in shaping the way that messages are received, a position closer to the view of hegemony adopted earlier by Gramsci that there will always be some room for a battle of ideas.

More recent work by Philo et al (2013) has applied this perspective to a study of the tone and language used by journalists in sections of the media reflecting views from the political establishment that have encouraged a stigmatisation of immigrants and asylum seekers amongst the public.

The view that audiences are highly vulnerable to the direct effect of mass media output is not exclusive to Marxist theory. In the United States during the 1950s, C Wright Mills developed an elite theory analysis of a mass society which challenged the pluralist view of a democratic society in which media diversity reflects the views of an engaged and active public that it serves in its pursuit of profit. For Mills, whilst once holding credibility, pluralism had become just an ideology of the powerful. He argued that through a concentration of big business and power elites, American society had undergone a collapse of a once politically active public sphere for there to remain a society of atomised individuals vulnerable to mass consumerist manipulation. The media has become pervasive big business in opinion management, setting its image of reality and its agenda from above. Through its preoccupation with trivia and the world of the individual consumer, it had depoliticised public thinking and obscured the ability of individuals to relate their personal troubles to serious social problems.

Pervasive effects of the media

In Britain, a view of the pervasive effect of the media has been adopted by moral elites, putting themselves forward as the guardians of moral standards. The focus of concern has tended to be what is regarded as the corrupting effect of the mass media, particularly in the form of pornography and violence, on public life through its disinhibiting effect. One such figure, Mary Whitehouse, the first president of a pressure group the National Viewers' and Listeners' Association, challenged the liberalisation of media content in the context of a more permissive society that was emerging from the mid-1960s. This position, which in part reflects the early ethos of the BBC, is elitist in the sense that public figures put themselves forward as moral entrepreneurs and paternalist protectors of the public, in the above case advocating media censorship of corrupting materials.

Gauntlett (Barlow & Mills ed., 2009, Ch.17) has criticised the position of moral elites for focussing on the media as the source of social ills. In effectively scapegoating the media, it was argued that they are conveniently turning public attention away from such social and economic influences as poverty and deprivation which are more important factors behind levels or crime and violence that should be tackled.

Direct effects of the media

A range of laboratory research conducted during the 1960s and 1970s (eg. that conducted by Eysenck and Nias and by Bandura) appeared to support the direct effects view of the media usually held by moral elites and taken as common sense by significant proportions of the public. Under controlled experimental laboratory conditions, it was claimed to have been shown that exposure to mass media violence can lead to violent tendencies or imitative violent behaviour. This was of particular concern regarding the effects of media content on the impressionable and vulnerable young, a concern which has periodically emerged in such cases as the murder of the toddler James Bulger by two youngsters in 1993.

The findings of such research have been strongly questioned, particularly because of the artificiality of the situation in which they are conducted. Gauntlett (Barlow & Mills ed., 2009, Ch.17) challenges the validity of experimental laboratory findings, such as Bandura's, in generalising the effect of the exposure to children of mass media violence measured in these conditions to that of natural settings which do not replicate an abstracted and artificial focus by participants on the effects of a singular exposure to the communication of violent content. This criticism would suggest the superiority of ethnographic research of media effects in everyday life situations where, for example, there may be a range of other distractions taking place and parents are likely to have some control over the environment of media access.

In a more contemporary setting, it could be counter argued though that parental control of social media may be far more precarious, with children often being better equipped in the use of high tech devices than their parents. With this criticism in mind, there have been calls for tighter policing of social media content by the media providers.

Gerbner has pointed out the importance of distinguishing between heavy and light viewers of television as well as placing greater emphasis on its long term effects than is possible under laboratory conditions (Jones and Jones, 1999, pp.164-165). Based on content analysis of American television, Gerbner found that this mediated reality portrayed an excessively violent view of the world and that for heavy viewers a mediated image of the world tended to prevail over their direct experiences as the real world.

Views of the direct negative effect of the media have been turned around by those, such as Feshbach and Singer, who have referred to its cathartic effect. The argument here is that it is the frustrations of everyday life which can lead to the build-up aggressive tendencies which the viewing of mass media violence can relieve through a form of living out the aggression. The build-up of aggression, the decision as to whether to view violent media output or not and the degree to which it can be lived out is likely to vary significantly between individuals. However, if there is some substance to this position, an important broader question is surely that of ascertaining the level and type of violent media content that would produce an overall positive effect and the point at which it becomes counterproductive.

Two step flow model of media effects

The direct effects and passive audience model has been strongly criticised as crude and over simplistic and a variety of alternatives have been proposed. One alternative which views audiences as more active in relationship to the media is the 'two step flow' model (see figure 2). This model emerged from research conducted by Lazarsfeld et al in the United States during the early 1940s, which looked at political opinion formation during the 1940 American presidential election, and was refined by Katz and Lazarsfeld in the 1960s.

This model still tends to emphasise the one way directional flow of information. However, a vital role in the two step process is taken by active intermediary opinion leaders who closely follow media output. These leaders have status within informal communities of followers through their acknowledged special competence and persuasiveness within particular issue or topic areas that are of interest to the followers. The role of opinion leaders is highly important for the filter that they apply to media information and pass on to followers.

Figure 2	Two Step Flow Model of Mass Media

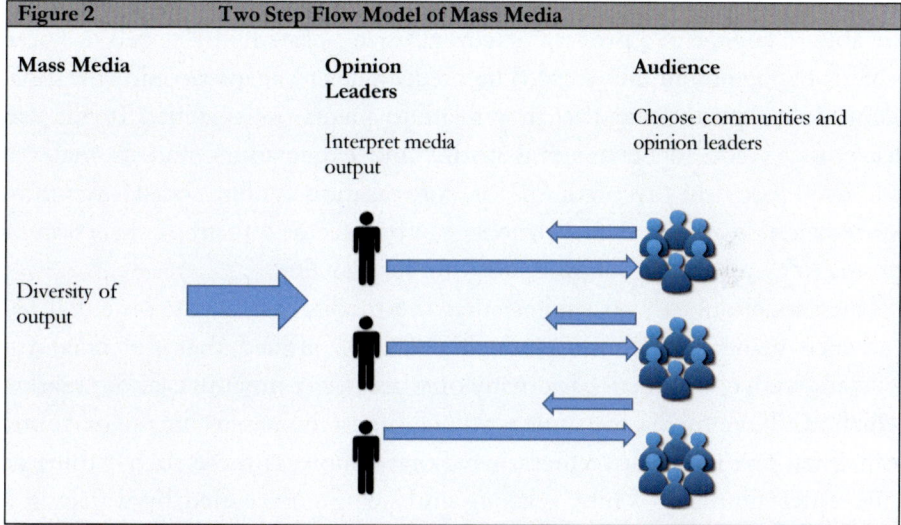

This model is critical of the mass manipulation model, especially in the form of a direct hypodermic syringe effect, which is regarded as lacking in awareness of the role of key active participants outside of the established media in the process of opinion formation. Moreover, even those who follow opinion leaders, although often not being as active, have made a choice regarding the opinion leaders and groups that they relate to and tend not to be regarded as passive individuals but as part of engaged opinion communities.

It is clear that advertisers and political parties often find it economical to have opinion leaders on board to convey their messages to a broader audience. Furthermore, although originally developed in the context of traditional mass media, more contemporary support for the two step model has been found in the opinion leadership of celebrities and bloggers who have large followings on such social media at Twitter.

Media gratification of audience needs

A number of writers, including E. Katz, D. McQuail, J. Blumler, J. Halloran, and J. Lull have attributed, through the 'uses and gratifications' approach, a more active and selective approach by individuals toward the media which is seen as relatively innocuous in its effects. According to this approach, audiences have socially shaped needs for psychological satisfaction which they turn to the media to satisfy.

McQuail has identified a number of key need satisfactions which the media provides (Long & Wall, 2009, pp. 244-245). Through the media, users are able to engage in a process of surveillance to satisfy their need to know what is happening in the world. The media helps to shape people's personal identity through the way that they relate to media personalities. It can also serve as a guide to behavioural norms and expectations and its material can itself provide the medium for conversation within social situations. Moreover, it is argued that the media can be used as a form of diversion or retreat to escape from the pressures of everyday life.

This model appears to suggest that the media has limited potential for audience manipulation. However, it could be argued that the need for relaxation is a consequence for many of work in a competitive labour market which can leave media consumers vulnerable to the passive intake of subtly influential or manipulative messages. For example, is there such a thing as pure entertainment? Whilst relaxing and being entertained by watching a soap such as Coronation Street may provide relief from a hard day's work, it may also, more subconsciously, be performing a political function in conveying the gratification that there is always someone else worse off than oneself.

Encoding and decoding of media messages

A further very valuable contribution toward understanding media effects has been provided by Stuart Hall. For Hall, the hypodermic syringe model of the media that has been espoused by some Marxists overstates its capacity for consciousness manipulation. If this were the case, oppositional ideas and groups would find no room to emerge. Instead, Hall proposed a model whereby senders of messages, as professional specialists in communication, engage in meaning production through which language and imagery are 'encoded' with an intended meaning to the message. However, audiences as recipients of messages, often do not passively absorb the intended meaning. They engage in an active process of message 'decoding' which can lead to different types of interpretation or reading. We should therefore make no assumption that content or semiotic analysis of a message will unlock a universal meaning that is received as such by all at the decoding end.

Hall theorised an ideal type of three main types of message decoding by audiences. One type of message reception may be to accept the intended meaning constructed by encoders. This Hall referred to as a 'dominant' reading. This alone would be the recognised outcome for advocates of the hypodermic syringe / mass manipulation model. However, for Hall, the world views and experiences of some may lead them to form an 'oppositional' interpretation of the message. In this case, whilst the intended meaning is understood, it is strongly opposed by an alternative viewpoint. A further response is that whereby the preferred meaning of the message is broadly taken on board but particular criticisms or alternative positions are adopted. In this case, a 'negotiated' position is taken up.

Hall regards that the type of message decoding that takes place will be shaped by the recipient's pre-existing knowledge and experience. This model therefore leads him to have a closer affinity to Gramsci's concept of hegemony which leaves far more room for ideological struggle of opposed interests than that of Althusser's ideological state apparatus or Adorno's and Horkheimer's mass manipulation model (Laughey, 2007, Ch.4). Moreover, any behaviourist views of direct media effect are regarded as crude misrepresentations.

David Morley, working within the framework developed by Stuart Hall, conducted empirical research into the reception of media messages, an approach referred to as 'reception analysis'. Two early pieces of research framed in this way were Morley's study of The 'Nationwide' Audience (1980) and his Family Television project (1986).

The first of these studies was of audience responses to a BBC magazine type programme called 'Nationwide'. In this research, a range of audience groups such as bank managers, shop stewards and students in further education were shown Nationwide footage followed by involvement in discussion. The research took place within institutional settings. Morley was able to identify a range of responses that could be classified across the dominant, oppositional and negotiated spectrum. However, he did discover some unexpected findings when relating a group's position in the social structure to the readings. For example, whilst it was not surprising that the group of bank managers adopted a dominant reading or that shop stewards took an oppositional reading, it was of interest that a group of working class apprentices accepted the dominant message.

Useful as Hall's model had been, it became clear to Morley that the meaning made by the recipient of the message is not determined and could not necessarily be predicted from knowledge of their position in the social structure (Morley, 1992, p.136). It was the outcome of a complex range of social structural influences and personal experiences. For example, it was likely that workers who had been directly involved in an industrial dispute would decode news coverage of it (and through this experience other industrial disputes) in different ways to workers in the same social structural position but who had not been involved in a dispute. For Morley, a position in between structural determinism and individual subjective uniqueness was necessary to form a sociological understanding of how mass media messages are read.

Morley also came to recognise some important deficiencies of the Nationwide study. He became aware that exposing groups with like structural backgrounds to media output that he had chosen for them to watch within an institutional setting would likely produce high levels of similarity within the groups and differences between them which may not surface to such a degree when reading messages from television programmes within a more natural setting such as their home environment. Morley subsequently adopted a more ethnographic approach in his Family Television research.

In the Family project, study of television use was observed within eighteen south London family households and family members were interviewed within their own homes. In this research, gender differences emerged as the main focus of attention and Morley acknowledged that there was some drift in his approach toward the uses and gratifications model as he was keen to identify the viewing preferences, choices, and controls which were taking place within the household. The research revealed that gender was a significant factor in viewing regarding programme preferences, degree to which it was combined with other tasks, and 'the politics of the living room' in terms of the male control of viewing (Trowler, 1996, p.180).

Commercial and public service broadcasting

In 1922, the British Broadcasting Company was formed and in that year the first public radio transmission was made from London. Radio broadcasting was established in the United States at about the same time, but the models of radio and later television communication would develop in somewhat different directions.

In Britain, the British Broadcasting Corporation, as a public corporation, was established in 1927. Although a public corporation, publicly funded through the license fee, the BBC was set up to operate independently from government control and run by its own board of directors. The model adopted at the time can be seen as in between that of a fully state controlled media, as in the Soviet Union, and a more thoroughgoing free enterprise approach taken in the United States. Its mandate was to provide a public service, a concept that needs to be viewed within the historical context of a class ridden society within which elites regarded themselves as the custodians of high moral and cultural standards. Through its first director, John Reith, this meant that the BBC had a responsibility for transmitting content aimed at enhancing cultural uplift, enriching the lives of viewers, and providing a service through a 'selfless commitment to doing good for people' (Long and Wall, 2009, p.177). As originally a monopoly provider, the mission of the BBC was one of promoting shared national cultural identity and impartial information for the public to assist democratic discussion in the public sphere. However, a measure of what this view of impartiality and public interest amounted to at the time can be seen in Reith's position regarding the 1926 General Strike; no content would be broadcast that would assist the strike and 'damage the nation' (Kuhn, 2007, p.43).

The BBC began television broadcasting in 1936 to a small and exclusive clientele in the London and immediately surrounding area, but shut down its broadcasts during the war. Post war, it initially operated as a public sector monopoly, delivering British programmes to a British audience, but in 1954 it faced competition from the first commercial broadcaster, ITV. Although financed by commercial funding, ITV also had to operate within a regulatory framework of public service requirements. Thus, although its originator, public service broadcasting was not strictly limited to the public sector institution of the BBC. Further broadcasters followed with a public service remit with the introduction of BBC 2 in 1964 and Channel 4 in 1982, but major changes were afoot from the 1980s with the election of a new right Conservative government. These changes were political, economic, social and technological, in particular:

1. A pervasive shift in political ideology in the direction of the virtues of the free market, private enterprise and deregulation. In this climate, the BBC was regarded as a privileged public sector institution which, for that reason, came in for political criticism. Its content was carefully scrutinised from

Conservative quarters for any possible bias against the government who were themselves criticised for introducing political bias in appointments to the board of governors ("World in Action", The Taming of the Beeb, 21/2/2019).

2. A recognition of growing diversity within the nation, which tallied with the idea of the need for greater diversity of choice in free market providers and content.

3. Technological advance in the form of satellite TV which, as well as adding to diversity of channels, added a more global dimension to media output through its capacity to transmit across national boundaries.

4. Within the reality of an increasingly consumer driven market, the old top down paternalistic model and comfortable public sector monopoly of the past became dated. Public service broadcasting would have to adapt. How can we conceptualise this?

Ang (Barlow, D.M. & Mills, B. ed., 2009, Ch.25) has identified different paradigms within which public service and commercial television operate with regard to their audiences. Ang argues that each of these forms of mass media have attempted to 'conquer' their audience in their own way. The traditional public service paradigm for doing so is that of a pubic to be served and enlightened. The model, as exemplified by the early BBC, is both a paternalistic and top down one with the service run on the basis that a culturally superior elite has a duty to inform and culturally enlighten the public by communicating knowledge, values and tastes to them from above. Its success is therefore not singularly driven and measured by competition for ratings but by achieving the aforementioned purposes.

By contrast, the driving force of commercial television is that within the free market programmes are made for profit. The key purpose of programmes is to maximise ratings to attract associated advertising revenue, viewing audiences as potential customers with products to be brought to their attention. The downside of the free market approach of commercial television is therefore the tendency toward an expansion of advertising time and the invasion of product placement into popular programmes; it relentlessly promotes the values of a consumer culture over responding to pre-existing public needs. This model has therefore often been criticised as having a negative effect on the cultural level by providing easy viewing bland entertainment to maximise its audiences – a characteristic not lost to Mills or early Frankfurt School adherents. However, audiences are not just an undifferentiated mass and quality programmes, accompanied by appropriate advertising, are produced for niche viewing markets. Advertising can thus be seen to link media output to a diverse market, as emphasised in pluralist theory.

Ang argues that the public service paradigm has been pulled in a competitive market direction as the expansion of private commercial television has provided a powerful competitive force for public service broadcasters to adapt their paradigm toward viewing their audience as a market and to compete for ratings. However, in the UK, this remains a mix somewhat different to that of the United States in that the publicly funded BBC remains part of that competitive environment.

New media – grounds for optimism or pessimism?

Traditional media refers to largely one way communication of standardised information to mass audiences, to which the term mass media has been applied. The main means of this communication have been newspapers and magazines, radio and television, and the technology has traditionally been in analogue form. Lister et al (2009, Ch.1) provide a useful definition of analogue technology. It is that through which information is converted in fixed form from one physical object to another. For example, the finished product of a printed newspaper as a fixed form physical object traditionally required hand written notes to be converted to metal type set up by a typesetter, the application of ink, a physical proof copy to be run off, typesetting corrections to be made, and the final copies to be run off. The relatively heavy technology used was typical of an era of standardised mass production, and it readily lent itself to centralised sources of production and communication to mass audiences.

From the latter decades of the twentieth century, advances in computing and the introduction of digital technology and the internet were seen by many to herald a revolution in media communications. Initially, digital technology enabled the manipulation and reassembly of information to be worked on and transmitted between computers. Computer technology facilitated changes in the working practices of journalists by enabling them to type in and manipulate newspaper content directly, ready for printing. However, its introduction was not without industrial conflict. Major industrial disputes involving opposition from print workers took place in 1986 when the new technology was introduced to produce newspapers at Warrington and Wapping by Eddy Shah and Rupert Murdoch respectively.

Digital technology subsequently enabled massive storage and manipulation of information. The driving force providing global and instantaneous communication of this information was the internet. Technological convergence and digitised power have added concentration of functions and enhanced capacity and mobility to media communications appliances used by media companies and consumers. As devices such as I pads and phones have become more affordable, there has been a phenomenal growth in people's electronic access to information and personal media communications when on the move. Through social media sites, skype etc., people have been able to communicate globally and instantaneously with many others.

What types of social changes have been associated with new media and to what extent is it viable to talk about a media 'revolution'? This question raises a number of others for discussion:

1. To what extent does the new media challenge or complement the traditional mass media, particularly as channels of communication from political elites?

New media can be viewed a threat to the type of information control which was arguably in the hands of media magnates and political elites whose views corresponded or to the communication of politically spin doctored messages through traditional media. The routines of newspaper production have been traditionally geared to daily cycles which seem quite slow compared to the continuous flow of social media where stories can emerge through the input of private individuals into the new media sphere and become viral very quickly. This, along with a decline in newspaper sales, would appear to disrupt the capacity for control of media output by the powerful.

However, it is not simply a matter of trade off. People obtain information from a multitude of media sources, including an increasing uptake of online newspapers. The content of these is often very similar to the printed form, and the press still often influence the agenda of social media discussion.

2. In what ways does new media enhance the democratic process?

It is argued that democratic accountability can be enhanced through active social media participation and the use of on line petitions. In fact, traditional and new media often interface. For example, moves to acquire signatures for a second UK referendum on whether or not to leave the European Union and a petition to revoke Article 50 were launched on social media and made news of in news 24 media and influencers may work in the other direction; what trends on Twitter may follow themes established in the traditional media. Moreover, use of social media was a crucial element in the organisation of protest movements to oppose undemocratic regimes, as evidenced by Castells (2012) in the Arab Spring protests.

However, there have also been accusations of the undermining of democracy through social media by manipulative involvement of foreign powers in elections. Further, social media may have enhanced the possibility of the creation of 'fake news'. Whilst the use of propaganda has always been at the heart of mass media communication, new media has raised the prevalence of mediated reality to such an extent that, as some postmodernists claim, our ability to distinguish between fact and fantasy has been fatally eroded.

3. How does new media relate to consumerism?
Electronic media has in many ways assisted the consumer to search the market, benefit from the use of comparison sites to get the best deals and order online for products to be delivered without needing to venture outside the home.

However, commercial culture has been invading the internet and social media sites that are dependent on advertising revenue. On line activity has enabled businesses to engage in consumer surveillance and targeted advertising. Arguably, the power of corporations has thus become more invasive and a culture of rampant consumerism and entertainment trivia has emerged across a media saturated by commercialism.

4. Has new media opened up new social divides?
Research has shown that social divisions do exist in terms of access to new media, particularly with poorer and older sections of the population and those living in more geographically remote areas suffering greater levels of exclusion in an information age.

However, as a new media saturation point in technologically advanced countries is approached, the excluded are declining in numbers. We need to look more globally for a divide, with the poorest sections of the poorest countries remaining the most excluded, indicative of a new form of poverty.

5. How are patterns of media use changing?
Bakker and Sadaba (Kung et al, 2008, Ch.5) have usefully distinguished

between first order and second order effects of increasing use of the internet on use of old media. First order effects are direct, as in the case of a 'substitution effect' when, for example, more time spent on the internet reduces time spent with other more traditional media. Research has suggested that this effect is quite pronounced in the United States but less so in Germany. Furthermore, when studied in the Netherlands, substitution was shown to be more significant amongst the young. However, the trade-off is not always straightforward since there is no necessary zero sum whereby an increase in the use of one leads to an equivalent reduction in the use of the other and people may multitask, as for example being on line whilst watching television.

Second order effects of new media refer to changing attitudes and expectations resulting from its take-up. For example, as on line newspapers have become available free of charge, such free availability has tended to become an expectation, especially amongst younger users, and with possible negative consequences for the sale of printed copies.

6. How is new media changing our behaviour?

An obvious behavioural change brought about by the internet is in the way that people shop. The internet provides the facility for comparing products and prices, shopping on line and ordering products for home delivery. The shopping experiences of consumers have thus become more depersonalised and shopping areas in town centres have sometimes become hollowed out.

Regarding the workplace, cyberspace has enabled more workers the freedom to work from home, thus avoiding cost and time factors of travel. However, with that freedom can come a blurring of boundaries between home life and the world of work, with an intrusion of the feeling that one is constantly on call for work purposes at home.

Smart phones, as mobile devices that combine various functions, can lead to addictive usage and can be a source of frequent interruption in the course of face-to-face conversations.

7. What are some of the key arguments regarding optimistic or pessimistic interpretations of the effect of new media?

A broad historical backdrop to an optimistic outlook on the introduction of new media relates to Enlightenment thinking that linked technological to social progress through its liberating effect. Optimists therefore tend to view the changes associated with new media as both revolutionary and beneficial and usually liberating and empowering. For example, technological changes have arguably decentralised the media and by enhancing a two way flow of information are seen to have reinvigorated the democratic process of political engagement. New media has provided new capacity for political input and organised activity including social media organised protest movements of potentially global magnitude.

This global characteristic means that abuses of political power by repressive regimes are now more difficult to hide from the outside world. Furthermore, sociologists such as Anthony Giddens argue that the forces of globalisation associated with new media can, through bringing different cultures together, enhance a climate of cosmopolitan tolerance.

As well as benefits to consumers, optimists point to positive changes in working arrangements with more workers now having the opportunity to work from home.

Those who adopt a more pessimistic view of new media tend to argue that 1) the changes that 'new media' has brought about are not as revolutionary as optimists maintain, and that 2) where the changes are substantial they can often be viewed negatively. For example, Cornford and Robins (Stokes and Reading ed., 1999, Ch.7) state that optimists often adopt a technologically deterministic viewpoint. Emphasising the thoroughgoing effect of technological novelty, they are inclined to lose sight of the fact that technological changes often remain encased within established social and power relationships rather than breaking the mould. Political parties and pressure groups, as top down organisations, may in fact have the capacity to enhance their influence through the use of financial, organisational and status assets that they have at their disposal. The potential for new democratic involvement and empowerment may therefore not be a great as the optimists suggest.

Social media emerged within the context of neoliberal globalisation, emphasising the virtues of private enterprise and deregulation. However, the freedoms of the new media have opened up new opportunities for hate crime and political extremism. For example, there has been a significant rise in new media related far right activity during 2019. Further, whilst the consequences of in line personal bullying are occasionally highlighted in more traditional media sources, politicians are often reluctant to go beyond requiring more effective self-regulation by social media providers.

For cultural pessimists, new media is awash with cheap entertainment and advertising content, thus lowering the level of culture and promoting an intensification of consumerism. At a more personal level, new media technology can lead to addictive habits such as smart phone addiction and social media encourages a preoccupation with trivia and narcissistic tendencies and may promote fragmented thinking and short attention spans.

McLuhan (2001), writing in the mid-1960s, offered some profound insights into the developing media of the day. However, we must firstly embrace his particular definitions of the concepts of 'ground conditions' and 'messages' (Federman, 6/3/2019). McLuhan was interested in the way that we are able to extend our powers through innovations and inventions. These inventions, often in the form of mechanical devices, have obvious properties in their use. For example, the invention of the printing press enabled a new level of media communication to be possible. In the everyday use of the term, they enhanced the capacity to spread written messages. However, such inventions bring about subtle and longer term unanticipated changes to the nature of our interactions that are not easily perceived at the time. McLuhan referred to these interactions as 'ground conditions'. He argued that it is often only in the fullness of time that changes in the ground conditions are relayed back to us as a 'message' of the nature of the innovation. The problem is that unintended detrimental effects of innovations may only become apparent a long way down the line. It is therefore essential that we look very carefully for any 'message' in changing 'ground conditions' which can alert us to emerging detrimental effects so that we can intervene as early as possible to control them.

We might apply this reasoning to the new medium of the internet and social media. For example, when applied to social media, the term message is typically only being used in an obvious and trivial way when referring to actual messages sent between people electronically. For McLuhan, it would be the change in social dynamics of the innovation which provides a 'message' in a more profound sense of changes brought about by the new medium. These changes may come to show themselves in new forms of crime and psychological problems associated with effects on peoples' sense of self-worth. The lesson is that we need to identify the 'message' as soon as possible to understand the workings of the new medium and calculate ahead to anticipate and head off any such negative effects before they become pervasive, a lesson which regarding anticipating these aspects of the new media seems to have passed us by.

Media representation of social categories: gender, age, class and ethnicity

The image portrayed of different groups in society by mainstream media tends to reflect dominant outlooks at particular times in history, but also reflects those back to mass media audiences and media users. However, the way in which images are portrayed, for example in different sections of the press alone, will vary according to the readership that they are appealing to. For example, sections of the tabloid press are notorious for conveying images through the use of simplified stereotypes. These stereotypes order the complex world into categories, apply generalisations to assist in the grasping of reality by readers, and are likely to have evaluative meaning.

On the issue of gender representation, male and female identity has been traditionally portrayed in terms of a binary division, meaning that distinct gender roles were viewed as the direct outcome of biological sex differences. This binary division tended to be strongly reinforced through the various media of educational materials, films, soaps and pop music. For example, in the 1950s, Janet and John primary school reading books portrayed John in adventurous and Janet in caring roles. Even through to more recent times, films that showed women in danger frequently required the happy ending of men to save them, and country music often conveyed messages on traditional male and female roles in the lyrics. Television tended to underrepresent the appearance of women and restrict and trivialise their activities; phenomena referred to by Tuchman et al through the powerful concept of 'symbolic annihilation'. Women were portrayed as seeking happiness and fulfilment in their 'natural' housewife roles and encouraged to aspire to certain images of beauty by the fashion and the cosmetics industry as consumers.

The traditional gendered outlook was conveyed to adolescent girls, as demonstrated in McRobbie's 1977 semiotic study of the content of 'Jackie' magazine. Her research found that Jackie provided for its young girl readers a conservative femininity of heterosexual romance, pursuit of the latest fashion and the adoration of male pop pinups. It was this 'conservative ideology of femininity' (Laughey, 2007, p.107) that second wave academic feminists and the protests of the women's movement were keen to highlight and challenge.

Social change brought about by the women's movement became reflected in mass media output, albeit often with an element of cultural delay, through adverts showing more assertive women in liberated roles and, during the 1990s, in the popular music genre of girl power in such girl groups as the Spice Girls. This latter phenomena suggested, in the superficial and relatively apolitical stance of pop music feminism, that new assertive roles for young women had become mainstream and that the battles fought by second wave feminists had been won.

However, despite challenging male power and privilege, second wave feminism had essentially remained rooted a viewpoint of binary male and female gender distinctions. Third wave feminism related gender identity to the postmodern condition within which, according to Judith Butler, individual gender identity is liberated from binary gender norms and biological based sex differences and is far more freely socially constructed. Popular culture pioneers exhibiting this performative fluidity in gender remaking have included David Bowie and Madonna.

Traditional male working class occupations and communities have long been in decline through economic modernisation. Compared to a post war era of patriarchal and macho dominance, both media and social imagery of masculinity have diversified, with male orientated magazines appearing from the 1980s and 1990s to cater for a range of images. Amongst the diversity of male gender images was one of the new man (projected by such media personalities as the footballer David Beckham who married Spice Girl Victoria Adams) who is empathetic and sensitive, and provided a new market for the fashion and cosmetics industry!

As well as growing diversity of lifestyles and imagery between and within genders, there has been some liberalisation of views on sexuality – that is the sexual identities and preferences of individuals – from the traditional view of the normality of biologically determined binary division of opposite sex attraction. Homosexuality was once only subtly hinted at in the media or used to reinforce traditional gender and sexual norms. Following the decriminalisation of homosexuality in England and Wales in 1967, gay characters were sometimes conveyed with humour in the media. Both Larry Grayson in *The Generation Game* and John Inman's role as Mr. Humphries in the department store sitcom *Are You Being Served*, which ran from the early 1970s to mid-80s, employed exaggerated culturally recognised gay characteristics as a source of humour.

Further social and moral changes, represented in legislation allowing same sex civil partnerships (2005) and marriages (2014), have been symbolised in the media through ceremonies involving high status media personalities such as Elton John. These changes opened up new market and revenue possibilities for magazines and advertisers aimed at the gay and lesbian market whose image construction they have assisted with, by the early twentieth century, much reduced risk of offending the heterosexual public. Gay, lesbian and heterosexual characters now appear as serious mainstream characters in soap entertainment programmes.

For Clare (Gauntlett, 2008, pp.8-10) broad social and cultural changes from a time when men as well as women knew their place in the binary division, have been particularly difficult to adjust to for many males and have left masculinity in a state of crisis. Gauntlett (2008, pp.279-280), acknowledges that in postmodern / high modern social conditions, people have to work on identity construction in the face of a bewildering array of lifestyles that are open to them. However, he doubts that this has quite brought a 'crisis' of masculinity. Instead, Gauntlett (2008, pp.281-283) argues that the range of recipes and role models available through the mass media provide (in for example men's magazines) navigation points to assist in the social construction of masculine identities.

In terms of age, media representation has been particularly unkind and ageist toward women. Older women are still likely to be side lined as television news presenters. In films, middle aged men are frequently accompanied by substantially younger female girlfriends, putting a premium on their youthful glamour the same of which does not apply to men. Women have also made their mark as young action characters.

Different age groups can also be seen as cohorts of similar age gradually working their way through the population over time. Each cohort is likely to share a generational cultural view acquired through the process of socialisation into the culture of the times when they were young and more impressionable. As society changes, older age cohorts are likely to encounter changed times as unfamiliar when viewed through the lens shaped by their earlier social and cultural environment. An important point here is that through the massive choice of media material that is now available, there are far more opportunities for older groups to use the mass media to reinforce a world outlook that is familiar and makes more sense to them in a contemporary world that they may find it difficult to relate to.

Mass circulation tabloid newspapers that aim their sales at a working class market on balance usually adopt a pro establishment viewpoint or support parties of the political right. Whilst royal populism is frequently promoted, issues of elitism and privilege are rarely raised. Elites have privileged access to the media as a source of authoritative comment and therefore their representations of society, often shared with media owners, editors and journalists, are likely to predominate. Thus, the massive rewards for business and financial leaders are often couched in terms of the damage to the economy that would result if their talent cannot be retained as being a reality of the free market, even though they may be highly rewarded for failure. Furthermore, a preoccupation with celebrity culture, even though celebrities themselves may have little talent, is encouraged by the media for trivial entertainment purposes. The concept of merit is often negatively applied to the poor when they are maligned for their own failings or labelled as benefit scroungers, with little attention paid to analysing the impact of socially structured inequalities of life chances on their lives. Most disparaged are those portrayed as an underclass in shows like *The Jeremy Kyle Show* as the morally degenerate remains of a once respectable working class. Overall, serious analysis of the social structure is conveniently largely absent.

Although Britain is regarded as a multicultural society, media portrayal of ethnic minorities has often been a negative and condescending one. According to Hall, it is based on what is viewed from the perspective of the 'white eye', as black ethnic minorities are seen as an inherently inferior racial group (Jones & Jones, 1999, pp.122-123).

In certain sections of the tabloid media in particular, emotive headlines fuelling anti-immigrant hostility have over the decades portrayed certain ethnic groups as an invading threat to the way of life of the nation and communities in terms of their alien cultures, access to precious public services, competition for employment and levels of crime and violence. Against this backdrop, during the 1960s and 1970s situation comedies such as *Till Death Us Do Part* and *Rising Damp* used race in comedy, making racial minority groups the target of humour. It has been suggested that this puts those who hold racist views at ease. However, it is important to recognise the context that in these comedies the racist invariably turns out to be seen as the fool and that there is a generational dimension whereby the racism of the older character is ridiculed by their younger counterparts, reflecting changing social attitudes.

Cottle (Stokes and Reading ed, 1999) suggests that to understand racist representations in the media, one needs to go behind the scenes to look at influences shaping journalistic output. These Cottle has included as the following: the select white middle class composition of the journalist profession, their perception of the racist views of their readers, working pressures placing high reliance on police sources of information and pressures to sensationalise content.

However, it does appear that negative representations of racial groups in the media are likely to have greater effect on communities where the stereotyped groups are absent, as their main benchmark is that of the mediated reality (Jones & Jones, 1999, p.129).

Real events can have their own dramatic effect. Post 9/11/2001 terrorist attacks in Manhattan and 2005 London bombings, the media has been criticised for fuelling a climate of 'Islamophobia' – the demonization of Muslim communities as a whole as the 'enemy within' from the actions of a small number of fanatical extremists (Jones, 2012).

Globalisation – the media and a shrinking world

The media has played a key role in the development of an awareness of a globally interconnected world which is experienced as being compressed in space and time through instantaneous global communication.

During pre-industrial times, communication tended to be primarily face-to-face and situational. This is referred to as dialogical. Whether verbally or when supplemented by printed form, information would travel only as fast as it could be physically transported and for many the world that they directly experienced revolved around their local communities.

Inventions of the industrial era in the form of telegraph and telephone, released dialogical communication from the limitations of face-to-face contact and vastly expanded the range and increased the rapidity of communication. Rantanen (2005) has referred to this form as mediated dialogical communication. These advances were changing people's consciousness of time and space.

During the twentieth century, technological advance in radio and television enabled a massive global expansion the mass media as mediated communication with a largely one directional emphasis. This is referred to as monological. An important consequence of the growth of the mass media has been the development of a global consciousness shaped by an increasingly mediated view of the world. As a manufactured product, this lacks the purity of direct non-mediated interaction but nevertheless feeds into the values, viewpoints and topics of our face-to-face communication. Consequently, Giddens (cited in Rantanen, 2005, p.10) states: 'locales are thoroughly penetrated by and shaped in terms of social influence quite distant from them. What structures the locale is not simply that which is present on the scene'.

Mass media globalisation has taken various forms. One is corporate. A small number of media organisations have grown onto massive global conglomerates. Through technological developments such as satellite broadcasting and on-line newspaper publication, giant media organisations operate beyond the territorial sphere of the state as global scale corporations which, in their search for their own profitability and that of advertisers, look to expand into growing markets throughout the world.

Another aspect of globalisation is that of world spectacle events such as of the Olympic Games and the World Cup which readily lend themselves to global coverage. Important in the conveyance of these events to global audiences is a projection of the face of the society in which they are taking place; an image to the world which is likely to emphasise a selective caricature of its cultural tradition.

What are the consequences of global media and how might we respond? For Habermas, an important consequence is for democracy which requires a public sphere of involvement in discussion and debate in a climate of diversity and persuasiveness of contribution. This, he argued, emerged during the seventeenth and eighteenth centuries as an open environment of face-to-face opinion formation. However, through contamination by a dominant mass media narrowing 'legitimate' viewpoints and preoccupying discussion with trivia, the public sphere as an arena of authentic formation of public opinion to feed into the democratic process has collapsed. Social media may be the vehicle through which the public sphere can be reclaimed in the contemporary world at a more global level if it can resist the colonisation of the dominant institutions of capital and political institutions.

McLuhan adopted a more optimistic stance. He suggested that a globalising media offered the possibility of the emergence of a global public sphere that could transcend the restrictive outlook of national cultures.

An early model of the impact of an increasingly global media was that of media and cultural imperialism, put forward by writers such as Galtung and Ruge (1965) and Schiller (1976). Through the global influence of western media, Marxists in particular have argued that an ideology of capitalist consumer culture was becoming instilled throughout much of the world. This follows from the analysis that a) capitalism is by its nature globally expansionist and that b) its accompanying ideology imposes itself top down on host populations that are relatively powerless to resist it. By such means, corporate and media interests, often working along past lines of imperial military and administrative domination, were able to develop new types of control taking the form of 'soft power'. Through the invasion of western mass media technology and content, cultures in countries regarded as lucrative areas for profitability were becoming inculcated by pro-western consumer capitalist values. The consequence was argued to be a negative one of a tendency toward cultural homogenisation across the world accompanying the spread of global capitalism.

A number of issues and criticisms have been raised by this model, including the following:

- The top down ideological dominance effect of the mass media is now seen as rather crude, simplistic and dated. A number of critics, including Smith (1990), have pointed out that cultures are in fact often deeply historically rooted and can therefore provide an environment of resistance to mass media invasion. This would suggest that global media will likely have limited impact before broader cultural changes have provided fertile ground for them to take root. Cultural imperialism theory was therefore wrong in tending to conflate media with culture and in reality there would likely be a whole range of accommodations between cultures and global media throughout the world.

- The view of western domination tended to be itself rooted in the world of the 1950s and 1960s. Western media faced powerful resistance from state broadcasting within Soviet block countries, but the soft power of images of western consumerism that were able to seep through eventually contributed to the collapse of austere communist systems. However, whilst western style consumerism has since been embraced, a diversity of cultural and religious nationalisms have emerged.

One form of national cultural resistance may come from the media itself. The continued existence of public service broadcasting in the UK and a number of European countries has provided a degree of guardianship of national cultural identity, even if from the viewpoint of the establishment as trustees of the national interest in, for example, the face of American style commercial television. The European Economic Community placed quotas on the influx of imported media output in 1989. However, with advances in global media technology since then this has been a form of defence that has been difficult to maintain and in the UK the BBC has had to adapt to the reality of a more deregulated market.

Boyd-Barrett (Rantanen, 2005, pp.78-79) developed further criticisms of the media imperialism model. Powerful as they may be, it was argued that it is incorrect to assume that corporations simply reflect national identities or that there is a single national interest for some countries to protect against the threat of a singular media or cultural invasion. It was further argued that focussing on the production of media content makes unjustifiable assumptions about the presumed effect on audiences who can in fact be more independent in their actions than the model suggests.

Some countries, Iran being an example, have successfully held the influence of the western media at bay and rapidly developing nations such as China and India have come to establish their own media technology and content, as witnessed by the emergence of Bollywood in India. Furthermore, a number of news channels in the west are now freely available that provide, for example, an Arabic or Russian slant on the news.

The homogenising and culturally dominating effect of the global media which cultural imperialists have claimed to be taking place can therefore be seriously challenged. Furthermore, even if the global media is eroding the diversity that comes with a variety of national cultural traditions, it can be argued that media imperialists put a romanticised slant on the process of this loss as it could promote liberation from repressive traditional cultures.

Rantanen (2005, Ch.5) has suggested that as anthropologists and cultural studies scholars have applied fieldwork methods to the study of globalisation, their findings have revealed a greater awareness of heterogeneity than homogeneity. Their focus is more at the level of individual free choice where people selectively appropriate from a diversity of media available that which most closely represents their familiar cultural setting. Moreover, Rantanen has argued that globalisation can be shaped by forces of indigenization. By this, it is meant that global media companies often find that they need to tailor their output to satisfy the needs of indigenous cultures. In addition, national media companies will indigenously select programmes from global media that they think will suit their audiences who will themselves make decisions on what suites them in their social and cultural setting.

Postmodernity and the media – liberation to the freedom of bewilderment

Postmodernity refers to changed social conditions that are identified and explained from the theoretical perspectives of postmodernism. Postmodernists are generally critical of the modern period which was driven by the application of rational thinking as an intellectual liberation from the constraints of the metanarrative of religious dogma. They argue that the scientific and industrial era that emerged imposed its own social structural and intellectual constraints on people. The intellectual constraints were the new metanarrative of scientific rationalism which predominated through to the early post war decades.

Up to this period, advanced societies remained quite heavily structured in terms of social class and the family, supported by a relative uniformity of moral standards and confidence in intellectual certainty. Marco social theory, both functionalist and Marxist, seemed to adequately explain these social conditions.

Within the mass media, few television stations existed. In Britain, the BBC, as a public service broadcaster, held a monopoly of television broadcasting to its audience and saw itself as an elite and paternalistic guardian of cultural and moral standards. A number of other countries had developed their own variants of public service broadcasting through which integrated meaning structures could be conveyed through standardised messages from a mass media hierarchy. Unsurprisingly, the mass manipulation model of a narcotised public held some credibility during this period which postmodernists regard as still being under the grip of the modernist metanarrative.

However, over the latter decades of the twentieth century, social structures were undergoing fundamental transformation. This was particularly evident in the breakdown of the class system, changing gender relationships and the growing diversity of family and individual lifestyles. These structural changes were accompanied by a fracturing of moral uniformity. In total, new freedoms appeared to be emerging from old declining structures.

For postmodernists, a key driving force accompanying these changes was growing plurality in the mass media. Within the framework of advanced capitalism, the expansion of the mass media took the form of increasing diversity of commercial television and radio channels and printed sources of media output. Society was becoming saturated with media imagery that promoted the consumerism and entertainment of more affluent times. Postmodernists argued that through these changes society was undergoing a fundamental transition from the modern to postmodern which would finally achieve the liberation of the individual that the modern period had failed to deliver.

A number of theorists have associated these changes with the emergence of an illusory cultural realm, with the expansion of the media as the key source. An early attempt to understand this phenomena from a Marxist perspective was provided by Guy Debrod. Debrod argued that the news media produces heavily pre-structured 'pseudo-events'. Celebrities preoccupy viewers with 'spectacle' in such a way that the world of consumption and fashion design hides the continuing class exploitation that is embedded in capitalist production, thereby supporting the prevailing social order (Laughey, 2007, pp.152-154).

Other writers have adopted a postmodern culturalist view of social change outside of the Marxist framework. Broad parameters of social change to postmodern society have been laid out by Lyotard. For Lyotard, modern societies were dominated by the metanarrative that science, rationality and education were progressive forces in that they liberated people from the grip of religious superstition that prevailed within traditional societies. However, it is only in postmodern society, within a media driven culture of consumerism as an end itself, that liberation is fully possible in undermining the constraints of the modern scientific metanarrative.

The nature of the postmodern condition has been most forcefully argued by Baudrillard. Baudrillard (Barlow and Mills ed., 2009, Ch.21) maintains that we live in a world in which we are engulfed by a cultural realm of media information that is often poorly contextualised, leading to information overload, confusion and loss of the capacity to judge events with the same degree of structured certainty that we once could when our experiences of the world were often more direct. The key to this change is the technological development of the mass media which, through advertisement saturation, is the driving force behind the transition of our primary self-image to that of consumers rather than producers as once was the case.

In the postmodern world, high tech media communications drives a playful and shallow consumer and entertainment culture. For Baudrillard, our perceptions become media saturated by 'third order' simulations (Laughey, 2007, pp.148-152). By this he means that signs which once represented an underlying reality have now lost that connection. They have become a disconnected reality of their own, forming a substituted 'hyperreality' in their own right which is so all-engulfing that it conceals its substitute nature. In a media saturated global world, we can now only recognise the world through these mass media virtual reality simulations as few other reference points exist.

What we feel we know is a consequence of images that no longer represent reality but have taken over as reality. For example, Baudrillard has made the highly contentious claim that the Gulf War didn't happen! What he actually meant by this was that the mass media portrayed this conflict in terms of the clinical effect of American technological superiority, with smart bombing conveyed to the public in images virtually identical to that of video games (Laughey, 2007, p.151, Barlow & Mills ed., 2009, p.216). Our distance from the media presented events and their similarity to video games distances us from any authentic reality of what was going on. It is in this sense that the Gulf War did not exist.

For Marxists, ideology powerfully influences mass false consciousness. The media play an important role in inducing mass passivity to perpetuate the economic arrangements of capitalism. Postmodernists such as Baudrillard posit the existence of a hyperreality as an even more all-engulfing cultural realm than ideology is for Marxists. From this postmodernist position, hyperreality opens up almost unlimited potential to individuals for active choice in consumption, their view of the world and self-construction, but within a world where illusion is the new reality.

Under postmodern conditions, socialisation is a far more fluid process and identity formation the result of massively enhanced individual choice. The superficiality and playfulness conveyed by the mass media finds its counterpart in social media where individuals are free to constantly manipulate and update their self-image. Postmodernists argue that in this world, the structural and macro theories of the modern era (in particular Marxism and functionalism) that emphasised the constraining uniformity of external social forces and analysed society in terms of large organising concepts such as the nuclear family and social class, are relics of that era.

If postmodernists are correct, there may be a number of reasons to be concerned. One is that liberation from a more structured environment into a world of hyperreality is in fact liberation into a hyper active relationship to chaotic world of fleeting images, information overload, uncertainty and fantasy with its attendant psychological problems.

Furthermore, absorption into this fluid world of superficial entertainment trivia and consumerism would make it difficult to see, let alone address, pressing social problems. In terms of nurturing the capacity to link personal troubles to public issues as a means of intervening to promote well-being, as advocated by Mills, even those who had developed the capacity would find it redundant and the younger generation would be socialised into a world where that capacity would be lost.

But such concerns are posited on the fact that postmodernist views are correct. If the technological determinism of culture by the media is a false premise, then the extent and nature of social change that they claim may be highly exaggerated. An alternative position is argued by those who adopt a high modernist vantage point.

High modernism – media to the identity rescue

High modernists such as Giddens and Beck do not deny that the condition of contemporary society is far more fluid than that of the first half of the twentieth century. Alongside this fluidity, past social structures have been eroded that once anchored people within class systems, standard family structures, particular work and industrial relations etc. Accompanying social fluidity has come increasing social diversity and rapid change.

One of the key challenges of this environment, according to Ulrich Beck, is the need to for people to adopt a reflexive view toward their personal identity which requires constant reappraisal as they navigate their lives through a rapidly changing environment. However, for high or late modernists, this does not mean that all navigation points with any grounding in authentic reality are lost in a world of hyperreality, as posited by some postmodernists. Instead, the media, in reflecting changes that are taking place in the world, can actually help in this reflexive process by providing assuring navigation points as guides to self-identity work through providing images and information about identities and relationships. This can involve a variety of content such as the characters and stories in films and soaps or the issues raised in discussion programmes. Ganutlett (2008, Ch.8) has emphasised the importance of media navigation with regard to the more open nature of gender and sexuality, for example in media output providing, through a range of men's magazines, different recipes to help construct identity in the context of greater diversity that has left some men experiencing a 'crisis of manhood'.

Chapter 12
Crime and Deviance

Abstract

Studying criminality sociologically can be fraught with the challenges of preconceived personal perceptions and the chapter opens by raising questions about what in the everyday sense we may claim to know about crime. The issue of the emotive nature of this topic area can be related to media sensationalism in shaping everyday stereotypes of crime and criminals and much content provides a mismatching impression compared to the best evidence available. To make the transition to studying crime sociologically, the reader is forewarned of the need to recognise that crime is relative to time and place, that evidence of crime levels is the outcome of a number of social processes, and that crime is itself, viewed sociologically, a social construct. To emphasise the social control backdrop to this topic area, the reader recommended to review briefly the contents of chapter 2, Sociology: Society and the Individual.

A number of key concepts in the subject area are introduced and defined, including the important accompanying concept of deviance.

The viewpoint that criminality is essentially a consequence of predispositions in the makeup of certain individuals is raised. The adequacy of this approach is challenged by the alternative sociological vantage point that crime levels are influenced by social factors. The following sections lay down key founding sociological explanations of crime through consideration of functionalist and Marxist perspectives, followed by symbolic interactionism, a perspective that moves the sociological focus of analysis from crime toward deviance. Some more subtle points of clarification regarding crime and deviance are then raised. The radical position of the New Criminology which attempted to combine elements of Marxism and interactionism is then introduced.

A range of problems associated with the measurement of crime are next covered, particularly regarding deficiencies in official police statistics. It is then considered how evidence of victims and perpetrators of crime may be improved through the use of surveys.

The social distribution of crime is analysed in terms of the social categories of class, gender, ethnicity and locality.

Which sections of society are more of less prone to be victims of crime? This question is considered in the following section, along with a consideration of the mismatch between risk levels and fear of crime.

Definitions of white collar and corporate crime are provided and consideration is given to the limited recognition of these types of crime amongst the general public as well as their under recording in crime statistics. The issue of the comparatively lenient treatment of the perpetrators of corporate crime is raised, after which sociological explanations of its prevalence are introduced and examples of the victims of corporate crime are provided.

The challenging issue of the social construction of crime is introduced and tackled, with particular focus on insights generated by the ethnomethodological perspective. This is followed up by reference to the effects of the media in shaping the social construction of crime and deviance.

'Realist' explanations of crime which provide frameworks for policy intervention from both right and moderate left positions on the political spectrum are explained and the subsequent section looks at the practical question of crime prevention and control. The question is later raised though about whether adequately combatting crime can be based on the assumption that crime is invariably rational and economically motivated.

The issue of surveillance as a form of crime control is introduced, its effectiveness considered, and the suggestion is made that surveillance extends into broader reaches of social control.

In viewing crime within a global perspective, attention is paid to cybercrime, state crime, organised crime and green crime, and the final sections of this chapter provide an overview of postmodern and high modern approaches to the topic area.

The sociological challenge

How can crime be defined? The answer to this question is seemingly obvious – it is behaviour that breaks the law of the land. The law of the land derives from the state in its capacity to pass legislation and it is implemented through the criminal justice system. It is a hallmark of contemporary democratic societies (in contrast for example to feudal societies) that all are treated equally before the law, that punishment is based on factual evidence of law breaking behaviour, that the law is impartially applied across society, and that the severity of the sentence is closely related to the severity of the crime. These are commonly perceived ideals.

Public imagery of crime often focusses on certain types of behaviour that break the law: acts of theft or violence that are directly experienced by individual victims and which can be loosely referred to as 'street crime'. Perpetrators may be viewed in terms of their individual pathology against which the law abiding public need to be protected. Such perceptions of criminality may be shaped at different levels, for example from direct personal experience, through knowledge of local levels and types of criminality or by a bigger picture still relayed through the media.

Statistics on crime tend to be conveyed via the media as factual evidence of crime trends and may be politicised as a reflection of a government's term in office. The media may also focus on singular crimes that are particular newsworthy and help to shape public definitions of crime.

To approach the study of crime sociologically, a number of preconceptions have to be challenged, new and broader definitions considered and new vantage points opened up. Furthermore, viewed sociologically, the very encouragement of restricted definitions and viewpoints on the subject amongst the public may itself be set within a social context of power and control in which the 'crimes' of some are either not recognised as such, remain largely hidden, and even if perpetrators are found guilty, sentencing would appear to be comparatively light. It is therefore important to raise a number of preliminary issues before embarking on a sociological journey of analysis of this topic area.

How public perceptions of crime and attitudes toward it shaped? As with other social phenomena which we 'know' about, much is influenced by the output of the media. Of particular interest here is the crime content of the mass circulation tabloid press which, in competition for newsworthy stories, tends to focus on dramatic and personal events which are easy to relate to and provide simplistic accounts with little analysis, which can equally encourage simplistic responses from their readership. Crimes of theft and violence often fit the bill. It will become apparent that such images of crime tend to hide more than they reveal.

There is likely to be far less newspaper sales mileage in covering highly complex crimes perpetrated by or within powerful corporations and political elites. This is at least in part because the links between political elites, corporations and the media may involve the use of power and financial influence aimed to keep the criminal acts of the wealthy and powerful off the media radar. Even without assuming that the mass media has the capacity to determine the public consciousness, it is hardly surprising that crimes more associated with the relatively powerless tend to figure large, along with simplistic suggestions of punitive solutions.

Deviance is also a topic of this chapter. Like crime, it refers to behavioural infringements, but not necessarily in the form of law breaking. Attempts to control behaviour viewed as deviant may therefore tend to take the form of moral judgements and pressures.

Adopting a sociological approach to the study of crime and deviance is likely to be challenging for a number of reasons. It requires:

1. A dispassionate stance toward emotive issues which may be particularly difficult if they have impinged on one's own experiences.
2. The ability to recognise that what we tend to take for granted as normal in terms of criminal or deviant behaviour is not fixed in stone. Acts of crime and deviance, as well as the nature of responses to them, vary between societies and change through history. To understand this variability requires the ability to stand back and locate crime and deviance within different cultures and changing broader social contexts and political climates.
3. An awareness that measuring the extent of crime in society is far from a simple fact finding exercise since much crime is hidden.
4. The ability to conceive that what counts as crime or deviance is a social construct. By this, it is meant that there is nothing intrinsic to behaviour that identifies it as universally criminal or deviant by its nature. This is probably one of the most challenging dimensions of the topic area to acknowledge.

As crime and deviance take place within an environment of laws, norms and values etc., the reader is advised to review the short chapter 2 of this text entitled Sociology: Society and the Individual for a preliminary appreciation of the social constraints and controls the impinge on individual behaviour.

Definition of main concepts

Social constraint refers to influences and pressures on individuals that emanate externally from the social environment and have a controlling effect on behaviour. **Formal** forms of **constraint** tend to be experienced as heavily structured controlling impositions, often of a coercive nature. Such controls would be exercised through the police, the courts of law, prisons and the military. Formal constraints may need to be imposed in certain situations of lawbreaking activity but often their very presence acts as a deterrent which confines behaviour within certain bounds. Either way, they provide a harder line of control which resides alongside **informal constraints** that derive from society's or particular group's moral values and social norms.

Some important points arise from these definitions. One is that the formal operation of the law at any particular point in time is codified and in contemporary democratic societies at least formally expected to be applied in an impartial and uniform way. Nevertheless, this framework which defines legal and illegal behaviour changes over time along with social changes so that a degree of social synchronicity with dominant social norms and values tends to be maintained.

Not all groups necessarily share dominant or conventional norms and values though. The behaviour of members of some groups may be guided by alternative guidelines that are seen from the point of view of mainstream society as deviant. Behaviour that is regarded as **deviant** by conventional standards may be within the law or illegal, examples respectively being wearing outlandish clothing and fraud. However, the boundaries between criminality, deviance and acceptability of particular behaviour are often not static. For example, whilst homosexuality was an illegal act in the UK prior to legislative changes in 1967 which largely decriminalised it, for many it subsequently remained viewed as deviant, whilst to some extent it has more recently become de-deviantised through the advance of more tolerant social values.

Everyday perceptions of crime held by the general public and influenced by media preoccupation, especially through the tabloid press, tend to relate to lawbreaking activity which is directly experienced and can be conveyed in graphic terms or straightforward messages. Under this heading would be various crimes of personal violence and theft, the incidence of which is often the focus of official **crime statistics**. These statistics refer to crime known to the police and recorded as such. Given the known but less certain mismatch between these statistics and actual levels of crime committed, self-report crime surveys are regularly conducted to provide an improved measure of criminal acts and victim surveys to provide more accurate evidence on the victims of crime. Nevertheless, it is acknowledged that there remains a **dark figure** of criminal activity – an unknown amount of crime that remains hidden.

Organised crime may share some common features with crime as defined above, but will be perpetrated through some form of organisational structure. In its traditional form, this may have included robbery and protection rackets, whilst more contemporary examples would include people smuggling and drugs trafficking.

A distinction can be made between **white collar** and **corporate crime,** although it is not always a clear cut one or one that is consistently followed by criminologists or sociologists. White collar crime can be defined as that which those working in white collar occupations partake in, often against their employers, whereas corporate crime can be viewed as that conducted by corporate professionals for the benefit of the organisation. Typical within the former category may be embezzlement from an employer, whereas the latter category may include the manipulation of bank rates, cost saving through illegal dumping, breaking health and safety legislation or tax evasion. An important area of contention regards the relative impunity of penalties for such crimes compared to personal crimes of violence and theft that are highlighted in the mass media and popular imagery.

Green crime, as conventionally defined, is any activity which breaks the law that is put in place to protect the environment. However, more **radical green criminologists** argue for a more inclusive view whereby damage to the environment is by definition a criminal act against nature whether formally recognised as a crime or not.

Most crime is defined as such by the state. However, in some cases, **crime is conducted by the state** itself through explicitly or implicitly condoning actions which infringe international law. Torture of prisoners would therefore come within this scope. Scrutiny therefore needs to be at a global level, with organisations such as Amnesty International adopting a vigilant role in highlighting such abuses.

It has been suggested, particularly from a Marxist influenced viewpoint, that **criminogenic** tendencies are built into capitalist societies. The law is seen as shaped to protect the interests of a powerful economic class. However, the dominant social values of acquisitiveness and striving and the competitiveness of corporate life to achieve ends may encourage behaviour which crosses the boundaries between that which is legal and illegal. Furthermore, the privations of the poorest in an economically polarised society may lead to crimes of desperation (but given where power lies these will be disproportionately penalised).

As used in sociology and criminology, the term victimisation has a slightly different meaning to its more common social use. It is to do with being the victim of crime. In the case of some crimes, such as physical assault, individual victims may be identified, although even in these cases, who the primary perpetrator or the victim is may not be entirely clear. In other crimes, such as tax evasion or those causing environmental damage, the victims may be far more diffuse and distant from the crime and the effects of these 'abstract crimes' on individuals more difficult to measure and not included in victim surveys.

Founding sociological perspectives on crime and deviance

Explanations of criminality sometimes focus on the characteristics of the individual. This tradition was prominent during the second half of the nineteenth century when Darwin provided a basis for an individualistic explanation of criminality within the confines of his theory of evolution. According to Darwin, the criminal individual was the product of the genetic outcropping of a reversion to a more savage evolutionary condition. A pioneering criminological theory that picked up on this approach was developed by the Italian physician and prison psychiatrist Cesare Lombroso. For Lombroso, the behaviour of criminal individuals could be explained in terms of their internal genetically based impediments. Indeed, he argued that this condition was often evidenced by facial and bodily characteristics and deformities which showed in criminals similarities to the lower primates. This throwback condition he referred to as 'atavism', a condition which tended to impel the individual toward criminal behaviour. Such individuals were therefore regarded as both helpless in their actions and beyond reform.

More recently, arguments which link propensity toward criminality to individual genetic makeup have been forwarded by Herrnstein and Murray

(1994). Their research indicated a statistical link between low levels of intelligence, as measured through IQ testing, and rates of criminality as indicated by incarceration figures. Since Herrnstein and Murray argued that intellectual levels are largely innate and determined more by genetic inheritance than environmental factors, there would appear to provide a genetic basis for criminality.

The emergence of gene chip technology has reignited interest in a hard line biological predisposition toward criminality in the belief that it may be possible to identify a criminal gene within individuals.

From a sociological viewpoint, there are a number of problems and limitations associated with this type of explanation of criminality. One is that, at least in an extreme or simplistic form, it is too genetically deterministic – it attempts to explain all or most of crime or deviance in terms of irresistible forces that reside within individuals to act in law breaking or deviant ways. The study of crime and deviance would therefore leave little or no room to measure the impact of social influences on behaviour. Consequentially, it would be very difficult to understand evidence of fluctuations in crime rates in relation to changing social conditions. Also, what is or is not a law breaking act varies between societies and changes over time. It is therefore difficult to argue that certain individuals are predisposed criminogenic behavioural types if what is defined as criminal is socially relative and not an intrinsic feature of certain types of behaviour.

Durkheimian functionalism – criminality related to the infringement of the collective consciousness

Emile Durkheim was one of the pioneers in challenging accounts of behaviour which were commonly regarded as biological or psychological in their origin. He emphasised that moral standards and social norms change over time and differ between societies and that they are social in the sense that they exist externally to the lives of individuals. Whatever these standards and norms may be, they universally perform a key social function; that of constraining individual behaviour. This takes place through their internalisation by individuals via the process of socialisation and ongoing social and moral pressures and constraints. Indeed, Durkheim took the most personalised act, that of suicide, which was then regarded as a crime in many societies and commonly perceived to be related to conditions of individual mental ill health, and through his analysis of official suicide statistics claimed to have shown that suicide rates can be related to characteristics of the social environment (Durkheim, 1970).

This sociological viewpoint which Durkheim pioneered made at least two key advances on individualistic approaches to crime. The first was to do with the normality and social functionality of crime, at least within 'moderate' levels. It may be expected that functionalists, who place social integration, order and control at the very centre of their analysis of social good health, would view crime as fundamentally dysfunctional for society. However, Durkheim argued that the criminal acts of a minority are beneficial to social cohesion because they promote a broad public reaction which reasserts collective values and helps to maintain in the public consciousness clear boundaries between acceptable and unacceptable behaviour. Since the law reflects and codifies dominant social values, the shame that is associated with its infraction (for example through ritualised humiliation in court, punishment and media coverage) serves a positive social and moral purpose.

The question of the functionality of 'normal' levels of crime raises an interesting issue. Crime levels may be quantified by using official statistics. If crime rates become excessively high compared to the norm for societies of that type, this would suggest that a society is in an unhealthy and dysfunctional condition where social constraints and controls on behaviour are too weak. On the other hand, given the functionality of crime as identified above, the implication would be that crime rates could not fall excessively low. This would be because society would refine its moral values and the law would change so that what were once either minor or non-infringements would come to constitute criminal acts or deviance. Thus, even in a society of saintly behaviour there would still need to be sinners!

Secondly, Durkheim argued that 'we must not say that an action shocks the common conscience because it is criminal, but rather that it is criminal because it shocks the common conscience' (Durkheim, 1964a, p.81). This is a profound criticism of approaches to crime that identify it as intrinsic to certain types of action. Instead, criminal action is that which is defined by society's response to certain actions. What is regarded as criminal (and how it is punished) is therefore variable between different types of society and will change over time.

Durkheim related social responses to the infringement of social and moral values to the nature of social integration. 'Primitive' societies constituted relatively small communities with a very limited division of labour. This social condition Durkheim referred to as 'mechanical solidarity' (Durkheim,

1964a). Given the similarity of its members, the limited extent of social integration based on mutual exchange and its small scale, social cohesion needed to be reinforced through a strongly imposed collective consciousness backed up by vengeful retribution to punish criminal or deviant actions.

By contrast, modern large scale industrial societies exhibit a far more elaborate and complex division of labour, advancing individualism and enabling social integration to be enhanced through exchange relationships. Durkheim referred to this different basis for social cohesion as 'organic solidarity', a social condition in which a more liberal collective consciousness accompanied the advance of individual liberties and the tolerance of greater individual diversity. These societies hold a less retributive response to infractions of moral values and the law and, given their industrial nature, the legal system becomes based more on the principle of restitution – that is, returning the parties involved in an infraction to an equitable situation.

For Durkheim, the transition to the modern society can be a painful one involving destabilisation of the social fabric, as in the case of the political, social and industrial revolutions of the late eighteenth and early nineteenth centuries. Such rapid change is likely to be accompanied by the confusion of moral uncertainty. High levels of disorder therefore reflect the fact that it is the social condition that is pathological. However, even when societies have transitioned to the modern type, the easing and liberalisation of moral norms can make individuals vulnerable to a condition of 'anomie' in which they experience detachment and aimlessness, indexed by Durkheim by a rise in anomic suicide rates.

Mertonian functionalism – crime as strain between aspiration and opportunity

Robert Merton in 1938 applied a functionalist perspective to American society and developed an explanation of crime referred to as 'strain theory', which, compared to Durkheim's use of the term anomie, put a new twist on the concept. The backdrop to Merton's theory was the image of the American dream and the view of an open social structure. He argued that American cultural values of material success are broadly embraced, but that opportunities to achieve this success by legitimate means vary with people's position within a social structure that provides different levels of barrier to their realisation. For some, the conformist route of hard work and application will bring the valued materialistic rewards and accompanying social status. However, for those within a lower social stratum, there will exist a far greater gap between the values of materialistic aspiration and opportunities for their achievement. For Merton, this represents an 'anomic' condition in which moral constraints on individual behaviour can become slackened. The temptation to strive for material success through non-legitimate means is likely to lead to higher levels of materialistically driven crime amongst people who are disadvantaged by their low position in the social structure – an explanation which seemed to tally with statistics on social class related crime levels.

Important implications can be drawn from this theory. One is the danger of excessive media driven preoccupation with conspicuous consumption as the means to social status and success as exacerbating strain based criminality. Another is the potential for crime reduction through improving the life chances for achievement through legitimate means amongst the poorest and most disadvantaged sections of society.

However, from a decade after Merton's writings on strain theory there became a greater awareness of the existence but more hidden nature of white collar and corporate crime. A more contemporary spin on Merton's theory might also explain these types of crime in terms of strain through lesser barriers of economic disadvantage but heightened aspirational values.

Marxism – the criminality of the powerless

Little was written by Marx and Engels directly on crime, but from the body of their works relatively straightforward extrapolations can be made regarding crime under capitalism.

From a Marxist perspective, the starting point is the class divided nature of capitalism that originates in the economic infrastructure and through which a minority capitalist class are the primary beneficiaries. The legal and criminal justice system, along with the mass media, religion and the church and the state education system, is part of the state superstructure, the combined purpose of which is to protect the economic infrastructure of capitalism. The ideological aspect of state legislation is that, in protection of the capitalist system which generates opposing social class interests, laws passed that primarily reflect the interests of a powerful economic class are represented as existing for the common good. It is possible to perpetuate this distortion by the need for occasional action against particular rogue capitalist interests, often as a last resort, to protect the wider integrity of the system.

The value system of capitalism normalises a life of materialistic self-interest. Whilst the ideological state superstructure may disguise the true nature of class exploitation, it is unable to eradicate a sense of injustice experienced by members of an exploited working class. Thus, the suppressed class conflict will tend to re-emerge in criminal activity amongst poorer sections of society as a type of incoherent response to grievances which are found difficult to articulate politically. As Chambliss argues, shaping general public perceptions of crime to correspond to that experienced within the working helps to divert attention away from exploitation and to enlist working class support for coercive law.

However, Marxists would argue that it is the rich and powerful whose crimes are more likely to evade the law or be punished relatively lightly given the extent of their consequences. Moreover, the ideological distortion of reality which reflects the power base of a capitalist class, renders invisible, from a legal point of view, a particular ongoing crime of theft – the exploitation of a proportion of the surplus value created in the production process by the labour input of workers.

Marx was also aware of the existence of a section of society that existed below the working class which he referred to as the 'lumpenproletariat', a similar social category to that more recently referred to by some from a political right perspective as an 'underclass'. This group were defined in terms of their lack of access to regular employment and were unsympathetically regarded by Marx as a vice ridden section of society often immersed in a parasitic lifestyle of criminality.

A key criticism is that Marxist theory adopts an over deterministic explanation of crime. This criticism refers to an excessive emphasis on the economic and power inequalities inherent within capitalism to structure a class society to such an extent that high crime levels of the poor and powerless are an inevitable outcome. Moreover, the shaping of the law (primarily to protect profitability and property interests), the way that crime is defined and the form that its suppression takes, is essentially seen as a form of class control. The main problem with this position is that it over predicts the degree of working class crime compared to its measured amount.

Mankoff (cited in Holdaway, 1992, pp.77-78) has identified a number of comparisons and contrasts between functionalist and Marxist perspectives on crime. Of relevance here is the point that whilst functionalists view a constant level of crime to be functional to both capitalist and communist societies at similar levels of development, for Marxists, the eradication of the class struggle under communism should vastly reduce the crime rate.

Symbolic interactionism – a refocussing toward deviance

Symbolic interactionism, a perspective pioneered in the United States in the early twentieth century by theorists such as Mead and Cooley, offered an essentially micro approach to the understanding of social interaction. This perspective emphasises that individuals actively attribute meaning to each other's actions which can influence the way that they see themselves in terms of the way that others view them. People make judgements of the actions of others which when communicated can have a profound influence on the self-perception of those judged.

From this rather philosophical base, symbolic interactionism found its sociological grounding in the form of labelling theory. Applying a label to a person's or group's behaviour is making a judgement of that behaviour. Interactionists have been keen to examine the processes and effects involved in the application of negative labels to those whose action is regarded as deviant by those who are able to successfully apply the label. The impact of this perspective therefore shifted the focus of attention from criminal acts, as defined by law, to that of deviance, as defined by audiences of behaviour.

We have already seen that for Durkheim the designation of an act as criminal is relative to its capacity to shock the collective conscience rather than as being something intrinsic in the act itself. In a society where moral standards have arguably become more diverse, through the study of deviance, interactionists have pushed the point of relativity to new level, arguing not only that deviance does not exist in the essence of any particular act, but also that it is the product of the ability that some people have to successfully label the acts of others as deviant.

Who, then, are more able to successfully apply the deviant label to others? For Howard Becker, the origin of and capacity to define behaviour as deviant often relates to broader questions of social power and status. Becker has argued that from within social elites, moral crusaders, which he referred to as 'moral entrepreneurs' (Becker, 1973, Ch.8) who see themselves as the guardians and protectors of moral standards, are able to combine their superior social status with their advocated superior moral position to proscribe the behaviour of others that departs from their own standards as deviant. Mary Whitehouse, who from the mid-1960s railed against the

BBC, claiming that the permissiveness of some of its programme content was corrupting the morals of the young, provides an example of one such moral entrepreneur.

To answer the question of which people tend to engage in deviant behaviour in the first place, Becker (1973, Ch.2) looked at social constraints rather than individual characteristics. He initially reversed the question of why some people engage in deviant behaviour and asked why, given the likely common and widespread existence of individual impulses toward deviant behaviour, those who conform do not follow through these impulses? The answer provided was that they are embedded within institutional structures and routines and a mesh of activities within which non-conformity is envisaged as having detrimental consequences that one would want to avoid.

By contrast, those more prone to deviant acts are more likely to have a) avoided such social embedding and b) developed techniques of neutralisation, rationalisations for their actions that neutralise social pressures to conform.

Edwin Lemert pointed out that being caught and publically labelled for committing a deviant act, often carries the impact of a 'master status', something similarly referred to by Goffman as 'spoiled identity'. For Lemert, although it is the act (or omission) that is labelled as deviant, the attached label can become the overriding characteristic by which the individual is defined. Such labelling can engulf the self-identity of the individual and the negativity of the process can become compounded by the lack of conventional opportunities which the labelled person many have open to them.

However, it is important to recognise that labelling takes place within social processes with often very indeterminate outcomes. In challenging the simplistic misconception that 'we become what we are labelled', Holdaway (1992, p.44) emphasises that

'Reflection on the question 'Who am I?' presents a person with a debate about the relevance of a label to their self-image and their actions. The debate extends, of course, from within an individual's mind to various groups who could confirm or deny a label. Messages can be confused, redefined; they change over time, they can be deflected, accommodated, refused, accepted. Labelling is an indeterminate process; all is flux and flow'.

Nevertheless, a significant responsibility for the potential effects of deviant labelling can be attributed to those who are able to impose deviant labels on the behaviour of others. The consequences of such labelling can both effect the future behaviour of those labelled and the responses of others to their behaviour. In some instances, these processes can take the form of a 'deviant career' and bring about a 'self-fulfilling prophecy'. For example, a deviant career may emerge through the successful imposition of the label 'delinquent' on a youngster for their wayward behaviour. This can lead to a greater likelihood of the person's association with like labelled others, immersion into a deviant subculture of 'outsiders', the internalisation of a delinquent identity and the acquisition of a shared stock of knowledge to support further delinquent activities. If this leads to criminality and a criminal record, others may condemn the individual and, even if they wish to 'go straight', restrict their opportunities for conformist behaviour, as in the case of denying them the opportunity for gainful employment. The temptation to return to crime brings about a self-fulfilling prophecy which confirms the correctness of the label. However, Becker was clear that these processes were not necessarily predetermined or irreversible.

Becker (1973, Chs. 3 & 4) applied an interactionist approach to the study marihuana users as both law breakers and deviants in 1950s America. As well as the threat of arrest, the potential first user faced a conventional morality that associated the use of the drug with debauchery and addiction, as well as likely moral condemnation by others whose friendship was valued should one be discovered. These concerns would often inhibit first use.

Should use be trialled, the user would be very keen to maintain secrecy against risk of being found in possession of the drug or it's behavioural effects being detected by valued others. This usually would mean use away from the presence of non-users and learning to control the effects of drug use in conventional situations. More frequent use would be likely to lead to a move more into the deviant group for ease of regular supply and use in ease of the company of others. Within the group, one was likely to acquire techniques of neutralisation that challenged conventional condemnatory stereotypes of the harmful effect of the substance use, pointed out beneficial effects and criticised more harmful practices such as alcohol abuse engaged in by non-users. By becoming a member of a secretive deviant group, both a supply of the substance would become more readily available and superior views of the initiated may support the continuation of the deviant activity.

In Jock Young's research (1971) into a hippy group in Notting Hill, it was the derogatory police views toward and treatment of the group that were seen as key in accentuating a hippy subculture that felt under attack. Young found that drug taking, initially a marginal pursuit, became a more central activity of hippy identity and defiance. Such a phenomena had been referred to by Wilkins as a process of 'deviance amplification'.

Stanley Cohen's study (1973) of the emergence of the deviant youth groups of mods and rockers from events in 1964 utilised the concept of deviance amplification. Cohen was particularly interested in the way that reporting deviant behaviour could spark a 'moral panic' in which deviant groups became demonised.

The term moral panic refers to a panicked response from the general public that their familiar social norms are being threatened. Populations are vulnerable to such panics during times of rapid social change. One such period in Britain was the 1960s when an older wartime generation were experiencing a challenge to their authority by a younger generation. Within this broader context, the fuse of a moral panic became lit by the national media who, following skirmishes and some acts of vandalism between motor cycle and scooter riding youths during a dreary 1964 Easter bank holiday in Clacton, exaggerated and sensationalised the behaviour as youths out of control by such headlines as 'Youngsters Beat up Town' (Cohen, 1973, p.30). The general public had little opportunity to check the veracity of this reporting which tallied with the broader theme.

Public and political concern focussed on the need to control such disturbances. The press speculated that future like 'invasions' would occur over bank holidays at seaside resorts. This fuelled the oppositional culture of the mods and rockers who developed their distinguishable regalia of leather jackets and parkers respectively. The police planned to be out in force to impose authority over these future periods and the media were ready to capture the anticipated events. Through these processes, much larger and more organised groups of mods and rockers were ready to act out these expectations for the media reporters, police and the public. What started as a minor event became amplified into ritualised conflicts at a number of seaside resorts throughout the remainder of the 1960s.

There have been various attempts to refine the concept of deviance. For example, Lemert has pointed out that not all behaviour that might be regarded as deviant is publically labelled as such. This could be the case with regard to more private forms of deviant activity such as secretly viewing pornography. Alternatively, deviant behaviour may be effectively rationalised to observers. In such cases where public labelling of deviant behaviour is absent, reference has been made by Lemert to 'primary deviance'. The type of effects referred to in the above paragraphs are only likely to arise when behaviour calls forth severe public censure which becomes subjectively internalised as the deviant 'me'. Deviance of this type was referred to by Lemert as 'secondary deviance'.

Lloyd (Ed. Matthewman et al, 2007, Ch.15) has introduced the term 'straying' to refer to a softer form of departure whereby individuals wonder from generally accepted societal norms. It is likely to comprise behaviour at the pre-labelling stage. Whilst straying can lead on to deviance, Lloyd argues that there are no general laws by which this progression is determined and even if the transition to labelled deviance takes place, individuals can resist becoming helpless victims and work back toward a controlled form of straying behaviour or even conformity. What is required, Lloyd argues, is detailed case studies of processes experienced by individuals.

Far less from the vantage point of the wronged underdog, and as an alternative to the focus on the negative effects of negative labelling of criminal or deviant behaviour, Braithwaite (Newburn, 2013, pp.225-227) has argued that 'shaming', whilst used as a form of disapproval of unacceptable behaviour, can be followed up by offering the shamed individual opportunities for the show of remorse, which if supported by approval for reformed behaviour can lead to managed mainstream social reintegration.

Crime and deviance – similarities, differences and relativity

Often what is a criminal act and what is generally perceived as deviant act overlap given that both relate to a background of shared norms and values. However, this is not always the case. In this brief section, simple illustrations will be provided that distinguish between crime and deviance and also point to the relativity of deviance.

The first example refers to tax evasion and tax avoidance. Tax evasion by companies is a criminal act. It is also likely to be broadly seen as highly deviant. However, whilst highly critical of tax evasion by companies, many people would think it at worst only marginally deviant to pay cash in hand for odd job work done, thus evading the payment of VAT.

On the other hand, tax avoidance takes place when companies manage to get around a country's tax laws rather than strictly speaking breaking them. This has particularly been the case with certain global companies that have managed to organise the payment of their tax bills in countries with lower corporate tax rates rather than higher tax countries where some of their profits have been made. Since this practice will be reducing funds available for public services, it would be of no surprise that the general public may view the practice as highly deviant. However, for some in the business community, this may be seen as legitimate letter of the law use of the tax law system.

As a second example, cheating in an exam, whilst not breaking the law, is viewed within educational institutions and official bodies as a highly deviant act of serious misconduct with severe penalties, such as dismissal from a profession. However, within a school subculture, a pupil may be awarded status for this same act.

Thirdly, deviance related to swearing can be relative to location. Swearing is usually regarded as acceptable within certain places, such as at the pub. However, when one crosses a physical boundary, this may also constitute a cultural boundary. Thus, were a higher education student to enter a seminar room and engage in swearing, this would be regarded as deviant behaviour.

In traditional coal mining communities, swearing, referred to as 'pit talk', was part of the working culture amongst miners. However, using pit talk in front of women was often regarded as a lapse into deviant behaviour, with the user reprimanded and expected to apologise. But such language itself could also be used to maintain boundaries. Where the social club was regarded as a place for male workers, pit talk could operate as a form of boundary maintenance to keep women away. Thus, if women were present in this situation, it would be more likely that their presence would be regarded as the deviant act rather than the men's use of pit talk language.

A fourth example refers to stealing from an employer which is a criminal offence. However, particularly amongst workers who feel that they have been short changed by their employer, the act may barely be seen as deviant, but as justifiable recompense or at worst 'pilfering'. Indeed, in some instances, for example amongst dock workers, theft has frequently been part of the work culture.

Another example relates to conducting experiments on animals. For scientific purposes and under properly controlled and licensed conditions, this not a crime. However, for many, such experiments are viewed as an unnecessary cruelty toward animals. Animal rights protesters have themselves engaged in actions which have been criminal or broadly viewed as deviant in support of their cause.

As a final example, in Britain breaking fast on Ramadan is certainly not a crime. However, it is likely to be regarded as a highly deviant act by many within the Islamic community.

The reader may find it a useful exercise to contemplate his or her own examples to complement those provided above.

The New Criminology

During the early 1970s, an attempt to construct a new all-embracing theory of crime by Taylor, Walton and Young, comprised a critical response to what Young referred to as 'administrative criminology' – a tradition which had uncritically accepted crime statistics as the basis for shaping social policy. The theoretical ingredients of this new critical approach were the structural framework of Marxism and the voluntarism of interactionism.

The new criminologists attempted to avoid a crude determinist strand of traditional Marxism, by regarding crime as a rational but not just automatic response of the working class to the inequalities of capitalism, a system protected by coercive state legislation.

The creative synthesis of Marxism and interactionism was applied by Stuart Hall to explain the 'black mugger' moral panic of the 1970s. Hall identified the broader context for the emergence of this phenomena as a reaction to the crisis of law and order and productivity which befell capitalism during the 1970s. Within this framework, the black mugger became the criminal scapegoat to bring onside public opinion to favour more repressive policing and heavier sentencing, thus comprising a successful hegemonic move by the authorities. As with Cohen's study of Mods and Rockers, the mass media played a key role in identifying the folk devils to gain the support of a public that were vulnerable to the message.

In contrast to Durkheimian functionalism which regarded crime as a functional necessity for all societies, advocates of the new criminology argued that through fundamental transformation of society from capitalism to socialism crime could be virtually eliminated a) along with the material inequalities that generate it and b) the re-designation of acts that constitute crime and deviance through greater tolerance of social diversity.

Measuring crime – the search for the 'full jigsaw'

Clearly, there are no official statistics available on the extent of deviance per se and the most productive research into this area has been of a small scale and qualitative nature employing in-depth interviewing, participant observation and documentary sources. By contrast, crime statistics in one form or another can be traced back many centuries. For example, Sharpe (accessed 8/12/2018), who focussed on the period 1550 – 1914, has suggested that some measure of crime levels can be gleaned from early local assize court records. These sources have shown that rises in property offences coincided with poor harvests, for example in the late sixteenth and seventeenth centuries. During the eighteenth century, as Britain became an increasing power on the world stage, periods of peace following conflicts found young male soldiers and sailors returning to communities with little means of support were accompanied by increases in property offences.

The first British national based official statistics on crime, related to sentencing, were compiled in 1856, whilst twenty years later police and court sources were combined. At the time, the focus of interest in such statistics for purposes of scientific analysis lay alongside a fascination in criminal types. Subsequently, statistical analysis shifted more toward measuring the incidence of crime itself within society. Official crime statistics were for long regarded as relatively objective facts, used by the police for lobbying political support and conveyed by politicians to shape both public opinion and policy on crime. Aggregated from police records submitted to the Home Office, these crime statistics provided, during the post war decades, a virtually singular and relatively unquestioned source of apparently factual data on the incidence and social distribution of crime in society. The study of crime reliant on these statistics tended to reflect a positivist type official mentality on the phenomena.

Within the discipline of sociology, ethnomethodologists were, by the 1960s, developing scathing criticisms of the apparent objectivity of official crime statistics. By the early 1980s, it became increasingly recognised that attempting to obtain an accurate measure of the level of crime, its extent within different crime categories, its distribution across different sections of the population and its changing nature is a very challenging business which these official statistics were not singularly well equipped to handle. With such concerns in mind, the Home Office developed an alternative means of measuring crime. From 1981-1982, the Home Office initiated a series of national crime victim surveys (victimisation surveys) then entitled the British Crime Survey. A key aim of the survey was to acquire detailed information from people who knew that they had been the victim of crime during the previous twelve months, as well as to record whether or not they had reported it to the police. The intention was to provide a more informative measure of crime levels than that provided by police statistics alone. Over time the survey sample was expanded from 10,000 to 40,000 and the survey was conducted on a rolling annual basis from 2000, becoming renamed the Crime Survey for England and Wales from 2012.

Official police statistics

It became clear that the survey was picking up on the significant extent of non-reported crime. Whilst crimes such as burglary that require a police case number for insurance purposes have had a particularly high reporting rate, overall, surveys indicated that under a half of crimes known to the victims were reported to the police. The credibility of police crime statistics was thus increasingly brought into question. There has subsequently become a growing recognition of a range of reasons for this underreporting, including the following:

- A criminal act may be unknown to the victim. For example, a person may think that they have lost their wallet when in fact it has been stolen. If reported to the police, it would be as lost property.
- Some crimes, such as those involving the loss of a small amount of money, may be regarded by the victim as too trivial to report or make them feel that they may be viewed as wasting police time.
- There may be poor relationships between some communities and the police that, along with community cultural pressures, put victims off coming forward. Perhaps relatedly, victims may have little faith in the effectiveness of the forces of law and order to investigate or to solve the crime.
- In some cases, victims may decide to 'sort it out themselves' and thus probably themselves engage in criminal activity.
- For other types of crime, the parties involved may feel that they mutually benefit from keeping it secret, as for example in the buying and selling of illegal drugs, in cases of bribery, through insider share dealing or even through tax evasion by paying for work cash in hand.
- The victim of a crime may fear the consequences of reporting it. This is particularly likely to be so regarding victimisation in certain violent crimes, especially those of domestic violence and rape where women are the main victims. The media have raised the profile of crimes of sexual harassment or assault during 2017 and 2018 with high profile celebrities speaking out regarding historical cases of abuse as part of

the #Me Too campaign. Any subsequent increase in those coming forward to report historical cases would not have been included in the statistics of allegations compiled at the time of the alleged offence.

- There are also crimes which perpetrators and certain others in the know regard as fair game, as for example in the case of pilfering from employers by employees, often supported by a workplace subculture of silence. Even if thefts or other workplace criminal misdemeanours are uncovered, a range of disciplinary actions may be taken internally.
- Other types of crime may only have a 'victim' in a more abstract sense, thus not figuring in individualised reports. Crimes of this nature would include some environmental crimes, the making of false insurance claims which push up insurance premiums across the board, and tax evasion which impacts on the public purse, public sector investment and the quality of public services.
- The complexity of a crime may leave it undetected or difficult to prove, as in the case of highly complex financial crimes, especially with the growth of financial sectors of advanced economies.

Of course, some of the above factors may work in combination. Overall, the police rely heavily on the reporting of crime which constitutes about 80% of their official measure.

As well as the public underreporting and police under detecting of crime, the police authorities themselves have sometimes been complicit in the manipulation crime statistics. These practices have often related to institutional workload or performance pressures. For example, the once widespread practice of subsequently classifying a reported act such as rape or domestic violence as a 'no crime' when it became clear that the case would not progress was sufficiently common during the early 1980s for the Home Office to suggest to police forces that its use be restricted. Meanwhile, following the Home Office introduction of performance indicators for detection and clear up rates in 1992, certain police forces have been found to have engaged in 'cuffing' – that is, in an attempt to improve clear up rates, offenders have been 'encouraged' to admit to crimes that they had not committed.

To help gather a more comprehensive and valid measure of the level of crime in society through police sources, during 1998 – 1999 the category of 'notifiable offences' (those in which data has to be supplied to the Home Office) was expanded by the Home Office to include categories of less violent crime. This change produced a break in the continuity of the data and a leap in the figures of violence against the person by then including over 250,000 crimes that would have previously been excluded (Maguire & McVie in Liebling et al ed, p.171).

Further, in 2002, new standards for recording crime, the National Crime Recording Standard, were introduced. These required the police to take more account of the viewpoint of the victim when deciding whether to log a reported event as a crime, thus reducing their use of discretion to write off crimes. The changes also further restricted the powers of police officers to subsequently 'no crime' a reported crime. Unsurprisingly, comparing the years 2000 – 2001 and 2003 – 2004, the percentage of reported crime logged as crime by the police increased from 62% to 75% (Maguire and McVie, in Liebling, A. et al ed., 2017, Ch7). Simply as a result of the above changes in counting practices and police procedures during this period, police recorded crime showed correlative increases.

The Crime Survey for England and Wales

A strength of the Crime Survey has been its own standardisation in the core modules of the questionnaire used over a series of surveys. This has provided direct comparability and continuity in the time series of information for establishing crime trends. The findings have therefore been used as a check against the effects of discontinuity in the official police statistics referred to above. Interestingly, from a peak around the mid-1990s in both survey and police statistics, whilst the figures for police recorded crime increased again at points coinciding with new methods of classifying and recording crime, Survey figures continued on a downward track to 2016.

With the aim of providing a more reliable and valid overall measurement of the rates of most categories of known crime, police official statistics and Crime Survey findings have been reported together from 2005, although direct comparison of data has sometimes not been possible due to lack of standardisation across the two approaches in terms of offence categories used and classification decisions made. For example, Newburn (2013, pp.68-69) refers to Krenshaw et al's calculation of only a three quarter overlap in offence categories and Muncie and McLaughlin (ed. 2002, p.27) provide an example of the same events possibly classified by the police as vandalism whereas in the Crime Survey they are identified as attempted burglary.

Further, although providing a useful corrective to official crime statistics, the survey data is likely to have its own deficiencies, some of which relate to the interview situation. For example, the demand characteristics of the interview may influence the information provided. Also, given that questions refer to victimisation during the previous twelve months, some respondents may struggle with accurate memory recall, including mistaking the time when the event took place. Again, given the interview setting, and despite the availability of computer assisted self-interviewing (CASI) questionnaire sections where answers to highly sensitive questions are not seen by the interviewer, respondents appear to be reluctant to report being the victims of such crimes as domestic violence or rape.

Another important point is that measuring crime levels in a standardised way from survey to survey to provide reliable information on trends may increasingly lose touch with new types of crime that emerge as society changes. The decrease in survey measured crime from the mid-1990s may therefore be at least in part a reflection of this deficiency. Both the increase in official statistics and the simultaneous decrease in Crime Survey measures of crime levels can therefore be related to weaknesses in each of the methods themselves, limiting the certainty as to what is really happening to overall crime levels.

Williams (2016) has speculated whether over recent decades a likely decline in street crime has been counterbalanced by a shift to cybercrime, such as that related to online banking and romance fraud, which appear to have been rapidly increasing. One problem is that, for reasons such as embarrassment or not knowing where or how to report such crimes, victimisation reports to officials would appear to be very low. And Williams is surely right to comment that, although this type of crime has grown with the technological means to commit it, from the first inclusion of experimental questions on such crimes in the Crime Survey for England and Wales in 2015, if this data were included in the count (which it was not), the sudden jump detected in this area of crime would have had much to do with the measuring of that which was previously hidden from the survey statistics. If included in the main Survey figures, it is doubtful whether the survey would have continued to measure a downward trend in the overall level of crime. This category of statistics has since been granted the standard of official recognition.

It should be noted that there are other weaknesses in the Crime Survey, some of which also impact of police statistics. For example, as it focusses on households, the Survey is very unlikely to pick up on victimisation that takes place within closed or total institutions such as army barracks, asylums or children's homes, or to register crimes against the homeless. Additionally, very little is likely to be revealed in terms of victimisation from state, white collar or corporate crime.

To gain a more detailed, thorough and accurate measurement and understanding the extent and changing nature of crime levels and types, it would appear that a growing diversity of methods need to be applied to what Maguire and McVie refer to as 'the search for the 'full jigsaw' (Liebling, et al, ed., 2017, p.182). What other approaches have been developed?

Small scale surveys

Smaller scale local surveys have been funded by a number of mainly Labour held local authorities to make available more detailed profiling of victimisation in their localities. A pioneering example has been the Islington survey of 1986 which was repeated in 2016. In comparing their findings, these studies have demonstrated a significant degree of diversity between localities and provided information on high levels of crime related to poverty levels or experienced by particular groups within deprived urban areas which has sometimes been very much at odds with averages derived from broad national surveys.

According to national data, high victimisation fears amongst the elderly and women appear to be irrational as they directly contradict the statistics on risk factors for these groups. However, in terms of local experience and knowledge, they may be highly rational. For example, Jones and Young (cited in Holdaway, 1992, pp.34-36) pointed out regarding the early Islington survey that local levels of street crime and burglary victimisation were substantially higher than those of national averages and that employing more sensitive interviewing techniques revealed far higher levels of sexual and domestic violence in the home compared to the national survey.

A different type of small survey, conducted on behalf of the government by Ipsos MORI, is the Commercial Victimisation Survey. For this survey, first run in 1994 and repeated annually from 2012, businesses rather than individuals or families are the basic units of analysis and the person responsible for security is usually the key source of information. A small number of different business sectors are focussed on each year and businesses randomly selected from the Government Business Register are sent a letter explaining the survey, followed by a short questionnaire completed either on line or in paper form. The information on the questionnaire is then used to provide guidance for a 20 minute phone call interview with a target of 1,000 interviews per sector. Evidence published in 2017 for the year 2016 has indicated that whilst transportation and premises crime had declined, fraud against businesses has increased.

Researching crime within closed institutions

Closed or 'total' institutions are those within which people live as inmates, largely confined from the outside world, good examples being army barracks and psychiatric hospitals. Obtaining detailed and reliable information on victimisation within closed institutions can be challenging given the detachment of the organisation and capacity for environmental regulation. Research and investigation may require the use of more qualitative methods, including in-depth interviewing of whistle blowers or past participants. Researcher entry to the institution may be necessary to observe first-hand the workings of the institution and how these may relate to criminal behaviour that remains hidden to the outsider. For this purpose, covert participant observation may be deemed necessary to reveal what official documentation may hide. Insights into criminal behaviour in such institutions have occasionally been uncovered through journalistic investigation such as MacIntyre's (1999) revelation of the use of physical abuse of people with mental disabilities residing in care homes.

An alternative form of in-depth research within total institutions is regarding those whose actual purpose is to warehouse those who have already been found guilty of engagement in criminal acts – prisons. Here, the sociologist will have at hand potential participants for in-depth interviewing that may be far more difficult and dangerous to locate in the outside world. There are certain caveats accompanying this type of research though:

Confidentiality would need to be agreed with the authorities and inmates convinced that it would be maintained to maximise the chances of inmate co-operation.

The findings could not be generalised to other criminals of the type studied given the likely small scale nature of the research and the fact that having been caught those interviewed are unlikely to constitute a representative sample as they may be dissimilar to those not caught.

Self-report surveys

Attempts have been made to obtain more broadly reliable and valid information on the perpetrators of crime, especially with regard to ascertaining their social distribution according to age, class, ethnicity and gender. Official statistics, compiled from courts and prisons data, provide information on convicted offenders, but this data alone is likely to be a highly deficient measure of all those who have engaged in crime. The fact that a crime has taken place needs to be known in the first place and the perpetrator has to have been apprehended and convicted impartially irrespective of their social characteristics. The proportion that escape justice even from known crimes can be roughly calculated, but by definition knowledge of their characteristics is virtually impossible to ascertain compared to that of those convicted. To reiterate, it is not valid to generalise the social characteristics of criminals from the unrepresentative sample of those that have been caught and convicted.

In an attempt to improve the validity of the data on people who have committed crime, self-report studies and surveys have been carried out. The aim of this type of research is to elicit information in confidence from interviewees on any crimes or delinquent acts they have committed over a specified time period such as the previous 12 months, or even during their entire lifetimes. Many of the studies have focussed on measuring juvenile delinquency and tracing changes in self-reported behaviour through a longitudinal approach, one example of which was Farrington's early 1960s initiated longitudinal study in south London of 411 working class males (Newburn, 2013, p.78). More recently, the Home Office commissioned Offending Crime and Justice Survey (Treadwell, 2013, pp.87-88, Hales et al, 30/11/2018) was a self-report survey of national scope, run annually between 2003 and 2006. Taking a sample of 10 – 25 year olds, its aim was to measure offending amongst young people and through longitudinal follow up of up to four interviews of a proportion of the sample identify transitions in offending.

Self-report studies clearly offer the advantage over official statistics on convicted criminals in that this information does not bear the imprint of official processes, performance indicator pressures and possible bias in the treatment of certain groups in the criminal justice system which may lay behind the official conviction statistics. It can therefore be used to improve the accuracy of official data on criminals and their social distribution, but like victim surveys is much dependent on the accuracy of the information provided, the honesty of the provider, and the avoidance of demand characteristics of the interview situation.

However, the one area where information on criminality is particularly thin is on the white collar and corporate type. Regarding the latter, information is available from the Ministry of Justice on the prosecution of corporations, but it must be born in mind that most business 'misdemeanours' are handled by investigative agencies and that given the disparity of resources available between the agencies and many business corporations, prosecution and conviction rates are relatively low.

A weighted measure of crime

It has further been questioned whether a simple aggregate approach to the measurement of crime, however accurate, is appropriate given the vast variations in the seriousness of different crimes and the fact that lesser crimes substantially outnumber more harmful ones. As an alternative approach, a scale that provides weightings in terms of the relative seriousness of or harm resulting from different crimes could be constructed and applied. The 'Cambridge Crime Harm Index' (Maguire and McVie, in Liebling, et al, ed., 2017, Ch.7) is a recent example of such an attempt. Although the evaluation of the 'seriousness' of crimes underpinning such scales may be open to debate, one might speculate that if corporate crimes were placed on such an index, some would have a very high weighting indeed.

A tentative summary of some crime trends

Clearly, pulling all of these and other sources of information together would be a monumental task. Here, the far more modest task of summarising some general trends through reference to large data sources of police generated official statistics and Crime Survey information will be attempted.

1. From 1876 to 1981, national crime statistics have been reliant exclusively on official police sources. These statistics show very low levels of crime up to the late 1920s with modest increases between then and the mid 1950s, from which time crime levels soared until the early 1990s. This mid 1950s crime take off period, particularly regarding burglaries, would appear to be related to a period of growing affluence and the acquisition of portable

goods within households which were left unoccupied for longer periods as more women were becoming employed outside of the home.

2. Following the introduction of the Crime Survey in 1981, trends from two different measures can be compared. Whilst Crime Survey data has consistently revealed far higher levels of crime than the police recorded statistics show, both trends showed a very similar upward path through to approximately the early to mid-1990s. There is therefore mutual corroborative evidence of an increase in the general crime level over this period which would appear to have substance.

3. From that point, the trends from the two sources diverged, with Crime Survey statistics showing a steady decline through to 2010, whereas police recorded statistics leapt with the introduction of new counting rules in the late 1990s and the National Crime Recording Standard in 2002. Interestingly, once these changes had bedded in, from 2004, the police statistics started to parallel the drop which the Crime Survey had continued to show. Allowing for the effects of these changes in the recording of police statistics outlines earlier in this chapter, a downward trend post mid-1990s would seem to be substantiated.

4. The Crime Survey continued to show a downward crime trend, the drop for 2016 – 2017 being 9% overall. The closing of some police stations and a decline in the number of front line police officers through austerity related public sector cutbacks might be expected to itself have had a downward effect on both the detection and reporting of crime. However, police statistics for the three years leading up to 2017 have shown overall increases of 5%, 7% and 13% consecutively, the last figure indicating an increase within most of the main crime categories. If there has been a 'crime fall' since the mid-1990s as indicated in Crime Survey findings, this data challenges Crime Survey data that the fall is continuing, even though the police statistics lost their 'national statistics' accredited status in 2014.

5. One area of crime that had substantial media coverage during early 2019 was that of knife crime which had been reported to have reached epidemic proportions. Official statistics available for England and Wales provided by the Office for National Statistics in this area are reliant on police recorded data which do not have National Statistics status. The recording of a

crime as a knife crime includes all crimes involving knives, whether used or not. For purposes of continuity, data from Greater Manchester Police are excluded due to undercounting prior to December 2017 resulting in a misleading figure of an increase of 145% between 2017 and 2018. The remaining national figures showed a 6% increase from 2017 to 2018. Over this period, figures for homicides from knife crime actually fell from 258 to 252. However, a growing proportion of these crimes were becoming concentrated in the category of young male perpetrator and victims.

6. The full introduction of cybercrime measures into the Crime Survey data will lead to a significant jump in its measure of the crime level. Whilst providing a break in the continuity of the data, it is one which will more closely attune the Survey findings to the changing nature of crime in the early twenty first century.

The social distribution of crime

Levels of criminality can be analysed in terms of key social characteristics of the population. These characteristics include social class, gender and ethnicity, and a further factor in the distribution of crime is that of locality. In this section, we will touch on some explanations of the social distribution of crime, with the important proviso that they tend to rely on the factuality of official crime statistics.

Criminality and the working class

Crime statistics have consistently suggested that delinquency and crime levels are higher amongst the working class. Why might this be so? Marxist theorists such as William Chambliss have argued that in capitalist societies the ruling class have the power to socially define crime as behaviour that would threaten their power and privilege. The laws of the land and the entire criminal justice system, whilst cloaked in the ideological appearance of neutrality and public interest, are predicated on the need to politically control the working class. Whilst in fact crimes of the politically powerful are endemic in capitalist society, the focus on its prevalence amongst the working class directs their attention toward the criminals in their midst as opposed to their oppressors above and can rally their support for draconian measures against working class perpetrators. From a Marxist perspective, in reality, capitalism as a system is criminogenic due to its materialistically motivated culture, surfacing either through deprivation or greed and corruption, in different proportions dependent on the position of perpetrators in the stratification system.

Merton's strain theory also related high levels of working class criminality to materialistic values and position in the social structure, but from a functionalist perspective. For Merton, commenting on the enterprise culture of American capitalism, the values of a materialistically aspirational society were regarded as broadly shared across the social structure. However, some sections of society whose chances of success are restricted or blocked due to their lowly position within the stratification system, suffer the pressure of strain between materialistic aspirations and their lack of opportunity to achieve them by legitimate means. Consequently, Merton argued that the temptation to strive for social status accompanying material success through criminal means is greater amongst poorer sections of the population.

Alternatively, advocates of subcultural theory have questioned the view that shared aspirational values are a driving force that explains higher levels of working class criminality. Pioneered by Albert Cohen, this type of explanation emphasised that those within poorer sections of society tend to experience 'status frustration'. Recognising their limited likelihood to effectively compete with the middle classes for social status can lead to their detachment from and rejection of middle class values of success through conformity. This rejection, which may start in school, is conducive to the formation of an environment within which individuals are able to gain status through embracing with like others subcultural values of non-conformity. Immersion into such a subculture was claimed to provide a better understanding of delinquent behaviour that was not motivated by conventional status aspiration for monetary gain but instead often took the form of a more destructive nature.

Understanding women's lesser criminality

The focus of much criminology has traditionally been on explaining the crimes of men and building theories of criminality on this basis. This is because official statistics have consistently shown far higher levels of offending by men. Such explanations have included 'doing masculinity' to explain the higher level of male violent crime.

However, a theory claiming to explain the misleading nature of these statistics regarding the level of women's criminality was developed by Otto Pollak in the 1950s. Analysing data from a number of countries, Pollak argued that official statistics substantially under reported the level of female crime. The essence of his argument was that women are more deceitful and manipulative than men, and that along with this, given their more privatised domestic role within family life or employment status, they are more able than men to 'mask' many of the crimes that they commit against their families and employers. When caught, it appeared that women had a higher propensity to commit crimes which were of a minor nature, such as shoplifting, and Pollak's so called 'chivalry thesis' postulated that in a patriarchal society, when women were brought before the male dominated criminal justice system they were treated more leniently than men.

What does official data on gender differences in criminality reveal? Essentially, it suggests that women are far less involved in criminal behaviour than men in all areas of criminal activity. Moreover, the crimes that they do commit tend to be of a less serious nature and mainly property related offences. Indeed, in one specific form of offence, that of shoplifting, women's crime levels, whilst lower than men's, are closer behind than in other types. However, even here, this evidence needs to be placed in the context of: a) shopping being a more predominant female activity, b) research showing that women shoplift fewer and less expensive items than men and c) that this and other property crime may reflect the 'feminisation of poverty', placing women in the role of providers in need.

Overall, more women than men have only one conviction and their criminal careers are shorter than men's. However, during the 1980s and 1990s, female offending was increasing, and by the early twentieth century evidence was emerging of a narrowing of the male and female offending gap. Writers such as Adler sought to argue that following the women's movement, a degree of women's liberation from repressive controls and improved opportunities for labour market participation would open up more legitimate and illegitimate opportunities. Both this position and Pollak's above interpretation have been strongly criticised by feminist criminologists such as Heidensohn.

If Pollak were correct, self-report studies would tend to reveal a substantial amount of hidden female crime that has not been picked up on in official statistics. In fact, whilst such studies have indicated a narrowing of the female to male crime rates, evidence on the different patterns of crime has remained remarkably similar.

Heidensohn (1996, Ch.9) has argued that understanding women's crime and its relatively low rates must be seen within the context of a patriarchal social structure which: a) on the one hand requires of them the responsibilities of important social control roles, especially through the soft power of nurturing the young within the domestic sphere, and b) on the other remains highly controlling of them through the use of patriarchal power. It is argued that women's low levels of crime are seen to reflect their highly ensnared position within control structures and that therefore understanding women's crime can best be approached through a control theory approach.

Women's expected role in the domestic sphere is that of providing a good moral upbringing of the young, irrespective of whether domestic commitments are doubled up with work commitments. Blame can therefore be steeped on mothers for apparently not having performed this role adequately during periods of rising levels of public disorder, as, for example, was the case during the 1980s.

Within communities, women play important informal networking roles through sharing customs and moral values and engaging in basic care tasks, and within lower professional welfare roles they act to soften state power. Overall, the perceived importance of their nurturing and soft control roles heightens the possibility of their criminal or deviant behaviour being viewed as particularly shameful, itself providing an element of constraint on their behaviour.

Heidensohn goes on to contend that women's own freedom is heavily constrained through patriarchal power. They are controlled within the domestic sphere through gendered attitudes and expectations which keeps them to their prescribed tasks. This constrains women's expectations and they may be further controlled by actual or threat of male coercive power in the form of domestic violence as victims of a form of still relatively hidden male crime.

In the public sphere, women's freedom of movement is restricted by fear of being potential victims of street violence, despite the fact that they are more at risk of forms of violent crime within their own homes, and if falling victim to street violence, they risk having contributory blame put on their shoulders for not heeding advice to restrict their movements. Further, girls and women risk potential loss of 'good reputation' in the eyes of males if they do not carefully monitor their sexually related behaviour.

Within the workplace, women's roles tend to be subordinate to males who hold more powerful positions. They are therefore vulnerable to sexual harassment which induces stress and sometimes resignation. Their lower level occupational roles also reduce the extent of serious female white collar crime and implication in corporate crime.

Social policies, based on gendered assumptions, are likely to reinforce the control of women. For example, care in the community policy can pressurise women to taking on a heavy domestic burden through the expectation that they will naturally provide that care free for those in need within the family.

Essentially, then, Heidensohn explains low levels of female criminality in terms of the gendered constraints placed on their lives through the burdensome commitments they find themselves engulfed in within a patriarchal society as both agents of soft the social control of others and being oppressed and confined by patriarchal control within domestic, public and work environments.

From this position, on the issue of rising levels of imprisonment of women in recent decades, an alternative explanation to the liberationist one could be that the traditional constraints that Heidensohn refers to might not have slackened that much, but that women have been disproportionately hit by harder sentencing policies influenced by right realist zero tolerance approaches which increase the likelihood of incarceration for the more minor offences that women tend to commit. Women's incarceration in British prisons increased threefold between 1990 and the early 2000s.

Race, ethnicity and crime

Data in Britain on crime levels has shown significant variability between different ethnic groups, with the highest conviction rates shown for Afro Caribbeans. Thus, although this group make up under 3% of the population, they comprise almost 14% of the prison population. Likewise, in the United States, incarceration levels of black Americans are remarkably high compared to those of whites. Accepted at face value, such figures would suggest far higher levels of Afro Caribbean criminality.

The pioneering work of Lombroso related evidence of different criminality rates to different biologically inbuilt racial characteristics, arguing that the black race had retained primitive characteristics within its genetic makeup that predisposed individuals toward crime. This genetic based view, along with associated eugenics thinking, although subsequently discredited, has found more contemporary echoes in arguments put by such writers as Herrnstein and Murray who have argued that blacks are less intelligent than whites and that lower intelligence level is associated with higher concentrations within the underclass and higher levels of criminality.

Most sociologists would strongly avoid explaining criminal behaviour in terms of racial characteristics and would seek explanations in terms of ethnicity and cultural and environmental influences. For example, even if the veracity of official crime statistics is accepted, it could be argued, as did left realists such as Lea and Young, that the extent of relative economic deprivation, marginality and discrimination experienced by ethnic groups can lead to a subculture of resentment which may be moderated by the effect of different ethnic cultures that may play a greater or lesser constraining influence on ultimate criminal behaviour. We thus see substantial differences in the crime rates of those of Afro Caribbean and Asian ethnic groups.

But in other ways we cannot avoid the concept of race since conviction and incarceration rates are the outcome of a long process of judgements and decision making that may start with targeting certain groups for stop and search and processing them through the criminal justice system in such a way that racial bias can influence the outcomes. For example, although figures have shown that in relation to their numbers in the population Afro Caribbeans have been about seven times more likely to be stopped and searched on the streets, the proportionate 'hit rate' of finding drugs or weapons etc. on them has been about the same as for other ethnic groups at below 10%. However, purely in terms of higher stop and search numbers, higher levels of criminality will be discovered.

There is also a suggestion of racial bias in sentencing. For example, research by Hood (1992) in the West Midlands found that 57% of Afro Caribbeans compared to 40% of whites received prison sentences, along with evidence of longer sentences for comparable crimes, although the latter could in part be explained as a consequence of a higher proportion of not guilty pleas.

Since the official statistics themselves are therefore a highly suspect measure of the comparative levels of criminality of different ethnic groups, alternative measurements have been taken through self-report surveys. These surveys include the Youth Lifestyles Survey and the Offending, Crime and Justice Survey. In essence, they have consistently shown that, with the exception of robbery, white respondents had higher acknowledged rates, with the rate of crime reported by black participants significantly lower and that of Asians lower still.

A persuasive explanation of the focus on Afro Caribbean criminality, combining social structural and interactionist approaches, was put forward by Stuart Hall. Hall studied the phenomena of the 'black mugger' in terms of the economic and hegemonic problems that British capitalism was facing during the early 1970s. He argued that immigrant groups were hit particularly hard by the recession and that their involvement in petty street crime did increase. The hegemonic crisis of questioning state authority surfaced in the troubles in Northern Ireland and growing student militancy and industrial action. In the midst of these problems, the image of the black mugger took the proportions of a moral panic, with the press often repeating police sources of information and the public demanding stronger policing against the perceived problem. During these troubled times, the black mugger served to focus attention on immigrants as the main problem and simultaneously divided the working class along racial grounds.

The effect of locality

Crime can also be studied in terms of locality. This 'social spatial' approach to criminality can be traced back to the work of the Chicago School of urban sociology. In the American context of mass migration of Europeans and black Americans into cities during the early twentieth century and the largely unplanned and market driven nature of city expansion, sociologists at the University of Chicago developed a model of the dynamics of city growth based on that of Chicago for which they claimed much broader application.

Chicago School pioneers such as Ernest Burgess developed a concentric circle model of urban growth. According to this model, growth naturally radiates out from a business and industrial centre to form distinctive concentric circles of residential zones. Robert Park likened this process to that of the ecology of the natural world whereby similarly to the ecological processes of competition, invasion and establishment that take place in the natural world, cities develop distinctive neighbourhoods through sorting processes of city populations.

The key area of urban interest in the Chicago School model was that surrounding the industrial centre, referred to as the 'zone of transition'. This area of once quite substantial properties that were built during an earlier phase of city development, had subsequently become run down and cheap accommodation as the city developed outward into more recent suburban middle class zones and a commuter belt. The typical dynamics of population movement were that the zone of transition would often provide housing for newly arrived migrants, some of whom in would in time become sufficiently successful to move outwards to the suburbs and upwards into the American middle classes.

This process left the zone of transition with a ghettoised and shifting population of low skilled and rootless workers comprising people of different cultural backgrounds living in conditions of poverty and deprivation. Official statistics indicated that levels of crime and delinquency were comparatively high in this zone. What could best explain this phenomena?

One approach was 'disorganisation theory', adopted by Shaw and McKay. They argued that it was the disorganisation inherent in the zone of transition environment associated with the lack of a singular body of integrating cultural norms which provided room for the emergence of delinquent cultural values and behaviour to take hold, a situation which could be contrasted with the social order, stability and lower crime rates of the outer middle class zones.

Refining Shaw and McKay's approach, Sutherland emphasised the importance of 'differential association', which explained propensity toward criminality in terms of the relative exposure of individuals to conformist or lawbreaking cultural values. However, what arguably tends to be under-acknowledged in these approaches is an understanding at an individual level of why people form the associations that they do in the first place. Moreover, whilst certain types of crime such as drug dealing and taking, prostitution and the activities of street delinquent gangs may have been more characteristic of the zone of transition, Sutherland himself came to emphasise the vast underestimation of crime amongst the middle classes in the form of 'white collar crime'.

In a somewhat more contemporary context, Ian Taylor has related variable local and regional crime rates to the variable impact of the forces of global modernisation. For Taylor, against the background of economic and structural modernisation dating from the late 1980s, 'the highest rates of increase in reported crime have occurred in those industrial areas, like South Yorkshire, with the most recent loss of what was locally assumed to have been a secure labour market' (cited in Carrabine et al, 2002, p.66).

Victimisation and fear of crime

From the 1980s, a political, social and academic climate was emerging within which more attention was being paid to the victims of crime. This was against a backdrop of growing criticism that during the 1970s, especially from radical left criminologists, too much attention had been paid to understanding the social distribution of the perpetrators of crime, along with a view that perpetrators could themselves be seen as the victims of social structural circumstances. A new right political environment that put greater emphasis on individual responsibility for one's actions was accompanied by a hardening of attitudes toward those who engaged in crime. Crime was becoming a more highly politicised issue, associated with the broader issues of the perceived need to challenge a growing disrespect for authority. The victims of crime, commonly regarded as vulnerable and innocent, were seen as deserving more attention and sympathy. This was the broader context of the introduction of the first major victimisation survey in Britain, the British Crime Survey, in 1981. Much of the findings regarding victimisation have been based on these surveys and their successor, the Crime Survey for England and Wales.

Before some general findings are summarised, some cautionary points can be raised:

1. Following Newburn (2013, Ch.17), the tendency to stereotype perpetrators and victims as two separate and distinct groups of individuals must be called into question. Broad ranging research carried out by Fattah (1991) indicated that criminals were themselves more likely to be the victims of crime than were non-criminals. Furthermore, violent crime victims were more likely to have significant criminal involvement.

2. Public sympathy for victims was not universal. An example of a less sympathetic response might be that sometimes given to female victims of sexual crimes. In their dress and demeanour or their 'negligence' in not avoiding certain localities and at particular times, women have sometimes been held, even by judges in court, as being at least in part personally culpable for their victimisation.

3. Before considering which groups are the most likely victims of crime, it is important to be aware that findings tend to be based on a restricted definition of crime in the form of direct personal encounters, one close to that by which crime is commonly perceived and loosely defined as street crime.

Those living in poor urban areas, being young males or from ethnic minority groups, categories which are by no means mutually exclusive, are the social and geographical characteristics that are associated with higher risks of being as victim of crime. The higher crime rate amongst those in poor areas indicates that crime here is of an intra class nature – that is, working class on working class. Local surveys have shown that, regarding for example burglary, victims and perpetrators often reside in the same poor localities as each other. Thus, those with the least property suffer the higher frequency of victimisation and are disproportionately likely to find their victimisation exacerbated by the absence of insurance cover.

Some victimisation may be of a repeat of ongoing nature. This can make it difficult to quantify in large surveys. Although women may be less likely overall to be the victims of crime than men, there is one clear exception which is that of domestic violence. As far as it has been possible to measure, domestic violence, usually but not exclusively against women by men, is a crime that remains quite hidden, highly underreported is a crime with a high repeat level.

Ethnic minorities are more likely to live in poor urban areas and can suffer the additional risk factor of racial victimisation in the form of racial abuse or harassment as an ongoing reality. The police have often had a poor track record in taking such crimes seriously or responding adequately. This matter was brought to a head with the racist murder of Stephen Lawrence in Eltham in 1993 and the subsequent findings of the Macpherson Report which uncovered institutional racism and incompetence in the Metropolitan Police Force.

According to research carried out by Newburn and Rock in three cities in the south east of England and published in 2006 (Newburn, 2013, Ch.17), the homeless are particularly vulnerable to victimisation from the general public, and are, of course, a group that are largely invisible (depending on how homelessness is defined) in national household based surveys.

Although elderly people are generally less prone to be the victims of crime than younger sections of the population, in particular men, there are circumstances where the elderly are vulnerable to crime or mistreatment, often in the form of abuse or neglect – that is within an institutional setting of care homes where such behaviour can often be covered up. It may require the use of covert research or whistle blowing to reveal such abuses in particular instances, but the totality can be difficult to calculate.

A further important point is that the, emotional, behavioural and psychological effects of victimisation may last long after the offence. Neither may the effects on the victim be restricted to themselves. If we are measuring victimisation by its effects, it is important to recognise the effects it can have on those close to the victim, a phenomena that is referred to as 'indirect victimisation'.

In terms of age and gender, those aged 65 and above and women have generally low rates of victimisation. Yet when measures are taken of the fear of crime, these groups rank amongst the highest. Does this mean that the fears of these groups are irrational? There are a number of reasons to question this interpretation or suggest not.

Firstly, national crime survey statistics provide essentially abstracted aggregate measurements of risk or fear. Findings from a number of local surveys have shown fear of crime to be a realistic response to the reality of living in deprived areas where the risk of crime to these groups may be far higher than the national average.

Secondly, it has been suggested that the measurement of fear needs to be more precisely and subtly operationalised (converted to precise measurement) and explicitly related to fear of crime. For example, a question from the British Crime Survey (Newburn, 2013, Ch.17) which asked 'How safe do you feel walking alone in this area after dark', with options ranging from 'very safe' to 'very unsafe' would seem to substantiate this point.

Thirdly, given the restricted view of crime, there may be little or no connection between crime that is experienced and, for example, fear going out at night if a person had been a victim of crime in the workplace.

Fourthly, the media often highlights sexual and violent crimes committed by strangers in public places out of all proportion to the relative risk of being a victim of such crimes, often effecting people's feeling of vulnerability.

White collar, corporate and organisational crime

The concept of 'white collar crime' can be traced back to the pioneering work of Edwin Sutherland, who, in 1949, following a lengthy research into the activities of 70 major American corporations and a smaller number of public utilities, published a book of that name. Whilst public perception of 'crime' had traditionally focussed on street crime and that of the lower social classes, who were therefore seen as more prone to criminality, Sutherland was keen to draw attention to the extent of corporate criminal activity conducted by those in positions of high corporate and social status in the course of their work and he defined white collar crime in these terms.

Sutherland was subsequently criticised for what became regarded as a too loose use of the term and one which more recently has been seen to be in need of refinement. Since the time of his research, a substantial expansion of lower level white collar employment has taken place. This has led to a decline in the power, exclusivity and status associated with much white collar work and the criminal behaviour of workers in these positions is likely to be of a different type to that which Sutherland exposed. As Blumer has argued, the term white collar has retained some worth, more as a general sensitising concept referring to a range of crime within or by businesses. However, a range of more precisely classified definitions have emerged.

It is now more common to distinguish between a redefined use of the term 'white collar crime' and that of 'corporate crime'. Thus, white collar crime can be defined as that conducted by white collar employees, usually working within organisations and undertaken against their employers. This may range from petty theft and involve those low down in the corporate structure to that of illegal activities conducted for self-gain by those in more powerful positions. By contrast (although the boundaries are now always entirely clear), corporate crime can be regarded as criminal behaviour partaken on behalf of the perceived interests of the organisation, usually by those in powerful positions, against either corporate employees, other businesses, the state, or that which affects the general public. This is in fact closer to Sutherland's earlier definition of white collar crime.

A further classificatory approach is referred to by Joyce (2009, p.36). In this case, the term 'occupational crime' is used to refer to criminal activity engaged in by any employees, white or blue collar, undertaken against their employer or customers. By contrast, the term 'organisational crime' is that in which law breaking activity is driven by those working within organisations who regard it to be in the interests of an organisation. Each of these types can be distinguished from 'middle class crime' which is here defined as that engaged in by those of middle class status but in settings separate from the workplace.

Alternatively, Carrabine et al, (2002, Ch.4) make the case for referring to 'organisational forms of crime' which are defined (p.81) as crimes

'by those holding positions in legal or illegal structures or associations that have an organisational basis or are part of a wider organisational framework, the purpose, exploitation or abuse of which can facilitate the pursuit of profit or power or both.'

By focussing on the organisational context, this approach provides a broad umbrella for classifying criminal behaviour at different levels within and in all forms of organisational structure including legitimate and illicit business, organised crime, public and private sector organisations, state crime, political corruption and crossovers between these areas.

However defined, this whole area of criminality is massive. It far surpasses the financial cost of street crime, its costs may not just be financial and its effects are both direct and indirect. The main focus of attention in this section will be on corporate crime.

Public attitudes toward corporate criminality have tended to remain far more relaxed than in the case of 'ordinary' street crime. There are a number of reasons why this may be so. With the assistance of media focus of street crime, corporate crimes are often off the public radar. Crimes that take place within formal organisational settings are conducted within a private sphere of routine business activity that is usually remote from public scrutiny. Here, 'misdemeanours' can often be handled internally for reputational damage limitation purposes (but are sometimes revealed by whistle blowers). Criminal activity, particularly within financial organisations, may be of a highly complex nature and difficult to uncover. Even if uncovered, within complex organisational structures, proof of individual complicity may be difficult to attribute for purposes of successful prosecution.

The effects of corporate crime, even when known, are sometimes diluted across the broad public rather than experienced directly in physical form as in the case of assault or theft. For example, whilst it is possible to calculate the effects on the environment of excessive pollution levels when car manufacturers manipulate downwards figures for car emissions and falsify economy test results, it is not possible to pin these effects on the damaged health of particular individuals.

A further part of the low profiling of corporate, organisational or white collar crime is that it tends to be neglected in official crime statistics, being virtually absent from police statistics or information picked up on in victim surveys. The 'misdemeanours' of business organisations are often policed by light touch regulatory agencies. These agencies are usually more geared toward rectifying wrongs and enforcing compliance than the pursuit of legal action. Thus, for example, inspectors who find that restaurants have broken health and hygiene regulations may provide a timescale within which specified improvements have to be made, followed by notified re-inspection, for the organisation to avoid legal action. In many cases, external regulatory agencies may have limited resources at their disposal to bring prosecutions compared to that available to larger corporations. Furthermore, some institutions, such as the London Stock Exchange, have traditionally been self-regulating, saving the cost of employing an external agency given the complexity of the challenge.

Explanations of corporate and white collar crime

What types of sociological explanations of white collar and corporate crime have been forthcoming? It may be useful to distinguish between micro and macro level explanations, whilst bearing in mind that in the real world these levels are not necessarily mutually exclusive. Micro explanations will tend to focus within institutions, particularly on institutional and workplace cultures. Sutherland's theory of 'differential association' is of this type. According to this theory, institutional workplace environments contain their own balance of cultural norms and values, some tending to inhibit and others to enhance deviant or criminal behaviour. The exposure of individuals to the mix of conformist or criminal cultures will vary according to their patterns of interaction, their durability and intensity. This will shape the likelihood of their engagement in conformist or criminal behaviour and may be powerful enough to overcome the barriers of professional ethics erected in occupations such as accountancy. When criminal behaviour is embarked upon, Matza and Sykes have referred to 'techniques of neutralisation' that may be used to rationalise it by justifying the action or disarming criticism of those caught.

A combination of an intensive profit culture and complacent oversight of employee activities can provide a toxic recipe for the criminality of rogue individuals, an infamous example of which was the self-interested fraudulent trading activities of Nick Leeson which brought down Barings Bank in 1995.

Occupational crime may exist amongst both white and blue collar workers within a subcultural environment that justifies petty pilfering from employers through the neutralisation technique of fair game in recompense for poor pay. In such cases, fiddling may even be 'overlooked' by employers if conducted by employees against customers, as revealed in Ditton's research which revealed fiddling by bread delivery men.

Corporate criminality may even flow from dominant corporate values, possibly influenced by the tone from the top, and even be sanctioned in employee training, as, for example, in the case of the financial incentives and training of salespersons evidenced in covert research conducted by consumer protection programmes such as the BBC's *Watchdog*.

Other explanations take on board a more macro framework, focussing on the broader political, economic and normative social environment. From a functionalist perspective, for Durkheim the structural changes of the advance of the division of labour that accompanied modernisation risked enhancing conditions of anomie (normlessness) whereby moral guidelines lessen their capacity to inhibit illegal behaviour. Picked up on by Merton in the form of strain theory, corporations may engage in innovative responses to pressures for profit maximisation in the form of criminality under these anomic conditions.

In many cases where acts of corporate criminality are brought to light, state penalties and punishments can be relatively modest given the magnitude and severity of the consequences of some of these crimes. For example, the worst that rogue employers who breach minimum wage legislation (an act effectively comparable to that of theft on a grand scale) have to face is making back payment (or an agency having to do so if they were used), paying a fine, and suffering some damage, possibly temporary, to their reputation. One argument given as to why the law seems to apply relatively leniently to corporate offences is that the motives for their crime are often closely connected to the ethics and core values of the free enterprise market. As such, for Marxists, corporate criminality and corruption driven by materialistic values and the quest for profit maximisation are endemic to capitalism. This perspective also explains the general public ambivalence toward corporate crime as resulting from the powerful effect of pro-business ideology.

Punishment – corporate and street crime disparity

If we were to place corporate and various forms of organisational crime on a scale of the seriousness of its repercussions (like the Cambridge Crime Harm Index scale), many such crimes would be placed in a very high position. Given the expected close relationship between the severity of crime, in terms of the seriousness of its consequences, and the severity of sentencing, we would also expect to find evidence of particularly high sentencing. In terms of these types of crime, this relationship seems to be conspicuously absent.

It can be argued that there is a massive disparity, both in terms of public perception and relative punishment, between corporate and 'everyday' crime. To indicate the favour that perpetrators of corporate crime tend to receive before the law compared to 'ordinary' criminals, Box devised a spoof letter which, based on the treatment of corporate criminals, might be sent to a burglar:

'Dear G E Rald,
We should like to take this opportunity to inform you that on 12th March this year you were seen entering empty handed into the private premises of Ms P C Edwards of Convent St, Folkestone, and leaving shortly afterwards with your hands full.

In our opinion, this constitutes a violation of the Theft Act 1968 subsection 32(c) and we would be grateful if you would consider the following advice: please stop going down Convent St and entering houses without the owners' permission.

We should warn you that next March 12th another police constable will be on foot duty in Convent St, and should he notice a repetition of your behaviour, we shall have to consider the possibility of taking even more stringent action than we have on this occasion.'

(Box, 1983, p.50, quoted by Hughes and Langan in Muncie and McLaughlin ed., p.258.)

Through enhanced media attention in recent decades to such corporate misdemeanours as financial scandals, public awareness of these activities, whether technically criminal or not, is likely to have risen. However, the question remains as to the extent to which regulations, prosecutions and penalties against perpetrators have increased and whether public opinion in this area has hardened in the longer term given political and media focus on defining crime in street crime terms and focussing on the poorer sections of society as the main perpetrators.

Victims of corporate crime

As documented by Hughes and Langan (Muncie & McLaughlin ed., 2002, Ch.6), the potential victims of corporate crime include employees, consumers, the general public, businesses and the state. Given what would appear to be the very modest risk of severe penalties for corporate misdemeanours or criminal infractions, it is not surprising that rational calculations of costs and benefits can lead to corporate decision making that can risk high levels of victimisation, as illustrated in the following examples.

Customers risk harm from unrecalled products that are known by manufacturers to be defective. Such decisions have been known to be based on costs and benefits analysis, one example of which was the sale of the cheap and dangerously defective Ford Pinto car during the 1970s. From tests conducted, it was known that the placing of the petrol tank could lead to highly dangerous combustion in certain types of accident. However, production went ahead based on the calculation that the costs of recall and correction were likely to outweigh the penalties risked by any harm caused by the faulty product. Although the product was claimed to be responsible for at least 500 deaths, the company was unsuccessfully prosecuted for 'reckless homicide', with the car only eventually being recalled.

Businesses that disregard or are lax regarding health and safety regulations will be endangering their employees, but those with decision making power may rationally calculate that the risk is worth taking if policing is slack, proof of culpability is difficult and the potential penalties are modest. To illustrate this, under highly dangerous conditions and within the circumstances of competitive pressures in the industry, 168 workers lost their lives when the Piper Alpha oil rig exploded in 1988. Weaknesses were identified in the enforcement of safety regulations and the judge overseeing the investigation made over 100 recommendations for improving health and safety in this type of environment. Neither the firm, Occidental Petroleum, nor any of its personnel, faced criminal sanction.

Communities will be at risk where corporations are working with dangerous and toxic substances. The most serious disaster resulting from such a hazard was the escape of gasses from a plant in Bhopal, India, in 1984. Thousands of people in the locality lost their lives (there is much variation in the figures claimed) and the health of many more was severely damaged for the long term. The parent company Union Carbide disputed claims of negligence and through managing to have the case heard in India, enabled its own executives to avoid prosecution, was able to limit compensation to $470 million, a derisory figure by American compensation standards, and has been criticised for failing to adequately clean up the site.

In 1987, 193 lives were lost when a roll-on roll-off ferry, the Herald of Free Enterprise, capsized shortly after leaving the Belgian port of Zeebrugge. Set on a tight schedule, the ship departed from the port with ballast in the tanks and the bow doors left open. Although the coroner recorded a verdict of 'unlawful killing' and a public inquiry found negligence at all levels of the company hierarchy, criminal prosecution of the company for 'corporate manslaughter' was unsuccessful as the events were found to not be attributable to a corporate controlling mind.

Self-interested business activities, whilst not necessarily illegal, could seriously threaten the very survival of other businesses. As an example, the grocery market watchdog revealed in 2014 the supermarket Tesco's excessive delay in paying suppliers in order to improve the appearance of their own financial position. This practice severely impacted on businesses reliant on payment.

Rates of pay below the legal minimum wage, as well as intimidating working conditions, were revealed at Sports Direct by undercover reporters from the Guardian newspaper in 2015. A vast majority of workers were employed through an employment agency, Best Connection. The employment agency was required to pay workers back pay for the shortfall and a penalty of just over half that total amount, which was itself halved for being paid within 14 days.

Corporate tax evasion defrauds the government out of funds which ultimately will impact on the provision of public services. This will be most felt by those most reliant on them and even tax avoidance could be seen as a moral crime with a similar impact when viewed from a broader social harm angle.

At a very broad level, if strictly legal, reckless activities within the financial sector, driven by a culture of excessive risk taking in a market that was being deregulated from the mid-1980s, have been in large part responsible for widespread suffering following the post 2008 severe recession. This massive social harm has seen very few prosecutions throughout the world.

Given all that has been said above, there may ultimately be some justification for a broadening out of how crime is viewed to include activities which are strictly speaking not illegal. Thus, Hughes and Langan have defined corporate crime as 'illegal or harmful activities – both acts of commission and omission – engaged in by business organizations or members of such organizations in pursuit of their goal of maximizing power and profit' (Muncie & McLaughlin ed., 2002, p.246). Defined in this way, corporate crime is viewed as a form of rationally and economically motivated activity conducted for the benefit of the corporation but with harmful effects.

How crime and deviance are socially constructed

Attempts to measure the level of crime and identify crime trends have conventionally relied heavily on the notion that crime levels can be measured objectively as solid facts, even if there is some dispute over the accuracy of the figures themselves. Moreover, many theories that have attempted to provide sociological explanations of crime levels and their social distribution have rested on the apparent factuality of crime data. Sociological approaches which measure criminality in this factual way to try and establish its causes are essentially adopting a positivist methodology.

Those who adopt a social constructionist view of crime and deviance tend to be critical of positivist approaches for overlooking the fact that crime and deviance are socially constructed phenomena. To appreciate this vantage point, it is necessary to step back from seeing the contemporary conceptions of criminal and deviant behaviour within one's society as solid and normal and recognise that there is nothing intrinsic in any behaviour itself by which it will necessarily be deemed criminal or deviant. This is because what counts as criminal behaviour is socially defined and variable over time and between places. For example, although the taking of life may be an abhorrent crime during peace time (although societies vary in using the death penalty), the same act may be rewarded as an act of duty or heroism during time of war.

In adopting a social constructionist viewpoint, the focus shifts away from trying to understand the causes of criminality reliant on crime statistics and questions the apparent distribution of crime levels within different sections of the population. Attention turns to examining the social processes involved whereby some acts are seen as criminal within social and cultural meaning contexts whilst others are not. This shifts attention from seeing criminality as inherent in the person or the act to that of examining the social processes involved in the designation of their criminality. Official crime statistics are then recognised as the outcome of processes within meaning systems and as such must be recognised as soft as opposed to hard data. Social constructionist positions are therefore taken up within the interpretive perspectives of symbolic interactionism and ethnomethodology.

From a constructionist viewpoint, there emerged debate over the relationship between social class and criminality. Whilst official statistics suggest that crime levels are higher amongst the working class, ethnomethodologists such as Cicourel pointed out that judgements made by the police and within the criminal justice system are influenced by stereotypes whereby behaviour that is potentially labelled as juvenile delinquency is more likely to be so labelled in working class neighbourhoods compared to the same type of behaviour taking place within middle class areas. The focus of concern was to show that the resulting data on patterns of delinquency between different the social groups should not be taken as a valid measurement of their different propensities toward delinquency since poorer sections of society are more likely to have their behaviour criminalised due to pre-existing negative stereotypical judgements of them. The resultant delinquency rates therefore tell us more about subjective judgements toward, rather than different objective levels of, delinquency between the social classes. Consequently, Cicourel argued that the real focus of attention needed to be directed toward the processes involved in the creation of the statistics rather than the assumption of their factuality for further analysis as tended to be largely assumed by positivists.

Even the recording of crime by the police has a socially constructed dimension since it is influenced by decisions made by victims as to whether to report it in the first place and whether the police accept and record it as such. One of the key purposes for the recording of crime is for the police to be held accountable for their performance. Practices of recording crime may therefore be shaped by this context. The focus of attention should be employed in applying qualitative research to study these interpretive processes.

Symbolic interactionists such as Howard Becker have identified moral entrepreneurs as those in positions of power and status who are able to influence the moral climate of the 'right thinking' public against the actions of others who are defined as deviant. These elite minorities, who claim to speak on behalf of a 'moral majority', often find their views disproportionately shared within the traditional media. According to Stanley Cohen, the public are particularly susceptible to labelling sections of society as deviant during times of dramatic change, social crisis and uncertainty. The function of this process it to reaffirm a common consensus against a labelled group who are scapegoated as responsible for the problem and who become placed in the firing line of repressive measures.

Cohen argued that as a result of moral panic, induced by the media, attention to the labelled group in question is out of all proportion to the extent of their deviance. However, as in the case of the Mods and Rockers in the mid-1960s, that attention, media anticipation of further trouble, and the presence of the media to witness the trouble, provide the circumstances for the groups to play out their deviant roles. In other words, media exaggeration of deviance can promote deviance amplification, and broader public outrage elicits a response of support for its suppression.

Through the media, often working in symbiotic relationship with political elites, an element of agenda setting is possible which can influence the public and political climate, crime related social policy, the passage of legislation and operational decisions, ultimately effecting the official crime statistics which are fed back to the public and often reported in the media as hard facts.

A social constructionist viewpoint raises questions about the broader distribution of power and how the behaviour of some sections of society tends to become criminalised for purposes of social control. Thus, through their social power and status, some groups are particularly able to shape the laws of the land and define (other's!) particular behaviour as criminal, whilst the deeds of the powerful and corporations may escape the designation of criminality, face modest penalties or be little seen as criminal in the public consciousness.

The social construction of crime can be heavily influenced by media preoccupation with certain types of crime, such as violent crime, that are newsworthy due to the ease of sensational and graphic portrayal and simplistic explanations in terms of individual stories. Crime reporting therefore provides as distorted picture of crime compared to that in the 'real world'. Filming of demonstrations tends to be from behind the safety of police lines and easy information may be gleaned from official police sources. Media preoccupation with violent crime can be highly disproportionate. For example Jewkes (2004, p.54) referred to research by Williams and Dickinson (1993) which found that 65% of crime reporting in the British press involved stories of 'interpersonal violence' compared to 6% of police recorded crime. Furthermore, an excessive media emphasis on violent crime in public places has arguably at least in part shaped a social construction of fear of crime at the hands of strangers that is out of proportion to statistical risk, whilst through little mention of criminality within the private world of the family and corporations helps to render crimes in these areas almost invisible.

Guidance for pragmatic intervention – realist explanations of crime

During the 1980s, in both Britain and the United States, parties of the political right were in power and setting the agenda across a range of policy issues. Touchstones to their political ideologies included a sharp focus on promoting individual rights and responsibilities within free market economies, where, it was argued, the state had taken too much responsibility for people's lives and their welfare. The consequence had been a breakdown of authority, respect for others and law and order. Governments were focussing on the measures for reasserting authority within a capitalist system that they were steering in a neoliberal direction.

Within this social and political context, 'realist' approaches in criminological thinking were emerging and right realism took a particularly hard-nosed form in the United States. For right realists, to combat spiralling levels of crime, it was argued that policy changes needed to be introduced which held individuals more accountable for their own actions. The most assertive positions tended to be adopted by writers such as James Wilson who were critical of those libertarians whom, it was claimed, had taken a soft approach to low level crime and deviance and had been, as a consequence, exacerbating the problem. The action of individuals was seen as driven by their rational calculation of those courses that on balance pay, and criminal behaviour was no exception. Since criminal action was regarded as a consequence of individual calculation which takes into account a balancing of benefits and risks in situations of opportunity, it was argued that the calculus had to be tilted against the temptation to engage in criminal behaviour. This could be best achieved through enhanced security and surveillance measures, the risk of stern penalties, a zero tolerance of low level crime and increasing use of incarceration.

Other right realists placed crime within the context of social class and ethnicity whilst also relating it to individual deficiencies. Thus, for Charles Murray, high levels of crime within deprived inner city areas were viewed in terms of cultural and moral deficiency. High crime rates within these areas were associated with the actions of a morally irresponsible underclass, encouraged by a culture of welfare dependency and allowed a lifestyle sustained by the taxation of those who supported themselves by gainful employment and adherence to the rules. From this position, generous welfare levels would not reduce crime. Instead, they enhanced dependency and moral irresponsibility at cost to others. The key to tackling high crime levels within such communities was therefore the sobering effect that enhancing individual moral responsibility for self-support by gainful employment would be best encouraged through reducing welfare levels.

Herrnstein and Murray evidenced that research had shown that those with lower IQs, taken as a measure of their intelligence, display higher levels of reported criminality. Greater proportions of the less able concentrated in the lower social classes explains high crime levels in deprived inner city areas. Likewise, a genetic link was claimed to exist between black ethnic minorities and their lower intelligence levels than the white population, as demonstrated in their lower IQ scores, which was then linked to their higher crime rates.

In an important right realist article by Wilson and Kelling entitled 'Broken Windows' (Newburn, 2013, pp.275-276), it was argued that the key to controlling crime in run down areas is a hardening of response to low level crime and the clearing up of the consequences of vandalism within neighbourhoods that would otherwise attract further acts of crime and vandalism. Later, Kelling and Coles (1997, Ch.7) went as far as arguing that a new paradigm is needed to tackle the blighting of city neighbourhoods resulting from rising street criminality amongst young males. In their work entitled 'Fixing Broken Windows', they argued that the old model of tackling street crime had been too fragmented between various agencies and lacked ownership by the communities themselves. To gain control of blighted communities, high profile proactive policing and the use of custodial sentencing was necessary to signal a strong message to both hardened and 'wannabe' criminals. This included a zero tolerance toward even minor criminality. However, once established, to retain control a broader social approach was necessary. This would comprise community policing applied in a cooperative and integrated way in conjunction with other institutions within and outside of the criminal justice system. In the longer term, the maintenance of order required citizens to take ownership of norm enforcement within their communities.

In Britain, the emergence of a left realist position on crime during the 1980s and 1990s, pioneered by Young, Lea and Matthews, can be seen in the context of a response to two very different positions on crime and law and order. One was to right realist thinking on crime that had gained much soundbite approval and populist support during these decades. The other was to the new and critical criminology of the Marxist influenced left of the 1970s that was combined with interactionism.

In response to right realist analysis, left realists argued that crime could not simply be understood and responded to at the level of individual free choice but had to take account of social structures, social inequality and expectations. The period of new right Conservative government in the UK had introduced policy reforms that aimed to invigorate an entrepreneurial culture, status striving consumerism and materialistic individualism. Economic inequality increased and although people were generally better off and had been lifted out of the absolute poverty of the immediate post war years, this condition enhanced grievance associated with the experience of relative deprivation within poor communities.

Poorer sections of society had become marginalised, not only from the economic benefits of greater wealth creation, but also socially excluded from the routines of mainstream activities through which people's lives are occupied and structured. These conditions heightened a sense of injustice, left realists claimed, which provided an environment within which crime was likely to flourish. Poorer communities therefore experienced higher levels of both criminality and victimisation. This meant, from the point of view of left realists, that the Marxist view of crime as a response of the victims of capitalism to their subjugation was utopian and out of touch with people's immediate and everyday fears of being the victims of street crime.

For Downs and Rock (2007, pp.276-279), Marxist influenced new criminology that had looked to solutions to crime in future socialist conditions became regarded by left realists as idealistic, especially given revelations of the tyrannical nature of eastern European communist regimes, and ill equipped to respond to people's immediate problems of victimisation. Furthermore, new criminology was criticised from feminists such as Carol Smart for ignoring the extent of victimisation suffered by women.

Whilst left realism emerged out of new criminology, it left the ideological radicalism behind. Having transitioned from the new criminology himself, Jock Young provided a left realist analysis (within the context of a high modernist perspective) that a key social change behind a rise in street crime had been a decline in local community life. This decline led to a weakening of the soft policing of moral boundary constraints on individual behaviour that communities once provided. Moreover, a reduction in community policing and a more vigorous top down stop and search approach, which was criticised for targeting certain groups, was seen to have eroded the valuable resource of provision of information and public cooperation with the police within the targeted groups.

Tackling crime, for left realists, had to be evidence based. This was demonstrated in the commissioning in the 1980s of local victimisation surveys within a number of left leaning local authorities. One of the most famous was that headed by Young in Islington in 1986. The purpose of such surveys was to provide people in deprived communities with a voice and acquire empirical evidence to assist analysis in the tackling of crime at a local level.

Left realists, compared to right realists, retained an iota of structural awareness in their explanation of criminality. Their ideas gained more political recognition when New Labour came to power in 1997 with the government mantra being 'tough on crime and tough on the causes of crime'. Whilst much was made of promoting social inclusion, the problem remained that economic inequalities further widened, despite the fact that resources were targeted toward poorer neighbourhoods. In reality, the second half of the mantra became somewhat watered down by the government.

Crime prevention and control

Crime control is an issue that, in varying degrees, has been a matter of public concern from the mid-1950s and became a more highly politicised matter from the 1980s. The best information available suggested that during this time period and through to the mid-1990 the crime rate was steadily and rapidly rising. Concern regarding the crime level was often highlighted in the mass media, with some sections of the tabloid press in particular focussing attention on street and violent crime and the need for a strong law and order response. As explained in the work of sociologists such as Stanley Cohen and Stuart Hall, public reaction had occasionally surfaced in the form of moral panics against a perceived upsurge of criminality within certain sections of the population, to which politicians, the police and the criminal justice system were expected to respond.

Viewed sociologically, we have seen that from a Durkheimian functionalist position, crime can never be fully prevented. Furthermore, from a Marxist perspective, crime is seen as endemic to capitalism. However, crime rates do significantly vary between societies as do responses to crime. Therefore, an important question is how, and to what extent, can the level of crime be controlled. Many of the ideas regarding crime control originate from and have been tested in the United States.

Newburn (2013, Ch.24) identifies 'social' and 'situational' approaches to control. Each of these approaches have been tested in research aimed at providing measurable data on crime reduction. The method often used has been that of experiment and control groups, through which the effects of interventions can be measured to provide policy makers with information by which they can judge their effectiveness and value for money. Research has therefore tended to be focussed at the micro level.

Socially based approaches have taken account of social conditions such as poverty levels, broken families and poor housing which have been seen as social risk factors behind crime levels. Research to measure the effects of compensatory intervention into such conditions was pioneered in the United States during the 1960s. In one such research design, the Perry Preschool Project in Michigan (Program: Perry Preschool Project, 18/01/2019), an experiment group of 58 three to four year old African American children from high risk backgrounds attended preschool classes in guided problem solving each weekday morning and weekly home visits were organised to involve mothers in the project. These interventions were not available to a comparable control group of 56 children. Reviewing data taken from participants in the two groups at the age of 27, it was found that the arrest rate of those in the experiment group was only half that of the control group. Combined with other advantageous comparisons with the control group, for example in levels of education and income achieved, the researchers concluded that the investment in these forms of early intervention was very good value for money.

Intervention in local communities has also been attempted with the purpose of reducing crime levels, especially with an emphasis on the police working with members and listening to their needs. However, the main weakness of such attempts has been in not managing to organise the necessary coordination between a broad body of relevant community groups, thus making prospective effects difficult to measure.

Another social based interventionist approach to reducing offending has been that of organised adult mentor guidance of youngsters. A Home Office evaluation of a range of such programmes in place internationally found that success in reducing offending was related to the duration and frequency of mentor meetings and the availability of support through other forms of intervention (Newburn, 2013, p.602).

Social approaches tend to emphasise the importance of reformist intervention and thus tend to be opposed by hard line right realists. Moreover, the key problem that they have faced is the requirement for quick returns on the substantial up-front investment needed to produce potential long term economic payback which does not rest comfortably on the shorter term democratic political cycles and public expectations for more draconian measures with immediate effect.

By contrast, situational approaches to crime reduction view the influence of social factors on crime as being relatively unimportant and see crime as an act of rational decision making undertaken by individuals tempted in situations of opportunity. It therefore figures strongly as a front line strategy of crime control favoured by right realists. For Felson, (Treadwell, 2013, pp. 64-65) the key characteristics of a crime prone situation are 1) a motivated potential offender, 2) a suitable target, and 3) the lack of a capable guardian of the target.

If we break this down, it can be argued that a combination of situational interventions can reduce the level of criminal acts, but the main focus of this approach tends to be on the above mentioned third characteristic – that of changing features of the environment to reduce opportunities for crime. One aspect is 'target hardening', which refers to such off putting target defensive measures as having adequate security arrangements, for example locks, alarms, lighting and cameras in place to act as guardian. The manipulation of other environmental factors could include the elimination of easy access and escape routes and hiding and loitering places. Felson, indeed, provided an example of the effectiveness of these changes in reducing the crime level at a New York bus station (Newburn, 2013, pp.593-595).

Opportunity reduction can therefore provide a defence against crime by affecting the calculus of the potential offender. A further factor that has been usually advocated is that of a toughening of penalties faced by the convicted criminal, with the purpose of impacting on decision making through fear of the consequences of being caught and convicted.

There has, however, been debate as to whether situational approaches can be effective in bringing down crime rates overall, with one key criticism being that criminality will simply be displaced from hardened target areas into softer ones. This criticism has been countered by the arguments that criminals prefer to work in areas with which they are intimately familiar, that off putting environmental changes can reduce crime levels beyond the area concerned through the broader messages that they send out, and that any crime levels resulting from displacement would be very difficult to measure and attribute to a displacement effect.

A further criticism of this type of approach is that in tending to ignore the impact of social factors on crime, it draws attention away from the need for a) broader reform of social conditions and b) the support identified in social approaches. It also tends to focus attention on the individual street criminal, the typical criminal of the common consciousness, but would be of less worth if applied to combatting corporate crime. It therefore adopts a hardnosed and repressive approach to the criminality of the less well of sections of society and, whilst emphasising the deterrent effect of incarceration, pays scant regard to what Goffman has referred to as the effects of prison culture on potential training in criminality.

Motivations for crime – rational or emotional?

We have seen that criminality has often been explained as primarily motivated by rational calculation for materialistic gain. For the street criminal, such as the burglar, this would be likely to require the identification of a suitable target, an assessment of the level of its vulnerability, knowledge of the local terrain, and an evaluation of the prospects of successful escape. This model of the rationally motivated individual lies at the heart of right realists' analysis of street crime and guides the nature of their response.

However, for cultural criminologists, a different type of motivation for crime can be the accompanying feelings of emotion and thrill associated with the act itself. This is a key component of what Lyng (1990) has referred to as 'edgework'. For Lyng, the attraction for engagement in some criminal acts is the experience of exhilaration. This exhilaration derives from the act undertaken in situations of risk. Risk can therefore be an important part of the motivation for criminal behaviour rather than a deterrent and feeling during the act more important than material gain as a result of the act.

Another explanation of emotional based criminality is provided by Mike Presdee (30/5/2019) through the phenomena of 'carnival'. A key characteristic of carnivals in the traditional sense is the acting out of a fantasy world in which the constraints of the normal world can be temporarily set aside, for example through the guise of new identities, which can be acted out in a parade. For Presdee, certain types of crime are motivated by participation in a theatrical type street event which seeks excitement and release in acts of subversion. Presdee viewed the crime of joy riding, which emerged on some poorer housing estates in the early 1990s, as a classic carnivalesque type of crime. He documented joy riding on an Oxford housing estate which had suffered substantial unemployment following redundancies at a local car manufacturer. Joy riding involved the theft of top range cars, their tuning up, and the performance of racing them round the streets for the thrill and as a show of skill. This carnival show represented a topsy-turvy world of car culture which enabled the temporary possession and destruction of consumer objects participants once made but could never afford to legitimately own.

These perspectives may better explain criminal or deviant acts which appear to be senseless when viewed for material gain motives, such as delinquent acts which destroy property. It would also suggest that attempting to control crime levels by tilting the rational calculation of risk against the potential offended is in such cases unlikely to have the anticipated effect.

Rational and emotional motivators may of course sometimes combine or evolve in criminal acts. For example, participation in the financial crime of insider trading may start out as motivated by an individual quest for monetary gain, but through participation the thrill of the risk involved in taking part may come to take over as an addictive type motivator.

Surveillance, crime and social control

Surveillance of the activities of others has long been recognised as a form of behavioural control. As in the case of Bentham's model prison design, this type of control is usually a form of top down monitoring of people's behaviour by others in a position of authority. People's knowledge of the very possibility of surveillance being carried out of their behaviour can bring about their self-controlled conformity. Where conformity does not result, surveillance may enable swift intervention to take place and it can also provide evidence of lawbreaking or 'inappropriate' behaviour for future prosecution or condemnation. The need for surveillance can therefore be conveyed to the general public as a necessity for friendly authorities to protect them from the misbehaviour of some and as a means of crime reduction.

The capacity and nature of surveillance are very much tied up with the new forms of technology which have made it an endemic feature of contemporary societies, operating at different levels of society and in a range of social contexts. One level is that of surveillance by the state over its population. Its history has been one of vigilance against those deemed to be disruptive social forces, an imperative which was raised in the early twenty first century as a result of major terrorist attacks. The security services have at their disposal a range of high tech apparatus for monitoring planned attacks and other activities deemed as threats.

At another level, close circuit TV is now an intrinsic part of many public places in the UK, especially modern cityscapes. Shops may have their own security cameras on display to warn off those considering potential criminal activity or to provide important evidence that can be used when a crime has been committed. Cameras are commonly installed in shopping malls to enable the behaviour of groups or individuals to be constantly observed. For the purpose of 'purifying' a consumerist environment where customers can feel at ease to be seduced by the products on show, surveillance either brings about behavioural self-control or enables the swift removal of unwanted individuals such as drunkards or the homeless (Aas, 2013, p.62).

Other areas that are monitored by CCTV included commercial premises and fortressed housing estates where private security guards are often employed. Various forms of surveillance have also become a significant feature of many workplaces, sometimes assisting and sometimes standing in the place of direct management. The activity of delivery people can be carefully tracked at a distance, the dealing with customers by call centre operatives can be monitored, and school and other institutional environments can be watched over.

As well as CCTV, other forms of surveillance can include tracking people's movements through their mobile phone use, their use of facilities through swipe cards and the monitoring of spending habits by stores and supermarkets through the use of bonus cards. Facial recognition technology and the use of high tech biometric passports can be used to track or restrict movement. Furthermore, as various sources of surveillance have become technologically integrated, Haggerty and Ericson have argued that a powerful form of 'survaillant assemblage' has emerged.

Within a neoliberal environment of free market individualism, it would appear that control from above by surveillance technology may be replacing the constraints of community, as, for example, leaner management structures have brought about a decrease in direct management at work and policing in the community has declined.

Even our more personal thoughts may be becoming vulnerable to supervision. Through social media sites, we are encouraged to reveal what is 'on our minds' in ways that might otherwise have remained more secret but could in theory be open to scrutiny for monitoring purposes by people other than those with whom we intend to share our thoughts, such as the state or potential employers.

All in all, this would appear to give credence to what Foucault has referred to as contemporary 'surveillance societies', with carceral type oversight of daily behaviour where surveillance saturation is intended to have a powerful effect on behavioural self-governance going well beyond crime control and operating in an essentially downward direction. Even surveillance taking place at a lateral level, as in the case of people using mobile phones to film antisocial behaviour in their neighbourhoods, is likely to take place with the purpose of filtering it back up the hierarchy.

Some forms of surveillance may operate in an upward direction though, at least to a modest extent. Thus, surveillance in the workplace may, as well as monitoring the behaviour of workers, provide an element of protection from abuse by their superiors, and police cameras may constrain the behaviour of patrol officers as well as members of the public that they come into contact with. Nevertheless, paralleling the lack of focus on the crimes of the powerful, there would appear to be few opportunities for long range upward surveillance.

Whilst manipulation of elements of the environment and the use of technology can have some controlling effect on crime levels and society more generally, the belief that the pervasive use of surveillance technology itself is the answer to control crime is a misleading form of technological determinism as humans have the capacity to evade or challenge control and the view that surveillance is just about crime control in the first place may be an ideological argument for stepping up invasive forms of social control.

Crime in the context of globalisation

A globalising world is one that is becoming increasingly interconnected. National boundaries have become more porous to the movement of people, products, information and value. A fundamental driving force of globalisation has been technological advance, especially in the form of the internet and the creation of a global cyberspace environment. Moreover, the growing power of our technological intervention has raised its impact on the natural environment to global proportions. The political, economic and cultural framework within which these global forces have become largely encapsulated has been that of neoliberal global free enterprise. The understanding of a whole range of phenomena therefore needs to be reconfigured outside of the geographical confines of countries and nation states. This section will touch on some of the issues related to criminality within a global context.

Cybercrime

Up to the post war decades, a vast majority of crime was perpetrated in physical space, often encompassing a face-to-face dimension. Through an explosion in connectivity to the global internet from the latter decades of the twentieth century and technological advances in public space security, a rebalancing of risks and opportunities seems to have brought about a degree of displacement of crime from the physical public place and into the anonymous and extended reach of the cyber world. This raises the further question of the extent to which cybercrime facilitates 'old' crimes and has enabled completely new types of crime to emerge. David Wall (2007, cited in Treadwell, 2013, p.141) has provided a classificatory scheme of cybercrime types on a scale as follows:

Traditional cybercrime is crime that may have flourished through the use of the internet, but would be able to continue in its traditional form without it. An example of this type would be that of child pornography.

At the other end of the scale is true cybercrime. This refers to crime which is restricted to the existence of cyberspace, without which it would not exist. Crimes of this nature include those designed to hack and attack computer systems.

Hybrid cybercrimes are those which can be placed in an intermediate position between the traditional and true types. Whilst they could continue to exist independent of cyberspace, the latter has enabled them to substantially evolve, as in the case of identity fraud.

Cybercrime may be perpetrated against individuals, organisations and states by criminal individuals, organisations or states. The motive may be that of accessing state or corporate information, but it is frequently that of extorting money. This may be through accessing people's computers and using fraudulent scams to extract money on line. True cybercrime could include incapacitating computer systems, as in the case of a cyberattack on the National Health Service computer system in 2017 when a ransomware programme was used to lock computers and demand payments. These types of attack have been launched from within or outside of the nations affected. To combat them requires not just sophisticated defence systems but also the global tracking and sharing of forensic intelligence which may prove difficult to pursue if the origin of the attack is itself a foreign state.

State crime

Crime is traditionally viewed from the perspective of infringements of the law of the land as established within sovereign states. However, since the passage of laws and their enforcement takes place through the apparatus of the state, national legislation becomes an inadequate framework for dealing with crimes by the state. Crimes perpetrated through or on behalf of the state have included state sponsored terrorism (for example by Iran), torture (for example of suspected terrorists by United States authorities at Guantanamo Bay), war crimes, genocide and crimes against humanity (Nazi Germany and the former Yugoslavia).

The prosecution of such crimes requires a global framework of standards and apparatus through which individuals carrying out such acts can be held accountable, as well as having the resources available for lengthy investigation. Post Second World War, Nuremberg Military Tribunals were set up to try Nazi war criminals. More recently, an institution of the United Nations, the International Criminal Court, based at the Hague, has been established since 2002 and has notably tried Ratko Mladic and Radovan Karadzic for their war crimes during the civil war in the former Yugoslavia. The United States and a number of other countries have failed to ratify the Court.

Another form of crime conducted through the state has been referred to by Grabosdky and Stohl as 'kleptocracy' (Aas, 2013, p.138); the use of the state by rulers to maximise their personal fortune. A prime example of this type was the authoritarian leader of the Philippines, Ferdinand Marcos, who used complex money laundering devices to amass a massive fortune, the full extent of which is unknown.

Another form of state related crime is the breaking of arms embargos. One case of this type in the mid-1980s under the American President Reagan involved the supplying of arms to Iran, despite an embargo, for Iran to assist in the freeing of American hostages in the Lebanon. More than half of the money supplied by the CIA for the weaponry was syphoned off for the illegal funding of Contra insurgents against the communist backed Nicaraguan government. Reagan was criticised for lack of oversight of these events and whilst a number of officials were found guilty they were later pardoned.

In the UK, the official government line during the war between Iran and Iraq in the 1980s was that weapons would not be exported to either side. In the early 1990s, executives of the company Matrix Churchill were charged with exporting equipment illegally to Iraq. It was discovered during the trial that from 1987 the government had secretly changed policy to encourage such exports.

Organised crime has a history of being located in local territories or patches, taking, for example, the form of gangland crimes such as 'bootlegging' during the prohibition period in the United States, or protection rackets, such as that of the Krays in the East End of London. It has also traditionally involved 'hands on' robberies, some of the most notorious of which have included the Great Train robbery in 1963 and more recently the 2015 Hatton Garden robbery. However, organised crime has also come to take on an increasingly global dimension, often operating with the same rational money driven efficiency as legal business activity and even interfacing with it.

The form of capitalism which globalisation has largely taken on, sometimes referred to as fast capitalism (Agger) or the end of organised capitalism (Lash and Urry), is a deregulated, free market, neoliberal form. Within this context, a combination of the deregulation of financial institutions and the use of global technology has arguably offered greater opportunity for the activity of 'money laundering'; a process whereby 'dirty' money made from criminal activities can be 'cleaned up' within the financial system. Dirty proceeds are often the result of criminal gangs involved in such activity as the trafficking of drugs and people across national borders, the latter case involving illegal immigration and often perpetual indebtedness into secretive forms of slavery employment such as prostitution, domestic service or farm labour work.

The collapse of Soviet Union in 1991 provides a fascinating example of the emergence of organised crime within the neoliberal global context. Following the collapse, pressure from the west for 'shock therapy' transition from state regulated communism to free market capitalism left a political vacuum which became partially filled by organised crime, with estimates suggesting that by the mid-1990s about 40% of the money circulating in Russia was from criminal activity (Hughes and Langan, in Muncie and McLaughlin ed., 2002). Ironically, given the increasingly global scope of organised crime, some of this activity is likely to have global repercussions.

Green crime

As scientific and technological intervention in the natural environment has become more powerful, risks become magnified and their effects stretched. The risks of mishaps have become increasingly dangerous and their effects geographically stretched with national boundaries providing no obstacle. Particular instances of widespread environmental damage have been evidenced in such events as major oil spills (Exxon Valdez, 1989) and the fallout from the Chernobyl nuclear reactor disaster in the Soviet Union in 1986. There therefore needs to be rules and safeguards in place with the aim of minimising the risk of accidents to protect the environment through criminalising certain actions (eg. discharging oil at sea) or omissions (eg. evading legal requirements regarding health and safety).

Viewed in a formal and legalistic sense, green crime refers to actions of omissions which break the law regarding environmental matters. These laws themselves are shaped by a number of factors. Traditionally, attitudes toward environmental protection have tended to be anthropocentric – seen from the vantage point of human centred consciousness. From this viewpoint, shaping the view of what constitutes green crime prioritises concern for human wellbeing (however short sighted) over that of other species. Moreover, some green criminologists have picked up on leads from critical theorists who point out that environmental laws are shaped by powerful corporate influences, inconsistently applied and policed, and even when broken usually only provide financial penalties which can be absorbed by business organisations and passed on to the consumer.

Perpetrators of green crime include individuals, businesses and governments. In an affluent, consumerist and throwaway society, individuals may be encouraged to fly tip unwanted goods and materials as a cheaper and easier method of disposal than abiding by legal requirements for safer disposal which include costs. Businesses, under pressure to minimise costs, may flout emissions and pollution regulations, especially if working in collusion with corrupt authorities. Or they may be attracted to operate in countries where regulatory control is lax, labour is cheap and compensation for damage to people and the environment is low, as did the American corporation Union Carbide which situated a factory in Bhopal, a chanty town in India, where an accident released toxic gas that killed upwards of a thousand local inhabitants and seriously injured the health of many thousands more. The poor and powerless are often found to suffer the highest rates of green crime victimisation.

Some green crimes are of broader and less dramatic impact but involve damage to the environment and the health of the public. Such a crime could include the illegal manipulation of car emissions test results by Volkswagen, uncovered in 2015, to make their vehicles appear to meet American and European Union emissions standards.

An area where public awareness of green crime can be advanced is through the media. However, under consumer capitalism, consumer appetite is constantly enticed by media advertising and the planned obsolescence of products aims to enhance its buoyancy. Meanwhile, the media tends to focus public consciousness on seeing crime primarily in terms of street crime.

Although green criminology has conventionally regarded green crime as action which breaks environmental laws, a more radical approach raises the key question of who defines environmental harm and who sets the laws and punishments which are supposed to protect the environment? This takes us back to the use of power. Since it is argued that corporations and states have much power in defining environmental harm, establishing environmental laws, and policing them in ways which may not sufficiently protect the environment, radical green criminologists such as Lynch and Stretsky have argued for a 'transgressive approach' in which activities that harm the environment but do not break the law should nevertheless be recognised as green crimes. A good example of legalised risk to the environment would be the granting of licences to use the technique of high pressure 'fracking' to release oil and natural gas deposits deep underground, a process accompanied by the danger of earth tremors and water pollution. Taking this radical green position into the area of pressure group activity, it can be argued that breaking the law to protect the environment from damaging actions which may not have broken the law may be justified.

To meet its recycling targets, Britain exports refuse for recycling to poorer countries that have inferior processing technology. From a social and environmental harm perspective, it could be argued that the exporting of waste from advanced to developing countries could constitute environmental crime in the above broader sense. This harm is likely to be exacerbated by the heightening of a global consumerist culture and the manufacturing practice of planned obsolescence.

Looking at the issue of green crime at the broadest level, there is evidence of a growing consciousness, especially amongst younger sections of the population in a number of countries, that serious action needs to be taken in the form of measures to combat the effects of global warming. Whether governments and industry can be forced to seriously take on board measures to combat environmental harm, whether consumers will change their lifestyle habits, and whether technological fixes may be part of the solution, only time will tell.

Postmodernism – we cannot know social causes of crime

For postmodernists, the defining characteristics of modern societies included a relatively high degree of moral unity and a widespread belief that progress could be brought about through rational analysis of and intervention in social structurers to bring about social improvement. It was believed that criminality could be understood in terms of causal influences running through social structures and criminologists placed faith in the capacity of the scientific analysis of hard data to provide evidence of crime trends and patterns to reveal underlying causes of criminality which could be tackled by interventions to reduce crime levels.

However, postmodernists have pointed to the inexorable rise in the crime rate from the mid-1950s to indicate the futility of such a quest. Furthermore, they have argued that even the possibility of modernist type understanding and control of social phenomena, including criminality, are becoming impossible with the breakdown of social structures, of moral uniformity and of the regulative capacity of the bureaucratic state under increasingly postmodern conditions of social diversity and complexity. As Young and Matthews (ed. 1992, p.11) explained, modernist theories of crime were criticised for their 'essentialism'; the apparently misleading attempt to reduce the understanding of a diversity of behaviour that breaks the law by means of a singular and all-embracing theory. Classic targets of postmodernists were therefore such grand theorists as Comte, Marx, Durkheim and Parsons.

Postmodernists have argued that contemporary society is transitioning toward a condition of growing diversity and relativity of lifestyles. This is celebrated as true liberation from the judgements and constraints of moral uniformity backed up by state power during the modern period. Consequently, the legal system as a standardised and overarching structure is becoming unable to adequately reflect this diversity. A number of implications flow from a postmodern perspective, including the following:

1. As a result of the breakdown of broad social structures and moral uniformity, the analytic study of the social causes of crime must give way to descriptive accounts of individual and unique circumstances. A plethora of micro ethnographic type studies would replace all embracing structural explanations of crime.

2. If the understanding of crime cannot be reduced to universal analysis, neither can responses to it. The control of crime therefore needs to be located within its more diverse and localised context. This could include a variety of public and private sector responses that are fine tuned to specific local and situational needs. The use of electronic surveillance systems and private security firms signify a fragmentation in crime prevention responses which can also be found in the growth of gated housing communities, greater use of individual security devices and neighbourhood watch schemes etc.

3. As argued by Henry and Milovanovic (1996), a society of diversity and tolerance of difference requires a whole reconceptualization of crime, one which is refocussed to include 'social harms' that result from actions of intolerance by some toward the difference of others. Some movement in this direction is arguably becoming evidenced through greater awareness of and response to hate crimes against others of different personal characteristics or lifestyle choices.

4. The prevalence of spectacle and consumerism in the postmodern world would seem to find highest form in the physical location of contemporary shopping malls which are designed to purify the consumerist experience. High tech surveillance enables control or exclusion of undesirable groups or individuals that may undermine this experience.

Given the postmodernists' emphasis on abandoning attempts to manage or control crime through rational analysis of the forces behind it, modernists are likely to retort with a number of criticisms. For example, postmodern analysis tends to:
1. ignore social forces that it can be argued continue to influence criminal behaviour, in particular socially structured poverty and deprivation and social exclusion.
2. avoid criticisms of the unfairness of socially structured inequalities and undermines faith in the capacity to manipulate these forces for purposes of social reform.

3. not seem able to explain the degree of ongoing social consensus that inhibits the majority from engaging in criminal behaviour. Given the emphasis on moral relativity, it would be difficult to see that there could be a moral consensus rallied by the media against deviant groups.

4. suggest that with a reconceptualization of crime to include social harms, infraction rates are likely to be high. In the absence of the rational analysis of causes as the basis for intervention, a 'what works' policy of repressive policing and high incarceration rates is likely. This response quite closely reflects the position of right realists and may be better understood through the dynamics of neoliberal capitalism producing a socially fragmented, materialistic, individualistic and privatised free enterprise society in which the state minimises its welfare intervention role and hardens its repressive role.

High modernism – controlling the risk of crime

For Muncie (Walton and Young ed., 1998, p.230), the implication of postmodernist criticisms of modernist approaches to understanding and controlling crime would be the abandonment of the concept of 'crime' altogether in the study of a diverse and broad range of social harm behaviour. The problem would then be that this area of behaviour would be left vaguely defined and open ended, a position destructive of enlightened understanding.

High or late modernists share some agreement with postmodernists that compared to the earlier phase of modernity, contemporary society has undergone social and technological change of a qualitative order. However, compared to postmodernists, they retain faith that these changes can be rationally understood and responded to, if more precariously. Adopting a high modernist type left realist position, Muncie has acknowledged the growing complexity of contemporary phenomena but has not seen this as destroying the possibility of providing improved theoretical understanding as a guide to social policy on crime. As a general point, he has argued that rejecting all-embracing causal theories should not necessarily lead to the abandonment of the search for causes but instead its refinement.

Garland (2001) has identified social and technological changes associated with late modernity to comprise the mass availability of goods of high value that have become more highly portable. Household material possessions might also be enhanced through the growing phenomena of dual career families but these lifestyle changes, in leaving more properties unattended, have reduced opportunities for capable guardianship. These changes were seen to relate to rising levels of property crime in the increasingly affluent decades of the second half of the twentieth century.

High modernists such as Jock Young have retained a left realist element of structural analysis which tends to be absent in postmodern accounts of consumer society. For Young, improved levels of consumer prosperity have also been accompanied by experiences of relative deprivation, particularly amongst unemployed youngsters who may be tempted toward property crime. Young has also argued that reliable data on criminality, victimisation and the fear of crime can provide the basis for rational analysis, but that given the degree of diversity in high modern society, the most appropriate level of analysis is through information derived from local surveys.

Ulrich Beck famously placed the phenomena of crime and responses to it within late modernist society referred to as 'risk society'. Beck has argued that the scientific and technological advances that have accompanied late modernity have produced conditions of growing uncertainty and unanticipated risks, increasingly with global consequences. The state has therefore had to prioritise crisis management at some expense to the engineering of social welfare. It is against this type of backdrop that Garland argues that a sense of crisis promotes a culture of the need for control and 'punitive populism' that emphasises strong oppression as a response to crime with less concern for rehabilitation of offenders.

Given the impact of neoliberal reforms, right realist rational choice explanations of crime, which focus choice and responsibility for criminal behaviour squarely on the shoulders of individuals and are myopic regarding social structural influences, have come to some prominence. As part of the state drive for cost effectiveness, 'new penology' approaches have attempted to manage crime by directing resources to the control of groups with regard to the seriousness of the risk that they pose.

Chapter 13

Sociology of Globalisation

Abstract

Because the term globalisation has become so commonly used, a key challenge for the sociologist is to distance oneself sufficiently from unreflective everyday usage to develop an awareness of the complexity required for the development of an academic definition of the concept and analysis of the processes involved. A very brief definition is initially provided.

Developing a definition of globalisation is next assisted by reference to key dimensions identified by David Held, following which a number of related concepts are identified and explained.

Whilst the reader is alerted to the limitations of founding theoretical perspectives in explaining contemporary globalisation, it is also suggested that the usefulness of these perspectives for this purpose should not be completely dismissed.

In a further section, a number of theories leading up to globalisation are touched on: Rostow's modernisation theory, Frank's dependency theory and Wallerstein's world system theory. Although global in their scope, these theories of the relationship between the developed and underdeveloped world are referred to as internationalist as opposed to globalist.

The forces of globalisation can be artificially divided into the realms of technology, economics, culture and politics. Globalisation in relation to each of these dimensions is explained, whilst the importance of recognising their interrelationship in the real world is emphasised.

David Held's classification of theoretical positions on globalisation is used as an organisational touchstone comprising the following positions. Globalists, particularly hyperglobalists, tend to adopt a highly optimistic position on the benefits of global free enterprise and free trade capitalism. However, neo-Marxists, whilst acknowledging the forces at play, adopt a critical and pessimistic interpretation of global capitalism. Traditionalists argue that globalists have overstated the extent to which the forces of globalisation have impacted, whilst transformationists adopt the position that these forces are real and risk running rampant if not intelligently controlled.

A more concrete approach to globalisation is taken in sections which refer to its effects on the workplace, the extent of poverty and inequality, concentrations of corporate power and the key role of global cities.

Finally, an overview raises some general questions on the development and inevitability of globalisation and the need to recognise its complex effects on the lives of individuals. Brief reference is made to global intersectionality theory and comments are made on the consequences for sociology following on from adopting different positions in Held's classificatory scheme.

The sociological challenge

The term 'globalisation' came to prominence in the 1990s and has since become part of everyday currency. In essence, it refers to processes of social change whereby the boundaries of geography and country have become assailed by technological, economic, political and cultural forces which have enabled the globe to become interconnected in real time. This definition and other associated terminology will be significantly developed as the chapter unfolds.

Common everyday usage of the term does raise certain problems for the sociologist. In particular, its definition is often left rather vague and it may be perceived as a mysterious and unstoppable force with regard to which strong feelings are likely to be evoked either for or against. These positions may be related to whether people feel themselves to be on the winning or losing side of the perceived processes. For the sociologist, the aim should be to develop a subtle understanding and nuanced approach to this highly complex area.

There is much debate about the timing of globalisation. This can often be related to varying definitions of the process and the fact that different viewpoints may be taken in the different subjects, for example geography, politics and economics, within which the term is applied. For example, Steger (2009, Ch.2) refers to globalisation as 'a long term phenomenon' in which he distinguishes five historical periods starting with the prehistoric, each divided by a step change in the pace and scope of social exchange. For the purpose of this text, given the definition that will be employed, it is Steger's 'contemporary period' (from the 1970s) that will be the main focus of our attention.

Within sociology, there has been extensive debate regarding the key forces behind globalisation, the nature and extent of their impact and how different forces, for example political and economic may feed into each other. Furthermore, there has been a substantial expansion in the terminology associated with globalisation, not all of which has been consistently applied. Most sociologists agree though that the processes involved are highly complex and for many the outcomes are uncertain. It is therefore particularly important to carefully define the term and introduce a number of key concepts that will provide an academic basis from which to study the processes involved.

Definition of main concepts

The writings of David Held (2002) offer a useful starting point for defining globalisation. Held has identified the key characteristics of globalisation as 1) the stretching of social relations, 2) the intensification of flows, 3) increasing interpenetration and 4) the emergence of global infrastructure. Taking each of these in turn:

1. **Social relations are stretched** globally when they are able to cut across and transcend prescribed national boundaries or geographical regions. Stretching can be evidenced by an increasing range of migration and labour movement and the improved retention of communication that migrants are able to maintain with people in their place of origin.

2. Flow refers to **extent, intensity and fluidity of communication** which increases the volume of stretched communication. It may involve the volume of migration, travel or information flows as communication (relationships?) can be detached beyond past limits of geographical space and time, now through immediate high tech global communication that enables an increase in mass and speed of carrying load.

3. **Interpenetration** refers to the complex relationship between the global and the local, the effects of which could include on the one hand increasing global uniformity and on the other growing local diversity. The impact of global uniformity, often perceived as the predominant effect of globalisation, can be illustrated by **McDonaldization**, a term coined by George Ritzer which referred to the setting up of McDonalds fast food outlets following very similar fast food work processes and recognised symbolism across the world. The tendency toward global uniformity in this instance is easy to recognise. However, to maximise its economic returns, McDonalds has had to improvise its product to cater for different cultural tastes.

Furthermore, globalisation can add to local diversity, a dynamic first summed up by Ronald Robertson in his use of the term **glocalisation**. For example, as many different food traditions become extended globally through food transportation, travel and migration, the overall crisscrossing effect is likely to add to diversity at the local level as can be witnessed in the array of food available in local supermarkets and the ethnic diversity of restaurants.

Different cultural settings can form the context for variations in consumer preferences. Large global corporations thus have to balance economic pressures for standardisation of goods, products and services with the satisfaction of different requirements in different countries and localities. Some financial institutions have picked up on the imagery of glocalisation in appealing to customers as institutions that combine global power with local expertise.

Environmental movements also provide examples of glocalisation by emphasising that although the effect of human behaviour on the environment is intrinsically global and requires a global response, action at the local level is also important in contributing toward tackling global environmental issues. For example, consumer preference for locally produced foodstuffs should be encouraged to help combat global pollution resulting from long range transportation.

4. **Global infrastructure** refers to the emergence of networks and institutions which may interface with and effect the policy options that are available to the state. This infrastructure could involve the power of transnational corporations to influence labour relations policy, the emergence of supra national organisations of global governance designed to tackle new global problems such as climate change, or the influence of such non-governmental organisations as Amnesty International who globally monitor abuses of human rights which arguably even the most secretive states would now find it difficult to hide through the advance of technological communication in the hands of citizens and journalists.

Overall, the world is becoming more interdependent. A key feature of globalisation, according to Anthony Giddens, is **time-space distanciation**. For Giddens, through the speed and reach of contemporary communications technology and transportation systems, past barriers of time and distance fall down and the world is subjectively experienced as if shrinking. For Harvey, from a more Marxist angle, the concept of **time-space compression** brings a step change in the speed and stretch of communication and capital movement that has the effect of shrinking the constraints of space and shortening the experience of time to that of global real time. The result is that human actions become sped up and intensified as global capitalism drives and utilises technological advances.

Cohen and Kennedy (2013, p.8) refer to the more subjective dimension of the growing awareness of globalisation as the experience of **globality**, whereas Steger (2009, p.10) refers to this subjective consciousness as the **global imaninary** and instead uses the term globality in referring to the social condition that the processes of globalisation bring about.

There is little doubt that we are becoming socialised into seeing the world as a much smaller place than people just two generations ago would have, let alone those who lived in pre-industrial times. An important consequence of advancing time-space distanciation is that decisions directly affecting people, for example corporate investment decisions, can be quickly made at ever increasing distance. The impact of such decisions can sometimes be destructive of local communities and opportunities; having been made from afar, they are **'disembedded'** from those who are affected.

An important distinction can be made between internationalisation and globalisation. Whilst internationalisation refers to the growing interconnectedness of discrete and bounded territorial states, globalisation involves forces that cut across, tend to undermine traditional territorial units and can appear as if operating in an ungrounded way. Thus, regarding the effects of globalisation, Cohen and Kennedy (2013, p.32) have used the term **'deterritorialization'** to refer to people's thinking and acting becoming uprooted from specific geographical locations. This is related to the fact that global processes such as environmental change and contagion in financial markets have broken free from territorial rooting and constraints.

This is, however, a contested concept. For example, Scholte (2005, p.77) argues that deterritoriailzation can suggest that global forces are relentlessly sweeping away all forms of territorial grounding, whereas in fact they touch down, remain shaped by and run through territorial influences and constraints such as built city structures and national cultures. Scholte therefore avoids use of the term. Instead, he refers to the spread of 'transplanetary' and 'supraterritorial' connections between people.

For Scholte globalisation refers to **transplanetary** forces in the development of linkages between people across the planet, reconfiguring their experience and perception of space as a result. As well as the idea of extension, these interlinkages have advanced in their density, but are still territorially grounded. **Supraterritoriality** refers to more advanced global processes that delink people from the constraints of territory, in particular through the instantaneous global reach of cyberspace communication. This takes the experience of a shrinking world to a qualitatively higher level. Scholte is keen to point out, however, that globalisation operates very much in terms of both processes. Whilst life in the world of strong container state governance and weighty agricultural and manufacturing economies was more territorially focussed, it would be inappropriate to signal the demise of **territoriality** in a globalising world. Such a view would mistakenly reify (mistakenly elevate to the status of an independent force in its own right) supraterritorial forces which even themselves must 'touch down' to work through banks, stock exchanges and cities etc.

Steger (2009, p.39) refers to the post war period of reconstruction as the 'golden age of **controlled capitalism'.** During these years, new international institutions were formed, such as the International Monetary Fund and the International Bank for Reconstruction and Development, the latter, initially created to assist European reconstruction, subsequently combined with other institutions to form the World Bank to provide capital assistance for developing countries. The economic theory of John Maynard Keynes, referred to as **Keynesianism**, provided much of the intellectual backdrop to this period of economic planning. The approach required governments to take responsibility for regulating their economies by timing the use of deficits or surpluses for the purpose of levelling out the cyclical booms and slumps that the capitalist free market tends to spontaneously generate. This required significant levels of taxation and investment in public utilities such as education, health services and transport infrastructure etc. to manage the economy.

Following poor economic performance in a number of western economies during the 1970s, this orthodoxy was becoming abandoned. By the 1980s, particularly in the United States and the UK, in its place was emerging the alternative of what has become referred to as **neoliberalism**. According to this approach, governments should ease back from their economic planning and interventionist role, reduce taxation, privatise nationalised industries wherever possible, enhance a cultural climate of entrepreneurial responsibility, and open up their economies to free trade and free market forces. Assistance given in the form of loans to developing countries from international institutions would now be based on them accepting **structural adjustment** of their economies in line with these new priorities.

Founding theorists and globalisation

Nineteenth century pioneers of sociology tended to adopt broad visions of social change, but from a Eurocentric viewpoint of modernisation and their evaluation of future advancement that was heavily shaped by a vantage point taken from within their own society. As Durrschmidt and Taylor (2007, p.10) comment 'the modern age was an age of meta-ideologies: total ideologies…... that defined past, present and future in terms of a linear trajectory towards a pre-defined utopia'. Societies were equated with territorially bound nations that could be arranged in linear form in degrees of advancement. For this reason, founding theorists have tended to be overlooked in discussions on globalisation. However, at least two salient points can be raised cautioning taking this position too far:

1. A number of the pioneering social theorists referred to in chapter 3 looked to the future in terms of global commonality – of societies converging to a particular social type as the end point of historical progress.

2. Marx in particular had analysed globalising dynamics which he claimed were built into capitalism, with the key forces being economic. In the Communist Manifesto, Marx commented that:

> 'The need of a constantly expanding market for its products chases the bourgeoisie over the whole surface of the globe. It must nestle everywhere, settle everywhere, establish connections everywhere' (Marx, 1973, p.71).

Toward theories of globalisation – internationalism

Although sociological thinking would eventually come to question the past emphasis on viewing societies as nationally bounded units, the focus on the nation state remained rooted throughout much of the twentieth century during which time two world wars had heightened nationalistic and patriotic sentiments. Post war theories adopting a worldwide remit tended to be cast within the political standoff of the cold war between the communist east and the capitalist west and the quest of each to align underdeveloped countries to their sphere of influence. With the forces of globalisation still gathering, key theories of worldwide view remained essentially pre-global or at best of a transitional nature. These will be briefly summarised as follows:

Modernisation theory, exemplified in the work of W.W. Rostow, retained a viewpoint of linear modernisation that located development in terms of stages to modernisation that the capitalist west had gone through and could assist underdeveloped countries to take the same pathway. Assistance therefore equated to alignment to the west.

It was argued that internally engendered traditions within underdeveloped societies were the main obstacles to their modernisation. These obstacles included closed stratification systems and cultural and religious values that impeded a work ethic. The injection of western technology and financial support, supplemented by the emergence of an achievement driven enterprise culture, were seen as prerequisites to promote the dynamism required to kick start the key stage of economic take-off and bring developing countries into the western capitalist sphere of influence.

Dependency theory, whose prime advocate was the Marxist influenced Andre Gunder Frank, adopted a position on the relationship between advanced capitalist societies and underdeveloped societies which was diametrically opposed to that of development theory. Frank argued that western capitalist involvement in underdeveloped countries was undertaken to its own advantage and had the effect of holding underdeveloped countries in a state of perpetual dependency as a source of raw materials and cheap labour. The impediments to development were therefore of external rather than internal origin and the temptation to accept western development aid should be resisted, the main internal beneficiaries being pro-western elites.

The basis of Wallerstein's Marxist influenced **world system theory** is that capitalism is inherently expansionist in the search to maximise profits. From as far back as the early sixteenth century, trade and expansionist tendencies were starting to pull countries into what in time would develop into a systemically ordered world hierarchy of nations. Capitalist countries that had developed strong state structures had been able to colonise less developed countries with weaker state structures and an abundance of natural resources and cheap labour for their benefit. This would eventually develop into a systemic world order comprising 'core' nations that were able to dominate societies of 'semi-peripheral' and 'peripheral' positioning, with possible positional movement over time, and the main beneficiaries of the world system would be the capitalist corporations in the core nations.

In summary, these theories, developed during the 1960s and 1970s, although adopting a worldwide vision, tended to do so from an internationalist stance which remained attached to the nation state as container model. The differences between this type of position and more contemporary theories of globalisation should become clear in the subsequent sections of this chapter.

Dimensions of globalisation

In academic circles, there has been much debate about the nature and extent of globalisation and varying emphasis placed on its technological, economic, cultural and political aspects. As a preliminary grounding, these categories will be separated out for purposes of definition and illustration. In the real world, of course, these influences overlap and interact in complex ways and it may also be that globalisation is taking contradictory paths in each of them. A more sophisticated understanding will therefore later require a more holistic view.

1. Technological

A key aspect of globalisation is the advance of technology. Early advances in the speeding up and stretching of communications involved the development of longer distance and faster shipping in the transportation of people, goods and written communication around the world. The invention and growing accessibility of telegraph communications during the nineteenth century and radio, television and air transport in the twentieth have all in their time contributed to the enhanced flow of communications and the movement of people. Subsequent developments in micro-processing and widespread usage of computer technology hooked up to the internet have enabled virtually instantaneous communication and transfer of information within and across national boundaries. This has made it possible for financial institutions which are globally linked to transfer money and investments from place to place at the press of a button. It allows news events to be instantly communicated globally and other mass media information to be broadly disseminated. And it enables global networks of communication to be established through social media. Modern communications technology has enabled call centres, particularly servicing people in western countries, to geographically disembed their location and then re-embed themselves in countries such as India where the advantages of cheap labour can be utilised. Rapid means of personal transportation over great distances are now accessible to more people as witnessed in pressures for airport expansion that raise environmental issues at both a local and global level.

However, technological changes have also often generated new problems, one of which is the vulnerability of computer systems of individuals, organisations or governments to security breaches, cyber-attacks, identity theft, cyber-bullying and cyber fraud.

Some of the changes enabled by technology generate opposition, as in the case of protests against the above mentioned airport expansion or consumer dissatisfaction with the use of overseas call centres; opposition that may itself rely heavily on modern technology for its organisation.

Important questions raised for sociologists include the extent to which technologically mediated communication is authentically 'social' and what influences its spread may have on people in their daily lives and on them psychologically?

2 Economic

The economic dimension of globalisation refers to the forces of the production of wealth and the institutions through which they operate. These institutions may be more or less geographically rooted or delimited in their activities; factors which themselves are closely related to technological developments. Essentially, advanced technology has enabled businesses to extend their reach and become more nimble footed on the global stage, especially in the case of financial institutions. In this sense, advanced economies tend to become more 'lightweight'.

A measure of economic globalisation is the emergence of industrial and service enterprises, often giants, with a base in more than one country. These are referred to as multinational or transnational corporations. Following definitions employed by Hirst and Thompson, multinationals have their headquarters firmly established in one country and are thus subject to regulation by their home government. Consequently, Hirst and Thompson have argued that they should be viewed as international rather than truly global corporations. Transnational corporations may be similar in scale to multinationals but differ in that they are relatively free to move their operations and even headquarters anywhere in the world in search of the most favourable conditions of operation and profitability. This potential mobility provides them with significant opportunities to influence the policies of national governments who compete to attract and retain inward investment.

For Hirst and Thompson, whilst multinational corporations point to an international economy, it is really only the activities of transnational corporations which are indicative of truly globalised economic forces. In reality, though, the difference between the two is often unclear and more a matter of degree. However classified, corporations such as Toyota, Coca-Cola and General Motors operate on a global scale.

From the 1980s, political decisions made in leading capitalist societies followed by the collapse of Eastern Block state communism have shaped global economic forces to work along neoliberal lines (associated with new right Conservative politics in the UK), essentially meaning that the predominant form that globalisation has taken has been one driven by the extension of private enterprise and free market competition. Advanced economies have seen an expansion in their service and financial sectors, which allied with advanced technology has enabled global corporations in these sectors to often benefit from locations in globally connected cities.

Manufacturing has had to adapt to free market driven rapidly changing tastes, fashions, conditions and opportunities, with advanced global communications enabling businesses to utilise up to date intelligence on the state of markets which they need to adapt innovatively to. In this environment, businesses have often found it necessary to employ flexible production techniques through which they can quickly change specialist runs of products based on the latest consumer demands in different parts of the world; a form of business organisation referred to by Piore as post-Fordism. Employees have therefore had to be increasingly prepared to respond to change in the form of retraining and adopting new working practices as well as facing the enhanced threat of redundancy or unemployment.

Strictly speaking, 'outsourcing' refers to a process whereby business activity which was traditionally performed within a company is farmed to an outside provider where benefit can be made from greater labour efficiency or lower costs, ultimately providing goods or services to consumers with a competitive price edge. Globalisation has enhance the range at which this process can work. As well as the above mentioned relocation of call centres in India, outsourcing has involved the production of goods for the garment industry through cheap sweatshop labour in countries such as Bangladesh and car making corporations relying on the manufacture of components in a number of countries.

As well as access to low labour costs, global corporations may be attracted to particular locations by a combination of specialist labour skills, restrictions on trade union activity, good urban infrastructure and global communications and low rates of corporation tax. Some global enterprises have even, through the practice of internal transfer pricing, managed to effectively transfer profits made in one country of higher corporation tax to another where the rate is lower, thus engaging in legal tax avoidance with the consequence of diminishing their contribution to public revenues in a country where the profit was made.

The financial sector has become a greatly expanded sector in many advanced economies since the 1980s and by the early twentieth century comprised about 40% of the American economy. Following Agger (1989), it has been argued that capitalism has reached a 'fast capitalism' stage. From this Marxist framed analysis, the financial sector is driven by the quest to obtain maximum return from short term financial speculation rather than the creation of real value, for example through manufacturing. Whilst it adds little wealth to the productive economy, the fast movement of investments and investment prices can through the global interconnectedness of financial institutions and markets become highly destabilising and cause major global economic damage, as in the case of the global post 2008 recession.

3. Cultural

In sociology, culture refers to an environment of meaning. It is conveyed through language and symbols and has been traditionally located in local environments and communicated by process of face-to-face contact. Culture is the means of conveying local and national traditions and heritage and it shapes people's values and understanding of the world.

Following Ritzer (2008, pp.579-589), key questions to be raised here are whether in a globalising world the integrity of traditional cultures can be maintained, whether cultural convergence, usually seen to be in the direction of western capitalist and consumerist values, is taking place, or whether new hybrid cultural forms are emerging. Moreover, culture arguably also has increasingly a technologically related aspect to its formation through the output of the mass media. A key question here is the degree and nature of the impact of a mass media of increasingly global range on national or local culture. Will it promote the spread of popular consumerist culture programming surrounded by 'advertisement clutter'? Is it likely to erode national cultural differences, perhaps into a global mush, or is its impact relatively superficial in the face of millennia of territorially rooted cultural traditions that can operate as a defensive shield? May it help to promote an enhanced cosmopolitan outlook and tolerance between peoples as their knowledge of different cultures is enhanced? Or may it provoke cultural reactions in the form of defensive assertions of national traditions or even the appeal of fundamentalism?

The position of Samuel Huntington (2002) is that cultural differences will be retained but that the main lines of configuration will be between the world's major civilisations. Civilisations are cultural heritages which straddle individual nations and provide a very broad sense of identity which is often related to religious traditions. For Huntington, certain historical civilisation differences became temporarily submerged beneath the economic, political and ideological animosity between the communist east and capitalist west during the post war cold war era. With the collapse of communism, global fault lines have reconfigured to those between civilisations. He goes on to argue that the most dangerous element of this is the 'clash of civilisations' between the Christian west, which has attempted to universalise its culture, and the resurgence of Islamic culture. Similar animosities may also emerge between cultural and ethnic groups within multicultural societies.

An alternative interpretation of the effects of globalisation is that of cultural convergence. This view suggests that globalisation is changing all cultures toward something similar. Convergence may well be driven by economic factors to do with the standardising effect of global capitalism. If this is the case, the convergence is likely to lean strongly in the direction of the values of western or American capitalism. In the strongest assertion of this position, it may be seen as 'converging' completely in this direction, either viewed negatively from a Marxist position in the form of 'cultural imperialism', with capitalist cultural dominance replacing military imperialism, or more positively by supporters of neoliberal global capitalism.

Arguably, 'hybridization' provides the most optimistic interpretation of the effect of globalisation on culture. A hybrid culture is a unique and creative outcome of the interplay between various cultural influences coming into global contact with each other. In this scenario, more societies are experiencing a growing cultural mix throughout the world that can lead to novel outcomes in such forms as popular music and religious belief systems – a recipe that chimes well with postmodernist theory.

4. Political

Politics is about the institutions of government but it is also about the distribution and use of power locally, nationally and globally. During the modern period, the key institutions of government were seen to operate through sovereign nation states and political conflicts between and within states. The idea of national sovereignty related to a world of countries demarcated as territorial containers. It refers to the capacity of the state to legislate and form policy at national level and to hold legitimate use of power within its own territorial boundaries. However, a number of questions bearing on national sovereignty arise with reference to globalisation. For example, to what extent may governments have to modify their policies to accommodate the wishes of powerful global corporations? How can governments best co-operate to respond to global crime and terrorism? How can governments work together in response to global environmental issues?

In a globalised world, there are many pressures on governments to compromise a degree of national sovereignty, ideally for the mutual benefit of their societies in tackling global problems. For this purpose, various supra national institutions have been created. One of these is the International Monetary Fund which provides loans for economies in trouble. In this case, when one looks at the playing field within which this institution has operated from the 1980s, it has become one of the imposition of conditions of free market reforms on recipient states. For example, following the deep economic recession from 2008, Greece had to compromise a degree of national sovereignty by forcing through unpopular austerity and privatisation reforms as part of an economic bailout deal in part supplied by the IMF to avoid its own economic collapse and the contagious effect that this would likely have on other economies in a globally interlinked world. This raises major questions regarding the sovereign outcome of its own internal democratic processes and the political response options available to its citizens.

Modern communications technology has enhanced the ability for protest movements to organise at a global level, often regarding global issues such as opposition to environmental destruction. More formal non-governmental civil society organisations representing, for example, workers' rights, religious groups and environmental groups also increasingly fill the global landscape.

Psychological identification with nationhood has far from disappeared though. During the second decade of the twenty first century, countries throughout Europe witnessed a rise in nationalist political sentiment and citizens of the UK voted to leave the European Union whilst under Donald Trump's 'America first' banner, more protectionist trade policies have been selectively introduced.

In conclusion, there may be a tendency to see these different dimensions of globalisation as discrete systems, even if interlocking and sometimes even following contradictory paths. A rather looser alternative has been proposed by Appadurai who uses the term 'scapes' to refer to the terrains of various swirling influences at the global level of ethnic culture, media, ideology, technology and finance. For Appadurai, these flows, in a state of flux, produce in combination, within a globalised environment, 1) varied and unpredictable form which 2) will be interpreted differently by people and groups from different vantage points (Aas, 2013, Ch.1, Ritzer, 2008, pp.588-589).

Held's classification of approaches to globalisation

Sociological analyses of the nature and extent of globalisation are varied. Following a review of a broad range of sociological contributions on the subject, David Held (2000a & b) devised a classificatory system of positions adopted. This classificatory system will here be used as an initial organisational reference point for the ideas of some key contributors to the debate and reference will be made to the above dimensions of globalisation.

1. Globalists and rampant global neoliberalism

Held applied the term globalists to those who view the process of globalisation as profound and inevitable. Globalisation can be measured in terms of the growing extent and frequency of flows of information, communication, trade and capital etc. To varying degrees, those who adopt a globalist position emphasise the eroding effect of these processes on national boundaries and the sovereign power of the state. Globalists can be differentiated into optimists, who adopt a positive stance toward the form that globalisation has taken under neoliberal capitalism, and pessimists who recognise this form of globalisation but are highly critical of it.

1a Optimists

A highly optimistic position is taken by the Japanese organisational theorist Kenichi Ohmae who emphasises the predominating effects of the economic dimension of globalisation over that of the political sphere; he adopts quite a strongly economic determinist position. Ohmae advocates the merits of global free enterprise capitalism naturally leading toward the complete opening up of national borders to the free flow of trade and finance. By such means, it is argued that businesses and consumers can benefit from specialisation in goods and services that are produced in their most advantageous locations and which when traded maximise the total global creation of wealth. Consumers, thus provided with maximum choice and value for money, are regarded as the main beneficiaries of unbounded globalisation. Ohmae argues that in an increasingly 'borderless world' economy, governments need to go with the grain of global free trade and free enterprise capitalism, enhancing the competitive edge of their workforce by encouraging employee flexibility and supporting retraining. It is argued that the wealth created will in time trickle down to poorer sections of society and to the poorest countries so long as free market reforms are embraced. Ohmae's position is quite an extreme one which Held has referred to as 'hyperglobalist'.

Related to the technological dimension of cultural production, the massive expansion of commercially funded satellite and cable television can be taken as a measure of globalisation. A positive slant was put on the emergence of a global media by Marshall McLuhan as far back as the 1960s. McLuhan emphasised that communications revolutions are the driving force for social change and that the electronic media revolution held the potential for bringing the world together in a 'global village' of shared information to which our sensory perceptions would adjust.

More recently, Ohmae sees the emergence of a common global enterprise culture accompanying the triumph of global free enterprise capitalism as positive change, with rampant consumerism buoying up global capitalism. The economics of the global free market is therefore the driving force of global cultural uniformity.

In the realm of politics, the forces of globalisation, as argued by Ohmae, render national governments relatively powerless to control their own economies. The mobility of capital tends to pressure states toward open market friendly policies by which they can benefit by attracting inward investment. For Ohmae, nationally self-interested government intervention in the form of the erection of protectionist barriers to free trade in a globalising world would be damaging to the process of global wealth creation by distorting the beneficial effect of free markets and free trade to allocate production to the most economically beneficial (usually cheapest and most efficient) locations.

1b Pessimists

A critical stance toward global capitalism is adopted by globalists taking a neo-Marxist slant. Although the global spread of free enterprise is recognised, here globalism is viewed in terms of the imposition of the interests of western capitalism and a global capitalist class throughout the world. The result is a deterioration in the terms and conditions of employment experienced by workers in the face of profit maximising mobile capital and increasing polarisation of levels of income and wealth both within most societies and between the richer and poorer nations.

Tunstall views global media control and its output in terms of the cultural imposition of western capitalist values on developing countries. From this perspective, the mass media has the power to impress on populations an external culture of consumerism against which indigenous cultures have little defence. This 'cultural imperialism' is a new form of invasion in support of capitalist interests that does not require the presence of armies and a costly administrative apparatus for its imposition.

Leslie Sklair also adopts a neo-Marxist position. He points to the growing economic turnover of transnational corporations as powerful evidence of a globalised world in which national boundaries are being eroded by the emergence of a transnational system that has risen above nation states. At this general level, there is some agreement with Ohmae. However, for Sklair, the main beneficiaries of this process are not consumers but a broadly defined transnational capitalist class including corporate executives, top professionals, pro-globalist politicians and bureaucrats and mass media producers. The almost complete global reach and pervasiveness of the mass media promotes an 'ideology of consumerism' – a powerfully dominant view that consumerism is natural and desirable. This ideology extends an appetite to consume from a growing array of goods and services that are available, with the effect of maintaining the buoyancy of transnational capitalism for its major beneficiaries.

Sklair argues that socialism may ultimately emerge out of capitalism to reshape globalisation. This is because the consequences of transnational capitalism are the crises of economic polarisation between and often within societies as well as the ecological damage caused through the ruthless corporate exploitation of natural resources. In response, anti-capitalist and environmental movements come to adopt an increasingly global stance of opposition to transnational capitalism and some governments are engaging in protectionist measures to defend their environment and ways of life.

2. Traditionalists – globalisation is overstated

In contrast to globalists, traditionalists, such as Hirst and Thompson, adopt a sceptical position regarding the extent to which the forces of globalisation have emerged and advanced. They are keen to differentiate between globalisation, as has been defined in this chapter, and internationalism, the latter taking the form of trade and communications between states which can be traced back through many centuries. They therefore maintain that the case for globalisation has been overstated and argue that state power and national culture within territorial boundaries remains substantial. In terms of economics, they point out that there is little new in the nature and extent of international trade. For example, Thompson offers evidence that the trade to gross domestic product ratio for many countries in 1995 was little changed from that of 1913. Moreover, he maintains that most international corporations are multinationals. With their headquarters rooted in one country, these organisations can be controlled by national governments. Very few businesses are strictly transnational corporations that can move freely between countries and by such means exert significant influence over government policy – the true index of economic globalisation.

From this perspective, it can be argued that whilst governments are keen to attract inward investment, they are able to be more protectionist in terms of major corporate takeovers from an external source. For example, in 2014, the American pharmaceutical giant Pfizer, which had previously closed a major plant in England, launched an attempt to take over the British pharmaceutical company AstraZeneca, prospectively becoming the largest takeover of a British company. At the time, the government claimed to be looking at whether the move would satisfy the public interest, which it defined in terms of British jobs and science. Whilst this might suggest evidence of national government resistance to unbounded economic globalisation, the capacity of the government to override the decision of shareholders if 1) it decided that a takeover was against the public interest but 2) shareholders nevertheless voted for the takeover (which they didn't) would have provided an interesting test case between the perspectives of traditionalists and globalists.

A traditionalist position on culture emphasises that national cultures are rooted in national traditions and are quite resistant to the more ephemeral effects of the global media. From this viewpoint, information crossing national boundaries is mediated through the prism of a national culture and mass media, especially in countries where national public service channels such as the BBC operate.

For traditionalists, the focus of political power remains strongly with national governments. Governments retain the ability to pass legislation, control their own economic and social policy and, where inclined, to defend the welfare state. Moreover, it could be argued that the development of modern technology in the form of information gathering and surveillance techniques has actually enhanced the power of the state. Governments retain their own armies, police and intelligence services and can maintain their own borders. Indeed, the issue of immigration control, along with nationalist and anti-European political establishment sentiments, figured prominently in the May 2014 European elections, with the success of parties of the political right sending a strong message to a number of national governments. Arguably, similar sentiments lay behind the Brexit outcome of the 2016 UK European Union Referendum.

3. Transformationists – globalisation must be steered

Those that can be placed within this position stand somewhere in between that of globalists and traditionalists, but in terms of recognition of the extent of global change, closer to the former. They maintain that profound globalising changes have been taking place but, unlike optimistic globalists, they see no single and inevitable beneficial direction to these changes which are very complex and can work themselves out differently in economic, cultural and political spheres. For writers such as Giddens and Beck, the challenges and risks associated with globalisation are great, sometimes new, and solutions uncertain. Consequently, a level of global governance is emerging and needs to be developed to help manage these problems. Although the state remains a powerful entity, it must increasingly work alongside a plethora of global, regional and local institutions to go with the grain of globalisation but also intervene, especially through regional and global institutions and agreements, to tame its excesses.

Those who adopt this position recognise some of the economic changes that have been highlighted by free enterprise globalists, but do not view them in terms of unmitigated success or disaster as optimistic and pessimistic globalists respectively tend to. Although the global economy is capable of producing great wealth, it is argued that if left unchecked in neoliberal capitalist form it could lead to a further polarisation between winners and losers within and between nations. However, for Giddens, the main nations which have lost out are in fact those that have been marginalised by the globalisation process rather than being its direct victims.

Writers in this tradition invariably adopt a high-modernist sociological stance. They tend to emphasise that it is possible and necessary to rationally intervene to tame global capitalism in such a way that international and national security and social justice can complement the benefits of economic efficiency and the creation of wealth that it provides. This is the key theme of Giddens' 'Runaway World' (2002), in which he likened the condition of the forces of capitalist globalisation when left unchecked to that of a juggernaut hurtling out of control and urgently requiring someone to grasp the steering wheel.

For transformationists, the impact of globalisation on culture is complex. Unlike neo-Marxists, transformationists argue that cultural flows from the mass media are not simply top down one-way influences of cultural imperialism and ideology of consumerism which are uniformly imposed on and passively absorbed by populations. Even if media output is becoming standardised, different readings are likely to form in the context of different cultures rather than there simply being a homogenising effect. From the transformationist position, it is argued that detailed research is necessary to establish the dynamics involved in each case in understanding the effects of media output in different cultural contexts.

Transformationists such as Giddens strongly emphasise the need to develop new institutions of 'global governance' to tackle problems that have taken on an increasingly global dimension, such as extreme inequalities in the distribution of wealth, international crime, the risk of destabilised financial markets and global economic collapse and environmental damage. Governments must be prepared to cede a degree of national sovereignty and perceived self-interest to supra-national institutions for the common benefit. Giddens saw the European Union as an important model in the direction of global governance, but one which needed to improve the democratic accountability of its institutions.

Globalisation and the workplace – new work, at a price

The decades of the 1950s and 1960s have been referred to as a period of Fordist prosperity in modern western societies. As economies emerged from post-war austerity, Fordist production systems applied to manufacturing made possible the mass production of standardised goods. Based on the early twentieth century work of efficiency expert F. W. Taylor, who pioneered scientific management techniques, the typical model of efficient manufacturing was becoming one of large scale production line work within hierarchical organisations in which management designed work tasks and measured worker productivity in the finest detail. For shop floor workers, although the technology was modern, this usually required training in low skilled and narrowly designated tasks with the repetitive work tempo regulated by the speed of the production line that they worked on. With wages tied to productivity, both would increase simultaneously and so mass production was buoyed up by increased purchasing power and mass consumption. Growing prosperity was complemented by governments tending to adopt a Keynesian approach to broader economic policy. This provided a degree of security through governments taking responsibility for regulation of the economy with the aim of minimising unemployment and committing to significant spending on welfare provision.

Although scientific management / Fordism were designed to disempower workers, government commitment to near full employment and growing trade union power led to a period of rising industrial disputes, higher wage demands and growing inflation. Coupled with economic competition from a resurgent Japan and a period of massive increases in world oil prices, western economies throughout the 1970s slowed.

In response, by the early 1980s a number of governments, in particular in Britain and the United States, were turning to neoliberal economic and social policy by introducing reforms which deregulated and opened up economies to global free market pressures. Policy included curbing public expenditure, breaking the political power of trade unions, privatising nationalised industries and restricting the money supply to curb inflationary pressures, even if (and when) the consequence was rising unemployment.

In this more competitive environment, many businesses were looking for more flexible and cheaper production models than those offered by Fordist mass production techniques. The pattern of adaptation often adopted came in the form of downsizing workforces to a core of workers and subcontracting out work to external organisations offering low paid and casualised work. For transnational corporations, solutions often included outsourcing work to or in part relocating in low wage countries.

Whilst many developing countries were expanding their manufacturing sectors, western economies were undergoing deindustrialisation. The knowledge economy was growing, information and communications technology developing and more women were working. Growing employment in the service sector was replacing that in manufacturing. This expanding sector included a large proportion of low skilled and low paid jobs in occupations such as catering, domestic work, leisure, healthcare, tourism, and fast food. Other service sector occupations comprised more highly skilled professionals such as architects, lawyers, accountants, stockbrokers, managers and those working in advertising and marketing, some of whom, especially those providing services for corporations in global cities, benefited substantially from globalisation. This category tended to be a male dominated one.

Taking these far reaching changes into account, writers such as Piore argued that advanced economies had entered a post-Fordist phase of production. In reality, the situation has remained a mixed one. Scientific management type systems of control still very effectively operate in some industries. Thus Ritzer, in reference to McDonaldization, has analysed fast food production processes in terms the global application of Weber's formal rationality to the workplace.

The global economy has undergone a process of financialisation from the late 1980s. Growth of the financial sector can be linked to neoliberalism in the deregulation of financial markets, arguably promoting what has been referred to as 'hypercapitalism' (Scholte, 2005, p.24) or 'fast capitalism' (Agger, 1989). The world of financial markets has grown and became increasingly interconnected, with global financial cities playing a key role. This, with the increasing mobility of capital investment, increased the risk of contagious financial destabilisation, possibly leading to economic destabilisation, something that came to be realised in the global banking crisis from 2007 which led to a deep and protracted global economic recession.

According to Castells, technological advances associated with the internet have brought about globally networked 'informational capitalism'. He has argued that those working with this technology are being reskilled rather than deskilled and are able to work with less monotony and greater autonomy within networked as opposed to hierarchical environments. Within high tech informational work environments, both institutions and individuals must take on higher levels of reflexivity – a change which arguably works against the collective culture associated with trade unions.

However, for Durrschmidt & Taylor (2007, pp.66-81), emblematic of the networked world is the restructuring and relocation of the workplace in the call centre industry. This 'customer care' work is often feminised. Women are frequently regarded as being endowed with caring qualities, amenable to part-time work, stereotypically regarded as relatively compliant and being a lowly unionised section of the workforce. With reference to research carried out by Callaghan and Thompson on a Scottish call centre (Durrschmidt & Taylor, 2007, pp.66-67) key characteristics of the workplace include the use of scripts to deal efficiently with telephone queueing systems, the perpetual uncertainty faced by workers of individual surveillance through managers listening in, and the management of performance data. High levels of stress and dissatisfaction usually surface in high rates of employee turnover.

Of particular interest regarding globalisation is the practice of outsourcing. An example of this is the 'disembedding' of call centre work, for example to India, where the government has tended to follow western neoliberal reforms. An Indian call centre study by Mirchandani (Durrschmidt & Taylor, 2007, pp. 76-77) found that 'scripting' rules were commonly used to standardise and structure conversation. Workers were even trained in the neutralisation of their Indian accent. This was likely to assist in 'locational masking' – the attempt to hide the global distance which existed in the communication and reduce the risk of workers being subjected to racist hostility. But it was 'synchronicity' which was particularly revealing regarding the globalised nature of this work. Given the global time differences involved in Indian call centres servicing American or British customers, call centre workers in India had to operate according to western time. This required substantial night shift work which tended to 'disembed' workers from family and community life in their local context, often impacting on their well-being.

Overall, the dynamics of neoliberal globalisation have tended to work against lower skilled and less educated workers who lack the geographical mobility of capital and face constant insecurity through the threat of capital movement to other locations where the cost of labour is even cheaper. Whilst it is often difficult to unravel the effects of neoliberal capitalism from globalisation, it could be argued that for a majority of the world's poorer workers, they combine in a toxic mix.

Globalisation – tackling poverty and stretching inequality

Applied at a global level, poverty is usually measured in absolute terms; that is around universally adopted criteria for basic subsistence living, often equated to a minimum daily income. From this position, effectiveness in combatting poverty can be measured in terms of changes in aggregate numbers or proportions of people living below this officially defined minimum. By contrast, inequality refers primarily to the distribution of wealth and income which can be measured in terms of changing profiles of its distribution. Clearly, there is much room for playing with statistics here to support particular arguments, but the fundamental point in this distinction made by Martell (2012, Ch.8) is that it is possible for people to be lifted out of absolute poverty whilst at the same time inequalities increase and the rich become much richer.

Neoliberalism has been associated with the most robust advance of globalisation. Although this form is the result of political decision making, it can be difficult to envisage globalisation other than in a capitalist neoliberal form since the ideology of neoliberalism, often conveyed through the western media, would have it that the two are irresistible and inextricably bound up forces. Disentangling the effects of globalisation per se from the neoliberal variant that it has predominantly come to take is a very difficult task.

The World Bank has become a key advocate of the neoliberal route to modernisation. Consequently, in the loans that it has made available to underdeveloped countries, it has attached requirements for economic restructuring in terms of privatisation and the opening up of economies to free trade. It is argued that in the long run, the wealth created by these reforms will sufficiently 'trickle down' to lift significant numbers out of absolute poverty.

Big data on the alleviation of absolute poverty has been provided by the World Bank to support the effectiveness of the neoliberal course that it has taken. Thus, between 1990 and 2000, a time coinciding with the impact of neoliberal reforms, the numbers globally existing in absolute poverty, here measured as those living on or below 1$ a day at the time, declined from 27.9% to 21.3% of the world's population (Martell, 2012, p.164) and the Gross Domestic Product of developing countries taken as a whole increased by 30% between 1981 and 2001 (Cohen & Kennedy, 2013, pp.106-107). The World Bank has also been able to claim an impressive record of investment in the education and training of women in the developing world during the late twentieth century (Scholte, 2005, p.339). This, along with programmes by organisations such as UNICEF and the World Health Organisation to expand child immunisation and improve the health and education of children in the poorer global south, is no mean feat, and such data is taken by supporters of neoliberal globalisation to support the effectiveness of structural reform in developing countries.

However there are a number of questions that need to be raised, including the following:

1. Which countries should be included in the data to support the neoliberal's case? A number of countries that have made the most rapid development, including China, South Korea and South Vietnam, may have latterly benefited a great deal by opening up their economies to the global free market, but in these cases only after strategic periods of state protected home growth which restricted imports until the economies were strong enough to compete to export effectively in the global market. For China, the protective growth period spanned the 1970s and much of the 1980s. From the end of the latter decade, the economy was exposed to global trade and has since made remarkable strides. Again, the Indian economy was protected by tariffs during the 1980s, and was only later able to take advantage of global free markets to make its own rapid development. Given their population size and growth of China and India, their achievements in taking people out of absolute poverty have been substantial, accounting in total for approximately all of the global improvement documented in the above figures on the decline in global poverty. A case has been put (for example by Cohen and Kennedy (2013, pp.107-108) and Martell (2012, Ch.8)) that since neoliberal globalisation cannot take full credit for these improvements, the statistics for these two countries should be taken out of the aggregate if assessing the impact of neoliberal capitalism on the reduction of absolute poverty.

Many areas of the developing world that have turned to World Bank and the International Monetary Fund to provide financial assistance have not been in the stronger position that India and China were when they entered the global market. For them, from a position of weakness and dependency, the imposition of structural adjustment programmes of privatisation and free trade that the lending institutions have attached to development loans has often led to the growing immiseration of large sections of the population as prioritising the servicing of debt repayment has stifled growth and drawn resources away from much needed investment in key public services such as healthcare and education. The prospects for such countries would appear to be the bleak one of long term servitude to their lenders and in some cases dashed promises of debt cancellation.

2. Focussing on figures for absolute poverty and GNP tells us nothing about levels of inequality within societies. Thus, although India and China have been very successful in lifting vast numbers out of absolute poverty, there has been a substantial syphoning of wealth upwards. For example, data provided by Ellwood (2015, p.131) refers to the fact that in 2005, 0.4% of China's population amassed 70% of the nation's total wealth. In Russia, following the collapse of communism and western insistence on rapid transition to free market capitalism, the income and working conditions of very many workers has significantly suffered whilst massive wealth has been concentrated in the hands of super rich oligarchs. These 'achievements' certainly can be more closely attributed to the effects of neoliberal global capitalism.

Whether in the developing or the developed world of neoliberal capitalism, a common pattern has emerged that economic inequalities have been stretched as a small minority have seen their income and wealth massively increased whilst for the vast majority it has stagnated. For example, Ellwood (2015, p.132) provides figures showing that in the United States, the percentage of wealth in the hands of the top 1% increased between 1973 and 2014 from 25% to 40%, and this in the context of overall wealth creation substantially increasing over this period.

3. In a free trade world, it tends to be the stronger, more advanced nations who are the main beneficiaries. Their corporations can exploit cheap labour and resources in developing countries and when it comes to protecting their own national interests, they do not always practice what they preach to others, showing themselves to be 'hypocritical globalizers' (Martell, 2012, p.182). By this, it is meant that whilst they preach to and

impose the virtues of free trade and the dismantling of subsidies on developing countries, they selectively ignore such requirements when it suites their own national interest. Such is the case, for example, of wheat subsidies paid to American farmers and the imposition of trade tariffs on the import of steel. Meanwhile, rural areas in developing countries have often been severely hit. Peasant farmers, unable to compete with invading efficiently run agribusinesses may have to face the option of offering their services in the free market for low paid agricultural labour or migrating to the precarious life of the growing shanty town slums.

4. The conditions of life of those living in developing countries cannot be adequately measured on the single dimension of monetary income alone. Instead, a broader multifactorial range of measures of standard of living and quality of life need to be taken into account. For example, people may lose access to common land bought up by agribusinesses. Privatisation, central to structural adjustment programmes linked to the conditions of loans, is likely to deplete the provision of public services such as housing and transport which poorer sections of society are disproportionately reliant on. Moreover, debt servicing has to be prioritised over the financing of public services.

5. Declining availability and / or quality of public services is likely to have a strongly gendered element to its impact; it is has been particularly severe on the lives of women, many of whom are forced back into more traditional caring and educating roles whilst also needing to be in employment. This has to be balanced against the positive effects of education and training initiatives for women sponsored by the World Bank.

6. The impact of neoliberal globalisation can be viewed in terms of social justice or social equity. Market liberals tend to emphasise that free market capitalism enhances opportunities for all. However, Scholte (2005, Ch.10), who analyses inequality related to neoliberal global capitalism in terms of social equity, finds that this position is difficult to sustain. By social equity, we need to examine the extent to which and ways that neoliberal globalisation has influenced life chances in terms of people gaining access to resources by which they can realise their capacities. Since the effect of neoliberal globalisation has been to reverse redistributive trends in taxation and cut welfare state and public sector provision, it has impacted especially on poorer and vulnerable sections of societies,

including unskilled workers and women. Scholte therefore concludes that a form of globalisation which has primarily benefited the wealthy and super wealthy has been inequitable. For Ellwood (2015, p.142), the track record of neoliberal globalisation leaves the need for 'an economic system more connected to real human needs and aspirations – and less geared to the anti-human machinations of the corporate-led free market'.

Globalisation and corporate power of mobility

Global corporations have been a key driving force in the broader process of globalisation, promoting a culture of free enterprise and consumerism, shaping national and global policy and impacting on the lives of people throughout the world. These corporations are often massive in the economic resources that they deploy across the globe and the neoliberal form that global capitalism has by and large taken usually finds much support from within these corporations. To give some idea of the concentration of wealth at the top global corporate level, research by the Institute for Policy Studies (Ellwood, 2015, p.70) found that 25% of the world's economic activity was conducted by the top 200 corporations. As much as a third of all goods traded globally moved between branches within global corporations.

Although some transnationals are emerging from the top rank of developing countries such as China, India, Brazil, Mexico and Malaysia, the majority of the largest ones are established in the developed northern capitalist economies. Top in the league table in sales value are Walmart (American based department and grocery stores), Royal Dutch Shell (a Dutch and UK based oil and gas corporation), Exxon (an American based petroleum corporation) and Toyota (the Japanese based motor vehicle manufacturer). The sales revenue for each of these corporations, and a number of others, is greater than the gross domestic product of a majority of the world's nations (Cohen and Kennedy, 2013, pp. 181-183).

Such corporations are argued to bring a number of benefits to developing countries. Those frequently identified include the diffusion of advanced technology and expertise from advanced economies that promote efficient production, provide employment opportunities, assist economic development and promote export potential.

However, the activities of global corporations can have a number of problematic effects, including the following:

1. In a globalised world where corporations locate their activities in a number of countries, and where distance becomes less of a barrier to the movement of investment, global corporations, especially transnationals, are in a strong position to take advantage of their capacity for actual or potential mobility in the quest for profit maximisation. They are able to play the governments of countries off against each other when substantial investment is at stake in the context of national competition for inward investment. As a result, there is massive pressure on governments, whose political elites may often be in the pocket of these powerful interests, to prioritise private enterprise friendly policies, often with a deleterious effect on resources available for the provision of public services, on the environment and on workplace conditions.

To attract inward investment, governments across the world have welcomed or been pressured toward corporate tax reduction. Neoliberal governments from the 1980s in the UK and the United States have driven tax reductions and by and large successfully promoted low tax tolerant cultures. The UK corporate tax rate of 52% in 1979 was substantially reduced during the period of new right Conservative governments to 31% when they left office in 1997. Under New Labour governments, the rate further declined to 28% and subsequent Conservative dominated coalition and Conservative governments cut the rate to 19% in 2017 and have planned further reductions to 17% for 2020. In the United States, the corporation tax rate in 1968 was set at 52.8% and has been reduced from 35% to 21% in 2018 under the Republican presidency of Donald Trump. Consequently, an increasing proportion of the tax take for pressurised public sectors is taken from income tax and tax on the sale of goods and services. In the case on income tax, rates in the UK fell significantly during the 1980s and especially at the top end, making the system less 'progressive', with increases in VAT having a similar effect.

2. Wealthy corporations are also able to employ the best accountants and legal experts to minimise their corporate tax bills. Transnational companies have been further able to reduce their tax liability through payment in a country of low taxation on profits made in other countries.

3. Governments in developing countries are often particularly keen to attract global corporate inward investment. On offer, as well as competitive levels of corporate taxation, wages are likely to be comparatively low, trade union

rights restricted or non-existent, terms and conditions of employment poor and health and safety protection for workers minimal. In the case of disasters such as Shell's catastrophic pollution of the Niger delta and the mass loss of life from the Union Carbide gas leakage in Bhopal, compensation is often miniscule by western standards, with corporations dragging out the process, as in the latter case where blame was placed on the actions of a subsidiary.

4. But the problem does not stop at the door of developing countries. Power is not just about doing something but also holding the capacity to threaten to do something. Thus, the threat to move investment to poorer developing countries can powerfully influence the pay and conditions that can be bargained for by workers in developed countries, placing trade unions on the back foot and workers, who usually do not have the degree of mobility that capital has, more at the mercy of the chill winds of competition with workers far away.

5. There would appear to be strong tendencies toward monopolisation in the global corporate world. The drive toward massive mergers and takeovers has helped produce this concentration of wealth and power at the top corporate end, with size of market share limiting competition. This has particularly been the case in the steel industry, the pharmaceutical industry, banking and finance and telecommunications.

For large global corporations, it can be the crushing of competition that is a key aim. Through their financial muscle and ability to cross subsidise their activities, these corporations can pose a major threat to smaller local companies by sustaining short term losses to drive them out of lucrative areas and then benefit from the resultant lack of competition by raising their prices. Cohen and Kennedy (2013, p.183) provide one such example from the intrusion of a fast food corporation in the Caribbean.

6. In their global pursuit of profits, the activities of transnational corporations can thus have a negative effect on cultural diet. They can also detrimentally affect health. With health campaigns, advertising and smoking restrictions and a substantial decline in smoking in the west, tobacco companies have moved into vast substitute markets of Asia and China where through advertising they have been able to associate smoking with the desirable status of a western lifestyle, much as they were able to in western societies themselves during the post war decades.

7. We must increasingly consider the role of banks and financial companies which as global high tech service sector organisations are particularly light and nimble movers on the world stage. Financialisation has been accompanied by deregulation since the 1980s, especially in Britain and the United States. A strong case can be made that perverse casino capitalism incentives of making quick monetary gain from financial speculation involving rapid movements of investment of money in money, rather than stable long term investment in manufacturing, have encouraged irresponsible individual and institutional activities within this growing sector. Whilst Cohen and Kennedy (2013, pp.180- 181) claim that this sector has contributed little of substance to the global economy, its virtual collapse, only averted through massive governmental cash injections, almost wrecked it and brought severe recession from 2008. With the effects still being felt in austerity programmes and public sector cutbacks, burdened publics have shown renewed interest in anti-establishment political parties and leaders.

8. Overall, the ideological power of the global corporate world is immense; arguably hegemonic. It holds the capacity to shape attitudes and values in its favour through constant and clever marketing and advertising campaigns which critics argue are promoting a homogenous western free enterprise consumerist culture throughout much of the world.

Meanwhile, the capacity of small shareholders to constrain the activities of global corporations, even if they were inclined to, is minimal since the majority of shareholding is held in institutional blocks. More effective can be citizen campaigning and protesting through which bad media publicity can damage the reputation of unscrupulous companies. International non-governmental organisations, such as Greenpeace, can act as pressure groups, highlighting environmental and moral issues and organising action. At a more micro level, individuals can make investment and consumer decisions – if they have access to information.

Global cities

1. The developed world – global control and command functions

The transition to from pre-industrial economies and societies to modern capitalism marked a change from the experience of time and space once locked more into nature and locality to the concentration of capital and workers into controlled and confined workplace space and urban settings. Such changes were of utmost interest to classical sociologists, who tended to view both national and unban life as quite territorially bounded. An important debate has more recently emerged regarding the degree to which the growing forces of globalisation have had a deterritorializing effect on economic, political and social life, operating as if territorially detached forces. A good testbed by which this may be assessed can be in the emergence of 'global cities', entities that are highly globally interconnected but also each uniquely geographically and historically grounded.

What are the key characteristics of global cities which distinguish them from other cities and urban centres? As well as their size and density of population, global cities concentrate cutting edge technology which provides the means of communication for the performance of command and control functions of global reach. Whilst large cities have been dominant on the world stage for millennia as powerful religious, military, trading and colonial locations, globally networked cities, reliant on advanced information and communications technology, enabling the location of key global functions in finance and banking and the provision of top level managerial and professional services, are of far more recent development. Following Sassen (2001), it is commonly recognised that there are three top level global cities in the performance of global functions: New York, London and Tokyo, followed by other global cities such as Paris, Hong Kong, Sydney and Los Angeles, which perform a lesser range of global functions.

Multinational and transnational manufacturing corporations are likely to be headquartered in global cities. A physical landscape of impressively rising glass tower blocks typically accommodate global banking and financial institutions from across the world who will have their head offices there. Global cities will also be the location of the major stock exchanges. For Short and Yeong-Hyun (1999) these institutions are key to the performance of command functions in the globally networked economic and financial world.

Massive infrastructure projects are a key feature of global cities. Of vital importance is the development of large international airports with heavy global traffic flows, sometimes creating a point of conflict between global pressures for expansion and local protest movements regarding quality of life and property values - witness, for example, the political difficulties in deciding on the location for extra airport capacity in the south east of England during the second decade of the twenty first century.

Global cities in the developed world are usually renown as cultural and entertainment centres, boasting the world's greatest museums and art galleries. They are the location of great shopping malls and some of the world's most iconic buildings. Sports stadia, along with supporting infrastructure, are used for hosting global sporting events.

Globalised telecommunications have become essential in providing networks of communication and control that enable and support the geographical dispersal of global companies. As well as reflecting a general change in advanced economies away from manufacturing, financial services drive and are driven by globalisation. And to run globally dispersed companies, financial or otherwise, their command and control functions require specialist marketing, accounting, advertising, legal and managerial services etc. These services have become increasingly outsourced in the post-Fordist era to smaller firms of specialist service providers. Having a substantial impact on the profitability of global companies, top service professionals are able to trade on their much needed expertise and geographical mobility to obtain high salaries. However, with the service sector also comprising a proliferation of low paid, casualised and low skilled support work in waitressing, cleaning and domestic employment etc., there is usually evidence of a very highly stretched hierarchy of incomes in the global city.

The degree of interconnectivity between global cities could be suggestive of an abstracted realm of forces whereby global cities converge into a globally interlinked city system, disconnected from their own regions and national territories. Whilst global cities often do develop a more cosmopolitan culture which distinguishes them from their national hinterlands, there are also reasons to be cautious of overplaying this image of deterritorialized and homogenising forces. Thus, Sassen (2001) argues that focussing our view on the physicality of global cities helps us to recognise the fact that the forces of globalisation are actually shaped by the grounded structures that they run through. Although often performing similar global functions, these cities are marked by their territorial variations in terms of the imprint of their geography, history, culture and institutions. Global forces work through these territorialized features and global cities are therefore often able to retain a significant degree of uniqueness.

This uniqueness can take the form of global cities developing their own key functional niches in the global network with some, for example, operating primarily as financial centres (London and New York) and others as manufacturing centres (Barcelona, Chicago and Detroit), features which will have been to some extent influenced by heritage. Other cities, such as Sydney and Los Angeles, occupy more of a role in connecting regions into the global economic system.

Although locked into co-operative networks, globalisation has also intensified the competition between major cities. Whilst New York, Tokyo and London comprise a first tier of global cities, below them competition for global recognition is intense. These cities have been referred to as 'wannabe cities', and the situation of competition between cities for global status has been referred to by Haider (1992) as 'place wars'.

Cultural globalisation with regard to the city in the context of place wars, like that of nations that attempt to develop powerful magnet economies to attract inward investment, invariably takes the form of competitive rebranding, primarily promoting a pro-business image to attract mobile capital by emphasising the existence of an entrepreneurial culture and excellent business infrastructure. In the process, cities themselves become repackaged, commodified and sold in brochures. Competition for investment is intense as in the lighter financialized and service sector economies of advanced capitalist societies its tie to natural resources and manufacturing plant tends to decrease.

However, rebranding can also place an emphasis on leisure, 'culture' and quality of life. Glasgow in 1990, for example, attempted such rebranding through its designation as a European City of Culture. Capital attracted by these means may include a larger proportion of 'circulating capital' coming with tourists and the hosting major world conferences and conventions.

Competitiveness to enter the top or at least second tier of world cities can be seen in the quest to hold major global sporting spectacles such as the World Cup and Olympic Games. Such 'wannabe' world cities as Seoul have competed intensively for these events, in this case staging both the Olympic Games and the World Cup, and cities in the developing world such as Mexico City have also occasionally managed to make their mark.

Overall, the enterprise and growth image has become the dominating ideology for city success in 'place wars'. There are corporation and executive winners from low taxation, but in the manipulation of image game, the plight of the poor tends to become screened out, as when streets are cleared of the homeless in the hosting of Olympic Games.

2. The developing world – the problems of mega city growth

Major cities in the developing world often suffer the most acute problems. The increased urban population in all developing countries is phenomenal at about 45 million extra people per year in total. Overall, the world is still urbanising, but at least 90% of this increase is accounted for by a rise in urban populations of large cities such as Mexico City, Delhi, Mumbai, Sao Paulo and Dhaka in developing countries. Potter and Lloyd-Evans (1998) have identified the key factors typically involved as a combination of high numbers migrating from rural locations to cities and high natural population increases resulting from improved life expectancy combined with remaining traditional patterns of high birth rates. This means that urban populations of such cities are increasing even more rapidly than was the case during the industrial revolutions of western societies.

The problem is often that in the developing world the rate of urbanisation runs substantially ahead of industrialisation and the 'carrying capacity' of the city – its ability to 'adequately' support its population. As a result, city peripheries are often populated with ghettoised areas where people rely heavily on the informal economy for work, live in overcrowded and insanitary housing conditions, suffer environmental degradation and high levels of pollution and lack access to adequate health, welfare and educational services. At a macro economic and political level, we have seen that these conditions have arguably been exacerbated by pressures toward free market liberal policies which are invariably attached to loans from such institutions as the World Bank.

Globalisation – an overview

Many issues can be raised regarding globalisation, a small number of which will be touched on here.

One question is just how new is the process of globalisation? For example, Holton (2011, p.19) has suggested that there have been early historical episodes of mini-globalisations, such as the reach of the Roman Empire two thousand years ago, which subsequently faltered, whilst Steger (2009, Ch.2) has identified key advances, particularly in technology, which have led to step changes toward contemporary globalisation. As with so much in sociology, the answer to such questions depends on definitions. If taken literally to mean the interconnectedness of the entire globe in the form of political and economic infrastructure and instantaneous global communication, it would be reasonable to conclude that globalisation is a uniquely recent and still somewhat uneven phenomena, perhaps having gathered pace with the emergence of international free trade organisations from the 1950s, satellite broadcasting from about the mid-1960s, the take-off of the internet from the latter decades of the twentieth century, and the collapse of the Soviet Union and Eastern European communist states between 1989 and 1991.

It has been argued by supporters of hyper globalisation such as Ohmae that allowing globalisation free rein would contribute to global peace as well as prosperity. This would be because as well as free trade, highly permeable national borders would substantially enhance investment across societies. In this event, countries would be reluctant to go to war with each other as to do so would destroy some of the resources of their companies abroad.

Arguably, however, this view of conflict has become somewhat dated in ways related to the very forces of globalisation. The permeable national borders and use of modern technology which enabled the 9/11 attack on the twin towers symbolised a new type of warfare which may not be limited by the above mentioned constraints. Hatred of America or the west has led to terrorist attacks in which the loss of property has not been a limiting factor.

However far reaching its effects have been, we should be cautious against viewing globalisation as a singular reified process bearing down its effects uniformly throughout the world. Globalisation is a highly complex process, working in different and unpredictable ways in the interconnected spheres of the economy, culture and politics and as well as bringing change to global cities operates through their structures (Sassen, 2001). It is not simply an overarching top down process moving the world in a single and inevitable direction. The thoughtful observer may therefore adopt a varied response to globalisation as it affects different aspects of their life. For example, opposition to the power of global multinationals may sit alongside support for global regulatory apparatus designed to constrain their abuses of power. For poorer sections of society in the developed world, as consumers, globalisation may bring within reach cheaper products such as clothes produced by cheap labour in developing countries. However, they may find that, as workers, their own terms, conditions and security of employment are eroded by the capacity of multi and transnational companies to easily withdraw resources in an open global market to invest in those very areas of cheap labour.

But how do the forces of global oppression and identity formation impact subjectively on individuals or groups? Global intersectionality theory is an approach which has attempted to enhance such an understanding. Pioneered by the American black feminist Kimberle Crenshaw in 1989, intersectionality theory grew out of criticism of mainstream white middle class feminism, arguing that the experiences of black females were usually quite different. Importantly, an understanding of these experiences could not simply be arrived at through an aggregation of gender, ethnicity and class oppressions. This is because the effect of the intersection of a range of oppressions is experienced holistically by individuals and groups and therefore has to be understood as such from their standpoint. For example, the experience of migrant ethnic minority women working as cleaners in a global city in the developed world requires an insight into the dimensions of migrant minority status, gender and occupational class as holistically experienced in their own identity formation. This immensely complicated form of analysis could be applied across a whole matrix of identity forming processes affecting the lives of oppressed people.

But just how relentlessness of is the process of globalisation? This has been questioned by writers such as Polanyi (Holton, 2011, p.228) who has argued that there are economically related phases of globalisation and deglobalisation. In this view, tendencies toward global free market deregulation eventually lead to social crisis and the need for interventionary responses. This could be in the form of the protection of home markets through import controls to safeguard home employment, as during the inter war years. Although a capitalist neoliberal variant of globalisation has become an increasingly dominant force from the 1980s, the early twentieth century has seen an upsurge of anti-globalisation sentiment and protest, particularly aimed at those institutions (the WTO, G8, G20) that symbolise neoliberal globalisation.

Following a deep and lengthy recession post 2008, the turn of political events has seen a rise in dissatisfaction with traditional political elites and nationalistic and anti-immigration sentiments throughout much of Europe. Ironically, economic support packages to save economies from the consequences of deregulated financial markets have been provided by global institutions which have required the countries in receipt of massive funds, such as Greece, to pursue deregulation in the form of free market reforms.

In 2016, the vote in for the UK to leave the European Union and the election of Donald Trump in the United States expressed measures of rejection of traditional globalising political elites, reassertions of national sovereignty and perceived protection of national self-interest. By 2018, Trump had introduced a broad range of protectionist tariffs, aimed particularly against the importation of Chinese steel and a range of manufactured products, but which also impacted on other countries including those of the European Union. Both China and the EU responded with retaliatory tariffs against a range of American products.

Globalisation and the role of sociology

Briefly returning to the Held's typology, it is possible to extract from the different positions on globalisation different consequences for the nature and role of sociology. For hyperglobists such as Ohmae, there is little that planned social intervention can or should do to stem the headlong process of deregulated global capitalism. From this position, sociology would be reduced to little more than the handmaiden of free market economics. For neo-Marxists, sociology can have a political role to play in highlighting the nature of consumerist ideology so as to enhance oppositional movements to transnational capitalism and challenge its neoliberal hegemony.

For traditionalists, a sociology similar to that developed by the founding theorists which tended to conceptualise society in terms of bounded nation states remains relatively valid. For transformationists, there is both the possibility of and need for enlightened human agency to influence the conditions of global capitalism and steer social change. Sociological theories and concepts are needed to guide human action, but the new and highly complex conditions of globalisation require their creative reworking rather than the retention of ideas fashioned in a different age of earlier modernism.

Chapter 14

Developments in Sociological Theory

Abstract

The purpose of this chapter is to pull together some developments in sociological theory which were signalled at the end of the third chapter and built upon at the end of subsequent topic area chapters. These developments are taken a little further and others introduced.

The emergence of contemporary sociological theory is related to conditions of a rapidly changing social world. The chapter highlights the key importance of technological advance and the role of information and the media as important drivers of increasingly rapid social change. It is emphasised that such changes bring about new opportunities and problems and with them a desire for the development of new theory to assist in their understanding. However, it will become clear that this is not just a matter of society speeding up but, depending on the perspective, identifying more fundamental social changes within or beyond the stage of modernity. Key conceptualisation and theories through which sociology is attempting to understand the contemporary world include globalisation, introduced in the previous chapter, a phenomena that can be linked to variants of postmodernism and high modernism.

Important social changes and associated social thinking in the form of post-industrial society, post Fordism and neo-Marxist situationism that tended to precede postmodern and high modern perspectives are introduced. Some of the key features of postmodern theory are explained and related to the social conditions behind its emergence. The idea of social control through discourse is introduced with reference to the thinking of Foucault, and queer theory is explained as providing a new approach to sexuality and gender identity within a postfeminist and postmodern context.

It is shown that whilst postmodernism, particularly in its more radical form, offers little hope of certain knowledge and positive rational intervention in society, high modernist approaches retain faith in our potential to understand new and complex challenges that confront us and in the capacity of renewed sociological theory to assist in rising to these challenges.

In trying to explain a rapidly changing world of extensive and immediate communication, some of the theory touched on in this chapter, such as informational society, hybrid society, manufactured risk and post-social world, is itself in the process of development. The reader may therefore find it more useful in terms of the questions and insights that it raises compared to the more firmed up but more dated analysis of the founding perspectives.

Introduction – a rapidly changing world

In chapter three, it was shown that sociology emerged as a response to the major social changes which formed the transformation from traditional pre-industrial to modern industrial societies. Theories were developed to explain the characteristics of the main social types and the processes, dynamics and direction of change involved. These theories explained how traditional societies, characterised by local communities and rural life, relatively closed social hierarchies, and the prevalence of religious thinking, were giving way to urban development, more open social hierarchies, greater geographical mobility and the advance of science. The development of social theory can be viewed in terms of a response to the need for 'ontological security' – the need to structure understanding of society brought about by times of unprecedented change.

To many contemporary observers, it appears that fundamental changes at least as profound as those involved in the emergence of modern industrial society are again afoot in the world. These changes are posing new challenges to our understanding of society. Sociologists who adopt this view tend to argue that new forms of conceptualising society are needed. There is, however, much debate on the nature of this society and how it can best be conceptualised, with the most radical positions asserting that society, as a structured and coherent entity that is amenable to rational analysis, no longer exists, and that sociology has therefore run its useful course.

Recent decades have been marked by the development and mass uptake of new technologies. Pioneering developments included satellite television and workplace use of computers. With the development of the internet, a phenomenal growth of home computers with global connectivity was taking place from the latter decades of the twentieth century. Video conferencing enabled the supplementation or replacement of face-to-face meetings by 'bringing together' participants who remained spatially separated. Now, in the form of I pads and I phones, technology has miniaturised, combined functions, increased speed of operation and capacity, and become a highly portable means of communication. The possibilities of holographic technology to transport talking images of people has been demonstrated. In schools, the internet is both an everyday educational aid and the use of information technology an essential skill for the workplace. We are living in a world in which, through the medium of advanced technology, it is increasingly commonplace that communication is both becoming instant and overcoming past barriers of distance.

How is the use of new technology affecting peoples' lives? It can help to provide more efficient private and public services. However, our reliance on modern technology is particularly evident when systems struggle to cope with the job for which they were designed. This was evident in the case of problems encountered with computer systems installed for the London Ambulance Service and Air Traffic Control. High tech communication can also leave individuals and organisations vulnerable to new forms of criminality.

Modern technology also gives organisations access to information about us as consumers and citizens and the authorities are equipped with improved surveillance techniques. There is more information stored on us than ever before. On the other hand, advances in technology have also enhanced people's capacity to organise direct political action by establishing networks of rapid and flexible communication. In the case of the direct action taken by farmers and lorry drivers in Britain in response to high fuel duty prices in 2000, the use of internet and mobile phone facilities initially seemed to catch the government on the back foot. Other forms of direct political action made possible by the use of modern communications technology have included more global based protests such as those timed to coincide with G8 summit meetings and the uprisings of the Arab Spring in 2011.

The prevalence of new technology raises issues of freedom and security. It has been used by governments to monitor communications between people and to store official secrets. Important issues of state security, public interest and freedom to know have been raised when some of this information has been accessed and made publically available, as, for example, through WikiLeaks, set up in 2006. Technology can be used as a weapon of sabotage through sending computer viruses and by terrorist groups recruiting and organising through the internet. Mobile phones have been used both to detonate explosives on a public transport system and also to track terrorists.

For all of its promise, modern technology introduces new risks into our lives. Such risks include the uncertain but potentially catastrophic effects of global warming and concerns regarding the introduction of genetically modified crops. Against these challenges, a key question is the extent to which technology may both help provide solutions and by so doing introduce further problems and risks for which it is again used to attempt to manage in a potentially never ending sequence.

From this brief introduction, the broader question to be considered in this chapter is the effect that recent changes are having on both society and people's lives. Whilst sociology can help to address these questions, it should also become evident that to do so sociologists must reflect on the theories and concepts that have been inherited from the period of the inception of the subject and be prepared to develop theories and concepts better able to shed light on contemporary conditions. It is in this context that some of the key issues surrounding the development of sociological theory will be reviewed in this chapter.

Toward contemporary theory

In this section, consideration will be given to some key theoretical insights into social change that would later be taken to a new level in postmodern and high modern social theory. The first theory of major social change to be considered is Daniel Bell's anticipation of a post-industrial society. Bell, developing his ideas from the early 1960s, extrapolated changes in the American economy and society to construct an image of a future society in which profit motive driven free enterprise capitalism based on manufacturing would give way to a predominantly service and knowledge orientated white collar professional middle class society.

The culture of modern capitalism in the form of the profit motive had been shaped by the economic base; this culture comprised the core values of a business owning capitalist class. However, Bell argued that a new service and information society would require highly trained and educated managers, technicians and scientists to head flexible organisational structures and university research institutes to promote innovation. Business reliance on the skills of rational planners and the use of high technology would promote a managerial revolution in which the ownership of enterprises would be separated from their control, with a substantial transfer of decision making power from those who owned capital to those with knowledge and expertise. The latter would comprise the emergence of a new 'knowledge class'.

In the post-industrial society, universities would take over from businesses as the core institution of innovation and provide the skills necessary to run a service economy. The service economy would include the provision of health, educational, financial and leisure services. The knowledge class would be a service class whose decisions made would be based on an ethic of service to the community rather than prioritising the profit motive. Through change in the economic base and the transference of power, in post-industrial society this co-operative ethic would broaden out into a new more general social culture. Whilst private ownership of enterprises would remain, the whole basis for old ideological opposition and class conflict would cease to exist.

This optimistic tone was enhanced by the view that technological advances would allow the length of the working week to decrease, leading to a society of increasing leisure time and consumer affluence in which the Calvinist self-restraint and work ethic of early capitalism would give way to present time orientation and instant gratification through the availability of instant credit and mass consumption. In effect, post-industrial society would deliver enhanced affluence to depoliticised consumers.

Although based on a model of trends in American capitalism, Bell envisaged that the economic aspects of a post-industrial society were part of a broad process of modernisation. Thus, despite the diversity of cultures and political systems in different societies, he argued that common features of post-industrial modernisation would reduce the ideological opposition between capitalist and communist systems of the cold war period of the industrial era.

Focussing on production and organisation of the workplace, Michael Piori and Charles Sabel were early exponents of the view that a major transition had been under way in the latter decades of the twentieth century in the form of a change from Fordist to post-Fordist production.

The model for workplace efficiency during the mass production industrial era was typified by the Henry Ford production line of the early twentieth century. This approach followed closely Frederick Taylor's scientific management principles. Taylor advocated that it was the responsibility of management to train production line workers to achieve maximum efficiency through carrying out narrowly designed, low skilled and highly repetitive work tasks. This hierarchical and prescriptive approach took no account of workers' need for job satisfaction but nevertheless appeared to be an ideal work system for the mass production of standardised products and was often incentivised by a piece work reward system.

Post-Fordists argue that Fordist production methods became an inappropriate model for the workplace in the context of rapidly changing global markets and post-industrial conditions of the latter twentieth century. They are too inflexible and rely on the economies of scale through mass standardisation. By contrast, fluid conditions of rapidly changing consumer taste and demand require firms to be highly attentive to changing markets for both goods and services. They must adopt highly flexible and responsive production techniques which can accommodate short term production runs of specialist goods. Consequently, rather than repetitiously following a single work task, workers need to develop a breadth of skills, be prepared to regularly retrain and be flexible. Businesses must be highly innovative. This requires collaborative rather than hierarchical relationships between workers and management, with work teams pooling skills and ideas to solve problems. Workers therefore work more autonomously, experience higher levels of satisfaction and gain in social status.

In reality, it would appear that post-Fordist production methods are part of a broader mix of approaches rather than simply taking the place of Fordist methods. There is therefore more continuity amongst change, as witnessed by the Fordist type production line practices still thriving in fast food chain workplaces.

Some accounts of change have adopted a neo-Marxist analysis which maintained that consumer capitalism had become the dominant means of social control and de-politicisation. For Guy Debord, a key figure in the French Situationist International movement of the 1950s and 1960s, modern technology, the media and advertising created product 'spectacles', forming systematic imagery which enticed consumers into a fantasy world of artificially created needs for the latest goods which were associated with images of happiness.

Situationists argued that in modern consumer capitalism, the world is fabricated by advertisements and images which entice people to live their lives through the objects of consumption, leading to a 'degradation of being into having' in which 'human fulfilment was no longer equated with what one was, but with what one possessed' (Debord, 1992, pp.10-11). Goods are desired and acquired for their status value. Identification with stars and celebrities, who themselves help give spectacle to consumer goods, offers some compensation for the very shallowness of these consumer orientated lives.

From this theoretical position, people's awareness of the class divided nature of capitalist society, which emanates from work based relations, becomes hidden behind consumerism which addresses all equally. The image of happiness associated with luxuries and the latest goods is open to all. By such means, social control is raised to a new level. Aiming for such happiness fantasies, workers become trapped into working harder to spend. Through the 'false consciousness' of achieving happiness through consumption, workers are not just exploited in the workplace but as consumers they are also the ultimate payers of the cost of media advertising. A further tie and burden is that of the cost of consumer debt. This pervasive form of domination renders workers de-politicised. As consumers, they abandon the trade union for the shopping mall.

In contrast to the classical Marxist position, this and other schools of post war Marxism tend to recognise a greater potency of the superstructure, especially in the form of mass media advertising, to encourage workers, as consumers, to embrace capitalism. The development of the mass media has provided an encapsulating effect on consciousness beyond that envisaged by Marx. Thus, although retaining a Marxist perspective, such writers are often less certain than Marx was regarding the immanent demise of capitalism. Postmodernists have since taken on board and developed further such insights into the effect of the media on society but have largely abandoned the Marxist framework of analysis.

Postmodernity or high modernity?

There has been much dispute over the nature of contemporary society relating to the types of changes identified earlier in this chapter. A key line of distinction can be drawn between those who maintain that modern society is being replaced by conditions of 'postmodernity' (for example Lyotard and Baudrillard) and others who refer to change taking place within modernity through reference to such terms as 'high modernity' (Giddens), 'second modernity' (Beck) or 'liquid modernity' (Bauman). Some commonality exists between the two main approaches, each of which emphasise the fluidity and uncertainty of contemporary life and there is a grey area in which it is difficult to classify a theorist as squarely in the modernist or postmodernist tradition (for example neo-Marxists such as Jameson and Harvey), and some writers, such as Bauman, have changed their position over time.

However, if one were to somewhat simplify matters at this stage, there is one fundamental difference between the various contemporary modernist theories and postmodern approaches. Whilst those who refer to conditions of advanced or high modernism believe that even in a complex and fluid contemporary global world it is possible to still rationally analyse social conditions with the assistance of developments in sociological theory and beneficially intervene in society, the more radical postmodernists (such as Baudrillard) claim that truth statements about contemporary social reality are not possible, that authentic society ceases to exist, and that sociology as a rational quest for truth about society and as a guide to intervention is now redundant. The break between modern and postmodern society is thus fundamental.

Postmodernism and the periodisation of history

Before the nature of the social condition advanced by a diverse body of thinkers commonly bracketed as postmodernists is outlined, it is necessary to review how they tend to periodise history leading up to the postmodern stage. The stages identified by Jean-Francois Lyotard are traditional, modern and postmodern.

Lyotard, an early exponent of postmodernism, emphasised the importance of the cultural dimension, in particular the understanding of the world through narratives. A narrative is a story conveyed by a narrator in a situation of discourse with others which holds a claim to truth. The nature of narratives defines historical stages. In traditional societies, narratives took the form of fables, religious stories and legends etc., and the legitimacy of the narrative was judged in terms of the status of the communicator and their perceived exclusive access to the truth. Others acceptance of narrative explanations reflected and was a source of social dominance and reinforced positions within a closed social structure. This situation pertained in one form or another up to the late Middle Ages.

The transition to modern society was paved particularly by Enlightenment thinking of the late seventeenth and the eighteenth century which applied rational criticism to attack traditional thinking. Especially important were French Enlightenment thinkers who scrutinised and undermined religious dogma through the application of reason (for example Diderot and d'Alembert) and challenged the veneration of antiquity and its thinkers (for example Fontonelle). For Enlightenment thinkers, reason held the prospect of liberation from the clutches of religious dogma and superstition and could be applied to establish universal truths, organise society and promote progress. Such thinking assisted the transition to modern societies by helping to create the intellectual conditions for scientific progress behind social, political and industrial revolutions.

Postmodernists refer to the single dominant system of scientific and rational thinking that came to accompany the modern era as a 'metanarrative'. A metanarrative is an all-embracing system of thinking. The modern metanarrative, derived from the Enlightenment, asserted that the establishment of scientific truth was superior to all other knowledge, was possible, was applicable to all areas of understanding, and was beneficial. It accompanied a more open social structure in which statements could be judged according to the universal, objective and impersonal criteria of scientific truth rather than from a person's privileged position in the social structure. Scientific understanding could now be applied to all realms of the world, including society, and those with scientific and professional expertise acquired the power and status to control people's lives. This is the social context of the birth of sociology in its positivist (pretensions to science) form in the theorists of progress: Comte, Spencer, Marx and Durkheim.

For Lyotard, the dominance of the metanarrative of science in the modern era failed to achieve the promised liberation. Instead, it created a sterile world of clinical efficiency, deficient of emotional intelligence and moral guidance. Technological advances accompanied by social disasters undermined faith in the superiority of scientifically established truth and spawned the conditions for the collapse of the scientific metanarrative as the context for superior knowledge and the transition to the postmodern world. Zygmunt Bauman, during his phase of postmodern writing, pointed out that the metanarrative of rational thinking, emphasising organisational efficiency, is by itself devoid of moral guidance. Associated with the modern propensity to try and create social utopia through social engineering, it had been put to use by totalitarian communist and fascist regimes applying totalizing ideology with catastrophic consequences.

According to postmodernists, the scientific metanarrative is collapsing and leading to 'societies' (the reason for the inverted commas will be evident later) characterised by a plurality of belief systems. Only in such a 'society' where the relativity of different belief systems as different approaches to knowledge replaces the metanarrative of science can liberation through choice amongst diversity of beliefs and lifestyles be more fully realised. This is the postmodern era. It is a high tech computer and internet world where knowledge becomes a battle ground for use (what it can do) rather than truth, which is illusive. The search for marketable knowledge eclipses the search for truth.

Radical postmodernism – the end of society

Jean Baudrillard depicts the postmodern condition as one in which high tech mass media promotes a fashion dominated populist consumer culture in post industrial leisure and information societies. Everyday life is characterised by the elevation of consumption over production. Furthermore, the prevalence of the mass media in an information and entertainment society has led to an explosion of signs and symbols to the extent that the exchange of symbolic meaning has taken over from the material production of goods as the dominant form of production. In 'societies' where the creation of wealth is no longer a problem to our survival, we are surrounded by consumer products and messages in shops and massive shopping centres which bring together products from many countries. This experience comes to dominate people's consciousness. Displays offer meanings to objects such as new lifestyle images and shopping experiences, rather than focussing on their individual utility, and combine objects with the aim of directing purchasing impulses toward networks of products. Objects once purchased for utility become more acquired for the status associated with brand image. This is the cultural dimension of consumerism. The products of consumption are from diverse parts of the world and with heightened obsolescence and rapidly changing fashion become abstracted from context, are part of a fluid and rapidly changing fashion and present orientated world, and give the feeling of a 'society' without history.

The sprawling mass media promotes a bewildering diversity of images and information. This brings about what Vattimo calls 'the dissolution of centralized perspectives'. A pluralistic world view undermines any notion of a single reality and a single truth and promotes the recognition of the contingency of all systems of thinking. In the postmodern world, in contrast to modern society, people reach emancipation not through scientific truth but from its singular dominance.

For Baudrillard, we are entering a postmodern stage in which a high tech mass media conveys self-referencing signs and images (simulacra) in which messages become interconnected and understood with reference to each other. Signs and images which once reflected an underlying reality to which they were connected have now exploded to such an extent that they have detached themselves from their material reference points and created a reality of their own. They no longer portray reality, but become a different type of reality – a virtual reality. They masquerade as reality and encapsulate people in a world where reality and truth are illusive. In this world, the 'real' is obscured by electronic images of simulated events and cannot be distinguished from the latter. This media generated world becomes the realm of experience to which Baudrillard applies the term 'hyperreal' which replaces the reference points of a 'real' world by media produced self-referencing signs. The 'hyperreal' kills the 'real' which it artificially resurrects through these self-referencing signs, rather like creating a theme park reality to replace authentic reality. Having no other reference point, the 'hyperreal' (illusion) fills the void as the 'real' world is lost to systems of signs and images. When we watch events on the television, they inter-reference with other events on the television and in the newspapers, and so on. In this way, emphasises Baudrillard, the Gulf War was experienced, by those not involved, at a clinical distance, rather like a simulated exercise, as a surgical operation of high tech precision bombing! But what really happened?

Baudrillard argues that the phase of modern capitalism described in the economic determinism of Marxist theory, in which power derives from economic production, has been largely transcended. In the postmodern era, power resides in 'hyperreality' – one-way media generated communication to politically passive and privatised consumers. In such a 'society', cultural production is everything and truth and reality are impossible to substantiate. This spells an end to sociology as an attempt to establish scientific truth about society and as a guide to tackling social issues. Since reality cannot be grasped, we are now beyond the point at which it can be constructively changed. People become abandoned to their worlds of personal troubles, unable to meaningfully relate them to broader social structures as authentic society ceases to exist.

In summary, according to this position, images become free floating in a world of make believe, leaving people helpless in ascertaining whether they bear any relationship with an underlying reality in a world where the cultural realm becomes dominant and all embracing.

Alternatively, it could be argued that the culture of media images has become a froth through which it is difficult to see an underlying reality rather than becoming a new reality itself.

Or capitalism in crisis?

Whilst many sociologists believe that profound changes are taking place in society and the world, many do not agree with postmodernist accounts, especially those as radical as Baudrillard's. Neo-Marxists attempt to explain some of the cultural features identified by postmodernists but within a Marxist framework. For example, Frederic Jameson recognises the emergence of simulacra, cultural superficiality and fragmentation, loss of historicity and the intensification of innovation. However, these cultural features are viewed as the products of 'late capitalism'. Therefore, despite these cultural changes, there is an underlying continuity between the modern and the postmodern as the essential economic structure of capitalism remains predominant across this period.

For Jameson, the development of new technology has helped to reinvigorate a waning capitalism by extending consumerism and the range of commodities from the production of goods to the entire culture through the reproductive technology of computers and television. The disorientating effect of postmodern culture is therefore not an out of control phenomena in its own right but a consequence of adjustments within capitalism. In contrast to the resignation of postmodernists, it is argued that this effect can be overcome if social theorists develop a neo-Marxist analysis which can provide people with 'cognitive maps' by which they can regain an understanding of the world, develop class consciousness and reacquire their capacity for political action.

David Harvey also adopts a neo-Marxist interpretation of postmodernity and relates social and cultural changes to the economic base of capitalism in crisis. According to this analysis, during the post second world war decades, capitalism had delivered growth through the application of production line systems. Workers had experienced rising living standards based on systems of mass production of standardised goods. These modern techniques of production, referred to as 'Fordism', operated within the confines of economies regulated by Keynesian economic intervention, comprising a Fordist – Keynesian period of capitalism referred to as 'organised capital accumulation'.

However, for Harvey, the oil crisis of 1973 brought a period of crisis to capitalism. The hiking of oil prices by the oil producer nations had a major impact on the economies of modern capitalist societies. Businesses had to be more inventive and dynamic in their quest for profit if they were to compete and survive. The model of organised capital accumulation was too inflexible to respond to these needs. New post-Fordist work organisation and production techniques were devised in which businesses became lean, flexible, high tech and responsive to specialised markets. Work practices were changed. For many, security of employment diminished, and, assisted by right wing governments in Britain and the USA during the 1980s, the power of trade unions was curtailed. Subcontracting and privatisation were further features of the post-Fordist approach to production within deregulated economies, ushering in a period of 'flexible capital accumulation'.

According to Harvey, the intensification of time and space through technological advances and tendencies toward globalisation were the result of an intensification of the work process as capitalist enterprises were driven by the quest for improved efficiency and profit in crisis conditions. Changing fashions were driven by free enterprise to buoy up consumer demand and achieve profitability by businesses showing superior versatility and innovation to that of their competitors. For Harvey, this economic imperative of the quest for profitability under new conditions of capitalist competition was the real dynamic behind the pace of life and cultural changes in terms of growing diversity of social fashions and interests which had been highlighted by postmodernists.

Adopting a neo-Marxist position, Harvey believed that the Enlightenment project of understanding and improving society by means of intelligent intervention remained possible. Indeed, his theory is a theory of the social conditions of emergence of postmodern theory explained from a neo-Marxist perspective which prioritised the effect of economic forces to explain cultural change rather than a postmodern theory per se.

The discourse of science and normative control

The work of Michel Foucault is not strictly postmodernist and certainly not high modernist. He is usually viewed as a post-structuralist who is critical of macro and structural theories such as functionalism and Marxism, regarding them as totalising theories that filter reality in conformity to their perspectives. He also opposes theoretical approaches which see history as unfolding in a logical direction which is viewed in terms of progress. This would include the progressiveness and humanitarianism built into Enlightenment thinking and the above mentioned sociological theories which followed in its tradition. This, and the centrality of discourse to his analysis, makes Foucault's position very close to that of the postmodernists. His work, though, is recognised as having evolved from more structuralist beginnings.

Central to Foucault's approach was the idea that knowledge and power are closely interrelated and that control operates in the context of discourses. A discourse is a way of thinking, writing and talking regarding a set of assumptions which are taken as the truth and forms a milieu of communication. In fact, discourses are the means by which power operates. Foucault was particularly interested in the way that discourses in the wake of the Enlightenment were implicated in new methods of social control rather than their professed humanitarianism and liberation.

These latter features may appear to be true on the surface as witnessed by changes in the treatment of criminals who in the Middle Ages suffered bodily torture and public humiliation compared to that of confinement and rehabilitation in modern societies. This self-evident view of improvement is because the discourses of the Enlightenment have their own inbuilt view of progress which appears to be natural to the participants of that era of discourse. But people are in fact prisoners of the discourse who are not conscious of their mental confinement. It thus takes a careful examination of history in terms of different discourses to help reveal what may otherwise remain invisible within the discourse of the current age.

For Foucault, predominant discourses change over time, but there is no single or purposeful direction to this change or means of establishing the superiority of one discourse compared to another. Foucault studied the discourses of different eras to show that in fact the heritage of the Enlightenment is an extension of control through the application of 'supposed' science to classify and distinguish the pathological from the normal and to extend interventions by professionals in the name of scientific based treatment to in fact suppress the pathological and regulate social normalcy. In other words, what passes as science is a new finely graded and more invasive form of control which is essentially morally based. Against this background, Foucault studied changes in discourse and its consequences regarding the mad, criminals and sexual deviance.

The emergence of the discourses of the human and social sciences are themselves a product of the Enlightenment. These sciences provided a justification for classifying and controlling populations in the guise of treatment and help. New interventions and knowledge, in the name of science, are in the hands of professionals – doctors, educators, psychiatrists, prison officials etc. In fact, science is essentially moral in that through it professionals impose normalising judgements on the behaviour of others, differentiating the normal from the pathological and providing 'helpful' interventions such as treatment and rehabilitation which enables professionals to impose moral and social control on others.

This can be illustrated in society's view of the mad. In the Middle Ages, the mad were cast from society, left free to roam, but were regarded as relatively harmless. The advance of rational thinking was bound up with the eighteenth century Enlightenment. Viewing phenomena from an increasingly rational point of view accentuated the distinction between the mad and the rational thinking and emphasised the extent to which the former was a threat to the latter. The mad, along with the destitute, left free could become a social order problem in a rationally organised society and so these groups tended to become commonly incarcerated and later separated. The advance of the sciences included the human and social sciences of psychology and psychiatry. The incarcerated mad were now viewed in confinement as 'mentally ill' and 'mental patients' requiring treatment by professionals versed in what Foucault regarded as an 'assumed' science. He questioned the extent to which psychiatry is a science and suggested that its interventions are morally based since the purpose of confinement and treatment was in fact a matter of social control with the aim of 'normalisation' of the 'pathological'.

A change in discourse also had implications for the treatment of criminals. Foucault's historical study of changes in the punishment of prisoners was intended to shed new light on the use of discipline but also on the technology of surveillance and control that has come to pervade society. Foucault showed that up to the middle of the eighteenth century, punishment of prisoners sometimes involved torture and public humiliation. The treatment of criminals up to this period of time was viewed from the Enlightenment perspective as barbaric and became replaced by rationally judged periods of confinement and the application of prison rules. The common view from within Enlightenment discourse is that this signified progress to a more humanitarian regime in which punishment was rationalised and routinized. But for Foucault, the aim was in fact to punish more invasively and effectively and to control criminals.

Here, the disciplinary power of surveillance is very important. The very potential for constant surveillance whilst in confinement enables control to run very deep. As the individual prisoner can never be sure of whether or not they are being observed, the very possibility of surveillance generates self-discipline. Foucault went on to argue that surveillance becomes a strategy for imposing self-control in a range of institutions including schools, psychiatric hospitals, and workplaces and is part of what could be more broadly called 'carceral society' in which activities are brought into regulation and surveillance by functionaries and professionals for purposes of social control. This extension of external control and its intrusion into self-control runs counter to the Enlightenment view of the progress of individual freedom. Enlightenment thinking therefore provides the self-contained delusion of freedom which is difficult to recognise when looking from within its own discourse.

Participants within institutions are judged by professional educators, psychiatrists, officers etc. as objects of knowledge. The discourse of the human sciences and the emergence of professionals has enabled power to be exerted by professional experts over others. It provided institutional discipline in the form of record keeping and surveillance. Rather than emphasising that the source of power, discipline and surveillance is uniquely focussed in the centralised state or a ruling class, Foucault emphasised that it is decentered into these numerous institutions with their own history and uncertain future trajectory of change.

Foucault also argued that the imposition of power can never be total but will always generate its own opposition and evasions. Discourse on sexuality provides a good example of this. With the development of twentieth century psychiatry, homosexuality became designated as pathological sexuality which treatment aimed to cure. For Foucault, the apparent science of psychiatry that was applied in treatments to bring about a moral 'normalisation' of behaviour was not dissimilar to moralising control through religious confession. Nevertheless, counter action by this persecuted minority has led to effective political opposition to the above viewpoint and the acquisition of new rights.

Queer theory

The issue of gender roles gained increasing prominence in both society and sociology from the late 1960s with the emergence of the women's movement and feminist thinking. Feminists attacked the use of patriarchal power over women throughout society and argued for equality of opportunity between the sexes. At a theoretical level, feminist academics were highly critical of the Parsonian model which emphasised the impact of early socialisation into gendered roles whereby women were expected to use their affective skills in the upbringing of children and men their instrumental skills in supporting the family unit.

From a postmodernist and postfeminist vantage point, despite its radical criticism at the time, feminism, like functionalism, was also a product of the modern era and its use of universal categories. Thus, although feminists recognised the role of socialisation in the formation of gender identity, they still saw gender in terms of a 'binary division' between female and male identities with females systematically subjected to patriarchal power. This universal binary division approach was reproduced by symbolic interactionists who studied homosexuality as a form of deviance from sexual norms.

Postfeminists such as Judith Butler have come to argue that gender identity can no longer be viewed in such binary male and female terms and regarded as the primary feature of a fixed self. Gender and sexuality are social constructions and as such are subject to change. Instead, within the context of cultural growing diversity, gender identity is an increasingly diverse and fluid individual accomplishment that is open to reflexive change. Furthermore, sexual identity is influenced by culture and discourse which in contemporary times is fragmented, multiple and shifting. This approach, which questions any essential normality to gender and sexuality, has been referred to as 'queer theory'.

In the context of postmodern studies, queer theory is not used as a derogatory term nor is it a form of gay or lesbian studies. Although, like gay and lesbian studies, it puts sexuality at the centre of analysis, it is critical of such studies for putting gays and lesbians at the centre of enquiry that emphasises a heterosexual / homosexual divide, oversimplifies sexuality as a fixed characteristic and legitimises heterosexuality as a norm. From the queer theory viewpoint, defining people in terms of a single collective binary sexual identity is inappropriate as this 1) silences a range of other characteristics of identity, all of which are 2) highly complex and fluid. Sexuality is not seen as a naturally embedded core of identity but something which is socially constructed and policed. Queer theorists bring this to light and emphasise that in the postmodern condition of diversity and tolerance of difference there is great subtlety and indeterminacy to sexual identity which cannot be reduced to a binary scale and can change in the individual over time. Hetero normality is simply a social construct, and an oppressive one at that under postmodern conditions should be challenged. Critics, however, are likely to question the free floating nature of gender and sexuality that queer theory argues.

High modernist theories

The term 'high modernity' is used here as a general umbrella for a group of like terms also including 'liquid modernity' 'late modernity' and 'second modernity' that have been identified in previous sections. To this we can also add Habermas' modernist view of the stage of 'late capitalism'.

1. Extending life world rationality

The social theory of late capitalism developed by Jurgen Habermas draws from a variety of theoretical sources. His work was shaped within the influence of first generation Frankfurt School of neo-Marxists such as Horkheimer and Adorno. Like them, he was critical of a strong deterministic tendency in Marx's writings regarding the course of history and predictive certainty of the future overthrow of capitalism and its succession by communism. However, he was less pessimistic than his Frankfurt School predecessors of the capacity of the masses to resist the impact of consumerist ideology and domination through instrumental rationalism. Likewise, although he built into his theory Weber's ideas regarding rationalisation and bureaucratisation, he was less pessimistic than Weber regarding the dehumanising effect of an all confining instrumental rationalism. Into these macro dimensions which focus on the social system, Habermas integrated phenomenological insights regarding processes of life world communication. Combined in Habermas' approach, these perspectives provide a powerful defence of modernism and the capacity for rational thought to be utilised to serve the public good. Habermas was therefore highly critical of postmodern thinking which tends to adopt a nihilistic attitude toward the prospects of social improvement through the application of rational thinking.

What are the purposes or ends to which rational action is directed and to what extent are these ends open to political debate? These questions are of central importance in Habermas' theory. In incorporating the above perspectives into his analysis, Habermas has analysed society in terms of 'social integration' and 'systems integration'. Social integration refers to the processes of the everyday life world in which consensus is built on discourse between actors who are able to engage in free and rational communication. System integration refers to the way that action is structured through the dominance of social institutions and the external imposition of rules, constraints and regulations. For Habermas, the 'public sphere' is a contested realm of free communication and debate and systematic institutional impositions, the latter being controlling and repressive, the former potentially liberating.

At both levels, the Enlightenment inheritance of rationality is evident, but tension is generated over the different types of rationality. In the sphere of system integration, action is directed by instrumental rationality. This type of rationality is evident in systems which operate through the efficient direction of practical action toward given ends which are unreflectively accepted. The motivating force of this imposition may be enterprises driven by the profit motive or the efficiency of government bureaucratic structures. The external imposition of systems which aim at achieving material wealth are key to realising standards of living. However, the way in which they operate is through the use of power and the imposition of sanctions.

By contrast, the rationality of social integration refers to everyday communication which takes place through shared meaning in an environment that is ideally open and free discourse. This discourse takes the form of the application of reasoned discussion in which individuals attempt to convince others, resulting in negotiated consensus. Issues therefore are to do with individual interests, social ends and quality of life. This form of rationality is referred to as substantive rationality in which rational communication is formative of public opinion. For Habermas, late capitalism has come to increasingly generate conflict between the levels of system integration and social integration rationality. To help understand this requires a historical detour back to the Enlightenment.

The eighteenth century Enlightenment was a period of the opening up of free discussion of contemporary issues and the development of critical rational thinking in the public sphere and beyond the control of the state. Free rational discourse undermined tradition and promoted revolutionary change in the form of emancipation of people from the servitude of feudal thinking and institutions and enhanced the democratic political institutions of modern western societies. The essential point for Habermas, though, and the one general point of agreement with the postmodernists, is that as modern societies progressed, the freedoms of substantive rationality were closed down. This was because the rationality of free and open public discourse became invaded by the instrumental rationality of the modern system, leading to the increasing bureaucratisation of public life, control by experts, the power of private enterprises, the dominance of mass media corporations in framing discussion and a mass consumerist culture, all for the benefit of efficient production and profitability.

In contrast to postmodernists, who are resigned to the inevitability of bland consumerism, Habermas argues that such conditions are a pathology of late capitalist modernisation, not an essential condition of a postmodern society. The excessive intrusion into the life world by the instrumental rationality of the system (referred to as colonisation), through, for example, sophisticated mass media techniques, has closed down the area of public debate. In doing so, it distorts life world communication to its own needs, where issues of standard of living prevail over quality of life and people tend to become controlled and passive consumers. The outcome is a shallow pseudo public sphere. And, under communist regimes, it was administrative structures and the state imposed ideology of 'sham comradeship' that invaded the public sphere to distort free communication and control criticism.

The key to regaining the emancipatory potential of the Enlightenment is for the emergence of resistance in the public sphere to system colonisation by pushing back the intrusions of instrumental rationality. The public sphere needs to develop the space to re-established open discussion and free discourse regarding society's ultimate values, undistorted by system imperatives. Only by so doing can rational public discussion freely debate issues of public good and develop a constraining criticism of the instrumental rationality of the system.

For Habermas, in these conditions of late capitalist modernisation, it is communication conflict between the two rationalities which has replaced class conflict of the capitalism of Marx's time. However, he is not as pessimistic as Weber that society will be engulfed by instrumental rationality. One reason for this is that the development of the welfare state has opened up areas of debate and interest group action regarding its operation and the constraints that it is under. Another is that however much it has been closed down, debate is necessary for the legitimacy of democracy and so there will always be an opening for more free discussion. Moreover, given the advance of technologically mediated communication, the possibilities for debate and organised resistance to system colonisation of the life world may have been enhanced, and new social movements raising issues of the quality of life have an important role to play here.

Habermas is relatively optimistic that late modern society can regain the more fully liberating potential of the Enlightenment. This requires a new balance of the life world and system spheres so that the fruits of prosperity resulting from the application of instrumental rationalism of the system can be enjoyed within societies in which open rational discussion generates effective public opinion regarding ultimate values of public good. In a truly free and democratic society, truth is not something that can be arrived at by experts within institutional settings and imposed on the rest of society. It emerges organically from dialogue between people in the life world. For Habermas, a situation whereby communication and argument free from the distorting and constraining effect of domination through the overpowering effect of the social system or the social status of the contributors is the ideal type through which truth and freedom converge. Whilst this ideal type may never be fully realised, it should act as a compass bearing for shaping institutional reform.

The main exception to this optimism is the United States where Habermas believes that the colonisation of the public sphere by instrumental rationalism and culture of consumerism are so complete that the liberating potential of true free public discussion is unlikely to emerge.

2. Liquid modernity and disembedding

Zygmunt Bauman's early works adopted a neo-Marxist orientation. However, the growing individualism and diversity that he observed to be taking place in advanced capitalism enhanced his dissatisfaction with the economic determinism and social categories built into Marxism. In the 1980s, Bauman come to recognise the merits of postmodernist approaches. In Gane's 'The Future of Social Theory' (2004), Bauman explains that his past postmodern stance was itself only a stopgap position. For Bauman, postmodernism had performed an important task of showing that the world was unlike the grid mapped by modernist grand theory such as Marxism and it alerted us to new uncertainties. However, Bauman announced that he was now abandoning postmodernism. He signified his change of position thus:

> 'The 'postmodern' has done its preliminary, site-clearing job: it aroused vigilance and sent the exploration in the right direction. It could not do much more, and so after that it outlived its usefulness; or, rather, it worked itself out of a job…..And we can now say more about the present-day world than it is unlike the old familiar one. We have, so to speak, matured to afford (to risk?) a positive theory of its novelty' (Gane, 2004, pp.17-18).

For Bauman, postmodernism was, on the one hand, too negative regarding the prospects of developing a coherent understanding of the contemporary world, and on the other, overly optimistic regarding the individual freedoms and pleasures enjoyed in contemporary consumer society.

Bauman now proposed a theory of 'liquid modernity' to explain the contemporary social condition. In using the term 'liquid', Bauman was referring to a situation of continuous fluidity in social relations, in signs and in information. How does he apply this concept of liquidity? For Bauman, the transition from traditional pre-industrial to modern industrial societies involved the rapid and far reaching change from one solid social structure, through temporary liquefaction, to another solid structure. The temporary period of liquefaction of social structures disembedded people (lifted them out) from the social constraints of a traditional society which had provided a fixed position in a hierarchy of feudal estates.

Once emerged, modern industrial society, referred to by Bauman as a phase of 'solid modernity', re-embedded people (placed them back) into a class stratified system in which position was not so ascribed but where acquiring social mobility depended on people learning rules of admission to another class. However, contemporary societies had, by the late twentieth century, entered a state of continuous fluidity with no prospect of this ending. In the society of liquid modernity, the structures and constraints of the phase of solid modernity have broken down and life is becoming individualised. People have experienced disembedding from the confines of the old class structure, but they have been cut adrift into a void of ever changing rules with no solid social structure for re-embedding. This new freedom is one of abandonment and uncertainty, which generates in the individual anxiety in the relentless quest for security and the self-construction of identity.

The structured past modern world of solid modernity was the world of Fordist production methods, top down organisational hierarchies, controlled workers, surveillance and imposed identity, established career paths and lasting marriages. It was a rational survival strategy, argues Bauman, to learn the rules and structure of society and adjust one's behaviour accordingly in the expectation that this would serve one's interests in the long term over which one could expect to continue in a line of work or plan a career. In the context of liquid modernity, attempting to apply this strategy would be detrimental. Survival in the contemporary situation requires an unending process of trials and errors, learning, unlearning and relearning, and the abandonment of the idea of a single occupation or life project.

During the phase of solid modernity, both workers and employers experienced relative immobility. Workers held a degree of power in this antagonistic relationship through their ability to disrupt the production process. However, under conditions of liquid modernity, capital had migrated to cyberspace. In doing so, it had achieved far greater freedom of mobility than workers who remained relatively tied to their locality, and with it the threat and power of possible disengagement of capital. Workers have thus become relatively disempowered, with old forms of stratification conflict eclipsed by 'space wars' in which the most globally mobile are the winners. Bauman thus argued that mobility or lack of it becomes the new basis for social polarisation. Contemporary societies are also arenas of 'identity wars' involving struggles to impose one's own and others' identity through whatever resources are available.

Referring, as Mills had, to the relationship between personal troubles and the broader social structure, for Bauman, in structured traditional societies, and to some extent in solid modern societies, the causes of private troubles were often obvious to the individual as they were experienced directly. For example, the cause of individual hunger was obvious enough – a lack of food – even though solution of the problem for them may not have been quite so straightforward. In contemporary liquid modernity, new socially generated risks, in particular globalisation leading to the dismantling of social bonds, safety networks, and collective projects and the effects of pollution, are not so directly seen or easily understood by the individual. The effects of individualisation are those of growing individual uncertainty and anxiety, whilst at the same time an understanding of the processes bringing this about is less easy to recognise through individual experiences. Individualisation in contemporary society increases the rift between private experiences of anxiety and the capacity to understand the broader and often increasingly distant social causes of it, promoting the tendency in individuals to retreat into a world of private concerns.

For Bauman, unlike postmodernists, rational sociological analysis and intervention can help remedy the situation. The current time is one of urgent need for a reinvigorated sociological imagination. Society has fundamentally changed, but sociology has been weighed down by the baggage of an earlier era. Detailed sociological understanding of the contemporary condition of liquid modernity is needed to help re-establish the connection between private experiences and their social causes and to guide remedial political action. This requires the creative development of new sociological theories and concepts applicable to the contemporary condition of liquid modernity, not the use of what Beck refers to as 'zombie terms' such as social class and the family which are more applicable to the conditions of past solid modernity.

3. Informational society

Manuel Castells has analysed the effect of the rise of new information technology, especially in the form of the internet, on contemporary life. He argues that the globalising impact of such technology is having a profound effect on both capitalism and individual identity. For Castells, capitalism remains the social driving force, but the form that it is taking is changing. A key factor in this change is the ever sprawling internet which gives rise to networked communication. Compared to old hierarchies of command, these high tech networks are flexible, adaptable and instantaneous in their global reach. In the face of such changes, old command economies have had to adapt, as in the case of China, or fall, as did the Soviet Union.

According to Castells, such technology is bringing about a new form of global capitalism, 'informational capitalism', in which the search for wealth shifts from an emphasis on industrial production to the maximisation of investment opportunities via instant access and response to the condition of global markets. Money has therefore to some extent become separated from production in a more impersonal world.

In the informational society, Castells sees social conflict becoming displaced from the class conflict of an earlier era. Under industrial capitalism, organised labour could sometimes check the power of capital as both were locked together and relatively immobile. Adopting a similar view to Bauman, for Castells, under informational capitalism, capital is global and mobile whereas labour remains more locally rooted. Labour has therefore become relatively powerless and conflict has been displaced from that between the classes of earlier capitalism to that of protest groups, themselves organised through the use of modern technology which generates a new type of capacity for opposition.

High tech informational capitalism is having a major effect on the capacity of the state to any longer act as a self-contained entity as viewed by the pioneering sociologists. For example, the capacity of states to protect their welfare programs tends to be undermined by the ease that informational capitalism provides for capital movement to gravitate toward the states with the lowest welfare costs. In the competition for inward investment, states have to adapt accordingly – there is overall downward pressure on welfare expenditure.

For Castells, the positive effects of informational capitalism include the creation of enhanced opportunities for individual enterprise and greater individual input into identity creation. However, a major concern is the capacity of the informational world to become an out of control automaton. In response, Castells adopts a modernist approach that through the application of human reason and will, the information revolution can be harnessed for human good, but time may be running out for our opportunity to shape its effects.

4. Hybrid societies and reconfigured relationships

The form taken by sociology in its formative period reflected the then close association between societies and nation states – sociology was the study of bounded societies. Founding sociological theory linked the social, society and human, and, even in positivist theory, established clear distinctions between the physical science of objects and the social science of societies. For John Urry, the impact of developments in technology has led to the emergence of new patterns of social life and communication, reconfigured humans and the need for a reconfigured sociology.

The advance of technological modernisation and globalisation have weakened the society / nation tie as new networks without centres, in particular based on the internet, have emerged to enhance communication across national borders. As well as a growing separation of the social from nation states, social 'relations' themselves are increasingly made up of a mix of human agency and material objects and technologies. Urry suggests that in this sense we cannot now talk about uniquely human societies but of 'hybrid societies' – networks of connection involving humans and technological objects which change the human experience in ways that we need to understand. Consequently, a change is needed in sociological focus to recognise 'reconfigured' humans – a reconfigured sociology is required to account for the impact of technology and objects on 'relationships' which makes them less authentically social.

The effect of technological developments on the senses can be illustrated through the simple example of the development of the automobile. The speed and insulation involved in travelling through a city by car provides a very different experience of the environment than one would have when walking, whilst the presence of traffic in the city will also affect the experience of walkers.

What form may a reconfigured sociology take? Urry speculates that what is needed is a move from the study of bounded society to the study of high tech globally networked communications as open and dynamic systems which cut across societies and can be analysed as structures and flows. Movement thus replaces location in the study of the social. Theories and methods need to be developed that enable the analysis of connections between human powers and material objects and that track the effect of communication flows through networks. As new technologies such as have enabled fast and distant travel and developed the internet and advanced mobile phone technology have accelerated the experience of time, analysis needs to take account of instantaneous time rather than the traditional exclusive preoccupation with clock time.

As globalisation enhances cosmopolitanism, it is likely that emerging global standards will effect how people think and behave. This will enhance reflective modernisation and sociology will need to reconfigure itself in a global and cosmopolitan way, making society a decreasing focal point of study.

5. Society of manufactured risk

This section will be focussing on theories put forward by Anthony Giddens and Ulrich Beck. Both of these writers tend to adopt a transformationist position on globalisation – they argue that globalisation is bringing about profound changes and new problems and risks, but remain optimistic that these changes can be rationally understood and that positive intervention to improve society is possible. This transformationist stance therefore links closely to their characterisation of contemporary society as 'high modern' or 'second modern' rather than postmodern.

Giddens, in 'Runaway World' (2002), periodises history into traditional, modern and high modern phases. Traditional societies were agricultural based. Life for most people was linked to working the land and lived out within small local communities. The tempo of life was dominated by the repetitions and constraints of the seasons and ritual played an important part in people's lives. Nature related work tasks at a local level moulded the measurement and perception of distance and time to season and locality.

The dawn of the modern era came in the seventeenth and eighteenth centuries with the Enlightenment. Science and rational thinking were applied to question the superstitions and social constraints of traditional societies. Faith in social progress was invested in the capacity of science to fashion a rationally based social order. Scientific advances included the development of mechanical devices that enabled time to be precisely divided up and universalised. With industrialisation, this standardised time became attached to new routines as work became extracted from the tempo of nature and the countryside and increasingly governed by man made tempo of the factory and the office. The effect of these changes was the experience of the compression of distance and time.

A process linked to the compression of distance and time was the disembedding of social relations. In traditional societies, social relations operated largely at a personal, face-to-face level within the context of small local communities. The development of impersonal institutions accompanied modernisation. These institutions mediated social relationships involving, for example, the exchange of news and money. News could be widely disseminated through printed materials and financial transactions mediated through the institution of banks. These changes allowed such exchanges to become extracted from direct involvement in social encounters between parties.

Giddens argues that the freeing of social relationships from the constraints of traditional society led to life becoming more 'reflexive'. Social relations in traditional societies held certainties in the sense that life was parochial and opportunities were limited. These certainties were upset by the processes of modernisation which brought change and opened up opportunity. Uncertainty encourages reflexivity – the need of people to continuously monitor and interpret their own behaviour and that of others as they make assessments of risks and possibilities that their environment offers. However, if tradition is viewed in terms of behavioural rituals and repetitions which give life form, modern society was also characterised by its own traditions. The need for reflexivity was thus limited.

For Giddens, what has transpired more recently is that change, uncertainty and risk have now reached a new level. The 1970s witnessed an advance in the interconnectedness of the world as advances in technology extended the range and speed of communications and travel. This further compression of distance and time was associated with globalisation and was the hallmark of a new stage in society which Giddens refers to as high modern. Now, accompanying globalisation, change, uncertainty and risk take on new dimensions. In an increasingly interconnected world, unexpected happenings in one part, such as currency fluctuations, can impact globally and heighten instability. For individuals, uncertainty and constant reflexivity are part of high modern globalised life which accompany an extension of individual autonomy.

Globalisation brings with it new risks. Giddens explains the changing nature of risk. Traditional societies were vulnerable to risks of nature such as drought, flood and storm. These dangers Giddens refers to as natural or 'external' risks. The drive and industriousness behind capitalist modernisation saw a leap in the imposition of human action onto nature, creating new problems such as pollution and contagious diseases associated with crowded and unhygienic living conditions in towns and cities. However, because life in modern society was still structured and constrained by its own traditions and routines, our knowledge of risks could be calculated and some degree of security could be made possible through insurance.

In the high modern global context, our enhanced level of intervention into nature has brought about new dangers in the form of 'manufactured' risk. Global warming and its likely consequences is one such manufactured risk and others include the unknown effects of genetic modification of crops and the possibility of economic meltdown. These risks are different from external risks in that there is no experience by which outcomes can be calculated and therefore against which insurance can be provided. We have created through our interventions in nature a fluid and uncertain environment which is at the 'end of nature' and traditions, and risks getting out of our control. Given the level of individual autonomy, risk and need for constant reflexivity in contemporary society, there is attraction for some in turning to compulsive behaviour or fundamentalist beliefs (phenomena have both been on the increase) as attempts to close down the uncertainties and anxiety of individual autonomy through retreat to forms of ritual and tradition.

It is to the challenge of this environment of man-made risks that new and enlightened responses and new policies and forms of governmental organisation are required. Reflexivity is necessary at a governmental and global level given the global nature of the risks faced. Difficult as it is, Giddens argues that appropriate new institutions and interventions can still be rationally guided by a sociology that is up to the mark. This development is an urgent social imperative.

Ulrich Beck's analysis of the contemporary social and sociological condition is a remarkably similar one to that of Giddens. Beck places the changing nature of risk at the centre of his analysis and divides modernity into two phases - first modernity and second modernity. Prior to first industrial modernity, the main risks to people, such as famine and disease, were a consequence of nature and largely beyond the control of man. Beck defined the first phase of modernity as pre-globalised industrialisation.

At this stage of development, scientific advances such as the introduction of new farming techniques and medical treatments assisted in the control of natural risk. However, the creation of wealth through technological intervention in nature created new by-product risks such as pollution. Within this first phase of modernisation, risk, like society itself, remained relatively localised and calculable. The scope for uncertain consequences of human intervention was limited.

At the theoretical level, society of the first modernity was adequately explained in the Parsonian functionalist model in which separate societies as nation states operated as systems which adjusted toward equilibrium and institutions such as the family and the church imposed a degree of certainty into people's lives.

A key feature of the second phase of modernity, from the latter decades of the twentieth century, is that uncertainty cannot so readily be reduced to calculated and controlled risk. This is because societies have reached the stage where scientific and technological advance and intervention has led to the creation of new manufactured uncertainties. An example here may be the health threats posed by the emergence of superbugs as a result of the use of antibiotics to combat diseases. And even technological developments attempting to solve manufactured risks introduce their own uncertainties or unanticipated undesirable consequences. As technological intervention in the context of globalisation has enabled an ever-increasing dominance of nature, the new risks created, such as radiation and global warming, take on a more challenging global dimension. The one certainty that we now have is that there will be as yet unknown future consequences and risks of our current interventions, including interventions that attempt to control risks.

Whilst the institutions of the family, social class, local community and religion constrained the lives of individuals during first stage modernity, they provided structure, a framework of identity and stability to people's lives. In second stage modernity, individual freedom has advanced as globalisation and cosmopolitanism have eroded these institutions and structures. This liberation from past constraints leaves individuals vulnerable to new insecurities. For all of the benefits that contemporary society brings, risk also becomes a growing feature of this liberation. Overall, it becomes so much a feature of life that we can characterise second phase modernity as 'risk society'. Risk society is so open that individuals are increasingly conscious that they often don't readily know or control the consequences of their actions. This can affect the very possibility of predicting or controlling their own life trajectories in a world of high levels of marital breakdown and highly flexible labour markets. Actors have to navigate their lives in new social conditions in which risks and uncertainties are transferred to the individual who has no socially handed down playscript for guidance. Life becomes an ongoing act of 'reflexivity' in which individuals are continuously weighing up circumstances and available options and adapting response strategies to attempt to promote a degree of security. This may include weighing up how one's behaviour can be changed to reduce global warming, considering whether it is safe at a particular time to travel by plane or considering precautions to avoid contracting sexually transmitted disease.

In response to risk, a new type of globally and environmentally aware politics has emerged. But in attempting to manage risk, do we trust the judgements of experts? Their calculations of risk are based on laboratory knowledge which first-hand experience may challenge. Whose interests do experts serve and can we trust what experts and politicians tell us? Risk society has thus seen the emergence of direct action protest movements aiming to influence or challenge decision making with regard to the risks accompanying technological intervention, as, for example, in the recent case of protests against the practice of fracking – the fracturing of rock formations to extract oil and gas.

For Beck, the world has moved on since that adequately explained by Parsonian functionalism with regard to the post war decades. Just as people's national experiences and perspectives have been eclipsed by global and cosmopolitan forces and perspectives, so sociology must move on from the 'methodological nationalism' of its founding fathers to 'methodological cosmopolitanism'. It can only do so through engaging in painstaking research across the world and developing theories able to conceptualise contemporary conditions. It must move beyond what have now become the 'zombie categories', such as the family, social class, career and the nation, that it has inherited from the first modernity period. By so doing, sociology may be able to provide analytical assistance to guide reflexivity in response to risk at both individual and governmental level.

6. A post-social world?

Technology is increasingly becoming the medium of communication, often squeezing out the need for direct face to face social contact. For example, computer technology and electronic communication has enabled work to be conducted in increasingly 'virtual organisations' in which telephone and e mail are the main means of contact and through the visual medium of video conferencing and Skype.

One's finances can now be conducted via internet banking and the use of cash machines. Furthermore, many high street banks have been closing and if one were to phone a bank or one of many other large organisations, it is often necessary to have to navigate through a system of automated responses, frequently encouraging internet contact, before possibly speaking to a person. Even transferring small amounts of money from person to person can now take place via mobile phone rather than the need for personal contact.

There has been a massive increase in online shopping where goods can be selected, ordered and delivered with personal communication reduced to the signing of a docket on delivery. If one shops at a supermarket or visits a petrol station, the only required contact is with a checkout assistant and even this can be avoided through the use of self-service checkouts or credit card usage at petrol pumps.

Computer technology can open up the possibility of cyber contact with people that one has never met personally. This can lead to new opportunities to develop personal friendships and relationships but can also entail risks associated with deception.

Through the use of advanced technology, the reach of possible contacts may be vastly extended at the same time as the experience of personal loneliness. Sociology will have to develop an understanding of the effects of a world of communication which is increasingly mediated by technology.

Chapter 15

Pioneers in Sociological Theory
Chapter 3 Extension Reading

Abstract

This chapter provides a more in-depth survey of the theoretical perspectives of pioneering sociologists that were introduced in chapter 3. The focus of interest is on the systems of thinking developed by Henri Saint Simon, Auguste Comte, Herbert Spencer and Karl Marx.

The social forces that each theorist maintained were shaping the condition of society and driving social change inexorably toward the future are examined.

For both Saint Simon and Comte, it is shown how belief systems explained the condition of society and provided the driving force for social change.

By contrast, the sections on Spencer explain his theory that social change is driven by survival of the fittest and that the condition of society depends on the evolution of its members' moral condition.

A further alternative is shown to be provided by Marx for whom the economy provided the engine room for social change and shaped opposing social class interests.

We have seen in chapter 3 that a major preoccupation of the pioneers of sociological thinking was to extract from broad sweeping views of social history a scientific understanding of social change by claiming to uncover the operation laws of social change. Each theorist developed a system that attempted to explain the key forces that shaped the condition of society, the direction of social change and the emergent characteristics of the future that laws of progress or evolution would bring about. In this chapter, we will probe in a little more depth these aspects of the theories of Saint Simon, Comte, Spencer and Marx.

Henri Saint Simon – belief systems drive change and shape the condition of society

The writings of Henri Saint Simon date from the early 1800s. He essentially argued that an appropriate diagnosis of the current social malaise of the protracted social and political turmoil experienced during the post French Revolution decades and the way forward was dependent on the study of social history. This study would have to adopt a high altitude vantage point to look at societies in the whole and delineate their direction of change over long periods of time. In pursuit of this task, Saint Simon adopted an 'idealist' approach. Idealism in this context (not to be confused with idealism as a value judgement which could also be applied to Saint Simon, as well as Comte, Spencer and Marx) emphasises that the condition of intellectual and belief systems within society determines the condition of society.

The study of changes in prevailing intellectual and belief systems would therefore explain changes in the condition of society. A single and widely shared world view which emphasises the duties of individuals to society would be highly conducive to promoting the conditions of social harmony and integration. By contrast, ideas that are critical of a single and integrated world view, which promote fragmented belief systems and emphasise individual rights and freedoms, would lead to social disruption, fragmentation and even possibly revolution.

Scanning history, Saint Simon characterised the feudal social order of the Middle Ages as a stable and integrated society with a clearly defined and established social hierarchy. He argued that Catholicism provided an integrated system of thinking and religious dogma that was a basis for moral authority, promoting social harmony and integration. Saint Simon referred to this condition of stability as an 'organic' period in history, meaning that society exhibited conditions of organic unity.

However, from an idealist perspective, intellectual progress will lead to social disruption if new thinking was critical of established systems of thinking without offering a united and constructive alternative. Saint Simon maintained that from the Middle Ages the church became a servant to the political powers and vested interests of the nobility. As such, it resisted intellectual change and fell behind the advances in science which increasingly passed into the hands of laymen. From the sixteenth century, the religious Reformation challenged the moral authority of Catholicism, and by the eighteenth century Enlightenment philosophers were developing systems of thinking which increasingly attacked religious dogma through the application of rational scrutiny to matters of faith. These challenges had a corrosive effect on the dominant religious belief system of Catholicism and with it the legitimacy of the privileges of the feudal social order that it supported. This fomented an erosion of authority and the undermining of social harmony and for Saint Simon provided the seedbed of social discontent which eventually culminated in the French Revolution.

The French Revolution liberated the majority from the suppression of feudal institutions which it swept away, but what had people been liberated to? Saint Simon argued that a period of intellectual and therefore social anarchy had stretched beyond the Revolution. New ideas of liberty, equality and fraternity which had clashed with the ideas of duty upon which the old order was based could not provide a single constructive alternative around which to reintegrate and reorganise society. In contrast to the past organic period, this period of intellectual, social and moral breakdown was referred to as a 'critical' period. For social and individual well-being, the critical period needed to be terminated and a higher organic phase of social order and stability instituted. The direction to the future and the new type of stable society that would emerge needed to be discovered by the analysis of history which would reveal laws of intellectual and social progress to provide guidance and assist the process of social reconstruction.

The advance of science to understand the laws of social change

What, from his overview of history, were these laws of change and what did they reveal regarding the future? For Saint Simon, a key feature of change was the advance of science. This precluded a return to the religion of the past as a cohesive system of thinking and basis for a new social and moral order. Saint Simon argued that a study of the advance of science in history revealed that, starting in the inorganic subject areas, it was advancing its methods and explanations into the life sciences. As society was viewed as the highest life form, science was destined to become the means by which society could be understood and regulated. This would require the empowerment of new elites with the appropriate expertise to do so. To drive progress, critical and rational philosophies had already performed the negative task of attacking religious dogma and undermining the old order. From the intellectual and social anarchy created, science now had to perform the positive task of supplying a new integrated belief system and the intellectual means of organisation to build the new social order.

The immanent new industrial society

What was to be the nature of this new social order and who were to be the new leaders? To answer these questions, Saint Simon utilised a 'militant' and 'industrial' typology. A typology is a simplified model which assists the understanding of something which in reality is far more complex by extracting its essential features. This can be applied to societies. For Saint Simon, militant type societies prevailed in the Middle Ages. They comprised social hierarchies that were politically dominated by the nobility who ruled the masses coercively. Such societies were organised primarily for warfare.

Industrial type societies, organised for peaceful productivity, would come to replace militant societies. This was because along with the advance of science, society was on the verge of undergoing industrial modernisation. In transition to the industrial society, science and industry would be applied to the pursuit of economic production which enabled the growth of wealth by peaceful means to replace wealth acquisition through the plunder of warfare. The new battle would be in utilising the resources of nature. To regulate such a society in an efficient way, scientific and industrial expertise, in the hands of scientists and managers, would be necessary. It was therefore fitting that in the new social order, scientists and industrialists would replace the nobility as the new elite. A key insight derived by Saint Simon was that in the new industrial society, these elites would be appointed on intellectual merit and industriousness as opposed to the principle of birthright under the old order.

In summary, for Saint Simon, the study of history revealed that there were scientific laws of social change which demonstrated that science and industry were the only progressive basis for establishing a new social order. The reorganisation of society according to scientific principles required the administrative application of a 'social physics' in the hands of proven experts to replace the old politics which, under feudalism, had taken the form of the coercion of the productive by the idle. Private property would be protected. The industrial society would be socialist in the limited sense of the need for central rational economic planning but anti-democratic in denying the masses, regarded as unworthy, access to power. A new social cohesion would emerge around the shared values of industry and science, with the masses being imbued in its culture and dogma as a type of this worldly religion which would constructively replace the old religion of Catholicism, and with the new elites taking on the role of intellectual governance (Pullinger, 2015, Ch.2).

Auguste Comte – belief systems drive change and shape the condition of society

Auguste Comte acted as secretary to Saint Simon until their acrimonious breakup. His key ideas were elucidated in writings from the early 1820s. Comte offered a similar diagnosis of the social and moral condition of post-Revolution France to that of Saint Simon, whose ideas he developed, modified and systematised. He also shared Saint Simon's idealism, arguing that the condition of society is essentially determined by the progress and nature of intellectual thinking and belief systems.

Like Saint Simon, Comte argued that post-Revolution France was suffering social instability associated with intellectual and moral chaos. Whilst large numbers of people had been consigned to great poverty, others lived unconcerned in considerable wealth. Comte viewed excessive and uncaring individualism as a negative consequence of the collapse of the old moral constraints of traditional society with no new socially binding intellectual outlook and morality yet emerging. To re-establish a sound social and moral order required a new integrated system of thinking which would provide a basis for the moral binding of individuals in social obligation, much as in feudal times under the dominant religious outlook of the Catholic Church.

Comte argued that he had discovered laws of intellectual and social change that anticipated the emergence of a new stable social order. This new order he referred to as the 'positivist' era (Comte was the first to use this term). In this society, widespread faith in science would provide the shared world view for integrating the masses, whilst scientific understanding of the laws by which society operated through the new science of 'sociology' (Comte also coined this term) would form the basis for scientifically informed social intervention by elites, enabling them to regulate society independently from any political party or sectional interests. Comte took it as his mission to attempt to prove that from what he saw as the current social chaos, the reintegrated and reconstructed positivist society was immanent. To this end, he argued that he had extracted from his overview of history two interrelated laws of progress which he referred to as the 'law of the three stages' and the 'hierarchy of the sciences'.

Comte's law of the three stages

Comte's law of the three stages signalled a break from the militant and industrial typology that has been used by Saint Simon to periodise social historical stages. This law posited that human understanding of all phenomena passes sequentially through three stages. These Comte referred to as the theological, the metaphysical and the positivist. The theological stage represents the infancy of knowledge in any subject area. At this stage, phenomena is viewed as created and controlled by divine beings and religious belief systems prevail. For Comte, the height of the influence of theological thinking in Europe was during the early Middle Ages when the world view and precepts of the Catholic Church formed the basis for intellectual and moral integration.

Whilst this system of thinking upheld social order, in time it became an obstacle to progress. At the metaphysical (philosophical) stage, belief in forces operating within phenomena challenges theological thinking which explains phenomena through the influence of external divine powers. These forces within the phenomena may still be of a mysterious nature, but the effect of metaphysical thinking is to confront and dissolve theological belief systems. In so doing, it dismantles theological obstacles to social progress but in subverting an integrated system of beliefs comes to undermine the social order that they supported. However, it provides a stepping stone enabling a transition to be made toward scientific understanding, which ultimately reveals the concrete laws by which Comte argued all phenomena operate in their own way.

Comte's hierarchy of the sciences

So, Comte maintained that all phenomena are governed by laws which in time will be revealed when, by understanding having progressed through the three stages, science will explain everything. To the law of the three stages, Comte added the idea of the hierarchy of the sciences to explain that the laws governing different phenomena become understood at different times. The hierarchy of the sciences was a law that indicated the sequencing by which scientific knowledge of laws that operate for different levels of phenomena are uncovered. For Comte, this sequencing is dependent on the level of complexity and generality of the phenomena in question. Scientific understanding is first possible with reference to the least complex and most general of phenomena. This is that of the physical realm to which mathematical analysis may be directly applied to demonstrate the laws by which the physical world is governed. The last frontier in which science is able to understand the laws that operate is that of the most complex and least general phenomena of the life sciences of the biological and social world which are the most challenging because they are the least reducible to mathematical analysis. The transition from theological understanding through metaphysical to positivist thus takes place in the subject sequence of mathematics, astronomy, physics, chemistry, biology and finally sociology, the scientific study of society.

The immanent new positivist society

As illustrated in the simplified chart in figure 1, combining these two laws shows that throughout history scientific understanding has been making advances up the hierarchy of the subjects, but at any point in time different subject areas may have reached different stages of understanding in their progression through the law of the three stages. For example, the lower science of astronomy was entering the scientific stage by the seventeenth century, yet as late as the nineteenth century political economists were applying to social phenomena a metaphysical view of society when referring to the mysterious 'invisible hand' of free market forces. However, scientific understanding had by then moved up to the life science of biology, immediately below that of sociology on the hierarchical scale. For Comte, this showed that science was on the verge of application to understanding the most complex of phenomena and thus discovering the laws by which society operated. When this transpires, all knowledge will have reached the scientific stage. Science will be able to explain all levels of phenomena, providing the foundation for a new integrated intellectual outlook and the means for a new level of social and moral integration and objective basis for social intervention. In this positivist society, the application of social science by positivist sociologists will enable the intelligent regulation of society and science will form the basis for the highest social consensus (Pullinger, 2015, Ch.3).

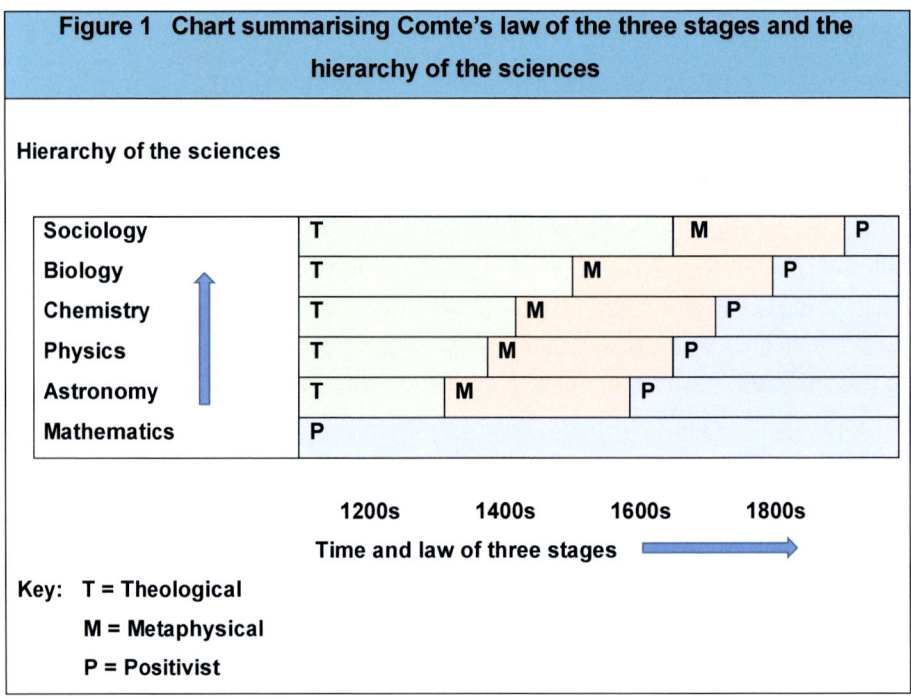

Figure 1 Chart summarising Comte's law of the three stages and the hierarchy of the sciences

Both Comte and Saint Simon argued that the future held the certain prospect of a highly regulated scientific and industrial society which would transcend what they viewed as the intellectual, moral and social chaos of the post-revolutionary period. For Comte, the positivist society would reunite social progress with social order. The triumph of science in establishing the most highly ordered society would signify the end point in history. However, other writers in this era also claimed scientific credentials for their theories but with very different conclusions regarding the forces and direction of social change and the type of society that would be the outcome. One such challenge came from the evolutionary theory of Herbert Spencer and another from the historical materialism of Karl Marx.

Herbert Spencer – the survival of the fittest drives change and the moral makeup of individuals shapes the condition of society

Although the Industrial Revolution in England had a profound effect on the way of life for many, England had not experienced in the eighteenth century the social and political turmoil of revolution, anarchy and political reaction that beset France in the late eighteenth and the early nineteenth century. By comparison at least, in England the social and political changes brought by the Industrial Revolution, though far reaching, were arguably less dramatic and extreme. Through these changes, an entrepreneurial class was emerging to challenge the social status, power and values of the aristocracy. This class were keen to establish a soundly based ethical justification for their new made wealth that would enhance their social standing – an ethical system which supported the institutions of free enterprise capitalism and the culture of individualism from which they were the main beneficiaries. Herbert Spencer, whose ideas on evolution and progress found their essential formulation by the late 1850s, proved to be a powerful intellectual advocate of such a justification.

For Spencer, the Enlightenment idea of progress as social improvement in terms of happiness maximisation could be found in the ideas of political economists such as Adam Smith. At the dawn of the Industrial Revolution, Smith analysed the conditions under which wealth creation and economic growth could be developed. He argued that a high division of workforce labour in terms of task specialisation would maximise efficiency of production and the creation of wealth. A high division of labour would necessitate production for exchange, as few people would be able to live just off the products that their labour contributed to produce. This would lead to the need for the extension of market exchange and competition between producers to achieve profitability and reinvestment. Such an environment would provide a catalyst for general economic growth – that is as long as production and markets remained free from government intervention. This model is referred to as 'political economy'.

Spencer took Smith's ideas on how a modern economy should run and broadened them out from an economic model into a model of a society of spontaneous co-operation, framed by contractual obligations between free individuals. Smith's ideas were radicalised by Spencer to provide a model society of the future. What were the social forces that Spencer argued would move society to that destination?

Spencer did not adopt the idealist position of Saint Simon and Comte. He strongly opposed the view that intellectual and belief systems determine the condition of society and provide a vehicle for progress. Instead, he argued that the range of workable social institutions is determined by the moral makeup of individuals as the units upon which the social fabric is built. Whilst this moral makeup can change through the impact of the social environment back onto individuals, this change, he claimed, can only happen very slowly as it takes the form of the inheritance of acquired characteristics. The slow rate and direction of social and moral change was explained by Spencer through his law of evolution.

Spencer's law of evolution

Evolution refers to a process of growth in the form of the unfolding of an inbuilt potential. If a common evolutionary process could be demonstrated as the natural order of change operating in all phenomena, it could be argued that a natural direction of social change with a clear outcome could be scientifically established. Consequently, a model of the evolutionary high point of society could be provided as guidance for progressive social reform. Spencer's ultimate aim was to demonstrate that the superiority of a social and ethical system derived from political economy could be justified through his formula of evolution.

Through comparison of society with biological entities, otherwise known as the biological analogy, Spencer attempted to show that, as in organisms, likewise in society, the natural direction of evolutionary change could be established. He explained these parallel evolutionary processes in terms of structure and function. For Spencer, evolutionary advance takes the form of structural differentiation. In biological organisms, this refers to growing complexity and specialisation of organs as organisms grow from infancy toward maturity and as shown in more highly evolved types. Spencer argued that as societies modernise and evolve, a parallel process takes place as they grow in size and develop increasingly specialised and interconnected institutions which perform their precisely allocated functions within the social structure.

But how does change occur and what is the driving force? Central to the dynamics of evolution is the idea of adaptation. Structural and functional adaptation refers to the capacity of an organism to respond to the demands of the surrounding environment. Biological organisms must adapt to their environment to survive. Likewise, society must develop those institutions which will assist it to do so or it will go under. The effect of this surrounding social environment of other societies on adaptive survival capacity can best be explained through reference to Spencer's use of the militant and industrial typology.

For Spencer, militant type societies (defined similarly to Saint Simon) have dominated much of social evolution. They are part of a broader hostile environment characterised by wars and conquests. Within this environment, societies that are highly regulated and have repressive political control mechanisms and rigid social hierarchies through which the powerful subjugate populations are best able to maximise the collective war effort in the battle for survival. The model of a military hierarchy and political coercion impacts on all other areas of the broader social structure. People living within such a barbaric social environment adapt a barbaric moral condition – given the freedom to do so, individuals would trample over the rights of others. Authoritarian control is thus necessary to avoid anarchy. Such societies comprise simple authoritarian structures through which rulers rule by might and individual rights are little recognised or respected.

However, through compounding by military conquest and by natural growth, societies grow in size. With growth, an advance in structural differentiation takes place in the form of the emergence of a growing range of specialist institutions and occupations. Specialisation promotes commercial transactions and trading which enhances the free exchange of goods and services between individuals. As peaceful industrial and commercial activities advance, the controls and suppressions of the militant society become impediments to the maximisation of wealth producing activity through free association. The evolutionary potential of large industrial societies is to develop a free social form of co-operating individuals in which the role of government retreats toward that of overseeing this process and restraining the declining number of recalcitrant members of society.

This change of social environment has a civilising effect on the moral nature of members of society. According to Spencer, through many generations of experience within this social setting, the moral characteristics of responsible individualism become developed and built in through inheritance. The moral nature of the individuals that constitute society gradually modifies and evolves from the condition of brutality within the barbaric conditions of militant society toward enlightened individualism in the industrial society. A very different from of industrial society to that envisaged by Saint Simon becomes the high point of social evolution and enlightened individualism becomes the correlative high point of moral evolution.

The immanent new industrial society

Spencer's image of the fully evolved industrial society is one of pure free enterprise capitalism. It takes the form of the highest level of individual specialisation and structural sophistication. Moral evolution to a state of enlightened individualism means that individual freedoms become mutually respected amongst members of society and external repressive control by the state becomes largely redundant. At this evolutionary high point, 'survival of the fittest' remains the driving force for innovation and change but becomes elevated from effectiveness in warfare to the competitive capacity for efficient economic production. This is only possible through a moral condition of enlightened economic individualism within society and the broader context of peaceful trade between nations. At this point, the fabric of society will come to comprise a network of contractual relationships, agreements and co-operations freely entered into and honoured by individuals of high moral rectitude. Those societies that evolve in this way will have adapted to the natural conditions of competition between industrial societies.

Spencer outlined the social fabric in terms of a society shaped by freely entered into co-operative business relationships:

'All trading transactions, whether between masters and workmen, buyers and sellers of commodities, or professional men and those they aid, are effected by free exchange..........This relation, in which the mutual rendering of services is unforced and neither individual subordinated, becomes the predominant relation throughout society in proportion as the industrial activities predominate. Daily determining the thoughts and sentiments, daily disciplining all in asserting their own claims while enforcing them to recognise the correlative claims of others........[such a society is] characterised throughout by the same individual freedom which every commercial transaction implies. The co-operation by which the multiform activities of society are carried on, becomes a voluntary co-operation' (Spencer, 1876, cited in Andreski, 1972, p.164).

Spencer's justification for minimal state intervention was related to the process of structural differentiation and growing social complexity leading to a delicate balance of finely interconnected free enterprise institutions and independent individuals. Within this type of society, to maximise both human happiness and wealth creation, a minimalist state should leave decision making to individuals who, in aggregate, would always make superior decisions, for example to satisfy their personal needs or invest profitably in enterprise, to those attempted on their behalf and imposed on them by the state. The latter would be a cumbersome and inefficient mechanism of intervention in an advanced and complex industrial society. Moreover, Spencer argued that even if state intervention could produce some planned desirable outcomes, the scope for unintended and often negative remote consequences within societies of high complexity and interconnectedness would outstretch the capacity of social scientific analysis to anticipate them and only require further intervention with its own unforeseen consequences to try and put right, and so on. Even state welfare intervention would therefore be counterproductive as well as an infringement of individual responsibility for self-support.

For Spencer, the workings of evolution would bring about a very different industrial society to the future centrally regulated industrial society predicted by Saint Simon and the positivist society of Comte. However, he counselled that the process was likely to be long and slow, with possible setbacks. The repressive and regulatory characteristics of militancy would re-emerge within industrial societies as a response of self-preservation if they were threatened by other hostile societies. Furthermore, although Spencer's future utopia of a deregulated capitalist industrial society was for him both the logical and desirable end product of history, for the maintenance of social order and stability, the retreat of state interventionism to make this possible should not run substantially ahead of the moral evolution of the population. Although the moral condition of populations is influenced by the social environment, Spencer argued that workable social institutions must ultimately reflect the stage of moral evolution of the individuals that make up society.

As, through the inheritance of acquired characteristics, people's moral condition can only evolve slowly, if state control retreats too quickly, the persistence of the moral traits of barbarism will mean that individual freedoms will be abused. In this situation, the only alternatives will be a retreat to greater regulation or the risk of growing social anarchy. Only when the moral nature of enlightened individualism, where individuals mutually respect each other's equal rights and freedoms is sufficiently widespread and advanced throughout society can the state safely largely withdraw its controls (Pullinger, 2015, Ch.7).

Karl Marx – the economy drives change and shapes the condition of society

Marxism is a theoretical perspective developed by Karl Marx and Frederick Engels at the height of English free enterprise capitalism around the middle of the nineteenth century. It provided a radical critique of capitalism and a theoretical alternative to Spencer's evolutionism which had charted the future toward a pure free enterprise capitalist society.

Marx placed economic forces at the centre of his social theory and provided a 'materialist' explanation of the causes of social change throughout history. Through a materialist interpretation of history, Marx emphasised that social change has as its driving force economic and material factors. This is in contrast to Saint Simon's and Comte's idealist view that changing intellectual and belief systems drive social and economic change. From Marx's materialist perspective, changing belief systems emerge mainly as a response to economic change. The values and outlook of those who hold economic power are likely to pervade society and take the form of justifications of social systems and hierarchies, benefiting the economically wealthy and powerful in their subjugation of the impoverished lower social orders. In the Manifesto of the Communist Party, Marx stated this precisely when he wrote

'What else does the history of ideas prove, than that intellectual production changes its character in proportion as material production is changed. The ruling ideas of each age have ever been the ideas of its ruling class' (Marx, 1973, p.85).

Related to this materialist position, Marxism is often interpreted as a form of 'economic determinism'. This means that the economy is the determining or at least powerfully shaping force around which the rest of society is organised. The economy and the distribution of wealth and power 1) structure society into relationships between social classes, arrangements which 2) are justified through dominant ideas and controlling institutions.

Put simply, economic forces shape cultural values and cultural values shape individual consciousness and action.

For Marx, work, as an economic activity, is the most fundamental social activity, without which society could not exist. Within society, therefore, the essential social relationships revolve around productive activity. These work relationships form distinct social classes which are central to the formation of social structures.

Economic relationships shape social class relationships

In his analysis of society, Marx utilised the following concepts:

- All production requires 'forces of production' which comprise levels of technology and machinery, production techniques, raw materials and labour power – all of which makes production possible.

- Of the forces of production, the 'means of production' are those that take the form of legally owned productive property, therefore excluding workers in capitalist societies who are free to seek alternative employment.

For economic production to take place, there must exist social relationships. The term 'relations of production' refers to the form, shaped by duties and obligations between the parties, which the social relationships that are necessary for production take. According to Marx, in all societies where the means of production are privately owned, these relationships mark out social class divisions. The fundamental feature of these social class divisions is that one class (under capitalism, a capitalist class) will own the means of production and also have at its disposal the only asset that the other class (the working class) owns and has to sell – its capacity to work, referred to as its 'labour power'. The utilisation of workers' labour power is necessary for the owners of the means of production to create value, extract profit and accumulate wealth, whilst the hiring out of their labour power by workers is necessary to provide them with a waged income. Built into this relationship is conflict between the classes over the allocation of value created by the productive process.

The term 'mode of production' is a very broad concept which specifies how production is organised and refers to levels of technological advancement and types of social relationships. For Marx, societies are differentiated by their mode of production and historical materialism refers to the forces that lead to changes in the dominant mode of production. These forces have effected the transition from feudal to capitalist societies and will impel a further transition to a future communist social order.

Private ownership of the means of production has been a feature of most of modern history. Indeed, when people were not free, such as slaves in slave societies, the entire forces of production were privately owned. It is the source of social power for the class owning them. Power derived from this economic source is the capacity that owners have to exert control over workers. From this perspective, power is a fundamental characteristic of the relations of production which exist between the social classes. It is through the utilisation of labour that value is added in the production process. However, for Marx, through their use of power, the owners of the means of production are able to expropriate or skim off an excessive proportion of that value. This means that those who have provided their labour are short changed in relation to the value it creates through the products produced and the price at which they are sold. The relations of production when the means of production are privately owned therefore give rise to, through the use of class power, the 'exploitation' of the subject working class.

The dynamics of the social transition from feudalism to capitalism

Contradictions can emerge between stages in the development of the means of production and the relations of production and ideological justifications. The emergence of new means of production, for example the rapid growth of an urban located capitalist factory mass production processes, and the decline of rural based agrarian production, will contradict old relations of production (between landowner and tied agricultural worker) and their supporting ideology (aristocratic superiority through lineage and required deference from social inferiors) which were suited to the old means of production (pre-industrial low level technology). As new relations of production emerge (contractual relationships between employer and formally free waged worker) which are appropriate to new means of production (factory technology), the system generates new ideological justifications (wealth of capitalists as proof of industriousness and enterprise, and therefore merited). Economic change thus drives revolutionary social transformation, but the consequence for workers is that all the time that the means of production are privately owned, one form of class oppression will simply be replaced by another.

This process of transition from feudal to capitalist modes of production can be reviewed a little more closely. Feudal society, at its height in Europe during the Middle Ages, is pre-industrial and largely agricultural based, typified by life in small rural communities. Religion and superstition are powerful sources of explanation and moral values. The means of production comprise land, agricultural buildings, machinery and implements of a low technological level (which may utilise wind and water power) and animals. Industrial production, conducted in small workshops, remains at a handicraft level, and working the land is the main means for the generation of wealth. Land ownership is concentrated largely in the hands of the nobility and the church, who therefore comprise the ruling class.

Various grades of commoner below the nobility and priesthood in the social hierarchy include craftsmen, traders and those who work the small areas of land that they own. At the bottom of the social scale reside a large stratum of impoverished and landless agricultural labourers known as serfs. For Marx, the defining class relationship in this type of society is the exploitation of the labour of serfs by a landowning nobility and church. These agrarian relations of production, which are a potential point of fracture between the classes in the social hierarchy, are maintained by force where necessary and by an ideology which emphasises the importance of deference and loyalty of the lower orders toward their lords who claim for themselves the virtues of superior social breeding through tracing their noble lineage. This 'natural' social order is sanctified by the established church in its religious teachings.

However, within the late feudal social order, new and more efficient means of production were being developed by enterprising artisans (craft workers) and inventors. In time, as industrial technology and machinery improve, industrial production expands but is restricted by feudal social relations. Both the feudal relations of production of serf bonded to master, based around land ownership, and the supporting ideology of superior social breeding of the nobility and deference and loyalty expected from serfs, begin to look antiquated. They are beginning to outlive their purpose. A point is eventually reached where, through private ownership and enterprising use of newly developing technology, a capitalist class emerges to gain sufficient wealth and power to eclipse the nobility and achieve social ascendancy. This industrial revolution is a bourgeois revolution, forcing the transition from feudal to capitalist society. Around the new means of factory mass production, new relations of production emerge which are appropriate to a dynamic capitalist economy. These are embodied in flexible wage labour contracts which benefit a new ruling class of capitalists employing waged workers.

This transformation from feudal to capitalist economy and social structure must bring forth a change in supporting ideological representations of society to disguise the new relationship of worker exploitation and dissipate conflict. Changes in the economic infrastructure thus drive and shape necessary changes in the superstructure as the old institutions and ideologies of the feudal superstructure no longer match the requirements of the new infrastructure of industrial capitalism. The new ideological values are those that correspond with the writers of political economy (and radicalised by Herbert Spencer) that the system is best left to self-regulate through forces of supply and demand and that workers are free to engage in contracts of employment with whom they wish. Moreover, position in society is now viewed as increasingly reflecting individual merit in a more open social structure.

From the Marxist perspective, the emergence of capitalism from feudalism simply replaces one form of class exploitation by another. Although the system has changed, private ownership of the means of production remains. Conflict of class interests over the allocation of value created in the production process therefore also remains and must in the long term come to the surface. The potential under capitalism is for that conflict to bring into opposition a minority exploiting capitalist class and a majority exploited working class.

Capitalism and the experience of alienation

Under capitalism, workers (referred to by Marx as the 'proletariat') are obliged to provide their one asset, their labour power, to capitalists (referred to as the 'bourgeoisie') in exchange for the wages that are necessary for their survival. But, Marx argued, as well as suffering economic exploitation, this relationship leads to the degradation of the worker who feels like a powerless object performing meaningless tasks, with the employer, driven by the competitive struggle to survive and quest to maximise efficiency and profit, controlling the work process. An advance in the division of labour in the pursuit of efficiency heightens the repetition of narrowly defined work tasks and renders the worker's experience of work as devoid of creative input and control. The resulting dehumanisation experienced by workers is referred to by Marx as 'alienation' – a malady deriving from the conditions of capitalist production.

Marx characterised the alienating conditions experienced by factory workers under conditions of industrial capitalism in the following way:

'Owing to the extensive use of machinery and to division of labour, the work of the proletarians has lost all individual character, and, consequently, all charm for the workmen. He becomes an appendage of the machine, and it is only the most simple, most monotonous, and most easily acquired knack, that is required of him......[Workers] are daily and hourly enslaved by the machine, by the overseer, and, above all, by the individual bourgeois manufacturer himself' (Marx, 1973, p.74).

The oppression of the working class under capitalism

As, for Marx, conflict lies at the heart of this relationship between the social classes, and given the vast numerical supremacy of the working class, why is open class conflict not a more common feature of this relationship? An understanding of this question requires reference to the distinction made by Marx between the 'infrastructure' and the 'superstructure'.

Together, Marx refers to the means of production and the relations of production as forming the 'economic base' of society or the infrastructure. It is here where social class relationships are located and tensions between the classes are generated.

The term superstructure, within the Marxist perspective, refers to society's dominant social values, beliefs, laws and institutions. These operate as controls within the relations of production and as broader social controls. Whilst class conflict is built into the economic infrastructure, the dominant ideas and institutions of the superstructure serve to hide or suppress this conflict of interests and minimise the likelihood of actual open class conflict emerging. Dominant ideas and institutions justify and support the unequal distribution of power within the workplace and society and therefore primarily benefit the owners of the means of production by emphasising the normality and inevitability of the prevailing situation. The laws of the land thus serve the needs of the dominant class, for example, for efficient and profitable production and the protection of private property, and workers are encouraged to accept the system and their position in it as natural, a view often supported by religious teachings.

Power and control can take the form of coercion. Coercion refers to the use or threat of the use of force. Within the superstructure, institutions of coercion, such as the armed forces, police, judiciary and prisons, impose social order and suppress discontent. But, for Marx, dominant social ideas also have a controlling effect. From Marx's power model, it follows that the prevailing ideas in society are the ideas conducive to the interests of the ruling economic class, i.e. the nobility under feudalism and the capitalist class under capitalism. These ideas aim to give legitimacy to the existing social order by providing credible justifications for it being so and hiding or disguising the reality of a conflict of class interests. This can only transpire via a systematically distorted image of reality, referred to by Marx as 'ideology'. Through the process of socialisation, an ideologically distorted view of society provides a 'false consciousness' of reality through which the compliance of the working class is gained. Ideological distortion of reality therefore often acts as a front line of social control, relieving the necessity for the relentless use of coercive force.

An illustration of the infrastructure and superstructure relationship is provided in figure 2 below.

Figure 2, illustrating the Marxist model of the generation and suppression of class conflict under capitalism

Superstructure

Institutions and ideas Suppress class conflict. Armed forces, police, legal system and prisons enforce **coercive** control. Church and religious belief systems, mass media and values of consumerism, education system and image of equality of opportunity, political parties and the view that the electorate have significant choice and power - all provide **ideological** distortions of reality with the effect of inducing subject class conformity through creating **false consciousness**.

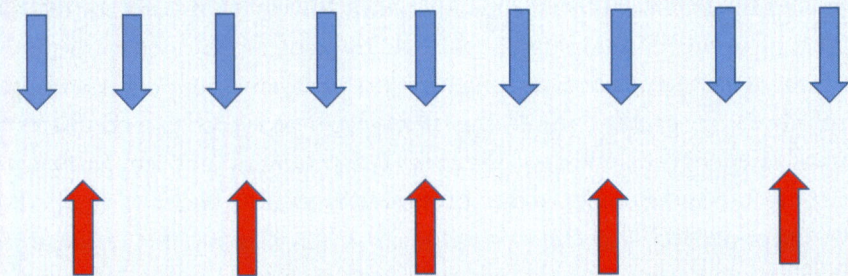

Infrastructure

Economic base Forms exploitative social class relations in the productive process and generates **class conflict**.

The dynamics of capitalism

Marx argued that the controlling forces of the superstructure can prevail for lengthy periods of time, but cannot indefinitely suppress inbuilt class conflict which is more likely to emerge during times of crisis in the capitalist system. Class exploitation, and the potential for conflict that it generates, can be hidden by ideological distortions, such as the notion of equality in terms of contracts freely entered into by both sides and the idea of a fair wage being provided for a fair days work. For Marx, these distortions help govern the relations of production. However, the capitalist system generates inbuilt tendencies toward overproduction. This is because in the competitive battle for survival and profit maximisation between capitalists, the survivors are those who are able to increase their efficiency and apply downward pressure on wages.

Consequently, the production of goods outstretches workers' limited purchasing power, making periodic economic recessions or depressions unavoidable. During these times great mass hardship, contradictions between ideology (fair wage) and reality (exploitation and unemployment) are more likely to become evident and the transparency of ideology could pave the way to class consciousness and mass opposition.

The transition from capitalism to communism

Marxists argue that free enterprise capitalism is essentially unstable. Tendencies toward a polarisation of wealth between the main classes and through the conditions of production under which capitalism brings together workers into larger aggregates in both the workplace and in the urban environment. These are conditions that enhance the possibility of the emergence of a common class consciousness that can lead to revolutionary action. Thus, in this system and productive process, capitalism has been assembling the troops of its own future destruction. Marx argued that the inbuilt mechanics of capitalism will in the long run drive the working class toward revolution.

Marx argued that the revolutionary overthrow of capitalism will be different from the revolutions that overthrew feudalism and brought the minority capitalist class to power. This is because the revolutionary class seizing power will now be the majority not a minority class. It will therefore take the means of production into common ownership, to be run in the common interest. Greed and selfishness, which appeared as universal features of human nature with life encapsulated in capitalist society, would give way within this new system to a nature shaped by the necessity of co-operation. The resulting communist society would be the product of the final revolutionary transformation of society since, as a classless society, it would resolve all class conflict.

Biblography

Aas, K.F. (2013) *Globalization & Crime*. London: Sage

Abbott, P. & Wallace, C. (1997) *An Introduction to Sociology*. London: Routledge

Abercrombie, N., Warde, A., Deem, R., Penna, S., Sayer, A., Soothill, K.L., Urry, J. & Walby, S. (2006) *Contemporary British Society*. Cambridge: Polity

Alam, M.S. (2002) *A Critique of Samuel Huntington. Peddling Civilizational Wars*. Available at: http://www.counterpunch.org/alampeddle.html (Accessed 27/3/2019)

Alam, M.S. "A Clash of Civilizations? Nonsense", *Journal of The Historical Society*, 2008 (2) Issue 3-4, pp.379-395

Alam, M.S. (2008) Clash within civilizations? *Revisiting Samuel Huntington's 'The Clash of Civilizations'*. Available at:: https://cafedissensusblog.com/2018/04/12/clash-within (Accessed 26/3/2019)

Aldridge, A. (2013) *Religion in the Contemporary World*. Cambridge: Polity

Allan, K. (2005) *Explorations in Classical Sociological Theory*. California: Pine Forge

Allen, M. (2013) *The Curriculum Great Reversal*. Available at: http://radicaled.wordpress.com/2013/05/01/the-curriculum-great-reversal/ (Accessed 19/6/2014)

Alvesson, M. (2002) *Postmodernism and Social Research*. Buckingham: Open University

Andreski, S. (1972) *Herbert Spencer*. London: Nelson

Apple, M.W., Ball, S.J. & Gandin, L.A. (ed) (2010) *The Routledge International Handbook of the Sociology of Education*. London: Routledge

Ariel, B., Sutherland A., Henstock, D., Young, J., Drover, P., Sykes, J.,

Megicks, S., & Henderson, R. " 'Contagious Accountability' A Global Multisite Randomized Controlled Trial on the Effect of Police Body-Worn Cameras on Citizens' Complaints Against the Police", *Criminal Justice and Behaviour*, 2016 (44) Issue 2, pp.293-316

Bilton, T., Bonnett, K., Jones, P., Lawson, T., Skinner, D., Stanworth, M., & Webster, A. (2002) Introductory Sociology. Basingstoke: Palgrave MacMillan

Ball, S.J. (ed.) (2004) *Sociology of Education*. London: Routledge Falmer

Barlow, D.M. & Mills, B. (eds.) (2009) *Reading Media Theory*. Harlow: Pearson

Barrington Moore Jr. (1969) *Social Origins of Dictatorship and Democracy*. Harmondsworth: Penguin

Beck, U. (1992) *Risk Society*. London: Sage

Becker, H.S. (1973) *Outsiders*. New York: The Free Press

Berger, P.L. (1969) *The Social Reality of Religion*. London: Faber & Faber

Berger, P.L. (1974) *Invitation to Sociology*. Harmondsworth: Penguin

Berry, M. *Understanding the role of the mass media in the EU Referendum*. www.referendumanalysis.eu/eu-referendum-analysis-2016/section-1 (Accessed 4/6/2019)

Bilton, T., Bonnett, K., Jones, P., Lawson, T., Skinner, D., Stanworth, M. & Webster, A. (2002) *Introductory Sociology*. Basingstoke: Palgrave MacMillan

Blackburn, R. (ed.) (1972) *Ideology in Social Science*. Fontana / Collins: UK

Blair, O. (2015) *Staying off Facebook can make you happier, study claims*. https://www.independent.co.uk/life-style/gadgets-and-tech/news (Accessed 25/6/2018)

Bolton, P. (a) (2012) *Education: Historical Statistics*. House of Commons Library. researchbriefings.files.parliament.uk/documents/SN04252/SN04252.pdf (Accessed 26/3/2019)

Bolton, P. (b) (2019) *Higher Education Student Numbers*. House of Commons Briefing Paper. https://researchbriefings.files.parliament.uk/documents/CBP-7857/CBP-7857.pdf (Accessed 26/3/2019)

Bott, E. (1957) *Family and Social Network*. London: Tavistock

Bottero, W. (2005) *Stratification: Social Divisions and Inequality*. Abingdon: Routledge

Brierley, P. (2014) *UK Church Statistics*, Number 2, 2010 to 2020. Tonbridge: ADBC

British Election Study - Questionnaire Wave 5. Available at: doc.ukdataservice.ac.uk/doc/8176/mrdoc/pdf/8176_bes2015_wave5re (Accessed 22/6/2018)

British Social Attitude Surveys, Available at: natcen.ac.uk (Accessed 28/7/2018)

Browne, K. (2006) *An Introduction to Sociology*. Cambridge: Polity

Bruce, S. (1995) *Religion in Modern Britain*. Oxford: Oxford University Press

Bryson, V. (2003) *Feminist Political Theory, An Introduction*. Basingstoke: Palgrave MacMillan

Calhoun, C., Gerteis, J., Moody. J., Pfaff. S., & Virk. I. (eds.) (2002) *Contemporary Sociological Theory*. Oxford: Blackwell

Cannadine, D. (2000) *Class in Britain*. London: Penguin

Carrabine, E., Cox, P., Lee, M., & South, N. (2002) *Crime in Modern Britain*. Oxford: Oxford University Press

Cassen, R. & Kingdom, G. (2007) *Tackling low Educational Achievement.* Available at: www.jrf.org.uk/sites/files/jrf/2063-education-schools (Accessed 18/6/2014)

Castells, M. (2012) *Networks of Outrage and Hope.* Cambridge: Polity

Cheal, D. (2002) *Sociology of Family Life.* Basingstoke: Palgrave MacMillan

Chitty, C. (2009) *Education Policy in Britain.* Basingstoke: Palgrave MacMillan

Clark, S., Mountford-Zimdars, A., & Francis, B. "Risk, Choice and Social Disadvantage: Young People's Decision Making in a Marketised Higher Education System", *Sociological Research Online*, 2015, 20 (3) 9

Clements, B. "Exploring Christian beliefs and practices in Britain", *Sociology Review*, 2015, 20 (1)

Cohen, R. & Kennedy, P. (2013) *Global Sociology.* Basingstoke: Palgrave MacMillan

Cohen, S. (1973) *Folk Devils & Moral Panics.* St. Albans: Paladin

Coser, L.A. (1977) *Masters of Sociological Thought.* New York: Harcourt Brace Jovanovich

Coxall, B., Robins, L., & Leach, R. (2003) *Contemporary British Politics.* Basingstoke: Palgrave MacMillan

Cremer, J. (2015) *Drop Facebook and be happy:* Danish study https://www.thelocal.dk/20151109/dropping-facebook-will-make-you (Accessed 25/6/2018)

Cromie, C. (6/7/2015) *Gay marriage now has overwhelming support in Northern Ireland – poll*, https://www.belfasttelegraph.co.uk/news/northern-ireland/ gay-marriage-now-has... (Accessed 11/10/2019)

Crompton, R. (2008) *Class & Stratification.* Cambridge: Polity Press

Cuff, E.C., Sharrock, W.W., & Francis, D.W. (2001) *Perspectives in Sociology.* London: Routledge

Dahrendorf, R. (1959) *Class and Class Conflict in Industrial Society.* London: Routledge & Kegan Paul

Davie, G. (2013) *The Sociology of Religion A Critical Agenda.* London: Sage

Debord, G. (1992) *Society of the Spectacle.* London: Rebel press.

Denzin, N.K. (1978) *Sociological Methods.* New York: McGraw-Hill.

Devine, F. & Heath, S. (eds.) (1999) *Sociological Research Methods in Context.* Basingstoke: Macmillan

Downes, D. & Rock, P. (2007) *Understanding Deviance.* Oxford: Oxford University Press

Durkheim, E. (1964a) *The Division of Labour in Society.* New York: Free Press

Durkheim, E. (1964b) *The Rules of Sociological Method.* New York: Free Press

Durkheim, E. (1970) *Suicide.* London: Routledge & Kegan Paul

Durkheim, E. (1976) *The Elementary Forms of the Religious Life.* London: George Allen & Unwin

Durrschmidt, J. & Taylor, G. (2007) *Globalization, Modernity and Social Change.* Basingstoke: Palgrave MacMillan

Dustmann, C., Frattini, T., & Theodoropoulos, N. (2009) *Ethnicity and Second Generation Immigrants.* Available at: www.ucl.ac.uk/~uctpb21/ Cpapers/Ethn_2gen_revision_C1.pdf (Accessed 30/8/2018

Ellwood, W. (2015) *Globalization Buying and Selling the World.* Oxford: New Internationalist

Engels, F. (1972) *The Origin of the Family, Private Property and the State.*

Lawrence & Wishart: London

Engels, F. (1974) *The Condition of the Working Class in England*. St Albans: Panther

Evangelical Alliance: *How many churches have opened or closed*. Available at: www.eauk.org/church/research-and-statistics/how-many-churches-have-opened-or-closed-in-recent-years.cfm (Accessed 28/7/2018)

Federman, M. *What is the Meaning of The Medium is the Message?* Available at: www.individual.utoronto.ca/markfederman/article_mediumisthemessage.htm. (Accessed 6/3/2019)

Flanagan, K. & Jupp, P.C. (eds.) (1999) *Postmodernity, Sociology and Religion*. Basingstoke: Macmillan

Flecha, R. & Soler, M. "Turning difficulties into possibilities: engaging Roma families and students in school through dialogic learning", *Cambridge Journal of Education*, 2013 (43) Issue 4, pp. 451–465

Flick, U. (2011) *An Introduction to Qualitative Research*. London: Sage

Ford, R. & Goodwin, M. (2014) *Revolt on the Right*. Abingdon: Routledge

Francis, B. (2000) *Boys, Girls and Achievement, Addressing the classroom issues*. London: Routledge Falmer

Frankenberg, R. (1973) *Communities in Britain*. Harmondsworth: Penguin

Fulcher, J. & Scott, J. (2011) *Sociology*. Oxford: Oxford University Press

Fuller, S. (2016) *Prolegomena to the Deep Sociology of Brexit: The Long Road Back to Pareto*. Available at: https://social-epistemology.com/2016/07/04/prolegomena-to-the-deep-sociology-of-brexit. (Accessed 14/10/2019)

Furlong, A., Cartmel, F., Biggart, A., Sweeting, H., & West, P. "Social class in an 'individualised' society", *Sociology Review*, April 2006 (15) Issue 4, pp.28-32

Furseth, I. & Repstad, P. (2010) *An Introduction to the Sociology of Religion.* Farnham: Ashgate

Gabb, J. (2010) *Family Lives and Relational Living: Taking Account of Otherness.* Available at: http://www.socresonline.org.uk/16/4/10.html (Accessed 8/6/2014)

Gane, N. (2004) *The Future of Social Theory.* London: Continuum

Gane, N. (2012) *Max Weber and Contemporary Capitalism.* Basingstoke: Palgrave Macmillan

Garfinkle, H. (1984) *Studies in Ethnomethodology.* Cambridge: Polity Press

Gauntlett, D. (2008) *Media, Gender and Identity, An Introduction.* Abingdon: Routledge

Geary, I. & Pabst, A. (eds.) (2015) *Blue Labour.* London: I. B. Tauris & Co. Ltd.

Gerth, H.H. & Mills, C. Wright (1977) *From Max Weber.* London: Routledge

Giddens, A. (1976) *New Rules of Sociological Method.* London: Hutchinson

Giddens, A. (1982) *Sociology, A Brief but Critical Introduction.* Basingstoke: MacMillan

Giddens, A. et al (ed) (1995) *The Polity Reader in Social Theory.* Cambridge: Polity Press

Giddens, A. (2000) *The Third Way and Its Critics.* Cambridge: Polity

Giddens, A. (2002) *Runaway World.* London: Profile

Giddens, A. (2009) *Sociology.* Cambridge: Polity

Grant, W. (1995) *Pressure Groups, Politics and Democracy in Britain.* Hemel Hempstead: Harvester Wheatsheaf

Gwynne, J. BBC NEWS | UK | Magazine | *Going undercover in the BNP* news.bbc.co.uk/2/hi/uk_news/magazine/3896213.stm (Accessed 24/6/2018)

Hales, J., Nevill, C., Pudney, S., & Tipping, S. *Longitudinal analysis of the Offending, Crime and Justice Survey 2003–06*. Available at: http://www.natcen.ac.uk/our-research/research/longitudinal-analysis-of-the-offending-crime-and-justice-survey/ (Accessed 30/11/2018)

Hall, D. & Hall, I. (2005) *Practical Social Research: Project Work in the Community*. Basingstoke: Macmillan

Hall, S., Held, D., & McGrew, T. (eds.) (1993) *Modernity and its Futures*. Cambridge: Polity

Haralambos, M. & Holborn, M. (2013) *Sociology Themes and Perspectives*. London: HarperCollins

Hayden, M. *Andrew Marr Show*, BBC 1, 20 May 2018.

Hedderman, C. "Gender and criminal justice", *Sociology Review*, 2015, 24 (3), pp.30-33

Heidensohn, F. (1996) *Women & Crime*. Basingstoke: Macmillan

Held, D. (ed) (2000a) *A Globalizing World?* New York: Routledge

Held, D. (2000b) *A Globalizing World? Culture, Economics, Politics* London: Routledge

Held, D. (ed) (2003) *The Global Transformations Reader*. Cambridge: Polity

Hennessy, P. (2014) *Establishment and Meritocracy*. London: Haus Publishing

Hesse-Biber, S.N. (ed) (2012) *The Handbook of Feminist Research*. London: Sage

Heywood, A. (1999) *Political Theory, An Introduction*. Basingstoke: Palgrave

Holdaway, S. (1992) *Crime and Deviance*. Walton-on-Thames: Nelson

Holton, R.J. (2011) *Globalization and the Nation State*. Basingstoke: Palgrave MacMillan

House of Commons Library (29/6/2016) - *Analysis of the EU Referendum results 2016* Available at: researchbriefings.parliament.uk/ResearchBriefing/Summary/CBP-7639 (Accessed 30/5/2018)

House of Commons Library - *General Election 2019: full results and analysis* Available at: https://researchbriefings.parliament.uk/ResearchBriefing/Summary/CBP-8749 (Accessed 6/2/2020)

House of Commons Library - *Social background of MPs 1979-2017* Available at: researchbriefings.files.parliament.uk/documents/CBP-7483/CBP-7483.pdf (Accessed 23/5/2018)

Hubbard, P. (2006) *City*. Abingdon: Routledge

Humanists UK, Religion and Belief: Some Surveys and Statistics. Available at: https://humanism.org.uk/campaigns/religion-and-belief-some-surveys-and-statistics/ (Accessed 27/7/2018)

Hunt, S.J. (2002) *Religion in Western Society*. Basingstoke: Palgrave

Hunt, S.J. (2005) *The Life Course*. Basingstoke: Palgrave MacMillan

Huntington, S. (2002) *The Clash of Civilisations and the Remaking of World Order*. London: Free Press

Jacobs, J. (1969) *"Symbolic Bureaucracy": A Case Study of a Social Welfare Agency*. Social Forces 47 (4): 413-421

Jäntti, M., Bratsberg, B., Røed K., Raaum, O., Naylor, R., Österbacka, E., Björklund, A., & Eriksson, T. (2006) *American Exceptionalism in a New Light: A Comparison of Intergenerational Earnings Mobility in the Nordic Countries, the United Kingdom and the United States*. Available at http://ftp.iza.org/ap1938.pdf (Accessed 10/3/2014)

Jewkes, Y. (2004) *Media & Crime*. London: Sage

Joint Council for Qualifications (2013) www.jcq.org.uk (Accessed 28/11/2013)

Johnes, G. & Soo, K.T. "Grades across universities over time", *Manchester School*, 2017 (85) Issue 1, pp.106-131

Jones, M. "Media Representation of Islam post 9/11", *Sociology Review*, 2012, 21 (3), pp.10-12

Jones, M. & Jones, E. (1999) *Mass Media*. Basingstoke: MacMillan

Joyce, P. (2009) *Criminology and Criminal Justice*. Abingdon: Routledge

Kelling, G.L. & Coles, C.M. (1997) *Fixing Broken Windows*. New York: Touchstone

Kirby, M., Kidd, W., Koubel, F., Barter, J., Hope, T., Kirton, A., Madry, N., Manning, P., & Triggs, K. (2000) *Sociology in Perspective*. Oxford: Heinemann

Kuhn, R. (2007) *Politics and the Media in Britain*. Basingstoke: Palgrave MacMillan

Kung, L., Picard, R.G. & Towse, R. (2008) *The Internet and the Mass Media*. London: Sage

Landale, J. (20/2/2016) *EU reform deal: What Cameron wanted and what he got*. www.bbc.co.uk/news/uk-politics-eu-referendum-35622105 (Accessed 1/6/2018)

Lauder, H., Brown, P., Dillabough, J., & Halsey, A.H. (eds.) (2006) *Education, Globalization & Social Change*. Oxford: Oxford University Press

Laughey, D. (2007) *Key Themes in Media Theory*. Maidenhead: Open University

Liebling, A., Maruna, S., & McAra, L. (eds.) (2017) *The Oxford Handbook of*

Criminology. Oxford: Oxford University Press

Lincoln, Y.S. & Denzin, N.K. (eds.) (2003) *Turning Points in Qualitative Research*. Oxford: Altamira Press

Lister, M., Dovey, J., Giddings, S., Grant, I., & Kelly, K. (2009) *New Media, A Critical Introduction Second Edition*. London: Routledge

Livesey, C. & Lawson, T. (2005) *AS Sociology for AQA*. Abingdon: Hodder Arnold

Lloyd, J. (2001) *The Protest Ethic*. London: Demos

Long, P. & Wall, T. (2009) *Media Studies, Texts, Production and Context*. Harlow: Pearson

McCall, G.J. & Simmons, J.L. (ed) (1969) I*ssues in Participant Observation*. London: Addison-Wesley

McIntosh, I. & Punch, S. (2005) *Get Set for Sociology*. Edinburgh: Edinburgh University Press

McKenzie, J. (2001) *Changing Education*. Harlow: Pearson

McLuhan, M. (2001) *Understanding Media*. Abingdon: Routledge

McNeill, P. & Chapman, S (2005) *Research Methods*. Abingdon: Routledge

Macionis, J. J. & Plummer, K., (2008) S*ociology, A Global Introduction*. Harlow: Pearson

Marsh, I. (ed) (2006) *Sociology, Making Sense of Society*. London: Pearson

Marshall, G., Rose, D., Newby, H., & Vogler, C. (1993) *Social Class in Modern Britain*. London: Routledge

Martell, L. (2012) *The Sociology of Globalization*. Cambridge: Polity Press

Marx, K. (1973) *The Revolutions of 1848*. Harmondsworth: Penguin

Matthewman, S., West-Newman, C.L., & Curtis, B. (eds.) (2007) *Being Sociological*. Basingstoke: Palgrave

Miliband, R. (1973) *The State in Capitalist Society*. London: Quartet

Miller, C.C., The Divorce Surge Is Over, but the Myth Lives On, *The New York Times*, www.nytimes.com/2014/12/02/upshot/the-divorce-surge-is-over-but-the-myth-lives-on.html (Accessed 18/7/2018)

Mills, C. Wright (1975) *The Sociological Imagination*. Harmondsworth: Penguin

Monahan, S.C. (ed) (2001) *Sociology of Religion*. New Jersey: Pearson

Morgan, D.H.J. (1996) *Family Connections, An Introduction to Family Studies*. Cambridge: Polity

Morley, D. (1992) *Television, Audiences and Cultural Studies*. Abingdon: Routledge

Muncie, J. & McLaughlin, E (eds.) (2002) *The Problem of Crime*. London: Sage

National Survey on Sexual Attitudes and Lifestyles. www.natsal.ac.uk/natsal-3.aspx (Accessed 22/6/2018)

Newburn, T. (2013) *Criminology*. Abingdon: Routledge

Niam, M. (2014) *The End of Power*. New York: Basic Books

Nisbet, R.A. (1970) *The Sociological Tradition*. London: Heinemann

Office for National Statistics, www.ons.gov.uk

Office for National Statistics (2018) *Crime Survey for England and Wales*. Available at: https://www.ons.gov.uk/peoplepopulationandcommunity/crime (Accessed 22/6/2018)

Orum, A.M. & Chen, X. (2003) *The World of Cities.* Oxford: Blackwell

Parker, S. (2004) *Urban Theory and the Urban Experience.* London: Routledge

Parker, S., Williams, L., & Aldridge, J. (2002) *The Normalization of 'Sensible' Recreational Drug Use: Further Evidence from the North West England Longitudinal Study.* Available at: www.brown.uk.com/brownlibrary/parker.pdf (Accessed 22/6/2018)

Parry, M. "Harvard Researchers Accused of Breaching Students' Privacy", *Chronicle of Higher Education*, 2011 (57) Issue 41

Parsons, T. & Shils, E.A. (1951) *Toward a General Theory of Action.* Cambridge: Harvard University Press

Payne, G. (ed) (2006) *Social Divisions.* Basingstoke: Palgrave Macmillan

Philo, G., Briant, E., & Donald, P. (2013) *Bad News for Refugees.* London: Pluto

Popper, K.R. (1972) *Conjectures and Refutations.* London: Routledge & Kegan Paul

Popper, K.R. (1974) *The Open Society and Its Enemies*, Vol.2. London: Routledge & Kegan Paul

Porta, D. (ed) (2009) *Social Movements in a Globalising World.* Basingstoke: Palgrave

Potter, R.B. & Lloyd-Evans, S. (1998) *The City in the Developing World.* Harlow: Longman

Presdee, M. *Chapter 3 from Carnival to the Carnival of Crime* https://blogs.kent.ac.uk/culturalcriminology/files/2011/03/presdee-carnival.pdf (Accessed 30/5/2019)

Program: Perry Preschool Project - CrimeSolutions.gov. Available at: www.crimesolutions.gov/ProgramDetails.aspx?ID=143 (Accessed 18/1/2019)

Pullinger, J.T. (2015) *Prophets of Progress, Saint Simon, Comte & Spencer.* Cambridge: Cambridge Academic

Punch, K.F. (2005) *Introduction to Social Research.* London: Sage

Ranilo, J. & Hermida, B. Gianni Vattimo and John Reader – *The meaning of the 'return to religion' in a postmodern setting.* Available at: people.stfx.ca/wsweet/00-PCT/Vol. 1 2002 Hermida.pdf (Accessed 12/11/2019)

Rantanen, T. (2005) *The Media and Globalization.* London: Sage

Ritzer, G. ed. (2003) *Major Contemporary Social Theorists.* Oxford: Blackwell

Ritzer, G. (2008) *Sociological Theory.* Boston: McGraw-Hill

Roberts, K. (2011) *Class in Contemporary Britain.* Basingstoke: Palgrave MacMillan

Robertson Elliot, F. (1996) *Gender, Family and Society.* Basingstoke: MacMillan Sassen, S. (2001) *The Global City.* Woodstock: Princeton

Saunders, P. (1990) *Social Class and Stratification.* London: Routledge

Savage, M., Devine, F., Cunningham, N., Taylor, M., Li, Y., Hjellbrekke, J., Le Roux, B., Friedman, S., & Miles, A. "A new model of social class? Findings from the BBC's Great British Class Survey Experiment". *British Sociological Association,* 2013, (47) Issue 2, pp.220-250

Scambler, G. "A new Marxist theory of social class?", *Sociology Review,* 2016 (25) Issue 4, pp.8-12

Schatzman, L. & Strauss, A.L. (1973) *Field Research.* New Jersey: Prentice – Hall

Scholte, J.A. (2005) *Globalization, a Critical Introduction.* Basingstoke: Palgrave MacMillan

Schutz, A. (1974) *The Structures of the Life-World.* London: Heinemann

Sclater, S.D. (2005) *Families*. London: Hodder & Stoughton

Seale, C. (ed) (2004) *Social Research Methods*. London: Routledge

Seldon, A. (ed) (2001) *The Blair Effect*. London: Little, Brown & Co.

Selfe, P. & Starbuck, M. (2003) *Religion*. London: Hodder & Stoughton

Sharpe, J. *The History of Crime in England, 1550 – 1914*. Available at: www. ehs.org.uk/dotAsset/afd80919-6736-4af1-bb24-2a1cebb45a28.pdf (Accessed 8/12/2018)

Short, J.R. & Yeong-Hyun, K. (1999) *Globalization and the City*. Harlow: Longman

Silverman, D. (2011) *Qualitative Research, Issues of Theory, Method and Practice*. London: Sage

Simmel, G. (1903) *The Metropolis and Mental Life*. Available at: www. blackwellpublishing.com (Accessed 26/11/2015)

Slater, A. & Tiggerman, M. "'Uncool to do sport' : A focus group study of adolescent girls' reasons for withdrawing from physical activity", *Psychology of Sport and Exercise*, 2010 (11) Issue 6

Slattery, M. (2003) *Key Ideas in Sociology*. Cheltenham: Nelson Thornes

Smart, C. (2007) *Personal Life*. Cambridge: Polity Press

Smith, A. (13/4/2009) *Can Marxism Explain the Financial Crash?* Available at: http://socialistworker.org/2009/04/13/marxism-and-the-financial-crash (Accessed 26/ 11/2013)

Sonner, B.S. "A is for "Adjunct" : Examining Grade Inflation in Higher Education", *Journal of Education for Business*, 2000 (76) Issue 1, pp.5-8

Speech to Conservative Party Conference - Margaret Thatcher https://www.margaretthatcher.org/document/107352 (Accessed 4/6/2019)

Stake, R.E. (1995) *The Art of Case Study*. London: Sage

Statistical First Release (24/1/2013) Available at: http://www.education. gov.uk/researchandstatistics/allstatistics/a00219200/gcse-and-equivalent-attainment (Accessed 20/11/2013)

Steel, L., Brown, A., & Kidd, W. (2012) *The Family*, Basingstoke: Palgrave MacMillan

Steger, M.B. (2009) *Globalization A Very Short Introduction*. Oxford: Oxford University Press

Stephens, M. & Becker, S. (eds.) (1994) *Police Force, Police Service*. Basingstoke: MacMillan

Stokes, J. & Reading, A. (eds.) (1999) *The Media in Britain*. Basingstoke: MacMillan

Stones, R. (ed) (2008) *Key Sociological Thinkers*. Basingstoke: Palgrave

Street, J. (2001) *Mass Media, Politics and Democracy*. Basingstoke: Palgrave

Strauss, A. & Corbin, J. (1998) *Basics of Qualitative Research*. London: Sage

Sutton Trust, Parliamentary Privilege - *The MPs 2017* https://www.suttontrust.com/research-paper/parliamentary-privilege (Accessed 23/5/2018)

Swingewood, A. (2000) *A Short History of Sociological Thought*. Basingstoke: Palgrave

Thompson, K. (1976) *Auguste Comte: The Foundation of Sociology*. London: Nelson

Tocqueville, A. de (1966) *The Ancien Regime and the French Revolution*. Manchester: Fontana

Toffler, A., (1971) *Future Shock*. London: Pan Books Ltd

Treadwell, J. (2013) *Criminology, the Essentials.* London: Sage

Trowler, P. (1996) *Investigating Mass Media.* Hammersmith: Collins

UK Media Ownership Report - Media Reform Coalition
www.mediareform.org.uk/wp-content/uploads/2015/10/Who_owns_
the_UK (Accessed 6/2/2019)

de Vaus, D.A. (1999) *Surveys in Social Research.* London: UCL Press

Vinnicombe, S., Atewologun, D. & Battista, V. *The Female FTSE Board
Report* - Cranfield University.
https://www.cranfield.ac.uk/som/expertise/changing-world-of-work/
gender-leadership-and...(Accessed 20/1/2020)

Vote 2014 Election Results for the EU Parliament UK
www.bbc.co.uk/news/events/vote2014/eu-uk-results (Accessed 30/5/2018)

Walton, P. & Young, J. ed. (1998) *The New Criminology Revisited.* Basingstoke:
Macmillan

Ward, S.C. (2014) *Neoliberalism and the Global Restructuring of Knowledge and
Education.* Abingdon: Routledge

Warren, T. "Work-time underemployment and financial hardship: class
inequalities and recession in the UK", *Work, Employment and Society,* 2015
(29) Issue 2, pp.191-212

Weber, M. (1958) *The City.* London: Collier MacMillan

Weber, M. (1978) *The Protestant Ethic and the Spirit of Capitalism.* London:
George Allen & Unwin

Weiner, J.W. (1981) *English Culture and the Decline of the Industrial Spirit.*
Cambridge: Cambridge University Press

Whyte, W.F. (1993) *Street Corner Society.* Chicago: University of Chicago
Press.

Williams, J. "The rise and rise of cybercrime", *Sociology Review,* 2016, 25 (4), pp.24-25

"World in Action" The Taming of the Beeb (TV Episode 1988)
https://www.imdb.com/title/tt2313123 (Accessed 21/2/2019)
Worsley, P. (1970) *Introducing Sociology*. Harmondswirth: Penguin

Wright, C. "Understanding black academic attainment", *Education Inquiry,* 2013 (4) Issue 1, pp. 87–102

Yin, R.K. (2009) *Case Study Research*. London: Sage

Young, J. & Matthews, R. (1992) *Rethinking Criminology: The Realist Debate*. London: Sage

Young, M. & Willott, P. (1974) *Family and Kinship in East London*. Harmondsworth: Penguin

Picture sources

Auguste Comte Facts, information, pictures, www.encyclopedia.com (Accessed 30 May, 2014)

Herbert Spencer Facts, information, pictures, www.encyclopedia.com (Accessed 30 May, 2014)

Karl Marx Facts, information, pictures, www.encyclopedia.com (Accessed 30 May, 2014)

Index

279, 280, 281, 283, 286, 287, 288, 292, 293, 294, 297, 304, 309, 310, 312, 316, 317, 318, 329, 330, 331, 332, 333, 334, 335, 339, 351, 352, 353, 354, 357, 358, 359, 362, 363, 364, 365, 366, 368, 369, 370, 375, 376, 377, 381, 386, 387, 402, 405, 408, 411, 419, 420, 424, 445, 447, 448, 449, 450, 451, 454, 462, 463, 489, 575, 603, 605, 617, 636, 654, 657, 739, 745, 746, 749, 763, 767, 784

social closure 253, 276, 292, 355, 444

social conflict 47, 51, 52, 53, 69, 269, 419, 424, 740

social consensus 44, 49, 185, 190, 233, 259, 260, 262, 322, 418, 558, 559, 560, 674, 756

social construction 178, 242, 245, 566, 575, 597, 608, 656

social contract 442

social control function 344, 360

social differentiation 253

social divisions 252, 258, 336, 591

social engineering 29, 43, 136, 174, 340, 360, 380, 469, 470, 522, 725

social harms 673, 674

social integration 46, 47, 71, 74, 150, 152, 300, 511, 514, 615, 616, 734, 735

socialisation 2, 12, 13, 14, 16, 19, 20, 21, 25, 41, 45, 49, 50, 64, 149, 179, 182, 185, 186, 188, 189, 190, 193, 207, 224, 228, 268, 310, 319, 354, 372, 445, 446, 447, 558, 597, 605, 614, 732, 768

social laws 36, 39, 147, 148, 150, 154

social mobility 169, 186, 187, 193, 249, 251, 253, 255, 257, 258, 260, 261, 264, 278, 279, 281, 283, 288, 289, 290, 291, 292, 294, 295, 296, 297, 313, 316, 318, 330, 348, 361, 364, 380, 385, 386, 401, 408, 425, 429, 445, 447, 448, 529, 738

Social Mobility and Child Poverty Commission 295

social order 19, 25, 30, 33, 34, 36, 37, 38, 40, 43, 44, 45, 48, 49, 69, 73, 162, 186, 188, 210, 230, 231, 259, 260, 308, 346, 347, 348, 349, 381, 415, 418, 438, 440, 508, 509, 511, 514, 543, 604, 643, 731, 742, 750, 751, 752, 753, 754, 756, 761, 764, 765, 768

social physics 753

social policy 1, 2, 5, 95, 136, 173, 177, 229, 230, 235, 237, 333, 341, 346, 360, 375, 442, 482, 625, 656, 674, 696, 698

social solidarity 46

social status 181, 187, 241, 251, 253, 254, 261, 271, 273, 274, 275, 276, 279, 280, 305, 310, 323, 330, 332, 346, 359, 530, 532, 542, 559, 561, 617,